PENGUIN BOOKS

The Emmys

Thomas O'Neil is a freelance journalist who lives in New York City where he writes for a variety of publications such as *Architectural Digest, Good Housekeeping, Travel & Leisure, The Boston Globe*, and *The San Francisco Examiner*. He's also a shameless TV junkie and admitted awards fanatic who had to forego watching vintage television in his spare time in order to write about it at length in this first book on the Emmy Awards in more than 20 years. His hope for the book is that it will guide TV programmers in filling up those dozens of empty cable channels with more of TV's finest hours, which he can enjoy watching now that this compendium is completed.

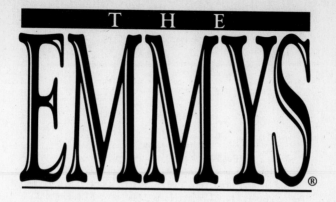

THE EMMYS

Star Wars, Showdowns,

and the Supreme Test

of TV's Best

Thomas O'Neil

Penguin Books

A WEXFORD PRESS BOOK

PENGUIN BOOKS

Published by the Penguin Group

Viking Penguin, a division of Penguin Books USA Inc.,

375 Hudson Street, New York, New York 10014, U.S.A.

Penguin Books Ltd, 27 Wrights Lane, London W8 5TZ, England

Penguin Books Australia Ltd, Ringwood, Victoria, Australia

Penguin Books Canada Ltd, 10 Alcorn Avenue, Suite 300,

Toronto, Ontario, Canada M4V 3B2

Penguin Books (N.Z.) Ltd, 182–190 Wairau Road,

Auckland 10, New Zealand

Penguin Books Ltd, Registered Offices:

Harmondsworth, Middlesex, England

First published in Penguin Books 1992

3   5   7   9   10   8   6   4   2

A Wexford Press Book

Design by Louis Cruz Creative Group, Inc.

"Emmy" is a registered trademark of the Academy of Television Arts
and Sciences and the National Academy of Television Arts and
Sciences. "Emmy" statuette copyright A.T.A.S. and N.A.T.A.S. This
book is not authorized or endorsed by A.T.A.S. or N.A.T.A.S.

LIBRARY OF CONGRESS CATALOGING IN PUBLICATION DATA

O'Neil, Thomas.

The Emmys: star wars, showdowns, and the supreme test of TV's
best / Thomas O'Neil.

p.   cm.

ISBN 0 14 01.6656 4

1. Emmy awards.   I. Title.

PN1992.55.054   1992

791.45'079—dc20   91–46977

Printed in the United States of America

Set in Times Roman

To Frank and Marge O'Neil

who are tuned in

to everything

Contents

TV as Art and Science:
What Does the Future Hold?

For the past 45 years I have had a love affair with a sociological movement that has been given various descriptions but is best known for its Emmy Awards. Alongside my love for my wife and daughter and my family and friends, this has occupied more than half of my 83 years. In this lively and entertaining book by Tom O'Neil, all the creativity known as the television arts and sciences passes in a parade, which, by bestowing awards of merit, created a standard of achievement that is the solid base of culture for 500 million television-set owners around the world.

Looking back over the 45 years that comprise the birth and growth of commercial television as an art form, I think of the Emmy Awards as a symbol of literally millions of hours of patience and extraordinary devotion to analysis and judgment by thousands of the judges of merit among actors, writers, directors, producers, editors, camerapersons, production artists, sound technicians, station executives (network and local), animation artists, talent agents, deal makers, and others affiliated with the television industry. Their efforts are part of the history of the present maturity of the "academe" movement and are evaluated regardless of whether our culture is in a state of rise or decline or of what the piece of art or performance may cost in money.

The dreamers who created the science and technology of the television arts and sciences go back more than 100 years to Paul Gottlieb Nikow and his 1884 patent for a television system. The state of the art in 1992 owes a debt to many nations' engineers who work to perfect satellites, microwaves, high-definition TV, video cassettes, videodiscs, theater television, and the further development outside entertainment and education of television as a tool of medicine and even space exploration.

The Emmys, developed during the beginning years of the Academy of Television Arts and Sciences, now has a permanent home in the West Coast town of motion pictures, Hollywood, where the moving image reached its greatest heights as a medium of culture. It has a second home, too, in New York, where the newborn television medium of the 1940s was able to tap the vast talent then working in radio and on Broadway and where industry leaders could turn to Madison Avenue advertisers to fund a grand new experiment in popular culture. But the "academe" movement is not restricted by geography. The television art form is recognized in many cities of the United States and around the world as a symbol of worth and achievement.

I think of the Emmy Awards as a symbol of literally millions of hours of patience and extraordinary devotion.

In less than 50 years the Emmys have helped television gain a critical stature. It did not take away criticism of the media and its content largely based on its commercial form. Instead, the Emmys have tried to present a measuring stick of TV's artistic mission, its entertainment potential, and its success at reporting world news in a fair and enlightening way. The

ix

award might take a beating if one doesn't agree with the choices, but one cannot escape the attempt to reach a high standard of excellence.

Today, with most of the world's developed nations having their own television systems, this mass communications revolution finds the Emmy in the position of being its oldest and most highly developed qualitative measurement as an awards honor. But certain questions must be asked: Have the Emmys created a vision of what television could do by seeking a consensus of our best television art? To what degree have the Emmys benefitted education? What are the futures of television and the Emmys? Debating the answers to these questions is as important as debating the results of who or what won which award. The Emmys are given away by academies for that reason: A.T.A.S. and N.A.T.A.S. invite the intellectual debate and hope to benefit from its conclusions.

Because the science of TV necessarily impacts its achievement as art, the task of the future is to deal with new emerging technologies that will continue to change the nature of TV and present more hurdles to measuring the best or most extraordinary programs worthy of an Emmy. And any prevailing cynicism, in the meantime, will have to give way to acceptance of future TV systems that promise to change television even more drastically than it's changed since an academy was first formed in 1946. The Emmys to date are a starting place for these next 100 years.

Tom O'Neil's book is a milestone in the history of the Emmys and a rewarding reading experience. It should be of interest to artists, writers, students of the great TV movement, and thousands of others in the arts and sciences of TV.

Syd Cassyd
Los Angeles

Syd Cassyd is the founder and fourth president of the original Academy of Television Arts and Sciences, recipient of the 1991 A.T.A.S. Syd Cassyd Founder's Award, the 1971 25th Anniversary Governors Award, and the 1955 President's Emmy.

NOTE: Because this volume is not an official publication of either of the two television academies, Syd Cassyd is participating as a journalist who has written professionally for more than 45 years about the evolution of television and his contribution to the legacy of the Emmy Award.

Acknowledgments

The two television academies deserve immense credit and enormous thanks for the honorable way they cooperated with this book, which was in no way an official or sanctioned endeavor. Quite sensibly, they applied a rule of standard procedure: I was dealt with on the same basis as any other journalist writing any other book, and my requests along the way were either denied or approved accordingly. Even when denied, they were handled most fairly.

Therefore, much appreciation to the A.T.A.S. staff, including Hank Rieger, Larry Stewart, Murray Weissman, James Loper, Leo Chaloukian, and John Leverence, and the N.A.T.A.S staff, including John Cannon, Trudy Wilson, Bob Blake, Fred Plant, Nick Nicholson, Alan Benish, David Beld, Bob Christie, Ed Eberling, Susana Hernandez, and Dick Thrall. Penguin and I are deeply grateful for that help.

Most profound thanks, though, go to the original academy's founder, Syd Cassyd, who initially lit the way for me through the dark, twisting vaults of Emmy history. He could have chosen to lead me astray whenever we came close to those skeletons in the catacombs ahead, but Cassyd is also a journalist who cares passionately about historical accuracy. To him and his wife Miriam, who once served dutifully as the original academy's first paid employee — its executive secretary — I hope I speak for all of us who will never win an Emmy but who care about those who do: hail, hail.

The keeper of those (unlocked) vaults is Shirley Kennedy, A.T.A.S.'s chief archivest and librarian. *Salante*, Shirley. Kennedy and her whole clan were ever professional, cheerful, and accommodating, and they include Paula Petrie, Louise Danton, Cesar Ramirez, KT Boyce, and Lisa Livoti. To Paula Petrie, a special thanks for her tireless and cheerful moonlighting.

In the libraries of New York and Washington, D.C., Edwin Gardner led the quest for periodical research. I could not have trusted myself to a more able pathfinder or, for that matter, have completed this task without him. Ed died just as this book was finished; his contribution to it was, though, to borrow one of his favorite phrases, his most glorious accomplishment of all.

In Los Angeles, it was Sherie Van Sanford who helped out as well, and skillfully so.

Hilary Marsh was a dogged professional and a champion of *le mot juste* while serving as this volume's copy editor.

Others who must be thanked include Brian Mangum, Catherine Miller (who pointed the way), Chandler Warren, Ty Wilson, Dianne Mangum, Jennifer Gottlieb Schwartzberg, Gary and Audrey Clark, Curtiss Anderson, Lara Davidson, Hana Dolgin, Dawn Reel, and Leko Singer. I would also like to thank a ghost I wish to be haunted by forever, Fred Birmingham, the late, great, former editor of *Esquire* who once rescued this writer from a journalist's plight in the Midwest and introduced him to Gotham and to how this craft really works. His wife, Franny, continues to inspire.

Other bows go to the many people who granted interviews, such as Walter Cronkite, Ed Asner, and Peter Falk among celebrities, and Bud Rukeyser and Linda Oken among TV industry veterans. At the networks, hats off go to Betty Hudson and Paul McGuire at NBC, George Schweitzer and Marty Silverstein at CBS, and Dick Connelly, Peter Murray, and Anne Farrell at ABC. Also, much appreciation to MTM Enterprises, 20th Century Fox, Hallmark Hall of Fame, MGM-UA, Orion, Columbia Pictures Television, Lucy Arnaz Enterprises, Time-Life Films, Paramount Television, World Vision, Masterpiece Theatre, and others for supplying crucial photographs. Ray Waylan and his worldly gang at Globe Photos worked especially hard and were particularly resourceful.

Louis Cruz and his very creative group were responsible for design and layout, making this volume about prizes a prize itself. To Louis and Pilar, Young Kim, Nick Koutoufas, and Rita Pocock: You know how to make *everything* look good. But especially yourselves.

One day, if I'm ever allowed to bestow my own Emmy, it will have to go to Caroline White, this volume's editor at Penguin. She cares deeply about books and television in a way that has helped to make a valuable contribution to both industries. The new award will be inscribed: "To Caroline White — for Outstanding Achievement in Publishing."

"I think television should be the visual counterpart of the literary essay, should arouse our dreams, satisfy our hunger for beauty, take us on journeys, present great drama and music, explore the sea and the sky and the woods and the hills. It should be our Lyceum, our Chautauqua, our Minsky's and our Camelot. It should restate and clarify the social dilemma and the political pickle. Once in a while it does — and you get a quick glimpse of its potential."

— E.B. White,
quoted by
Alexander Kendrick,
Prime Time, *1969*

How She Grew:
TV's Original "Golden Girl"

For more than 30 years, and long before the appearance of a popular television show with a similar name, the Emmy Award was known throughout the show business world as TV's "Golden Girl."

But how golden is she really in this ongoing Golden Age of Television? Or, more to the point, how tuned in are America's top television awards?

The answer can be found in weighing the shows that have won the most. At this writing, among prime-time programs, it's *The Mary Tyler Moore Show*, which holds the record with 29 awards. *MTM* was more than just great programming: It pioneered the genre of sophisticated realistic comedies that revolutionized TV in the 1970s and then encouraged other shows like *All in the Family* to follow. But *MTM* only won its top program prize three times. Six prime-time series have won it on four occasions, all are thus far tied for the record, and each of them is indisputably an example of superior television: *The Dick Van Dyke Show, All in the Family, Hill Street Blues, L.A. Law, Cheers,* and *Upstairs, Downstairs* (which won three times as best drama series and once as best limited series).

Now it seems inevitable that *Cheers,* with 26 Emmys, will soon overtake the *MTM* record of 29 someday, since it still ranks high in the Nielsen ratings as well as with Emmy voters. Also, like the still-running *L.A. Law,* it could also break the six-way tie among the best series winners and establish a supreme champ once and for all. Whatever happens, the result, measured purely in terms of how it reflects in Emmy's golden eye, should be something to cheer about.

In the daytime competition, the award has also tracked program achievement fairly well among soap operas. In 1981, for example, when *General Hospital* producer Gloria Monty endeavored, according to the show's director, to "change the look of daytime drama," sources like *The Los Angeles Times* declared the overhauled, number-one-ranked series "innovative," "complex," and "ingratiating." The Emmy for Outstanding Daytime Drama Series soon followed.

The biggest winner in the daytime contest is actually a children's show, which also proves that the golden girl at least has had 24-karat tastes consistently. *Sesame Street* (the best contribution to childhood since the invention of Oreos — but don't tell the Cookie Monster) has been voted best in its field a record 12 times. Outside the series competitions, the *ABC Afterschool Specials* are the record-holders and, like *Sesame Street*, are superb examples of entertaining shows that are also enlightening and informative. It's impossible to calculate how many young people may have been spared problems with alcohol and drug abuse, for example, thanks to what they learned while watching such prize-winning *Afterschool* dramas as "The Late Great Me" (about a schoolgirl's drinking problem) and "Stoned" (about a boy's addiction to marijuana).

The news and documentary Emmys have consistently gone to more than just the obvious investigative coverage of major news events like Watergate. They've also rewarded thoughtful essay segments by the likes of Bill Moyers, who strived to put such issues into thoughtful perspective. "Can the World

Be Saved?" is a good example of a deserving news segment winner: "World" probed the environmental crisis long before any White House announcement of a "green revolution" in the land. In sports, producer Roone Arledge is the clear champion among Emmy trophy holders, and it's safe to say that his prizes invariably followed some of his greatest professional accomplishments, particularly his early development of Olympics television coverage back "when no one else wanted it," as he once pointed out at the Emmys ceremony. It's Arledge's *ABC's Wide World of Sports* that has been named best series or best program more often than any other show, regardless of category — a record 15 times. The sports Emmys have had their share of problems, but in general they've been regarded well enough that in 1981 baseball legend Johnny Bench pulled that year's honored broadcaster, Dick Enberg, aside backstage and said, "Now you know what it feels like to win the World Series."

Other Emmys include Trustees, Governors, Founder's, Public Service, Community Service, and A.T.A.S. Hall of Fame awards. Religious and international shows have their own prizes, too, the latter bestowed by the International Council, which operates under the authority of the National Academy of Television Arts and Sciences, one of the two TV academies that bestow Emmy Awards (the other being the Academy of Television Arts and Sciences). The international council's purpose is to acknowledge "that, in an age of satellite communications, no one country stands alone in terms of television communications," and it includes the participation of more than a dozen countries from

First president Edgar Bergen (left) with founder Syd Cassyd: Their new academy would support the "cultural, educational, and research aims" of TV.

around the world. Beyond all of the above, hundreds of additional Emmy Awards are given away each year to local stations for program excellence, although there are so many of the regional variety that they could not all be covered in this book.

In toto, nearly 5,000 national Emmys have been awarded to date, a number so staggering that the *L.A. Times* once asked, "Who but the blessed winners themselves can recall winners from previous years?" Critics argue that the huge number dilutes the importance of the individual prizes; defenders say still more are needed to reward the hundreds of thousands of people who toil in the television field every day. The numbers have been cut back often — and drastically — in the past, but they always seem to be reinstated. The reason: Whole fields like the engineering awards are so vital that they now have their own separate awards banquets, and deservedly so. Achievements in engineering may be boring to the average TV viewer, but without them, he or she might be watching *Roseanne* through the fuzzy hues of kinescope today — and without a remote control to silence the commercials (or Roseanne Arnold at her bawdiest). Engineering Emmys have been awarded for such revolutionary contributions as the development of the video graphic generator and RCA's tricolor picture tube, everything but the one breakthrough that turned television into our true National Pastime — AT&T's transcontinental microwave relay system that made live coast-to-coast broadcasts possible. It was nominated in 1951, but lost.

Despite such occasional and obvious oversights, the Emmys are actually the most accurate of all entertainment awards. The Oscars, Tonys, and Grammys, by comparison, are decided by large votes of their organizations' members and the wide input invariably yields choices reflecting broad popular tastes. In the case of the Oscars, they can also be blind choices. It's hard to believe that all Oscar voters see every one of the scores of films nominated each year, which they should do, theoretically, if the award's results are to be honest and fair. It's somewhat controversial among those who believe strongly in majority rule, but, after the members of the two TV academies vote to decide who the prime-time and daytime nominees will be, the winners are determined by judging panels made up of about 6 to 75 industry peers. All panelists are required to view all nominated material before they cast their votes. The difference was important to George C. Scott in 1971. One month after he refused to accept his Oscar for *Patton*, he accepted his Emmy for starring in Arthur Miller's *The Price* on *Hallmark Hall of Fame*. The Oscars, he said, were a degrading popularity contest pitting actors against each other; he considered the Emmys a far truer reflection of performance excellence.

In addition, the Emmys have made valuable contributions to the industry they honor. Producer/writer Steven

Bochco has been quick to acknowledge the impact they had on saving his *Hill Street Blues* series, which went on to become one of the top three Emmy-winning shows in prime time, having won 26 awards. (It also holds the records for winning the most prizes in a series' first season as well as in any single season: eight.) Winning major awards also helped to save *Cagney & Lacey* and *Mission: Impossible. The Andy Williams Show* had been canceled in 1963, but was picked up as a weekly series again after it won outstanding variety show that year. *The $20,000 Pyramid* won the Emmy *several* times after it was dropped by various host networks, and each time the prize helped to keep the show alive.

But the Emmys have a history of embracing the pedigree underdog, even when the results turned out to be ironic or amusing. Emmys have bravely gone to canceled but first-rate series so frequently, for example, that newspaper TV columnists have nicknamed the award "the kiss after death" and even "the black kiss after death." Such canceled shows include *The Defenders, The Seven Lively Arts, The Bob Newhart Show, Van Dyke and Company, The Mary Tyler Moore Show, My World and Welcome to It, The Julie Andrews Hour, Barney Miller, Captain Kangaroo, Crossroads,* and *Woman to Woman*. Unlike *Hill Street Blues*, however, none of them was resurrected after receiving TV's highest rating.

The Emmy Awards broadcast helped to make Bob Newhart a TV star and household name. His *Button Down Mind* albums were high on the record charts in 1960, but he was still relatively unknown to television audiences when he was invited to perform on the Emmy ceremony that year. Luckily for him, an especially irreverent skit by Mike Nichols and

Elaine May was axed just before air time and he was asked to extend his routine to fill the time. The result was so impressive that a year later he had his own show and a year after that it was named best comedy series of 1961–62. (It's also lucky for Newhart that he has a professional-size sense of humor. NBC dropped the show just before it got the "black kiss" — or top award.)

Peter Falk credits the Emmy Awards with giving him his first big career boost. He was just another unknown actor who had been out in Hollywood for little more than a year when he was named Best Actor of 1961 for starring in an episode of *The Dick Powell Theatre*. More choice parts followed. Then Falk found a wrinkled raincoat in his closet one day, they both found the *Columbo* series, and more winged Emmys descended.

By studying the Emmys, you can observe popular writing trends taking their biggest shift in the history of U.S. culture. The serious wordy dramas of early TV necessarily echoed the talky favorites popular for decades on Broadway, but eventually they had to give way to the minimalist realism of shows like *Hill Street Blues*. But many of those early talky dramas were excellent ones such as *Playhouse 90*'s *Requiem for a Heavyweight* and *The Comedian*. Both were named Best Single Program of the Year (back when "best" was still kept in the award titles; now the winning shows are merely "outstanding") regardless of category and both, coincidentally, were also written by Rod Serling, who was rewarded with scriptwriter's gold for each show. The Emmys have also reflected the broad shifts in program preferences. When America grew nostalgic over its prairie past and yearned for escapist drama, westerns swept TV's evening lineups and *Gunsmoke* and *Maverick* swept the Emmys. (The genre was so popular in 1957 that *Gunsmoke* beat out two other westerns to win best drama series.) In the 1970s and '80s, when viewers decided that they preferred cops and robbers to cowboys and Indians, shows like *Police Story*, *Barney Miller*, *Cagney & Lacy*, and *Hill Street Blues* copped the best-series laurels.

The Jack Benny Show was the top comedy series in 1960–61 and its victory marked the end of that era of funny shows. After Newhart's victory the next year (whose program was largely a variety/humor series), the mold that cast hit comedy shows was broken in 1962-63 by *The Dick Van Dyke Show*, which had a new, contemporary format and attitude, and would also break all past records for Emmy triumphs. For four unprecedented years *DVD* reigned over the comedy field and presaged a new kind of sophisticated humor that would dominate the best of television once Van Dyke's costar Mary Tyler Moore got her own show and got the joke just right by adding a bite of realism and a new irreverent attitude. Frivolous programs continued to flourish in the category, such as *The Monkees* and *Get Smart*, but then in the 1970s comedy suddenly got serious again when Emmy was honoring *All in the Family* and *M*A*S*H*, two very dramatic comedy series that bravely examined sensitive social and political issues. After that, Hollywood wanted to play it safe with more formatted (although albeit good) comedies like some of the Emmy victors that followed, such as *Taxi* and *The Golden Girls*.

The drama series category has gone through its own cycle and now seems to be favoring thoughtful programming, just as in Emmy's earliest days when anthology shows like *Studio One*, *The U.S. Steel Hour*, *Producers' Showcase*, and *Playhouse 90* kept reaping the honors. After their decline, *The Defenders* was the first of the regular drama series, as we know them today, to stand out; it monopolized its slot for the three years between 1962 and 1964 by taking occasional chances while still delivering the (safe) dramatic goods. What followed then in the category were occasional high-brow programs like *N.E.T. Playhouse*, *Masterpiece Theatre*'s *Elizabeth R*, and *Upstairs, Downstairs*, but for the most part the champion dramas in between and after them were sometimes good and even great, but will probably never be shown in an art house: *The Fugitive*, *Mission: Impossible* (twice), *Marcus Welby, M.D.*, *The Waltons*, *Police Story*, and *The Rockford Files*.

The awards pattern changed in 1979 when the best dramas became more realistic and therefore more genuinely dramatic. All the shows were so good that they even became repeat winners: *Lou Grant* (twice), *Hill Street Blues* (four times), *Cagney & Lacey* (twice), and *L.A. Law* (four times). But it wasn't the Emmys that changed. The best of television simply got better and the Emmys bravely acknowledged the development.

Throughout Emmy history, winners from all these shows have made their triumphant jaunts up to the podium to collect the most coveted prize of their profession while Americans watched on with unabashed relish. In the 1950s, the suspense sometimes centered on simple matters: Would Lucille Ball attend the ceremony this year? She stayed home in 1956 (for the 1955 awards) because she was still pouting over her loss the previous year. (And, naturally, she ended up winning.) In 1958, her sponsor kept her homebound because of a conflict with the Emmys' underwriter. (It didn't matter. She lost.) On one more recent occasion, the question actually became: Would any star appear? In 1980, Hollywood actors were on strike and decided to boycott the Emmys in order to increase the pressure on the networks. Only one celebrity winner showed up — actor Powers Booth, who admitted to the

audience, "This is either the most courageous moment of my career or the stupidest." It was certainly courageous.

It's been up at the podium that many stars have really shone. Acceptance speeches can be the most telling things about award shows, since that's when actors speak up without their scripts, thereby revealing their true character — or else inviting disaster. Shelley Winters made the worst flub of all in 1964 when she passionately thanked "the whole motion picture academy." Lily Tomlin was intentionally, we must only suppose, hilarious when she said in 1974, "This is not the greatest moment in my life because on Friday I had a really great baked potato at Niblick's on Wilshire." Valerie Harper thanked her analyst. Melvyn Douglas thanked God and "the president for keeping the enemies far from our shore." Dan Rowan and Dick Martin thanked "Laurel and Hardy and all the others we've stolen things from," while *Saturday Night Live* producer Lorne Michaels credited, of all people, a place — New York City "for providing the rejection and alienation that keeps the comedy spirit alive." Charming personal moments have occurred, too, when, for example, *All My Children*'s Julia Barr addressed her daughter watching at home and said,

You can chart a shift in popular writing trends by studying Emmy history: Those early, talky drama series later yielded to the minimalist realism of shows like **Hill Street Blues.**

"Yes, Allison, mom won the enemy award." But Betty White had one of the all-time toppers. As *The New York Times* noted, White was "absolutely adorable as she sweetly thanked the 'evil, wonderful, nasty' business of television." Compare these performances with that of *Ironside*'s Barbara Anderson who, when she won in 1968, was much more dramatic: She was literally speechless. Despite her brevity, the Emmycast still ran into overtime that year.

Tony Randall and William Windom were among those who seized the moment of having everyone's attention and asked for a job when they were out of work. ("I am sober, have tux, and will travel," said Windom.) Sometimes it even worked, as in the case of Martin Charnin who won awards in 1972 for directing and producing *Jack Lemmon in 'S Wonderful, 'S Marvelous, 'S Gershwin*. When he picked up his first one, Charnin let the audience know that he was unemployed. By the time he returned to the podium a few minutes later to pick up his second, he told the crowd, "I just got a job offstage!"

And just the act of getting to the podium has been the source of heightened drama. Daytime actress Kim Zimmer once lost a shoe in her jubilant scurry to pick up her statuette. Barbara Stanwyck was so delirious over her own first victory that her dress got ripped en route to the stage. On occasion such outbursts of joy even revealed a star's hidden talents. Who knew, for example, that Alan Alda was so adept at doing cartwheels before he celebrated one of his five Emmy victories by doing one down the aisle on his way to collect a scriptwriter's award for *M*A*S*H*?

The award may have gladdened the hearts of many, but still Emmy, despite her appearance, is no angel. Offstage infighting among academy members has sometimes resembled a barroom brawl on *Cheers*. "It wouldn't be the Emmys if there weren't some stormy controversy attendant to the annual ceremony," the *L.A. Times* once wrote.

Controversies date back to the award's earliest years when Ed Wynn spilled the beans at the 1949 awards and told everyone that he knew he'd won even before the announcement was made. (It was in the days before accounting firms got involved in awards shows. The winner's list got leaked a few hours before the ceremony and everyone stayed graciously mum about it but Wynn.) A similar snafu occurred in 1984 at the daytime ceremony when *The New York Post* broke an embargo on a press release that contained the names of winners and had the news on the street before the event even began. Now all winners are revealed only when the envelope is opened at the podium.

Other controversies have had different issues at stake. The year following the Ed Wynn incident the ruckus got particularly nasty — and personal — when comedian Alan Young was voted best actor. To his credit, Young beat out Oscar-winner Jose Ferrer and even the voice of puppet-show character Cecil the Sea-Sick Sea Serpent, but sometimes Emmy critics insist that only actors (read serious actors) are supposed to win the performance awards. Comedians, even leading comic actors, are apparently entitled only to get laughs, as evidenced by Dick Van Dyke's experience when he took a critical lashing for winning among "actors and performers" in 1964–65. At least Young and Van Dyke were lucky enough to win at all. Jackie Gleason never won an Emmy and was sore about it throughout his career. Meantime, his *Honeymooners* sidekick Art Carney won six (five for his work with Gleason), and kept them all in a closet at home, reputedly out of respect for the feelings of television comedy's

"Great One."

Dancers get a good kick now and then, too, since they aren't taken seriously as actors either, at least in the case of the infamous "Astaire Affair." On the awards night in 1959 the "Old Dad" watched in proud amazement as his *An Evening with Fred Astaire* special swept up a record total of nine Emmys, including one for Astaire for giving the year's Best Single Performance by an Actor. Then the carping started. "There was no acting in it!" cried one letter writer to the editor of the *L.A. Times*. Another called Astaire's victory a "travesty." Even past academy president Ed Sullivan denounced the award and demanded that the ballots be impounded. But the ever-charming Astaire kept his cool and suffered the outcry nobly, even offering to return the statuette. (The academy refused.) And Astaire bore no ill will. He returned to the Emmys the following year as host and the academy voters apparently bore no continuing grudge either. They heaped two more Emmys on Astaire during his TV career — and, ironically, both of them performance awards, one even for Outstanding Actor in a Drama Special in 1978.

Boycotts, like the biggest one in 1980, have plagued the Emmys whenever the academy infighting got particularly heated. One of the most ironic was led in part by Mary Tyler Moore in 1974 when someone at the academy came up with the (not quite so stupid) idea of initiating "Super Emmys." The thought was intriguing: Advocates wanted to pit all those best actors and actresses in a given year — for dramas, comedies, and limited series — against each other for, for example, an "Actor of the Year – Series" award. Mary Tyler Moore said it was like comparing apples and oranges and she was among the hundreds of Hollywood stars who threatened not to participate in the show if the new awards

A.T.A.S

Dorothy McManus, wife of the designer, was the model for the Emmy statuette. Photo shows her as she looked then.

were introduced. Luckily for the academy, the stars backed down shortly before the Emmycast. Unluckily for Mary Tyler Moore, she won a Super Emmy. The award was then dropped, so the academy said, forever.

The most serious boycott of all occurred from 1964 to 1967 when CBS News chief Fred Friendly denounced the procedure for selecting news winners as being "unrealistic, unprofessional, and unfair" and refused to participate. The entire staff of then-third-ranked ABC, which wasn't faring well with either the Emmys or the Nielsen ratings anyway, backed Friendly and together the two networks nearly killed off the "golden girl" once and for all. Peace was made only after the academy made considerable changes in the awards procedure and after Friendly resigned from CBS as a result of an unrelated matter. NBC led a different boycott — in the early to mid-1980s of the sports and news awards — and again it was over the issue of how they were administered. N.A.T.A.S. made considerable changes as a result of suggestions by NBC and others, but still the disagreement dragged on for a painfully long time.

There has been such fierce factionalism behind the Emmy Award that it's frankly a wonder that it's survived at all. Past academy president Rod Serling was among those who never thought it would. After a year in office, he was so disgusted by the acrimony around him that he told *Variety* that the academy's demise was imminent. "It is an organization of disparate parties with no common view," he said. "I don't think it will be missed." Technically, Serling turned out to be wrong, of course, but the problems he faced as president resulted, if not in the death of the academy, then in an outcome that many consider equally tragic. Inner factionalism would eventually lead to a split into *two* academies.

*****

The original Academy of Television Arts and Sciences was founded in 1946 by Syd Cassyd, who was then working as a reporter for a TV trade magazine while also moonlighting as a grip on Paramount's back lot. As he watched the new broadcast medium grow, it occurred to him one day that just what it needed was an organization similar to the Academy of Motion Picture Arts and Sciences. Similar, that is, but not exactly the same. Cassyd actually wanted his group to be much more academic in nature. He foresaw a professional forum equivalent to the French Academy of Sciences and the National Academy of Science in Washington where ideas could be openly discussed and debated and position papers exchanged between members.

After preliminary meetings with Klaus Landsberg, Paramount's TV engineer, and Professor Paul Sheets of U.C.L.A. (who was also president of the Audio-Visual Educational Association of America), Cassyd gathered together seven associates in an exploratory meeting held in the offices of S.R. Rabinoff, an F.C.C. attorney who ran a TV school and other operations behind the 20th Century-Fox studios on Sunset Boulevard. In order to pull off their mission, the group decided they needed a big name behind them, and Cassyd, who had been designated the group's first chairman, went after one of the biggest in show business. As a result, on January 7, 1947, famed ventriloquist Edgar Bergen was elected the new academy's first president and one year later the organization was formally incorporated as a nonprofit organization with its chief aim being "to promote the cultural, educational, and research aims of television." The incorporation papers were filed by Bergen, Ray Monfort (of *The Los Angeles Times*'s TV operations), and Donn Tatum, who was soon to become chairman of the board of Walt Disney Studios.

Emmy Awards were first given away in 1949 for the 1948 broadcast year and were named by the president of the Society of Television Engineers — Harry Lubcke — who would later serve as the academy's third president. Originally, the Emmys were to be called "Ikes," a short form for the television iconoscope tube, but the nickname had problems, particularly the fact that it was associated in the public mind with a certain past war hero (and future U.S. President). Lubcke then volunteered his successful alternative, a feminization of "Immy," a term commonly used for the early image orthicon camera tube. The design for the prize's statue was chosen from the last of 48 entries submitted by industry contestants. The winner was Louis

McManus, an engineer at Culver City's Cascade Pictures, who used his wife, Dorothy, to model the form of the winged woman triumphantly holding up the universal symbol of the electron.

When the TV academy was born, the TV industry was still in its infancy and most programming was still generated locally. The country would not be linked with a coast-to-coast hookup via microwave transmission until AT&T did so in 1951, and so therefore the earliest Emmys were bestowed mostly to local heroes. The first one ever awarded went to Shirley Dinsdale, a young ventriloquist with a popular L.A. puppet show.

For a program to win one of the first six Emmys, it had to have been produced in Los Angeles. By the award's second year, the requirement was only that it had to be aired over an L.A. station and suddenly the winners included prominent New York names like Milton Berle and Ed Wynn. Some authorities like academy founder Cassyd claim that the awards had a national scope right from the beginning. His reasoning: Many of Hollywood's programs were being seen all over the U.S. on kinescope, which used 16-millimeter cameras to film what appeared on a TV tube. The films were then shipped out to St. Louis, Boston, and elsewhere for local airing.

But St. Louis and Boston were also getting kinescope shows out of New York where the entertainment industry was presided over by Broadway columnist Ed Sullivan, who also had a top-rated radio show and a new hit television program. In 1950, Sullivan and his friends set up their own rival TV awards — called the Michaels, reputedly in reference to microphones — but the Academy of Radio and Television Arts and Sciences, which bestowed them, was in actuality a magazine instead of a membership organization and the awards died after they were given out

for the last time in 1953. (*TV Guide, Look* magazine, and the Sylvania electronics company all had their own TV awards during the 1950s, too, but they met the same fate.)

In 1955, the Emmys were shown on national television for the first time, and it was suddenly apparent to Sullivan that the rival, L.A.-based awards had become an established success. Reportedly furious, he called together his "Committee of 100," comprised of New York's TV elite, and petitioned for his own East Coast chapter of the nine-year-old California academy. He prevailed that June, but still felt overshadowed by Hollywood's clout and began a campaign for a completely new academy, one with Hollywood and New York designated as equal "founding chapters." Exactly two years later, the original Academy of Television Arts and Sciences was

Emmy was named after "Immy," a nickname for the early image orthicon camera tube.

supplanted by the new National Academy of Television Arts and Sciences, and Sullivan was elected its first president. Throughout it all, the Emmy pageant continued to be broadcast every year, apparently without the viewing public knowing anything about the intrigue off stage.

Sullivan's battle with Hollywood didn't end with his victory, however; instead it called attention to a growing East–West war that would eventually tear the academy in two. "There have been rumblings of discontent inside the television academy since it began as a Hollywood-based organization," Dick Adler of the *L.A. Times* once wrote. "New York appears to have always looked upon Hollywood as the sausage factory, the place where canned comedy and cop shows came from. Hollywood's attitude toward its eastern colleagues was equally derisory: They were elitist snobs who thought that their involvement in news and live drama gave them special status."

From the outset of the New York–L.A. war, the New York television industry did indeed have considerable advantage with those news programs and live dramas. Shrewdly, it tapped the best of Broadway writing and acting talent for *Playhouse 90*, *Studio One*, and *Hallmark Hall of Fame* productions. Gotham also had additional big guns just a few streets over, on Madison Avenue, where the commercials were being made that funded the new medium. Because TV's money was in New York, so were its network executives, and, just down the hall from them, the staffs that made those superb news and documentary programs. Hollywood's munitions were measly by comparison. The town's leading movie producers originally scorned the small screen in favor of the big one and its bigger dollars, just as its top stars did. The lead parts were therefore left to lesser names to fill, like Lucille Ball, who had never lacked for work in Hollywood, but never made it big either.

Except for 1954, the Emmy Awards have been televised every year. At first the ceremony was aired only in southern California, but as the event became more lavish and costly, the financially limited L.A. broadcasters decided to drop it just as the national networks became interested. In 1955, when the awards show went national, the issue of whether Hollywood or New York would host the program was resolved amicably by giving it to both, even before Ed Sullivan got involved to insist on equal treatment for Easterners. In a ambitious gesture of technological daring, the Emmys were shown from 1955 to 1971 in "simul-cast," which involved cameras cutting back and forth dizzily between the bicoastal ceremonies, often leaving perplexed viewers at home in front of screens that stayed blank for as long a minute. But the boldness of the effort only added to its irresistible drama, and the Emmys enjoyed rating shares that surpassed virtually every show they honored. The next day, however, *Variety* and the newspapers in L.A. and New York invariably began their coverage, not with who won the golden trophies, but with who was winning the East–West war. Typical of the times was *Variety*'s headline in 1957: "N.Y. Outpoints Hollywood 15–4," followed the next year by Hollywood's revenge, as also noted by *Variety* — "Coast Wins Over East."

The early ceremonies usually included dinner and lavish musical spectacles that were popular on Hollywood sets and Broadway stages. It was a flamboyant display of TV's sudden might and one that eventually drew in top film stars like Laurence Olivier, Helen Hayes, and Bette Davis, all of whom finally shucked their reluctance to appear on TV and were rewarded with Emmys to take home to pair off with their Oscars. As America watched on, it was not just the Emmys anymore. It looked like both the Emmys and Oscars, a twin entertainment extravaganza.

But as Emmy grew up, Hollywood television grew in prominence, aided by the death of live TV in New York. The simulcast continued for a while without bias. Throughout the 1960s, the two- and three-hour-plus awards shows allowed sufficient time to acknowledge New York's news and documentary programs, a few of which even won Program of the Year, as *The Tunnel* did in 1963 and David Wolper's *The Making of the President 1960* did in 1964. New Yorkers like Walter Cronkite continued to serve as academy presidents, trading off with Hollywood titans like CBS West Coast executive Harry Ackerman and Thomas Sarnoff of NBC. Meanwhile, as TV shows continued to multiply, and with them the number of Emmy Awards, pressures mounted to keep the telecast no more than two hours long, which suggested trimming the number of prizes bestowed on the air.

The academy responded with a fateful mistake, even if it was one that had the best of intentions. Emmy-show watchers clearly tuned in for Hollywood glitz over New York's gutsy news, but the academy insisted on including the news awards in the same show. As a result, New York's awards were downplayed so blatantly that in 1968 the news and documentary winners were not even welcomed up to the stage to be acknowledged by their peers. Instead, they were asked to stand up en masse in the audience where the Emmys were distributed to them at their tables. New York's defeat seemed not only total. It was humiliating.

The academy ultimately solved the problem with an idea it probably should have tried earlier, by giving the news, documentary, daytime, and sports awards their own ceremonies, as they have today. By the time the solution was tried, however, New York's academy members were back at their old battle stations. The peace was kept temporarily by the networks, who gave the New York–based news and documentary awards their own prime-time shows in 1973 and 1974, but the ratings were poor and the telecast was dropped. In 1970, the organization's East Coast half of its national co-headquarters was closed. One year later, that year's awards-show broadcaster, NBC, announced that the East Coast end of the simulcast would be dropped as a cost-cutting measure. New York seemed powerless to fight back.

Meanwhile, outlying cities were organizing affiliated academy chapters — in Seattle, Atlanta, Chicago, Washington, D.C., Columbus, Dayton and Cincinnati, Ohio, and elsewhere. As their numbers and influence grew, some Hollywood members got increasingly resentful that all academy members had an equal vote in determining the winners of the best shows being made in Hollywood. Wasn't the point of these awards, after all, they asked, for professionals to be judged by their peers? Hollywood had outgrown the other chapters and now wanted the power and privilege of its rank. But the smaller chapters had a considerable ally who had been helping them to grow and prosper from their natal days — New York — and New York still had some fighting spirit left.

"As time goes by, there is an adjustment to the fact that Hollywood is the center of the entertainment world of television," N.A.T.A.S. president John Cannon says. "It is. And that's fine. But a national academy should be truly national and should involve all the chapters." Back in 1976, however, the Hollywood contingent disagreed passionately. Larry Stewart was president of the Hollywood chapter when the split in the academy occurred and soon thereafter became the first president of the newly formed A.T.A.S. Referring to many members of the local academy chapters, he says, "They were in the broadcasting business, yes, but not in the manufacture of television programs on a national scale. When they joined, they got to vote among their peer groups for the Emmy Awards. Suddenly, a news cameraman in Dayton, Ohio, had a vote equal to the cinematographer in Hollywood for the work on *Roots* and this cameraman in Dayton had never even seen a 35-millimeter camera, much less shot one. Mr. Bobo of Seattle's morning children's show was voting for the best actor.

Local television performers were suddenly voting on a national scale. In addition to that, there were so many chapters with so many votes that Hollywood, the founding place of the academy, was being outvoted on almost every issue."

Cannon counters: "To the best of my knowledge, all of that is a myth. There was really very little voting of people out there who weren't qualified. I don't see anything wrong with the station manager in Cleveland voting on the programs that come over his station and other stations."

The dispute within the academy is known today in Emmy circles simply as "the war." The two sides had their obvious differences, but they might not have led to an eventual battlefield had an initial gunshot not been fired. That blast came in 1976 when the post of the academy's presidency came up for a vote. Californians backed Robert Lewine, a former network executive who had served as the academy's president once before, in 1961–63, and as its executive director for most of the 1970s. New York — and with it the outlying local chapters — backed Cannon. When Cannon prevailed, the Californians sued for a dissolution of the academy.

It took a year to sort out all the lawsuits and counter-suits, but in the end the warring factions made peace. There would now be two academies, they decided. The National Academy of Television Arts and Sciences, based in New York, would manage the daytime, sports, news and documentary, international, and local awards, while the new, separate Academy of Television Arts and Sciences in California would bestow the prime-time prizes.

Strangely, the breakup of the academy actually helped to improve the Emmy Award. Once the warring factions took their attention off each other, they concentrated on their own turf and seeded it. Without the breakup and the new delegation of authority, it's unlikely that the Emmy would have evolved as much as it has. "There have been tremendous benefits from all this," Cannon admits. "There has been so much more development and growth."

Following the split, Hollywood's prime-time awards grew again in prestige once they were returned predominantly to Hollywood voters (although A.T.A.S. certainly invites — and indeed encourages — other qualified professionals to join from outside California). The new academy opened a library and archives, established a speakers bureau, set up student internships and scholarships, and founded *Emmy Magazine*. Meanwhile, New York's N.A.T.A.S. continued to publish *Television Quarterly*, which had been established during Walter Cronkite's tenure as president. It also offered student internships and scholarships and continued to cultivate the growth of the local chapters (doubling their number under Cannon's stewardship). These many years after the breakup, there is even a sense of cooperation growing between the two old warring parties. In the past few years, both academies have joined hands to produce the newly revitalized daytime awards, so rejuvenated and slick that its ceremony was aired for the first time in prime time in 1991 and did so well that it topped the Nielsen ratings that the prime-time awards got the year before.

But will the two academies ever get back together again? Editor of *Emmy Magazine* and former A.T.A.S. president Hank Rieger says that A.T.A.S. wants to and is ready to negotiate at any time. N.A.T.A.S. president John Cannon responds to the question by saying, "I don't think so. We ended up making an omelet and you can't put the eggs from an omelet back in the shells once you're done." The man who founded the original TV academy has a long-term, historical view. "Reunification is inevitable," Syd Cassyd says. "When the people who were involved in the war are no longer in power and the 15,000 members of both academies — who are the economic and creative leaders of this industry — discuss the problem in a democratic forum, we'll have one academy again."

*****

CBS

The Emmys' biggest oversight: Jackie Gleason (left) never won, while supporting star Art Carney (second from left) took five for The Honeymooners.

"Things haven't changed 1949–1991," Syd Cassyd had scribbled on a press release he sent this writer in the mail one day as this book was being compiled. The release was from A.T.A.S. and attempted to answer some controversial questions surrounding the 1990–1991 prime-time Emmys just before they went on the air. Why was *The Simpsons* competing as an animated series and not a comedy? Why are certain awards bestowed off the air? What was the celebrated series *The Civil War* doing nominated against *Entertainment Tonight*? (One smug answer to the last question could be suggested by the title of the also-nominated *Unsolved Mysteries*.)

Although peace has finally been established between the two coasts, new controversies continue to erupt. The most ongoing public drama continues to be: Will daytime star Susan Lucci ever win that Emmy? It's too late for Gleason — or, for that matter, Gracie Allen, Judy Garland, and Ed Sullivan — but there's got to be hope for Lucci, Angela Lansbury, Roseanne Arnold, and others who are still vital in the industry, right? But to answer that, one has to consider the nature of show-business awards. They're quirky, and that's what keeps us watching them. Compare these obvious Emmy oversights to ones involving other show

business awards: Richard Burton went to his grave without an Oscar; Diana Ross, Rod Stewart, and the Beach Boys have never won Grammys. Neil Simon went without a Tony Award for so long that it wasn't funny, even to him.

But the Emmy has a severe disadvantage compared to other prizes. When the Oscars declare a Best Actor of the year, the title has an exciting ring to it. The Emmy's equivalent acting designation, when judged just by its name, is hard to get so worked up over: Outstanding Lead Actor in a Miniseries or a Special. The top male acting honor has been called many things over time, including Best Actor, Outstanding Single Performance by an Actor in a Drama, and Actor of the Year, which points to another problem: The titles change all the time. So how can you have an honest competition in which the categories, and with them the rules, fluctuate — and often drastically so — from year to year?

It's also a game that's played two different ways, which hardly seems fair to some. If you're a nominated drama series writer, you're at least assured that someone in your category will win. But if you're a writer of another sort — of a program's theme music — you're not. That's an "area" award, a prize classification in which the nominees compete against an ideal standard of excellence instead of each other, and often there are no winners at all, which invariably causes groans from the audience at the celebratory banquet where the voting results are announced.

The following disciplines are judged on an "area" basis today: the crafts or creative arts (makeup, costumes, electronic camera work, and the like) for the prime-time, daytime, and sports awards, plus all areas of news and documentary programming. All other Emmys are selected in a competitive system in which one winner is always picked among actors, directors, writers, and so on. "The concept of the area award is excellence that's being judged on its own merits against a standard of excellence," N.A.T.A.S. president Cannon says. "It's not a horse race. It's not one against the other. The news people, for example, really don't want to run anchorman against anchorman and I think this is a good solution."

But why not run all the awards the same way? "You *do* need horse races," Cannon says, arguing that both the TV industry and the general public want to see them in the chief entertainment categories. And he may have a powerful point, even if it means tolerating an obvious inconsistency. Few people would volunteer to handle the Emmys' switchboard the day following the announcement that there was no winner, let's say, in the category of Outstanding Comedy Series this year — although if any category deserves to be judged so seriously, it's that slot brimming with often frivolous sitcoms.

What the academies are reserving for themselves by bestowing area awards at all is the ultimate heady authority of making a competition's cruelest — and sometimes its most responsible — judgment: the opportunity of saying to all nominees that none of them has measured up. But how do you deliver such bad news? The Tony Awards resolved this problem years ago by just eliminating whole categories if the voters felt that way. In 1985, to cite one year, the Tonys announced early on that there would be no categories for Best Actor or Best Actress in a Musical or for Best Choreographer. The problem with the Emmys is that same announcement is presently deferred to the last possible minute. To wait to deliver the bad news of no winners in a certain category at an industrywide banquet, where the nominees are all gathered cheerfully with their peers while awaiting good news for *somebody,* seems harsh.

The area awards, however, do represent one aspect of the academy that is still academic in nature, since it applies a lofty intellectual standard. But in the opinion of at least two important persons — A.T.A.S. founder Syd Cassyd and past president and multiple Emmy winner Walter Cronkite — the academies are still not academic enough.

Cronkite is emphatic on the point, in fact, still wanting them to harken back to their original model of the French Academy — "of a bunch of wise men and women," he says, "who sat in judgment of their peers." He adds: "It was a matter of great argument in the early days of the academy. I spoke up vociferously for this and I was shouted down by the huge majority — the *huge* majority — [who were] principally motivated with the idea of giving awards each year and putting on a good show. But I have not changed my position in the years since I was president, and I didn't last very long in the higher echelon of the academy affairs because of my views. I've always thought the academy should be a real academy and should be interested in the furtherance of the arts and sciences of television. In that regard, the awarding of prizes for performance should be very definitely limited to outstanding contributions and should not perhaps even be given on a regular basis." Cassyd agrees: "The original purpose of A.T.A.S. was to give America a standing in the arts and sciences, not just to compliment an industry."

But the academies do have an obvious responsibility to compliment their industry by rewarding excellence within it. So the question must be asked: At the very least, how good a job have the academies done at the task they consider their primary one — bestowing the Emmy Awards? Television is a radically evolving industry, which means that the Emmys have had to evolve right alongside the medium they honor. It's a credit to what academic aspirations the TV academies still maintain, in fact, that they've suffered the year-to-year tumult over changes in awards procedure in the intellectual spirit of getting it right — and many believe they have. No one has ever been a more credible or more objective authority on the Emmys than TV columnist Cecil Smith, who covered them in the *L.A. Times* for more than two decades (and criticized them often). He ultimately concluded: "The system of selecting winners is still the most intelligent used by any entertainment medium ... [The Emmys] may be the only awards system, including the Oscars, the Tonys, and particularly the Pulitzers, where the judges actually vote for the things they have seen, not just things that they have heard about or read about or the waiter at the bistro told them about .... One looks back through the years and the argument is valid that most of the time what was best on television won an Emmy — from *The Tunnel* to *Upstairs, Downstairs*, and *Roots*."

One aspect of the Emmy Awards that the academies may not have gotten quite right, though, is the full and equal inclusion of cable TV programming, which was not allowed to participate in the prime-time competition until 1987. (N.A.T.A.S., by comparison, allowed cable to participate a little earlier; the Turner Broadcasting Station first competed for the sports trophies in 1986.) The delay led to the almost inevitable creation of the alternative Awards for Cable Excellence (or A.C.E. Awards).

Cable's number of prime-time nominations and wins has grown steadily in the past few years, but it still only gets a little more than 10% of both today, which seems slight. One A.T.A.S. official who does not want to be identified says the academy voters, not the academies, are to blame since, in the case of the prime-time and daytime prizes, it's the members who determine the nominees. The source adds, "You have to remember that a lot of our members are old-timers. They're fiercely loyal to the broadcast industry and many of them are on fixed incomes like Social Security, which means they may not even have cable at home." Past A.T.A.S. president Larry Stewart disagrees, and says that it's chiefly a matter of program sophistication. "Cable has not caught up to the quality [of broadcast] as yet," he says. "They don't spend the amount of money to attract the top producers. They're making good stuff, but they only have a limited ability to do so." Another past president, Hank Rieger, says it's more quantitative. Cable may represent dozens of new channel options for viewers, he says, but it actually comprises only "a small percentage of the original programming on TV.

"But it's getting better," he adds. "Maybe in another few years cable will win as many awards as the others. Maybe more." At N.A.T.A.S., president John Cannon insists, "In the sports and news and documentary categories cable is well represented. We go out of our way to get their product." That's true, but N.A.T.A.S. is still not immune to criticism, as evidenced by the outcry that followed the omission of any Cable News Network nominations at the 1990 news awards.

*****

"Poor Emmy has been so battered and bruised with post mortems following her annual parties, she'd have been in a booby hatch by now if she'd been a human rather than a symbol," *Hollywood Reporter* columnist Hank Grant once wrote. "It appears to us that all of the academy's so-called mistakes result from its honest effort to satisfy the demands of everyone — its members, the public, and the critics. Without exception, the many radical changes in awards structure have been made as a result of post-Emmy criticism."

The *L.A. Times*'s Cecil Smith echoed Grant's lament in 1969 when he addressed how "battered" poor Emmy had really become, but asserted that the show must go on. "Seldom has a lady been so mocked and scorned and maligned and boycotted as this golden statuette for television achievement," he wrote. "And she has not only survived but managed to remain the most significant award in television, the only one that means a damn to the viewing public or the industry."

But does the industry really care? Phil Silvers, for one, seems to. He once said, "Having an Emmy is like having a gold searchlight in a sea of confusion, reminding you to rehearse, rehearse, rehearse!" Jane Fonda once said that she was never as nervous about winning an Oscar as she was about winning her Emmy in 1984. Daytime stars like Joan Rivers and Bob Barker care so much about winning Emmys that they've both publicly bemoaned the fact that it took them more than 20 years in TV to get one. ("I always had a fantasy as a child that I'd win one of these," Rivers said in 1990 when she finally had one in her grasp.)

"The unusual thing about winning is that the more Emmys I have, the more important they become," said Mary Tyler Moore, who has six. "I keep thinking I've done it all, and then suddenly there's another Emmy." Celebrities, at the very least, have always cared. "Most people cry when they win an Emmy," Jack Benny once said. "I cry when I lose."

*****

Lastly, a word is in order about this book's heavy reliance on newspaper and trade-paper quotes, particularly those from *The Los Angeles Times, The Los Angeles Herald Examiner, Variety, The Hollywood Reporter, The Washington Post,* and *The New York Times.* To paint a realistic picture of events long ago, a writer needs lots of local color, and mine, happily, came from the ancient inks of a dozen or more publications that did an outstanding job of recording what happened on the scene each year as the Emmys drama unfolded. I could have chosen to say the same things in equally colorful or opinionated ways, but it wouldn't have been the same as hearing from those who were there when the "Astaire Affair" happened or the night Milton Berle pulled his "floperoo." Today, looking back over the lists, we can all see who won the awards. What reactions those victories caused, and how they were perceived, come chiefly from the people just inches offstage, watching and gaping, just as we star-watch, gape, and applaud today.

Thomas O'Neil
March 1992

The Emmys
Year by Year

The First Hurrah

The first awards banquet was held at the old Hollywood Athletic Club on Sunset Boulevard, which was draped with banners for the occasion. Outside the club, searchlights pointed skyward to draw Hollywood's brightest stars to the 600-seat ceremony that would honor a total of six original Emmy winners. Tickets cost $5 each and were sold out long before the show.

Few stars, though, came out that night. Instead, the audience was made up mostly of academy members new to television, a few local political lords, and 75 members of the press. In his booklet *Emmy Awards Confidential*, academy founder and its fourth president Syd Cassyd remembered: "The program wasn't televised nationally — indeed there weren't as many as 50,000 television sets in all of Los Angeles, compared to a total of only one million throughout the country. Our first banquet celebrities included such people as the assistant chief of police from the City of Los Angeles, the mayor, and a county supervisor." Mayor Fletcher Bowron declared it TV Day — January 25, 1949.

The ceremony was broadcast on local station KTSL beginning at 9:30 p.m. Former academy secretary Rudy Vallee was scheduled to emcee, but another headline entertainer of the day, Walter O'Keefe, was asked to take over at the last minute when Vallee was called out of town. Also conspicuously missing was Edgar Bergen. Bergen had served the academy as its first president in 1947, but he couldn't be on hand now because he was summoned to the White House by Harry Truman to be a guest at the President's inauguration cermonies. Entertainment

Shirley Dinsdale, the first person to win an Emmy, with puppet Judy Splinters.

was provided by singers Frankie Laine and Herb Jeffries, dancer Frank Veloz, and radio comedian Bill Constance.

Trophies were given out only to shows produced in Los Angeles County and subsequently aired over one of the four L.A. TV stations then competing. Five hundred academy members voted for three awards, the technical committee bestowed a plaque, the academy honored the designer of the new statuette, and the general public voted by postcard ballots for the most popular program.

The first Emmy ever bestowed went to 20-year-old ventriloquist Shirley Dinsdale of KTLA for being the Most Outstanding Television Personality. The honor was no doubt intended in part, too, for her puppet sidekick, Judy Splinters, who, in one of the five-day-a-week, 15-minute broadcasts, sat on a throne and imagined herself a queen. "The applause which greeted the announcement" of the winner, noted the *L.A. Herald-Express*, "indicated sincere and hearty approval of the results of the secret ballot. This award brought more applause than did any other."

After Dinsdale won, Mike Stokey, host of *Pantomime Quiz* and a loser in the personality category, was overheard gasping, "I've been robbed!" but then *Quiz* (which featured celebrities playing charades) was chosen Emmy's first Most Popular Television Program. Stokey went on to become such a favorite in academy circles that he followed Cassyd as the academy's fifth president in 1951.

In honor of the first Emmy Awards, the mayor declared it TV Day.

The prize for Best Film Made for Television went to *The Necklace*, a half-hour adaptation of a Guy de Maupassant short story that was produced for $9,000 as part of Lucky Strike's *Your Show Time* series. Its sponsorship was somewhat ironic, considering that cigarette smoking was banned at the first Emmys banquet.

KTLA was given an award for outstanding overall achievement. It was accepted by station manager Klaus Landsberg, who was also the West Coast director of Paramount's television operations. Charles Mesak of Don Lee Television won a plaque for his invention of the phasefader used in TV cameras, a device that changes the colors on title cards from white on black to black on white. A special award was given to the designer of the new Emmy symbol, artist Louis McManus, who used his wife, Dorothy, as a model for the image of the winged "golden girl" who stands on a cutout section of the globe and holds up the symbol of an electron. Ironically, McManus was honored with a plaque — not one of his own prized statuettes.

In its very first year, many New York critics dismissed the awards as a provincial L.A.-only affair because of the stipulation that nominated programs had to have been both made and broadcast in Los Angeles. Founder Cassyd has always maintained, however, that the awards were national in scope right from their start. "You've got to remember that while only Hollywood shows and stars were eligible for an Emmy in the beginning, Hollywood was providing programs for other parts of the country," he says. "*The Necklace* was one of those shows filmed in Hollywood that was then seen throughout the nation and the world."

Commenting on the first awards ceremony, *Variety* columnist Jack Hellman wrote prophetically, "In years to come, the Emmy will have attained [as much] recognition in and out of the industry as the world-acclaimed Oscar. [The awards ceremony] was an ambitious undertaking and paid off exceedingly well in prestige and advancement of the new art form."

A.T.A.S.

Six hundred people paid $5 each to attend the first Emmys show, which was held at the old Hollywood Athletic Club.

Awards presented on January 25, 1949, at the Hollywood Athletic Club and broadcast on KTSL-TV, Los Angeles.

MOST POPULAR TELEVISION PROGRAM
• *Pantomime Quiz.* KTLA.
Armchair Detective KTLA.
Don Lee Music Hall. KTSL.
Felix de Cola Show. KTLA.
Judy Splinters. KTLA.
Mabel's Fables. KTLA.
The Masked Spooner. KTSL.
The Treasure of Literature. KFI-TV.
Tuesday Varietie. KTLA.
What's the Name of that Song? KTSL.

BEST FILM MADE FOR TELEVISION
• *The Necklace* (*Your Show Time* series), Marshall Grant-Realm Productions.
Christopher Columbus, Emerson Film Corporation.
Hollywood Brevities, Tele-Features.
It Could Happen to You, Vallee Video.
The Tell Tale Heart, Telepak.
Time Signal, Centaur Productions.

MOST OUTSTANDING TELEVISION PERSONALITY
• Shirley Dinsdale and puppet Judy Splinters. KTLA.
Rita LeRoy. KTLA.
Patricia Morrison.
Mike Stokey. KTLA.
Bill Welsh. KTLA.

TECHNICAL AWARD
• Charles Mesak, Don Lee Television for introduction of the phasefader.

STATION AWARD
• KTLA for outstanding achievement in 1948.

SPECIAL AWARD
• Louis McManus, original designer of the Emmy Award statuette.

Campaigns in Hollywood

"The Emmys seemed to be a success right from the beginning," academy founder Syd Cassyd wrote years later. "Starting in 1949, campaigning was right out in the open. There was trade paper advertising and rebroadcasting of nominated television programs. There were party invitations to meet the various nominees, or anyone who *wanted* to be nominated."

This year's contenders were determined by the combined input of television station heads and advertising executives, while the winners were chosen by the academy's membership. Press speculation over who would win began as early as the second awards year, too. Calling upon "a combination of wild rumors and some solid facts," *Los Angeles Daily News* writer Paul Price predicted: "You can bet the house and lot that *Time for Beany* will be named the best children's show." It was. The popular puppet program about a boy in a propeller cap who sailed the world aboard the "Leakin' Lena" even surpassed the now more-remembered puppet classic *Kukla, Fran & Ollie*, which came in second place in the voting.

"Just bet the automobile on this one," Price added, "but it is generally conceded that Klaus Landsberg's station (KTLA) will get the award for best public service on its coverage of the Kathy Fiscus rescue." The Fiscus show was a docu-drama that followed the tragedy of a girl who had fallen down a well, but assuming that it would win the public service prize risked turning L.A. into a pedestrian city. A documentary about Gen. Dwight Eisenhower's military struggles in World War II, *Crusade in*

Best Children's Show Time for Beany *triumphed over* Kukla, Fran & Ollie.

Europe, won instead. KTLA did take the station achievement award, however, for the second year in a row.

Variety made its own forecasts, too, and was generally right, except for the same mistake underestimating *Crusade in Europe.* The trape paper also predicted that USC–UCLA football would nab Best Sports Coverage, which it may or may not have done. Official academy records maintain that a wrestling program won in its place, but contemporary press reports — including *Variety, L.A. Times, L.A. Herald-Express,* and *L.A. Mirror* — recount a win for college pigskin. The confusion may be understandable in light of wrestling's immense popularity. In 1949–50, it was also the most-watched programming in the greater Los Angeles area. The academy's first paid employee, who was also its original executive secretary (and the founder's wife), Miriam Cassyd, remembers, "It was such a surprise, you couldn't believe it — women over 50 just got into wrestling and made up most of the audience. Of course, it was staged, but wrestling was *the* topic of conversation in those days."

After the first year, the Emmys quickly extended their reach by dropping the requirement that all shows must be made in Hollywood. Contenders did have to be aired over Los Angeles TV stations, but those shows suddenly included a host of new national talent thanks to the availability of kinescope programs out of New York, Chicago and elsewhere. A 40-year-old Milton Berle, who even then was called a "video veteran gagster" in one press account, won Most Outstanding Kinescope Personality. Pabst Blue Ribbon's "televersion" of *The Life of Riley* was named Best Film (over second-place winner *Lone Ranger*) and starred, not William Bendix, who was known for playing the role on radio and who later did so on the syndicated show, but Jackie Gleason. Gleason gave a powerful performance as Chester A. Riley and would have been a strong contender

Milton Berle, king of kinescope, as Queen Cleopatra on his comedy show.

to win an award himself, but it wasn't until Emmy's third year that acting categories were included in the lineup. As a result of this and other bad luck, winning an Emmy Award would elude

Gleason for a lifetime.

Prior to the early 1950s, microwave transmissions out of New York could reach only as far west as St. Louis. Kinescope was the method by which syndicated shows could be seen nationally. "What they did in New York was shoot the picture appearing on a TV tube with a 16 mm or 35 mm camera and then made a print and sent it out here to L.A. by air so we had it the next

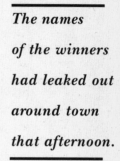

The names of the winners had leaked out around town that afternoon.

day," Cassyd recalls. "It was done all over the country the same way." The Best Kinescope Show of 1949 turned out to be Milton Berle's *Texaco Star Theater*, which edged out such tough competition as *The Goldbergs* and *Studio One* and was the third most-watched show in L.A. after wrestling and *Hopalong Cassidy*.

Ed Wynn's CBS program won Best Live Show and Wynn himself was named Most Outstanding Live Personality, the latter being an appropriate distinction since Wynn was among the live talent performing at the Emmy Awards dinner in the Embassy Room of the Ambassador Hotel that night of January 27, 1950. Wynn proved himself masterful as a comic entertainer, but a bad sport as a prize recipient. The names of the winners had leaked out around town that afternoon. "Even the pretense of the 'top secret' envelopes was shattered when Ed Wynn came to the floor to receive his Emmy," reported *Variety*. "Wynn came on gagging about having known he had won over five weeks ago, but later stated that he was only kidding. 'I just learned about it 20 minutes ago,' Wynn said. Wynn's slip, however, was the only one of the evening. Other award winners

Double winner Ed Wynn couldn't keep a secret at the 1949 awards ceremony.

played thesp to the end, emitting surprise and astonishment at being picked to receive the golden Emmy."

As of their second ceremony, the fledgling awards were quickly growing more sophisticated. *TV*, a trade publication, noted: "The affair was staged with all the kliegs and fanfare of a Hollywood premiere. The audience in attendance at the banquet was augmented by viewers at home who may have numbered close to a million. KFI-TV facilities and personnel were used to put the program on the air, with the six other Los Angeles stations sharing the expense of the two-hour telecast." Despite the fact that the Emmy show had no commercials, they still played a part in the evening ceremony when Lucky Strike was named the year's Best Commercial, a category that would never again be considered on a single-episode basis. "After the 1949 awards, we dropped the category," Cassyd says. "There were just too many commercials to be considered."

There were two people in the audience that night of particular significance to the bestowing of entertainment awards. One was Charles Brackett, president of the Academy of Motion Picture Arts and Sciences, who no doubt had more than just a passing interest in seeing how these new show-biz awards were going. The other was Lloyd Dunn, an ad agency executive who later went on to become a vice-president of Capitol Records. "Dunn saw how important an award could be in the entertainment industry," Cassyd says. "He then applied the idea to recorded music and became one of the principal people who started the Grammys."

1949

Awards presented on January 27, 1950, at the Ambassador Hotel in Los Angeles and broadcast on KFI-TV, Los Angeles.

BEST LIVE SHOW
• *The Ed Wynn Show*. KTTV (CBS).
Pantomime Quiz. KTTV (CBS).
Your Witness. KECA-TV (ABC).

OUTSTANDING LIVE PERSONALITY
• Ed Wynn. KTTV (CBS).
Tom Harmon. KFI-TV, KECA-TV (ABC), KTTV (CBS).
Mike Stokey. KTTV (CBS), KTLA.
Bill Welsh. KFI-TV, KTLA.

BEST KINESCOPE SHOW
• *Texaco Star Theater*. KNBH (NBC).
Fred Waring. KTTV (CBS).
The Goldbergs. KTTV (CBS).
Studio One. KTTV (CBS).

MOST OUTSTANDING KINESCOPE PERSONALITY
• Milton Berle. KNBH (NBC).
Fran Allison. KNBH (NBC).
Arthur Godfrey. KTTV (CBS).

BEST FILM MADE FOR & VIEWED ON TELEVISION
• *The Life of Riley*. KNBH (NBC).
Guiding Star. KTTV (CBS).
The Lone Ranger. KECA-TV (ABC).

Time Bomb. KNBH (NBC).
Vain Glory. KNBH (NBC).
Your Show Time. KNBH (NBC).

BEST CHILDREN'S SHOW
• *Time for Beany.* KTLA.
Cyclone Malone. KNBH (NBC).
Kukla, Fran & Ollie. KNBH (NBC).

BEST SPORTS COVERAGE
• *USC–UCLA Football.* KECA-TV
(ABC). (Press accounts designated as
winner.)
• *Wrestling.* KTLA. (Official A.T.A.S.
winner.)
Amateur Boxing. KTLA.
Baseball. KLAC.
College Basketball. KTTV (CBS).
Ice Hockey. KTLA.

**BEST PUBLIC SERVICE, CULTURAL, OR
EDUCATIONAL PROGRAM**
• *Crusade in Europe.* KECA-TV (ABC)
and KTTV (CBS).
Ford News & Weather. KNBH (NBC).
Kathy Fiscus Rescue. KTLA.
Man's Best Friend. KTLA.
Nuremberg Trials. KTSL.
Teleforum. KTLA.

TECHNICAL AWARD
• Harold W. Jury of KTSL, Los Angeles,
for the synchronizing coordinator device
that allows superimposition from different
locations.

BEST COMMERCIAL MADE FOR TELEVISION
• Lucky Strike. N.W. Ayer for American
Tobacco Co.

STATION ACHIEVEMENT
• KTLA, Los Angeles.
(Honorable mention to KECA-TV.)

Groucho Kidnaps Emmy!

As the awards grew in prestige during their early years, so did the number of them given out. By 1950, there were 15 prizes to bestow, with new categories added (*finally*, some said) for actors and such popular emerging programs as game shows. *Truth or Consequences* won the first Emmy ever given in the latter category.

In accepting the award for *Consequences*, show host Ralph Edwards set the mood of the 1950 ceremony, which took place on an unusually muggy January night, saying, "It's with great humidity that I accept this symbol of the

Groucho: Going for laughs, he grabbed the presenter instead of the statuette.

Academy of Television Arts and Scientists!" Such clowning and shenanigans prevailed all evening, and especially over the new best actor category in which veteran theatrical and screen talent Jose Ferrer was competing against Stan Freberg's voice as Cecil the Sea-Sick Sea Serpent, a character from the puppet show *Time for Beany*. "How silly can we get?!" cried one reporter. The answer was in the category's eventual

winner — Alan Young — and it wasn't funny at all. That a comedian won instead of an accomplished dramatic actor caused such an outcry that the award categories for acting had to be recast again the following year. In 1951 and 1952, separate awards would be given for actors and comedians.

But the night's funniest moment belonged to one of America's funniest men. The last award of the evening went to Groucho Marx, who accepted the honor as TV's Most Outstanding Personality in front of a sedate audience that included California Governor Earl Warren and L.A. Mayor Fletcher Bowron. Appearing to confuse the duo with a certain past New York governor (and later U.S. President) and a fictitious radio and TV character, Groucho said, feigning dementia, "Ladies and gentlemen, Governor Roosevelt and Mayor Aldrich, this is no surprise to me. I deserve it!" Next to him on stage were academy founder Syd Cassyd and Rosemary LaPlanche, a former Miss America who had also been named Miss Emmy for the occasion. Cassyd remembers, "When he accepted his Emmy, Groucho picked up Miss Emmy and carried her off the stage, leaving his golden statuette behind him on the table."

In the Emmys' first two years, local TV stations paid the cost of broadcasting the ceremonies, but by the awards' third year, the academy had to look for outside help. At least the lighthearted spirit of the 1950 awards was consistent with the show's first commercial underwriter. "I had to go out and have a dog food company be the sponsor," academy founder and that year's president Syd

Cassyd recalls. "Dr. Ross's Dog Food donated a thousand dollars so I could hire a station with three cameras and everything."

In between the dog food commercials came the rest of the awards, some for programming of such high artistic standards as *Pulitzer Prize Playhouse* (Best Dramatic Show); others for new categories like Best Variety Show, which was won by *The Alan Young Show*. *Time for Beany* once again beat out *Kukla, Fran & Ollie* in the competition for Best Children's Show, a prize the latter would finally win in 1953.

This year's chief controversy centered on the wins in the top acting cate-

Syd Cassyd (center) with Consequences' *Ralph Edwards (left) and "Dr. Ross" backer D.B. Lewis.*

gories. Best Actor Alan Young was a Canadian-born performer most remembered today for being the human foil to a talking horse on the popular *Mr. Ed* series. The acting he did on his 1950 program was for the most part equally frothy. Best Actress Gertrude Berg won for playing Molly in *The Goldbergs*, a comedy about a loud-mouthed Bronx family that Berg also wrote. Champions of dramatic acting bristled at comedic talent prevailing over such famous theatrical and film stars as Jose Ferrer, Judith Anderson, and Helen Hayes. But they had little to complain about, really. All three were relatively new to television. Anderson and Hayes were nomi-

nated for their TV debuts and both would go on to win Emmys in future years.

The night's biggest winner was Klaus Landsberg, manager of L.A. station KTLA, which took five awards — for station achievement, public service, special events, children's show, and news programming. Landsberg's own show *City at Night* won the public service award and was an ambitious piece of production work for its time.

"Klaus was a genius," Cassyd says. "Back then, cameras weren't as sensitive to darkness as they are today, but Klaus had his team filming all over Los Angeles at night — in the factories, people's homes, and public places like restaurants. He thought nothing, for instance, of flying a helicopter out on a story. *City at Night* was bold, beautiful documentary work."

Award eligibility rules continued to be controversial in 1950. A New York–based program could be nominated, but it had to air over a California TV station. *Hollywood Reporter* columnist Dan Jenkins cried: "That the Academy considers itself a national organization seems apparent in its recognition of two New York–originated shows among the winners. Yet while its left hand is proclaiming Mrs. Berg as the outstanding actress in all television, its right hand is arbitrarily limiting eligibility for the station achievement award to precisely 7 of the nation's 107 operating stations. Fish, flesh or fowl, gentlemen — what's it going to be?"

Syndicated writer Hal Humphrey also observed a preference for local winners and wrote in the *L.A. Mirror*, "Although the A.T.A.S. remains a little vague about its own policy, it does pretend to be national in scope. The fact that 13 of its

15 Emmy awards went to either local stations, personalities or shows revealed how provincial A.T.A.S. has become." Then Humphrey added, prophetically, "To ignore New York, the present center of video production, is simply leaving the door open for that city to set up its own trophy-awarding organization.

"A.T.A.S. would do well to limit itself to the local video scene — at least until the coast-to-coast TV network is completed."

That trans-American link was coming soon.

1950

Awards presented on January 23, 1951, at the Ambassador Hotel in Los Angeles and broadcast on KLAC-TV, Los Angeles.

BEST DRAMATIC SHOW
• *Pulitzer Prize Playhouse*. KECA-TV (ABC).
Fireside Theatre. KTLA.
I Remember Mama. KTTV (CBS).
Philco TV Playhouse. KNBH (NBC).
Studio One. KTTV (CBS).

BEST VARIETY SHOW
• *The Alan Young Show*. KTTV (CBS).
Four Star Revue. KNBH (NBC).
Ken Murray. KTTV (CBS).
Texaco Star Theater. KNBH (NBC).
Your Show of Shows. KNBH (NBC).

BEST CULTURAL SHOW
• *Campus Chorus and Orchestra*. KTSL.
Designed for Women. KNBH (NBC).
Sunset Service. KNBH (NBC).
Vienna Philharmonic. KTTV (CBS).
The Woman's Voice. KTTV (CBS).

BEST GAME AND AUDIENCE PARTICIPATION SHOW
• *Truth or Consequences*. KTTV (CBS).
Kay Kyser's Kollege of Musical Knowledge. KNBH (NBC).
Life With Linkletter. KECA-TV (ABC).
Pantomime Quiz. KTTV (CBS).
You Bet Your Life. KNBH (NBC).

BEST CHILDREN'S SHOW
• *Time for Beany*. KTLA.
Cisco Kid. KNBH (NBC).
Jump Jump. KTTV (CBS).
Kukla, Fran & Ollie. KNBH (NBC).
The Lone Ranger. KTLA.

Daredevil producer Klaus Landsberg of KTLA dominated the early awards.

BEST SPORTS PROGRAM
• *Rams Football*. KNBH (NBC).
College Basketball Games. KTTV (CBS).
College Football Games. KTTV (CBS).
Hollywood Baseball. KLAC.
Los Angeles Baseball. KFI-TV.

BEST NEWS PROGRAM
• *KTLA Newsreel*. KTLA.
Clete Roberts. KLAC.
Fleetwood Lawton. KTSL.
Ford News and Weather. KNBH (NBC).

BEST EDUCATIONAL SHOW
• *KFI-TV University*. KFI-TV.
Kieran's Kaleidoscope. KECA-TV (ABC).
Know Your Schools. KFI-TV.
Magazine of the Week. KTLA.
Zoo Parade. KNBH (NBC).

SPECIAL EVENTS
• *Departure of Marines for Korea.*
KFMB-TV, San Diego, and KTLA.
Arrival of Cruiser from Korea. KTLA.
Commissioning of Hospital Ship Haven.
Election Coverage. KECA-TV.
Tournament of Roses. KECA-TV (ABC).

BEST PUBLIC SERVICE
• *City at Night.* KTLA.
Classified Column. KTTV (CBS).
Community Chest Kickoff.
In Our Time. KTTV (CBS).
Marshall Plan. KECA-TV (ABC).
Teleforum. KTLA.

MOST OUTSTANDING PERSONALITY
• Groucho Marx. KNBH (NBC).
Sid Caesar. KNBH (NBC).
Faye Emerson. KTTV (CBS) and KECA-TV (ABC).
Dick Lane. KTLA.
Alan Young. KTTV (CBS).

BEST ACTOR
• Alan Young. KTTV (CBS).
Sid Caesar. KNBH (NBC).
Jose Ferrer.
Stan Freberg (as voice of Cecil the Sea-Sick Sea Serpent). KTLA.
Charles Ruggles. KECA-TV.

BEST ACTRESS
• Gertrude Berg. KTTV (CBS).
Judith Anderson.
Imogene Coca. KNBH (NBC).
Helen Hayes. KECA-TV (ABC).
Betty White. KLAC.

STATION ACHIEVEMENT
• KTLA.

TECHNICAL ACHIEVEMENT
• Orthogram TV Amplifier by KNBH (NBC).

NBC: "Nothing But Citations"

In mid-1951, *Variety* ran the grabber headline "Tele Academy Liberalizes System of Picking Emmys." The accompanying article began: "After the beating the Academy took in the press and from the industry over its selections last year, a committee was set up to develop an awards system national in its scope .... The committee agreed to mail ballots to TV editors in all TV markets and let the press make the nominations." As in the past, winners would be decided by the vote of academy members.

Suddenly, it was no longer a contest determining how many awards were won by local stations (specifically by KTLA and manager Klaus Landsberg, who dominated the early years). Now what mattered most was how the networks — based in New York — fared instead. NBC was clearly the big winner of 1951, taking five out of the six major categories. The network's sweep was so devastating, in fact, that comedian Red Skelton even told the audience of 700 gathered at the Cocoanut Grove in the Ambassador Hotel that NBC's call letters really stood for "Nothing But Citations."

Skelton himself was voted Best Comedian while his series was named best comedy show. *The Hollywood Reporter* noted, "This fourth dinner was marked by something that had been lacking in the past. Call it heart for lack of a better word." The reason was one of Skelton's acceptance speeches.

"There was hardly a dry eye in the house," observed the *Reporter* when Skelton accepted the comedian's Emmy from presenter Zsa Zsa Gabor and told the audience in a quiet, humble voice, "I think this should have gone to Lucille

Best Comedian Red Skelton: "I think this should have gone to Lucille Ball."

A.T.A.S.

Ball." Ball was the ceremony's hostess that night, along with cohost (and costar and husband) Desi Arnaz, but neither of them was to take home an Emmy until the following year. Skelton's win should not have seemed like such a misplaced honor, though. In 1951, *I Love Lucy* was still in its first year on TV and while it lost to a program that was also in its premiere TV season, *The Red Skelton Show* and its host had been big on radio since 1941. Lucy had made 67 films while at MGM, but she'd never distinguished herself as a superstar prior to her TV show.

The other NBC awards were all for *Your Show of Shows*, which took Best Variety Show and also elevated Sid Caesar and Imogene Coca to status of Best Actor and Actress soon after they each, like Lucy, lost the comedian's crown to Skelton. But the stars hardly needed the lift. *The Washington Post* TV critic Tom Shales once described *Your Show of*

Shows, from the vantage point of the sit-com-reigning 1980s, as "a weekly comedy classic which made Caesar and Coca at least as famous in their time as Caesar and Cleopatra were in theirs."

Neither Caesar nor Coca could attend the dinner, but they were waiting anxiously by their phones in New York for the academy to call in case they won. Presenter Ed Wynn had a devil of a time reaching Coca at first because of trouble he was having with the long-distance operator. Exasperated, the show biz legend tried to impress the operator by identifying himself. It didn't work. Finally, he blurted out, "Ed Wynn, you know — Keenan's father!"

Wynn's call to Caesar went a lot more smoothly. Once linked with the awards group via the phone line, Caesar acknowledged the tribute by saying that the award was actually his second in two days. Winning an Emmy followed by one day the addition to his family of a newborn son named Richard. Ironically, the episode of *Your Show of Shows* that was viewed by voters to determine that category's winner showed Caesar as a crazed father-to-be in a maternity ward waiting room.

The one non-NBC show to win a top award was CBS's *Studio One*, the classic dramatic anthology series that was presenting one-hour dramas such as *Of Human Bondage*, starring Charlton Heston, and *The Storm* with Margaret Sullavan. *Studio One* was hailed as the year's Best Dramatic Show.

Senator Estes Kefauver was honored for the Watergate-style broadcast of his U.S. Senate probe into organized crime. Unable to attend the Emmys ceremony in person, Kefauver had the trophy accepted on his behalf by two friends who happened to live in Los Angeles: Ellie Arnold, the daughter of political columnist Drew Pearson, and her husband George, son of F.D.R.'s "trust-buster" Thurman Arnold. When he was declared a winner, Kefauver was up in New Hampshire campaigning for the 1952 presidential nomination and was not near a telephone, but he was still able to address the Los Angeles audience when the state police hooked him up to a phone line via their wireless.

In September, 1951, AT&T took the credit for linking the east and west coasts with a microwave relay system so that television could finally be viewed nationwide, but the company lost the Special Achievement Award to Kefauver, whose

Best Actor Caesar and Best Actress Coca in 1951's Best Variety Program.

crusade against the Mafia must have seemed more immediately compelling to academy voters. Nonetheless, as a result of this and other pioneering efforts, television was fast becoming a national force, just as the Emmy Awards were, as they strove to keep pace.

Some academy members were outraged by Emmy becoming a truly national award. As the 1951 Emmys evening was about to begin, *The Los Angeles Times* reported, "One discord mars tonight's celebrations. Last week managers of five of the seven local television stations ... announced they are withdrawing their support from the

Academy because they felt the organization no longer is primarily concerned with the progress of television in Hollywood as distinguished from other areas."

In a bizarre twist, the same article noted, however, that one of the mutinying stations, ABC-affiliate KECA-TV, would nonetheless "carry the award ceremonies from 9 to 10 p.m. tonight as a public service."

1951

Awards presented on February 18, 1952, at the Cocoanut Grove in Los Angeles and broadcast on KECA-TV (ABC), Los Angeles.

BEST DRAMATIC SHOW
• *Studio One*. CBS.
Celanese Theatre. ABC.
Philco-Goodyear TV Playhouse. NBC.
Pulitzer Prize Playhouse. ABC.
Robert Montgomery Presents. NBC.

BEST VARIETY SHOW
• *Your Show of Shows*. NBC.
All Star Revue. NBC.
Comedy Hour. NBC.
The Fred Waring Show. CBS.
Toast of the Town. CBS.

BEST COMEDY SHOW
• *Red Skelton Show*. NBC.
The George Burns and Gracie Allen Show. CBS.
The Herb Shriner Show. ABC.
I Love Lucy. CBS.
You Bet Your Life. NBC.

BEST ACTOR
• Sid Caesar.
Walter Hampden.

Charlton Heston.
Robert Montgomery.
Thomas Mitchell.
Vaughn Taylor.

BEST ACTRESS
• Imogene Coca.
Helen Hayes.
Maria Riva.
Mary Sinclair.
Margaret Sullavan.

BEST COMEDIAN OR COMEDIENNE
• Red Skelton. NBC.
Lucille Ball. CBS.
Sid Caesar. NBC.
Imogene Coca. NBC.
Jimmy Durante. NBC.
Dean Martin and Jerry Lewis. NBC.
Herb Shriner. ABC.

SPECIAL ACHIEVEMENT AWARDS
• U.S. Senator Estes Kefauver for his outstanding public service on television.
American Telephone and Telegraph Company for the transcontinental Microwave Relay System.
Jack Burrell of station KNBH, Los Angeles, for the development of an independent transmission mobile unit.

A.T.A.S.

The most festive and elegant early ceremonies were held at the Cocoanut Grove.

Everybody Loves Lucy

"Gee, Desi, we got it!" Lucille Ball roared with delight to husband and costar Desi Arnaz as she clutched their first Emmy Award up on stage. The duo had been disappointed the year before when they lost to Red Skelton, but now they had two trophies in hand — one for their number-one-rated sitcom, which was then pulling an amazing 67.3% audience share (and which would stay numbber one for three more seasons) and one just for the carrot-topped clown herself for being officially designated America's favorite comedienne.

The dinner ceremony marked the first time that Lucy had left home for any social function since the birth of little Desi just two weeks before. Now she was exasperated and confessed to the audience of 1,500 people gathered in the Pacific Ballroom of the new Hotel Statler in L.A., "I'm a nervous wreck!"

She was also favored to win in the category of Most Outstanding Personality, but lost to someone with considerably more clout — Bishop Fulton J. Sheen. Sheen's ABC show *Life is Worth Living* (later renamed *The Bishop Sheen Program*) was surprisingly simple and no-frills. On the air, he worked with a blackboard behind him and addressed home audiences like a high cardinal condescending to teach a parochial school class. But despite its stark quality and lofty tone, the show prospered and even survived heavy competition, such as Milton Berle's

After I Love Lucy *lost last year, Best Comedienne Lucille Ball finally saw it voted top comedy show.*

Texaco Star Theater (Berle used to quip: "We both work for the same boss — Sky Chief!") because of Sheen's powerful personal style. "He was a great actor," says academy founder Syd Cassyd, remembering him. "All great priests, great rabbis, great ministers are great actors, and he was one of the best."

Other winning shows that night included at least one "sure thing," according to the *L.A. Mirror* — *Dragnet*. Its director and star, Jack Webb (who played Sergeant Joe Friday), was on hand to take home the award for the newly minted category Best Mystery, Action, or Adventure Program. The Best Public Affairs Program was *See It Now*, the CBS world news show hosted by Edward R. Murrow. Puppet program *Time for Beany* took Best Children's Show for the third time in four years.

For the second year in a row *Your*

Show of Shows won the Emmy for Best Variety Show — the last Emmy it would win. During the four years of the program's reign (1950–54), it was one of the most popular shows ever, incorporating the silly vaudevillian slapstick of yesteryear with the daring and imaginative comedy of the future. When the program folded in 1954, Coca left to star in her own variety series, while stalwarts Carl Reiner and Howard Morris followed their Caesar onto *Caesar's Hour*. The entire gang would not get back together again until 1967 — for a CBS special that would win the Emmy for Outstanding Variety Special.

Among the individual performers honored for 1952 were "the versatile Thomas Mitchell," said United Press, "who played a variety of roles on several networks and was selected as best actor of the year." Best Actress Helen Hayes had previously won an Oscar for her lead role in *The Sin of Madelon Claudet* and so now became the first performer in entertainment history to win awards from both the television and motion picture academies. She was not on hand to accept the prize, however, since she was acting that night in a play on Broadway called *Mrs. McThing*. Jimmy Durante wasn't present either. Emmy's Best Comedian was busy performing in a Miami nightclub.

"I'm a nervous wreck!" Lucy told the crowd.

The 1952 awards marked a major turnaround for Academy of Television Arts and Sciences. Before that evening's ceremony, the problem of how to mend divisions within the academy seemed overwhelming. Hollywood wanted its awards to keep their strong L.A. emphasis while New York and the rest of the U.S. wanted America's television awards to become truly national in scope. In an effort to accommodate the latter's wish, the academy seemed to be losing its L.A. base. "By 1952," remembers Syd Cassyd, "membership went down to 92." An academy letter pleaded to past members: "Those of you who resigned or did not renew your memberships because of the handling of certain affairs are urged to rejoin as the new board is correcting all these former actions." Few responded.

A fair solution seemed to be to honor local shows and talent separately. It wasn't the first time it was done. When San Francisco members of the TV industry formed an affiliated academy chapter a few years earlier, the group bestowed silver Emmys to local winners. That chapter no longer existed by 1952, but the precedent of giving local champs their own awards had been set and the idea suddenly worked well as a solution to the new problem in Los Angles. And these new L.A. winners wouldn't be given silver awards. Local honorees such as Liberace and Betty White took home the same 14-karat versions of Emmy that the national winners did.

The plan worked. The 1952 awards ceremony was such a success that membership soon boomed again to more than 500. The evening also gave, according to one local press account, the "definite indication that the Academy of Television Arts and Sciences is a healthy adolescent, bound to be with us for some time."

The academy would be needed, too. The same day that the Emmy winners were announced, a small article appeared on the front page of *The Hollywood Reporter* with the following headline: "21,234,100 TV Sets in Homes as of Jan. 1." The number represented a whopping 5 percent increase over the number of sets in America just 30 days earlier. Television — and the Emmys — were taking off together.

Presented on February 5, 1953, at the Statler Hotel in Los Angeles and broadcast on KLAC-TV, Los Angeles.

BEST DRAMATIC PROGRAM
• *Robert Montgomery Presents*. NBC.
Celanese Theatre. ABC.
Kraft Television Theatre. NBC.
Philco-Goodyear TV Playhouse. NBC.
Studio One. CBS.

BEST SITUATION COMEDY
• *I Love Lucy*. CBS.
Amos 'n' Andy. CBS.
The George Burns and Gracie Allen Show. CBS.
Mr. Peepers. NBC.
Our Miss Brooks. CBS.
The Adventures of Ozzie & Harriet. ABC.

BEST MYSTERY, ACTION OR ADVENTURE PROGRAM
• *Dragnet*. NBC.
Big Story. NBC.
Foreign Intrigue. Syndicated.
Martin Kane, Private Eye. NBC.
Racket Squad. CBS.

BEST VARIETY PROGRAM
• *Your Show of Shows*. NBC.
Arthur Godfrey and His Friends. CBS.
Colgate Comedy Hour. NBC.
The Jackie Gleason Show. CBS.
Toast of the Town. CBS.

BEST PUBLIC AFFAIRS PROGRAM
• *See It Now*. CBS.
Life Is Worth Living. Du Mont.
Camel News Caravan. NBC.
Meet the Press. NBC.
Victory at Sea. NBC.

BEST CHILDREN'S PROGRAM
• *Time for Beany*. KTLA.
Big Top. CBS.
Gabby Hayes.
Howdy Doody. NBC.
Kukla, Fran & Ollie. NBC.
Super Circus. NBC.
Zoo Parade. NBC.

BEST AUDIENCE PARTICIPATION, QUIZ, OR PANEL PROGRAM
• *What's My Line?* CBS.
Down You Go. Du Mont.
This Is Your Life. NBC.
Two for the Money. NBC.
You Bet Your Life. NBC.

BEST ACTOR
• Thomas Mitchell.
John Forsythe.
Charlton Heston.
John Newland.
Vaughn Taylor.
Jack Webb.

BEST ACTRESS
• Helen Hayes.
Sarah Churchill.
June Lockhart.
Maria Riva.
Peggy Wood.

BEST COMEDIAN
• Jimmy Durante. NBC.
Sid Caesar. NBC.
Wally Cox. NBC.
Jackie Gleason. CBS.
Herb Shriner. ABC.

BEST COMEDIENNE
• Lucille Ball. CBS.
Eve Arden. CBS.
Imogene Coca. NBC.
Joan Davis. NBC.
Martha Raye. NBC.

MOST OUTSTANDING PERSONALITY
• Bishop Fulton J. Sheen. Du Mont.
Lucille Ball. CBS.
Arthur Godfrey. CBS.
Jimmy Durante. NBC.
Edward R. Murrow. CBS.
Donald O'Connor. NBC.
Adlai Stevenson. NBC.

Make Room for Danny
... and Lucy (Again)

Considering that America's top TV newspaper editors were again choosing the Emmy nominees, it's surprising how poorly some of them did at predicting the eventual winners. Offering his forecasts in *The San Diego Union*, columnist Donald Freeman was wrong 10 out of 14 times, adding, "Last year *I Love Lucy* and *Dragnet* — and their respective stars, Lucille Ball and Jack Webb — swept the field. The odds are against a repeat performance."

But *I Love Lucy* and *Dragnet* did come back. *Lucy* was still the highest-rated show in the country and took Best Situation Comedy, while the L.A. detective show *Dragnet* triumphed again easily in its own category.

Other returning winners from last year also included *See It Now*, Edward R. Murrow's crusading telejournalism program that was then taking on Senator Joseph McCarthy's red hunt. *See It Now*'s most controversial 1953 episode — and the most likely reason the show won its second Emmy — was called "The Case Against Milo Radulovich A0589539" and told the story of a University of Michigan student asked to resign his post as an Air Force Reserve lieutenant because his father and sister were suspected of communist sympathies. On the program, Radulovich asked poignantly, "If I am going to be judged by my relatives, are my children going to be asked to denounce me? I see a chain reaction that has no end." After the show aired, U.S. Air Force Secretary Harold Talbott halted the probe, saying that Radulovich was not a security risk and would be "retained in his present status." McCarthy cried foul and

Danny Thomas: Proud "Daddy" of the Best New Program of the year.

denounced Murrow as "the leader and the cleverest of the jackal pack which is always found at the throat of anyone who dares to expose individual communists and traitors."

Murrow was also named Most Outstanding Personality, beating out Bishop Fulton Sheen, who had topped him the previous year in the same category.

A fourth show that reprised its victorious status in 1953 was *What's My Line?*, which began on TV in 1950 with the unusual but popular format of a blindfolded panel of New York's glibbest glitterati trying to guess the one thing they know least about: what work people did for a living. It tied with *This is Your Life*, NBC's live surprise biography show, to make the second tie at the Hollywood Palladium awards ceremony that night.

The first tie involved the Best New Program category, itself new. Winner *Make Room for Daddy* was an instant hit when it was launched in September, and was one of the first shows depicting an "average" American family coping with "average" problems. The show's extraordinary difference was that Daddy was a nightclub performer. In real life, Thomas was home so seldom that, when he did drop by, his kids' bedrooms got shuffled around to make room for him, thus giving the show its name.

Co-winner *U.S. Steel Hour* was an admirable effort to bring Broadway-caliber drama to the home screen, including *Hedda Gabler* starring Tallulah Bankhead, and *No Time for Sergeants* with Andy Griffith.

The Best Actor and Actress categories of 1952 became Best Male/Female Star of a Regular Series in 1953. Ex-vaudevillian and veteran film actor Donald O'Connor won his one career Emmy for being the periodic host of *The Colgate Comedy Hour.* Eve Arden won her single Emmy for the role she created on CBS radio in 1948, then on television as *Our Miss Brooks* — the hip, flip English teacher of Madison High School.

This was the first year that actors were acknowledged in supporting-role categories. Art Carney won the first of the five Emmys he'd win for his portrayal of Ed Norton on *The Jackie Gleason Show* and *The Honeymooners*, and Vivian Vance won the only Emmy of her career for playing Ethel Mertz on *I Love Lucy*, a role that rewarded her well over a lifetime. She was fond of saying as she got older, "Look how rich I got making a fool of myself!"

Kukla, Fran & Ollie finally won its bid for best children's show after losing out three times before. Other winners included Best Public Affairs Program *Victory at Sea*, the 26-part World War II documentary narrated by Leonard Graves and scored triumphantly by Richard Rodgers. Best Variety Program *Omnibus* was an eclectic hodgepodge of drama, music, documentary, and even ballet segments that were made exciting by such name stars as Orson Welles playing King Lear and Victor Borge playing the piano.

For the first and only time in the academy's history, the awards presentation was not telecast. Los Angeles tele-

CBS program chief Harry Ackerman (left) with the Best Situation Comedy gang: Lucille Ball, Desi Arnaz, and Best Supporting Actress Vivian Vance.

vision stations were no longer eager to pick up the increasingly high cost of broadcasting the ceremony. Meantime, however, as local interest in showing the festivities declined, national interest was peaking. In late 1954, academy president Don DeFore would sign an agreement with NBC that would not only put the Emmys back on the air, it would beam them across the country — simultaneously from both coasts.

Awards presented on February 11, 1954, at the Hollywood Palladium. No telecast.

BEST NEW PROGRAM
• *Make Room for Daddy*. ABC.
• *U.S. Steel Hour*. ABC.
Adventure. CBS.
Ding Dong School. NBC.
A Letter to Loretta. NBC.
Person to Person. CBS.

BEST DRAMATIC PROGRAM
• *U.S. Steel Hour*. ABC.
Kraft Television Theatre. NBC.
Philco-Goodyear TV Playhouse. NBC.
Robert Montgomery Presents. NBC.
Studio One. CBS.

BEST SITUATION COMEDY
• *I Love Lucy*. CBS.
The George Burns and Gracie Allen Show. CBS.
Mr. Peepers. NBC.
Our Miss Brooks. CBS.
Topper. CBS.

BEST MYSTERY, ACTION OR ADVENTURE PROGRAM
• *Dragnet*. NBC.
Foreign Intrigue. Syndicated.
I Led Three Lives. Syndicated.
Suspense. CBS.
The Web. CBS.

BEST VARIETY PROGRAM
• *Omnibus*. CBS.
Colgate Comedy Hour. NBC.
The Jackie Gleason Show. CBS.
Your Show of Shows. NBC.
Toast of the Town. CBS.

BEST PROGRAM OF NEWS OR SPORTS
• *See It Now*. CBS.
Camel News Caravan. NBC.
Gillette Calvacade of Sports. NBC.
NCAA Football Games. NBC.
Pabst Blue Ribbon Bouts. CBS.
Professional Football. Du Mont.

BEST PUBLIC AFFAIRS PROGRAM
• *Victory at Sea*. NBC.
Adventure. CBS.
Life is Worth Living. Syndicated.
Meet the Press. NBC.
Person to Person. CBS.

BEST AUDIENCE PARTICIPATION, QUIZ, OR PANEL PROGRAM
• *This is Your Life*. NBC.
• *What's My Line?* CBS.
Adventure. CBS.
I've Got a Secret. CBS.
Two for the Money. CBS.
You Bet Your Life. NBC.

BEST CHILDREN'S PROGRAM
• *Kukla, Fran & Ollie*. NBC.
Big Top. CBS.
Ding Dong School. NBC.
Super Circus. NBC.
Zoo Parade. NBC.

MOST OUTSTANDING PERSONALITY
• Edward R. Murrow. CBS.
Arthur Godfrey. NBC.
Martha Raye. NBC.
Bishop Fulton J. Sheen. Syndicated.
Jack Webb. NBC.

BEST MALE STAR, REGULAR SERIES
• Donald O'Connor, *Colgate Comedy Hour*. NBC.
Sid Caesar, *Your Show of Shows*. NBC.
Wally Cox, *Mr. Peepers*. NBC.
Jackie Gleason, *The Jackie Gleason Show*. CBS.
Jack Webb, *Dragnet*. NBC.

BEST FEMALE STAR, REGULAR SERIES
• Eve Arden, *Our Miss Brooks*. CBS.
Lucille Ball, *I Love Lucy*. CBS.
Imogene Coca, *Your Show of Shows*. NBC.
Dinah Shore, *The Dinah Shore Show*. NBC.
Loretta Young, *Letter to Loretta*. NBC.

BEST SERIES SUPPORTING ACTOR
• Art Carney, *The Jackie Gleason Show*. CBS.
Ben Alexander, *Dragnet*. NBC.
William Frawley, *I Love Lucy*. CBS.
Tony Randall, *Mr. Peepers*. NBC.
Carl Reiner, *Your Show of Shows*. NBC.

BEST SERIES SUPPORTING ACTRESS
• Vivian Vance, *I Love Lucy*. CBS.
Bea Benedaret, *The George Burns and Gracie Allen Show*. CBS.
Ruth Gilbert, *Texaco Star Theater*. NBC.
Marion Lorne, *Mr. Peepers*. NBC.
Audrey Meadows, *The Jackie Gleason Show*. CBS.

West Meets East

When the Emmys were first bestowed in 1949 for the 1948 awards, there were only a million TV sets in America. Six years later, on the night of the Emmy's first national broadcast, there were 25 million sets. And the show was seen by at least that number of viewers.

The program was also historic in another way: it was simultaneously broadcast across the country from the Moulin Rouge nightclub in L.A. and Nino's LaRue restaurant in New York City, thus reflecting what had finally taken place off camera. The New York television industry was at last working officially with the academy in California.

Past Emmy winner Edward R. Murrow (left) with his trademark cigarette.

With one exception. Since 1950, Ed Sullivan had been competing against the Emmys with his own set of New York-based TV awards called the Michaels. The threat he posed was serious: In the mid-1950s, Sullivan was a powerful Broadway newspaper columnist who also had his own hit TV program. But his Michael Awards never quite caught on and by 1955, soon after the Emmys were broadcast on national television for the first time, Sullivan switched tactics and went after the Academy of Television Arts and Sciences to try to break its strong Los Angeles hold.

"The Sullivan coup took over the academy in 1955," founder Syd Cassyd recalls. Early that year, Sullivan called together a group of key television and A.T.A.S. leaders at Toots Shor's, a famous New York restaurant. In attendance that day were producer Walt Disney, future academy president Johnny Mercer, and current president Don DeFore. Sullivan reportedly ranted and raved, then finally got what he'd want-

ed: his own new, New York chapter, which would have equal status with the Los Angeles one.

The L.A. host of the twin Emmy ceremonies was Steve Allen, who told the 1,000 people gathered that he'd "decided to get laughs, but would settle for respect." When the audience responded with hearty cackling, he said he'd "go back to trying to get laughs." Dave Garroway hosted the New York show, which was far more sedate.

NBC paid $110,000 for the transcontinental hookup and ended up tying CBS for most wins. Its biggest champs included *Dragnet*, which prevailed for the third year in a row; *This is Your Life*, which won this time without tying in its category; and George Gobel for the Most Outstanding New Personality. "Lonesome George's" program writers were also honored — with one of the first two awards ever given to TV scribblers.

Veteran scriptwriter Reginald Rose took the other Emmy for writers, for *Twelve Angry Men*, which was shown on

Studio One. The show also won acknowledgment for a director for the first time (Franklin Schaffner) and gave Robert Cummings an Emmy for Best Actor in a Single Performance. The good news came with some bad: Cummings had wagered $100 that he'd lose. After paying up and after toiling one more year in Hollywood, a most happy Cummings would have his own hit comedy show as a result of his sudden TV ascendancy.

Angry Men lost out, however, for the new honor of Best Individual Program of the Year, which went to an episode of *Disneyland*, also winner of Best Variety Series. The one-hour show was the start of the longest-running prime-time network series in TV history and was the first program produced by a major Hollywood film studio since most of them were still leary of the new airwave medium. But the later-renamed *Walt Disney's Wonderful World of Color* was a quick success made up of cartoon, documentary, and adventure or nature segments and introduced such future spin-offs as *Davy Crockett*.

Other notable winners: Danny Thomas harvested trophies for himself and his show; *Omnibus* reprised its 1953 win; Gillette struck a championship blow for boxing on its *Cavalcade of Sports*; and Judith Anderson won her first Emmy for portraying Lady Macbeth on *Hallmark Hall of Fame*. She would win again for the same role when *Hallmark* remade *Macbeth* in 1960-61.

Three performers who would win big in future years won their first awards this time around. Dinah Shore won initially for her twice-weekly, 15-minute music show that filled in the last half of the NBC evening news broadcast. She would go on to win seven more, distinguishing herself as the all-time Emmy champ among performers and actors. Perry Como also won for his singing abilities and would take home three more in his career. A most

fashionable Loretta Young won her first of three for the show that took her full name this year, after previously being called *A Letter to Loretta*.

All-time Emmy loser Jackie Gleason had been a favorite to win in 1954, but neither he nor another "shoo-in," Jack Webb, took any trophies home. Their shows did win three Emmys each, though. Gleason's costar Art Carney won in the supporting actor's category for a second time and Audrey Meadows won, for the first and only time, in the female supporting race. Gleason's head hoofer June Taylor took the new prize for choreography. *Dragnet* took sound editing and original music honors, in addition to Best

Judith Anderson with her first Macbeth *Emmy. She repeated the win in 1961.*

Mystery or Intrigue Series.

An occasional technical award had been bestowed in the past, but 1954 was the first year that the academy gave away a full range of prizes in science-related fields, recognizing film and sound editing, art direction, and technical and engineering achievements. The nomination procedure also changed. Consideration for programs and personalities was now determined exclusively by the full A.T.A.S. membership. In the

*Emmy's most honored performer: Dinah
Shore with her first of eight awards.*

more technical categories, each of the
professional groups chose the contenders from their own disciplines.

But how did the awards reflect the
preferences of the new Emmy-watchers
at home? *I Love Lucy, Gleason,
Dragnet, Disneyland,* and *Gobel* were
all among the 10 most-watched shows at
the end of 1954. *Lucy* was still number
one and was up for five prizes, but surprisingly it ended up with scratch. Shortly after the awards, Philip Morris withdrew as the show's sponsor and Lucille
Ball was livid.

"It was a bitter loss for Lucy," academy founder Syd Cassyd recalls. "For a
while she was very angry with the academy and claimed that, because of us, the
show was almost pulled off the air."

1954

Awards presented March 7, 1955, at the
Moulin Rouge in Hollywood and Nino's
LaRue in New York. The first Emmy's
show to be broadcast coast to coast was
shown on NBC.

BEST INDIVIDUAL PROGRAM OF THE YEAR
• "Operation Undersea," *Disneyland.*
ABC.
Diamond Jubilee of Light. Four networks.
"White is the Color," *Medic.* NBC.
"A Christmas Carol," *Shower of Stars.*
CBS.
Twelve Angry Men, Studio One. CBS.

BEST DRAMATIC SERIES
• *U.S. Steel Hour.* ABC.
Four Star Playhouse. CBS.
Medic. NBC.
Philco TV Playhouse. NBC.
Studio One. CBS.

BEST SITUATION COMEDY SERIES
• *Make Room for Daddy.* ABC.
The George Burns and Gracie Allen Show.
CBS.
I Love Lucy. CBS.
Mr. Peepers. NBC.
Our Miss Brooks. CBS.
Private Secretary. CBS.

BEST MYSTERY OR INTRIGUE SERIES
• *Dragnet.* NBC.
Foreign Intrigue. Syndicated.
I Led Three Lives. Syndicated.
Racket Squad. Syndicated.
Waterfront. Syndicated.

BEST WESTERN OR ADVENTURE SERIES
• *Stories of the Century.* Syndicated.
Annie Oakley. Syndicated.
Death Valley Days. CBS.
The Roy Rogers Show. NBC.
The Adventures of Wild Bill Hickok. Syndicated.

BEST CULTURAL, RELIGIOUS,
OR EDUCATIONAL PROGRAM
• *Omnibus.* CBS.
Life is Worth Living. Du Mont.
Meet the Press. NBC.
Person to Person. CBS.
See It Now. CBS.

BEST VARIETY SERIES,
INCLUDING MUSICAL VARIETIES
• *Disneyland.* ABC.
The George Gobel Show. NBC.
The Jack Benny Show. CBS.
The Jackie Gleason Show. CBS.
Toast of the Town. CBS.
Your Hit Parade. NBC.

BEST DAYTIME PROGRAM
• *Art Linkletter's House Party*. CBS.
The Betty White Show. NBC.
The Bob Crosby Show. CBS.
The Garry Moore Show. CBS.
Robert Q. Lewis. CBS.

BEST AUDIENCE, GUEST PARTICIPATION OR PANEL PROGRAM
• *This is Your Life*. NBC.
Masquerade Party. ABC.
People Are Funny. NBC.
What's My Line? CBS.
You Bet Your Life. NBC.

BEST CHILDREN'S PROGRAM
• *Lassie*. CBS.
Art Linkletter and the Kids. Syndicated.
Ding Dong School. NBC.
Kukla, Fran & Ollie. ABC.
Time for Beany. Syndicated.
Zoo Parade. NBC.

BEST SPORTS PROGRAM
• *Gillette Cavalcade of Sports*. NBC.
Pabst Blue Ribbon Bouts. CBS.
Forest Hills Tennis Matches. NBC.
Greatest Moments in Sports. NBC.
NCAA Football. ABC.
Professional Football. Du Mont.

BEST ACTOR STARRING IN A REGULAR SERIES
• Danny Thomas, *Make Room for Daddy*. ABC.
Richard Boone, *Medic*. NBC.
Robert Cummings, *My Hero*. Syndicated.
Jackie Gleason, *The Jackie Gleason Show*. CBS.
Jack Webb, *Dragnet*. NBC.

BEST ACTRESS STARRING IN A REGULAR SERIES
• Loretta Young, *The Loretta Young Show*. NBC.
Eve Arden, *Our Miss Brooks*. CBS.
Gracie Allen, *The George Burns and Gracie Allen Show*. CBS.
Lucille Ball, *I Love Lucy*. CBS.
Ann Sothern, *Private Secretary*. CBS.

BEST SUPPORTING ACTOR IN A REGULAR SERIES
• Art Carney, *The Jackie Gleason Show*. CBS.
Ben Alexander, *Dragnet*. NBC.
Don DeFore, *The Adventures of Ozzie and Harriet*. ABC.
William Frawley, *I Love Lucy*. CBS.
Gale Gordon, *Our Miss Brooks*. CBS.

BEST SUPPORTING ACTRESS IN A REGULAR SERIES
• Audrey Meadows, *The Jackie Gleason Show*. CBS.
Bea Benaderet, *The George Burns and Gracie Allen Show*. CBS.
Jean Hagen, *Make Room for Daddy*. ABC.
Marion Lorne, *Mr. Peepers*. NBC.
Vivian Vance, *I Love Lucy*. CBS.

BEST ACTOR IN A SINGLE PERFORMANCE
• Robert Cummings, *Twelve Angry Men*, *Studio One*. CBS.
Frank Lovejoy, *Double Indemnity*, *Lux Video Theatre*. CBS.
Fredric March, "A Christmas Carol," *Shower of Stars*. CBS.
Fredric March, *Royal Family*, *Best of Broadway*. CBS.
Thomas Mitchell, *Good of His Soul*, *Ford Theatre*. NBC.
David Niven, *The Answer*, *Four Star Playhouse*. CBS.

BEST ACTRESS IN A SINGLE PERFORMANCE
• Judith Anderson, *Macbeth*, *Hallmark Hall of Fame*. NBC.
Ethel Barrymore, "The 13th Chair," *Climax*. CBS.
Beverly Garland, "White Is the Color," *Medic*. NBC.
Ruth Hussey, "Craig's Wife," *Lux Video Theatre*. NBC.
Dorothy McGuire, "The Giaconda Smile," *Climax*. CBS.
Eva Marie Saint, "Middle of the Night," *Philco TV Playhouse*. NBC.
Claire Trevor, "Ladies in Retirement," *Lux Video Theatre*. NBC.

BEST MALE SINGER
• Perry Como. CBS.
Eddie Fisher. NBC.
Frankie Laine. Syndicated.
Tony Martin. NBC.
Gordon MacRae. NBC.

Best Female Singer
• Dinah Shore. NBC.
Jane Froman. CBS.
Peggy King. NBC.
Gisele Mackenzie. NBC.
Jo Stafford. CBS.

Most Outstanding New Personality
• George Gobel. NBC.
Richard Boone. NBC.
Walt Disney. ABC.
Tennessee Ernie Ford. CBS.
Preston Foster. Syndicated.
Michael O'Shea. NBC.
Fess Parker. ABC.

Best News Reporter or Commentator
• John Daly. ABC.
Douglas Edwards. CBS.
Clete Roberts. Syndicated.
Eric Sevareid. CBS.
John Cameron Swayze. NBC.

Best Direction
• Franklin Schaffner, *Twelve Angry Men*, *Studio One*. CBS.
Robert Florey, *The Loretta Young Show*. NBC.
Clark Jones, *Your Hit Parade*. NBC.
Roy Kellino, *Four Star Playhouse*. CBS.
Ted Post, *Waterfront*. Syndicated.
Alex Segal, *U.S. Steel Hour*. ABC.

Best Written Dramatic Material
• Reginald Rose, *Twelve Angry Men*, *Studio One*. CBS.
Paddy Chayefsky, *Philco TV Playhouse*. NBC.
David Dortort, *Climax*. CBS.
Leonard Freeman, *Four Star Playhouse*. CBS.
James Moser, *Medic*. NBC.

Best Written Comedy Material
• James Allardice, Jack Douglas, Hal Kanter, Harry Winkler, *The George Gobel Show*. NBC.
George Balzer, Milt Josefsberg, Sam Perrin, John Tackaberry, *The Jack Benny Show*. CBS.
James Fritzell, Everett Greenbaum, *Mr. Peepers*. NBC.
Jackie Gleason and staff writers, *The Jackie Gleason Show*. CBS.
Jess Oppenheimer, Robert G. Carroll, Madelyn Pugh, *I Love Lucy*. CBS.
Danny Thomas and staff writers, *Make Room for Daddy*. ABC.

Best Original Music Composed for TV
• Walter Schumann, *Dragnet*. NBC.
Bernard Hermann, *Shower of Stars*. CBS.
Gian Carlo Menotti, *Hallmark Hall of Fame*. NBC.
Victor Young, *Diamond Jubilee of Light*. Four networks.
Victor Young, *Medic*. NBC.

Best Scoring of a Dramatic or Variety Program
• Victor Young, *Diamond Jubilee of Light*. Four networks.
Buddy Bregman, "Anything Goes," *Colgate Comedy Hour*. NBC.
Gordon Jenkins, *Shower of Stars*. CBS.
Nelson Riddle, *Satins and Spurs*.
Walter Scharf, "Here Comes Donald," *Texaco Star Theater*. NBC.

Best Choreographer
• June Taylor, *The Jackie Gleason Show*. CBS.
Rod Alexander, *Max Liebman Spectaculars*. NBC.
Tony Charmoli, Bob Herget, *Your Hit Parade*. NBC.
Louis Da Pron, "Here Comes Donald," *Texaco Star Theater*. NBC.

OTHER AWARD WINNERS
Best Direction of Photography
• Lester Shorr, *Medic*. NBC.

Best Technical Achievement
• John West, Color TV Policy, Burbank Color. NBC.

Best Engineering Effects
• Robert Shelby, Four Quadrant Screen, 1954 national election coverage. NBC.

Best Television Sound Editing
• George Nicholson, *Dragnet*. NBC.

Best Television Film Editing
• Grant Smith, Lynn Harrison, *Disneyland*. ABC.

Best Art Direction of a Live Show
• Bob Markell, *You Are There*. CBS.

Best Art Direction of a Filmed Show
• Ralph Berger, Albert Pyke, *Shower of Stars*. CBS.

A Gold Rush for Silvers

"Emmy Is a Big Girl Now," said a headline in the *L.A. Mirror*. The fete in her honor was equally big, with 4,000 people attending the bicoastal parties at Hollywood's Pan Pacific auditorium and the ballroom of the Waldorf-Astoria Hotel in New York. The shows were broadcast simultaneously again by NBC, with Art Linkletter hosting out west and John Daly as emcee back east. Huge TV monitors were scattered throughout the audiences to show the podium doings up close, an apt complement for an evening designed to pay tribute to the tube.

The night turned out to be a salute to TV's Sergeant Bilko, Phil Silvers, who was named both best actor and best comedian (irreconcilable opposites, some critics cried) while the program bearing the star's name and the subtitle *You'll Never Get Rich* was richly rewarded with a gold statue for top honors as well. After his personal triumph, *TV Guide* reported: "Silvers puts a special value on his trio of gilt idols. He keeps them on a gleaming, black-marble shelf in front of a mirror in his foyer. A visitor who enters the Silvers household with abandon is in danger of becoming impaled upon six needle-sharp wings." Silvers told the magazine, "Having an Emmy Award is like having a gold searchlight in a sea of confusion, reminding you to rehearse, rehearse, rehearse!" *The Phil Silvers Show* also won for comedy writing and direction.

Silvers' daring-for-its-day program was an irreverent farce that had premiered only the previous September. When trying to come up with the show idea for Silvers, producer/director Nat Hiken was looking for an unconventional

Best Actor and Best Comedian Phil Silvers as "goldbrick" Sergeant Bilko.

approach at the outset. He once explained, "We watched television and the characters who maneuvered through the bright, chintzy modern living rooms .... They were mostly young couples, lovable, honest, upstanding. That left us with only one choice for Phil. He had to be a finagler, a goldbrick, and a charlatan. In other words, Sergeant Bilko was born and Phil was stuck with him — along with a platoon of associated characters in long underwear and other G.I. issue. As Phil nonchalantly said at the start, 'This is the best we can do. If we're wrong, so what? I'll just kill myself.'"

Silvers' amazing survival seemed to be shared by the man who was once the academy's nemesis, the oft-deadpan Ed Sullivan, who was now head of its New York chapter (formed in June 1955). Sullivan ultimately smiled that night in

Manhattan as he witnessed his Sunday night showcase being named Best Variety Series. He himself would never win an Emmy in voter competition, but he would be given a Trustees Award in 1971.

The leading lady of the 1955 TV awards was one who made her mark, as she had previously on Broadway, playing a boy. On the night of March 7, 1955, Mary Martin flew across America's small screens in the role of Peter Pan and landed in that never-never land of television's historic live broadcasts. The very mobile Martin was not on hand to claim her award, but it was accepted by daughter Heller Halliday (so named, Martin once said, because "prenatally, she kicked like mad") who told Emmy watchers that her mom, contrary to jestful rumor, was not grounded. She said, "Phil Silvers told me to say that my mother would have been here, but the wire broke."

Peter Pan was shown on *Producers' Showcase*, which was also named Best Dramatic Series and won a music award for the Sammy Cahn/James Van Heusen song "Love and Marriage."

The other leading-lady-of-the-night, Nanette Fabray, won two Emmys, one for Best Comedienne and the other for outstanding supporting actress on *Caesar's Hour*, which she'd retired from the week before. She was a sentimental favorite to take honors that night and her wins reaped the loudest applause. "Stunning in a black and aquamarine evening gown," said one press account, Fabray thanked former costar Sid Caesar tearfully. Afterward, syndicated TV columnist Hal Humphrey teased her with a warning: "See what happened to Imogene Coca when she was no longer with Caesar?!" (Coca had left *Your Show of Shows* for her own variety program, which was canceled in 1955.)

Aside from Mary Martin, the night's other most-missed no-show was Lassie, star of the Best Children's Series. *The*

Hollywood Reporter groused: "The [academy] board said they didn't want to cheapen the affair by having an animal present, so we're starting a campaign to have one dog at [next] year's ceremonies. At the Peabody Awards presentations, Lassie won, ran up to the podium, barked and walked proudly back to his table with the award in his mouth!" It would take two more years, but Lassie would eventually make it up to Emmy's dais, too.

Lucille Ball was also noticeably absent, still smarting from her loss the previous year, but the academy made it up to her this time around, and *Lucy* writer Madelyn Pugh ended up accepting the prize for Best Actress in a Continuing Performance on Ball's behalf. Ball's grudge seemed strange to some, especially since her costar/husband Desi Arnaz had never even been nominated in the male category. But Arnaz never complained. He once said, "I'm waiting for them to put in a category of bongo drummer and if they have one and don't nominate me, then I'll squawk!"

Winning game show $64,000 Question would become embroiled in an infamous scandal.

Lucy had been America's number one show for three years, but finally lost the distinction to *The $64,000 Question*, which now also reaped Emmy's Best Audience Participation Series. The quiz show's new king-of-the-hill status was achieved more or less by ambush, too. It was first aired less than a year before, but captured its huge audience share by being the first show ever to offer huge dollar sums, paying out nearly a million dollars in its first season. It also offered substantial proof that inflation was loose

Mary Martin as Peter Pan *gives flying lessons in the Program of the Year.*

in the land or at least in TV land. The show had began on radio as *The $64 Question*. It would end up on TV broke — and beaten, the casualty of the most notorious scandal ever involving a game show when it was revealed that some participants knew the answers to questions before the show.

After the ceremonies, *The Hollywood Reporter* said, "The only surprise about the Emmy Awards was that there were no surprises." But that was hardly so. Early favorites to win included *Disneyland,* George Gobel, and Jackie Gleason, but only *Disneyland* prevailed, while loser Gobel good-naturedly participated as an awards presenter, and the academy continued its contagious-disease distance from the self-anointed "Great One," Jackie Gleason. Gleason's sewer-worker sidekick on his show, Art Carney, won in the Best Supporting Actor's category for the third straight year and immediately put his prize in storage. Perhaps because of embarrassment over his opposite luck with Emmy voters, Carney always claimed he kept his total of six awards at home in a closet.

Other repeat winners from the year

before included *Omnibus* and Edward R. Murrow. Perry Como, like Dinah Shore, won vocalist recognition again this year and then, in an upset, was also named Best M.C. or Program Host. Also among the newly honored were *Your Hit Parade*, the Best Music Series that played America's best — or most popular — songs. It was an ominous time for its victory. The show was beloved for celebrating tuneful romantic ballads and hummable orchestral favorites, but significant inroads were then being made by that other hit music just then hitting the scene: rock 'n' roll.

Although the academy was no longer recognizing single commercials for awards, it did honor Ford for its commercial series. The prize was not given away on the broadcast, however, because the academy said "there just wasn't time." Critics said it was because the show's chief sponsor was Oldsmobile. Other winning shows included *Matinee Theatre*, an hour-long daytime drama that was one of the first programs broadcast in color, and coverage of the Yucca Flats atomic tests that decimated such competition as the previous year's Emmy broadcast, which was also nominated for Best Special Event or News Program.

Controversies of 1955 included the omission of such TV titans as George Burns, Bishop Sheen and Arthur Godfrey among the nominees. Danny Thomas was originally omitted, too, but he was rescued by a late, although eventually unsuccessful, consideration thanks to a widespread write-in campaign. Jerry Lewis was stewing at home because he and Dean Martin weren't nominated either and consequently refused, "in no uncertain terms," an invitation to host the awards ceremony. The reason for the Lewis and Martin omission from the ballot, said incoming academy president Johnny Mercer after the show, was simply that "nobody nominated them."

Mercer had pleaded with the industry ahead of time for "charity and tolerance" since the voting was complicated by 7,000 programs competing in 41 categories, but he was still met with periodic intolerance. Jack Webb withdrew his director's nomination for 1955, he said, because "I'm so terribly confused by the academy's method of nominations and choice of categories that the only solution I can see is to withdraw." More specifically, he was upset that the show for which he was being considered as best director of a filmed series was a repeat of a *Dragnet* Christ-mas episode from 1953. Mercer blamed Webb. "He submitted the wrong program himself" for consideration, the new A.T.A.S. president said.

Other problems persisted over the awards, too. Writing winner Paul Gregory was so "embarrassed" to receive an award he thought should have gone to Herman Wouk that he refused to accept it. Outgoing academy president Don DeFore was prepared before the ceremonies for the hoopla ahead. He opened the evening telecast with the comment, "Good evening, ladies and gentlemen and rebels without cause. This is a bulletproof vest I'm wearing."

1955

Awards presented March 17, 1956, at the Pan Pacific Auditorium in Hollywood and the Waldorf-Astoria Hotel in New York. Broadcast on NBC.

BEST SINGLE PROGRAM OF THE YEAR
• *Peter Pan, Producers' Showcase*. NBC.
"The American West," *Wide Wide World*. NBC.
The Caine Mutiny Court-Martial, Ford Star Jubilee. CBS.
"Davy Crockett and River Pirates," *Disneyland*. ABC.
No Time for Sergeants, The U.S. Steel Hour. ABC.
"Peter Pan Meets Rusty Williams," *Make Room for Daddy*. ABC.
The Sleeping Beauty, Producers' Showcase. NBC.

BEST DRAMATIC SERIES
• *Producers' Showcase*. NBC.
The Alcoa Hour/Goodyear Playhouse. NBC.
Climax. CBS.
Studio One. CBS.
U.S. Steel Hour. ABC.

BEST COMEDY SERIES
• *The Phil Silvers Show*. CBS.
The Jack Benny Show. CBS.
The Bob Cummings Show. CBS.
Caesar's Hour. NBC.
The George Gobel Show. NBC.
Make Room for Daddy. ABC.

BEST ACTION OR ADVENTURE SERIES
• *Disneyland*. ABC.
Alfred Hitchcock Presents. CBS.
Dragnet. NBC.
Gunsmoke. CBS.
The Lineup. CBS.

BEST VARIETY SERIES
• *The Ed Sullivan Show*. CBS.
The Dinah Shore Show. NBC.
Ford Star Jubilee. CBS.
The Perry Como Show. NBC.
Shower of Stars. CBS.

BEST MUSIC SERIES
• *Your Hit Parade*. NBC.
Coke Time with Eddie Fisher. NBC.
The Dinah Shore Show. NBC.
The Perry Como Show. NBC.
The Voice of Firestone. ABC.

BEST SPECIAL EVENT OR NEWS PROGRAM
• *A-Bomb Test Coverage*. CBS.
Academy of Motion Picture Arts & Sciences Awards. NBC.
Academy of Television Arts & Sciences Awards. NBC.
Football — Rose Bowl. NBC.
Baseball — World Series. NBC.

BEST DOCUMENTARY PROGRAM (RELIGIOUS, INFORMATIONAL, EDUCATIONAL, OR INTERVIEW)
• *Omnibus.* CBS.
Meet the Press. NBC.
Person to Person. CBS.
See It Now. CBS.
Wide Wide World. NBC.

BEST CONTRIBUTION TO DAYTIME PROGRAMMING
• *Matinee Theatre.* NBC.
The Bob Crosby Show. CBS.
The Garry Moore Show. CBS.
Home. NBC.
Today. NBC.

BEST AUDIENCE PARTICIPATION SERIES (QUIZ, PANEL, ETC.)
• *$64,000 Question.* CBS.
I've Got a Secret. CBS.
People Are Funny. NBC.
What's My Line? CBS.
You Bet Your Life. NBC.

BEST CHILDREN'S SERIES
• *Lassie.* CBS.
Ding Dong School. NBC.
Howdy Doody. NBC.
Kukla, Fran & Ollie. ABC.
The Mickey Mouse Club. ABC.
The Pinky Lee Show. NBC.

BEST ACTOR—SINGLE PERFORMANCE
• Lloyd Nolan, *The Caine Mutiny Court-Martial, Ford Star Jubilee.* CBS.
Ralph Bellamy, *Fearful Decision, The U.S. Steel Hour.* CBS.
Jose Ferrer, *Cyrano de Bergerac, Producers' Showcase.* NBC.
Everett Sloane, *Patterns, Kraft Television Theatre.* NBC.
Barry Sullivan, *The Caine Mutiny Court-Martial, Ford Star Jubilee.* CBS.

BEST ACTRESS—SINGLE PERFORMANCE
• Mary Martin, *Peter Pan, Producers' Showcase.* NBC.
Julie Harris, *Wind From the South, The U.S. Steel Hour.* CBS.
Eva Marie Saint, *Our Town, Producers' Showcase.* NBC.
Jessica Tandy, *The Fourposter, Producers' Showcase.* NBC.
Loretta Young, "Christmas Stopover," *The Loretta Young Show.* NBC.

BEST ACTOR—CONTINUING PERFORMANCE
• Phil Silvers, *The Phil Silvers Show.* CBS.
Bob Cummings, *The Bob Cummings Show.* CBS.
Jackie Gleason, *The Honeymooners.* CBS.
Danny Thomas, *Make Room for Daddy.* ABC.
Robert Young, *Father Knows Best.* CBS.

BEST ACTRESS—CONTINUING PERFORMANCE
• Lucille Ball, *I Love Lucy.* CBS.
Gracie Allen, *The George Burns and Gracie Allen Show.* CBS.
Eve Arden, *Our Miss Brooks.* CBS.
Jean Hagen, *Make Room for Daddy.* ABC.
Ann Sothern, *Private Secretary.* CBS.

BEST ACTOR IN A SUPPORTING ROLE
• Art Carney, *The Honeymooners.* CBS.
Ed Begley, *Patterns, Kraft Television Theatre.* NBC.
William Frawley, *I Love Lucy.* CBS.
Carl Reiner, *Caesar's Hour.* NBC.
Cyril Ritchard, *Peter Pan, Producers' Showcase.* NBC.

BEST ACTRESS IN A SUPPORTING ROLE
• Nanette Fabray, *Caesar's Hour.* NBC.
Ann B. Davis, *The Bob Cummings Show.* CBS.
Jean Hagen, *Make Room for Daddy.* ABC.
Audrey Meadows, *The Honeymooners.* CBS.
Thelma Ritter, *A Catered Affair, The Alcoa Hour/Goodyear Playhouse.* NBC.

BEST COMEDIAN
• Phil Silvers. CBS.
Jack Benny. CBS.
Sid Caesar. NBC.
Art Carney. CBS.
George Gobel. NBC.

BEST COMEDIENNE
• Nanette Fabray. NBC.
Gracie Allen. CBS.
Eve Arden. CBS.
Lucille Ball. CBS.
Ann Sothern. CBS.

BEST MALE SINGER
• Perry Como. NBC.
Harry Belafonte. NBC.
Eddie Fisher. NBC.
Gordon MacRae. NBC.
Frank Sinatra. NBC.

BEST FEMALE SINGER
• Dinah Shore. NBC.
Rosemary Clooney. Syndicated.
Judy Garland. CBS.
Peggy Lee.
Gisele Mackenzie. NBC.

BEST MC OR PROGRAM HOST (MALE OR FEMALE)
• Perry Como. NBC.
Alistair Cooke. CBS.
John Daly. ABC.
Dave Garroway. NBC.
Alfred Hitchcock. CBS.

BEST NEWS COMMENTATOR OR REPORTER
• Edward R. Murrow. CBS.
John Daly. ABC.
Douglas Edwards. CBS.
Clete Roberts. CBS.
John Cameron Swayze. NBC.

BEST SPECIALTY ACT—SINGLE OR GROUP
• Marcel Marceau. NBC.
Harry Belafonte. NBC.
Victor Borge.
Sammy Davis, Jr.
Donald O'Connor. NBC.

BEST PRODUCER—LIVE SERIES
• Fred Coe, *Producers' Showcase*. NBC.
Herbert Brodkin, *The Alcoa Hour/Goodyear Playhouse*. NBC.
Hal Kanter, *The George Gobel Show*. NBC.
Martin Manulis, *Climax*. CBS.
Theatre Guild, *The U.S. Steel Hour*. CBS.
Barry Wood, *Wide Wide World*. NBC.

BEST PRODUCER—FILM SERIES
• Walt Disney, *Disneyland*. ABC.
James D. Fonda, *You Are There*. CBS.
Paul Henning, *The Bob Cummings Show*. CBS.
Nat Hiken, *The Phil Silvers Show*. CBS.
Frank La Tourette, *Medic*. NBC.

BEST DIRECTOR—LIVE SERIES
• Franklin Schaffner, *The Caine Mutiny Court-Martial, Ford Star Jubilee*. CBS.
John Frankenheimer, *Portrait in Celluloid, Climax*. CBS.
Clark Jones, *Peter Pan, Producers' Showcase*. NBC.
Delbert Mann, *Our Town, Producers' Showcase*. NBC.

Alex Segal, *No Time for Sergeants, The U.S. Steel Hour*. CBS.

BEST DIRECTOR—FILM SERIES
• Nat Hiken, *The Phil Silvers Show*. CBS.
Rod Amateau, *The Bob Cummings Show*. CBS.
Bernard Girard, *You Are There*. CBS.
Alfred Hitchcock, *Alfred Hitchcock Presents*. CBS.
Sheldon Leonard, *Make Room for Daddy*. ABC.
Jack Webb, *Dragnet*. NBC.

BEST ORIGINAL TELEPLAY WRITING
• Rod Serling, *Kraft Television Theatre*. NBC.
David Davidson, *The Alcoa Hour/Goodyear Playhouse*. NBC.
Robert Alan Aurthur, *Philco TV Playhouse*. NBC.
Paddy Chayefsky, *The Alcoa Hour/Goodyear Playhouse*. NBC.
Cyril Hume, Richard Maibaum, *The U.S. Steel Hour*. CBS.

BEST COMEDY WRITING
• Nat Hiken, Barry Blitser, Arnold Auerbach, Harvey Orkin, Vincent Bogert, Arnold Rosen, Coleman Jacoby, Tony Webster, Terry Ryan, *The Phil Silvers Show*. CBS.
Hal Kanter, Howard Leeds, Everett Greenbaum, Harry Winkler, *The George Gobel Show*. NBC.
Jess Oppenheimer, Madelyn Pugh, Bob Carroll, Jr., Bob Schiller, Bob Weiskopf, *I Love Lucy*. CBS.
Sam Perrin, George Balzer, Hal Goldman, Al Gordon, *The Jack Benny Show*. CBS.
Mel Tolkin, Selma Diamond, Larry Gelbart, Mel Brooks, Sheldon Keller, *Caesar's Hour*. NBC.

BEST TELEVISION ADAPTATION
• Paul Gregory, Franklin Schaffner, *The Caine Mutiny Court-Martial, Ford Star Jubilee*. CBS.
David Dortort, *The Ox-Bow Incident, The 20th Century-Fox Hour*. CBS.
John Monks, Jr., *Miracle on 34th Street, The 20th Century-Fox Hour*. CBS.
Rod Serling, *The Champion, Climax*. CBS.
David Shaw, *Our Town, Producers' Showcase*. NBC.

BEST COMMERCIAL CAMPAIGN
• Ford Motor Co.
Bank of America
Chrysler Corp.
Hamm's Beer Co.
Piel's Beer Co.

OTHER AWARD WINNERS
BEST MUSICAL CONTRIBUTION
• Sammy Cahn, James Van Heusen, "Love and Marriage," from *Our Town, Producers' Showcase*. NBC.

BEST CHOREOGRAPHER
• Tony Charmoli, *Your Hit Parade*. NBC.

BEST CINEMATOGRAPHY FOR TELEVISION
• William Scikner, *Medic*. NBC.

BEST CAMERA WORK—LIVE SHOW
• T. Miller, *Studio One*. CBS.

BEST EDITING OF A TELEVISION FILM
• Edward W. Williams, *Alfred Hitchcock Presents*. CBS.

BEST ART DIRECTION—LIVE SERIES
• Otis Riggs, *Playwrights '56* and *Producers' Showcase*. NBC.

BEST ART DIRECTION—FILM SERIES
• William Ferrari, *You Are There*. CBS.

BEST ENGINEERING OR TECHNICAL ACHIEVEMENT
• RCA Tricolor Picture Tube, which made the commercial color receiver practical.

GOVERNORS AWARD
• President Dwight D. Eisenhower, for his use and encouragement of television.

A "No, No" for Nanette

A month before the usual awards ceremony the academy inaugurated a second Emmys broadcast, this one to announce the nominations. A "helluva" script was written by Rod Serling, said awards chairman Ed Sullivan, and the show was telecast on February 16, 1957 — in color, an Emmy first. "For the most part, it proved to be a good show," *Radio-TV Daily* commented afterward. "A well-meaning effort was made to combine entertainment with the more somber business." The entertainers who did their jobs so well included Steve Allen, Sid Caesar, Phil Silvers, Danny Thomas, and musician/songwriter/academy president Johnny Mercer. The highlight proved to be a Burr Tillstrom song called "TV Rating Blues," which went, in part: "The applause was great/ And the sales were, too/ But you drop two points, buddy/ and you're thru ... Got those TV rating/ got those TV rating blues."

After such a celebratory unveiling of the nominees came the morning-after blues. As invariably happens, certain high-profile stars and programs were overlooked, such as Groucho Marx, George Burns, *Dragnet*, *The Arthur Godfrey Show*, *The Lineup*, and *The Millionaire*. Lawrence Welk and his show weren't nominated either and Welk made his displeasure known, complaining that he never even received a ballot so that he could vote for himself. Sullivan and Mercer released a joint statement: "The [nominating] method has been improved each successive year and we will continue to work to perfect it."

Actress Ann Sothern, another critic, was not placated. Her television show *Private Secretary* also failed to make the competition and, like Welk, she claimed she never got a nominating ballot. (N.A.T.A.S. looked into the matter and learned it was sent to her business manager's office.)

"I'm on the warpath!" Sothern persisted. "Out of the list of 20 series [nominated], my show has beaten more than half of them in the ratings. It's most unfair .... Who remembers you if you're not on the list? I think the academy should be investigated." It wasn't, and,

Caesar's crowning hour: Winners Sid Caesar, Nanette Fabray, Pat Carroll, and Carl Reiner.

NBC/GLOBE PHOTO

ironically, while the actress's show was not named an Emmy contender, Ann Sothern herself had been nominated — as a comedienne. She lost.

The awards program took place, just as the nomination show had, at NBC's East and West Coast studios and was beamed nationwide in color for the first time. CBS won 14 trophies, NBC 13, and ABC 1. New York won big, too. *Variety* noted: "For the second consecutive year, New York dominated the awards, taking 15 to Hollywood's 14." Part of the reason for the Big Apple success was because of its virtual monopoly of the medium's live broadcasts. "And again live TV won over film," *Variety* added, "with 19 Emmys going to live shows, nine to vidfilmed programs."

The night's heaviest hitter was *Playhouse 90*, which had been nominated for six awards and ended up winning them all, five for *Requiem for a Heavyweight*. *Playhouse 90* had just premiered that season and *Heavyweight* was only its second program — but clearly it was already the champ of all live dramatic anthology series. *Playhouse* won prizes for both Best Single Program of the Year and Best New Program Series. Last year's writing winner Rod Serling was honored for his script that was destined to become a classic. Jack Palance played the boxer and won the prize for Best Single Performance by an Actor. The show also took best direction and art direction.

Sid Caesar's show had been falling in the ratings recently, no doubt causing him to watch out for industry execs telling him the afore-sung "Buddy, you're thru!" but *Caesar's Hour* was given a sudden boost by its five awards. It was named Best Series of One Hour or More. Caesar himself was honored as best comedian and Carl Reiner and Pat Carroll were recognized for their supporting roles on the show. The Best Continuing Performance by a Comedienne in a Series was also given to a show costar, a result that triggered a horrific outcry.

Last year's winner Nanette Fabray had retired from *Caesar's Hour* and therefore had not starred in a single episode during the previous season. When she was nonetheless awarded the Emmy for giving the Best Continuing Performance by

a Comedienne in a Series, certain awards fans were suddenly telling Nanette "no, no." "There was much griping," *Variety* reported. "Those beefing pointed out Miss Fabray left Caesar's show at the end of last season, yet she won over such stalwarts as Lucille Ball, Gracie Allen and Ann Sothern. Miss Fabray seemed

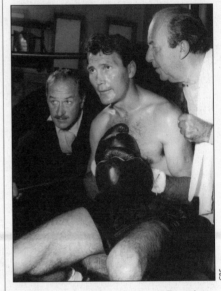

CBS

Jack Palance in Rod Serling's Requiem for a Heavyweight, *Program of the Year.*

just as astonished at winning her Emmy." A few days later the Emmy Board of Governors announced that it considered Fabray's award legitimate since the voting period covered January 1 to December 31, 1956 instead of the network season spanning autumn, 1956 to spring, 1957. Since the awards were determined on a calender year-basis, they said, Fabray was therefore eligible because she was still on the show through late spring, 1956.

Lucille Ball stayed home for the 1955 awards after she'd lost for 1954, but was on hand this year. It was another big disappointment. *I Love Lucy* was nominated for three Emmys, but failed to take any. Ball's twin consolations:

Lucy was once again the top-rated show after losing that status for a year to *The $64,000 Question*. And husband Desi Arnaz was the Emmy's L.A. emcee.

Silvers came back a winner again this year with his show named Best Series of a Half Hour or Less. It also triumphed in comedy writing. Perry Como and Dinah Shore came back big, too, as did Loretta Young, Edward R. Murrow, and Murrow's highly regarded series *See It Now*. Murrow's year-end news wrap-up was also honored. Claire Trevor was credited with giving the Best Single Performance by an Actress and Robert Young was saluted for doing his best on *Father Knows Best*.

Before the night's results were known, *The Hollywood Reporter* took a stab at predicting the outcome. It did well calling the evening's champ,

Awards chairman Ed Sullivan (left) with presenter Lucille Ball and show emcee Desi Arnaz, who never won an Emmy.

Requiem for a Heavyweight, adding "but we like *A Night to Remember*." It then went on to prophesy in 17 more slots. It was right in six.

1956

Awards presented March 16, 1957, at NBC's Burbank studios in California and the Colonial Theatre in New York. Broadcast on NBC.

BEST SINGLE PROGRAM OF THE YEAR
• *Requiem for a Heavyweight*, Playhouse 90. CBS.
A Night to Remember, Kraft Television Theatre. NBC.
"Leonard Bernstein," *Omnibus*. CBS.
"Secret Life of Danny Kaye," *See It Now*. CBS.
The Victor Borge Show. CBS.

BEST NEW PROGRAM SERIES
• *Playhouse 90*. CBS.
Air Power. CBS.
The Dinah Shore Chevy Show. NBC.
The Ernie Kovacs Show. NBC.
The Steve Allen Sunday Show. NBC.

BEST SERIES—ONE HOUR OR MORE
• *Caesar's Hour*. NBC.
Climax. CBS.
The Ed Sullivan Show. CBS.
Omnibus. CBS.
The Perry Como Show. NBC.

BEST SERIES—HALF HOUR OR LESS
• *The Phil Silvers Show*. CBS.
Alfred Hitchcock Presents. CBS.
Father Knows Best. NBC.
The Jack Benny Show. CBS.
Person to Person. CBS.

BEST PUBLIC SERVICE SERIES
• *See It Now*. CBS.
Meet the Press. NBC.
NBC Opera Theatre. NBC.
Wide Wide World. NBC.
You Are There. CBS.

BEST SINGLE PERFORMANCE
BY AN ACTOR
• Jack Palance, *Requiem for a Heavyweight*, Playhouse 90. CBS.
Lloyd Bridges, *Tragedy in a Temporary Town*, The Alcoa Hour/Goodyear Playhouse. NBC.
Fredric March, *Dodsworth*, Producers' Showcase. NBC.
Sal Mineo, *Dino*, Studio One. CBS.
Red Skelton, *The Big Slide*, Playhouse 90. CBS.

BEST SINGLE PERFORMANCE BY AN ACTRESS
• Claire Trevor, *Dodsworth, Producers' Showcase.* NBC.
Edna Best, *This Happy Breed, Ford Star Jubilee.* CBS.
Gracie Fields, *Old Lady Shows Her Medals, The U.S. Steel Hour.* CBS.
Nancy Kelly, *The Pilot, Studio One.* CBS.
Evelyn Rudie, *Eloise, Playhouse 90.* CBS.

BEST CONTINUING PERFORMANCE BY AN ACTOR IN A DRAMATIC SERIES
• Robert Young, *Father Knows Best.* NBC.
James Arness, *Gunsmoke.* CBS.
Charles Boyer, *Four Star Playhouse.* CBS.
David Niven, *Four Star Playhouse.* CBS.
Hugh O'Brien, *The Life and Legend of Wyatt Earp.* ABC.

BEST CONTINUING PERFORMANCE BY AN ACTRESS IN A DRAMATIC SERIES
• Loretta Young, *The Loretta Young Show.* NBC.
Jan Clayton, *Lassie.* CBS.
Ida Lupino, *Four Star Playhouse.* CBS.
Peggy Wood, *Mama.* CBS.
Jane Wyman, *Fireside Theatre.* NBC.

BEST CONTINUING PERFORMANCE BY A COMEDIAN IN A SERIES
• Sid Caesar, *Caesar's Hour.* NBC.
Jack Benny, *The Jack Benny Show.* CBS.
Bob Cummings, *The Bob Cummings Show.* CBS.
Ernie Kovacs, *The Ernie Kovacs Show.* NBC.
Phil Silvers, *The Phil Silvers Show.* CBS.

BEST CONTINUING PERFORMANCE BY A COMEDIENNE IN A SERIES
• Nanette Fabray, *Caesar's Hour.* NBC.
Edie Adams, *The Ernie Kovacs Show.* NBC.
Gracie Allen, *The George Burns and Gracie Allen Show.* CBS.
Lucille Ball, *I Love Lucy.* CBS.
Ann Sothern, *Private Secretary.* CBS.

BEST SUPPORTING PERFORMANCE BY AN ACTOR
• Carl Reiner, *Caesar's Hour.* NBC.
Art Carney, *The Jackie Gleason Show.* CBS.
Paul Ford, *The Phil Silvers Show.* CBS.
William Frawley, *I Love Lucy.* CBS.
Ed Wynn, *Requiem for a Heavyweight, Playhouse 90.* CBS.

BEST SUPPORTING PERFORMANCE BY AN ACTRESS
• Pat Carroll, *Caesar's Hour.* CBS.
Ann B. Davis, *The Bob Cummings Show.* CBS.
Audrey Meadows, *The Jackie Gleason Show.* CBS.
Mildred Natwick, *Blithe Spirit, Ford Star Jubilee.* CBS.
Vivian Vance, *I Love Lucy.* CBS.

BEST MALE PERSONALITY— CONTINUING PERFORMANCE
• Perry Como. NBC.
Steve Allen. NBC.
Leonard Bernstein. CBS.
Tennessee Ernie Ford. NBC.
Alfred Hitchcock. CBS.
Bishop Fulton J. Sheen. ABC.

BEST FEMALE PERSONALITY— CONTINUING PERFORMANCE
• Dinah Shore. NBC.
Rosemary Clooney. Syndicated.
Faye Emerson. CBS.
Arlene Francis. CBS.
Gisele Mackenzie. NBC.

BEST COVERAGE/ NEWSWORTHY EVENT
• *Years of Crisis,* year-end report with Edward R. Murrow and other correspondents. CBS.
Andrea Doria Sinking. CBS.
Andrea Doria Survivors Arrive in New York. NBC.
National Political Conventions. ABC.
National Political Conventions. NBC.

BEST NEWS COMMENTATOR
• Edward R. Murrow. CBS.
Walter Cronkite. CBS.
John Daly. ABC.
Douglas Edwards. CBS.
Chet Huntley. NBC.

BEST DIRECTION—ONE HOUR OR MORE
• Ralph Nelson, *Requiem for a Heavyweight, Playhouse 90.* CBS.
Lewis Allen, *Child of the Regiment, The 20th Century-Fox Hour.* CBS.
Bob Banner, *The Dinah Shore Chevy Show.* NBC.
Kirk Browning, *La Bohème, NBC Opera Theatre.* NBC.
John Frankenheimer, *Forbidden Area, Playhouse 90.* CBS.
George Roy Hill, *A Night to Remember, Kraft Television Theatre.* NBC.

Multiple past Emmy winner Walter Cronkite acted as presenter this year.

BEST DIRECTION—HALF HOUR OR LESS
• Sheldon Leonard, *The Danny Thomas Show*. ABC.
George Archainbaud, *Tales of the 77th Bengal Lancers*. NBC.
Herschel Gaugherty, *The Road That Led Afar*, *General Electric Theater*. CBS.
William Russell, *You Are There*. CBS.
Clay Yurdin, *As I Lay Dying*, *Camera Three*. CBS.

**BEST TELEPLAY WRITING—
HALF HOUR OR LESS**
• James P. Cavanagh, *Alfred Hitchcock Presents*. CBS.
Morton Fine, David Friedkin, *Frontier*. NBC.
Richard Morris, *The Loretta Young Show*. NBC.
John Nesbitt, *Telephone Time*. CBS.
Dan Ullman, *The Life and Legend of Wyatt Earp*. ABC.

**BEST TELEPLAY WRITING—
ONE HOUR OR MORE**
• Rod Serling, *Requiem for a Heavyweight*, *Playhouse 90*. CBS.
Louis Peterson, *Joey*, *The Alcoa Hour/ Goodyear Playhouse*. NBC.
George Roy Hill, John Whedon, *A Night to Remember*, *Kraft Television Theatre*. NBC.
Elick Moll, *Sizeman and Son*, *Playhouse 90*. CBS.
Reginald Rose, *Tragedy in a Temporary Town*, *The Alcoa Hour/Goodyear Playhouse*. NBC.

BEST COMEDY WRITING—VARIETY OR SITUATION COMEDY
• Nat Hiken, Billy Friedberg, Tony Webster, Leonard Stern, Arnold Rosen, Coleman Jacoby, *The Phil Silvers Show*. CBS.
Goodman Ace, Jay Burton, Mort Green, George Foster, *The Perry Como Show*. NBC.
Ernie Kovacs, Louis M. Heyward, Rex Lardner, Mike Marmer, *The Ernie Kovacs Show*. NBC.
Sam Perrin, George Balzer, Hal Goldman, Al Gordon, *The Jack Benny Show*. CBS.
Mel Tolkin, Gary Belkin, Mel Brooks, Sheldon Keller, Neil Simon, Larry Gelbart, Mike Stewart, *Caesar's Hour*. NBC.

OTHER AWARD WINNERS
BEST CINEMATOGRAPHY FOR TELEVISION
• Norbert Brodine, *The Loretta Young Show*. NBC.

BEST EDITING OF A FILM FOR TELEVISION
• Frank Keller, "Our Mr. Sun," *Bell Telephone Science Series*. CBS.

BEST MUSICAL CONTRIBUTION FOR TELEVISION
• Leonard Bernstein, "Composing, Conducting," *Omnibus*. CBS.

BEST LIVE CAMERA WORK
• *A Night to Remember*, *Kraft Television Theatre*. NBC.

**BEST ART DIRECTION—
HALF HOUR OR LESS**
• Paul Barnes, *Your Hit Parade*. NBC.

**BEST ART DIRECTION—
ONE HOUR OR MORE**
• Albert Heschong, *Requiem for a Heavyweight, Playhouse 90*. CBS.

BEST ENGINEERING OR TECHNICAL ACHIEVEMENT
• Development of video tape by Ampex and further development and practical applications by CBS. (Dual entry.)

A Second Decade, A New Academy

The Ed "Sullivan coup" of 1955 was overtaken two years later by what A.T.A.S. founder Syd Cassyd calls Sullivan's "ultimate coup" — the abolition of the old academy in favor of a new one with the word "National" in front of its name. Its charter gave New York more than just equal chapter status with the former Hollywood-based academy, too. The new N.A.T.A.S. was headquartered both in New York and L.A. while other chapters were also springing up in Chicago and Washington. And Sullivan smiled again. He was named the new academy's first president.

The N.A.T.A.S.'s first awards marked the 10th Emmy ceremony. Out in Hollywood the night of April 15, 1958, dinner and dancing were restored to the functions that took place at the Ambassador Hotel's Cocoanut Grove and the banquet ceremony out east, said one press account, "was unceremoniously staged in several overcrowded NBC studios." The dual-broadcast's home viewership was gauged by the Trendex ratings firm, which reported 73.4 percent of the nation's television audience tuned in — Emmy's highest rating to date.

CBS went into the evening with more than a dozen nominations over NBC and emerged with 15 1/2 wins compared to the latter's 11 and 1 1/2 for ABC. (An award shared by two networks was counted as one-half for each.) In the past two years, New York pulled more awards than L.A., but this time Hollywood beat Gotham 17 to 11.

The nominees, according to the International News Service, comprised "a slate dominated by cowboys and crooners." Cowboys were conquering the new

A "shaken" Polly Bergen won Best Actress for The Helen Morgan Story.

terrain of TV in a dramatic way in the 1957–58 season. Of America's 10 most-watched series, five were westerns. *Gunsmoke* was the only show of the genre that scored so high the previous year, and this time it became the first western ever to win a major Emmy — an achievement that would occur only once more in academy history when *Maverick* would ride just as high in the saddle in 1958. *Gunsmoke*, in 1957, was the country's number-one show and won Best Dramatic Series with Continuing Characters — and Best Editing.

Playhouse 90 garnered the most awards (five), including Best Dramatic Anthology Series, Best Live Camera Work, and Best Actress for Polly Bergen's performance in *The Helen Morgan Story*. It was a vote of vindication for Bergen. She had personally purchased the television rights to the story of the torch singer's struggles with love and liquor and then made a deal with CBS to air it. When she accepted her award, *Variety* said Bergen was "probably more shaken with emotion than any other Emmy winner" and tearfully thanked Mrs. Lulu Morgan, "who had the courage to let me do her daughter's story."

Playhouse 90's fourth award went to Rod Serling (his third successive writing prize) for *The Comedian*, also voted Program of the Year. "In a bit of irony, Milton Berle presented [Serling's] Emmy," wrote the *L.A. Herald-Express*. "The program, obviously based on Berle's struggles in the medium, represented the trials of a TV comic and his nervous strain in growing up. Berle, in making the announcement, ad-libbed: 'I wonder who they wrote that about?'" Berle was portrayed by Mickey Rooney who was favored to win a statuette, too, but he was usurped by an emerging industry upstart. *Variety* reported: "When Peter Ustinov was named the winner as Best Actor for a Single Performance, for *Samuel Johnson*, there was an audible sigh of disappointment in the Grove." But the upstart was simply establishing himself as a favorite Emmy dark horse: Ustinov would shock pundits again in 1967 by beating both Lee J. Cobb and Hal Holbrook.

Berle upstaged everyone that night in 1958. The former burlesque king delivered part of the evening's entertainment — "an unmistakable floperoo," said the *Herald-Express*. Among the jokes he tossed off was "I had my nose fixed, now my mouth doesn't work," but that was hardly so. "Too Much Talk 'Dims Out' Emmys" was the paper's banner, page-one headline the next day. Berle had hogged the small screen for so long that Jack Benny, in Hollywood, "actually was prepared to do a five-minute session, but had to trim it to nothingness."

Danny Thomas, emcee of the West Coast telecast, obviously burned throughout the rest of the show." Its directors, the paper added, "were ready to revive the old vaudeville hook."

The night's biggest surprise winner was the short-lived *Seven Lively Arts*, which edged out odds-on-favorite *Maverick* for Best New Program Series of the Year. The program included brilliant adaptations of short stories by the likes of Ernest Hemingway and tackled such controversial subjects as evangelism, but it died for lack of a sponsor shortly after it premiered and has been called, as the *L.A. Times* once noted, "one of TV's finest hours and finest flops."

The Best Comedy Series for the third straight year was *The Phil Silvers Show*, which also took honors for comedy writing. Silvers was the East Coast show's emcee and so was up on stage when his writers approached their own Sergeant Bilko for something more than rations. "I can't understand this!" Silvers told the audience, looking befuddled. "You know I ad-lib!" Silvers was also responsible for part of the night's formal entertainment and got one of his biggest laughs when the troops from his hit series stormed the stage in New York while keeping in step with the marching tune from *The Bridge on the River Kwai*. "You don't know what they've been up against!" Silvers cried, making apologies for their ragtag appearance. "*M Squad*, the first half of *Cheyenne* ...!"

Other returning winners included "crooner" Dinah Shore — for the fourth

Program of the Year The Comedian by Rod Serling was clearly based on Milton Berle's early TV career.

Double winner Jack Benny got a double kiss from Eve Arden and Jane Wyatt.

A.T.A.S.

year in a row. Her show was also named top musical program and had the best director for broadcasts of one hour or more. More Emmy familiars followed, including Carl Reiner for his supporting role on the "dearly departed" *Caesar's Hour* and Edward R. Murrow for Best News Commentary.

Although he'd been on TV since 1950, Jack Benny had never won an Emmy. He took it all good-naturedly, too, once joking, "I'm trying to talk the Emmy people into giving an award for best violin soloist. I'll kill myself if Henny Youngman wins!" Before the Emmy hoopla started this year, *Variety* had made an issue of it, writing, "Call it electioneering or what you will, but there must be something cockeyed about Emmy voting when such great talents as Jack Benny and Bob Hope have never carried off one of the baubles." The academy decided to make up for the oversight and awarded Benny its first-ever Trustees Award "for his contributions to the field and his excellence as a

performer." The eternally 39-year-old Benny accepted, saying, "I have an eerie feeling you want me to retire, but I'm not going to quit until I'm 50 and then I'll have to because I'll be 80!" In what the *Herald-Express* then called a double-cross to the trustees, Emmy membership voted Benny an award in a competitive category — for being the year's most outstanding performer who "Essentially Plays Himself."

The top awards for actors essentially playing other characters went to the couple known to America as James and Margaret Anderson on *Father Knows Best*. The *Herald-Express* said, "One of the most well-received presentations in Hollywood was to the 'family togetherness' team of Robert Young and Jane Wyatt" who both received best acting honors and standing ovations as well. Wyatt hardly expected the tribute. The most surprised winner of the night was actually outside the Grove talking to reporters in the press tent when her victory was announced and had to dash back inside to collect the honor. She would win again in 1959 and 1960. Young would win his third in 1970, as Marcus Welby, M.D.

Speculation over whether or not the easily slighted Lucille Ball and husband Desi Arnaz would attend the Emmy shows usually kept Hollywood and its gossip columnists buzzing before the ceremony each year. But this time the matter was decided for them by the couple's advertising bosses, who kept them at home because of a sensitive sponsor conflict. *I Love Lucy* was sponsored by Ford. The Emmys broadcast was underwritten, in part, by Plymouth.

The absence of Lassie outraged some Emmy watchers and collie lovers two years before, but this time the heroic canine came — and rescued the evening's entertainment. The top dog was part of a skit led by host Danny

Thomas, whose tax problems were then well known to the home viewing audience. He and his new best friend marched on stage along with *The Danny Thomas Show*'s costars Rusty Hamer and Angela Cartwright and a fellow dressed like Abe Lincoln. "I have no money for a pilot," Thomas pleaded, "so I'm going to do a pilot right here tonight called *Rover the Talking Dog!*"

1957

Awards presented April 15, 1958, at the Cocoanut Grove in Hollywood and NBC's studios in New York. Broadcast on NBC.

BEST SINGLE PROGRAM OF THE YEAR
• *The Comedian, Playhouse 90.* CBS.
Edsel Show. CBS.
The Green Pastures, Hallmark Hall of Fame. NBC.
The Helen Morgan Story, Playhouse 90. CBS.

BEST NEW PROGRAM SERIES OF THE YEAR
The Seven Lively Arts. CBS.
Leave it to Beaver. CBS.
Maverick. ABC.
The Jack Paar Tonight Show. NBC.
Wagon Train. NBC.

BEST DRAMATIC SERIES WITH CONTINUING CHARACTERS
• *Gunsmoke.* CBS.
Lassie. CBS.
Maverick. ABC.
Perry Mason. CBS.
Wagon Train. NBC.

BEST COMEDY SERIES
• *The Phil Silvers Show.* CBS.
The Bob Cummings Show. CBS, NBC.
Caesar's Hour. NBC.
Father Knows Best. NBC.
The Jack Benny Show. CBS.

BEST DRAMATIC ANTHOLOGY SERIES
• *Playhouse 90.* CBS.
Alfred Hitchcock Presents. CBS.
Climax. CBS.
Hallmark Hall of Fame. NBC.
Studio One. CBS.

BEST MUSICAL, VARIETY, AUDIENCE PARTICIPATION, OR QUIZ SERIES
• *The Dinah Shore Chevy Show.* NBC.
The Ed Sullivan Show. CBS.
The Perry Como Show. NBC.
The Steve Allen Show. NBC.
The Jack Paar Tonight Show. NBC.

BEST PUBLIC SERVICE PROGRAM OR SERIES
• *Omnibus.* ABC, NBC.
Bell Telephone Science Series. NBC.
Person to Person. CBS.
See It Now. CBS.
Wide Wide World. NBC.

ACTOR — BEST SINGLE PERFORMANCE— LEAD OR SUPPORT
• Peter Ustinov, *The Life of Samuel Johnson, Omnibus.* NBC.
Lee J. Cobb, *No Deadly Medicine, Studio One.* CBS.
Mickey Rooney, *The Comedian, Playhouse 90.* CBS.
David Wayne, *Heartbeat, Suspicion.* NBC.
Ed Wynn, *On Borrowed Time, Hallmark Hall of Fame.* NBC.

ACTRESS — BEST SINGLE PERFORMANCE—LEAD OR SUPPORT
• Polly Bergen, *The Helen Morgan Story, Playhouse 90.* CBS.
Julie Andrews, *Cinderella.* CBS.
Helen Hayes, *Mrs. Gilling and the Skyscraper, The Alcoa Hour.* NBC.
Piper Laurie, *The Deaf Heart, Studio One.* CBS.
Teresa Wright, *The Miracle Worker, Playhouse 90.* CBS.

BEST CONTINUING PERFORMANCE (MALE) IN A SERIES BY A COMEDIAN, SINGER, HOST, DANCER, MC, ANNOUNCER, NARRATOR, PANELIST, OR ANY PERSON WHO ESSENTIALLY PLAYS HIMSELF
• Jack Benny, *The Jack Benny Show.* CBS.
Steve Allen, *The Steve Allen Show.* NBC.
Sid Caesar, *Caesar's Hour.* NBC.
Perry Como, *The Perry Como Show.* NBC.
Jack Paar, *The Jack Paar Tonight Show.* NBC.

Best Continuing Performance (Female) in a Series by a Comedienne, Singer, Hostess, Dancer, MC, Announcer, Narrator, Panelist or Any Person Who Essentially Plays Herself

• Dinah Shore, *The Dinah Shore Chevy Show*. NBC.
Gracie Allen, *The George Burns and Gracie Allen Show*. CBS.
Lucille Ball, *I Love Lucy*. CBS.
Dody Goodman, *The Jack Paar Tonight Show*. NBC.
Loretta Young, *The Loretta Young Show*. NBC.

Best Continuing Performance by an Actor in a Leading Role In a Dramatic or Comedy Series

• Robert Young, *Father Knows Best*. NBC.
James Arness, *Gunsmoke*. CBS.
Bob Cummings, *The Bob Cummings Show*. CBS, NBC.
Phil Silvers, *The Phil Silvers Show*. CBS.
Danny Thomas, *The Danny Thomas Show*. ABC, CBS.

Best Continuing Performance by an Actress in a Leading Role in a Dramatic or Comedy Series

• Jane Wyatt, *Father Knows Best*. NBC.
Eve Arden, *The Eve Arden Show*. CBS.
Spring Byington, *December Bride*. CBS.
Jan Clayton, *Lassie*. CBS.
Ida Lupino, *Mr. Adams and Eve*. CBS.

Best Continuing Supporting Performance by an Actor in a Dramatic or Comedy Series

• Carl Reiner, *Caesar's Hour*. NBC.
Paul Ford, *The Phil Silvers Show*. CBS.
William Frawley, *I Love Lucy*. CBS.
Louis Nye, *The Steve Allen Show*. NBC.
Dennis Weaver, *Gunsmoke*. CBS.

Best Continuing Supporting Performance by an Actress in a Dramatic or Comedy Series

• Ann B. Davis, *The Bob Cummings Show*. CBS, NBC.
Pat Carroll, *Caesar's Hour*. NBC.
Verna Felton, *December Bride*. CBS.
Marion Lorne, *Sally*. NBC.
Vivian Vance, *I Love Lucy*. CBS.

Best Coverage of an Unscheduled Newsworthy Event

• Coverage of the Rikers Island, New York, plane crash, *World News Round-up*. CBS.
Four newsmen interview Governor Orval Faubus of Arkansas in Little Rock. ABC.
News coverage of the integration story in Little Rock and other southern cities. NBC.
Coverage of the Little Rock school riot, as presented on *Little Rock, 1957*. CBS.
News coverage of first Russian sputnik, the U.S. satellite launching efforts and Vanguard failure. NBC.

Best News Commentary

• Edward R. Murrow, *See It Now*. CBS.
John Daly, *News.* ABC.
Douglas Edwards, *News*. CBS.
Chet Huntley, David Brinkley, *News*. NBC.
Eric Sevareid, *World News Roundup*. CBS.

Best Direction—One Hour or More

• Bob Banner, *The Dinah Shore Chevy Show*. NBC.
John Frankenheimer, *The Comedian*, *Playhouse 90*. CBS.
George Roy Hill, *The Helen Morgan Story*, *Playhouse 90*. CBS.
Arthur Penn, *The Miracle Worker*, *Playhouse 90*. CBS.
George Schaefer, *The Green Pastures*, *Hallmark Hall of Fame*. NBC.

Best Direction—Half Hour or Less

• Robert Stevens, "The Glass Eye," *Alfred Hitchcock Presents*. CBS.
Bill Hobin, *Your Hit Parade*. NBC.
Clark Jones, *The Patrice Munsel Show*. ABC.
Sheldon Leonard, *The Danny Thomas Show*. ABC, CBS.
Peter Tewksbury, *Father Knows Best*. NBC.

Best Teleplay Writing— One Hour or More

• Rod Serling, *The Comedian*, *Playhouse 90*. CBS.
Marc Connelly, *The Green Pastures*, *Hallmark Hall of Fame*. NBC.
William Gibson, *The Miracle Worker*, *Playhouse 90*. CBS.
Arthur Hailey, *No Deadly Medicine*, *Studio One*. CBS.
James Lee, *The Life of Samuel Johnson*, *Omnibus*. NBC.

Best Teleplay Writing— Half Hour or Less

• Paul Monash, *The Lonely Wizard*, *Schlitz Playhouse of Stars*. CBS.
Joe Connelly, Bob Mosher, *Leave it to Beaver*. CBS.
John Meston, *Gunsmoke*. CBS.

Roswell Rogers, *Father Knows Best*. NBC.
Morton Wishengrad, *Frontiers of Faith*.
NBC.

BEST COMEDY WRITING
• Nat Hiken, Billy Friedberg, Phil Sharp,
Terry Ryan, Coleman Jacoby, Arnold
Rosen, Sidney Zelinka, A.J. Russell, Tony
Webster, *The Phil Silvers Show*. CBS.
Ernie Kovacs, *The Ernie Kovacs Show*.
NBC.
Sam Perrin, George Balzer, Al Gordon,
Hal Goldman, *The Jack Benny Show*. CBS.
Mel Tolkin, Larry Gelbart, Mel Brooks,
Neil Simon, Sheldon Keller, Mike Stewart,
Gary Belkin, *Caesar's Hour*. NBC.
Roswell Rogers, Paul West, *Father Knows
Best*. NBC.

BEST MUSICAL CONTRIBUTION FOR TELEVISION
• Leonard Bernstein, "Conducting and
Analyzing Music of Johann Sebastian
Bach,"*Omnibus*. ABC.

OTHER AWARD WINNERS

BEST ENGINEERING OR TECHNICAL ACHIEVEMENT
• Engineering and camera techniques on
Wide Wide World. NBC.

BEST LIVE CAMERA WORK
• *Playhouse 90*. CBS.

BEST CINEMATOGRAPHY FOR TELEVISION
• Harold E. Wellman, "Hemo the Magnifi-
cent," *Bell Telephone Science Series*.
NBC.

BEST EDITING OF A FILM FOR TELEVISION
• Mike Pozen, *Gunsmoke*. CBS.

BEST ART DIRECTION
• Rouben Ter-Arutunian, *Twelfth Night,
Hallmark Hall of Fame*. NBC.

TRUSTEES AWARD
• Jack Benny

The Notorious "Astaire Affair"

Once again the academy displayed amazing accordion skills when it came to playing with the nominations procedure. This time there would be 43 awards, compared to 29 the previous year. (They had been cut back from 40-plus to 20-plus in 1956 in order to keep the ceremony short.) Academy president Harry Ackerman said, "The expanded list will now allow everyone in the industry to compete in his appropriate field and should result in the most complete awards program in the history of the academy." After this awards ceremony, the count would yet again be compressed dramatically to 20-plus.

The New York chapter had asked for more news awards, L.A. for more honors for actors. Both got what they wanted. New categories were also added for "one shots" to acknowledge, for instance, best single program and the amazing popularity of westerns, now given their own strike at the gold. In early 1959, there were 25 westerns on TV, 8 of them crowding Nielsen's top-10 rankings list. The category, however, would become a casualty in next year's nominations squeeze and then vanish forever into that smoky sunset of the genre.

Nominations this year were determined by "preferential ballots" sent directly to the academy membership instead of various unions and guilds as had been done occasionally in the recent past. "As expected, the Emmy nominations created more squawks than a peacock invading a duck farm," said *The Hollywood Reporter*, noting the outcry that followed. In another change, the eligibility period was stretched to 14 months in an effort to change over grad-

Fred Astaire with his controversial Best Actor Emmy for his Evening *special, one of a record-setting nine awards.*

NBC/ GLOBE PHOTO

ually from calendar-year awards to ones spanning the actual TV season.

The night's sweepstakes winner was a dancer's first television special. *An Evening with Fred Astaire* won all nine of the awards for which it was nominated, thereby establishing an Emmy record. *The San Diego Union* TV columnist was among its detractors, however, grousing, "You do get the idea that the members of the TV academy were unable to differentiate between honoring a deserving show and deifying it."

It was the Most Outstanding Single Program of the Year as well as the Best Special Musical or Variety Program. *Evening* was also honored for its direction, writing, camerawork, art direction, music, choreography, and the acting performance of its star. Upon accepting the statuette for the last of these, Astaire sighed happily and said softly, "This is a great night for the Old Dad." After the ceremonies at the Moulin Rouge, the fleet-footed winner celebrated, appropriately enough, by commandeering the nightclub's dance floor, choosing as his partners *Evening* costar Barrie Chase and screen vixen Kim Novak.

It was only the start of what would be remembered in entertainment awards history as the notorious "Astaire Affair." Past academy president Ed Sullivan was among those protesting the win the loudest and asked that the ballots be impounded. The TV columnist for the *L.A. Times* reported receiving a "flood of mail" from Emmy-watchers crying foul, too. One *Times* reader wrote: "The judges must have had confetti for brains when they gave Fred Astaire the best acting award. We loved his show and are happy it got the award for best single program of the year, but let it go at that — there was no acting in it!" Another reader called the win "ridiculous, humiliating and a travesty." Less than a week after his victorious night, a humbled Astaire offered to return the one award he won personally for his triumphant *Evening*. The academy politely refused. Its board of governors, reported *Variety*, "has ended the 'Astaire Affair' by declaring that Fred Astaire rightfully won his Emmy and will have to keep it."

Maverick proved it was top gun by outdueling number-one rated *Gunsmoke* in the new Best Western category, but, strangely, it took no other awards. *Gunsmoke* evened the score, at least by number, with an Emmy for Dennis Weaver. The night's other high-scoring champ was *Little Moon of Alban*, a *Hallmark Hall of Fame* production of an original drama about a love-torn Irish lass who seeks comfort in a convent. Its star, Julie Harris, was named best actress, and the show won three more prizes — for Best Special Dramatic Program and for its direction and writing.

> *Ed Sullivan railed against Astaire's Emmy and demanded the ballots be impounded.*

Past winners reappeared at the podium all night. *Playhouse 90, Omnibus,* and *What's My Line?* proved their staying power; old favorites Perry Como, Edward R. Murrow, Jane Wyatt, Ann B. Davis, and Loretta Young claimed new prizes. Dinah Shore continued her record-setting five-year winning streak, too. *The Beverly Hills Citizen* reported, erroneously, "Her mantel bows under the weight of six awards to date." She really had just one per year. The extra one counted by the *Citizen* was actually for her program, which was named Best Musical or Variety Series in 1957.

Jack Benny also came back, responsible in part for his show's three victories — for best actor, best comedy series, and best comedy writing. When accepting his own statuette, Benny seemed relieved and deadpanned, "Most people cry when they win an Emmy. I cry when I lose." The recipient of last year's new Trustees Award had the honor of bestowing the second one — to Bob Hope "for bringing laughter to all the people of the world and selflessly enter-

Best Actress Julie Harris finds sanctuary from love in Little Moon of Alban.

Bob Hope finally received an Emmy in another banner year for Jack Benny.

taining American troops in every corner of the globe." (Hope's best gag of the night referred to the *Evening with Fred Astaire* show as "the *Gigi* of TV.")

Besides Hope, other new winners included Best Dramatic Series *The Alcoa Hour/Goodyear Playhouse,* a dramatic anthology show that featured episodes with such forbidding titles as "In the Dark" and "Ten Miles to Doomsday." Barbara Hale was hailed for her superior secretarial, sleuthing, and dramatic skills in her supporting role on *Perry Mason* and Raymond Burr took his first of two Emmys as her boss. *The Huntley-Brinkley Report* was fast becoming an American — and Emmy — mainstay and was recognized as the Best News Reporting Series.

For the first time ever, the Emmy galas were staged in, and broadcast from, three different locations. In addition to the Moulin Rouge in Hollywood, the ceremonies originated from the Ziegfeld Theatre in New York and the Mayflower Hotel in Washington, D.C., where Vice President Richard Nixon helped to present the news, documentary, and public service awards. On the night of May 6th, 1959, the entrance of each place was picketed by striking NBC technicians who, most considerately, wore formal attire. Inside — "amazingly," said the academy later — the broadcasts proceeded without technical difficulty.

1958–59

For programs telecast between January 1, 1958, and February 28, 1959. Awards presented May 6, 1959, at the Moulin Rouge in Hollywood, the Ziegfeld Theatre in New York, and the Mayflower Hotel in Washington, D.C. Broadcast on NBC.

MOST OUTSTANDING SINGLE PROGRAM OF THE YEAR
• *An Evening with Fred Astaire.* NBC.
Child of Our Time, Playhouse 90. CBS.
Little Moon of Alban, Hallmark Hall of Fame. NBC.
The Old Man, Playhouse 90. CBS.

BEST DRAMATIC SERIES—ONE HOUR OR LONGER
• *Playhouse 90.* CBS.
The U.S. Steel Hour. CBS.

BEST DRAMATIC SERIES— LESS THAN ONE HOUR
• *The Alcoa Hour/Goodyear Playhouse.* NBC.
Alfred Hitchcock Presents. CBS.

General Electric Theater. CBS.
The Loretta Young Show. NBC.
Naked City. ABC.
Peter Gunn. NBC.

BEST SPECIAL DRAMATIC PROGRAM— ONE HOUR OR LONGER
• *Little Moon of Alban, Hallmark Hall of Fame.* NBC.
The Bridge of San Luis Rey, DuPont Show of the Month. CBS.
Hamlet, DuPont Show of the Month. CBS.
The Hasty Heart, DuPont Show of the Month. CBS.
Johnny Belinda, Hallmark Hall of Fame. NBC.

BEST COMEDY SERIES
• *The Jack Benny Show.* CBS.
The Bob Cummings Show. NBC.
The Danny Thomas Show. CBS.
Father Knows Best. CBS, NBC.
The Phil Silvers Show. CBS.
The Red Skelton Show. CBS.

BEST WESTERN SERIES
• *Maverick.* ABC.
Gunsmoke. CBS.
Have Gun Will Travel. CBS.
The Rifleman. ABC.
Wagon Train. NBC.

BEST MUSICAL OR VARIETY SERIES
• *The Dinah Shore Chevy Show.* NBC.
The Perry Como Show. NBC.
The Steve Allen Show. NBC.

BEST SPECIAL MUSICAL OR VARIETY PROGRAM—ONE HOUR OR LONGER
• *An Evening with Fred Astaire.* NBC.
Art Carney Meets Peter and the Wolf. ABC.

BEST PUBLIC SERVICE PROGRAM OR SERIES
• *Omnibus.* NBC.
Bold Journey. ABC.
Meet the Press. NBC.
Small World. CBS.
The Twentieth Century. CBS.
Young People's Concert. CBS.

BEST NEWS REPORTING SERIES
• *The Huntley-Brinkley Report.* NBC.
Douglas Edwards with the News. CBS.
John Daly and the News. ABC.

BEST SPECIAL NEWS PROGRAM
• *The Face of Red China.* CBS.
"American GIs in Lebanon," *Outlook.* NBC.
Election Night Returns. CBS.
Projection '59. NBC.
"The Story of Atlas 10B," *Chet Huntley Reporting.* NBC.
Where We Stand II. CBS.
Years of Crisis. CBS.

BEST PANEL, QUIZ, OR AUDIENCE PARTICIPATION SERIES
• *What's My Line?* CBS.
I've Got a Secret. CBS.
Keep Talking. CBS.
The Price is Right. NBC.
This is Your Life. NBC.
You Bet Your Life. NBC.

BEST ACTOR IN A LEADING ROLE (CONTINUING CHARACTER) IN A DRAMATIC SERIES
• Raymond Burr, *Perry Mason.* CBS.
James Arness, *Gunsmoke.* CBS.
Richard Boone, *Have Gun Will Travel.* CBS.
James Garner, *Maverick.* ABC.
Craig Stevens, *Peter Gunn.* NBC.

Efrem Zimbalist, Jr., *77 Sunset Strip.* ABC.

BEST ACTRESS IN A LEADING ROLE (CONTINUING CHARACTER) IN A DRAMATIC SERIES
• Loretta Young, *The Loretta Young Show.* NBC.
Phyllis Kirk, *The Thin Man.* NBC.
June Lockhart, *Lassie.* CBS.
Jane Wyman, *Jane Wyman Theatre.* NBC.

BEST ACTOR IN A LEADING ROLE (CONTINUING CHARACTER) IN A COMEDY SERIES
• Jack Benny, *The Jack Benny Show.* CBS.
Walter Brennan, *The Real McCoys.* ABC.
Bob Cummings, *The Bob Cummings Show.* NBC.
Phil Silvers, *The Phil Silvers Show.* CBS.
Danny Thomas, *The Danny Thomas Show.* CBS.
Robert Young, *Father Knows Best.* CBS, NBC.

BEST ACTRESS IN A LEADING ROLE (CONTINUING CHARACTER) IN A COMEDY SERIES
• Jane Wyatt, *Father Knows Best.* CBS, NBC.
Gracie Allen, *The George Burns and Gracie Allen Show.* CBS.
Spring Byington, *December Bride.* CBS.
Ida Lupino, *Mr. Adams and Eve.* CBS.
Donna Reed, *The Donna Reed Show.* ABC.
Ann Sothern, *The Ann Sothern Show.* CBS.

BEST SINGLE PERFORMANCE BY AN ACTOR
• Fred Astaire, *An Evening with Fred Astaire.* NBC.
Robert Crawford, *Child of Our Time*, *Playhouse 90.* CBS.
Paul Muni, *Last Clear Chance*, *Playhouse 90.* CBS.
Christopher Plummer, *Little Moon of Alban*, *Hallmark Hall of Fame.* NBC.
Mickey Rooney, *Eddie*, *Alcoa-Goodyear Theatre.* NBC.
Rod Steiger, *A Town Has Turned to Dust*, *Playhouse 90.* CBS.

BEST SINGLE PERFORMANCE BY AN ACTRESS
• Julie Harris, *Little Moon of Alban*, *Hallmark Hall of Fame.* NBC.

Judith Anderson, *The Bridge of San Luis Rey*, *DuPont Show of the Month*. CBS.
Helen Hayes, *One Red Rose for Christmas*, *The U.S. Steel Hour*. CBS.
Piper Laurie, *The Days of Wine and Roses*, *Playhouse 90*. CBS.
Geraldine Page, *The Old Man*, *Playhouse 90*. CBS.
Maureen Stapleton, *All the King's Men*, *Kraft Television Theatre*. NBC.

BEST SUPPORTING ACTOR (CONTINUING CHARACTER) IN A DRAMATIC SERIES
• Dennis Weaver, *Gunsmoke*. CBS.
Herschel Bernardi, *Peter Gunn*. NBC.
Johnny Crawford, *The Rifleman*. ABC.
William Hopper, *Perry Mason*. CBS.

BEST SUPPORTING ACTRESS (CONTRIBUTING CHARACTER) IN A DRAMATIC SERIES
• Barbara Hale, *Perry Mason*. CBS.
Lola Albright, *Peter Gunn*. NBC.
Amanda Blake, *Gunsmoke*. CBS.
Hope Emerson, *Peter Gunn*. NBC.

BEST SUPPORTING ACTOR (CONTINUING CHARACTER) IN A COMEDY SERIES
• Tom Poston, *The Steve Allen Show*. NBC.
Richard Crenna, *The Real McCoys*. ABC.
Paul Ford, *The Phil Silvers Show*. CBS.
Maurice Gosfield, *The Phil Silvers Show*. CBS.
Billy Gray, *Father Knows Best*. CBS, NBC.
Harry Morgan, *December Bride*. CBS.

BEST SUPPORTING ACTRESS (CONTINUING CHARACTER) IN A COMEDY SERIES
• Ann B. Davis, *The Bob Cummings Show*. NBC.
Rosemary DeCamp, *The Bob Cummings Show*. NBC.
Elinor Donahue, *Father Knows Best*. CBS, NBC.
Verna Felton, *December Bride*. CBS.
Kathy Nolan, *The Real McCoys*. ABC.
Zasu Pitts, *Oh! Susanna*. CBS.

BEST PERFORMANCE BY AN ACTOR (CONTINUING CHARACTER) IN A MUSICAL OR VARIETY SERIES
• Perry Como, *The Perry Como Show*. NBC.
Steve Allen, *The Steve Allen Show*. NBC.
Jack Paar, *The Tonight Show*. NBC.

BEST PERFORMANCE BY AN ACTRESS (CONTINUING CHARACTER) IN A MUSICAL OR VARIETY SERIES
• Dinah Shore, *The Dinah Shore Chevy Show*. NBC.
Patti Page, *The Patti Page Show*. ABC.

BEST NEWS COMMENTATOR OR ANALYST
• Edward R. Murrow. CBS.
John Daly. ABC.
Chet Huntley. NBC.

BEST DIRECTION OF A SINGLE DRAMATIC PROGRAM—ONE HOUR OR LONGER
• George Schaefer, *Little Moon of Alban*, *Hallmark Hall of Fame*. NBC.
George Roy Hill, *Child of Our Time*, *Playhouse 90*. CBS.
John Frankenheimer, *A Town Has Turned to Dust*, *Playhouse 90*. CBS.

BEST DIRECTION OF A SINGLE PROGRAM, DRAMATIC SERIES—UNDER ONE HOUR
• Jack Smight, *Eddie*, *Alcoa-Goodyear Theatre*. NBC.
Herschel Daugherty, *One is a Wanderer*, *General Electric Theater*. CBS.
Blake Edwards, "The Kill," *Peter Gunn*. NBC.
Alfred Hitchcock, "Lamb to the Slaughter," *Alfred Hitchcock Presents*. CBS.
James Neilson, *Kid at the Stick*, *General Electric Theater*. CBS.

BEST DIRECTION OF A SINGLE PROGRAM OF A COMEDY SERIES
• Peter Tewksbury, "Medal for Margaret," *Father Knows Best*. CBS.
Hy Averback, "Kate's Career," *The Real McCoys*. ABC.
Seymour Berns, *The Jack Benny Show* (with guest star Gary Cooper). CBS.
Richard Kinon, "The Interview," *Mr. Adams and Eve*. CBS.
Sheldon Leonard, "Pardon My Accent," *The Danny Thomas Show*. CBS.

BEST DIRECTION OF A SINGLE MUSICAL OR VARIETY PROGRAM
• Bud Yorkin, *An Evening with Fred Astaire*. NBC.
Clark Jones, *The Perry Como Show* (with Maureen O'Hara, Robert Preston). NBC.
Gower Champion, Joe Cates, *Accent on Love*, *Pontiac Star Parade*. NBC.

Best Writing of a Single Dramatic Program—One Hour or Longer
• James Costigan, *Little Moon of Alban*, *Hallmark Hall of Fame*. NBC.
Horton Foote, *The Old Man*, *Playhouse 90*. CBS.
J.P. Miller, *The Days of Wine and Roses*, *Playhouse 90*. CBS.
Irving Gaynor Neiman, *Child of Our Time*, *Playhouse 90*. CBS.
Rod Serling, *A Town Has Turned to Dust*, *Playhouse 90*. CBS.

Best Writing of a Single Program of a Dramatic Series—Less Than One Hour
• Alfred Brenner, Ken Hughes, *Eddie*, *Alcoa-Goodyear Theatre*. NBC.
Roald Dahl, "Lamb to the Slaughter," *Alfred Hitchcock Presents*. CBS.
Blake Edwards, "The Kill," *Peter Gunn*. NBC.
Christopher Knopf, *The Loudmouth*, *Alcoa-Goodyear Theatre*. NBC.
Samuel Taylor, *One is a Wanderer*, *General Electric Theater*. CBS.

Best Writing of a Single Program of a Comedy Series
• Sam Perrin, George Balzer, Hal Goldman, Al Gordon, *The Jack Benny Show* (with guest star Ernie Kovacs). CBS.
Billy Freidberg, Arnie Rosen, Coleman Jacoby, "Bilko's Vampire," *The Phil Silvers Show*. CBS.
Paul Henning, Dick Wesson, "Grandpa Clobbers the Air Force," *The Bob Cummings Show*. NBC.
Roswell Rogers, "Medal for Margaret," *Father Knows Best*. CBS.
Bill Manhoff, "Once There Was a Traveling Salesman," *The Real McCoys*. ABC.

Best Writing of a Single Musical or Variety Program
• Bud Yorkin, Herbert Baker, *An Evening with Fred Astaire*. NBC.
Goodman Ace, Mort Green, George Foster, Jay Burton, *The Perry Como Show* (with guest stars Pier Angeli, Andy Griffith, Helen O'Connell). NBC.
Larry Gelbart, Woody Allen, *Sid Caesar's Chevy Show* (with guest stars Shirley MacLaine, Art Carney, Jo Stafford). NBC.
J. Russell, *Art Carney Meets Peter and the Wolf*. ABC.

Leonard Stern, Stan Burns, Herb Sargent, Bill Dana, Don Hinkley, Hal Goldman, Larry Klein, *The Steve Allen Show* (with guest stars Peter Ustinov, Louis Armstrong, Van Cliburn). NBC.

OTHER AWARD WINNERS
Best Musical Contribution to a Television Program
• David Rose, for the musical direction of *An Evening with Fred Astaire*. NBC.

Best Choreography for Television
• Hermes Pan, *An Evening with Fred Astaire*. NBC.

Best Cinematography for Television
• Ellis W. Carter, "The Alphabet Conspiracy," *Bell Telephone Special*. NBC.

Best Live Camera Work
• *An Evening with Fred Astaire*. NBC.

Best Editing of a Film for Television
• Silvio D'Alisera, "Meet Mr. Lincoln," *Project 20*. NBC.

Best Art Direction in a Television Film
• Claudio Guzman, "Bernadette," *Desilu Playhouse*. CBS.

Best Art Direction in a Live Program
• Edward Stephenson, *An Evening with Fred Astaire*. NBC.

Best Engineering or Technical Achievement
• Industry-wide improvement of editing video tape as exemplified by ABC, CBS, and NBC.

Best On-the-Spot Coverage of a News Event
• Cuban Revolution: Jack Fern, film director. Stuart Novins, Richard Bate, reporters. Frank Donghi, coordinator. Paul Rubenstein, Ralph Santos, Larry Smith, cameramen. CBS.

Trustees Award
• Bob Hope

Heavyweight Bouts

Scaling back the number of categories — from 43 to 24 this year — the academy explained, was "to preserve the prestige, news value, and audience interest in the awards." The two prizes formerly given out for the finest drama and comedy series were also cut, to one in each category and the best "single program of the year" was eliminated entirely. Other awards were slashed, too, including the supporting acting prizes. Even the award titles themselves were altered with the substitution of the word "outstanding" for "best."

"A British knight, a Swedish beauty and the first member of the Negro race to win an Emmy captured the top awards," wrote *The Los Angeles Times* the next day. The winning shows and performances marked the first time that either Laurence Olivier or Ingrid Bergman had performed on American television and the actors were quickly rewarded for Olivier's "soul-twisting performance of a tortured painter" based on Paul Gauguin, in W. Somerset Maugham's *The Moon and Sixpence*, and for Bergman's portrayal of the haunted governess in Henry James's *The Turn of the Screw*. Harry Belafonte had been seen frequently on TV in variety specials throughout the 1950s and was even Emmy-nominated for one in 1955, but this was the year he would make awards history by being the first black to take one home — for his "outstanding" performance in *Tonight with Belafonte.*

Neither Olivier nor Bergman could be on hand to accept their statuettes. Olivier, in fact, had asked his show's costar Hume Cronyn to accept on his behalf if he won, and even cabled his prepared thank-you remarks to Cronyn for the

Past Gleason Show *winner Art Carney holds the trophy for his* V.I.P. *special.*

occasion. But in a major snafu, broadcaster NBC asked Charlton Heston to do the honors. Then the network flip-flopped and asked Cronyn to stand in. Cronyn agreed on the condition that the decision was final. NBC said it was. Cronyn then went to the Ziegfeld Theatre where the New York ceremonies were being held, took an aisle seat, and waited for the show to begin. He then learned that Heston would be taking over — and he walked out.

The Olivier/Bergman/Belafonte victories spawned further disgruntlement — among the press, too — since none of the shows in which the winners starred took its respective program award. "If Olivier is the best actor of the year in *The Moon and Sixpence* and Bob Mulligan is the best director of the year for *The Moon and Sixpence*, then why isn't *Moon and Sixpence* the best drama?" asked the *L.A. Times* after the fact. *Sixpence* and *Screw* in fact, lost the drama distinction to *Playhouse 90*, which one of its own producers even admitted had had a "disaster" of a season. *Tonight with Belafonte* lost to the backward-glancing *Fabulous Fifties* review show on CBS, which, to compound the irony, also beat out *Another Evening with Fred Astaire*. The first Astaire *Evening* had caused enough commotion. Its sequel took no awards.

The night's big sweepstakes winner was, gratefully, beyond such swiping. *The Untouchables* took four trophies, three for technical achievements and one for its star Robert Stack, who played the unreproachable Eliot Ness. Before the show became a weekly hit on Thursday nights, Stack had distinguished himself as an accomplished actor in some of the best dramatic anthology shows on TV. *The Untouchables* even grew out of one of them, having been produced originally as an episode on *Desilu Playhouse*.

The only show in the Nielsen ratings' top ten to take an Emmy this year was *Father Knows Best*, whose actress Jane Wyatt received her third in a row. Other popular programming was singled out, though, including *The Huntley-Brinkley Report*, which proved once and for all that two talking heads were better than one, since it triumphed over the news show Chet Huntley did solo for NBC. Art Carney had won three Emmys in the past for his supporting role as Ed Norton on the Gleason show, but this year he had his own special about famous people — *V.I.P.* — which was acknowledged for its Outstanding Program Achievement in the Field of Humor. Also up for laughs — and laurels— was the first syndicated program *and* the first cartoon series ever to win an Emmy Award. Producers William Hanna and Joseph Barbera accepted the prize for best children's show for *Huckleberry Hound*.

Outstanding Program Achievement in the Field of Public Affairs and Education went to *The Twentieth Century*, the CBS documentary program narrated by Walter Cronkite that would run more than a dozen years as it chronicled historic moments in the century's politics, arts, and other key areas. As the new academy president, however, Cronkite was the Invisible Man of the Night at the Emmys since just prior to the show, he was summoned to Tokyo to chronicle President Eisenhower's impending trip, which was then canceled at the last minute due to rioting.

But Cronkite at least appeared at the ceremonies on a film clip to review academy news and to emphasize the seriousness of N.A.T.A.S.'s commitment to the television industry and the general public. It was also a big night for Cronkite's employer, CBS. The network won more than half (14) of the accolades,

> **The Emmycast ushered in a new TV star: Bob Newhart.**

including a Trustees Award, which was given to CBS President Frank Stanton whose "forthright and courageous action ... advanced immeasurably the freedom of television as an arm of the free press."

"The one award that seemed completely foreordained [sic]," wrote the *L.A. Times*, "was the musical award to Leonard Bernstein and his New York Philharmonic concerts on CBS for the best musical program of the year.

"The writing awards *were* rather a surprise," though, the paper added. A 35-year old Rod Serling took home his fourth prize, but not for another superlative script written for the dramatic anthology shows. It was for writing "various episodes" of his classic *Twilight Zone* series. Gag-spinners for *The Jack Benny Show* also won. Both were CBS programs, too.

The Emmys ceremonies, said *Variety*, set a record for "showmanship, excellence, skill and timing." In charge that night as emcees were Arthur Godfrey out east and, in Hollywood, the "Old Dad" Fred Astaire. Astaire, who took such a beating the year before over the much-ballyhooed "Astaire affair," took charge of this year's proceedings in a gentlemanly fashion when he opened the broadcast saying that he was chosen "to be the Alfred Hitchcock" of the night's suspense. Entertainment was provided by actor Joe Flynn of *The Steve Allen Show* and singer Mahalia Jackson.

Everyone, however, was upstaged by another entertainer, who, added *Variety*, "just about grabbed the laurels and ran." "The show managed to usher in a new comedy star: Bob Newhart," said the *L.A. Times*. The young comedian "who was unknown six months ago, bumbled through a hilarious discussion of life in the Navy ... and (another) hilarious portrait of a TV director blocking out the Krushchev arrival in Washington." Newhart was given more air time than he'd been allotted ahead of time because of the last-minute cancellation of an appearance by Mike Nichols and Elaine May. NBC announced that the comic couple "withdrew" from the program "by mutual agreement" because "they were not satisfied with their material," but Nichols denied that. The duo had prepared a skit involving digs at home permanents and TV producer David Susskind that was to be aired just before a commercial for Lilt's similar hair-care product. The skit was deemed "inappro-priate" and yanked. Susskind later told friends, "Mike and Elaine can be pretty lethal."

"There was none of the fanfare" usually surrounding the award ceremonies, the *L.A. Times* wrote. "No bleachers full of screaming fans, no klieg lights, no long lines of limousines discharging beautiful mink-clad cargo of the most famous personalities on earth." Instead, the seating areas that actually looked like bleachers contained mostly the night's nominees such as Teresa Wright and Donna Reed. There was no podium either. A "cyclorama" was substituted, "a curtain affair that will seem to draw the audience in on the show."

The home audience was comprised of 60 million viewers — at least in part. *The New York Times* explained: "In untold numbers of homes on Monday evening, the radio was tuned in to the Floyd Patterson-Ingemar Johansson fight while the television set, with the sound off, was adjusted to see the annual ceremony of the Emmy prizes. If what the ear heard and the eye saw were allowed a measure of traditional interrelationship, there was a risk of concluding that Mr. Patterson had won the Emmy for cinema photography and that Jack Benny's writers were working for Howard Cosell at ringside."

The Emmys show acknowledged its heavyweight competition and the viewing audience's interest in it when Fred Astaire interrupted the proceedings at one point to announce that Patterson had just reclaimed his boxing championship by knocking out Johansson at the Polo Grounds in New York.

1959–60

For programs telecast between March 1, 1959, and March 31, 1960. Awards presented June 20, 1960, at NBC's Burbank Studios and the Ziegfeld Theatre in New York. Broadcast on NBC.

OUTSTANDING PROGRAM ACHIEVEMENT IN THE FIELD OF DRAMA
• *Playhouse 90*. CBS.
Ethan Frome, DuPont Show of the Month. CBS.

The Moon and Sixpence. NBC.
The Turn of the Screw, Ford Startime.
NBC.
The Untouchables. ABC.

**OUTSTANDING PROGRAM ACHIEVEMENT
IN THE FIELD OF HUMOR**
• *Art Carney Special.* NBC.
The Danny Thomas Show. CBS.
Father Knows Best. CBS.
The Jack Benny Show. CBS.
The Red Skelton Show. CBS.

**OUTSTANDING PROGRAM ACHIEVEMENT
IN THE FIELD OF VARIETY**
• *The Fabulous Fifties.* CBS.
Another Evening with Fred Astaire. NBC.
The Dinah Shore Chevy Show. NBC.
The Garry Moore Show. CBS.
Tonight with Belafonte, The Revlon Revue.
CBS.

**OUTSTANDING PROGRAM ACHIEVEMENT
IN THE FIELD OF PUBLIC AFFAIRS AND
EDUCATION**
• *The Twentieth Century.* CBS.
Meet the Press. NBC.
"The Population Explosion." *CBS Reports.*
CBS.
Small World. CBS.
Winter Olympics. CBS.

**OUTSTANDING PROGRAM ACHIEVEMENT
IN THE FIELD OF NEWS**
• *The Huntley-Brinkley Report.* NBC.
Chet Huntley Reporting. NBC.
Douglas Edwards with the News. CBS.
Journey to Understanding. NBC.
Khrushchev's arrival, appearance at
National Press Club, and speech to the
nation, *Journey to Understanding.* NBC.

**OUTSTANDING PROGRAM ACHIEVEMENT
IN THE FIELD OF MUSIC**
• *Leonard Bernstein and the New York
Philharmonic.* CBS.
The Bell Telephone Hour. NBC.
*The Green Pastures, Hallmark Hall of
Fame.* NBC.
"The Music of Gershwin," *The Bell
Telephone Hour.* NBC.
Young People's Concerts. CBS.

**OUTSTANDING ACHIEVEMENT IN THE
FIELD OF CHILDREN'S PROGRAMMING**
• *Huckleberry Hound.* Syndicated.
Captain Kangaroo. CBS.
Lassie. CBS.

Quickdraw McGraw. Syndicated.
Watch Mr. Wizard. NBC.

**OUTSTANDING PERFORMANCE
BY AN ACTOR IN A SERIES (LEAD
OR SUPPORTING)**
• Robert Stack, *The Untouchables.* ABC.
Richard Boone, *Have Gun Will Travel.*
CBS.
Raymond Burr, *Perry Mason.* CBS.

**OUTSTANDING PERFORMANCE
BY AN ACTRESS IN A SERIES (LEAD OR
SUPPORTING)**
• Jane Wyatt, *Father Knows Best.* CBS.
Donna Reed, *The Donna Reed Show.*
ABC.

N.A.T.A.S.

*After losing in 1955, Harry Belafonte
won at last for* Tonight with Belafonte.

Loretta Young, *The Loretta Young Show.*
NBC.

**OUTSTANDING SINGLE PERFORMANCE
BY AN ACTOR—LEAD OR SUPPORTING**
• Laurence Olivier, *The Moon and
Sixpence.* NBC.
Lee J. Cobb, *Project Immortality,
Playhouse 90.* CBS.
Alec Guinness, *The Wicked Scheme of
Jebal Deeks, Ford Startime.* NBC.

**OUTSTANDING SINGLE PERFORMANCE
BY AN ACTRESS LEAD OR SUPPORTING**
• Ingrid Bergman, *The Turn of the Screw,
Ford Startime.* NBC.
Julie Harris, *Ethan Frome, DuPont Show*

of the Month. CBS.
Teresa Wright, *The Margaret Bourke-White Story*, *Breck Sunday Showcase.* NBC.

Outstanding Performance in a Variety or Musical Program or Series
• Harry Belafonte, *Tonight with Belafonte, The Revlon Revue.* CBS.
Fred Astaire, *Another Evening with Fred Astaire.* NBC.
Dinah Shore, *The Dinah Shore Chevy Show.* NBC.

Outstanding Directorial Achievement in Drama
• Robert Mulligan, *The Moon and Sixpence.* NBC.
John Frankenheimer, *The Turn of the Screw, Ford Startime.* NBC.
Phil Karlson, "The Untouchables," *Desilu Playhouse.* CBS.

Outstanding Directorial Achievement in Comedy
• Ralph Levy, Bud Yorkin, *The Jack Benny Hour Specials.* CBS.
Seymour Berns, *The Red Skelton Show.* CBS.
Sheldon Leonard, *The Danny Thomas Show.* CBS.

Outstanding Writing Achievement in Drama
• Rod Serling, *The Twilight Zone.* CBS.
James Costigan, *The Turn of the Screw, Ford Startime.* NBC.
Loring Mandel, *Project Immortality, Playhouse 90.* CBS.

Outstanding Writing Achievement in Comedy
• Sam Perrin, George Balzer, Al Gordon, Hal Goldman, *The Jack Benny Show.* CBS.
Dorothy Cooper, Roswell Rogers, *Father Knows Best.* CBS.
Nat Hiken, *The Ballad of Louie the Louse.* CBS.

Outstanding Writing Achievement in the Documentary Field
• Howard K. Smith, Av Westin, "The Population Explosion." *CBS Reports.* CBS.
James Benjamin, "From Kaiser to Fuehrer," *The Twentieth Century.* CBS.
Richard F. Hanser, "Life in the Thirties," *Project 20.* NBC.

OTHER AWARD WINNERS
Outstanding Achievement in Cinematography for Television
• Charles Straumer, "The Untouchables," *Desilu Playhouse.* CBS.

Outstanding Achievement in Electronic Camera Work
• *Winter Olympics.* CBS.

Outstanding Achievement in Film Editing for Television
• Ben H. Ray, Robert L. Swanson, *The Untouchables.* ABC.

Outstanding Achievement in Art Direction and Scenic Design
• Ralph Berger, Frank Smith, "The Untouchables," *Desilu Playhouse.* CBS.

Outstanding Engineering or Technical Achievement
• The new General Electric supersensitive camera tube permitting colorcasting in no more light than is needed for black and white.

Trustees Award
• Dr. Frank Stanton, president, the Columbia Broadcasting System, Inc.

Trustees Citations
• The Ampex Corp.
• The Radio Corporation of America
• Michael R. Gargiulo
• Richard Gillaspy.

A Bloodless Coup
for *Macbeth*

A successful power play by *Macbeth* to be this year's Emmys king was expected from the outset. "It was quite obvious," wrote TV columnist Cecil Smith of *The Los Angeles Times* when the nominations were announced, "that the two really superior efforts in television this year — the *Hallmark Macbeth* and the ABC-Screen Gems's Winston Churchill series — would nab their share of nominations." Smith also cheered another vote-getter: "I was delighted by the nomination of a very fine actor whose talent usually is unrecognized — Cliff Robertson for his starring role in *The Two Worlds of Charlie Gordon* on the *Steel Hour*." *Variety* applauded the first recognition that Bob Hope received from academy voters. His *Buick Show* special on NBC was up for outstanding humor program, although the *Times* predicted the cartoon series *The Flintstones* would best it come awards night. And there were the predictable complaints, too. "Yes," said *The Hollywood Reporter*, "as we did last year, we take umbrage at the fact there was no reinstatement of the 'Outstanding Comedian' categories." Others were upset that Ronald Reagan was overlooked for his work on *G.E. Theatre*.

Awards night was hosted by Dick Powell in Hollywood and Joey Bishop in New York and reflected an academy precedent: It was first time that the eligibility period for the prizes directly paralleled the television networks' yearly season. And, as expected, the evening turned out to be a private party for William Shakespeare.

The *Hallmark Hall of Fame*'s *Macbeth* swept five awards, one for each

nomination it received. The tale of the bloody deeds of the Thane of Cawdor had been presented live by *Hallmark* before, in 1954, and with the same lead cast, but this one was a more ambitious production. Filmed on location in Scotland for $750,000 and broadcast later in a special two-hour, color presentation, it is considered by many television historians to have been the first true made-for-TV movie. It was also shown in "art houses" in the U.S. and in film theaters overseas, and was entered by its British co-producer in contests such as the Berlin Film Festival. At the TV awards ceremonies, its American producer George Schaefer "kept bouncing up to the stage

Hallmark's lavish remake of Macbeth *is considered the first made-for-TV movie.*

to collect *Macbeth* Emmys" all night out in New York, wrote the *L.A. Times*, including one for himself as its director. It was the second time that Schaefer received an Emmy for directing a *Hallmark* presentation. His first was for *Little Moon of Alban* in 1958–59.

In addition to being named Outstanding Program in the Field of Drama and taking the director's prize, *Macbeth* also took the most coveted distinction of all, the newly reinstated category of Program of the Year. Honors went as well to its star Maurice Evans, who hadn't been nominated for his performance in the 1954 version, but this time beat out the young Cliff Robertson, who would later win an Oscar for portraying the same Charlie Gordon character in the film *Charly*. Judith Anderson had won her first Emmy for playing *Hallmark*'s Lady Macbeth in 1954 and this time she triumphed again, becoming the first person in Emmy history to win a prize

 PHOTOS: HALLMARK HALL OF FAME

The first Macbeth *in 1954 was spartan. Anderson won Emmys for both versions.*

twice for the same role in two different feature productions. In her acceptance speech, she thanked the one important contributor who took no Emmy nominations or trophies, not even posthumously — William Shakespeare.

As if it expected the perfect timing of the *Macbeth* triumph, the academy decided before the awards show to acknowledge the drama's financial benefactor with a special prize. Greeting card company founder J.C. Hall was given a Trustees Award for "uplifting the standards of television through complete sponsorship over a 10-year period

of *Hallmark Hall of Fame*, which has brought many enriching hours of entertainment to the viewing public." "Mr. Hall has done more for television than any individual who has ever appeared on the little screen," Cecil Smith commented in the *L.A. Times*. "It might be well to hand out an award to an enlightened sponsor every year (though I suppose you'd run out of them in a couple of years)."

ABC's *Winston Churchill — The Valiant Years* was expected to win Outstanding Program Achievement in the Field of Public Affairs and Education, but was upset by the 1959–60 champ, Walter Cronkite's *The Twentieth Century*. *Churchill* did, however, take a trophy for documentary writing. Contrary to Smith's prediction, *The Flintstones* lost, too — and to the popular winner of Emmy's Best Comedy Series of 1958–59, *The Jack Benny Show*. Benny's program may have been acknowledged as the funniest on TV, but his writers lost to Red Skelton's and the directing award in comedy went to Sheldon Leonard of *The Danny Thomas Show*. Strangely, neither of the latter two shows were nominated against Benny's for the outstanding humor program — "one of those TV academy imponderables," whined the *Times*.

Since prizes for comedians had been suspended, Benny was not up for one himself, but he did want to be on hand on awards night in the event his program won. He didn't show, though, because of a tragedy that also cast a noticeable gloom over those who did attend. Ten hours before the start of the Emmycast, funeral services in Hollywood were held for actor Gary Cooper at the Church of the Good Shepherd, which was crammed with 500 mourners. Benny had been a pallbearer and, according to his show's producer, Irving Fine, who accepted the comedy program award on his behalf, "didn't feel it would be right to come to a happy affair at the end of such a day."

Fine was given the statuette by the obviously cheerful news team of Chet Huntley and David Brinkley, who also gave an award to George Judd, Jr., on behalf of Leonard Bernstein's *Young People's Concert*, which upset NBC's *The Shirley Temple Show* in the children's program competition. America's favorite news duo was obviously pleased because the night's show opened with their own program winning in the broadcast journalism category for the third year in a row. (It would continue to dominate the slot for successive years to come — eventually triggering two networks' "mutiny" in 1964.) Comedienne Carol Burnett had the honor of giving them their newest trophy, referring to the pair teasingly as "Nuntley-Hunkley."

Another repeat winner from last year was Rod Serling, whose second win for his *Twilight Zone* scripts seemed to sound a death knell separate from Gary Cooper's that day and of a different sort. Serling won over Reginald Rose, his distinguished peer and longtime nemesis in past competitions over writing TV's best live dramas. Rose's dramatic script this year, based on the Sacco and Vanzetti spy case, was expected to triumph, but lost to the more commercial kind of writing that Serling was now running through his typewriter. TV observers — including the television academy, which sponsored a special seminar on the subject six months after the awards night — wondered aloud if this meant that live television was dead. Bemused and perplexed industry insiders were also concerned that Hallmark's *Macbeth* had been shot on tape instead of being broadcast live, as all past *Hallmark* specials had been. They pointed for further evidence of live TV's infirm condition to the vast, cavernous, and costly studios that both NBC and CBS had recently built in Hollywood, but which now

stood empty. No one came up with a definitive answer, but it could probably be found in what soon happened to Rose. He turned away from the "live" medium, too, and soon went on to write scripts for the TV series *The Defenders*, which grew, ironically, out of an episode he once wrote for *Studio One*.

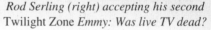

Rod Serling (right) accepting his second Twilight Zone *Emmy: Was live TV dead?*

A Harry Belafonte TV special was expected to take the Outstanding Variety Program of 1960–61 just as one did the year before, but academy members had a change of heart and had old business to settle, too. They gave it to *Astaire Time*, which again teamed up the "Old Dad" with dancer Barrie Chase and the David Rose Orchestra, and recognized its once-maligned star, not for his acting skills this time, but for his outstanding performance in a variety show. "If Fred Astaire keeps it up," commented the *L.A. Times*, "his Emmys and Walt Disney's Oscars could start a new race."

Raymond Burr won his second Emmy as Perry Mason. Barbara Stanwyck won the first of her three career statuettes for performing on her short-lived TV show made up mostly of pilots intended to become future series. (None made it.) Stanwyck, though, was so excited to win the award that, in her race to the podium to accept it, she ripped her evening gown. An awkward delay followed while someone tried to help her on with her coat. When Stanwyck finally got to the stage, said the *L.A. Times*, she "was greeted with an ovation that shook TV sets." New York host Joey Bishop tried to dispel the embarrassing seriousness of the situation later on by quipping "The guy who helped Barbara Stanwyck with her coat was on camera longer than I was!"

An award for supporting actor or actress was reinstated this year. Don Knotts would go on to win five of them throughout his career for his portrayal of Deputy Sheriff Barney Fife on *The Andy Griffith Show* (compared to none for Griffith, an irony mirrored by the fates of Art Carney and Jackie Gleason in earlier years), but it was his first that impressed him most. His acceptance speech in 1961 was comprised mostly of his admission that he was "a prepared loser" and therefore didn't know what to say. Roddy McDowall had nothing at all to say for winning in the supporting actor's category for a single show (*Equitable American Heritage*'s *Not Without Honor*). He was busy that night performing on stage in *Camelot*, so his statuette was accepted by Piper Laurie in New York.

The entertainment of the night included Lorne Greene and Dan Blocker playfully mimicking what *Bonanza* might look like performed on English and Japanese TV; the *My Three Sons* boys did a skit of what a film would look like if there were no editors cutting them back. But in what was variously called "the most inspired moment of the program" and "the hit of the show," Dennis Weaver delivered a farcical tribute to the man of the night — William Shakespeare — which was comprised of a hilarious parody of the *Hamlet* soliloquy. "With a throbbing drumbeat in the background and all the shadows and paraphernalia that ordinarily accompany an appearance of the melancholy Dane," reported the *L.A. Times*, "Weaver with dead seriousness read, 'TV or not TV, that is the question. Whether 'tis nobler to suffer the slugs and arrows of *Bonanza* ... or switch to *Perry Mason* ....'" The paper's TV columnist Cecil Smith concluded, "It was wonderful."

Smith added: "Strictly as entertainment, I thought Tuesday night's Emmy Awards show a delightful 90 minutes. It will be criticized, I suppose, because so much of it was on tape and film and included canned laughter, but ... the Oscar shindig might take some lessons!"

The viewing public seemed to agree. The Emmys show pulled a 33.9 Nielsen rating and became the most-watched show of its week, beating out popular runners-up *Candid Camera*, *The Ed Sullivan Show*, and even *The Untouchables*.

1960–61

For programs telecast between April 1, 1960, and April 15, 1961. Awards presented May 16, 1961, at the Moulin Rouge in Hollywood and the Ziegfeld Theatre in New York. Broadcast on NBC.

PROGRAM OF THE YEAR
• *Macbeth, Hallmark Hall of Fame.* NBC.
Astaire Time. NBC.

Convention Coverage. NBC.
An Hour with Danny Kaye. CBS.
Sacco-Vanzetti. NBC.

OUTSTANDING PROGRAM ACHIEVEMENT IN THE FIELD OF DRAMA
• *Macbeth, Hallmark Hall of Fame.* NBC.
Naked City. ABC.
Sacco-Vanzetti. NBC.

The Twilight Zone. CBS.
The Untouchables. ABC.

**OUTSTANDING PROGRAM ACHIEVEMENT
IN THE FIELD OF HUMOR**
• *The Jack Benny Show.* CBS.
The Andy Griffith Show. CBS.

*Brinkley and Huntley: Their news show
dominated the airwaves and the Emmys.*

The Bob Hope Buick Show. NBC.
Candid Camera. CBS.
The Flintstones. ABC.

**OUTSTANDING PROGRAM ACHIEVEMENT
IN THE FIELD OF VARIETY**
• *Astaire Time.* NBC.
Belafonte. CBS.
The Garry Moore Show. CBS.
An Hour with Danny Kaye. CBS.
The Jack Paar Tonight Show. NBC.

**OUTSTANDING PROGRAM ACHIEVEMENT
IN THE FIELD OF PUBLIC AFFAIRS
AND EDUCATION**
• *The Twentieth Century.* CBS.
CBS Reports. CBS.
Project XX. NBC.
"The U-2 Affair," *NBC White Paper.*
NBC.
Winston Churchill — The Valiant Years.
ABC.

**OUTSTANDING PROGRAM ACHIEVEMENT
IN THE FIELD OF NEWS**
• *The Huntley-Brinkley Report.* NBC.
Convention Coverage. NBC.
Douglas Edwards with the News. CBS.
Eyewitness to History. CBS.
*President Kennedy's Live News
Conferences.* ABC, CBS, NBC.

**OUTSTANDING ACHIEVEMENT IN THE
FIELD OF CHILDREN'S PROGRAMMING**
• "Aaron Copland's Birthday Party,"
Young People's Concert. CBS.
Captain Kangaroo. CBS.
Huckleberry Hound. (Syndicated.)
The Shari Lewis Show. NBC.
The Shirley Temple Theatre. NBC.

**OUTSTANDING PERFORMANCE
BY AN ACTOR IN A SERIES (LEAD)**
• Raymond Burr, *Perry Mason.* CBS.
Jackie Cooper, *Hennesey.* CBS.
Robert Stack, *The Untouchables.* ABC.

**OUTSTANDING PERFORMANCE
BY AN ACTRESS IN A SERIES (LEAD)**
• Barbara Stanwyck, *The Barbara
Stanwyck Show.* NBC.
Donna Reed, *The Donna Reed Show.* ABC.
Loretta Young, *The Loretta Young Show.* NBC.

**OUTSTANDING SINGLE PERFORMANCE
BY AN ACTOR IN A LEADING ROLE**
• Maurice Evans, *Macbeth, Hallmark Hall
of Fame.* NBC.
Cliff Robertson, *The Two Worlds of
Charlie Gordon, The U.S. Steel Hour.* CBS.
Ed Wynn, *The Man in the Funny Suit,
Westinghouse-Desilu Playhouse.* CBS.

**OUTSTANDING SINGLE PERFORMANCE
BY AN ACTRESS IN A LEADING ROLE**
• Judith Anderson, *Macbeth, Hallmark
Hall of Fame.* NBC.
Ingrid Bergman, *24 Hours in a Woman's
Life.* CBS.
Elizabeth Montgomery, "The Rusty Heller
Story," *The Untouchables.* ABC.

**OUTSTANDING PERFORMANCE
IN A SUPPORTING ROLE BY AN ACTOR
OR ACTRESS IN A SINGLE PROGRAM**
• Roddy McDowall, *Not Without Honor,
Equitable's American Heritage.* NBC.
Charles Bronson, *Memory in White,
General Electric Theatre.* CBS.
Peter Falk, "Cold Turkey," *The Law and
Mr. Jones.* ABC.

Star Evans and producer/director Schaefer juggle their Macbeth *booty.*

OUTSTANDING PERFORMANCE IN A SUPPORTING ROLE BY AN ACTOR OR ACTRESS IN A SERIES
• Don Knotts, *The Andy Griffith Show.* CBS.
Abby Dalton, *Hennesey.* CBS.
Barbara Hale, *Perry Mason.* CBS.

OUTSTANDING PERFORMANCE IN A VARIETY OR MUSICAL PROGRAM OR SERIES
• Fred Astaire, *Astaire Time.* NBC.
Harry Belafonte, *Belafonte N.Y.* CBS.
Dinah Shore, *The Dinah Shore Chevy Show.* NBC.

OUTSTANDING DIRECTORIAL ACHIEVEMENT IN DRAMA
• George Schaefer, *Macbeth, Hallmark Hall of Fame.* NBC.
Sidney Lumet, *Sacco-Vanzetti.* NBC.
Ralph Nelson, *The Man in the Funny Suit, Westinghouse-Desilu Playhouse.* CBS.

OUTSTANDING DIRECTORIAL ACHIEVEMENT IN COMEDY
• Sheldon Leonard, *Danny Thomas Show.* CBS.
Jack Shea, Richard McDonough, *The Bob Hope Buick Show.* NBC.
Peter Tewksbury, *My Three Sons.* ABC.

OUTSTANDING WRITING ACHIEVEMENT IN DRAMA
• Rod Serling, *The Twilight Zone.* CBS.
Reginald Rose, *Sacco-Vanzetti.* NBC.

Dale Wasserman, "The Lincoln Murder Case," *DuPont Show of the Month.* CBS.

OUTSTANDING WRITING ACHIEVEMENT IN COMEDY
• Sherwood Schwartz, Dave O'Brien, Al Schwartz, Martin Ragaway, Red Skelton, *The Red Skelton Show.* CBS.
Richard Baer, *Hennesey.* CBS.
Charles Stewart, Jack Elinson, *The Danny Thomas Show.* CBS.

OUTSTANDING WRITING ACHIEVEMENT IN THE DOCUMENTARY FIELD
• Victor Wolfson, *Winston Churchill — The Valiant Years.* ABC.
Arthur Barron, Al Wasserman, "The U-2 Affair," *NBC White Paper.* NBC.
Fred Friendly, David Lowe, Edward R. Murrow, "Harvest of Shame," *CBS Reports.* CBS.

OTHER AWARD WINNERS
OUTSTANDING ACHIEVEMENT IN THE FIELD OF MUSIC FOR TELEVISION
• Leonard Bernstein, *Leonard Bernstein and the New York Philharmonic.* NBC.

OUTSTANDING ACHIEVEMENT IN CINEMATOGRAPHY FOR TELEVISION
• George Clemens, *The Twilight Zone.* CBS.

OUTSTANDING ACHIEVEMENT IN ELECTRONIC CAMERA WORK
• "Sounds of America," *The Bell Telephone Hour.* RED-EO-TAPE Mobile Unit for NBC.

OUTSTANDING ACHIEVEMENT IN FILM EDITING FOR TELEVISION
• Harry Coswick, Aaron Nibley, Milton Shifman, *Naked City.* ABC.

OUTSTANDING ACHIEVEMENT IN ART DIRECTION AND SCENIC DESIGN
• John L. Lloyd, *Checkmate.* CBS.

OUTSTANDING ENGINEERING OR TECHNICAL ACHIEVEMENT
• Radio Corporation of America and Marconi's Wireless Telegraph Company, Ltd., English Electric Valve Company Ltd.

TRUSTEES AWARDS
• National Educational Television and *Radio Center* and its affiliated stations.
• Joyce C. Hall, president of Hallmark Cards, Inc.

Hallmark Regina

In a significant change in the voting procedure, academy members now submitted their nominations on a monthly basis while the competing shows and star performances were still fresh in their minds. This year there were also new awards given for outstanding daytime television and original music composed for TV, and the gender classifications were reinstated in the supporting acting categories. Heading into the Emmycast night of May 22, 1962, *Hallmark Hall of Fame*'s *Victoria Regina* and *Ben Casey* were tied with the most nominations each — eight.

By evening's end, *Victoria Regina* would reign with three awards, includ-

Nominee James Donald and winner Julie Harris in Program of the Year Victoria Regina, *which failed to be voted Outstanding Drama Program.*

ing Program of the Year and a trophy for Julie Harris's We-Are-Moved-But-Not-Amused performance as the crusty British queen in the 90-minute adaptation of Laurence Housman's play. In her acceptance speech out in New York, Harris said that the credit really belonged to her director George Schaefer who "has guided me through so many wonderful roles. I think this is for George." *Victoria* also picked up a prize for Pamela Brown's supporting performance as the Duchess of Kent.

Although *Victoria Regina* was named Program of the Year, it failed to win the Outstanding Drama Program prize, causing an outcry reflected by the opinion of *The New York Times*, which wrote, "Under such circumstances, how can the voting procedure fail to be suspect? A program not deemed worthy of finishing first in its own category nonetheless is declared the finest accomplishment irrespective of category."

But at least it lost to the program that would come to dominate the category for years to come — *The Defenders* — a courtroom drama that premiered only the previous September, but did so to rave critical notices. Unlike *Ben Casey*, which lost in every single category in which it was nominated, *The Defenders* suffered no defeats, taking one award for each of its four nominations, including acting honors for E.G. Marshall and trophies for Reginald Rose's scripts and Franklin Schaffner's direction.

The top male acting award went to Peter Falk, who would go on in later years to take several more Emmys as the popular, squinty-eyed TV detective Columbo. His first one, though, went to acknowledge Falk's performance as a "dees-and-dems" Greek truck driver who picks up a pregnant hitchhiker in an episode of *Dick Powell Theatre* called "The Price of Tomatoes." *Powell Theatre* began the night with seven nominations, but lost them all except for the statuette for Falk. Among the six losers was scriptwriter-nominee Richard Alan Simmons, to whom Falk deferred in his acceptance speech. "I have to talk about Dick Simmons," he said. "Dick conceived the show, produced the show, and wrote the show. I must give him the credit."

> Carl Reiner said, "I wish somebody told me [I'd win]. I'd have worn my hair!"

The first award of the night was presented in New York by Arlene Francis, who gave the new daytime Emmy to the *Purex Specials* that were then tackling such weighty issues of concern to housewives as their feelings of being trapped, abandoned, and frigid. Another daytime show made Emmy history, too, when *Search for Tomorrow* saw one of its stars nominated in the acting competition. Mary Stuart lost, but at least she did so to the accomplished Shirley Booth, who portrayed America's favorite sassy maid who never seemed trapped or weighted down on her show, *Hazel*, by the housekeeping chores she performed around the Baxter residence. It was a historic win for Booth. In 1950, she had won the Tony Award and, in 1952, the Oscar for her portrayal of the pathetic wife of an alcoholic in William Inge's *Come Back, Little Sheba*. She was now matched only by Helen Hayes in having an Emmy, an Oscar, and a Tony. And she would win again as *Hazel* next year.

Bob Newhart, who first came to national prominence on the Emmy Awards telecast just two years earlier, now watched his own show receive the top prize for outstanding humor series. The irony was compounded by another one, though, that was no laughing matter: *The Bob Newhart Show* had just been canceled.

In years past, Carl Reiner had won two Emmys for acting on *Caesar's Hour*, but now came back for comedy writing credit for *The Dick Van Dyke Show*, an honor he would receive twice more in as many years, along with two more prizes for producing the show. This *Van Dyke* award was presented to him by Lucille Ball. Reiner accepted, saying, "I wish somebody would have told me. I'd have worn my hair!" Ball also gave a comedy trophy to Nat Hiken (creator of *The Phil Silvers Show*) for directing *Car 54, Where Are You?*

Somebody well known for his hair came up heads above the competition in the variety program category. Garry Moore had his own show throughout the 1950s, for a while in prime time and at other periods shown in a daytime slot, but by the early 1960s it was back on in the evenings and was so popular that it easily garnered the variety show award. *The Garry Moore Show* also earned a statuette for its young emerging costar Carol Burnett, who got her first big break in show business for being zany and outrageous alongside a staid and serious Moore, whose conservative look was punctuated with his signature crew cut and bow tie.

Repeat champs included Don Knotts and Emmy-winning veterans Leonard Bernstein for his televised concerts for young people and the Japanese, and David Brinkley for his *Journal* and *The Huntley-Brinkley Report*. Brinkley was given the first award in Washington, D.C., by Presidential press secretary Pierre Salinger and the second by Senator Warren Magnuson, who was chairman of the Interstate and Foreign Commerce Committee, which oversaw the laws affecting television.

The politicos really turned out in Washington for that segment of the first three-location broadcast attempted since 1959, counting among the presenters such notables as Associate Justice of the Supreme Court William O. Douglas. Lady Bird Johnson was on hand to accept a special honor on behalf of the camera-shy Jacqueline Kennedy, who was being honored for giving her historic tour of the White House to CBS that season. FCC Chairman Newton Minow recently had denounced TV as "a vast wasteland," but didn't seem to mind pushing past the carnage on the small screen to appear there himself in order to praise the academy for its crusading role in "rewarding distinguished achievement in television." *The New York Times* was outraged, commenting, "For public figures to lend the stature of their positions to the TV industry's calculated exercise in honoring itself may be another characteristic manifestation of an era of unrestrained press agentry."

This year's awards ceremonies tried something new. Shortly before the show, academy president Robert Lewine announced, "In as many categories as possible, we'll have film clips of all nominated shows. This should heighten interest for viewers, refreshing the memories of those who'd seen the shows and certainly a major point of interest for those who hadn't seen certain shows." *The Los Angeles Times* called the film-clip introductions "most impressive" and everyone else seemed to love them, too, so much so that a future Emmy tradition was born. Film clips were also used to invigorate the whole night, showing highlights from the past year, including scenes of Mrs. Kennedy's White House tour, Jack Paar's farewell speech, coverage of the John Glenn space shot, gripping closeups of Judy Garland singing, and a few affectionate glimpses of Ernie Kovacs, who had died recently in a car accident on a rainy night. Kovacs was given a posthumous award for Outstanding Achievement in Electronic Camera Work, which was accepted by his tearful

In 1960, the Emmy telecast made Bob Newhart a TV star. Then he won one for his new series, which NBC canceled.

widow Edie Adams. Later on, after watching a film clip of Kovacs performing, Adams became so distraught that she had to be ushered from the room and treated by a physician.

"The proceedings at the Palladium were conducted without the cheering crowds and frou-frou that usually accompanies such gatherings," the *L.A. Times* noted of the Hollywood end of the three-location gala. "Stars arrived early in evening clothes, leaving their limousines in the sun-drenched parking lot. There were no bleachers, no mobs, just a few squealing teenagers at the parking lot entrance.

"Stars and nominees strolled in as if arriving at a friendly party," the *Times* added. "Ethel Waters walked from her car into the building while an attendant followed with her wheelchair.

"Fred Astaire, winner of more Emmys than any other performer, strolled along from his Rolls-Royce to a rear entrance to take part in the show. Eddie Fisher escorted nominee [for her half-hour variety series *Here's Edie*] Edie Adams."

The night's excitement was kept up best by the grinning politicos gathered in Washington and a festive group out in New York headed up by emcee Johnny Carson who opened the show, confessing, "We want the people [viewing at home] to see show people as we really are — jealous!"

1961–62

For programs telecast between April 16, 1961, and April 14, 1962. Awards presented on May 22, 1962, at the Hollywood Palladium, the Astor Hotel in New York, and the Sheraton-Park Hotel in Washington, D.C. Broadcast on NBC.

THE PROGRAM OF THE YEAR
• *Victoria Regina*, *Hallmark Hall of Fame*. NBC.
"Biography of a Bookie Joint," *CBS Reports*. CBS.
The Judy Garland Show. CBS.
Vincent Van Gogh: A Self-Portrait. NBC.
"Walk In My Shoes," *Bell and Howell Closeup*. ABC.

OUTSTANDING PROGRAM ACHIEVEMENT IN THE FIELD OF DRAMA
• *The Defenders*. CBS.
Ben Casey. ABC.
Dick Powell Theatre. NBC.
Naked City. ABC.
People Need People, *Alcoa Premiere*. ABC.
Victoria Regina, *Hallmark Hall of Fame*. NBC.

OUTSTANDING PROGRAM ACHIEVEMENT IN THE FIELD OF HUMOR
• *The Bob Newhart Show*. NBC.
The Andy Griffith Show. CBS.
Car 54, Where Are You? NBC.
Hazel. NBC.
The Red Skelton Show. CBS.

OUTSTANDING PROGRAM ACHIEVEMENTS IN THE FIELDS OF VARIETY OR MUSIC
(Variety)
• *The Garry Moore Show*. CBS.
Here's Edie. ABC.
The Judy Garland Show. CBS.
The Kraft Music Hall. NBC.
Walt Disney's Wonderful World of Color. NBC.

(Music)
• *Leonard Bernstein and the New York Philharmonic in Japan*. CBS.
The Bell Telephone Hour. NBC.
NBC Opera. NBC.
The Thief and the Hangman. ABC.

OUTSTANDING PROGRAM ACHIEVEMENT IN THE FIELD OF NEWS
• *The Huntley-Brinkley Report*. NBC.
Capital Cities Broadcasting for the Eichmann Trial. Syndicated.
Douglas Edwards with the News. CBS.
Eyewitness with Walter Cronkite. CBS.
NBC-TV Gulf Instant News Specials. NBC.

OUTSTANDING PROGRAM ACHIEVEMENT IN THE FIELD OF EDUCATIONAL AND PUBLIC AFFAIRS PROGRAMMING
• *David Brinkley's Journal*. NBC.
ABC's Wide World of Sports. ABC.
Bell and Howell Closeup. ABC.
CBS Reports. CBS.
Howard K. Smith – News and Comment. ABC.
NBC White Paper. NBC.

OUTSTANDING DAYTIME PROGRAM
• *Purex Specials for Women*. NBC.
Art Linkletter's House Party. CBS.
Calendar. CBS.
Today. NBC.
The Verdict is Yours. CBS.

OUTSTANDING PROGRAM ACHIEVEMENT IN CHILDREN'S PROGRAMMING
• *New York Philharmonic Young People's Concerts with Leonard Bernstein*. CBS.
Captain Kangaroo. CBS.
1, 2, 3—Go! NBC.
The Shari Lewis Show. NBC.
Update. NBC.
Walt Disney's Wonderful World of Color. NBC.

OUTSTANDING CONTINUED PERFORMANCE BY AN ACTOR IN A SERIES (LEAD)
• E.G. Marshall, *The Defenders*. CBS.
Paul Burke, *Naked City*. ABC.
Jackie Cooper, *Hennesey*. CBS.
Vincent Edwards, *Ben Casey*. ABC.
George Maharis, *Route 66*. CBS.

The *Defenders*'s *E.G. Marshall: best
actor in the year's best drama series.*

OUTSTANDING CONTINUED PERFORMANCE BY AN ACTRESS IN A SERIES (LEAD)
• Shirley Booth, *Hazel*. NBC.
Gertrude Berg, *The Gertrude Berg Show*. CBS.
Donna Reed, *The Donna Reed Show*. ABC.
Mary Stuart, *Search for Tomorrow*. CBS.
Cara Williams, *Pete and Gladys*. CBS.

OUTSTANDING SINGLE PERFORMANCE BY AN ACTOR IN A LEADING ROLE
• Peter Falk, *Dick Powell Theatre*. NBC.
Milton Berle, *Dick Powell Theatre*. NBC.
James Donald, *Victoria Regina*, *Hallmark Hall of Fame*. NBC.
Lee Marvin, *People Need People*, *Alcoa Premiere*. ABC.
Mickey Rooney, *Dick Powell Theatre*. NBC.

OUTSTANDING SINGLE PERFORMANCE BY AN ACTRESS IN A LEADING ROLE
• Julie Harris, *Victoria Regina*, *Hallmark Hall of Fame*. NBC.
Geraldine Brooks, *Bus Stop*. ABC.
Suzanne Pleshette, *Dr. Kildare*. NBC.
Inger Stevens, *Dick Powell Theatre*. NBC.
Ethel Waters, *Route 66*. CBS.

OUTSTANDING PERFORMANCE IN A SUPPORTING ROLE BY AN ACTOR
• Don Knotts, *The Andy Griffith Show*. CBS.
Sam Jaffe, *Ben Casey*. ABC.
Barry Jones, *Victoria Regina*, *Hallmark Hall of Fame*. NBC.
Horace McMahon, *Naked City*. ABC.
George C. Scott, *Ben Casey*. ABC.

OUTSTANDING PERFORMANCE IN A SUPPORTING ROLE BY AN ACTRESS
• Pamela Brown, *Victoria Regina*, *Hallmark Hall of Fame*. NBC.
Jeanne Cooper, *Ben Casey*. ABC.
Colleen Dewhurst, *Focus*. NBC.
Joan Hackett, *Ben Casey*. ABC.
Mary Wickes, *The Gertrude Berg Show*. CBS.

OUTSTANDING PERFORMANCE IN A VARIETY OR MUSICAL PROGRAM OR SERIES
• Carol Burnett, *The Garry Moore Show*. CBS.
Edie Adams, *Here's Edie*. ABC.
Perry Como, *The Kraft Music Hall*. NBC.
Judy Garland, *The Judy Garland Show*. CBS.
Yves Montand, *Yves Montand on Broadway*. ABC.

OUTSTANDING DIRECTORIAL ACHIEVEMENT IN DRAMA
• Franklin Schaffner, *The Defenders*. CBS.
Arthur Hiller, *Naked City*. ABC.
Buzz Kulik, *Dr. Kildare*. NBC.
George Schaefer, *Victoria Regina*, *Hallmark Hall of Fame*. NBC.
Alex Segal, *People Need People*, *Alcoa Premiere*. ABC.
Jack Smight, *Come Again to Carthage*, *Westinghouse Presents*. CBS.

OUTSTANDING DIRECTORIAL ACHIEVEMENT IN COMEDY
• Nat Hiken, *Car 54, Where Are You?* NBC.
Seymour Berns, *The Red Skelton Show*. CBS.
Dave Geisel, *The Garry Moore Show*. CBS.
John Rich, *The Dick Van Dyke Show*. CBS.
Bud Yorkin, *Henry Fonda and the Family*. CBS.

Shirley Booth (TV's sassiest maid, Hazel) gives her first outstanding lead actress award a professional buff and polish.

OUTSTANDING WRITING ACHIEVEMENT IN DRAMA
• Reginald Rose, *The Defenders.* CBS.
Henry F. Greenberg, *People Need People,* *Alcoa Premiere.* ABC.
Jack Laird, *Ben Casey.* ABC.
Rod Serling, *Twilight Zone.* CBS.
Richard Alan Simmons, *Dick Powell Theatre.* NBC.

OUTSTANDING WRITING ACHIEVEMENT IN COMEDY
• Carl Reiner, *The Dick Van Dyke Show.* CBS.
Stan Freberg, *Chunking Chow Mein Hour.* ABC.
Nat Hiken, Tony Webster, Terry Ryan, *Car 54, Where Are You?* NBC.
Roland Kibbee, Bob Newhart, Don Hinkley, Milt Rosen, Ernie Chambers, Dean Hargrove, Robert Kaufman, Norm Liebman, Charles Sherman, Howard Snyder, Larry Siegel, *The Bob Newhart Show.* NBC.
Ed Simmons, David O'Brien, Marty Ragaway, Arthur Phillips, Al Schwartz, Sherwood Schwartz, Red Skelton, *The Red Skelton Show.* CBS.

OUTSTANDING WRITING ACHIEVEMENT IN THE DOCUMENTARY FIELD
• Lou Hazam, *Vincent Van Gogh: A Self-Portrait.* NBC.
Arthur Holch, "Walk in My Shoes," *Bell and Howell Closeup.* ABC.
George Lefferts, *Purex Specials for Women.* NBC.
Jay McMullen, "Biography of a Bookie Joint," *CBS Reports.* CBS.
Al Wasserman, Arthur Zegart, "Battle of Newburgh," *NBC White Paper.* NBC.

OTHER AWARD WINNERS
OUTSTANDING ACHIEVEMENT IN ORIGINAL MUSIC COMPOSED FOR TELEVISION
• Richard Rodgers, *Winston Churchill — The Valiant Years.* ABC.

OUTSTANDING ACHIEVEMENT IN CINEMATOGRAPHY FOR TELEVISION
• John S. Priestley, *Naked City.* ABC.

OUTSTANDING ACHIEVEMENT IN ELECTRONIC CAMERA WORK
• Ernie Kovacs, *The Ernie Kovacs Show.* ABC.

OUTSTANDING ACHIEVEMENT IN FILM EDITING FOR TELEVISION
• Hugh Chaloupka, Aaron Nibley, Charles L. Freeman, *Naked City.* ABC.

OUTSTANDING ACHIEVEMENT IN ART DIRECTION AND SCENIC DESIGN
• Gary Smith, *The Kraft Music Hall.* NBC.

OUTSTANDING ENGINEERING OR TECHNICAL ACHIEVEMENT
• ABC Video Tape Expander, or VTX (slow-motion tape developed by ABC), Albert Malang, chief engineer, Video Facilities. ABC.

TRUSTEES AWARDS
• CBS News, for the special program *A Tour of the White House.*
• Jacqueline Kennedy
• The heads of the News Departments of ABC, CBS, and NBC. (Space coverage)
• Brigadier General David Sarnoff

The *(Van) Dyke* Breaks

"It's hard to quarrel with the major awards," said Cecil Smith of the *L.A. Times*, referring to the high quality programming that took 1962–63's highest TV honors. One of the biggest winners was *The Defenders*, which defended its lofty spot as last year's outstanding drama program and took four more statuettes as well — for star E.G. Marshall, director Stuart Rosenberg, film editor Sid Katz, and scriptwriters Reginald Rose and Robert Thom. *The Defenders* was one of those rare crowd pleasers, an intelligent and insightful courtroom drama about father-son lawyers that was a darling of critics and the public alike.

The Beverly Hillbillies — another early odds-on favorite — was ranked number one in the Nielsens. "The hillbilly show is the most successful series of the season," the *L.A. Times* wrote, and it was expected to hog-tie all of the top comedy trophies. On the evening of the awards, though, a quite different trend could be seen breaking early on. When "hillbillies" Buddy Ebsen, Irene Ryan, and Max Baer, Jr., were presenting the prize for comedy writing, they, and everyone else, expected it to go to their show's Paul Henning. But when the actual winner was announced, it signaled a major upset in the making — or, to be more precise, a *Dyke* breaking. Carl Reiner came back from last year to win again for *The Dick Van Dyke Show*. ("The crowd seemed delighted," the *L.A. Times* reported.) John Rich then took the Emmy for directing the show. Ultimately, the program that dealt with what goes on behind the scenes of a TV comedy show was named the top comedy show itself. It was a victory that would be repeated three more years in a row, an Emmy win-

The DVD Show*'s Carl Reiner scored a startling triumph over the writer of the number one-ranked* Beverly Hillbillies.

ning streak matched only by *All in the Family* and *Hill Street Blues* in future years. "This proves these awards are voted for merit," said one CBS executive.

The Emmys, it seemed, were reaching for newer and higher standards of excellence in all award categories. To underscore the point perhaps, and for the first time in Emmy history, the paramount prize — Program of the Year — went to a news show: *The Tunnel*, a 90-minute documentary about 57 East Germans who fled Communist rule by escaping through a 450-foot cavity dug under the Berlin Wall.

Ironically, *The Tunnel* had trouble seeing TV daylight at first. It was originally scheduled to run in November, but because of another real-life drama involving Communism, the Cuban missile crisis, it was shelved and then aired the following month. Its eventual award victory, said *Emmy Magazine* years later, "symbolized the fact that news and public affairs were no longer simply adjuncts to network program schedules." The show was also named outstanding documentary program of the season.

The host for the Hollywood ceremonies, Joey Bishop, got his biggest laugh of the night when he said, "We'd better hurry and give the winners their Emmys before their shows are canceled." The joke was a throwback to last year's top laugh- and vote-getter, *The Bob Newhart Show*, which picked up its pink slip just before it picked up its prize for outstanding comedy show. This year's outstanding variety program was a surprise winner — and loser, too. Just before its victory, *The Andy Williams Show* was canceled by NBC. Its producers did promise, though, that it would be back as irregularly scheduled specials. One of those producers was Bob Finkel, who accepted the *Williams Show* award on another show that he produced — that night's Emmys. Soon after the broadcast, he announced that the *Williams Show* was once again scheduled for regular weekly viewing.

The Tunnel was the first documentary ever to be voted Program of the Year.

Kim Stanley was named outstanding actress in a single performance for her portrayal of a drug addict in a two-part drama on *Ben Casey* called "A Cardinal Act of Mercy." The award was presented by the star of a different medical show, Richard Chamberlain, TV's *Dr. Kildare*. The very urbane Trevor Howard was judged outstanding actor for his portrayal of the equally urbane British Prime Minister Benjamin Disraeli in *The Invincible Mr. Disraeli* on *Hallmark Hall of Fame*. ("Certainly, the performances of Kim Stanley and Trevor Howard were marvelous moments in the electronic theater," agreed the *Times*'s Cecil Smith.)

Carol Burnett's performance with Julie Andrews at Carnegie Hall made her an Emmys favorite again and *Julie and Carol at Carnegie Hall* was named best music program. *Walt Disney's Wonderful World of Color* was named best children's show.

College Bowl was the last game show to win the category of Panel, Quiz, or Audience Participation, which was dropped after this year. Game shows, in fact, would compete for Emmys only on rare occasions when the whole spectrum of daytime TV began to be recognized over the following decade. They would finally reappear with their own category in 1974 when the daytime awards would be given their own complete program.

"In many of the other Emmy classifications, the industry's big show [the awards broadcast] had the look of one of its summer reruns," said the *L.A. Times*. Repeat winners included Shirley Booth, Don Knotts, *Huntley-Brinkley*, and *David Brinkley's Journal*. A new award was given to a local TV station (WCBS in New York for its *Superfluous People* show) and an international production (*War and Peace*, produced by Granada TV of Britain). Trustee citations or awards were given to President John F. Kennedy, who frequently made himself available for televised press conferences, and AT&T "for conceiving and developing Telstar 1 and Telstar 2" satellites. The Emmys show was supposed to begin with a live broadcast from England via one of the satellites, but the opener had to be put on film and shipped over because neither of the two satellites was in the proper position for the transmission.

A Trustees Award was also given in the memory of Dick Powell, who had recently died of cancer. It was accepted by Powell's business partners and close

CBS

After The Dick Van Dyke Show *pulled an upset to win best comedy show, a CBS executive said, "This proves these awards are voted for merit."*

renowned in the film world for her crying scenes on screen, remained in the audience as she watched the tribute and was now crying for real.

All in all, the night's show was another good one, although columnist Cecil Smith had a few complaints to air: "Some of the presenters were unpardonably inept — particularly [presenter] Danny Thomas reeling off the names of the shows he owns while the camera was giving us clips of the nominees for Program of the Year, and [presenter] Sid Caesar stumbling over which show won the musical program award, finally getting it right on the third try. Said Joey Bishop: 'Do you get the idea in New York that if the winner isn't popular, you give them another one?'"

friends David Niven and Charles Boyer. The star's widow, June Allyson,

1962–63

For programs telecast between April 15, 1962, and April 14, 1963. Awards presented May 26, 1963, at the Hollywood Palladium, the Americana Hotel in New York, and the Sheraton-Park Hotel in Washington, D.C. Broadcast on NBC.

THE PROGRAM OF THE YEAR
• *The Tunnel.* NBC.
The Danny Kaye Show with Lucille Ball. NBC.
"The Madman," *The Defenders.* CBS.
"The Voice of Charlie Pont," *Alcoa Premiere.* ABC.

OUTSTANDING PROGRAM ACHIEVEMENT IN THE FIELD OF DRAMA
• *The Defenders.* CBS.
Alcoa Premiere. ABC.
The Dick Powell Show. NBC.
The Eleventh Hour. NBC.
Naked City. ABC.

OUTSTANDING PROGRAM ACHIEVEMENT IN THE FIELD OF HUMOR
• *The Dick Van Dyke Show.* CBS.

The Beverly Hillbillies. CBS.
The Danny Kaye Show with Lucille Ball. NBC.
McHale's Navy. ABC.

OUTSTANDING PROGRAM ACHIEVEMENT IN THE FIELD OF VARIETY
• *The Andy Williams Show.* NBC.
Carol & Company. CBS.
The Garry Moore Show. CBS.
Here's Edie. ABC.
The Red Skelton Hour. CBS.

OUTSTANDING PROGRAM ACHIEVEMENT IN THE FIELD OF MUSIC
• *Julie and Carol at Carnegie Hall.* CBS.
The Bell Telephone Hour. NBC.
Judy Garland. CBS.
The Lively Ones. NBC.
NBC Opera. NBC.

OUTSTANDING PROGRAM ACHIEVEMENT IN THE FIELD OF PANEL, QUIZ, OR AUDIENCE PARTICIPATION
• *College Bowl.* CBS.

Password. CBS.
To Tell the Truth. CBS.

**OUTSTANDING PROGRAM ACHIEVEMENT
IN THE FIELD OF DOCUMENTARY
PROGRAMS**
• *The Tunnel.* NBC.
"Emergency Ward," *The DuPont Show of
the Week.* NBC.
"He is Risen," *Project 20.* NBC.
The River Nile. NBC.
Shakespeare: Soul of an Age. NBC.

**OUTSTANDING PROGRAM ACHIEVEMENT
IN THE FIELD OF CHILDREN'S
PROGRAMMING**
• *Walt Disney's Wonderful World of Color.*
NBC.
Captain Kangaroo. CBS.
Discovery '62–'63. ABC.
The Shari Lewis Show. NBC.
Update. NBC.
Watch Mr. Wizard. NBC.

**OUTSTANDING ACHIEVEMENT
IN THE FIELD OF NEWS**
• *The Huntley-Brinkley Report.* NBC.
*CBS News Evening Report with Walter
Cronkite.* CBS.
Eyewitness. CBS.
*NBC Special News Reports, Gulf Oil
Corporation.* NBC.

**OUTSTANDING PROGRAM ACHIEVEMENT
IN THE FIELD OF NEWS COMMENTARY OR
PUBLIC AFFAIRS**
• *David Brinkley's Journal.* NBC.
Bell and Howell Closeup. ABC.
CBS Reports. CBS.
Howard K. Smith, News and Comment.
ABC.
The Twentieth Century. CBS.

**OUTSTANDING ACHIEVEMENT
IN INTERNATIONAL REPORTING
OR COMMENTARY**
• Piers Anderton, *The Tunnel.* NBC.
John Rich, *Germany: Fathers and Sons.*
NBC.
Marvin Kalb, Moscow correspondent,
for general reporting. CBS.
James Robinson, Southeast Asia,
for general reporting. NBC.
John Secondari, "The Vatican," *Bell and
Howell Closeup.* ABC.

**OUTSTANDING CONTINUED PERFORMANCE
BY AN ACTOR IN A SERIES (LEAD)**
• E.G. Marshall, *The Defenders.* CBS.
Ernest Borgnine, *McHale's Navy.* ABC.
Paul Burke, *Naked City.* ABC.
Vic Morrow, *Combat.* ABC.
Dick Van Dyke, *The Dick Van Dyke Show.*
CBS.

**OUTSTANDING CONTINUED PERFORMANCE
BY AN ACTRESS IN A SERIES (LEAD)**
• Shirley Booth, *Hazel.* NBC.
Lucille Ball, *The Lucy Show.* CBS.
Shirl Conway, *The Nurses.* CBS.
Mary Tyler Moore, *The Dick Van Dyke
Show.* CBS.
Irene Ryan, *The Beverly Hillbillies.* CBS.

**OUTSTANDING SINGLE PERFORMANCE
BY AN ACTOR IN A LEADING ROLE**
• Trevor Howard, *The Invincible Mr.
Disraeli, Hallmark Hall of Fame.* NBC.
Bradford Dillman, "The Voice of Charlie
Pont," *Alcoa Premiere.* ABC.
Don Gordon, *The Defenders.* CBS.
Walter Matthau, "Big Deal in Laredo,"
The DuPont Show of the Week. NBC.
Joseph Schildkraut, *Sam Benedict.* NBC.

**OUTSTANDING SINGLE PERFORMANCE
BY AN ACTRESS IN A LEADING ROLE**
• Kim Stanley, *Ben Casey.* ABC.
Diahann Carroll, *Naked City.* ABC.
Diana Hyland, "The Voice of Charlie
Pont," *Alcoa Premiere.* ABC.
Eleanor Parker, *The Eleventh Hour.* NBC.
Sylvia Sidney, *The Defenders.* CBS.

**OUTSTANDING PERFORMANCE
IN A SUPPORTING ROLE BY AN ACTOR**
• Don Knotts, *The Andy Griffith Show.*
CBS.
Tim Conway, *McHale's Navy.* ABC.
Paul Ford, *Teahouse of the August Moon,
Hallmark Hall of Fame.* NBC.
Hurd Hatfield, *The Invincible Mr. Disraeli,
Hallmark Hall of Fame.* NBC.
Robert Redford, "The Voice of Charlie
Pont," *Alcoa Premiere.* ABC.

**OUTSTANDING PERFORMANCE
IN A SUPPORTING ROLE BY AN ACTRESS**
• Glenda Farrell, *Ben Casey.* ABC.
Davey Davison,*The Eleventh Hour.* NBC.
Nancy Malone, *Naked City.* ABC.
Rose Marie, *The Dick Van Dyke Show.*
CBS.

Kate Reid, *The Invincible Mr. Disraeli*, *Hallmark Hall of Fame*. NBC.

OUTSTANDING PERFORMANCE
IN A VARIETY OR MUSICAL PROGRAM
OR SERIES
• Carol Burnett, *Julie and Carol at Carnegie Hall* on CBS and *Carol & Company*. CBS.
Edie Adams, *Here's Edie*. ABC.
Merv Griffin, *The Merv Griffin Show*. NBC.
Danny Kaye, *The Danny Kaye Show with Lucille Ball*. NBC.
Andy Williams, *The Andy Williams Show*. NBC.

OUTSTANDING DIRECTORIAL
ACHIEVEMENT IN DRAMA
• Stuart Rosenberg, *The Defenders*. CBS.
Fielder Cook, "Big Deal in Laredo," *The DuPont Show of the Week*. NBC.
Robert Ellis Miller, "The Voice of Charlie Pont," *Alcoa Premiere*. ABC.
Sydney Pollack, *Ben Casey*. ABC.
George Schaefer, *The Invincible Mr. Disraeli, Hallmark Hall of Fame*. NBC.

OUTSTANDING DIRECTORIAL
ACHIEVEMENT IN COMEDY
• John Rich, *The Dick Van Dyke Show*. CBS.
Seymour Berns, *The Red Skelton Hour*. CBS.
Frederick DeCordova, *The Jack Benny Show*. CBS.
David Geisel, *The Garry Moore Show*. CBS.
Richard Whorf, *The Beverly Hillbillies*. CBS.

OUTSTANDING WRITING
ACHIEVEMENT IN DRAMA
• Robert Thom, Reginald Rose, *The Defenders*. CBS.
Sidney Carroll, "Big Deal in Laredo," *DuPont Show of the Week*. NBC.
Norman Katkov, *Ben Casey*. ABC.
James Lee, *The Invincible Mr. Disraeli, Hallmark Hall of Fame*. NBC.
Halsted Welles, "The Voice of Charlie Pont," *Alcoa Premiere*. ABC.

OUTSTANDING WRITING
ACHIEVEMENT IN COMEDY
• Carl Reiner, *The Dick Van Dyke Show*. CBS.

Sam Perrin, George Balzer, Hal Goldman, Al Gordon, *The Jack Benny Show*. CBS.
Paul Henning, *The Beverly Hillbillies*. CBS.
Nat Hiken, *Car 54, Where Are You?* NBC.
Ed Simmons, Dave O'Brien, Martin A. Ragaway, Arthur Phillips, Larry Rhine, Mort Greene, Hugh Wedlock, Red Skelton, Bruce Howard, Rich Mittleman, *The Red Skelton Hour*. CBS.

OTHER AWARD WINNERS
OUTSTANDING ACHIEVEMENT
IN COMPOSING ORIGINAL MUSIC
FOR TELEVISION
• Robert Russell Bennett, "He is Risen," *Project 20*. NBC.

OUTSTANDING ACHIEVEMENT
IN CINEMATOGRAPHY FOR TELEVISION
• John S. Priestley, *Naked City*. ABC.

OUTSTANDING ACHIEVEMENT
IN ELECTRONIC CAMERA WORK
• *The Invincible Mr. Disraeli, Hallmark Hall of Fame*. NBC.

OUTSTANDING ACHIEVEMENT IN FILM
EDITING FOR TELEVISION
• Sid Katz, *The Defenders*. CBS.

OUTSTANDING ACHIEVEMENT IN ART
DIRECTION AND SCENIC DESIGN
• Carroll Clark, Marvin Aubrey Davis, *Walt Disney's Wonderful World of Color*. NBC.

INTERNATIONAL AWARD
• *War and Peace,* Granada TV Network, Ltd. of England.

STATION AWARD
• *Superfluous People*. WCBS-TV, New York.

TRUSTEES AWARDS
• Dick Powell
• American Telephone and Telegraph Co., for conceiving and developing Telstar 1 and Telstar 2.

TRUSTEES CITATION
• President John Fitzgerald Kennedy. For news conferences and in honor of his continued recognition of television's importance to a free society.

A "Friendly" Mutiny

"I've never played a mutiny!" Johnny Carson quipped to the home viewing audience, trying to add levity to the gloom cast over the Emmycast. CBS and ABC had both withdrawn their support of the awards just two weeks before they were to be given away on NBC and the two networks encouraged their employees to boycott the show. All throughout the awards night the performing talent tried to make the best of the situation, beginning with the opening remarks from Hollywood host Joey Bishop, who said, "I guess we're going through with it. I bid you welcome to one of the greatest fights of the century. The NBC peacock got its feather in CBS's eye. Should NBC decide to pull out tonight, there'll be immediate dancing. Win or lose, the secret word is jealousy!"

CBS News president Fred W. Friendly had denounced the awards procedures as being "unrealistic, unprofessional, and unfair." ABC president Thomas W. Moore backed up his call for a boycott, adding, "ABC does not think that the awards granted by the Academy of TV Arts and Sciences are determined by the merits of the programs."

Joey Bishop's suggestion that jealousy may have prompted the mutiny was the real feather in the CBS eye. CBS News was clearly irked that NBC's Chet Huntley and David Brinkley dominated the news awards throughout the early 1960s. ABC was also mad, but mostly because it seemed to fare poorly in almost all Emmy categories year after year, just as it suffered in the Nielsen ratings. NBC's exclusive contract to air the telecast, which it held since it first broadcast the ceremonies nationally in

Jealousy over Chet Huntley and David Brinkley's success with the news awards was rumored to trigger the CBS boycott.

1955 for the 1954 awards, frustrated both rival networks further since they certainly wanted to be involved in, and profit from, TV's highest honors. Friendly also quarreled with how the news awards were grouped and questioned the professional credentials of those who determined the winners. He even implied that NBC might be guilty of block voting. NBC denied the charges and said the boycott was "a classic of sham and hypocrisy with amusing overtones."

Soon after the controversy broke, the academy promised a "massive and agonizing" reappraisal of its awards procedures, but the pledge came too late to appease the networks before air time.

Before the show started, Joey Bishop predicted, "The entire Emmy affair may consist of just me and Price Waterhouse," but he and both boycotting networks miscalculated. "It was extremely gratifying to see the TV industry ignore the phony-baloney boycott of a few New York nabobs and attend the Emmy Awards Monday night en masse," *The Los Angeles Times*'s Cecil Smith wrote. "The Hollywood Palladium was packed with as enthusiastic a black-tie mob as I can ever recall. Although CBS canceled 10 tables for the affair and ABC 6, there were 1,456 performers, technicians, craftsmen, and executives who showed up, only slightly less than last year's 1,492." Out on the other coast, 4,000 persons packed New York's World's Fair Music Hall for that end of the simulcast, the largest number ever recorded. (There was no hookup to Washington, D.C., this year, as there had been in 1959, 1962, and 1963.)

All night the boycott stole the limelight — and the laughs. The show opened with an announcement that it was being broadcast on the rebellious CBS, causing the Palladium audience to scream with laughter. Cast members from the satirical revue show *That Was the Week That Was* did a skit bestowing "party pooper" awards to Fred Friendly and Thomas Moore. Carl Reiner and Mel Brooks sang an original tune to CBS and ABC: "Why do you pout? Why do you shout? Take your Emmy and shut your mouth!" and then added, "Don't spoil our wingding, CBS!" Clearly, the mutiny was triggering a counter mutiny and everyone seemed to be caught up in the frenzy. Shelley Winters was so flustered, in fact, that when she accepted her award for outstanding actress in a single role, she said, "I'd like to thank the whole motion picture academy."

The absurd quality of the 1963–64 awards actually started early. "Canceled TV Show Leads in Nominations for Emmys," said a headline in the *L.A.*

Times more than a month before. The program *East Side, West Side*, which featured George C. Scott as a social worker, led with eight nominations and caused comedian Mel Brooks to whine: "Do you really want me to comment on television, where they cancel *East Side, West Side* and still allow *Petticoat Junction* to keep rolling?" (*East Side* ended up taking only one award — for director Tom Gries.) Other canceled programs that received nominations included *Arrest and Trial*, *Breaking Point*, and Judy Garland's, Garry Moore's, and Richard Boone's eponymous shows. Meantime, the number one show in America, *The Beverly Hillbillies*, received only one nomination, for actress Irene Ryan, who played Granny. Number-two ranked *Bonanza* received none at all.

But it was America's number three show — and a CBS favorite — that took the Emmy sweepstakes this year. *The Dick Van Dyke Show* won five awards in all, including outstanding comedy program and honors for top actor, actress, comedy writers, and director. Van Dyke himself wiped his cheeks dry as he accepted his stat-

The CBS News chief called the awards "unrealistic, unprofessional, and unfair."

uette, saying, "I'm crying! I don't believe this!" When she heard her own name announced, Mary Tyler Moore raced up to the podium with her hand over her mouth in shocked disbelief and said, in her characteristic gee-whiz manner, "Oh, I thank you so very, very much!"

"The Danny Kaye Show, which was a new attraction this season and had the freshest quality and writing in popular variety entertainment, finished with a

Program of the Year The Making of the President 1960 *tracked John F. Kennedy's climb to the presidency.*

highly respectable total of four Emmys," noted *The New York Times*. It was voted outstanding variety program, and also won for Kaye as best variety show performer, for director Robert Scheerer, and for its electronic photography. Kaye couldn't be at the awards because he was performing in Las Vegas at the Desert Inn, but, as the *L.A. Times* noted, he still "went out of his way to crash the boycott." Kaye flew to L.A. the previous Sunday and performed in a special sequence that was later shown on tape. Back out in Vegas on awards night, Kaye learned of his win by phone just seconds before he stepped out on stage.

The Defenders began the evening with six nominations and ended up prevailing in three categories. In its third season, the show was widely considered to be television's finest weekly drama, and again it won the Emmy, making the opinion official. The program, featuring E.G. Marshall as Lawrence Preston, the head of a family law firm, boldly tackled some of the most controversial issues of recent times, including the practice of blacklisting show business talent for being sympathetic to communism. It was for its episode entitled "Blacklist" that Jack Klugman was named outstanding actor and Ernest Kinoy was credited with having written

the best original teleplay.

Chrysler Theater also took three Emmys: for Shelley Winters's performance as a frustrated spinster in *Two is the Number*, for supporting actor Albert Paulsen, and for Rod Serling's script adaptation of the John O'Hara short story "It's Mental Work." *Hallmark Hall of Fame* won two — for art direction and for Ruth White's supporting role in a remake, again starring Julie Harris, of Emmy's 1958–59 Oustanding Special Dramatic Program, *Little Moon of Alban. The Bell Telephone Hour* hit the high note in music, upstaging past maestro Leonard Bernstein in the category. *Discovery* was voted Outstanding Achievement in Children's Programming, "a show long applauded for its imaginative concept of entertainment for the younger set," according to *Emmy Magazine*. The Station Award went to KSD-TV of St. Louis for a special about the problems facing young people in Kinloch, Missouri.

"The CBS News division, for the second year, drew a blank across the board," *The New York Times* reported, "which inevitably is going to make the anti-Emmy blast of Fred Friendly, division president, look like prescient sour grapes." NBC won in the news commentary/public affairs category for its two *White Papers* on Cuba, one on the Bay of Pigs invasion and the other on the missile crisis. But worse for Friendly, NBC's *Huntley-Brinkley* was voted outstanding news program for the sixth year in a row. Chet Huntley accepted, referring to his Emmy as "a somewhat maligned and slandered young lady." He added: "We shall attempt to give her a good home."

One of Friendly's chief gripes was his opinion that news programming didn't receive enough serious attention from the Emmys, but for the second year in a row a news special was acclaimed Program of the Year. It was also named outstanding documentary and won for its film editing and original music, too. *The Making of the President 1960* was adapted from the Pulitzer Prize–winning book by Theodore H. White and traced John F. Kennedy's dramatic rise to power. "The victory of *Making of the President* as the Program of the Year was particularly gratifying," said Cecil Smith of the *L.A. Times*. "It marked a milestone for independent documentary production. Producer David Wolper has long battled for network acceptance of his independent productions, usually without success. Both NBC and CBS turned down *Making of the President* with the snide comment that 'we make our own documentaries.'"

At the end of the Emmy evening, Smith declared the event "a delight" and the boycott "a dud," adding, "not a single golden statuette was left unclaimed." When the final awards count was tallied, the big network winner was, oddly, Friendly's CBS with 13 trophies, also-mutinying ABC with 5, and NBC with 9.

1963–64

For programs telecast between April 15, 1963, and April 12, 1964. Awards presented on May 25, 1964, at the Hollywood Palladium and the Music Hall of the Texas Pavilion at the World's Fair in New York. Broadcast on NBC.

THE PROGRAM OF THE YEAR
• *The Making of the President 1960*. ABC.
The American Revolution of '63. NBC.
"Blacklist," *The Defenders*. CBS.
The Kremlin. NBC.
Town Meeting of the World. CBS.

OUTSTANDING PROGRAM ACHIEVEMENT IN THE FIELD OF DRAMA
• *The Defenders*. CBS.
Bob Hope Presents the Chrysler Theater. NBC.
East Side, West Side. CBS.
Mr. Novak. NBC.
The Richard Boone Show. NBC.

OUTSTANDING PROGRAM ACHIEVEMENT IN THE FIELD OF COMEDY
• *The Dick Van Dyke Show*. CBS.
The Bill Dana Show. NBC.
The Farmer's Daughter. ABC.
McHale's Navy. ABC.
That Was the Week That Was. NBC.

OUTSTANDING PROGRAM ACHIEVEMENT IN THE FIELD OF VARIETY
• *The Danny Kaye Show*. CBS.
The Andy Williams Show. NBC.
The Garry Moore Show. CBS.
The Judy Garland Show. CBS.
The Tonight Show Starring Johnny Carson. NBC.

OUTSTANDING PROGRAM ACHIEVEMENT IN THE FIELD OF MUSIC
• *The Bell Telephone Hour*. NBC.
The Lively Ones. NBC.
New York Philharmonic Young People's Concerts with Leonard Bernstein. CBS.

OUTSTANDING PROGRAM ACHIEVEMENT IN THE FIELD OF NEWS REPORTS
• *The Huntley-Brinkley Report*. NBC.
CBS Evening News with Walter Cronkite. CBS.
NBC Special News Reports. NBC.
Ron Cochran with the News. ABC.

OUTSTANDING PROGRAM ACHIEVEMENT IN THE FIELD OF NEWS COMMENTARY OR PUBLIC AFFAIRS
• "Cuba: Parts I and II – The Bay of Pigs and the Missile Crisis," *NBC White Paper*. NBC.
The American Revolution of '63. NBC.
CBS Reports. CBS.
Chronicle. CBS.
Town Meeting of the World. CBS.

OUTSTANDING PROGRAM ACHIEVEMENT IN THE FIELD OF DOCUMENTARY PROGRAMS
• *The Making of the President 1960*. ABC.
Greece: The Golden Age. NBC.
The Kremlin. NBC.
"Manhattan Battleground," *DuPont Show of the Week*. NBC.
Saga of Western Man. ABC.
The Twentieth Century. CBS.

NBC/ GLOBE PHOTO

A flustered Shelley Winters thanked "the whole motion picture academy."

OUTSTANDING PROGRAM ACHIEVEMENT CHILDREN'S PROGRAMMING
• *Discovery '63–'64.* ABC.
Exploring. NBC.
NBC Children's Theatre. NBC.
Science All-Stars. ABC.
Wild Kingdom. NBC.

OUTSTANDING CONTINUED PERFORMANCE BY AN ACTOR IN A SERIES (LEAD)
• Dick Van Dyke, *The Dick Van Dyke Show.* CBS.
Richard Boone, *The Richard Boone Show.* NBC.
Dean Jagger, *Mr. Novak.* NBC.
David Janssen, *The Fugitive.* ABC.
George C. Scott, *East Side, West Side.* CBS.

OUTSTANDING CONTINUED PERFORMANCE BY AN ACTRESS IN A SERIES (LEAD)
• Mary Tyler Moore, *The Dick Van Dyke Show.* CBS.
Shirley Booth, *Hazel.* NBC.
Patty Duke, *The Patty Duke Show.* ABC.
Irene Ryan, *The Beverly Hillbillies.* CBS.
Inger Stevens, *The Farmer's Daughter.* ABC.

OUTSTANDING SINGLE PERFORMANCE BY AN ACTOR IN A LEADING ROLE
• Jack Klugman, *The Defenders.* CBS.
James Earl Jones, *East Side, West Side.* CBS.

Roddy McDowall, *Arrest and Trial.* ABC.
Jason Robards, Jr., *Abe Lincoln in Illinois, Hallmark Hall of Fame.* NBC.
Rod Steiger, *A Slow Fade to Black, Bob Hope Presents the Chrysler Theater.* NBC.
Harold J. Stone, *The Nurses.* CBS.

OUTSTANDING SINGLE PERFORMANCE BY AN ACTRESS IN A LEADING ROLE
• Shelley Winters, *Two is the Number, Bob Hope Presents the Chrysler Theater.* NBC.
Ruby Dee, *The Nurses.* CBS.
Bethel Leslie, *The Richard Boone Show.* NBC.
Jeanette Nolan, *The Richard Boone Show.* NBC.
Diana Sands, *East Side, West Side.* CBS.

OUTSTANDING PERFORMANCE IN A SUPPORTING ROLE BY AN ACTOR
• Albert Paulsen, *One Day in the Life of Ivan Denisovich, Bob Hope Presents the Chrysler Theater.* NBC.
Sorrell Booke, *Dr. Kildare.* NBC.
Conlan Carter, *Combat.* ABC.
Carl Lee, *The Nurses.* CBS.

OUTSTANDING PERFORMANCE IN A SUPPORTING ROLE BY AN ACTRESS
• Ruth White, *Little Moon of Alban, Hallmark Hall of Fame.* NBC.
Martine Bartlett, *Arrest and Trial.* ABC.
Anjanette Comer, *Arrest and Trial.* ABC.
Rose Marie, *The Dick Van Dyke Show.* CBS.
Claudia McNeil, *The Nurses.* CBS.

OUTSTANDING PERFORMANCE IN A VARIETY OR MUSICAL PROGRAM OR SERIES
• Danny Kaye, *The Danny Kaye Show.* CBS.
Judy Garland, *The Judy Garland Show.* CBS.
Barbra Streisand, *The Judy Garland Show.* CBS.
Burr Tillstrom, *That Was the Week That Was.* NBC.
Andy Williams, *The Andy Williams Show.* NBC.

OUTSTANDING DIRECTORIAL ACHIEVEMENT IN DRAMA
• Tom Gries, *East Side, West Side.* CBS.
Paul Bogart, *The Defenders.* CBS.
Sydney Pollack, *Something About Lee*

Wiley, *Bob Hope Presents the Chrysler Theater*. NBC.
Stuart Rosenberg, *The Defenders*. CBS.
George Schaefer, *The Patriots, Hallmark Hall of Fame*. NBC.

OUTSTANDING DIRECTORIAL ACHIEVEMENT IN COMEDY
• Jerry Paris, *The Dick Van Dyke Show*. CBS.
Sidney Lanfield, *McHale's Navy*. ABC.
Paul Nickell, William Russell, Don Taylor, *The Farmer's Daughter*. ABC.
Richard Whorf, *The Beverly Hillbillies*. CBS.

OUTSTANDING DIRECTORIAL ACHIEVEMENT IN VARIETY OR MUSIC
• Robert Scheerer, *The Danny Kaye Show*. CBS.
Roger Englander, "A Tribute to Teachers," *New York Philharmonic Young People's Concerts with Leonard Bernstein*. CBS.
Bob Henry, *The Andy Williams Show*. NBC.
Marshall Jamison, *That Was the Week That Was*. NBC.
Clark Jones, Sid Smith, *The Bell Telephone Hour*. NBC.

OUTSTANDING WRITING ACHIEVEMENT IN DRAMA—ORIGINAL
• Ernest Kinoy, *The Defenders*. CBS.
Arnold Perl, *East Side, West Side*. CBS.
David Rayfiel, *Something About Lee Wiley, Bob Hope Presents the Chrysler Theater*. NBC.
Allan Sloane, *Breaking Point*. ABC.
Adrian Spies, *Dr. Kildare*. NBC.

OUTSTANDING WRITING ACHIEVEMENT IN DRAMA—ADAPTATION
• Rod Serling, *It's Mental Work, Bob Hope Presents the Chrysler Theater*. NBC.
James Bridges, "The Jar," *The Alfred Hitchcock Hour*. CBS.
Robert Hartung, *The Patriots, Hallmark Hall of Fame*. NBC.
Walter Brown Newman, *The Richard Boone Show*. NBC.

OUTSTANDING WRITING ACHIEVEMENT IN COMEDY OR VARIETY
• Carl Reiner, Sam Denoff, Bill Persky, *The Dick Van Dyke Show*. CBS.
Herbert Baker, Mel Tolkin, Ernest Chambers, Saul Ilson, Sheldon Keller, Paul Mazursky, Larry Tucker, Gary Belkin, Larry Gelbart, *The Danny Kaye Show*. CBS.
Robert Emmett, Gerald Gardner, Saul Turtletaub, David Panich, Tony Webster, Thomas Meehan, Ed Sherman, *That Was the Week That Was*. NBC.
Steven Gethers, Jerry Davis, Lee Loeb, John McGreevey, *The Farmer's Daughter*. ABC.

OTHER AWARD WINNERS
OUTSTANDING ACHIEVEMENT IN COMPOSING ORIGINAL MUSIC FOR TELEVISION
• Elmer Bernstein, *The Making of the President 1960*. ABC.

OUTSTANDING ACHIEVEMENT IN CINEMATOGRAPHY FOR TELEVISION
• J. Baxter Peters, *The Kremlin*. NBC.

OUTSTANDING ACHIEVEMENT IN ELECTRONIC PHOTOGRAPHY
• *The Danny Kaye Show*. CBS.

OUTSTANDING ACHIEVEMENT IN FILM EDITING FOR TELEVISION
• William T. Cartwright, *The Making of the President 1960*. ABC.

OUTSTANDING ACHIEVEMENT IN ART DIRECTION AND SCENIC DESIGN
• Warren Clymer, *Hallmark Hall of Fame*. NBC.

INTERNATIONAL AWARD
• *Les Raisins Verts*. Radiodiffusion Television Francais.

STATION AWARD
• *Operation Challenge — A Study in Hope*. KSD-TV, St. Louis.

Emmys for Art's Sake

"No more horse race!" said academy president Rod Serling at the Emmycast as he explained this year's awards procedure, which was revamped following CBS's and ABC's boycott of the competition last year. Now competition itself would be minimized. Instead, "excellence is honored whenever or wherever it occurred," Serling added, noting that multiple winners in each category, where appropriate, would occur. The 27 national categories of 1963–64 were reduced to four general ones: Outstanding Program and Outstanding Individual

HALLMARK HALL OF FAME

Lynn Fontanne and Alfred Lunt as Mr. and Mrs. Oliver Wendell Holmes in the year's top show, Magnificent Yankee.

Achievements in Entertainment and program and individual awards in the fields of news, documentaries, information, and sports. Blue-ribbon panels made up of no fewer than five judges "of the highest accomplishment in their respective fields" would determine the winners. Furthermore, for the first time

since 1955, NBC would no longer have an exclusive lock on broadcasting the awards. Beginning next year, the honor would rotate between all three networks. The drastic overhaul proved to CBS's and ABC's chief executives that the academy was serious about addressing their past concerns, and all of them agreed to rejoin the contest.

Except one. "The angriest man in television is the misnamed Fred W. Friendly," wrote *The San Gabriel Valley Tribune,* who is "furious because the academy won't mold the awards system that guarantees he and his playmates in the 'news' department will win loads and loads of awards more than Chet and David." The reference, of course, was to Chet Huntley and David Brinkley, who dominated the news awards in the past, and to Friendly's alleged jealousy over their success. Friendly was determined to continue the CBS News division's private boycott even though the rest of his network was rejoining the fold. He reasoning: There were no nominations this time for *any* newsmen *at all,* or, to use Friendly's words, "for those reporters and legmen who make the news organizations what they are." Also overlooked were "programs on contemporary issues or problems." The academy responded, saying, "We agree heartily. It's regrettable. But the plain fact is no ABC or NBC entries received a sufficient vote by the nominating committees and the CBS entries which did were disqualified by the CBS News position that its programs and personnel could not be viewed and judged for nomination."

There were gripes over other nominations, too. The academy's New York chapter reported a "furor" when members noticed the absence of the Outstanding Actor or Actress in a Comedy Series categories. "Also completely blanked out in the nominations were femme series stars," *The Hollywood Reporter* said. *Variety* pointed to a revolt among Hollywood's film editors, "whose importance to the industry has been relegated to a small place in the basement where they can scarcely be heard." (New York's film editors dominated the nominees.) Added ire came from *The Beverly Hills Citizen*, which wrote, "There are more than twice as many craftsmen with whom viewers have little or no identification up for Emmys as there are players and stars" and noted that not one sports show — "not even the World Series!" — was nominated. Also missing from the lineup were 16 of the top 20-rated shows in America.

"It's time we became not just an industry, but an art form," Rod Serling had said before the Big Event. His clarion call was answered with what UPI writer Vernon Scott called "a pretentious stab at rewarding 'art'" when it was revealed that nearly half of the nominations were dominated by such artistic programming as *Hallmark Hall of Fame, Chrysler Theater*, New York Philharmonic concerts, and specials on the Louvre Museum and Leonardo da Vinci. But the number-ten ranked *The Dick Van Dyke Show* was also nominated, as were such other favorites to win as *The Man from U.N.C.L.E.*, *Walt Disney's Wonderful World of Color*, and *The Tonight Show Starring Johnny Carson*. (None of the latter three shows would prevail.)

What did end up striking gold were three one-shot programs that took more than half (17) of the night's 29 national trophies: *The Louvre, Hallmark Hall of Fame*'s *The Magnificent Yankee*, and Barbra Streisand's TV special *My Name is*

Barbra. Hallmark Hall of Fame won an additional Emmy in the category of art and set direction for its *Holy Terror* episode about the life of nurse Florence Nightingale. The final score was: *Hallmark,* seven; *Louvre,* six; and *Barbra,* five.

The Louvre was a documentary that probed the Paris museum's galleries at night, giving viewers, in the words of its Emmy-winning director John J. Sughrue, the chance to have "the Louvre as everyone has always wanted to have it — all to himself." In addition to Sughrue's award, the show also took honors for being an outstanding documentary program and for its writer, film editor, cinematographer, and music director. *The Hollywood Reporter* thought it was overkill: "*The Louvre* was a good show worthy of an Emmy, but SIX that virtually swamped the wins in two out of three categories?" Comedian Don Rickles agreed, writing in *Variety,* "The cry used to be, 'Break up the Yankees!' After this year's Emmy show, it could be changed to 'Break up *The Louvre!*' One had to wonder ... could it be that the entire production was merely a plot to make De Gaulle like us again?"

Hallmark's *Magnificent Yankee*, based on Emmet Lavery's Broadway play about the life of Supreme Court Justice Oliver Wendell Holmes, was singled out as an Outstanding Program in Entertainment and also won statuettes for art and set direction, makeup, lighting, and the performances of its two accomplished stars, Alfred Lunt and wife Lynn Fontanne as the justice and Mrs. Holmes. For Lunt, the TV film was, said TV columnist Cecil Smith in the *L.A. Times*, "perhaps the last

> *Three specials* **(Yankee, Barbra,** *and* **Louvre)** *reaped most of the awards.*

major performance of his glorious career." Broadway's regal acting couple — who considered appearing in motion pictures undignified but enjoyed working in television because they felt its productions were more like theatrical shows — were not on hand to accept the honors, but watched the show from their home in Genesee Depot, Wisconsin. "We are awfully pleased," said the 72-year-old Lunt the next day, "even though it was way past our bedtime" by the time their wins were announced on TV.

One of the few victorious performers who did show up was another big Broadway star, Barbra Streisand, who took a break from performing in *Funny Girl* to acknowledge her win and, in an acceptance speech aside, a run in her stocking, too. She added, breathlessly, "This is too fantastic. When I was a kid — I mean a younger kid — my favorite shows were the Oscars and Emmys. I didn't care who won then, just how they looked. Television is a marvelous business. This is my first experience with it. I figured out that I would have to work 58 years in *Funny Girl* to reach as many people as I did in one [TV] show." Her TV special was also named an outstanding entertainment program and won recognition for its music director, art director, set director, and for its "conception, choreography, and staging." *The Hollywood Reporter* had trouble with this program's generous success as well: "*My Name is Barbra* was a very good show worthy of an Emmy, but that it should get FIVE Emmys while the Danny Thomas special *That Wonderful World of Burlesque* should get none is at least a disparity to ponder." The Thomas special was favored to sweep the awards, but lost in all its nomination categories except for technical direction.

Danny Thomas was again the host for the New York end of the ceremonies — opposite Sammy Davis, Jr., out in Holly-wood — and, unlike past years, was lambasted in the press afterward for his bad comedy material and bad delivery. He opened the show saying, "Only in America could an Arab and a Jew be on the same program." ("Reaching!" cried *The New York Post*.) But it was another of his opening remarks that set the tone of the awards night when he confessed to the audience, "We don't have the kind of suspense we had in the past."

The least suspenseful win of the night came as a major relief to some: the number-seven Nielsen-ranked *Dick Van Dyke Show* won the top award in its field for the third year in a row. It was a welcome outcome because the show was the one regularly scheduled TV series to win an outstanding program prize. Van Dyke also won an individual achievement award, which was accepted by his brother Jerry from a befuddled Jimmy Durante, who didn't seem to know who he was. (Jerry Van Dyke was just then gaining recognition as the star of the new TV series *My Mother the Car*.)

Leonard Bernstein's Philharmonic concert specials came back as a winner again this year, as did *The Defenders*, which had had its final broadcast just three days earlier. David Karp and Paul Bogart were the only writer and director to win awards for individual achievement in entertainment. They'd collaborated on *Defenders* winning episode "The 700-Year-Old Gang," which was described by *The New York World-Telegram-Sun* as "a touching program on the sensitive subject of a young couple on the rise who have their aging parents with them." In his acceptance speech, Karp referred to "Gang" star Jack Gilford's omission from the list of acting nominees as "a gyp!"

"He's right and Gilford isn't the only one who was gypped," cried *Radio-TV Daily*. The trade paper was referring to a gathering consensus that the television industry and the American public were cheated out of an exciting Emmys show this time. For one thing, the broadcast was plagued with technical difficulties. At one point the TV picture, alternating between L.A. and New York, was lost for almost a full minute. What did get aired wasn't well presented either: The comedy routines were lame and the dancing, featuring the *Hullabaloo* and *Shindig* dancers, was inadvertently funny. Frustrated by the delays, the constant flubs and the unnerving waiting backstage, awards presenter Mary Tyler Moore was overheard saying (prophetically), "Next year I've just got to be a winner. It's too tough being a presenter!"

"Instead of bubbling like champagne, it was like molasses from the deep freeze," said Hedda Hopper about the show in her column the next day, adding, "Dick Van Dyke must have known something — he didn't show." Other media critics were far more critical. "The worst fiasco in Emmy Awards history," said *The Hollywood Reporter*.

But it was the absence of suspense over what and who would win in many diverse categories, as occurred in the past, that was the biggest problem. Rod Serling admitted his awards overhaul failed. "It was a calculated risk and we lost," he said. "We just took the wrong road." He also regretted the show's entertainment and technical failures, saying, "I was bored, dismayed, unhappy, and appalled at the proceedings, but, unfortunately, I have to bear the responsibility." He then added, bravely, and with a gifted scriptwriter's sense of the dramatic: "I'll take my place in the dock."

Despite the "fiasco," more than 50 million Americans watched the show at home on TV. Among them was a woman who had not been heard from in a long time: Shirley Dinsdale, the first person ever to win an Emmy. Now calling herself Mrs. Frank Layburn, she tuned in from her home in Annandale, Virginia, and told reporters who had hunted her down that she was retired from television and was now "just another housewife." Her puppet sidekick Judy Splinters was, according to the *L.A. Herald Examiner*, "in a senior citizens' home for retired ventriloquists' dummies."

1964–65

For programs telecast between April 13, 1964, and April 30, 1965. Awards presented September 12, 1965, at the Hollywood Palladium and the New York Hilton. Broadcast on NBC.

All awards were determined on an area basis with the possibility of multiple award winners, one winner, or none in each area.

OUTSTANDING PROGRAM ACHIEVEMENTS IN ENTERTAINMENT
• *The Dick Van Dyke Show.* Carl Reiner, producer. CBS.
• *The Magnificent Yankee, Hallmark Hall of Fame.* George Schaefer, producer. NBC.
• *My Name is Barbra.* Richard Lewine, producer. CBS.
• "What is Sonata Form?," *New York*

Philharmonic Young People's Concerts with Leonard Bernstein. Roger Englander, producer. CBS.
The Andy Williams Show. Bob Finkel, producer. NBC.
Bob Hope Presents the Chrysler Theater. Dick Berg, producer. NBC.
The Defenders. Bob Markell, producer. CBS.
Hallmark Hall of Fame. George Schaefer, producer. NBC.
The Man from U.N.C.L.E. Sam Rolfe, producer. NBC.
Mr. Novak. Leonard Freeman, producer. NBC.
Profiles in Courage. Robert Saudek, executive producer. NBC.
Walt Disney's Wonderful World of Color. Walt Disney, executive producer. NBC.
That Wonderful World of Burlesque.

Star turn: Broadway sensation Streisand's first TV special, My Name is Barbra, *nabbed five awards.*

OUTSTANDING INDIVIDUAL ACHIEVEMENT AWARDS IN ENTERTAINMENT
(Actors and performers)

• Leonard Bernstein, *New York Philharmonic Young People's Concerts with Leonard Bernstein.* CBS.
• Lynn Fontanne, *The Magnificent Yankee, Hallmark Hall of Fame.* NBC.
• Alfred Lunt, *The Magnificent Yankee, Hallmark Hall of Fame.* NBC.
• Barbra Streisand, *My Name is Barbra.* CBS.
• Dick Van Dyke, *The Dick Van Dyke Show.* CBS.
Julie Andrews, *The Andy Williams Show.* NBC.
Johnny Carson, *The Tonight Show Starring Johnny Carson.* NBC.
Gladys Cooper, *The Rogues.* NBC.
Robert Coote, *The Rogues.* NBC.
Richard Crenna, *Slattery's People.* CBS.
Julie Harris, *The Holy Terror, Hallmark Hall of Fame.* NBC.
Bob Hope, *The Bob Hope Special.* NBC.
Dean Jagger, *Mr. Novak.* NBC.
Danny Kaye, *The Danny Kaye Show.* CBS.
David McCallum, *The Man from U.N.C.L.E.* NBC.
Red Skelton, *The Red Skelton Hour.* CBS.
(Writers)
• David Karp, *The Defenders.* CBS.
William Boardman, Dee Caruso, Robert Emmett, David Frost, Gerald Gardner, Buck Henry, Joseph Hurley, Tom Meehan, Herb Sargent, Larry Siegel, Gloria Steinem, Jim Stevenson, Calvin Trillin, Saul Turtletaub, *That Was the Week That Was.* NBC.
Robert Hartung, *The Magnificent Yankee, Hallmark Hall of Fame.* NBC.
Coleman Jacoby, Arnie Rosen, *That Wonderful World of Burlesque.* NBC.
Carl Reiner, *The Dick Van Dyke Show.* CBS.

George Schlatter, producer. NBC.
Xerox Specials — "Carol for Another Christmas," Joseph L. Mankiewicz, producer; "Who Has Seen the Wind?" George Sidney, producer. ABC.

OUTSTANDING PROGRAM ACHIEVEMENTS IN NEWS, DOCUMENTARIES, INFORMATION, AND SPORTS
• "I, Leonardo da Vinci," *Saga of Western Man.* John H. Secondari, Helen Jean Rogers, producers. ABC.
• *The Louvre.* Lucy Jarvis, producer; John J. Sughrue, coproducer. NBC.
NBC Convention Coverage. Reuven Frank, producer. NBC.
"The Decision to Drop the Bomb," *NBC White Paper.* Fred Freed, producer. NBC.

(Directors)
• Paul Bogart, *The Defenders*. CBS.
Dwight Hemion, *My Name
is Barbra*. CBS.
George Schaefer, *The Magnificent Yankee,
Hallmark Hall of Fame*. NBC.

INDIVIDUAL ACHIEVEMENT AWARDS
IN NEWS, DOCUMENTARIES, INFORMATION,
AND SPORTS
(Narrators)
Richard Basehart, *Let My People Go*.
Syndicated.
Charles Boyer, *The Louvre*. NBC.
(Directors)
• John L. Sughrue, *The Louvre*. NBC.
Frank De Felitta, *Battle of the Bulge*. NBC.
Marshall Flaum, *Let My People Go*.
Syndicated.
Tom Priestley, *John F. Kennedy
Remembered*. NBC.
Helen Jean Rogers, "I, Leonardo da
Vinci," *Saga of Western Man*. ABC.
(Writers)
• Sidney Carroll, *The Louvre*. NBC.
John H. Secondari, "I, Leonardo de Vinci,"
Saga of Western Man. ABC.
(Musicians)
• Norman Dello Joio, *The Louvre*. NBC.
Ulpio Minucci, composer, "I, Leonardo
de Vinci," *Saga of Western Man*. ABC.
Rayburn Wright, "I, Leonardo de Vinci,"
Saga of Western Man. ABC.
(Film editors)
• Aram Boyajian, *The Louvre*. NBC.
Walter Essenfeld, Nils Rasmussen,
"I, Leonardo da Vinci," *Saga of Western
Man*. ABC.
Angelo Farina, Ben Schiller, *Battle of the
Bulge*. NBC.
(Cinematographers)
• Tom Priestley, *The Louvre*. NBC.
Dexter Alley, Richard Norling, *The
Journals of Lewis and Clark*. NBC.
William B. Hartigan, "I, Leonardo da
Vinci," *Saga of Western Man*. ABC.

OTHER AWARD WINNERS
ART DIRECTORS AND SET DECORATORS
• Warren Clymer, *The Holy Terror,
Hallmark Hall of Fame*. NBC.
• Tom John, art director. Bill Harp, set
decorator, *My Name is Barbra*. CBS.

MUSICIANS
• Peter Matz, music director, *My Name is
Barbra*. CBS.

CONCEPTION, CHOREOGRAPHY,
AND STAGING
• Joe Layton, *My Name is Barbra*. CBS.

COSTUME DESIGNER
• Noel Taylor, *The Magnificent Yankee,
Hallmark Hall of Fame*. NBC.

MAKEUP ARTIST
• Robert O'Bradovich, *The Magnificent
Yankee, Hallmark Hall of Fame*. NBC.

COLOR CONSULTANT
• Edward Ancona, *Bonanza*. NBC.

CINEMATOGRAPHERS
• William Spencer, *Twelve O'Clock High*.
ABC.

SPECIAL PHOTOGRAPHIC EFFECTS
• L.B. Abbott, *Voyage to the Bottom of the
Sea*. ABC.

TECHNICAL DIRECTOR
• Clair McCoy, *That Wonderful World of
Burlesque*. NBC.

LIGHTING DIRECTOR
• Phil Hymes, *The Magnificent Yankee,
Hallmark Hall of Fame*. NBC.

INTERNATIONAL AWARD
• *Le Barbier de Seville*. Canadian
Broadcasting Corp.

STATION AWARD
• *Ku Klux Klan*. WDSU-TV, New Orleans.

"A Straight, Safe Act" ... A Compact Show

After the "fiasco" of last year's Emmycast, the awards were overhauled yet again, returning about half of them to their old format that allowed only one winner per category. The rest continued to be awards within "areas of achievement" in which there could be many winners, one or none. "All in all," said *The Hollywood Reporter*, "even TV's bitterest detractors must concede that the new awards structure is a step in the right direction."

If nothing else, the new setup also introduced or resurrected separate categories for sports, daytime programs, children's shows, music, and, added the *Reporter*, "virtually every behind-the-cameras activity from make-up to videotape editing." The awards were also broadcast on a network other than NBC for the very first time — and on the "mutinous" CBS, of all alternatives, whose news division actually continued its private boycott despite the obvious irony that it was now snubbing itself. That the boycott continued was also considered strange because CBS News chief and boycott crusader Fred W. Friendly had resigned earlier in the year over his network's initial reluctance to air the Senate hearings on the Vietnam War. In the end, CBS did interrupt daytime reruns of *I Love Lucy* to broadcast the Senate proceedings — as did NBC, which, unlike CBS (thanks to its boycott), would win a news program Emmy for it.

The award ceremonies this year, said its executive producer Bob Banner, "would be handled as an event, not as an entertainment special." The comic monologues and interchanges were played down and the song-and-dance

Carol Burnett spies Emmycast cohost Bill Cosby's first statuette for I Spy. *Cosby: "I was the sentimental favorite."*

acts scrapped entirely. Danny Kaye was tapped to be host at the Hollywood Palladium, Bill Cosby at the ballroom of New York's Americana Hotel. Going into the night's competition, shows favored to win included the heavily nominated *Hallmark Hall of Fame* segments *Eagle in a Cage* and *Inherit the Wind*, *I Spy*, *The Man From U.N.C.L.E.*, *Chrysler Theater*, *Bewitched*, *Batman*, *The Julie Andrews Show*, and Streisand's latest special, *Color Me Barbra*.

Right away *The Andy Williams Show*, which was last underestimated in 1962–63, returned as the surprise winner of Outstanding Variety Series. More shocks followed, including the loss of *The Julie Andrews Show* in the race for Outstanding Variety Special to Bob Hope's Christmas special, although

Andrews did end up with Emmys for its director and video-tape editors. *I Spy* and *U.N.C.L.E.* were relative newcomers to prime time and were overtaken in the category of Outstanding Dramatic Series by *The Fugitive,* which had been on the air and on the run since 1963. America's newest singing sensation Barbra Streisand lost to "Chairman of the Board" Frank Sinatra, and the only prize *Inherit the Wind* would take was for its technical director. *Batman* was so popular that it was broadcast twice a week in the 1965–66 season and was thus ranked both fifth and tenth in the Nielsen ratings, but it ended up taking no Emmys despite its three nominations, including one for Outstanding Comedy Series.

The latter award went instead to Emmy's comedy champ of the past several years. "In one way, the Emmy Awards seemed like a television rerun," said *The New York Times.* "*The Dick Van Dyke Show* garnered four more Emmys last night. It was considered a hail and farewell gesture, since this is the last season for the show." Van Dyke himself had canceled the program, saying, "We wanted to quit while we were still proud of it."

The Dick Van Dyke Show also won trophies for Van Dyke, costar Mary Tyler Moore, and writers Bill Persky and Sam Denoff.

Hallmark Hall of Fame and *Bob Hope Presents the Chrysler Theater* did end up prevailing, as predicted. *Hallmark*'s *Eagle in a Cage,* which dramatized Napoleon's exile on the island of St. Helena, took Emmys for its supporting actor James Daly and for its writer, Millard Lampell. The latter used his acceptance speech as an occasion to inform the audience that he had suffered a form of exile in his career, too. "Everybody ought to know that I was blacklisted for 10 years!" he said. One week later, the *L.A. Times* reported, "Since the Emmy show,

Lampell's telephone has not stopped ringing; he said the reaction has been overwhelmingly favorable."

Chrysler Theater won three Emmys, including one for Simone Signoret, who had recently lost her Oscar bid for Best Actress in the film *Ship of Fools.* Two of the show's Emmys were for an episode called "The Game," one for its director Sydney Pollack, the other for actor Cliff Robertson, who came close to winning the top acting Emmy in 1960–61. Now Robertson had, literally, come a long way to try again; he learned of his nomination while on a polar bear hunt in Alaska during the filming of ABC's *American Sportsman.* He'd just finished complaining of the cold when the news came and he replied, "All of a sudden, it's 40 degrees warmer up here!"

Of the other early Emmy favorites to win, *Bewitched* pulled a respectable two statuettes, one for its director William Asher (also husband of star Elizabeth Montgomery) and one for the actress who first played the Stevens' nosey neighbor, Gladys Kravitz. Alice Pearce had died of cancer the previous March. Her supporting actress award was accepted by her husband, agent Paul Davis, who led the banquet members in a toast to "the most wonderful wife a man ever had." Two other posthumous awards were given away that night. A standing ovation greeted the bestowing of a Trustees Award to Edward R. Murrow, who died in 1965 but now was saluted as "a symbol to colleagues and

The Fugitive, which had been on the air and on the run since 1963, finally won Outstanding Drama Series.

The DVD Show's "hail and farewell": four trophies, including an outstanding series prize for a fourth year in a row.

the public alike of the complete broadcast journalist." And one of the top news and documentary awards went to a special on the Ku Klux Klan produced by the late David Lowe.

I Spy may have lost its top series prize to *The Fugitive*, but it still scored a major victory when show costar and Emmycast cohost Bill Cosby won the drama series acting honors. Cosby had said in an Associated Press interview after the event, "I was the sentimental favorite. I'm a Negro," but his win had hardly been assured. Only one other black had ever won a major Emmy — Harry Belafonte in 1959–60 for performing in his own musical variety special. Cosby, furthermore, was the first black ever to have a lead role in a regular weekly drama series. In his acceptance speech, he referred to his network's courage in casting him by saying, "I'd like to thank NBC for having guts," then graciously thanked his fellow nominee and costar Robert Culp, too, saying, "He

lost this because he helped me."

Other shows to win the top awards included the Outstanding Dramatic Program of the year — *The Ages of Man*, a David Susskind production that featured John Gielgud musing on the stages of man's maturity by quoting verse from Shakespeare. Susskind used his time at the podium to remind the audience that he and his coproducers weren't always successful. Referring to a flop he packaged for CBS, he said, "Remember, we also produced *Mr. Broadway!*"

Don Knotts was no longer a regular on *The Andy Griffith Show,* but he nonetheless picked up an Emmy in the category of supporting actor, saying, "Would you believe this?" *The Hollywood Reporter* explained: "It must be presumed that Don Knotts himself felt a little awkward at grabbing his fourth Emmy for his Barney Fife role in the Andy Griffith series, this last time for a 'guest' return performance after he'd quit the series."

Under the latest awards system, *The Hollywood Reporter* now said that "a *Peyton Place* actor has as much chance at grabbing an Emmy in a separate series category as has a *Hallmark Hall of Fame* actor in a 'specials' category." *Peyton Place*'s Lee Grant fulfilled that potential by being named outstanding supporting actress in a drama. When her name was announced, "the whole audience stood up and tore the house down," future academy president Larry Stewart remembers. Grant then gave what Stewart calls "the greatest acceptance speech I've ever heard" when she responded by just saying "the feeling's mutual" and walked off the stage.

Another *Peyton Place* actress, Barbara Parkins, lost in the category of drama series top actress — to Barbara Stanwyck (in *The Big Valley*), who said *Radio-TV Daily*, may have been "shut out in four tries for an Oscar, [but she] made it two for two in the Emmys, having won for *The Barbara Stanwyck Show* in 1960–61." Parkins was hardly a gracious loser. "I was hurt," she told TV columnist Hal Humphrey, "but if I had to lose, I was glad it was to Barbara Stanwyck, who is a grand lady and a fine actress." She then added: "I would have hated to lose to Anne Francis [of *Honey West*]. I don't care much for her work."

In the reinstated and new award categories, *A Charlie Brown Christmas* was named outstanding children's program; *Camera Three* and *Wild Kingdom* were acknowledged for their "Achievements in Daytime Programming." Separate sports categories acknowledged *ABC's Wide World of Sports*, *The CBS Golf Classic*, and *Shell's Wonderful World of Golf*.

The 18th Annual Emmy Awards had been played very safe — and worked. "Some half-hearted attempts were made at comedy," said *Broadcasting*, "but for the most part the 1965–66 Emmy awards were a straight act." One of its producers, Julio Di Benedetto, had said ahead of time, "We're going for 90 minutes for a tight, compact show." In the end, it ran only 14 minutes overtime.

The telecast also caused no widespread outcry once it was over. Anticipating that it might, however, and preparing for the opportunity to challenge Emmy's preeminence as the medium's top award, a group of 12 TV critics had banded together ahead of time to form the Critics' Consensus, which, they said, would bestow four more accurate awards of their own for the period of mid-May, 1965, to mid-May, 1966. Their winners: NBC for "exceptional contribution by a network" (NBC also won the bulk of Emmys this year, winning 20 compared to 13 for CBS and 9 for ABC); the Xerox Corporation for its enlightened sponsorship of quality programs (it was honored with a special Emmy, too); Fred Friendly, for his "exceptional contribution by an individual" to TV; and David Susskind's production of *Death of a Salesman*. *Salesman* had been broadcast only three weeks earlier and was not eligible for an Emmy until next year — when the academy would agree with the Critics' Consensus by naming it Outstanding Dramatic Program.

1965–66

For programs telecast between May 1, 1965, and April 10, 1966. Awards presented May 22, 1966, at the Hollywood Palladium and the Americana Hotel in New York. Broadcast on CBS.

PRIME-TIME PROGRAM AWARDS
OUTSTANDING DRAMATIC SERIES
• *The Fugitive*. Alan Armer, producer. ABC.
Bonanza. David Dortort, producer. NBC.
I Spy. David Friedkin, Mort Fine, producers. NBC.
The Man from U.N.C.L.E. Norman Felton, executive producer. NBC.
Slattery's People. Irving Elman, producer. CBS.

OUTSTANDING DRAMATIC PROGRAM— SINGLE PROGRAM
• *The Ages of Man*. David Susskind, Daniel Melnick, producers. CBS.
Eagle in a Cage, *Hallmark Hall of Fame*. George Schaefer, producer. NBC.
Inherit the Wind, *Hallmark Hall of Fame*. George Schaefer, producer. NBC.
"Rally 'Round Your Own Flag, Mister," *Slattery's People*. Irving Elman, producer. CBS.

OUTSTANDING COMEDY SERIES
• *The Dick Van Dyke Show*. Carl Reiner, producer. CBS.
Batman. Howie Horwitz, producer. ABC.
Bewitched. Jerry Davis, producer. ABC.
Get Smart. Leonard Stern, producer. NBC.
Hogan's Heroes. Edward H. Feldman, producer. CBS.

Outstanding Variety Series
• *The Andy Williams Show.* Bob Finkel, producer. NBC.
The Danny Kaye Show. Bob Scheerer, producer. CBS.
The Hollywood Palace. William O. Harbach, Nick Vanoff, producers. ABC.
The Red Skelton Hour. Seymour Berns, producer. CBS.
The Tonight Show Starring Johnny Carson. Art Stark, producer. NBC.

Outstanding Variety Special
• *Chrysler Presents the Bob Hope Christmas Special.* Bob Hope, executive producer. NBC.
An Evening with Carol Channing. Bud Yorkin, producer. CBS.
Jimmy Durante Meets the Lively Arts. Alan Handley, Bob Wynn, producers. ABC.
The Julie Andrews Show. Alan Handley, producer. NBC.
The Swinging World of Sammy Davis, Jr. Stan Greene, producer. Syndicated.

Outstanding Musical Program
• *Frank Sinatra: A Man and His Music.* Dwight Hemion, producer. NBC.
The Bell Telephone Hour. Barry Wood, executive producer. NBC.
The Bolshoi Ballet. Ted Mills, producer. Syndicated.
Color Me Barbra. Joe Layton, Dwight Hemion, producers. CBS.
New York Philharmonic Young People's Concerts with Leonard Bernstein. Roger Englander, producer. CBS.

Outstanding Children's Program
• *A Charlie Brown Christmas.* Lee Mendelson, Bill Melendez, producers. CBS.
Captain Kangaroo. Al Hyslop, producer. CBS.
Discovery '64–'65. Jules Power, executive producer. ABC.
"The Further Adventures of Gallagher," *Walt Disney's Wonderful World of Color.* Walt Disney, Ron Miller, producers. NBC.
"The World of Stuart Little," *NBC Children's Theatre.* George Heinemann, producer. NBC.

PERFORMANCE, DIRECTING, AND WRITING
Outstanding Continued Performance by an Actor in a Leading Role in a Dramatic Series
• Bill Cosby, *I Spy.* NBC.
Richard Crenna, *Slattery's People.* CBS.
Robert Culp, *I Spy.* NBC.
David Janssen, *The Fugitive.* ABC.
David McCallum, *The Man from U.N.C.L.E.* NBC.

Outstanding Continued Performance by an Actress in a Leading Role in a Dramatic Series
• Barbara Stanwyck, *The Big Valley.* ABC.
Anne Francis, *Honey West.* ABC.
Barbara Parkins, *Peyton Place.* ABC.

Outstanding Continued Performance by an Actor in a Leading Role in a Comedy Series
• Dick Van Dyke, *The Dick Van Dyke Show.* CBS.
Don Adams, *Get Smart.* NBC.
Bob Crane, *Hogan's Heroes.* CBS.

Outstanding Continued Performance by an Actress in a Leading Role in a Comedy Series
• Mary Tyler Moore, *The Dick Van Dyke Show.* CBS.
Lucille Ball, *The Lucy Show.* CBS.
Elizabeth Montgomery, *Bewitched.* ABC.

Outstanding Single Performance by an Actor in a Leading Role in a Drama
• Cliff Robertson, *The Game, Bob Hope Presents the Chrysler Theater.* NBC.
Ed Begley, *Inherit the Wind, Hallmark Hall of Fame.* NBC.
Melvyn Douglas, *Inherit the Wind, Hallmark Hall of Fame.* NBC.
Trevor Howard, *Eagle in a Cage, Hallmark Hall of Fame.* NBC.
Christopher Plummer, *Hamlet.* Syndicated.

Outstanding Single Performance by an Actress in a Leading Role in a Drama
• Simone Signoret, *A Small Rebellion, Bob Hope Presents the Chrysler Theater.* NBC.
Eartha Kitt, *I Spy.* NBC.
Margaret Leighton, *Dr. Kildare.* NBC.
Shelley Winters, *Back to Back, Bob Hope Presents the Chrysler Theater.* NBC.

**OUTSTANDING PERFORMANCE
BY AN ACTOR IN A SUPPORTING ROLE
IN A DRAMA**
• James Daly, *Eagle in a Cage, Hallmark
Hall of Fame.* NBC.
David Burns, *Trials of O'Brien.* CBS.
Leo G. Carroll, *The Man from U.N.C.L.E.*
NBC.

**OUTSTANDING PERFORMANCE
BY AN ACTRESS IN A SUPPORTING ROLE
IN A DRAMA**
• Lee Grant, *Peyton Place.* ABC.
Diane Baker, *Inherit the Wind, Hallmark
Hall of Fame.* NBC.
Pamela Franklin, *Eagle in a Cage,
Hallmark Hall of Fame.* NBC.
Jeanette Nolan, *I Spy.* NBC.

**OUTSTANDING PERFORMANCE
BY AN ACTOR IN A SUPPORTING ROLE
IN A COMEDY**
• Don Knotts, *The Andy Griffith Show.*
CBS.
Morey Amsterdam, *The Dick Van Dyke
Show.* CBS.
Frank Gorshin, *Batman.* ABC.
Werner Klemperer, *Hogan's Heroes.* CBS.

**OUTSTANDING PERFORMANCE
BY AN ACTRESS IN A SUPPORTING ROLE
IN A COMEDY**
• Alice Pearce, *Bewitched.* ABC.
Agnes Moorehead, *Bewitched.* ABC.
Rose Marie, *The Dick Van Dyke Show.*
CBS.

**OUTSTANDING DIRECTORIAL
ACHIEVEMENT IN DRAMA**
• Sidney Pollack, *The Game, Bob Hope
Presents the Chrysler Theater.* NBC.
Sheldon Leonard, *I Spy.* NBC.
George Schaefer, *Eagle in a Cage,
Hallmark Hall of Fame.* NBC.
George Schaefer, *Inherit the Wind,
Hallmark Hall of Fame.* NBC.

**OUTSTANDING DIRECTORIAL
ACHIEVEMENT IN COMEDY**
• William Asher, *Bewitched.* ABC.
Paul Bogart, *Get Smart.* NBC.
Jerry Paris, *The Dick Van Dyke Show.* CBS.

**OUTSTANDING DIRECTORIAL
ACHIEVEMENT IN VARIETY OR MUSIC**
• Alan Handley, *The Julie Andrews Show.*
NBC.

The Andy Griffith Show's *Don Knotts with
his fourth Emmy: "Can you believe this?"*

Greg Garrison, *The Dean Martin Show.*
NBC.
Dwight Hemion, *Frank Sinatra: A Man
and His Music.* NBC.
Dwight Hemion, *Color Me Barbra.* CBS.
Bob Henry, *The Andy Williams Show.*
NBC.

**OUTSTANDING WRITING
ACHIEVEMENT IN DRAMA**
• Millard Lampell, *Eagle in a Cage,
Hallmark Hall of Fame.* NBC.
Morton Fine, David Friedkin, *I Spy.* NBC.
S. Lee Pogostin, *The Game, Bob Hope
Presents the Chrysler Theater.* NBC.

**OUTSTANDING WRITING
ACHIEVEMENT IN COMEDY**
• Bill Persky, Sam Denoff, *The Dick Van
Dyke Show.* CBS.
Mel Brooks, Buck Henry, *Get Smart.*
NBC.
Bill Persky, Sam Denoff, *The Dick Van
Dyke Show.* CBS.

**OUTSTANDING WRITING
ACHIEVEMENT IN VARIETY**
• Al Gordon, Hal Goldman, Sheldon
Keller, *An Evening with Carol Channing.*
CBS.

Ernest Chambers, Pat McCormick, Ron Friedman, Larry Tucker, Paul Mazursky, Billie Barnes, Bernard Rothman, Norman Barasch, Carrol Moore, *The Danny Kaye Show*. CBS.
Bill Persky, Sam Denoff, *The Julie Andrews Show*. NBC.

THE AREAS
Each area has the possibility of multiple award winners, one winner, or no winner. Winners are listed.

ACHIEVEMENTS IN NEWS AND DOCUMENTARIES
(Programs)
• *American White Paper: United States Foreign Policy*. Fred Freed, producer. NBC.
• "KKK — The Invisible Empire," *CBS Reports*. David Lowe, producer. CBS.
• *Senate Hearings on Vietnam*. Chet Hagan, producer. NBC.

ACHIEVEMENTS IN DAYTIME PROGRAMMING
(Programs)
• *Camera Three*. Dan Gallagher, producer. CBS.
• *Wild Kingdom*. Don Meier, producer. NBC.

ACHIEVEMENTS IN SPORTS
(Programs)
• *ABC's Wide World of Sports*. Roone Arledge, executive producer. ABC.
• *The CBS Golf Classic,* Frank Chirkinian, producer. CBS.
• *Shell's Wonderful World of Golf*. Fred Raphael, producer. NBC.

ACHIEVEMENTS IN EDUCATIONAL TELEVISION
(Individuals)
• Julia Child, *The French Chef*. NET.

ACHIEVEMENTS IN MUSIC
(Composition)
• Laurence Rosenthal, *Michelangelo: The Last Giant*. NBC.

INDIVIDUAL ACHIEVEMENTS IN ART DIRECTION AND ALLIED CRAFTS
(Art direction)
• James Trittipo, *The Hollywood Palace*. ABC.
(Cinematography)
• Winton C. Hoch, *Voyage to the Bottom of the Sea*. ABC.
(Cinematography: Special)
• L.B. Abbott, Howard Lydecker for photographic effects, *Voyage to the Bottom of the Sea*. ABC.
(Film editing)
• David Blewitt, William T. Cartwright, *The Making of the President 1964*. CBS.
• Marvin Coil, Everett Douglas, Ellsworth Hoagland, *Bonanza*. NBC.
(Audio engineering)
• Laurence Schneider, "Seventh Annual Young Performers Program," *New York Philharmonic Young People's Concerts with Leonard Bernstein*. CBS.
(Video-tape editing)
• Craig Curtis, Art Schneider, *The Julie Andrews Show*. NBC.
(Lighting)
• Lon Stucky, *Frank Sinatra: A Man and His Music*. NBC.
(Technical director)
• O. Tamburri, *Inherit the Wind, Hallmark Hall of Fame*. NBC.

SPECIAL CLASSIFICATIONS OF INDIVIDUAL ACHIEVEMENTS
• Burr Tillstrom, "Berlin Wall" hand ballet, *That Was the Week That Was*. NBC.

ENGINEERING DEVELOPMENT
• Stop Action Playback. MVR Corp. and CBS.
• Early Bird Satellite. Hughes Aircraft Co. and Communications Satellite Corp.

(No awards to individuals in daytime programming, sports, and news and documentary. No awards for music conducting or arranging, set decoration, costume design, wardrobe, makeup, sound editing, video control, electronic cameramen, or special electronic effects.)

SPECIAL AWARDS
THE INTERNATIONAL AWARD
(Nonfiction)
• "Wyvern at War—No. 2," *Breakout*. Westward Television Limited, Plymouth, England.
(No fiction winner)

STATION AWARD
• *I See Chicago*. WBBM-TV, Chicago.

TRUSTEES AWARDS
• Edward R. Murrow
• Xerox Corporation.

Caesar's Old Guard, and Lucille Ball, Bounce Back

"Now that Dick (Van Dyke) and his brood are retired temporarily from the TV screen," wrote *The Los Angeles Times*, "it's a whole new guessing game." *The Dick Van Dyke Show* had dominated the Emmys over the previous four years, but now that it was off the air, anything was possible and surprises were inevitable. Contrary to what the *Times* said, though, the brood hadn't vanished altogether. In fact, they were up for another award this year for a recent Van Dyke variety special that was pitted against a different Emmy-winning gang that virtually invented the variety format.

Variety champs Howard Morris, Sid Caesar, Carl Reiner, and producer Jack Arnold: "The good old days and talents of TV remain the best."

TV industry insiders believed that now that the Van Dyke series was out of the way, old losers *Bewitched*, *Get Smart*, and *Hogan's Heroes* all had a better chance this year in the top comedy competition, and all of them were nominated. None of them won. Instead, a new show came from behind to win best humor program — *The Monkees* — "the only comedy series of the season to take off in a direction other than that pursued by the overdone situation type," said the *Times*. The show was based, at least in spirit, on the 1964 Beatles film *A Hard Day's Night*, and it combined elements of impish slapstick with genuinely sophisticated humor full of outrageous double entendres. *The Monkees*, in fact, made a much better TV show than a rock band. Two of its members (Davy Jones and Mickey Dolenz) couldn't even play musical instruments. But the show had such a fresh style and avant-garde look (packed with fast- and slow-motion sequences, freeze frames, and montage tricks) that it also earned an Emmy for its director. When James Frawley accepted his trophy for his own monkeeing around with cast and cameras, he thanked the quartet of "really funny guys — Harpo, Chico, Groucho, and Gummo." "It was just that sort of evening," said *The Los Angeles Herald Examiner* of the Emmy ceremonies.

Get Smart did win two important awards, though, including one for its writers. But it was the show's second award that proved how smart the star portraying Maxwell Smart really was — if for nothing more than hanging on. Last year Don Adams lost the honors for comic acting to Van Dyke, but this year — and as his character would say, "Would you believe?" — he did prevail. And would continue to do so. Like Van Dyke before him, Adams would now

Past dark horse victor Peter Ustinov pulled off yet another upset to win best actor as Socrates in Barefoot in Athens.

dominate the acting category for three years running.

The winner of the funniest female on TV sparked "the only unexpected occurrence" of the night, said *The Hollywood Reporter* (overlooking, among other shockers, the surprise caused by *The Monkees'* win) and proved that an old law of physics also applied to the Emmys: Some balls can bounce back as long as they stay in the game. "Miss Ball Helps Save Dull Emmy Show" said the headline in *The Chicago Tribune*. It was Lucille Ball's first Emmy in more than a decade, and winning it for her role on *The Lucy Show* obviously caught her off guard. She wept openly as she accepted the statuette, telling the audience, "I can't believe it. I don't have one thing prepared to say, because it's been a long, long time. The last time I won I thought I got it because I had had a baby. That baby is 14 years old now." She was referring (mistakenly) to the year she gave birth to little Desi Arnaz, Jr., on

and off the little screen on the same day, January 19, 1953. The show did win Best Situation Comedy that year, but Ball was mistaken because the last time she'd won an Emmy was actually in 1956 when she was named 1955's Best Actress in a regular series. And she would win an outstanding actress nod one more time — next year, again for *The Lucy Show*.

In comedy's supporting-acting categories, Don Knotts won his fifth — and last — prize for portraying Barney Fife on *The Andy Griffith Show* and Frances Bavier won her first and only for playing the show's honey-sweet Aunt Bee.

The Times felt compelled to add this commentary: "Perhaps the TV academy's voting this time also reflects what the public generally might be thinking, namely, that the good old days and talents of TV remain the best." Nothing proved that point more than the brood that bested this year's Van Dyke program for best variety special: *The Sid Caesar, Imogene Coca, Carl Reiner, Howard Morris Special*. This comic quartet had worked together on Emmy's 1951 and 1952 Best Variety Show *Your Show of Shows* and two or three of them had hooked up at various times for *Caesar's Show*, *Sid Caesar Invites You,* and *The Caesar Hour* over the years, but there was never a complete reunion until this special — and the TV critics, the public, and the academy's blue-ribbon panel award voters all welcomed them back with warm enthusiasm. The special also won a prize for variety show writing, naming the likes of Reiner and Mel Brooks among the winners.

For the second year in a row, the year's Outstanding Variety Series was *The Andy Williams Show*, but just like the first time it won the distinction, in 1962–63, the show was canceled shortly before it took its highest honors. Back in 1963, however, the show was reinstated immediately after it won its Emmy. It was not so fortunate this time around and, in fact, two years would pass before Williams would be back on TV in a regular time slot.

Going into the Emmy Awards show this year, two specials led the way — *Death of a Salesman* with 10 nominations and *Brigadoon* with eight. *Salesman*, produced by David Susskind, was a historic telecast. It starred the original Broadway cast headed by Lee J. Cobb and Mildred Dunnock, and, said the *L.A. Times*, "brought new life to television drama and turned the 1966–67 season into a vintage dramatic year for TV viewers." The production ended up winning three awards, one for Arthur Miller, who adapted his own Pulitzer Prize–winning stage script for the small screen, another for its director, Alex Segal, and one for being the Outstanding Dramatic Program of the year. Picking up the latter prize, Susskind thanked CBS for its "gutty, courageous" decision to schedule the program even before it had a sponsor.

But something was noticeably absent from the *Salesman*'s dramatic awards sweep: namely, the salesman. Star Lee J. Cobb had been shooting a movie on location in Spain, but he flew to New York to be on hand at the Emmycast to accept the prize that everyone — including the academy, which paid for his airline ticket — was sure he'd win. When Cobb lost, it was considered especially sad since it mirrored his earlier failure to win the Tony Award in 1949 after he created the classic role of Willy Loman on stage. Cobb's bad luck with the award would even continue. When the 1951 film version was being cast, he was passed over in favor of Fredric March while Mildred Dunnock was invited to reprise her stage role for celluloid.

Cobb was upstaged by what *The New York Daily News* called the most surprising development of the night: Peter Usti-

nov's win for playing Socrates in *Barefoot in Athens* on *Hallmark Hall of Fame*. Ustinov had not even been considered a likely dark horse. *Daily News* columnist Ben Gross was among the TV critics who predicted Cobb would win, adding that if anyone was going to pull an upset, it would be Hal Holbrook for playing the lead in *Mark Twain Tonight!* Ustinov had pulled an equally surprising win, however, back at the 1957 awards competition when he overcame front-runner Mickey Rooney and, of all possible other contenders, Lee J. Cobb.

Mildred Dunnock lost to Geraldine Page, who played the spinster cousin in Truman Capote's *A Christmas Memory*, which also won an Emmy for Capote and cowriter Eleanor Perry. Supporting awards for dramatic acting went to Eli Wallach in a Xerox-sponsored special about the international narcotics trade called *The Poppy is Also a Flower* and to Agnes Moorehead for playing a socialite caught up in a series of mysterious murders on a two-part episode of *The Wild, Wild West*. Moorehead was also nominated this year for best actress (against Lucille Ball) for her role as Endora, *Bewitched*'s bewitching matriarch.

Lucy wept when she won: "It's been a long, long time."

As predicted, *Brigadoon* took quite a number of awards on this night, too — with five prizes, it was the evening champ. The ABC special presentation of the Lerner and Lowe musical starred Robert Goulet and won awards for being the Outstanding Musical Program of the year and for its director, technical director, lighting director, and electronic cameramen.

I Spy began the evening with the most series nominations — six — but it ended up with only one statuette, a repeat win for last year's "sentimental favorite" Bill Cosby, who couldn't accept his prize personally this year because he was out of town. Still, Cosby's win sparked what one press account called "a roar of acclaim" when it was announced, and probably because it was another of the "predictable" evening's many surprises. Martin Landau in *Mission: Impossible* and David Janssen in *The Fugitive* had been considered the category's front-runners.

But Landau at least had a consolation prize. After losing to Cosby, he sat back and watched his wife and costar Barbara Bain win best actress in a dramatic series, beating odds-on favorite Barbara Stanwyck. Landau grinned noticeably as Bain accepted the trophy saying, "There is a gentleman here I want to thank, but I'll do that privately." *Mission: Impossible*

Winners of the Outstanding Comedy Series prize monkee-ed around backstage with Jimmy Durante (right) and Family Affair*'s Anissa "Buffy" Jones.*

had already pulled off another improbable task that year just by staying on the air. The new show was doing poorly in the ratings (opposite the popular *Get Smart* on Saturday nights) and therefore was considered an Emmy longshot. But it ended up taking Outstanding Dramatic Series, in addition to its awards for Bain, its writer, and film editors.

In other categories, Gene Kelly's production of *Jack and the Beanstalk*

was cited as best children's show; Mike Douglas was named outstanding daytime individual; Art Carney won an area award for his work with Jackie Gleason; *ABC's Wide World of Sports* took the athletic competition; *Wild Kingdom* repeated its win of last year; and NBC vice president Sylvester "Pat" Weaver was given a Trustees Award for 18 years of contributions to the television industry, but especially as a champion of the *Today* and *Tonight* shows.

In the news and documentary categories, winners included *China: The Roots of Madness* which reunited maverick independent producer David Wolper and Pulitzer Prize–winning writer Theodore H. White, the same team behind the Emmy's 1963–64 Program of the Year *The Making of the President 1960*. *President* was initially turned down by both NBC and CBS and then was shown on ABC in a terrible time slot. This time all three networks turned down *China* and it was offered instead to individual stations across the country on a syndicated basis. Other documentary winners were *Hall of Kings*, which provided a camera tour of Westminster Abbey, and *The Italians*, produced by CBS News, which was still stubbornly boycotting the Emmys all by itself.

But not for long. One week after the Emmycast, *The Hollywood Reporter* splashed the following headline across its front page: "29 Tuners Sound Sour Note." That many composers and musicians had just resigned from the academy en masse (including Nelson Riddle and Lennie Hayton) because, in some of these new, noncompetitive "craft and programming areas," no one won a musical award even though such greats as Aaron Copland were nominated. The resignation letter called it a "disgrace," adding, "When other arts and crafts can receive recognition for their members, and music cannot, then there is something unhealthy about the awards program itself." In a courageous and speedy response, the academy's Board of Governors agreed, saying that the musicians' protest "justified strong and corrective action." The protest would lead to yet another revamping of the awards structure and one that assured the musicians that they would be among the winners next year. It was a promise that would be upheld.

This year's Emmys were broadcast on ABC for the first time ever and originated from both the Century Plaza Hotel in Los Angeles, where Joey Bishop played host (it was his fourth time performing the honors), and the Americana Hotel in New York, where Hugh Downs presided. Bishop opened the show by complaining that the celebrants out in New York were provided with a full-course dinner "while we're still sitting here waiting for Chicken Delight." However, other than Bish-

op's occasional barbs and a hilarious appearance by "The Schnoz" Jimmy Durante (who at one point rubbed noses with Anissa "Buffy" Jones of *Family Affair* — "an awesome experience," said *The Chicago Tribune*), the telecast was more serious than showy. A few taped excerpts of the nominated variety programs were aired as usual, but there were no singing or dancing acts again this year. Unlike the Oscars show the previous April, however, this awards telecast did take time out to honor the late Walt Disney whose *Disneyland* had been an early Emmy victor.

What the telecast lacked in glitz it made up for in celebrity. Except for Cosby, there were few no-shows this year. "It was a big night for TV," said the *Daily News*. "Stars, stars, stars. That's what Americans like to see." And tune in America did. The good news was that the Emmys ended up on top of the Nielsen ratings for its two-week period. The bad news was that it shared the spot for the first time ever — tying with two reruns of *The Dean Martin Show*.

1966–67

For programs telecast between March 25, 1966, and April 16, 1967. Awards presented on June 4, 1967, at the Century Plaza Hotel in Hollywood and the Americana Hotel in New York.

PRIME-TIME PROGRAM AWARDS
OUTSTANDING DRAMATIC SERIES
• *Mission: Impossible.* Joseph Gantman, Bruce Geller, producers. CBS.
The Avengers. Julian Wintle, executive producer. ABC.
I Spy. David Friedkin, Mort Fine, producers. NBC.
Run for Your Life. Jo Swerling, Jr., producer. NBC.
Star Trek. Gene Coon, Eugene Roddenberry, producers. NBC.

OUTSTANDING DRAMATIC PROGRAM
• *Death of a Salesman.* David Susskind, Daniel Melnick, producers. CBS.
A Christmas Memory, ABC Stage 67. Frank Perry, producer. ABC.
The Final War of Olly Winter, CBS Playhouse. Fred Coe, producer. CBS.
The Glass Menagerie, CBS Playhouse. David Susskind, producer. CBS.
The Love Song of Barney Kempinski, ABC Stage 67. Marc Merson, producer. ABC.
Mark Twain Tonight! David Susskind, producer. CBS.

OUTSTANDING COMEDY SERIES
• *The Monkees.* Bert Schneider, Bob Rafelson, producers. NBC.
The Andy Griffith Show. Bob Ross, producer. CBS.
Bewitched. William Froug, producer. ABC.

Get Smart. Arnie Rosen, producer. NBC.
Hogan's Heroes. Edward H. Feldman,
producer. CBS.

OUTSTANDING VARIETY SERIES
• *The Andy Williams Show.* Edward
Stephenson, Bob Finkel, producers. NBC.
The Dean Martin Show. Greg Garrison,
producer. NBC.
The Hollywood Palace. Nick Vanoff,
William O. Harbach, producers. ABC.
The Jackie Gleason Show. Ronald Wayne,
producer. CBS.
The Smothers Brothers Comedy Hour.
Saul Ilson, Ernest Chambers, producers.
CBS.
*The Tonight Show Starring Johnny
Carson.* Art Stark, producer. NBC.

OUTSTANDING VARIETY SPECIAL
• *The Sid Caesar, Imogene Coca, Carl
Reiner, Howard Morris Special.* Jack
Arnold, producer. CBS.
*Chrysler Presents the Bob Hope Christmas
Special.* Bob Hope, executive producer.
NBC.
*A Time for Laughter: A Look at Negro
Humor in America, ABC Stage 67.* Phil
Stein, producer. ABC.
Dick Van Dyke. Byron Paul, Jack
Donohue, producers. CBS.

OUTSTANDING MUSICAL PROGRAM
• *Brigadoon.* Fielder Cook, producer.
ABC.
*Frank Sinatra: A Man and His Music, Part
II.* Dwight Hemion, producer. CBS.
"Toscanini: The Maestro Revisited," *The
Bell Telephone Hour.* Gerald Green,
producer. NBC.

OUTSTANDING CHILDREN'S PROGRAM
• *Jack and the Beanstalk.* Gene Kelly,
producer. NBC.
Charlie Brown's All Stars. Lee Mendelson,
Bill Melendez, producers. CBS.
Discovery '66–'67. Jules Power, executive
producer. ABC.
It's the Great Pumpkin, Charlie Brown.
Lee Mendelson, Bill Melendez, producers.
CBS.

PERFORMANCE, DIRECTING, AND WRITING
**OUTSTANDING CONTINUED PERFORMANCE
BY AN ACTOR IN A LEADING ROLE IN A
DRAMATIC SERIES**
• Bill Cosby, *I Spy.* NBC.
Robert Culp, *I Spy.* NBC.

Inger Stevens (left) and Peter Falk with
Mission: Impossible*'s Barbara Bain.*

Ben Gazzara, *Run for Your Life.* NBC.
David Janssen, *The Fugitive.* ABC.
Martin Landau, *Mission: Impossible.* CBS.

**OUTSTANDING CONTINUED PERFORMANCE
BY AN ACTRESS IN A LEADING ROLE IN A
DRAMATIC SERIES**
• Barbara Bain, *Mission: Impossible.* CBS.
Diana Rigg, *The Avengers.* ABC.
Barbara Stanwyck, *The Big Valley.* ABC.

**OUTSTANDING SINGLE PERFORMANCE
BY AN ACTOR IN A LEADING ROLE
IN A DRAMA**
• Peter Ustinov, *Barefoot in Athens,
Hallmark Hall of Fame.* NBC.
Alan Arkin, *The Love Song of Barney
Kempinski, ABC Stage 67.* ABC.
Lee J. Cobb, *Death of a Salesman.* CBS.
Ivan Dixon, *The Final War of Olly Winter,
CBS Playhouse.* CBS.
Hal Holbrook, *Mark Twain Tonight!* CBS.

**OUTSTANDING SINGLE PERFORMANCE
BY AN ACTRESS IN LEADING ROLE
IN A DRAMA**
• Geraldine Page, *A Christmas Memory,
ABC Stage 67.* ABC.
Shirley Booth, *The Glass Menagerie, CBS
Playhouse.* CBS.

Mildred Dunnock, *Death of a Salesman.* CBS.
Lynn Fontanne, *Anastasia, Hallmark Hall of Fame.* NBC.
Julie Harris, *Anastasia, Hallmark Hall of Fame.* NBC.

OUTSTANDING CONTINUED PERFORMANCE BY AN ACTOR IN A LEADING ROLE IN A COMEDY SERIES
• Don Adams, *Get Smart.* NBC.
Bob Crane, *Hogan's Heroes.* CBS.
Brian Keith, *Family Affair.* CBS.
Larry Storch, *F Troop.* ABC.

OUTSTANDING CONTINUED PERFORMANCE BY AN ACTRESS IN A LEADING ROLE IN A COMEDY SERIES
• Lucille Ball, *The Lucy Show.* CBS.
Elizabeth Montgomery, *Bewitched.* ABC.
Agnes Moorehead, *Bewitched.* ABC.
Marlo Thomas, *That Girl.* ABC.

OUTSTANDING PERFORMANCE BY AN ACTOR IN A SUPPORTING ROLE IN A DRAMA
• Eli Wallach, *The Poppy is Also a Flower, Xerox Special.* ABC.
Leo G. Carroll, *The Man from U.N.C.L.E.* NBC.
Leonard Nimoy, *Star Trek.* NBC.

OUTSTANDING PERFORMANCE BY AN ACTRESS IN A SUPPORTING ROLE IN A DRAMA
• Agnes Moorehead, *The Wild, Wild West.* CBS.
Tina Chen, *The Final War of Olly Winter, CBS Playhouse.* CBS.
Ruth Warrick, *Peyton Place.* ABC.

OUTSTANDING PERFORMANCE BY AN ACTOR IN A SUPPORTING ROLE IN A COMEDY
• Don Knotts, *The Andy Griffith Show.* CBS.
Gale Gordon, *The Lucy Show.* CBS.
Werner Klemperer, *Hogan's Heroes.* CBS.

OUTSTANDING PERFORMANCE BY AN ACTRESS IN A SUPPORTING ROLE IN A COMEDY
• Frances Bavier, *The Andy Griffith Show.* CBS.
Nancy Kulp, *The Beverly Hillbillies.* CBS.
Marion Lorne, *Bewitched.* ABC.

OUTSTANDING DIRECTORIAL ACHIEVEMENT IN DRAMA
• Alex Segal, *Death of a Salesman.* CBS.
Paul Bogart, *The Final War of Olly Winter, CBS Playhouse.* CBS.
Paul Bogart, *Mark Twain Tonight!* CBS.
George Schaefer, *Anastasia, Hallmark Hall of Fame.* NBC.

OUTSTANDING DIRECTORIAL ACHIEVEMENT IN COMEDY
• James Frawley, *The Monkees.* NBC.
William Asher, *Bewitched.* ABC.
Earl Bellamy, *I Spy.* NBC.
William Russell, *Family Affair.* CBS.
Maury Thompson, *The Lucy Show.* CBS.

OUTSTANDING DIRECTORIAL ACHIEVEMENT IN VARIETY OR MUSIC
• Fielder Cook, *Brigadoon.* ABC.
Greg Garrison, *The Dean Martin Show.* NBC.
Dwight Hemion, *Frank Sinatra: A Man and His Music, Part II.* CBS.
Bob Henry, *The Andy Williams Show.* NBC.
Bill Hobin, *The Sid Caesar, Imogene Coca, Carl Reiner, Howard Morris Special.* CBS.

OUTSTANDING WRITING ACHIEVEMENT IN DRAMA
• Bruce Geller, *Mission: Impossible.* CBS.
Robert Culp, *I Spy.* NBC.
Ronald Ribman, *The Final War of Olly Winter, CBS Playhouse.* CBS.

OUTSTANDING WRITING ACHIEVEMENT IN COMEDY
• Buck Henry, Leonard Stern, *Get Smart.* NBC.
Edmund Hartmann, *Family Affair.* CBS.
Sidney Sheldon, *I Dream of Jeannie.* NBC.

OUTSTANDING WRITING ACHIEVEMENT IN VARIETY
• Mel Brooks, Sam Denoff, Bill Persky, Carl Reiner, Mel Tolkin, *The Sid Caesar, Imogene Coca, Carl Reiner, Howard Morris Special.* CBS.
Harry Crane, Rich Eustis, Lee Hale, Paul Keyes, Al Rogers, *The Dean Martin Show.* NBC.
Marvin Marx, Walter Stone, Rod Parker, *The Jackie Gleason Show.* CBS.

THE AREAS
Each area has the possibility of multiple award winners, one winner, or no winner. Winners are listed.

PROGRAM ACHIEVEMENTS IN NEWS AND DOCUMENTARIES
• *China: The Roots of Madness.* Mel Stuart, David Wolper, producers. Syndicated.
• *Hall of Kings.* Harry Rasky, producer. ABC.
• *The Italians.* Bernard Birnbaum, producer. CBS.

INDIVIDUAL ACHIEVEMENTS IN NEWS AND DOCUMENTARIES
• Theodore H. White, writer, *China: The Roots of Madness.* Syndicated.

PROGRAM ACHIEVEMENTS IN DAYTIME PROGRAMMING
• *Mutual of Omaha's Wild Kingdom.* Don Meier, producer. NBC.

INDIVIDUAL ACHIEVEMENTS IN DAYTIME PROGRAMMING
• Mike Douglas, *The Mike Douglas Show.* Syndicated.

PROGRAM ACHIEVEMENTS IN SPORTS
• *ABC's Wide World of Sports.* Roone Arledge, executive producer. ABC.

INDIVIDUAL ACHIEVEMENTS IN ART DIRECTION AND ALLIED CRAFTS
(Costume design)
• Ray Aghayan, Bob Mackie, *Alice Through the Looking Glass.* NBC.
(Makeup)
• Dick Smith, *Mark Twain Tonight!* CBS.
(Photographic special effects)
• L.B. Abbott, *The Time Tunnel.* ABC.
• L.B. Abbott, *Voyage to the Bottom of the Sea.* ABC.
• Darrell Anderson, Linwood G. Dunn, Joseph Westheimer, *Star Trek.* NBC.

INDIVIDUAL ACHIEVEMENTS IN FILM AND SOUND EDITING
• Paul Krasny, Robert Waits, film editors, *Mission: Impossible.* CBS.
• Don Hall, Dick Legrand, Daniel Mandell, John Mills, sound editors, *Voyage to the Bottom of the Sea.* ABC

INDIVIDUAL ACHIEVEMENTS IN ELECTRONIC PRODUCTION
(Technical directors)
• A.C. Cunningham, *Brigadoon.* ABC.
(Lighting directors)
• Leard Davis, *Brigadoon.* ABC.
(Audio engineering)
• Bill Cole, *Frank Sinatra: A Man and His Music, Part II.* CBS.
(Electronic cameramen)
• Robert Dunn, Gorm Erickson, Ben Wolf, Nick Demos, *Brigadoon.* ABC.

INDIVIDUAL ACHIEVEMENTS IN ENGINEERING DEVELOPMENT
• Plumbicon Tube, N.V. Philips, Gloeilampenfabrieken.
• High-Band Video Tape Recorder, Ampex Corp.

SPECIAL CLASSIFICATIONS OF INDIVIDUAL ACHIEVEMENTS
• Art Carney, performer, *The Jackie Gleason Show.* CBS.
• Truman Capote, Eleanor Perry, adaptation, *A Christmas Memory*, *ABC Stage 67.* ABC.
• Arthur Miller, adaptation, *Death of a Salesman.* CBS.

(No winners of awards for music composition, conductors, arrangers, sound recording, choral direction ,video tape editing, cinematography, mechanical special effects, art direction, or individual achievement in sports.)

INTERNATIONAL AWARDS
(Documentary)
• *Big Deal at Gothenburg.* Tyne Tees Television Limited, Newcastle-upon-Tyne, England.
(Entertainment)
• *The Caretaker.* Rediffusion Television Limited, England.

STATION AWARD
• *The Road to Nowhere*, KLZ-TV, Denver, Colorado.

TRUSTEES AWARD
• Sylvester L. "Pat" Weaver, Jr.

Laugh-In Gets
Serious (Recognition)

It was "a swinging, sock-it-to-me ceremony," said *The Los Angeles Times*, that
brought the night's big champ *Laugh-In*
a lot more than laughs. Thanks to winning multiple Emmys, the naughty new
humor program ended up with sudden
respectability, too.

Rowan and Martin's Laugh-In had
been on the air less than four months
when it entered the Emmys race. The
series had been launched in January as a
mid-season replacement show after it had
premiered as a popular special the previous September. Now it was zooming to
the top of the Nielsen chart and Emmy
voters' ballots as well, with seven nominations. The reason: At a time of civil
unrest, the Vietnam war, and the Robert
Kennedy and Martin Luther King, Jr.,
assassinations, many people were upset
and wanted (to use one of the show's
most popular phrases) to sock it to someone else, and *Laugh-In* happily did it for
them, and in an appropriately irreverent
but innovative way. On Tuesday morn-
ings throughout the late 1960s, the office
and factory scuttlebutt across America
was invariably about what happened the
night before on *Laugh-In*.

On Emmys night, the show ended up
with four awards. Two of them were for
the September special that introduced
the madcap program to America, one
for its tape editor and the other for
being the Outstanding Variety Special
of the year. The two other awards were
for Outstanding Variety Series and
kudos for its crazy gang of writers.
When accepting one of the two top variety prizes, Dan Rowan and Dick Martin
thanked Laurel and Hardy "and all the
others we've stolen things from." But

*Laugh-In jokers Dan Rowan, Alan Sues,
and Dick Martin had a sweepstakes
night, but really won only four awards.*

the victorious duo had been robbed, in a
sense, too, of the one award that would
have given them a clean sweep in the
variety programs category if their director Bill R. Foster had also prevailed.
Jack Haley, Jr., won the director's trophy instead for his NBC special *Movin'
with Nancy* (Sinatra).

Other major awards looked like a
rerun of last year's Emmycast. *Mission:
Impossible* started out with 11 nominations and ended up taking two wins,
including Outstanding Dramatic Series.
All of the top series actors came back
this year as well, an Emmy first (and
last): *Mission: Impossible*'s Barbara
Bain as best actress in a dramatic series;
I Spy's Bill Cosby as top actor; *Get
Smart*'s Don Adams as TV's funnyman;
and even Lucille Ball as best comedienne one more time. ("We all love
Lucy," whined *L.A. Times* columnist
Joyce Haber about the latter, "but
enough is enough!") Acknowledging her
fourth and final Emmy won in competi-

tion, Lucy said, humbly, "Last year was a surprise. This is a shock."

For Bill Cosby this was his third victory in a row. The first black to have a leading role in a regular series now greeted the audience sporting a new moustache and a recently emboldened attitude, saying, "Let the message be known to bigots and racists that they don't count!" It was a fiery farewell for Cosby. *I Spy* had just been canceled, but it did end up taking one more Emmy — for its composer Earle Hagen, who was one of the 29 musicians to resign from the academy last year over the failure of any musician to win an Emmy.

Strangely, last year's champ *The Monkees* wasn't even nominated for best comedy program, which enabled *Get Smart* to get lucky. *Get Smart* ended up with three top honors: Outstanding Comedy Series, the acting award for Adams, and a director's statuette for Bruce Bilson. It lost two others, though, one for actress nominee Barbara Feldon and another for its writers. The writing award went instead to a show that lasted only a year, *He & She*, about a TV cartoonist and his social-worker wife, which starred real-life spouses Richard Benjamin and Paula Prentiss. During one of the Emmy-cast's comic interludes, Pat Paulsen of *The Smothers Brothers Comedy Hour* pretended to quote a CBS executive saying, "*He & She* was the finest show we ever canceled!"

In the categories of supporting comic roles, the award went to Werner Klemperer as Colonel Wilhelm Klink on *Hogan's Heroes*. The week before the

All of last year's best series actors repeated their wins, an Emmy first (and last).

show, Klemperer had told a local journalist, "I'm beginning to feel like Richard Nixon. Every year since I've been on this series, I've been nominated, but I never win." Marion Lorne, the ever-befuddled Aunt Clara on *Bewitched* had been up for a supporting-acting award in the past, too, but now, sadly, it came too late. At the age of 82, Lorne died less than two weeks before her Emmy victory. It was accepted by *Bewitched* star (and losing nominee for best actress in a comedy series) Elizabeth Montgomery, who said, "I think she deserves it, and we owe her a big thank-you for all the happiness she brought us ... and I wish she were here."

Supporting-acting awards for drama series went to Milburn Stone, who was also overdue to win. He'd been playing the scruffy, sage "Doc" on *Gunsmoke* for 14 years. Conversely, Barbara Anderson was in her first TV season when she won the Emmy as Officer Eve Whitfield on *Ironside*. When she accepted it, she was so surprised and overwhelmed that she was literally speechless.

Again the top dramatic program of the year was a *Hallmark Hall of Fame* special. *Elizabeth the Queen*, the story of the British monarch's battle with Lord Essex over affairs of state and the heart, was written by playwright Maxwell Anderson and starred Dame Judith Anderson as Elizabeth and Charlton Heston as Essex, a distinguished trio that failed to win any Emmys for themselves. In the case of the two Andersons (not related), Dame Judith was beaten by Maureen Stapleton, who won for her role in a Xerox-sponsored special *Among the Paths to Eden*, a Truman Capote teleplay about a spinster's quest for love, and the prize for dramatic writing went to Loring Mandel for the *CBS Playhouse* production of *Do Not Go Gentle Into That Good Night*.

Good Night was the night's most

honored special, going in with six nominations and ending up with three awards, one for its electronic camerawork, the one for its writer, and one for leading man Melvyn Douglas. Douglas portrayed a retired carpenter who was placed in a nursing home reluctantly by his family. Accepting the honor, Douglas thanked his mother, God, "the president for keeping the enemies so far from our shore," writer Mandel, and producer-director George Schaefer. *CBS Playhouse* also won a fourth award, for Paul Bogart, director of *Dear Friends*.

Among the remaining awards, there were two other repeats from last year: Art Carney and the *ABC's Wide World of Sports*. *Today* was honored for daytime achievement and Pat Paulsen for his work on *The Smothers Brothers Comedy Hour*. In the end, CBS got 20 Emmys, NBC received 19, and, for the first time in the awards history, national public television took a batch, too — four — which compared respectfully with the six won by ABC.

This was the first year since 1964 that CBS News didn't maintain its private boycott. It was richly rewarded with eight trophies in the news and documentary fields. The move, however, may have been premature. After this year's awards, all three networks' news staffs would threaten to pull out again. None of their most recent awards was bestowed up at the podium where the winners could be acknowledged in front of their industry peers. Instead, telecast producer Greg Garrison, who was also the producer of *The Dean Martin Show*, had them passed out, all at the same time, to bewildered winners as they remained at their dinner tables in New York. *TV Guide* was among those upset that "the Emmycast could kiss these [winners] off but find time for a Don Rickles routine and film clips of variety-show nominees with Dean Martin well represented." "Where," asked irate ABC News chief Elmer Lower, "is the TV academy's sense of values?"

Other controversies were building, too. Independent documentary producer David Wolper claimed there was "a serious inequity in the nominations" procedure and implored the academy to take some action. Costume designers cried out that they were not included at all in the nominations and asked the academy what it planned to do about that in the future. In the meantime, rumors were flying that the International Radio & Television Society was considering launching its own awards. N.A.T.A.S.'s answer to all of the above: It would revamp the Emmys yet again next year.

Producer Garrison had said, cynically, before the show, "It'll be fun to put on what each year is called the dullest show on TV." He hardly knew what he was saying. Instead of being dull, the Emmys were headed toward another one of those "fiasco" years. *TV Guide* reported afterward: "If ever talent was wasted, it was in Hollywood where Frank Sinatra struggled valiantly against impossible odds to keep the show going and, in New York, where Dick Van Dyke alternated between embarrassment and panic as the production goofs piled up." Those "goofs" were described by *L.A. Times*'s Joyce Haber, cynically, as "small snafus like missing teleprompters, invisible idiot cards and at a time a total absence of sound." An exasperated Van Dyke didn't seem able to cope with it all, threw up his hands, and said to the viewing audience, "To think I've been out of TV only two years!"

For programs telecast between March 27, 1967, and March 6, 1968. Awards presented on May 19, 1968, at the Hollywood Palladium and the Americana Hotel in New York. Broadcast on NBC.

PRIME-TIME PROGRAM AWARDS
OUTSTANDING DRAMATIC PROGRAM
• *Elizabeth the Queen, Hallmark Hall of Fame.* George Schaefer, producer. NBC.
Do Not Go Gentle Into That Good Night, CBS Playhouse. George Schaefer, producer. CBS.
Dear Friends, CBS Playhouse. Herbert Brodkin, producer. CBS.
Dr. Jekyll and Mr. Hyde. Dan Curtis, producer. ABC.
Uncle Vanya, NET Playhouse. Sir Laurence Olivier, producer. NET.
Luther, Xerox Special. Michael Style, Trevor Wallace, producers. ABC.

OUTSTANDING DRAMATIC SERIES
• *Mission: Impossible.* Joseph E. Gantman, producer. CBS.
The Avengers. Albert Fennell, Brian Clemens, producers. ABC.
I Spy. Morton Fine, David Friedkin, producers. NBC.
NET Playhouse. Curtis Davis, executive producer. NET.
Run for Your Life. Roy Huggins, executive producer. NBC.
Star Trek. Gene Roddenberry, executive producer. NBC.

OUTSTANDING COMEDY SERIES
• *Get Smart.* Burt Nodella, producer. NBC.
Bewitched. William Asher. ABC.
Family Affair. Edmund Hartmann, producer. CBS.
Hogan's Heroes. Edward Feldman, producer. CBS.
The Lucy Show. Tommy Thompson, producer. CBS.

OUTSTANDING MUSICAL OR VARIETY PROGRAM
• *Rowan and Martin's Laugh-In Special.* George Schlatter, producer. NBC.
Frank Sinatra. Robert Sheerer, producer. NBC.

Dick Van Dyke clowning with Maureen Stapleton, honored for Capote's Eden.

Chrysler Presents the Bob Hope Christmas Special. Bob Hope, executive producer. NBC.
"Five Ballets of the Five Senses," *Lincoln Center/Stage 5.* Jac Venza, producer. NET.
The Fred Astaire Show. Fred Astaire, Gil Rodin, producers. NBC.
Herb Alpert and the Tijuana Brass Special. Gary Smith, Dwight Hemion, producers. CBS.

OUTSTANDING MUSICAL OR VARIETY SERIES
• *Rowan and Martin's Laugh-In.* George Schlatter, producer. NBC.
The Bell Telephone Hour. Henry Jaffe, executive producer; Robert Drew, Michael Jackson, Mel Stuart, producers. NBC.
The Carol Burnett Show. Joseph Hamilton, producer. CBS.
The Dean Martin Show. Greg Garrison, producer. NBC.
The Smothers Brothers Comedy Hour. Saul Ilson, Ernest Chambers, producers. CBS.

PERFORMANCE, DIRECTING, AND WRITING
OUTSTANDING CONTINUED PERFORMANCE BY AN ACTOR IN A LEADING ROLE IN A DRAMATIC SERIES
• Bill Cosby, *I Spy.* NBC.
Raymond Burr, *Ironside.* NBC.
Robert Culp, *I Spy.* NBC.
Ben Gazzara, *Run for Your Life.* NBC.
Martin Landau, *Mission: Impossible.* CBS.

**OUTSTANDING CONTINUED PERFORMANCE
BY AN ACTRESS IN A LEADING ROLE
IN A DRAMATIC SERIES**
• Barbara Bain, *Mission: Impossible*. CBS.
Diana Rigg, *The Avengers*. ABC.
Barbara Stanwyck, *The Big Valley*. ABC.

**OUTSTANDING SINGLE PERFORMANCE
BY AN ACTOR IN A LEADING ROLE
IN A DRAMA**
• Melvyn Douglas, *Do Not Go Gentle Into
That Good Night, CBS Playhouse*. CBS.
Raymond Burr, *Ironside*. NBC.
Van Heflin, *A Case of Libel*. ABC.
George C. Scott, *The Crucible*. CBS.
Eli Wallach, *Dear Friends, CBS
Playhouse*. CBS.

**OUTSTANDING SINGLE PERFORMANCE
BY AN ACTRESS IN A LEADING ROLE
IN A DRAMA**
• Maureen Stapleton, *Among the Paths to
Eden, Xerox Special*. ABC.
Dame Judith Anderson, *Elizabeth the
Queen, Hallmark Hall of Fame*. NBC.
Genevieve Bujold, *Saint Joan,
Hallmark Hall of Fame*. NBC.
Colleen Dewhurst, *The Crucible*. CBS.
Anne Jackson, *Dear Friends, CBS
Playhouse*. CBS.

**OUTSTANDING CONTINUED PERFORMANCE
BY AN ACTOR IN A LEADING ROLE
IN A COMEDY SERIES**
• Don Adams, *Get Smart*. NBC.
Richard Benjamin, *He & She*. CBS.
Sebastian Cabot, *Family Affair*. CBS.
Brian Keith, *Family Affair*. CBS.
Dick York, *Bewitched*. ABC.

**OUTSTANDING CONTINUED PERFORMANCE
BY AN ACTRESS IN A LEADING ROLE
IN A COMEDY SERIES**
• Lucille Ball, *The Lucy Show*. CBS.
Barbara Feldon, *Get Smart*. NBC.
Elizabeth Montgomery, *Bewitched*. ABC.
Paula Prentiss, *He & She*. CBS.
Marlo Thomas, *That Girl*. ABC.

**OUTSTANDING PERFORMANCE
BY AN ACTOR IN A SUPPORTING ROLE
IN A DRAMA**
• Milburn Stone, *Gunsmoke*. CBS.
Joseph Campanella, *Mannix*. CBS.
Lawrence Dobkin, *Do Not Go Gentle Into
That Good Night, CBS Playhouse*. CBS.
Leonard Nimoy, *Star Trek*. NBC.

**OUTSTANDING PERFORMANCE
BY AN ACTRESS IN A SUPPORTING ROLE
IN A DRAMA**
• Barbara Anderson, *Ironside*. NBC.
Linda Cristal, *The High Chaparral*. NBC.
Tessie O'Shea, *Dr. Jekyll and Mr. Hyde*.
ABC.

**OUTSTANDING PERFORMANCE
BY AN ACTOR IN A SUPPORTING ROLE
IN A COMEDY**
• Werner Klemperer, *Hogan's Heroes*.
CBS.
Jack Cassidy, *He & She*. CBS.
William Demarest, *My Three Sons*. CBS.
Gale Gordon, *The Lucy Show*. CBS.

**OUTSTANDING PERFORMANCE
BY AN ACTRESS IN A SUPPORTING ROLE
IN A COMEDY**
• Marion Lorne, *Bewitched*. ABC.
Agnes Moorehead, *Bewitched*. ABC.
Marge Redmond, *The Flying Nun*. ABC.
Nita Talbot, *Hogan's Heroes*. CBS.

**OUTSTANDING DIRECTORIAL
ACHIEVEMENT IN DRAMA**
• Paul Bogart, *Dear Friends, CBS Play-
house*. CBS.
Lee H. Katzin, *Mission: Impossible*. CBS.
George Schaefer, *Do Not Go Gentle Into
That Good Night, CBS Playhouse*. CBS.
Alex Segal, *The Crucible*. CBS.

**OUTSTANDING DIRECTORIAL
ACHIEVEMENT IN COMEDY**
• Bruce Bilson, *Get Smart*. NBC.
Danny Arnold, *That Girl*. ABC.
James Frawley, *The Monkees*. NBC.

**OUTSTANDING DIRECTORIAL
ACHIEVEMENT IN MUSIC OR VARIETY**
• Jack Haley, Jr., *Movin' with Nancy*.
NBC.
Bill R. Foster, *Rowan and Martin's
Laugh-In Special*. NBC.
Greg Garrison, *The Dean Martin Show*.
NBC.
Dwight Hemion, *Herb Alpert and the
Tijuana Brass Special*. CBS.
Gordon W. Wiles, *Rowan and Martin's
Laugh-In*. NBC.

**OUTSTANDING WRITING
ACHIEVEMENT IN DRAMA**
• Loring Mandel, *Do Not Go Gentle Into
That Good Night, CBS Playhouse*. CBS.

Allan Balter, William Read Woodfield, *Mission: Impossible*. CBS.
Don M. Mankiewicz, *Ironside*. NBC.
Reginald Rose, *Dear Friends, CBS Playhouse*. CBS.

OUTSTANDING WRITING ACHIEVEMENT IN COMEDY
• Allan Burns, Chris Hayward, *He & She*. CBS.
Danny Arnold, Ruth Brooks Flippen, *That Girl*. ABC.
Milt Josefsberg, Ray Singer, *The Lucy Show*. CBS.
Leonard Stern, Arne Sultan, *He & She*. CBS.

OUTSTANDING WRITING ACHIEVEMENT IN MUSIC OR VARIETY
• Chris Beard, Phil Hahn, Jack Hanrahan, Coslough Johnson, Marc London, Paul Keyes, Allan Manings, David Panich, Hugh Wedlock, Digby Wolfe, *Rowan and Martin's Laugh-In*. NBC.
Bill Angelos, Stan Burns, Don Hinkley, Buz Kohan, Mike Marmer, Gail Parent, Arnie Rosen, Kenny Solms, Saul Turtletaub, *The Carol Burnett Show*. CBS.
Larry Hovis, Paul W. Keyes, Jim Mulligan, David Panich, George Schlatter, Digby Wolfe, *Rowan and Martin's Laugh-In Special*. NBC.
Ted Bergman, Allan Blye, Sam Bobrick, Ernest Chambers, Ron Clark, Gene Farmer, Hal Goldman, Al Gordon, Saul Ilson, Jerry Music, Mason Williams, *The Smothers Brothers Comedy Hour*. CBS.

OTHER AWARD WINNERS
OUTSTANDING ACHIEVEMENT IN MUSICAL COMPOSITION
• Earle Hagen, *I Spy*. NBC.

OUTSTANDING ACHIEVEMENT IN ART DIRECTION AND SCENIC DESIGN
• James W. Trittipo, art director, *The Fred Astaire Show*. NBC.

OUTSTANDING ACHIEVEMENT IN CINEMATOGRAPHY
• Ralph Woolsey, *It Takes a Thief*. ABC.

OUTSTANDING ACHIEVEMENT IN ELECTRONIC CAMERA WORK
• A.J. Cunningham, technical director, Edward Chaney, Robert Fonorow, Harry Tatarian, Ben Wolfe, cameramen, *Do Not*

Go Gentle Into That Good Night, CBS Playhouse. CBS.

OUTSTANDING ACHIEVEMENT IN FILM EDITING
• Peter Johnson, "The Sounds and Sights of Chicago," *The Bell Telephone Hour*. NBC.

THE AREAS
Each area has the possibility of multiple award winners, one winner, or no winner. Winners are listed.

OUTSTANDING ACHIEVEMENT IN DAYTIME PROGRAMMING
(Programs)
• *Today*. Al Morgan, producer. NBC.

OUTSTANDING ACHIEVEMENT IN SPORTS PROGRAMMING
(Programs)
• *ABC's Wide World of Sports*. Roone Arledge, executive producer. ABC.
(Individuals)
• Jim McKay, sports commentator, *ABC's Wide World of Sports*. ABC.

SPECIAL CLASSIFICATION OF INDIVIDUAL ACHIEVEMENTS
• Art Carney, performer, *The Jackie Gleason Show*. CBS.
• Pat Paulsen, performer, *The Smothers Brothers Comedy Hour*. CBS.

OUTSTANDING INDIVIDUAL ACHIEVEMENT IN ELECTRONIC PRODUCTION
• Arthur Schneider, tape editor, *Rowan and Martin's Laugh-In Special*. NBC.

(There were no winners of achievement in children's programming, music, or visual arts. No individuals were named for daytime achievement.)

NEWS & DOCUMENTARY AWARD WINNERS
OUTSTANDING ACHIEVEMENT IN NEWS DOCUMENTARIES
(Programs)
• *Africa*. James Fleming, executive producer. ABC.
• "Summer '67: What We Learned." *NBC News Special*. Fred Freed, producer. NBC.
(Individuals)
• Harry Reasoner, writer, "What About Ronald Reagan?" *CBS Reports*. CBS.
• Vo Huynh, cameraman, *Same Mud, Same Blood*. NBC.

OTHER NEWS AND DOCUMENTARY
ACHIEVEMENTS
(Programs)
• *The 21st Century*. Isaac Kleinerman,
producer. CBS.
• "Science and Religion: Who Will Play
God?" *CBS News Special*. CBS.
(Individuals)
• Georges Delerue, composer, "Our
World." NET.

OUTSTANDING ACHIEVEMENT WITHIN
REGULARLY SCHEDULED NEWS
PROGRAMS
(Programs)
• "Crisis in the Cities," *Public Broadcast
Laboratory*. Av Westin, executive
producer. NET.
(Individuals)
• John Laurence, CBS News
correspondent, Keith Kay, CBS News
cameraman, *CBS Evening News with
Walter Cronkite*. CBS.

OUTSTANDING ACHIEVEMENT
IN COVERAGE OF SPECIAL EVENTS
(Individuals)
• Frank McGee, commentator, satellite
coverage of Adenauer's funeral. NBC.

OUTSTANDING ACHIEVEMENT
IN CULTURAL DOCUMENTARIES
(Programs)
• "Eric Hoffer: The Passionate State of
Mind," *CBS News Special*. Harry Morgan,
producer. CBS.
• "Gauguin in Tahiti: The Search for
Paradise," *CBS News Special*. Martin Carr,
producer. CBS.
• *John Steinbeck's "America and
Americans."* Lee Mendelson, producer.
NBC.

• "Dylan Thomas: The World I Breathe,"
NET Festival. Perry Miller Adato,
producer. NET.
(Individuals)
• Nathaniel Dorsky, art photography,
"Gauguin in Tahiti: The Search for
Paradise," *CBS News Special*. CBS.
• Harry Morgan, writer, "Who, What,
When, Where, Why with Harry Reasoner,"
CBS News Hour. CBS.
• Thomas A. Priestley, director of
photography, Robert Loweree, film editor,
*John Steinbeck's "American and
Americans."* NBC.

SPECIAL AWARDS
INTERNATIONAL AWARDS
(Documentary)
• *La Section Anderson*, Office de
Radiodiffusion Télévision Francaise,
O.R.T.F., Paris, France.
(Entertainment)
• "Call Me Daddy," *Armchair Theatre*,
ABC Television Limited, Middlesex,
England.

OUTSTANDING ACHIEVEMENT
IN ENGINEERING DEVELOPMENT
• British Broadcasting Corporation. For the
Electronic Field-Store Colour Television
Standards Converter.

THE STATION AWARD
• *Now is the Time*, WCAU-TV,
Philadelphia.

SPECIAL CITATIONS
• *The Other Side of the Shadow*, WWL-
TV, New Orleans.
• *The Other Washington*, WRC-TV,
Washington, D.C.

TRUSTEES AWARD
• Donald H. McGannon

A Big Night
for Network Losers

As Emmy turned 21, she put on the show of a lifetime. *The Hollywood Reporter* described the broadcast as "a technically faultless, entertainment-loaded program" that aimed to make up for last year's disastrous ceremony. *The Los Angeles Times* even called this year's event, "the smoothest, most professional telecast ever offered by Emmy."

But Emmy at 21 also had her share of new adult problems. In November, 1968, the academy announced two new rules, the first of which had been contemplated for some time as a solution to the year-to-year repetition of winners. The repeats had happened in a dramatic way the previous year when all of the major awards for series actors went to the champs of the year before. Now new programs and their stars, said the academy, would be eligible for prizes only in their first two seasons. Secondly, once a show wins an award, it could no longer be considered for another. Hollywood howled. Producers like *Mission: Impossible*'s Bruce Geller, *The Virginian*'s Joel Rogosin, and *Gomer Pyle*'s Aaron Ruben called the changes, respectively, "ludicrous," "idiotic," and "ridiculous." The academy withdrew the new guidelines immediately.

There were other new rules that did stick. Comic and dramatic performers were bunched together in the categories for supporting-acting honors. Another "big change we made this year is that we have the possibility of no awards, like Pulitzers," academy president Seymour

Presenters Irene Ryan (left) and Sebastian Cabot (right) with winners Don Adams of Get Smart *and Hope Lange of* The Ghost and Mrs. Muir.

Berns told *Broadcasting*. "I pray that it doesn't happen. We might get a hell of an explosion." Categories that always had one winner in the past no longer had that guarantee, like area awards.

Berns's predicted explosion followed inevitably when it was learned, before the Emmycast began, that no winner was chosen for directing a comedy or variety program. The three nominated directors all resigned from the academy as a result, and the American Federation of Television and Radio Artists lodged a formal complaint asking N.A.T.A.S. to reconsider the rule next year, which it agreed to do. "There is no point in kidding ourselves," Berns added. "What is happening now is reaction to a less-than-brilliant show [last year], and people are overreacting."

This year's "smooth," "faultless" show emanated from the Santa Monica Auditorium, where Bill Cosby hosted, and from Carnegie Hall in New York, where Merv

Griffin emceed. Early on in the evening, Griffin ribbed the networks, saying, "CBS has four new series starting this season. They would have had more, but NBC had no more they wanted to sell."

What he was referring to were some erratic program maneuvers made recently by NBC, which had canceled the popular *Get Smart* (picked up consequently by CBS) and the new *Ghost and Mrs. Muir* (picked up by ABC). Both shows would be big Emmy champs this year. So would other programs dropped by their networks, leading some industry insiders to think that, contrary to an old maxim, you could win for losing. "It was like in order to win you had to be canceled!" cried columnist Joyce Haber.

Among those bidding TV audiences farewell was Carl Betz, who won the statuette for Outstanding Lead Actor in a Dramatic Series. Betz was lauded for playing the cool criminal lawyer on *Judd for the Defense*, recently axed by ABC. Also dropped by its network was the winner of the trophy for best writing on a comedy, variety, or music show: *The Smothers Brothers Comedy Hour*. Tom and Dick Smothers had been feuding with CBS for four months over censorship. Finally, the network just despaired of — and dropped — the offbeat and irreverent hit show and replaced it with *Hee Haw*.

Also departing this year was *Mission: Impossible*'s Barbara Bain, who was named best actress for the third year in a row. On the same day as the Emmy ceremonies, Bain resigned from the series and issued a statement saying that the show's producers had broken her heart. "She will not be back on the series," reported *The New York Times*, "because her husband, Martin Landau, could not reach a contract with the producers." In her acceptance speech, she said, "This is a bittersweet moment. There are a lot of people who I'd like to

thank. There are a couple of people I'd like not to thank. Since they each know their names, I won't mention them."

Mission: Impossible began with eight nominations, but ended up with only two wins, the second shared by the show's art and set directors. The series was favored to take top drama series, too, but was upset by what *L.A. Times* called the "very uneven" *NET Playhouse*. One of the new drama winner's problems was that it was not exclusively a dramatic program, since it also included segments such as jazz and classical music features.

Get Smart's repeat triumph as Outstanding Comedy Series was another surprise of the night. The favorite to win was *Julia*, the popular new show featuring Diahann Carroll as a nurse and single

"It was like in order to win you had to be canceled!"

mother who had been widowed when her husband was killed in the Vietnam war. But *Get Smart* beat the odds and also won a third trophy for its star Don Adams.

As she picked up the award for Outstanding Comic Actress, Hope Lange thanked ABC for saving her new series, *The Ghost and Mrs. Muir*, which was based loosely on the 1947 movie of the same name starring Rex Harrison and Gene Tierney. The program was up for several top Emmys, including ones for best comedy and for its lead stars, Lange, who played the cheery widow Mrs. Muir, and Edward Mulhare, who portrayed the grumpy ghost who haunted her new home. In the categories of supporting series actors, the prizes went to last year's winner Werner Klemperer for his role as Colonel Klink on *Hogan's Heroes* and to Susan Saint James, who was cast as a reporter on *The Name of the Game*. Saint James was so delirious all night over her win that the *L.A. Times* said she "also got the award for evening's best basket case."

What was no surprise was that last year's Outstanding Variety Series returned for the prize again. *Laugh-In*, said the *L.A. Times*, was "still the most dazzling show of its kind" and entered the night with the most nominations: 11. The show's Arte Johnson also took an area award for variety performances (as did *The Carol Burnett Show*'s Harvey Korman, who later confessed to Johnson backstage, "I wish I were as funny as you!"). The statuette for Outstanding Variety or Musical Program went to *The Bill Cosby Special* on NBC, which dealt with issues of children growing up and was filmed in Cosby's boyhood neighborhood in South Philadelphia.

The Outstanding Dramatic Program of the Year turned out to be *Teacher, Teacher*, a *Hallmark Hall of Fame* production about a mentally retarded boy trying to cope with his handicap and school education. The boy was played by Billy Schulman, who was retarded in real life and who became the focus of a minor controversy when he (and the other two nominees) failed to win the prize for best supporting actor in a single performance. Producer George Lefferts was particularly upset and bitter about the loss and, while accepting the award for best drama, he apologized to Schulman for not "being allowed to compete and to win or lose with dignity." What Lefferts didn't seem to know was that the academy had planned a special presentation to the boy when it was learned that there'd be no winner in the category. Soon after Lefferts sat down, Billy Schulman was asked to rise from his seat to acknowledge a special citation awarded to him "almost immediately after Mr. Lefferts made his angry acceptance speech," noted *Broadcasting*.

Other winners in the drama categories

Hogan's Heroes's Werner Klemperer won best supporting actor twice in a row playing the bumbling Nazi Col. Klink.

included *CBS Playhouse*'s production of *The People Next Door*, about drug addiction in suburbia, that took three Emmys: for writing, directing, and its electronic camerawork. The acting laurels went to Geraldine Page for Truman Capote's *The Thanksgiving Visitor*. It was the second time Page had won the award — and for the same role. Her last victory was two years ago when she portrayed the same spinster, Miss Sookie, in Capote's *A Christmas Memory*. Paul Scofield was named the finest actor in a single leading role for playing a philandering lawyer in *The Male of the Species*. Anna Calder-Marshall won the supporting-acting award for her portrayal of the young woman he seduces.

The new best daytime program was *The Dick Cavett Show*, which had been canceled by ABC after only one season. Cavett, however, had this advantage over other Emmy winners/network losers: ABC dropped his daytime show in favor of trying Cavett out in a new nighttime slot. In other Emmy contests, two sports trophies went to ABC's summer Olympics coverage and were awarded by the former "bad boy of the New York Jets" Joe Namath, who also handled one of the funniest segments of the show. At one point Namath introduced a film montage showing football players slamming into each other while "The Nutcracker Suite" played in the background. Said *Variety*: "The choice of music ... was not to be ignored by the cognoscenti."

For the first time in the history of the Emmys, the news and documentary awards were announced two weeks prior to the telecast. This break with tradition helped to rectify a problem encountered last year when the awards were simply passed out to the winners as they remained at their dinner tables. It also helped to resolve another, gradually overwhelming issue, too. This year there were 253 Emmy nominations, 156 of which were for what academy president Seymour Berns called "the most important area of television" — news and documentary programs. "We can now select large segments of the winning programs to show the public on the Emmy telecast," Berns explained, "which would be impossible if we did not know in advance who the winners are."

Participating in the presentation of these awards was Coretta Scott King, widow of the slain civil rights leader Martin Luther King, Jr. Mrs. King presented awards to Wallace Westfeldt, executive producer of a special on hunger in America aired on *The Huntley-Brinkley Report*; John Laurence, correspondent for the "Police After Chicago" segment on the *CBS Evening News*; and Charles Kuralt, Robert Funk, and James Wilson for Kuralt's "On the Road" series, also on the *CBS Evening News*. She then presented a statuette to CBS for "its intensive and sobering coverage" of her husband's assassination.

Mrs. King commented: "No matter how you measure it, 1968 was a most extraordinary year." It included, she noted, the presidential election, "the shock and tragedy of two assassinations, the violence of riots and demonstrations, the first rays of hope for peace, and the first orbit of the moon.

"What made it still more extraordinary for the American people was the fact they virtually participated in every event by virtue of television news."

A Trustees Award was given to some of those same people behind one of those extraordinary events: the Apollo space missions. Said *The New York Daily News*: "It was the astronauts Tom Stafford, John Young, and Gene Cernan in New York who stole the show."

Together Mrs. King and the astronauts, said the *News*, "brought the excitement of real life" to the Emmys.

1968–69

For programs telecast March 7, 1968, to March 16, 1969. Awards presented on June 8, 1969, at the Santa Monica Civic Auditorium and Carnegie Hall in New York. Broadcast on CBS.

PRIME-TIME PROGRAM AWARDS
OUTSTANDING DRAMATIC PROGRAM
• *Teacher, Teacher, Hallmark Hall of Fame.* George Lefferts, producer. NBC.
"The Execution," *Mission: Impossible.*
William Read Woodfield, Allan Balter, producers. CBS.
Heidi. Frederick Brogger, James Franciscus, producers. NBC.
A Midsummer Night's Dream. Lord Michael Birkett, producer. CBS.
The People Next Door, CBS Playhouse. Herbert Brodkin, producer. CBS.
Talking to a Stranger, NET Playhouse. Michael Blakewell, producer. NET.

Outstanding Dramatic Series
• *NET Playhouse.* Curtis Davis, executive producer. NET.
The F.B.I. Charles Larson, producer. ABC.
Ironside. Cy Chermak, executive producer. NBC.
Judd for the Defense. Harold Gast, producer. ABC.
Mission: Impossible. Bruce Geller, executive producer. CBS.
The Name of the Game. Richard Irving, Leslie Stevens, David Victor, producers. NBC.

Outstanding Comedy Series
• *Get Smart.* Burt Nodella, producer. NBC.
Bewitched. William Asher, producer. ABC.
Family Affair. Edmund Hartmann, producer. CBS.
The Ghost and Mrs. Muir. Stanley Rubin, producer. NBC.
Julia. Hal Kanter, executive producer. NBC.

Outstanding Musical or Variety Program
• *The Bill Cosby Special.* Roy Silver, executive producer. Bill Cosby, star. NBC.
Barbra Streisand: A Happening in Central Park. Robert Scheerer, producer. Barbra Streisand, star. CBS.
"Duke Ellington Concert of Sacred Music," *NET Playhouse.* Richard Moore, Ralph J. Gleason, producers. Duke Ellington, star. NET.
Francis Albert Sinatra Does His Thing. Saul Ilson, Ernest Chambers, producers. Frank Sinatra, star. CBS.
"The Rite of Spring," *NET Festival.* Robert Foshko, producer. Zubin Mehta, conductor. NET.
Rowan and Martin's Laugh-In. Paul W. Keyes, Carolyn Raskin, producers. Dan Rowan, Dick Martin, Marcel Marceau, stars. NBC.
Vladimir Horowitz: A Television Concert at Carnegie Hall. Roger Englander, producer. Vladimir Horowitz, pianist. CBS.

Outstanding Musical or Variety Series
• *Rowan and Martin's Laugh-In.* Paul W. Keyes, Carolyn Raskin, producers. Dan Rowan, Dick Martin, stars. NBC.
The Carol Burnett Show. Joseph Hamilton, producer. Carol Burnett, star. CBS.

The Dean Martin Show. Greg Garrison, producer. Dean Martin, star. NBC.
The Smothers Brothers Comedy Hour. Allan Blye, George A. Sunga, producers. Tom Smothers, Dick Smothers, stars. CBS.
That's Life. Marvin Marx, Stan Harris, producers. Robert Morse, star. ABC.

PERFORMANCE, DIRECTING, AND WRITING
Outstanding Single Performance by an Actor in a Leading Role
• Paul Scofield, *Male of the Species, Prudential's On Stage.* NBC.
Ossie Davis, *Teacher, Teacher, Hallmark Hall of Fame.* NBC.
David McCallum, *Teacher, Teacher, Hallmark Hall of Fame.* NBC.
Bill Travers, *The Admirable Crichton, Hallmark Hall of Fame.* NBC.

Outstanding Single Performance by an Actress in a Leading Role
• Geraldine Page, *The Thanksgiving Visitor.* ABC.
Anne Baxter, *The Name of the Game.* NBC.
Lee Grant, *Judd for the Defense.* ABC.

Outstanding Continued Performance by an Actor in a Leading Role in a Dramatic Series
• Carl Betz, *Judd for the Defense.* ABC.
Raymond Burr, *Ironside.* NBC.
Peter Graves, *Mission: Impossible.* CBS.
Martin Landau, *Mission: Impossible.* CBS.
Ross Martin, *The Wild, Wild West.* CBS.

Outstanding Continued Performance by an Actress in a Leading Role in a Dramatic Series
• Barbara Bain, *Mission: Impossible.* CBS.
Joan Blondell, *Here Come the Brides.* ABC.
Peggy Lipton, *The Mod Squad.* ABC.

Outstanding Continued Performance by an Actor in a Leading Role in a Comedy Series
• Don Adams, *Get Smart.* NBC.
Brian Keith, *Family Affair.* CBS.
Edward Mulhare, *The Ghost and Mrs. Muir.* NBC.
Lloyd Nolan, *Julia.* NBC.

OUTSTANDING CONTINUED PERFORMANCE BY AN ACTRESS IN A LEADING ROLE IN A COMEDY SERIES
• Hope Lange, *The Ghost and Mrs. Muir.* NBC.
Diahann Carroll, *Julia.* NBC.
Barbara Feldon, *Get Smart.* NBC.
Elizabeth Montgomery, *Bewitched.* ABC.

OUTSTANDING SINGLE PERFORMANCE BY AN ACTOR IN A SUPPORTING ROLE
(No winner)
Ned Glass, *Julia.* NBC.
Hal Holbrook, *The Whole World is Watching.* NBC.
Billy Schulman, *Teacher, Teacher,* *Hallmark Hall of Fame.* NBC.

OUTSTANDING SINGLE PERFORMANCE BY AN ACTRESS IN A SUPPORTING ROLE
• Anna Calder-Marshall, *Male of the Species, Prudential's On Stage.* NBC.
Pamela Brown, *The Admirable Crichton,* *Hallmark Hall of Fame.* NBC.
Irene Hervey, *My Three Sons.* CBS.
Nancy Kovack, *Mannix.* CBS.

OUTSTANDING CONTINUED PERFORMANCE BY AN ACTOR IN A SUPPORTING ROLE IN A SERIES
• Werner Klemperer, *Hogan's Heroes.* CBS.
Greg Morris, *Mission: Impossible.* CBS.
Leonard Nimoy, *Star Trek.* NBC.

OUTSTANDING CONTINUED PERFORMANCE BY AN ACTRESS IN A SUPPORTING ROLE IN A SERIES
• Susan Saint James, *The Name of the Game.* NBC.
Barbara Anderson, *Ironside.* NBC.
Agnes Moorehead, *Bewitched.* ABC.

OUTSTANDING DIRECTORIAL ACHIEVEMENT IN DRAMA
• David Green, *The People Next Door,* *CBS Playhouse.* CBS.
Paul Bogart, *Secrets, CBS Playhouse.* CBS.
Fielder Cook, *Teacher, Teacher,* *Hallmark Hall of Fame.* NBC.

OUTSTANDING DIRECTORIAL ACHIEVEMENT IN COMEDY, VARIETY, OR MUSIC
(No winner)
Greg Garrison, *The Dean Martin Show.* NBC.

Bill Hobin, *The Bill Cosby Special.* NBC.
Gordon W. Wiles, *Rowan and Martin's Laugh-In.* NBC.

OUTSTANDING WRITING ACHIEVEMENT IN DRAMA
• J.P. Miller, *The People Next Door, CBS Playhouse.* CBS.
Allan E. Sloane, *Teacher, Teacher,* *Hallmark Hall of Fame.* NBC.
Ellen M. Violett, *The Experiment, CBS Playhouse.* CBS.

As a presenter, Coretta King brought the "excitement of real life" to the Emmys.

OUTSTANDING WRITING ACHIEVEMENT IN COMEDY, VARIETY, OR MUSIC
• Alan Blye, Bob Einstein, Murray Roman, Carl Gottlieb, Jerry Music, Steve Martin, Cecil Tuck, Paul Wayne, Cy Howard, Mason Williams, *The Smothers Brothers Comedy Hour.* CBS.
Paul W. Keyes, Hugh Wedlock, Jr., Allan S. Manings, Chris Beard, David Panich, Coslough H. Johnson, Marc London, David M. Cox, Jim Carlson, Jack Mendelsohn, James Mulligan, Lorne D. Michaels, Hart Pomerantz, Phil Hahn, Jack Hanrahan, *Rowan and Martin's Laugh-In.* NBC.
Arnie Rosen, Stan Burns, Mike Marmer, Hal Goldman, Al Gordon, Don Hinkley, Kenny Solms, Gail Parent, Bill Angelos, Alan Kohan, *The Carol Burnett Show.* CBS.

OTHER AWARD WINNERS

**OUTSTANDING ACHIEVEMENT
IN MUSICAL COMPOSITION**
• John T. Williams, *Heidi.* NBC.

**OUTSTANDING ACHIEVEMENT
IN ART DIRECTION AND SCENIC DESIGN**
• William P. Ross, art director, Lou Hafley, set decorator, *Mission: Impossible.* CBS.

**OUTSTANDING ACHIEVEMENT
IN CINEMATOGRAPHY**
• George Folsey, *Here's Peggy Fleming.* NBC.

**OUTSTANDING ACHIEVEMENT
IN ELECTRONIC CAMERAWORK**
• A.J. Cunningham, technical director, Nick DeMos, Bob Fonarow, Fred Gough, Jack Jennings, Dick Nelson, Rick Tanzi, Ben Wolf, cameramen, *The People Next Door, CBS Playhouse.* CBS.

**OUTSTANDING ACHIEVEMENT
IN FILM EDITING**
• Bill Mosher, *Judd for the Defense.* ABC.

THE AREAS
*Each area has the possibility
of multiple award winners, one winner,
or no winner. Winners are listed.*

**OUTSTANDING ACHIEVEMENT
IN DAYTIME PROGRAMMING
(Programs)**
• *The Dick Cavett Show.* Don Silverman, producer. ABC.

**OUTSTANDING ACHIEVEMENT
IN SPORTS PROGRAMMING
(Programs)**
• *19th Summer Olympic Games.* Roone P. Arledge, executive producer. ABC.
(Individuals)
• Bill Bennington, Mike Freedman, Mac Memion, Robert Riger, Marv Schlenker, Andy Sidaris, Lou Volpicelli, Doug Wilson, directors, *19th Summer Olympic Games.* ABC.

**SPECIAL CLASSIFICATION ACHIEVEMENTS
(Programs)**
• *Firing Line.* Warren Steibel, producer. Syndicated.
• *Wild Kingdom.* Don Meier, producer. NBC.

(Individuals – Variety performances)
• Arte Johnson, *Rowan and Martin's Laugh-In.* NBC.
• Harvey Korman, *The Carol Burnett Show.* CBS.

**OUTSTANDING INDIVIDUAL
ACHIEVEMENT IN MUSIC**
• Mort Lindsey, musical director, *Barbra Streisand: A Happening in Central Park.* CBS.

(No winners in the areas of children's programming, visual arts, special photographic effects, electronic production, or individual achievement in daytime programming.)

NEWS & DOCUMENTARY AWARD WINNERS

**OUTSTANDING NEWS DOCUMENTARY
PROGRAM ACHIEVEMENT
(Programs)**
• "CBS Reports: Hunger in America," *CBS News Hour.* Martin Carr, producer. CBS.
• "Law and Order," *Public Broadcast Laboratory.* Frederick Wiseman, producer. NET.
(Individuals)
• Perry Wolff and Andy Rooney, writers, "Black History: Lost, Stolen or Strayed—Of Black America," *CBS News Hour.* CBS.

**OUTSTANDING CULTURAL DOCUMENTARY
AND "MAGAZINE-TYPE" PROGRAMS
OR SERIES ACHIEVEMENT
(Programs)**
• "Don't Count the Candles," *CBS News Hour.* William McClure, producer. CBS.
• "Justice Black and the Bill of Rights," *CBS News Special.* Burton Benjamin, producer. CBS.
• "Man Who Dances: Edward Villella," *The Bell Telephone Hour.* Robert Drew, Mike Jackson, producers. NBC.
• "The Great American Novel," *CBS News Hour.* Arthur Barron, producer. CBS.
(Individuals)
• Walter Dombrow, Jerry Sims, cinematographers, "The Great American Novel," *CBS News Hour.* CBS.
• Tom Pettit, producer, "CBW: The Secrets of Secrecy," *First Tuesday.* NBC.
• Lord Snowdon, cinematographer, "Don't Count the Candles," *CBS News Hour.* CBS.

Talk show host and future Emmy winner Merv Griffin acted as ceremony cohost.

OUTSTANDING ACHIEVEMENT WITHIN REGULARLY SCHEDULED NEWS PROGRAMS
(Programs)
• "Coverage of Hunger in the United States," *The Huntley-Brinkley Report.* Wallace Westfeldt, executive producer. NBC.
(Individuals)
• Charles Kuralt, correspondent, James Wilson, cameraman, Robert Funk, soundman, "On the Road," *CBS Evening News with Walter Cronkite.* CBS.
• John Laurence, correspondent, "Police After Chicago," *CBS Evening News with Walter Cronkite.* CBS.

OUTSTANDING ACHIEVEMENT IN COVERAGE OF SPECIAL EVENTS
(Programs)
• "Coverage of Martin Luther King Assassination and Aftermath," *CBS News Special Reports and Special Broadcasts.* Robert Wussler, Ernest Leiser, Burton Benjamin, Don Hewitt, executive producers. CBS.

(No awards bestowed in the area of individual achievement in coverage of special events.)

INTERNATIONAL AWARD WINNERS
DOCUMENTARY
• *The Last Campaign of Robert Kennedy.* Swiss Broadcasting and Television, Zurich, Switzerland.

ENTERTAINMENT
• "A Scent of Flowers," *CBC-TV Festival.* Canadian Broadcasting Corporation.

SPECIAL AWARDS
SPECIAL CITATION
• *Assignment: The Young Greats.* WFIL-TV, Philadelphia.

CITATIONS
• Billy Schulman. For extraordinary achievement in *Teacher, Teacher,* presented by *Hallmark Hall of Fame.*
• CBS. For the development of the Digital Control Technique used in the Minicam miniaturized television color camera.

OUTSTANDING ACHIEVEMENT IN ENGINEERING DEVELOPMENT
• Eastman Kodak Co. For the ME-4 color film developing process.

STATION AWARD
• *Pretty Soon Runs Out.* WHA-TV, Madison, Wisconsin.

TRUSTEES AWARDS
• William D. McAndrew, 1914–1968, reporter, editor, and NBC News president.
• Apollo VII, VIII, IX, and X Space Missions. Astronauts: William A. Anders, Frank Borman, Walter Schirra, Donn Eisele, Walter Cunningham, James A. Lovell, Jr., James A. McDivitt, Russell L. Schweickart, David R. Scott, Thomas B. Stafford, Eugene A. Cernan, John W. Young.

Color TV Focuses
on Black and White

As the 1960s ended, and more Americans than ever were watching color television, they were also facing a bold new image of their nation in black and white. A decade of racial unrest had resulted in breakthroughs in social integration, and nowhere could the bigger picture be seen better than on America's small screens.

Emmy's Outstanding New Series of the year, for example, centered on an integrated California high school. *Room 222* was the surprise winner of the brand-new new series award (beating odds-on favorite *Sesame Street*) and centered on a hip black history teacher (Lloyd Haynes) and the rainbow of students he helped to educate. The show also won two best supporting acting awards, one for Michael Constantine as the school's wise and easygoing principal and another for Karen Valentine, who played a bubbly and naive student teacher. Valentine's reaction to her win was even more effervescent than her character and was matched by the response of the winner of the best supporting actress award in the dramatic series category, whose win also enhanced the night's theme of apparent racial harmony in TV land: Gail Fisher, the black secretary on *Mannix. The New York Daily News* referred to the two elated — and shocked — winners as "gushing" and "almost hysterical."

The Outstanding Dramatic Program of the year also continued the integration theme and earned Peter Ustinov his third trophy as one of Emmy's favorite actors. *A Storm in Summer,* written by Rod Serling, was about a curmudgeonly white storekeeper who battles, befriends, and gives shelter to a black ghetto youth.

ABC

Clockwise from upper left: Room 222 *stars Denise Nicholas, Karen Valentine, Lloyd Haynes, and Michael Constantine.*

A highly rated world-premiere drama, *My Sweet Charlie* ("the first time that a TV movie had received such recognition," said the *Daily News* about its viewership), received eight nominations, the most of any single show. It ended up with three prizes — for writing, film editing, and for Patty Duke's performance as a pregnant runaway from the South who hides out with a black New York City lawyer wanted for murder.

Duke "accepted her Emmy with a vacant and glassy-eyed stare" and uttered "a very few, very incoherent words," *Broadcasting* reported. *The Los Angeles Times* was less diplomatic: "Patty Duke's acceptance speech is still in the code room being deciphered."

After she'd picked up her statuette, Duke threw a fit backstage over costar Al

Freeman, Jr., not winning an award, too. In her memoirs, *Call Me Anna,* she remembers, "I was up on a platform answering questions angrily and accusingly, telling the world I was rejecting the award. I said I was getting out of show business. I was going to be a doctor. It was as if some other creature took over inside me and was picking answers out of the air, the more outrageous the better."

To explain her bizarre conduct Duke now says that she was suffering from severe manic depression, a condition for which she'd be treated successfully later in life. But of 1970, she writes, "accepting the Emmy I won turned into a nationally televised nightmare."

Meantime, back out on stage and at Carnegie Hall in New York, too, were the black-and-white hosts of the dual-coast broadcast: Bill Cosby and Dick Cavett. "Cosby was as good as usual," said the *L.A. Times,* "but the East Coast's Cavett was better and faster with the ad libs." Cavett's best line of the night was, "This is the show that each year asks the vital question: Is radio really improved by the addition of pictures?"

Both men were also Emmy nominees. Cosby had the most at stake since his second TV special and his new series had a total of five nominations. Cavett's talk show was up against *The David Frost Show* and *Laugh-In* in the only category, said Cavett, that didn't include "a widow, a dog, or Walter Cronkite." *The David Frost Show* won. Both Cavett and Cosby went home empty handed.

Another big loser was the number one show in America, which began the race with seven nominations. "*Laugh-In,* which had won so lavishly in its first two years," complained the *L.A. Herald Examiner,* "didn't get a single hunk of hardware for the showcase!" Also missing was last year's comedy series winner *Get Smart,* which would get taken off the air by the end of the year.

Instead, the Emmy contest turned out to be a dramatic sweep for new shows, not old pros. *Marcus Welby, M.D.* was only in its first season, but it started out on awards night with more nominations than *Laugh-In.* Out of a possible eight, *Welby* ended up with three wins, including Outstanding Dramatic Series, a supporting actor's triumph for James Brolin, and more laurels for its star. Robert Young had won two Emmys for his lead role on *Father Knows Best* during the 1950s. Later, at age 62, he took on the role of a kindly doctor in a popular 1969 TV movie that led to his second series and third Emmy. His win distinguished Young as the first person to win a best-acting prize in both comedy and drama series.

Two other new shows also won big. The Outstanding Comedy Series of the year turned out to be a program NBC had just canceled — *My World and Welcome To It* — which was based loosely upon the writings, cartoons, and everyday life of humorist James Thurber. William Windom played the Thurberesque character, who actually lived in *two* worlds, one real and humdrum, the other surreal and fantastic (and animated in Thurber's crude cartoon style). Windom was named best comic actor, too. In his acceptance speech, the now out-of-work winner informed the Hollywood audience, "I am sober, have tux, and will travel."

Also out of work — and for a second time in as many years — was Hope Lange, whose pink slips seemed to be followed regularly by her golden Emmy statuettes. Last year she was voted best comic actress right after her series *The*

> *Patty Duke's best actress victory became a "nationally televised nightmare."*

Best actor Peter Ustinov played a crusty white shopkeeper who helps a black ghetto boy in the year's best drama program A Storm in Summer.

Ghost and Mrs. Muir was axed by NBC. ABC picked up the series, then dropped it, too, just before Lange won again.

In the category of variety shows, the one that clearly stood out in the past year was *Annie, the Women in the Life of a Man*, featuring Anne Bancroft in a series of dramatic and comic vignettes. Said the *L.A. Herald Examiner* of the double-winner (best variety program, best variety writing): "Nobody dared to dispute the distinction that fell to the first-rate CBS special." Also undisputed were the three awards won by the show expected to win best new series. *Sesame Street* at least ended up being named outstanding children's program, in addition to being honored for its music and writers.

Trustees Awards went to the 3M Company for its special programs and to the presidents of the three network news divisions for "safeguarding the public right to full information." The latter was widely seen as a jab at U.S. Vice-President Spiro Agnew, who had been publicly accusing the network news chiefs of biased reporting.

A Trustees Award was also given to NASA for its television coverage of the Apollo 11 moon landing, even though it was widely reported that its color camera had failed to work once the "Eagle" landed on the lunar surface. Dick Cavett drew guffaws from the audience when he claimed the award was for NASA's black-and-white camera work.

Apollo coverage swept the news and documentary awards, too. Walter Cronkite won as an individual reporter for his CBS commentary on the moon mission; NBC won for its overall coverage. Both networks also took awards for special reports on their evening news programs: CBS for its evening news segment on the ecology "Can the World Be Saved?" and NBC for its four-day examination of teenage drug addiction. And three specials won two awards each: a profile of pianist Artur Rubinstein, a CBS look at "The Japanese," and "Hospital" on *NET Journal*. Just like last year, all the news and documentary winners were announced weeks before the Emmycast to allow time, said the *L.A. Times*, "to prepare a presentation to show the TV audience what the shouting is all about and to give this 'proudest face we show the world' its proper dignity."

As of 1970, the nighttime broadcast could no longer accommodate the expanding number of awards that were being given away to honor accomplishments in the industry. For the first time ever, and beginning what would become a tradition in the future, technicians and other crafts people were acknowledged at separate creative arts (or crafts) awards banquets, which were held at the Hollywood Palladium (where Danny Thomas was host) and at the Americana Hotel in New York (where David Frost presided). The prime-time TV cameras were not on hand for the functions, but television's top celebrities were. Mary

Tyler Moore, Bill Cosby, Shirley Jones, Patty Duke, and Frank Gorshin were among the stars who privately honored television's top costume designers, composers, choreographers, camera-men, and film editors. Said the *L.A. Times*: "It was the first time in the 22-year history of the Emmys that the backstage crews had a chance to steal the applause rather than share in it."

1969–70

For programs telecast between March 17, 1969, and March 15, 1970. Awards presented on June 7, 1970, from the Century Plaza Hotel in Hollywood and Carnegie Hall in New York. Broadcast on ABC.

PRIME-TIME PROGRAM AWARDS

OUTSTANDING NEW SERIES
• *Room 222.* Gene Reynolds, producer. ABC.
The Bill Cosby Show. William H. Cosby, Jr., executive producer.
Marvin Miller, producer. NBC.
The Forsyte Saga. Donald Wilson, producer. N.E.T.
Marcus Welby, M.D. David Victor, executive producer. David J. O'Connell, producer. ABC.
Sesame Street. David D. Connell, executive producer. Sam Gibbon, Jon Stone, Lutrelle Horne, producers. N.E.T.

OUTSTANDING DRAMATIC PROGRAM
• *A Storm in Summer, Hallmark Hall of Fame.* M.J. Rifkin, executive producer, Alan Landsburg, producer. NBC.
David Copperfield. Frederick Brogger, producer. NBC.
"Hello, Goodbye, Hello," *Marcus Welby, M.D.* David Victor, executive producer. David J. O'Connell, producer. ABC.
My Sweet Charlie. Bob Banner, executive producer. Richard Levinson, William Link, producers. NBC.

OUTSTANDING DRAMATIC SERIES
• *Marcus Welby, M.D.* David Victor, executive producer. David J. O'Connell, producer. ABC.
The Forsyte Saga. Donald Wilson, producer. N.E.T.
Ironside. Cy Chermak, executive producer. Douglas Benton, Winston Miller, Joel Rogosin, Albert Aley, producers. NBC.
The Mod Squad. Danny Thomas, Aaron Spelling, executive producers. Tony Barrett, Harve Bennet, producers. ABC.
The Name of the Game. Richard Irving, executive producer. George Eckstein, Dean Hargrove, Norman Lloyd, Boris Sagal, producers. NBC.
NET Playhouse. Jac Venza, executive producer. NET.

OUTSTANDING COMEDY SERIES
• *My World and Welcome To It.* Sheldon Leonard, executive producer. Danny Arnold, producer. NBC.
The Bill Cosby Show. William H. Cosby, Jr., executive producer. Marvin Miller, producer. NBC.
The Courtship of Eddie's Father. James Komack, producer. ABC.
Love, American Style. Arnold Margolin, Jim Parker, executive producers. Bill D'Angelo, producer. ABC.
Room 222. Gene Reynolds, producer. ABC.

OUTSTANDING VARIETY OR MUSICAL PROGRAM
(Variety and popular music)
• *Annie, the Women in the Life of a Man.* Joseph Cates, executive producer. Martin Charnin, producer. Anne Bancroft, star. CBS
"The Friars Club 'Roasts' Jack Benny," *The Kraft Music Hall.* Gary Smith, Dwight Hemion, producers. Jack Benny, star. NBC.
The Second Bill Cosby Special. Roy Silver, executive producer. Bruce Campbell, Roy Silver, producers. Bill Cosby, star. NBC.
Sinatra. Frank Sinatra, executive producer. Carolyn Raskin, producer. Frank Sinatra, star. CBS.
"The Sound of Burt Bacharach," *The Kraft Music Hall*. Gary Smith, Dwight Hemion, producers. Burt Bacharach, star. NBC.
(Classical music)
• *Cinderella.* National Ballet of Canada. John Barnes, Curtis Davis, executive producers. Norman Campbell, producer. N.E.T.
S. Hurok Presents – Part III. Jim Krayer,

executive producer. Roger Englander, producer. CBS.
Sounds of Summer (The Blossom Music Center with Pierre Boulez). Craig Gilbert, executive producer. Jack Sameth, producer. NET.
The Switched-On Symphony. Pierre Cossette, Burt Sugarman, executive producers, Jack Good, producer. NBC.

Outstanding Variety or Musical Series
• *The David Frost Show*. Peter Baker, producer. David Frost, star. Syndicated.
The Carol Burnett Show. Joe Hamilton, producer. Carol Burnett, star. CBS.
The Dean Martin Show. Greg Garrison, producer. Dean Martin, star. NBC.
The Dick Cavett Show. Jack Rollins, executive producer. Tony Converse, producer. Dick Cavett, star. ABC.
Rowan and Martin's Laugh-In. George Schlatter, executive producer. Carolyn Raskin, Paul Keyes, producers. Dan Rowan, Dick Martin, stars. NBC.

PERFORMANCE, DIRECTING, AND WRITING
Outstanding Single Performance by an Actor in a Leading Role
• Peter Ustinov, *A Storm in Summer*, *Hallmark Hall of Fame*. NBC.
Al Freeman, Jr., *My Sweet Charlie*. NBC.
Sir Laurence Olivier, *David Copperfield*. NBC.

Outstanding Single Performance by an Actress in a Leading Role
• Patty Duke, *My Sweet Charlie*. NBC.
Dame Edith Evans, *David Copperfield*. NBC.
Shirley Jones, *Silent Night, Lonely Night*. NBC.

Outstanding Continued Performance by an Actor in a Leading Role in a Dramatic Series
• Robert Young, *Marcus Welby, M.D.* ABC.
Raymond Burr, *Ironside*. NBC.
Mike Connors, *Mannix*. CBS.
Robert Wagner, *It Takes a Thief*. ABC.

Outstanding Continued Performance by an Actress in a Leading Role in a Dramatic Series
• Susan Hampshire, *The Forsyte Saga*. N.E.T.
Joan Blondell, *Here Come the Brides*. ABC.

Peggy Lipton, *The Mod Squad*. ABC.

Outstanding Continued Performance by an Actor in a Leading Role in a Comedy Series
• William Windom, *My World and Welcome To It*. NBC.
Bill Cosby, *The Bill Cosby Show*. NBC.
Lloyd Haynes, *Room 222*. ABC.

Outstanding Continued Performance by an Actress in a Leading Role in a Comedy Series
• Hope Lange, *The Ghost and Mrs. Muir*. ABC.
Elizabeth Montgomery, *Bewitched*. ABC.
Marlo Thomas, *That Girl*. ABC.

Outstanding Performance by an Actor in a Supporting Role in Drama
• James Brolin, *Marcus Welby, M.D.* ABC.
Tige Andrews, *The Mod Squad*. ABC.
Greg Morris, *Mission: Impossible*. CBS.

Outstanding Performance by an Actress in a Supporting Role in Drama
• Gail Fisher, *Mannix*. CBS.
Barbara Anderson, *Ironside*. NBC.
Susan Saint James, *The Name of the Game*. NBC.

Outstanding Performance by an Actor in a Supporting Role in Comedy
• Michael Constantine, *Room 222*. ABC.
Werner Klemperer, *Hogan's Heroes*. CBS.
Charles Nelson Reilly, *The Ghost and Mrs. Muir*. ABC.

Outstanding Performance by an Actress in a Supporting Role in Comedy
• Karen Valentine, *Room 222*. ABC.
Agnes Moorehead, *Bewitched*. ABC.
Lurene Tuttle, *Julia*. NBC.

Outstanding Directorial Achievement in Drama
• Paul Bogart, *Shadow Game*, *CBS Playhouse*. CBS.
Buzz Kulik, *A Storm in Summer*, *Hallmark Hall of Fame*. NBC.
Lamont Johnson, *My Sweet Charlie*. NBC.

Outstanding Directorial Achievement in Comedy, Variety, or Music
• Dwight A. Hemion, "The Sound of Burt Bacharach, " *The Kraft Music Hall*. NBC.
Seymour Berns, *The Second Bill Cosby Special*. NBC.
Roger Englander, "Berlioz Takes a Trip," *New York Philharmonic Young People's Concerts*. CBS.

Outstanding Writing Achievement in Drama
• Richard Levinson, William Link, *My Sweet Charlie*. NBC.
George Bellak, *Sadbird*, *CBS Playhouse*. CBS.
Don M. Mankiewicz, *Marcus Welby, M.D.*, *ABC Wednesday Night Movie*. ABC.

Outstanding Writing Achievement in Comedy, Variety, or Music
• Gary Belkin, Peter Bellwood, Herb Sargent, Thomas Meehan, Judith Viorst, *Annie, the Women in the Life of a Man*. CBS.
Paul W. Keyes, David Panich, Marc London, Coslough Johnson, Jim Carlson, Jim Mulligan, John Carsey, Gene Farmer, Jeremy Lloyd, John Rappaport, Stephen Spears, Jack Douglas, Allan Manings, *Rowan and Martin's Laugh-In*. NBC.
Allan Manings, David Panich, Coslough Johnson, John Carsey, Stephen Spears, John Rappaport, Jim Carlson, Marc London, Chet Dowling, Jim Abell, Barry Took, Jack Douglas, Jim Mulligan, Gene Farmer, Jeremy Lloyd, *Rowan and Martin's Laugh-In* . NBC.

OTHER AWARD WINNERS
Outstanding Achievement in Music Composition
(First year series program)
• Morton Stevens, *Hawaii Five-0*. CBS.
(Special program)
• Pete Rugolo, *The Challengers*, *CBS Friday Night Movie*. CBS.

Outstanding Achievement in Music, Lyrics, and Special Material
• Arnold Margolin, Charles Fox, *Love, American Style*. ABC.

Outstanding Achievement in Music Direction of a Variety, Musical, or Dramatic Program
• Peter Matz, "The Sound of Burt Bacharach," *The Kraft Music Hall*. NBC.

NBC/GLOBE PHOTO

Cohost Dick Cavett and presenter Big Bird on Sesame Street's *first big night.*

Outstanding Achievement in Choreography
• Norman Maen, *This is Tom Jones*. ABC.

Outstanding Achievement in Art Direction or Scenic Design
(Dramatic program or feature film)
• Jan Scott, art director, Earl Carlson, set decorator, *Shadow Game*, *CBS Playhouse*. CBS.
(Musical or variety series program)
• E. Jay Krause, art director, *Mitzi's 2nd Special*. NBC.

Outstanding Achievement in Costume Design
• Bob Mackie, *Diana Ross and the Supremes and the Temptations on Broadway*. NBC.

Outstanding Achievement in Makeup
• Ray Sebastian, Louis A. Phillippi, *The Don Adams Special: Hooray for Hollywood*. CBS.

Outstanding Achievement in Cinematography
(Series program)
• Walter Strenge, *Marcus Welby, M.D.* ABC.

(Special program)
• Lionel Lindon, *Ritual of Evil, NBC Monday Night at the Movies.* NBC.

OUTSTANDING ACHIEVEMENT IN TECHNICAL DIRECTION AND ELECTRONIC CAMERAWORK
• Heino Ripp, technical director, Al Camoin, Gene Martin, Donald Mulvaney, Cal Shadwell, cameramen, "The Sound of Burt Bacharach," *The Kraft Music Hall.* NBC.

OUTSTANDING ACHIEVEMENT IN FILM EDITING
(Series program)
• Bill Mosher, *Bracken's World.* NBC.
(Special program)
• Edward M. Abroms, *My Sweet Charlie.* NBC.

OUTSTANDING ACHIEVEMENT IN VIDEO-TAPE EDITING
• John Shultis, "The Sound of Burt Bacharach," *Kraft Music Hall.* NBC.

OUTSTANDING ACHIEVEMENT IN FILM SOUND EDITING
(Tie)
• Douglas H. Grindstaff, Alex Bamattre, Michael Colgan, Bill Lee, Joe Kavigan, Josef E. Von Stroheim, *The Immortal, Movie of the Week.* ABC.
• Richard E. Raderman, Norman Karlin, *Gunsmoke.* CBS.

OUTSTANDING ACHIEVEMENT IN FILM SOUND MIXING
• Gordon L. Day, Dominick Gaffey, *Mission: Impossible.* CBS.

OUTSTANDING ACHIEVEMENT IN LIVE OR TAPE SOUND MIXING
• Bill Cole, Dave Williams, *The Switched-On Symphony.* NBC.

OUTSTANDING ACHIEVEMENT IN LIGHTING DIRECTION
• Leard Davis, Ed Hill, *Appalachian Autumn, CBS Playhouse.* CBS.

THE AREAS
Each area has the possibility of multiple award winners, one winner, or no winner. Winners are listed.

OUTSTANDING ACHIEVEMENT IN DAYTIME PROGRAMMING
(Programs)
• *Today.* Stuart Schulberg, producer. NBC.

OUTSTANDING ACHIEVEMENT IN CHILDREN'S PROGRAMMING
(Programs)
• *Sesame Street.* David D. Connell, executive producer. Sam Gibbon, Jon Stone, Lutrelle Horne, producers. NET.
(Individuals)
• Joe Raposo, Jeffrey Moss, music and lyrics, "This Way to Sesame Street," *Sesame Street.* NET.
• Jon Stone, Jeffrey Moss, Ray Sipherd, Jerry Juhl, Dan Wilcox, Dave Connell, Bruce Hart, Carole Hart and Virginia Schone, writers, "Sally Sees Sesame Street," *Sesame Street.* NET.

OUTSTANDING ACHIEVEMENT IN SPORTS PROGRAMMING
(Programs)
• *The NFL Games.* William Fitts, executive producer. CBS.
• *ABC's Wide World of Sports.* Roone Arledge, executive producer. ABC.
(Individuals)
• Robert R. Forte, film editing, "Pregame Program," *Pro-Bowl Games.* CBS.

SPECIAL CLASSIFICATION OF OUTSTANDING PROGRAM AND INDIVIDUAL ACHIEVEMENT
(Programs)
• *Wild Kingdom.* Don Meier, producer. NBC.

(There were no winners in the areas of outstanding achievement in creative technical crafts, individual achievements in daytime programming, or special classification.)

NEWS & DOCUMENTARY AWARD WINNERS
OUTSTANDING ACHIEVEMENT IN NEWS DOCUMENTARY PROGRAMMING
(Programs)
• "Hospital," *NET.Journal.* Frederick Wiseman, producer. NET.
• *The Making of the President 1968.* M.J. Rifkin, executive producer. Mel Stuart, producer. CBS.

(Individuals)
• Frederick Wiseman, director, "Hospital," *NET Journal.* NET.

OUTSTANDING ACHIEVEMENT IN MAGAZINE-TYPE PROGRAMMING
(Programs)
• *Black Journal.* William Greaves, executive producer. NET.
(Individuals)
• Tom Pettit, reporter-writer, "Some Footnotes to 25 Nuclear Years," *First Tuesday.* NBC.

OUTSTANDING ACHIEVEMENT WITHIN REGULARLY SCHEDULED NEWS PROGRAMS
(Programs)
• "An Investigation of Teenage Drug Addiction—Odyssey House," *The Huntley-Brinkley Report.* Wallace Westfeldt, executive producer. Les Crystal, producer. NBC.
• "Can the World Be Saved?" *CBS Evening News with Walter Cronkite.* Ronald Bonn, producer. CBS.

OUTSTANDING ACHIEVEMENT IN COVERAGE OF SPECIAL EVENTS
(Programs)
• *Apollo: A Journey to the Moon.* James W. Kitcheil, executive producer. NBC.
• *Solar Eclipse: A Darkness at Noon.* Robert Northshield, executive producer. Walter Kravetz, producer. NBC.
(Individuals)
• Walter Cronkite, reporter, *Man on the Moon: The Epic Journey of Apollo XI.* CBS.

OUTSTANDING ACHIEVEMENT IN CULTURAL DOCUMENTARY PROGRAMMING
(Programs)
• *Artur Rubinstein.* George A. Vicas, producer. NBC.
• "Fathers and Sons," *CBS News Hour.* Ernest Leiser, executive producer. Harry Morgan, producer. CBS.
• "The Japanese," *CBS News Hour.* Perry Wolff, executive producer. Igor Oganesoff, producer. CBS.
(Individuals)
• Edwin O. Reischauer, commentator, "The Japanese," *CBS News Hour.* CBS. Artur Rubinstein, commentator, *Artur Rubinstein.* NBC.

(There were no awards to individuals for outstanding achievement within regularly scheduled news programs.)

Competitive awards. Winners are listed.
OUTSTANDING ACHIEVEMENT IN CINEMATOGRAPHY
(Regularly news programs and special events coverage)
• Edward Winkle, "Model Hippie," *The Huntley-Brinkley Report.* NBC.
(Documentary, magazine-type, or mini-documentary)
• Thomas A. Priestley, *Sahara: La Caravane du Sel.* NBC.

OUTSTANDING ACHIEVEMENT IN FILM EDITING
(Regularly news programs and special events coverage)
• Michael C. Shugrue, "The High School Profile," *The Huntley-Brinkley Report.* NBC.
(Documentary, magazine-type, or mini-documentary)
• John Soh, "The Desert Whales," *Undersea World of Jacques Cousteau.* ABC.

SPECIAL AWARDS
OUTSTANDING ACHIEVEMENT IN ENGINEERING DEVELOPMENT
• Apollo color television from space. For NASA's Video Communication Division and for the camera developed by the Westinghouse Electric Corporation.

STATION AWARD
• *Slow Guillotine.* KNBC-TV, Los Angeles.

SPECIAL CITATION
• *The Other Americans.* WJZ-TV, Baltimore.

CITATION
• Ampex Corporation. For developing the HS-200 color TV production system.

THE TRUSTEES AWARD
• Presidents of the news divisions.

TRUSTEES CITATIONS
• NASA. For television coverage of the Apollo 11 moon landing.
• 3M Company. For its art, cultural, scientific, and entertainment programs.

A *Family* Affair

All in the Family was suddenly all the rage because it was about an unlikely hero. Archie Bunker (played by Carroll O'Connor) was created as a real-life reflection of the Average (White) Working American who felt threatened by the "jungle bunnies," "spics," and others around him who were newly asserting their civil rights. Archie was angry, opinionated, outrageous, and sometimes (uh-oh) likeable.

As the prize ceremony opened, a specially prepared skit showed him at home being prodded by his family into watching the Emmy Awards. Archie grumbled, characteristically, and dismissed it as "just another dumb show!" but the feeling was hardly mutual. Later that night *All in the Family* was voted Outstanding New Series in addition to the prize it would sweep for four years in a row: Outstanding Comedy Series. It would then tie *The Dick Van Dyke Show*'s record for the most number of series awards. *Cheers* would make it a three-way tie among comedies in 1991.

But if it was Archie's night, and it was, he was noticeably absent from the winner's circle. The award for best comic actor went instead to *The Odd Couple*'s Jack Klugman, who had won an Emmy once before as best actor for *The Defenders* (1964). But while Emmy voters may have been reluctant to vote for the loud-mouthed bigot of America's new number one show, they were quick to embrace his lovable, bungling wife. It was the first of three Emmys Jean Stapleton would win as Edith Bunker. In her acceptance speech, she thanked "everyone involved," said *Variety*, "and it was a long count."

Another new comedy show that

Best actress Jean Stapleton and losing nominee Carroll O'Connor in the daring new best comedy show All in the Family.

swept the prizes also had its star overlooked. "Everyone on *The Mary Tyler Moore Show* seemed to win an award," said *The New York Times*, "except Mary Tyler Moore." Moore played the sweet, insecure assistant producer of a Minneapolis TV news show who probably deferred too often to her domineering boss played by Ed Asner and bossy best friend played by Valerie Harper. She would defer to them once more at this Emmy Awards. Asner won his first of three trophies for his supporting role as the cantankerous news editor Lou Grant. It was also the first of three Emmys for Harper as smart aleck pal Rhoda Morgenstern. Writers James L. Brooks and Allan Burns were also honored. The show would go on to reap so many Emmys that it would ultimately set a new record for winning more than any other prime-time series (29).

In terms of noticeably absent stars, the question of the night involved just one award: Would George C. Scott accept the Emmy if he wins? Scott had just snubbed the Oscar crowd one month before when they named him Best Actor for *Patton*. Now he was up for Emmy's top acting honor for playing the self-sacrificing brother in Arthur Miller's *The Price* on *Hallmark Hall of Fame*. Scott was mum about whether or not he'd accept the Emmy. He hadn't said no ahead of time like he did before the Oscars, but he also wasn't at the Hollywood Palladium on awards night. All the intrigue prompted the host of the very formal black-tie event, Johnny Carson, to quip, "Did it ever occur to you the reason George C. Scott doesn't come is because he doesn't own a tuxedo?"

A double-decker banner headline on the front page of the next day's *L.A.Times* proclaimed "SCOTT WINS EMMY — HE'LL KEEP IT." But how could Scott embrace the Emmy, while scorning the Oscar? some asked. The Oscars were a popularity contest to be dismissed, he answered, while the Emmys were more serious awards because they were bestowed by panels of experts. Scott's Emmy was accepted on his behalf by Jack Cassidy, who was nominated against him for his role in *The Andersonville Trial*, in which Cassidy was directed by George C. Scott. Said Cassidy afterward: "I think George is rather tired of the harassment. He doesn't believe in competition with other actors and I agree with him." Another winning actor for *The Price* was David Burns for his supporting role as an old furniture dealer and appraiser. Burns had died recently, but his trophy was accepted by his widow. Director Fielder Cook also won.

The Andersonville Trial had already won the year's Peabody Award and now was named Emmy's Outstanding Single Program. *Andersonville* told the story of the 1860s trial of a Confederate captain (played by Richard Basehart) who is held responsible for the deaths by starvation, disease, and neglect of more than 14,000 Union soldiers at a prisoner-of-war camp in Andersonville, Georgia, during the Civil War. Saul Levitt won a statuette, too, for adapting his hit Broadway play for TV.

Lee Grant, who had won a supporting actress award in 1966 for *Peyton Place*, was now back to accept a leading lady prize for *The Neon Ceiling*, an NBC drama about an unhappily married woman who runs off to a gas station-café in the desert. Grant was competing against Colleen Dewhurst (then Mrs. George C. Scott in real life) and herself as well since she had also been nominated for another NBC made-for-TV movie.

Hallmark Hall of Fame's *Hamlet* began the night the most nominattions (13) and ended up with five statuettes, including a best supporting actress trophy for Margaret Leighton as Queen Gertrude and four more for achievements in art direction, costume design, sound mixing, and lighting. What was noticeably absent, though, even from the nominations, was any acknowledgment for Richard Chamberlain as the Melancholy Dane — yet another example of the star missing from his or her winning program. In this case, suggested columnist Cecil Smith, it was particularly bad, since it was *"Hamlet* without a Hamlet."

Among series, the night's biggest winner was also the Outstanding Dramatic

The suspense was riveting: Would George C. Scott accept an Emmy?

Producer Roone Arledge established his early preeminence over the sports awards with ABC's Wide World of Sports.

Series: *The Senator* portion of *The Bold Ones*, which was comprised of rotating segments that also included *The Lawyers* and *The New Doctors*. Of its three parts, one got canceled — the winning one — but it at least it reaped five Emmys as farewell mementoes. Star Hal Holbrook (previously nominated for his portrayal of Mark Twain) won his first TV award for playing the crusading young politician of the title. In his acceptance speech, he said, "Although we were defeated, I'm tremendously proud of what we did."

Emmy's new Outstanding Variety Series was America's number two-ranked program, *The Flip Wilson Show*. Wilson "has done a lot for the black man," quipped host Johnny Carson. "He put him in a dress." Carson's joke referred to one of Wilson's popular characters, Geraldine, the 1970s's ultra-liberated woman whose jealous off-screen boyfriend was called "Killer." (On his show, Wilson was flip about most serious subjects, including religion, when he assumed the role of the Reverend Leroy, pastor of the Church of What's Happenin' Now.)

Among other variety shows, number-13-ranked *Laugh-In*, which won no prizes at all last year, took a trophy this year for Mark Warren, who became the first black director ever to win an Emmy. *Singer Presents Burt Bacharach* was named Outstanding Single Variety or Musical Show and also won an award for writing achievement.

David Frost reprised his win for the top talk show; *Sesame Street* came back as the best children's program. Another repeat winner was Susan Hampshire, who was named best actress last year in a single dramatic role for *The Forsyte Saga* and won this time for her performance in *The First Churchills* on *Masterpiece Theatre*. Other winners included an *ABC Movie of the Week, Tribes*, which won three awards — for film editing, film sound mixing, and writers Tracy Keenan Wynn and Marvin Schwartz. *The Carol Burnett Show*'s Harvey Korman was singled out for Outstanding Individual Achievement in the area awards, but refused to accept it because it was bestowed at the crafts ceremony that took place off camera. "He didn't like being considered in a secondary status," *Variety* explained.

In the news and documentary categories, Walter Cronkite, Bruce Morton, and Mike Wallace all prevailed, as did "The Tragedy of the Red Salmon," an episode of *The Undersea World of Jacques Cousteau* that won two awards. But the most notable winner of all newsworthy specials was "The Selling of the Pentagon," the CBS News exposé of the Defense Department that was drawing fire from Vice President Spiro Agnew. Said Agnew after its TV award win: "If the judges honestly thought that program merited an Emmy and didn't award it out of spite, then I'm surprised. They didn't vote an Emmy for costume design to the producers of *Oh, Calcutta!*"

This was the first time since 1953 that the Emmys were not broadcast simultaneously from both coasts. The New York link-up was finally dropped, but that did not mean the academy was foresaking Gotham's biggest TV giants. Foremost among them was Ed Sullivan, who flew out to the Hollywood Palladium to receive the one single honor that had eluded him throughout his career: an Emmy. The former N.A.T.A.S president had never won one in open competition, but now, as his long-running TV show was going off the air, he received a Trustees Award for "his showmanship, tastes, and personal commitment in entertaining a nation for 23 years."

Shirley Dinsdale was back, too. The first person ever to win an Emmy was flown by the academy to Hollywood to attend her first awards ceremony in more than 20 years. "It was so different then," she said, referring to the days when she reigned as a popular ventriloquist over Los Angeles television airwaves. "I didn't know what an Emmy was before I got it," she added. "And I didn't understand it afterward."

1970–71

For programs telecast between March 16, 1970, and March 16, 1971. Awards broadcast on NBC on May 9, 1971, from the Hollywood Palladium.

PRIME-TIME PROGRAM AWARDS

OUTSTANDING SINGLE PROGRAM— DRAMA OR COMEDY
• *The Andersonville Trial, Hollywood Television Theatre.* Lewis Freedman, producer. PBS.
Hamlet, Hallmark Hall of Fame. Cecil Clarke, executive producer. George LeMaire, producer. NBC.
The Price, Hallmark Hall of Fame. David Susskind, producer. NBC.
"They're Tearing Down Tim Riley's Bar," *Night Gallery, Four-in-One.* Jack Laird, producer. NBC.
Vanished, World Premiere NBC Monday and *Tuesday Night at the Movies.* David Victor, executive producer. David J. O'Connell, producer. NBC.

OUTSTANDING NEW SERIES
• *All in the Family.* Norman Lear, producer. CBS.
The Flip Wilson Show. Monte Kay, executive producer. Bob Henry, producer. NBC.
The Mary Tyler Moore Show. James L. Brooks, Allan Burns, executive producers. David Davis, producer. CBS.
The Odd Couple. Jerry Belson, Gary Marshall, executive producers. Jerry Davis, producer. ABC.
The Senator, The Bold Ones. David Levinson, producer. NBC.

OUTSTANDING SERIES—DRAMA
• *The Senator, The Bold Ones.* David Levinson, producer. NBC.
The First Churchills, Masterpiece Theatre. Donald Wilson, Christopher Sarson, producers. PBS.
Ironside. Cy Chermak, executive producer. Doulgas Benton, Winston Miller, Joel Rogosin, Albert Aley, producers. NBC.
Marcus Welby, M.D. David Victor, executive producer. David J. O'Connell, producer. ABC.
NET Playhouse. Jac Venza, executive producer. PBS.

OUTSTANDING SERIES—COMEDY
• *All in the Family.* Norman Lear, producer. CBS.
Arnie. Rick Mittleman, producer. CBS.
Love, American Style. Arnold Margolin, Jim Parker, executive producers. Bill Idelson, Harvey Miller, William P. D'Angelo, producers. ABC.
The Mary Tyler Moore Show. James L. Brooks, Allan Burns, executive producers. David Davis, producer. CBS.
The Odd Couple. Jerry Belson, Gary Marshall, executive producers. Jerry Davis, producer. ABC.

OUTSTANDING SINGLE PROGRAM— VARIETY OR MUSICAL
• *Singer Presents Burt Bacharach.* Gary Smith, Dwight Hemion, producers. Burt Bacharach, star. CBS.
Another Evening with Burt Bacharach. Gary Smith, Dwight Hemion, producers. Burt Bacharach, star. NBC.
Harry and Lena. Chiz Schultz, producer. Harry Belafonte, Lena Horne, stars. ABC.

HALLMARK HALL OF FAME

George C. Scott in The Price: *He scorned Oscar but embraced Emmy.*

(Classical music)
• "Leopold Stokowski," *NET Festival.* Curtis W. Davis, executive producer. Thomas Slevin, producer. Leopold Stokowski, star. PBS.
"Queen of Spades," *Fanfare—NET Opera Theatre.* Peter Herman Adler, producer. PBS.
"Swan Lake," *Fanfare—NET Opera Theatre.* Curtis W. Davis, John Barnes, executive producer. Norman Campbell, producer. PBS.

OUTSTANDING VARIETY SERIES—MUSICAL
• *The Flip Wilson Show.* Monte Kay, executive producer. Bob Henry, producer. Flip Wilson, star. NBC.
The Carol Burnett Show. Joe Hamilton, executive producer. Arnie Rosen, producer. Carol Burnett, star. CBS.
Rowan and Martin's Laugh-In. George Schlatter, executive producer. Carolyn Raskin, producer. Dick Martin, Dan Rowan, stars. NBC.

OUTSTANDING VARIETY SERIES — TALK
• *The David Frost Show.* Peter Baker, producer. David Frost, star. Syndicated.
The Dick Cavett Show. Jack Rollins, executive producer. John Gilroy, producer. Dick Cavett, star. ABC.
The Tonight Show Starring Johnny

Carson. Fred DeCordova, Rudy Tellez, producers. Johnny Carson, star. NBC.

PERFORMANCE, DIRECTING, AND WRITING
OUTSTANDING SINGLE PERFORMANCE BY AN ACTOR IN A LEADING ROLE
• George C. Scott, *The Price, Hallmark Hall of Fame.* NBC.
Jack Cassidy, *The Andersonville Trial, Hollywood Television Theatre.* PBS.
Hal Holbrook, *A Clear and Present Danger, World Premiere NBC Saturday Night at the Movies.* NBC.
Richard Widmark, *Vanished, World Premiere NBC Monday* and *Tuesday Night at the Movies.* NBC.
Gig Young, *The Neon Ceiling, World Premiere NBC Monday Night at the Movies.* NBC.

OUTSTANDING SINGLE PERFORMANCE BY AN ACTRESS IN A LEADING ROLE
• Lee Grant, *The Neon Ceiling, World Premiere NBC Monday Night at the Movies.* NBC.
Colleen Dewhurst, *The Price, Hallmark Hall of Fame.* NBC.
Lee Grant, *Ransom for a Dead Man, World Premiere NBC Monday Night at the Movies.* NBC.

OUTSTANDING CONTINUED PERFORMANCE BY AN ACTOR IN A LEADING ROLE IN A DRAMATIC SERIES
• Hal Holbrook, *The Senator, The Bold Ones.* NBC.
Raymond Burr, *Ironside.* NBC.
Mike Connors, *Mannix.* CBS.
Robert Young, *Marcus Welby, M.D.* ABC.

OUTSTANDING CONTINUED PERFORMANCE BY AN ACTRESS IN A LEADING ROLE IN A DRAMATIC SERIES
• Susan Hampshire, *The First Churchills, Masterpiece Theatre.* PBS.
Linda Cristal, *The High Chaparral.* NBC.
Peggy Lipton, *The Mod Squad.* ABC.

OUTSTANDING CONTINUED PERFORMANCE BY AN ACTOR IN A LEADING ROLE IN A COMEDY SERIES
• Jack Klugman, *The Odd Couple.* ABC.
Ted Bessell, *That Girl.* ABC.
Bill Bixby, *The Courtship of Eddie's Father.* ABC.
Carroll O'Connor, *All in the Family.* CBS.
Tony Randall, *The Odd Couple.* ABC.

OUTSTANDING CONTINUED PERFORMANCE BY AN ACTRESS IN A LEADING ROLE IN A COMEDY SERIES
• Jean Stapleton, *All in the Family*. CBS.
Mary Tyler Moore, *The Mary Tyler Moore Show*. CBS.
Marlo Thomas, *That Girl*. ABC.

OUTSTANDING PERFORMANCE BY AN ACTOR IN A SUPPORTING ROLE IN DRAMA
• David Burns, *The Price, Hallmark Hall of Fame*. NBC.
James Brolin, *Marcus Welby, M.D.* ABC.
Robert Young, *Vanished, World Premiere NBC Monday* and *Tuesday Night at the Movies*. NBC.

OUTSTANDING PERFORMANCE BY AN ACTRESS IN A SUPPORTING ROLE IN DRAMA
• Margaret Leighton, *Hamlet, Hallmark Hall of Fame*. NBC.
Gail Fisher, *Mannix*. CBS.
Susan Saint James, *The Name of the Game*. NBC.
Elena Verdugo, *Marcus Welby, M.D.* ABC.

OUTSTANDING PERFORMANCE BY AN ACTOR IN A SUPPORTING ROLE IN COMEDY
• Ed Asner, *The Mary Tyler Moore Show*. CBS.
Michael Constantine, *Room 222*. ABC.
Gale Gordon, *Here's Lucy*. CBS.

OUTSTANDING PERFORMANCE BY AN ACTRESS IN A SUPPORTING ROLE IN A COMEDY
• Valerie Harper, *The Mary Tyler Moore Show*. CBS.
Agnes Moorehead, *Bewitched*. ABC.
Karen Valentine, *Room 222*. ABC.

OUTSTANDING DIRECTORIAL ACHIEVEMENT IN DRAMA
(Special program)
• Fielder Cook, *The Price, Hallmark Hall of Fame*. NBC.
Peter Wood, *Hamlet, Hallmark Hall of Fame*. NBC.
Joseph Sargent, *Tribes, Movie of the Week on ABC*. ABC.
James Goldstone, *A Clear and Present Danger, World Premiere NBC Saturday Night at the Movies*. NBC.

OUTSTANDING DIRECTORIAL ACHIEVEMENT IN DRAMA
(Single program of a series)
• Daryl Duke, *The Senator, The Bold Ones*. NBC.
Bob Sweeney, *Hawaii Five-0*. CBS.
John M. Badham, *The Senator, The Bold Ones*. NBC.

OUTSTANDING DIRECTORIAL ACHIEVEMENT IN COMEDY
(Single program of a series)
• Jay Sandrich, *The Mary Tyler Moore Show*. CBS.
Alan Rafkin, *The Mary Tyler Moore Show*. CBS.
John Rich, *All in the Family*. CBS.

OUTSTANDING DIRECTORIAL ACHIEVEMENT IN VARIETY OR MUSIC
(Single program of a series)
• Mark Warren, *Rowan and Martin's Laugh-In* . NBC.
Art Fisher, *The Andy Williams Show*. NBC.
Tim Kiley, *The Flip Wilson Show*. NBC.

OUTSTANDING DIRECTORIAL ACHIEVEMENT IN COMEDY, VARIETY, OR MUSIC
(Special program)
• Sterling Johnson, *Timex Presents Peggy Fleming at Sun Valley*. NBC.
Walter C. Miller, Martin Charnin, "George M!" *The Bell System Family Theatre*. NBC.
Roger Englander, "The Anatomy of a Symphony Orchestra," *New York Philharmonic Young People's Concerts*. CBS.

OUTSTANDING WRITING ACHIEVEMENT IN DRAMA
• Joel Oliansky, *The Senator, The Bold Ones*. NBC.
David W. Rintels, *The Senator, The Bold Ones*. NBC.
Jerrold Freedman, *The Psychiatrist, Four-In-One*. NBC.

OUTSTANDING WRITING ACHIEVEMENT IN DRAMA, ORIGINAL TELEPLAY
• Tracy Keenan Wynn, Marvin Schwartz, *Tribes, Movie of the Week on ABC*. ABC.
William Read Woodfield, Allan Balter, *San Francisco International Airport, World Premiere NBC Tuesday Night at the Movies*. NBC.

David Karp, *The Brotherhood of the Bell,*
CBS Thursday Night Movies. CBS.

**OUTSTANDING WRITING ACHIEVEMENT
IN DRAMA, ADAPTATION**
• Saul Levitt, *The Andersonville Trial,*
Hollywood Television Theatre. PBS.
John Barton, *Hamlet, Hallmark Hall
of Fame.* NBC.
Dean Riesner, *Vanished, World Premiere
NBC Monday and Tuesday Night at the
Movies.* NBC.

**OUTSTANDING WRITING
ACHIEVEMENT IN COMEDY**
• James L. Brooks, Allan Burns, *The Mary
Tyler Moore Show.* CBS.
Norman Lear, *All in the Family.* CBS.
Stanley Ralph Ross, *All in the Family.*
CBS.
Bob Carroll, Jr., Madelyn Davis, *Here's
Lucy.* CBS.

**OUTSTANDING WRITING ACHIEVEMENT
IN VARIETY OR MUSIC**
• Herbert Baker, Hal Goodman, Larry
Klein, Bob Weiskopf, Bob Schiller,
Norman Steinberg, Flip Wilson,
The Flip Wilson Show . NBC.
Arthur Julian, Don Hinkley, Jack
Mendelsohn, Stan Hart, Larry Siegel,
Woody Kling, Roger Beatty, Arnie Rosen,
Kenny Solms, Gail Parent, *The Carol Bur-
nett Show* . CBS.
Danny Simon, Marty Farrell, Norman
Barasch, Carroll Moore, Tony Webster,
Coleman Jacoby, Bob Ellison, "The
Kopykats Kopy TV," *The Kraft Music
Hall.* NBC.

**OUTSTANDING WRITING ACHIEVEMENT
IN COMEDY, VARIETY, OR MUSIC**
(Special program)
• Bob Ellison, Marty Farrell, *Singer
Presents Burt Bacharach.* CBS.
Hal Goldman, Al Gordon, Hilliard Marks,
Hugh Wedlock, Jr., *Timex Presents Jack
Benny's 20th TV Anniversary Special.*
NBC.
Saul Ilson, Ernest Chambers, Gary Belkin,
Alex Barris, *The Doris Mary Ann
Kappelhoff Special.* CBS.

OTHER AWARD WINNERS
OUTSTANDING MUSIC COMPOSITION
(Series program)
• David Rose, *Bonanza.* NBC.

(Special program)
• Walter Scharf, *The Undersea World of
Jacques Cousteau.* ABC.

**OUTSTANDING MUSIC, LYRICS
AND SPECIAL MATERIAL**
• Ray Charles, *The First Nine Months Are
the Hardest.* NBC.

**OUTSTANDING MUSIC DIRECTION
OF A VARIETY, MUSICAL,
OR DRAMATIC PROGRAM**
• Dominic Frontiere, *Swing Out, Sweet
Land.* NBC.

OUTSTANDING CHOREOGRAPHY
(Series or special program)
• Ernest O. Flatt, *The Carol Burnett Show.*
CBS.

**OUTSTANDING ART DIRECTION
OR SCENIC DESIGN**
(Drama, special, or series)
• Peter Roden, *Hamlet, Hallmark Hall of
Fame.* NBC.
(Music or variety special or series)
• James W. Trittipo, art director, George
Gaines, set decorator, *Robert Young and
the Family.* CBS.

OUTSTANDING COSTUME DESIGN
• Martin Baugh, David Walker, *Hamlet,
Hallmark Hall of Fame.* NBC.

OUTSTANDING MAKEUP
• Robert Dawn, *Mission: Impossible.* CBS.

OUTSTANDING CINEMATOGRAPHY
(Series program)
• Jack Marta, *The Name of the Game.*
NBC.
(Special or feature) (Tie)
• Lionel Lindon, *Vanished, World
Premiere NBC Monday and Tuesday Night
at the Movies.* NBC.
• Bob Collins, *Timex Presents Peggy
Fleming at Sun Valley.* NBC.

**OUTSTANDING TECHNICAL DIRECTION
AND ELECTRONIC CAMERAWORK**
• Gordon Baird, technical director, Tom
Ancell, Rick Bennewitz, Larry Bentley
and Jack Reader, cameramen, *The
Andersonville Trial, Hollywood Television
Theatre.* PBS.

OUTSTANDING FILM EDITING
(Series)
• Michael Economou, *The Senator, The Bold Ones.* NBC.
(Special)
• George J. Nicholson, *Longstreet, Movie of the Week on ABC.* ABC.

OUTSTANDING VIDEO-TAPE EDITING
• Marco Zappia, *Hee Haw.* CBS.

OUTSTANDING FILM SOUND EDITING
• Don Hall, Jr., Jack Jackson, Bob Weatherford, Dick Jensen, *Tribes, Movie of the Week on ABC.* ABC.

OUTSTANDING FILM SOUND MIXING
• Theodore Soderberg, *Tribes, Movie of the Week on ABC.* ABC.

OUTSTANDING LIVE OR TAPE SOUND MIXING
• Henry Bird, *Hamlet, Hallmark Hall of Fame.* NBC.

OUTSTANDING LIGHTING DIRECTION
• John Rook, *Hamlet, Hallmark Hall of Fame.* NBC.

THE AREAS
Each area has the possibility of multiple award winners, one winner, or no winner. Winners are listed.

OUTSTANDING ACHIEVEMENT IN DAYTIME PROGRAMMING
(Programs)
• *Today.* Stuart Schulberg, producer. NBC.

OUTSTANDING ACHIEVEMENT IN CHILDREN'S PROGRAMMING
(Programs)
• *Sesame Street.* David D. Connell, executive producer. Jon Stone, Lutrelle Horne, producers. PBS.
(Individuals)
• Burr Tillstrom, performer, *Kukla, Fran & Ollie.* PBS.

OUTSTANDING ACHIEVEMENT IN SPORTS PROGRAMMING
(Programs)
• *ABC's Wide World of Sports.* Roone Arledge, executive producer. ABC.
(Individuals)
• Jim McKay, commentator, *ABC's Wide World of Sports.* ABC.

• Don Meredith, commentator, *NFL Monday Night Football.* ABC.

SPECIAL CLASSIFICATION OF OUTSTANDING PROGRAM AND INDIVIDUAL ACHIEVEMENT
(Individuals)
• Harvey Korman, performer, *The Carol Burnett Show.* CBS.

OUTSTANDING ACHIEVEMENT IN ANY AREA OF CREATIVE TECHNICAL CRAFTS
• Lenwood B. Abbott, John C. Caldwell, special photographic effects, *City Beneath the Sea, World Premiere NBC Monday Night at the Movies.* NBC.
• Gene Widhoff, graphic art—courtroom sketches, Manson trial, *The Huntley-Brinkley Report.* NBC.

(There were no awards to individuals for daytime programming or to programs for special classification.)

NEWS & DOCUMENTARY AWARD WINNERS

OUTSTANDING ACHIEVEMENT IN NEWS DOCUMENTARY PROGRAMMING
(Programs)
• "The Selling of the Pentagon," *CBS News.* Perry Wolff, executive producer. Peter Davis, producer. CBS.
• "The World of Charlie Company." *CBS News.* Ernest Leiser, executive producer. Russ Bensley, producer. CBS.
• *NBC White Paper: Pollution is a Matter of Choice.* Fred Freed, producer. NBC.
(Individuals)
• John Laurence, correspondent "The World of Charlie Company." *CBS News.* CBS.
• Fred Freed, writer, *NBC White Paper: Pollution is a Matter of Choice.* NBC.

OUTSTANDING ACHIEVEMENT IN MAGAZINE-TYPE PROGRAMMING
(Programs)
• Gulf of Tonkin segment, *60 Minutes.* Joseph Wershba, producer. CBS.
• *The Great American Dream Machine.* A.H. Perlmutter, Jack Willis, executive producers. PBS.
(Individuals)
• Mike Wallace, correspondent, *60 Minutes.* CBS.

**OUTSTANDING ACHIEVEMENT
WITHIN REGULARLY SCHEDULED
NEWS PROGRAMS
(Programs)**
• Five-part investigation of welfare, *NBC
Nightly News*. Wallace Westfeldt,
executive producer. David Teitelbaum,
producer. NBC.
(Individuals)
• Bruce Morton, correspondent, reports
from the Lt. Calley trial, *CBS Evening
News with Walter Cronkite*. CBS.

**OUTSTANDING ACHIEVEMENT
IN COVERAGE OF SPECIAL EVENTS
(Programs)**
• *CBS News Space Coverage for 1970–71:
Aquarius on the Moon: The Flight of
Apollo 13* and *Ten Years Later: The Flight
of Apollo 14*. Robert Wussler, executive
producer. Joan Richman, producer. CBS.
(Individuals)
• Walter Cronkite, correspondent, *CBS
News Space Coverage for 1970–71:
Aquarius on the Moon: The Flight of
Apollo 13* and *Ten Years Later: The Flight
of Apollo 14*. CBS.

**OUTSTANDING ACHIEVEMENT
IN CULTURAL DOCUMENTARY
PROGRAMMING
(Programs)**
• "The Everglades," *NBC News*. Craig
Fisher, producer. NBC.
• *The Making of "Butch Cassidy and the
Sundance Kid."* Ronald Preissman,
producer. NBC.
• *Arthur Penn, 1922 – : Themes and
Variants*. Robert Hughes, producer. PBS.
(Individuals)
• Nana Mahomo, narrator, "A Black View
of South Africa," *CBS News*. CBS.
• Robert Guenette, Theodore H. Strauss,
writers, *They've Killed President Lincoln*.
NBC.
• Robert Young, director, *The Eskimo:
Fight for Life*. CBS.

Competitive awards. Winners are listed.
**OUTSTANDING ACHIEVEMENT
IN CINEMATOGRAPHY
(Regular news program/ Special events
coverage)**
• Larry Travis, "Los Angeles —
Earthquake," (Sylmar V.A. Hospital) *CBS
Evening News with Walter Cronkite*. CBS.
• Jacques Renoir, *The Undersea World of
Jacques Cousteau*. ABC.

**OUTSTANDING ACHIEVEMENT
IN FILM EDITING
(Regular news program/ Special events
coverage)**
• George L. Johnson, "Prisons,"*NBC
Nightly News*. NBC.
**(Regular news program/ Special events
coverage)**
• Robert B. Loweree, Henry J. Grennon,
"Cry Help!" *An NBC White Paper on
Mentally Disturbed Youth*. NBC.

SPECIAL AWARDS
**OUTSTANDING ACHIEVEMENT
IN ENGINEERING DEVELOPMENT**
• The Columbia Broadcasting System. For
the development of the color corrector.
• The American Broadcasting Company.
For the development of an "open-loop"
synchronizing system.

CITATIONS
• General Electric. For the development
of the portable earth station transmitter.
• *Stefan Kudelski*. For his design of the
NAGRA IV sound recorder.

STATION AWARD
• *If You Turn On*. KNXT, Los Angeles.

TRUSTEES AWARD
• Ed Sullivan

"An Evening with Norman Lear"

Anticipating a repeat sweep by last year's comedy champ, Emmy host Johnny Carson predicted at the outset that the ceremony could easily be subtitled, "An Evening with Norman Lear." Carson was right. Producer Lear's number-one ranked *All in the Family* had been on the air only a year and a half, but it took three of the top prizes last year, including best comedy and best new show. This year it was up for 11, of which it would take home an impressive 7.

All in the Family was back as the Outstanding Comedy Series and again won a prize for Jean Stapleton as Edith Bunker. Stapleton expressed her thanks by using one of TV husband Archie's favorite words, saying that she felt "truly stifled by the generosity of the academy and the whole community." Nobody stifled Archie Bunker this time. Emmy voters did so last year, but now, finally, Carroll O'Connor (who played "America's favorite bigot," said *Variety*) was named best actor in a comedy series, an honor he called "an enormous pleasure ... for myself and the others whom I love." Sally Struthers, as his on-air daughter, tied with Valerie Harper of *The Mary Tyler Moore Show* in the supporting-actress category and said with amazement and gratitude in her acceptance remarks that the last time she'd won an award was in seventh grade when she starred in a class play. Other winners included the show's director, writer, and sound mixer.

The only principal member of the Norman Lear *Family* to be shut out was Rob Reiner, Archie's "meat head" son-in-law (and Carl Reiner's real-life son), who lost to Ed Asner of *The Mary Tyler*

Producer Norman Lear had a victorious night when All in the Family *swept up nearly all of the leading comedy awards.*

Moore Show. The gruff-acting and -looking Asner acknowledged his award saying that, without the talented gang he worked with, "I'd just be another pretty face." Of the three awards Asner earned for the series, this was his favorite, he said in an interview for this book. "I remember my joy at winning," he added, "because my [pretty face] speech was pretty good and I felt the award substantiated the first Emmy I won and didn't make it seem like such a fluke."

Asner gives Moore most of the credit for all three wins. "I don't think any of us could have operated so beautifully, so nicely, so humorously without her being the phenomenal spoke that she was," he said.

But Asner also added: "We felt robbed that Mary didn't win." For the second successive year, Moore lost the best comic actress trophy to Stapleton. It was a difficult loss to abide. Moore's

Glenda Jackson won dual acting honors for Elizabeth R, *which was voted both best drama series and best new series.*

show was one of the pioneers of the new sophisticated humor programs that were becoming so popular. CBS West Coast chief Perry Lafferty had even told the *L.A. Times* a few months earlier, "*The Mary Tyler Moore Show*, in a sense, broke the new ground to be trodden upon by *All in the Family*. When we put *Mary Tyler Moore* on, it was a comedy mature in theme and realistic in execution, not the sort of comedies that had been making it. When *Mary* was a smash, a little bong went off in our heads .... We put on *All in the Family* and ... after people found it, they loved it."

All in the Family was patterned in part after a British TV comedy hit called *Till Death Us Do Part*. The 1972 Emmys therefore took on a distinct British accent considering that and many of the other victors, too. The Outstanding New Series and Outstanding Drama Series awards were both won by *Elizabeth R*, which chronicled the long, dramatic reign of Britain's "Virgin Queen,"

Elizabeth I. Two of the series's five trophies were claimed by Glenda Jackson who had just won an Oscar for *Women in Love* and now won dual acting Emmys for her leading role in a single episode of *Elizabeth R* (competing against herself in another episode) and for her performance in the entire, limited-run series. The elaborate costume drama produced by the BBC also won a statuette for costume design.

The prize for Outstanding Single Performance by an Actor in a Leading Role was won by Keith Michell, who played Queen Elizabeth's father in a separate BBC series about the Tudors called *The Six Wives of Henry VIII*. The BBC also won two area awards for its *Search for the Nile* docu-drama series.

Tied with *All in the Family* for the most nominations of the night (11) was what film critic Leonard Maltin once called "a milestone of excellence in made-for-TV movies," *Brian's Song*, the film adaptation of Chicago Bear Gale Sayers's book *I Am Third*. The immensely popular television movie starred Billy Dee Williams as Sayers and recounted his friendship with teammate Brian Piccolo (James Caan), an N.F.L. running back felled by cancer. Its victory as Outstanding Single Program of the year was met with a response worthy of a Super Bowl upset: The announcement rocked the Hollywood Palladium with deafening cheers. *Brian's Song* also won an acting award for Jack Warden (accepted by Gale Sayers on behalf of the absent actor), a prize for film editing, and one for screenwriter William Blinn.

The dramatic series that had the most nominations was *Columbo* (with 10) a show that wasn't really a series in the traditional sense. It was part of the *NBC Mystery Movie*, which was also comprised, alternately, of episodes of *McMillan and Wife* and *McCloud*.

Columbo was by far the most popular of the three and starred Peter Falk, Emmy's new best actor in a dramatic series, as the clever, squinty-eyed detective. Falk had won once before, in 1961–62 for his lead role in an episode of *Dick Powell Theatre*, and would win again in the future as Lieutenant Columbo. This time the self-confident actor claimed his prize with an air of humorous smugness, saying, "I am trying to figure out some way to appear humble. It's not going to work." The show won three other trophies, — for writing, cinematography, and film editing. It lost the director's award to *The Lawyers* segment of *The Bold Ones*, a similar "umbrella" show that had just been canceled.

The night's biggest surprise came in the variety categories when *The Carol Burnett Show* was named the outstanding series. Burnett's program had been nominated in the category each of the four years that it was on the air, but lost in the past to David Frost's talk show, *Laugh-In*

Outstanding Drama Program Brian's Song, *with James Caan (left) and Billy Dee Williams, set new standards of excellence for made-for-TV films.*

ABC/ COLUMBIA PICTURES TELEVISION

(twice), and last year to *The Flip Wilson Show*. Wilson was expected to win again, but Burnett ended up nabbing the first of three Emmys she'd eventually receive for having the best variety program. The evergreen star who won her first TV

award for *The Garry Moore Show* (1961–62) and a second for her performance in a variety special with Julie Andrews at Carnegie Hall (1962–63) now thanked the Palladium audience saying, "I won my first Emmy 10 years ago and here I am one year older."

Her program featured some song and dance numbers, but it was known primarily for its comedy skits that earned the show's writers a collective Emmy. The skits included a parody of soap operas called "As the Stomach Turns" and a poke at typical family infighting called "Ed and Eunice," which would go on to become a popular spin-off series called *Mama's Family*. "Ed and Eunice" starred Harvey Korman as Ed and earned him a third trophy for his work on the *Burnett Show*. Last year he refused to accept his second award because it was bestowed off camera at the separate crafts awards luncheon. This year it was to be given at the evening broadcast, so the previously miffed Korman vouchsafed to accept his third. The Emmycast ran overtime, however, and two award presentations had to be cut at the last minute. One of them was Korman's.

The director's honors for a variety series went to Art Fisher of *The Sonny and Cher Comedy Hour* while those for a single variety program went to Martin Charnin of *Jack Lemmon in 'S Wonderful, 'S Marvelous, 'S Gershwin*, which also won for its choreography, music direction and one award for its technical director and cameramen. While thanking the academy for his director's statuette, Charnin said, "This is wonderful, especially when you're out of work." A few minutes later, *'S Wonderful* was also named Outstanding Single Program — Variety or Musical, and Charnin, as the show's producer as well as its director, returned to the podium and said, "It *is* wonderful. I just got a job offstage!"

The Dick Cavett Show was designated Outstanding Variety Series — Talk. *The New York Daily News* had reported earlier that Cavett's network had given him a 90-day ultimatum "to bolster his show, or else." Now, *The New York Times* said, the winning Cavett "may decide his Emmy is made of cast irony if ABC cancels his talk show at summer's end." It went off the air the following December.

Among new categories added this year was one for Outstanding Achievement in Daytime Drama, the first time the Emmys ever acknowledged the category with an award all its own. NBC's *The Doctors*, which chronicled the life, death, and romantic dramas in and around fictitious Hope Memorial Hospital, became the first soap opera ever to win a series award. Prizes for religious programming were also bestowed for the first time and went to the musical director of *And David Wept* and the lighting director of *A City of the King. Sesame Street* was again named best children's show.

> **The Doctors** *was the first soap opera ever to win a series award.*

A Trustees Award went to the late William Lawrence, national affairs editor of ABC News, for "dedicating more than four decades of his life to reporting the news of the nation." Another trustee winner was CBS president Frank Stanton for his "defense of our industry under attack," a reference to Stanton's responses to White House allegations that broadcast journalism was biased.

Entertainment for the evening surely would have been approved by the Washington administration since it included the Johnny Mann Singers whipping up patriotic fervor with a high-stepping rendition of "You're a Grand Old Flag" as an enormous Old Glory unfurled behind them. At the end of the number, Mr. Mann looked meaningfully into the camera and told the home audiences suffering from years of battle fatigue throughout the Vietnam conflict, "We're all partners and, partner, this is no time to sell out." Host Johnny Carson obviously thought the number was overkill and added a wry period to its grandiose patriotic statement when he told the Palladium audience after it was over: "War bonds will be sold in the lobby." *The New York Times* thought it was Carson's funniest line of the Emmycast and added: "The high point of the evening, as it turned out, was political."

The news and documentary awards were given away on the same day at a luncheon in Los Angeles and a dinner in New York. All three networks won prizes for covering key events of the past year: NBC for its special report on the Supreme Court's decision ordering the White House to release the Pentagon Papers, ABC for covering President Richard Nixon's historic trip to China, and CBS for its coverage of the Apollo XV space mission. NBC also won two Emmys for "Defeat of Dacca" and Mike Wallace of CBS was awarded an individual achievement prize for his work on *60 Minutes. The Undersea World of Jacques Cousteau* won three trophies, including two for Outstanding Documentaries.

Raymond Burr presided over the proceedings in L.A. and gave a "stirring and highly deserved tribute to the men and women who work behind the scenes in this vast industry," said the *L.A. Times.*

For programs telecast between March 17, 1971, and March 12, 1972. Awards broadcast on CBS on May 14, 1972, from the Hollywood Palladium.

PRIME-TIME PROGRAM AWARDS
OUTSTANDING NEW SERIES
• *Elizabeth R, Masterpiece Theatre.* Christopher Sarson, executive producer. Roderick Graham, producer. PBS.
Columbo, NBC Mystery Movie. Richard Levinson, William Link, executive producers. Everett Chambers, producer. NBC.
Sanford and Son. Bud Yorkin, executive producer. Aaron Ruben, producer. NBC.
The Six Wives of Henry VIII. Ronald Travers, Mark Shivas, producers. CBS.
The Sonny and Cher Comedy Hour. Allan Blye, Chris Bearde, producers. CBS.

OUTSTANDING SINGLE PROGRAM— DRAMA OR COMEDY
• *Brian's Song, ABC Movie of the Week.* Paul Junger Witt, producer. ABC.
"Jane Seymour," *The Six Wives of Henry VIII.* Ronald Travers, Mark Shivas, producers. CBS.
"The Lion's Cub," *Elizabeth R, Masterpiece Theatre.* Christopher Sarson, executive producer. Roderick Graham, producer. PBS.
"Sammy's Visit," *All in the Family.* Norman Lear, producer. CBS.
The Snow Goose, Hallmark Hall of Fame. Frank O'Connor, producer. NBC.

OUTSTANDING SERIES—DRAMA
• *Elizabeth R, Masterpiece Theatre.* Christopher Sarson, executive producer. Roderick Graham, producer. PBS.
Columbo, NBC Mystery Movie. Richard Levinson, William Link, executive producers. Everett Chambers, producer. NBC.
Mannix. Bruce Geller, executive producer. Ivan Goff, Ben Roberts, producers. CBS.
Marcus Welby, M.D. David Victor, executive producer. David J. O'Connell, producer. ABC.
The Six Wives of Henry VIII. Ronald Travers, Mark Shivas, producers. CBS.

OUTSTANDING SERIES—COMEDY
• *All in the Family.* Norman Lear, producer. CBS.
The Mary Tyler Moore Show. James L. Brooks, Allan Burns, executive producers. David Davis, producer. CBS.
The Odd Couple. Jerry Belson, Garry Marshall, executive producers. Jerry Davis, producer. ABC.
Sanford and Son. Bud Yorkin, executive producer, Aaron Ruben, producer. NBC.

OUTSTANDING SINGLE PROGRAM— VARIETY OR MUSICAL
(Variety and popular music)
• *Jack Lemmon in 'S Wonderful, 'S Marvelous, 'S Gershwin.* Joseph Cates, executive producer. Martin Charnin, producer. Jack Lemmon, star. NBC.
The Flip Wilson Show. Monte Kay, executive producer. Robert Henry, producer. Flip Wilson, star. NBC.
Julie and Carol at Lincoln Center. Joe Hamilton, producer. Julie Andrews, Carol Burnett, stars. CBS.
The Sonny and Cher Comedy Hour. Allan Blye, Chris Bearde, producers. Sonny Bono, Cher, stars. CBS.
(Classical music)
• *Beethoven's Birthday: A Celebration in Vienna with Leonard Bernstein.* James Krayer, executive producer. Humphrey Burton, producer. Leonard Bernstein, star. CBS.
"Heifetz," *The Bell System Family Theatre.* Lester Shurr, executive producer. Paul Louis, producer. Jascha Heifetz, star. NBC.
The Peking Ballet: First Spectacular from China. Lucy Jarvis, producer. NBC.
"The Trial of Mary Lincoln," *N.E.T. Opera Theater.* Peter Herman Adler, executive producer. David Griffiths, producer. PBS.

OUTSTANDING VARIETY SERIES — MUSICAL
• *The Carol Burnett Show.* Joe Hamilton, executive producer. Arnie Rosen, producer. Carol Burnett, star. CBS.
The Dean Martin Show. Greg Garrison, producer. Dean Martin, star. NBC.
The Flip Wilson Show. Monte Kay, executive producer. Robert Henry, producer. Flip Wilson, star. NBC.
The Sonny and Cher Comedy Hour. Allan

Blye, Chris Bearde, producers. Sonny
Bono, Cher, stars. CBS.

OUTSTANDING VARIETY SERIES—TALK
• *The Dick Cavett Show.* John Gilroy,
producer. Dick Cavett, star. ABC.
The David Frost Show. Peter Baker,
producer. David Frost, star. Syndicated.
The Tonight Show Starring Johnny Carson.
Fred DeCordova, producer. Johnny Carson,
star. NBC.

PERFORMANCE, DIRECTING, AND WRITING
OUTSTANDING SINGLE PERFORMANCE BY AN ACTOR IN A LEADING ROLE
• Keith Michell, "Catherine Howard," *The
Six Wives of Henry VIII.* CBS.
James Caan, *Brian's Song, ABC Movie of
the Week.* ABC.
Richard Harris, *The Snow Goose,
Hallmark Hall of Fame.* NBC.
George C. Scott, *Jane Eyre.* NBC.
Billy Dee Williams, *Brian's Song, ABC
Movie of the Week.* ABC.

OUTSTANDING SINGLE PERFORMANCE BY AN ACTRESS IN A LEADING ROLE
• Glenda Jackson, "Shadow in the Sun,"
Elizabeth R, Masterpiece Theatre. PBS.
Glenda Jackson, "The Lion's Cub,"
Elizabeth R, Masterpiece Theatre. PBS.
Helen Hayes, *Do Not Fold, Spindle or
Mutilate, ABC Movie of the Week.* ABC.
Patricia Neal, *The Homecoming.* CBS.
Susannah York, *Jane Eyre.* NBC.

OUTSTANDING CONTINUED PERFORMANCE BY AN ACTOR IN A LEADING ROLE IN A DRAMATIC SERIES
• Peter Falk, *Columbo, NBC Mystery
Movie.* NBC.
Raymond Burr, *Ironside.* NBC.
Mike Connors, *Mannix.* CBS.
Keith Michell, *The Six Wives of Henry
VIII.* CBS.
Robert Young, *Marcus Welby, M.D.* ABC.

OUTSTANDING CONTINUED PERFORMANCE BY AN ACTRESS IN A LEADING ROLE IN A DRAMATIC SERIES
• Glenda Jackson, *Elizabeth R,
Masterpiece Theatre.* PBS.
Peggy Lipton, *The Mod Squad.* ABC.
Susan Saint James, *McMillan and Wife,
NBC Mystery Movie.* NBC.

OUTSTANDING CONTINUED PERFORMANCE BY AN ACTOR IN A LEADING ROLE IN A COMEDY SERIES
• Carroll O'Connor, *All in the Family.*
CBS.
Redd Foxx, *Sanford and Son.* NBC.
Jack Klugman, *The Odd Couple.* ABC.
Tony Randall, *The Odd Couple.* ABC.

OUTSTANDING CONTINUED PERFORMANCE BY AN ACTRESS IN A LEADING ROLE IN A COMEDY SERIES
• Jean Stapleton, *All in the Family.* CBS.
Sandy Duncan, *Funny Face.* CBS.
Mary Tyler Moore, *The Mary Tyler Moore
Show.* CBS.

OUTSTANDING PERFORMANCE BY AN ACTOR IN A SUPPORTING ROLE IN DRAMA
• Jack Warden, *Brian's Song, ABC Movie
of the Week.* ABC.
James Brolin, *Marcus Welby, M.D.* ABC.
Greg Morris, *Mission: Impossible.* CBS.

OUTSTANDING PERFORMANCE BY AN ACTRESS IN A SUPPORTING ROLE IN DRAMA
• Jenny Agutter, *The Snow Goose,
Hallmark Hall of Fame.* NBC.
Gail Fisher, *Mannix.* CBS.
Elena Verdugo, *Marcus Welby, M.D.*
ABC.

OUTSTANDING PERFORMANCE BY AN ACTOR IN A SUPPORTING ROLE IN COMEDY
• Edward Asner, *The Mary Tyler Moore
Show.* CBS.
Ted Knight, *The Mary Tyler Moore Show.*
CBS.
Rob Reiner, *All in the Family.* CBS.

OUTSTANDING PERFORMANCE BY AN ACTRESS IN A SUPPORTING ROLE IN COMEDY
(Tie)
• Valerie Harper, *The Mary Tyler Moore
Show.* CBS.
• Sally Struthers, *All in the Family.* CBS.
Cloris Leachman, *The Mary Tyler Moore
Show.* CBS.

OUTSTANDING ACHIEVEMENT BY A PERFORMER IN MUSIC OR VARIETY
• Harvey Korman, *The Carol Burnett
Show.* CBS.
Ruth Buzzi, *Rowan and Martin's
Laugh-In.* NBC.

Lily Tomlin, *Rowan and Martin's Laugh-In.* NBC.

OUTSTANDING DIRECTORIAL ACHIEVEMENT IN DRAMA
(Single program)
• Tom Gries, *The Glass House, New CBS Friday Night Movies.* CBS.
Paul Bogart, *Look Homeward, Angel, CBS Playhouse 90.* CBS.
Fielder Cook, *The Homecoming.* CBS.
Patrick Garland, *The Snow Goose, Hallmark Hall of Fame.* NBC.
Buzz Kulik, *Brian's Song, Movie of the Week.* ABC.

OUTSTANDING DIRECTORIAL ACHIEVEMENT IN DRAMA
(Series program)
• Alexander Singer, *The Lawyers, The Bold Ones.* NBC.
Edward M. Abroms, *Columbo, NBC Mystery Movie.* NBC.
Daniel Petrie, *The Man and the City.* ABC.

OUTSTANDING DIRECTORIAL ACHIEVEMENT IN COMEDY
(Series program)
• John Rich, *All in the Family.* CBS.
Peter Baldwin, *The Mary Tyler Moore Show.* CBS.
Jay Sandrich, *The Mary Tyler Moore Show.* CBS.

OUTSTANDING DIRECTORIAL ACHIEVEMENT IN VARIETY OR MUSIC
(Series program)
• Art Fisher, *The Sonny and Cher Comedy Hour.* CBS.
Tim Kiley, *The Flip Wilson Show.* NBC.
David Powers, *The Carol Burnett Show.* CBS.

OUTSTANDING DIRECTORIAL ACHIEVEMENT IN COMEDY, VARIETY, OR MUSIC
(Special program)
• Walter C. Miller, Martin Charnin, *Jack Lemmon in 'S Wonderful, 'S Marvelous, 'S Gershwin.* NBC.
Roger Englander, "Liszt and the Devil," *New York Philharmonic Young People's Concerts.* CBS.
David P. Powers, *Julie and Carol at Lincoln Center.* CBS.

OUTSTANDING WRITING ACHIEVEMENT IN DRAMA, ORIGINAL TELEPLAY
(Single program)
• Allan Sloane, *To All My Friends on Shore.* CBS.
John D.F. Black, *Thief, Movie of the Weekend.* ABC.
Jack Sher, *Good-bye, Raggedy Ann.* CBS.

OUTSTANDING WRITING ACHIEVEMENT IN DRAMA, ADAPTATION
(Single program)
• William Blinn, *Brian's Song, Movie of the Week.* ABC.
Paul W. Gallico, *The Snow Goose, Hallmark Hall of Fame.* NBC.
Earl Hamner, Jr., *The Homecoming.* CBS.
Tracy Keenan Wynn, *The Glass House, The New CBS Friday Night Movies.* CBS.

OUTSTANDING WRITING ACHIEVEMENT IN DRAMA
(Series program)
• Richard L. Levinson, William Link, *Columbo, NBC Mystery Movie.* NBC.
Steven Bochco, *Columbo, NBC Mystery Movie.* NBC.
Jackson Gillis, *Columbo, NBC Mystery Movie.* NBC.

OUTSTANDING WRITING ACHIEVEMENT IN COMEDY
(Series program)
• Burt Styler, *All in the Family.* CBS.
Burt Styler, Norman Lear, *All in the Family.* CBS.
Philip Mishkin, Alan J. Levitt, *All in the Family.* CBS.

OUTSTANDING WRITING ACHIEVEMENT IN VARIETY OR MUSIC
• Don Hinkley, Stan Hart, Larry Siegel, Woody Kling, Roger Beatty, Art Baer, Ben Joelson, Stan Burns, Mike Marmer, Arnie Rosen, *The Carol Burnett Show.* CBS.
Herbert Baker, Hal Goodman, Larry Klein, Bob Schiller, Bob Weiskopf, Sid Green, Dick Hills, Flip Wilson, *The Flip Wilson Show.* NBC.
Phil Hahn, Paul Wayne, George Burditt, Coslough Johnson, Bob Arnott, Steve Martin, Bob Einstein, Allan Blye, Chris Bearde, *The Sonny and Cher Comedy Hour.* CBS.

OUTSTANDING WRITING ACHIEVEMENT IN COMEDY, VARIETY, OR MUSIC
(Special program)
• Anne Howard Bailey, "The Trial of Mary Lincoln," *NET Opera Theater*. PBS.
Martin Charnin, *Jack Lemmon in 'S Wonderful, 'S Marvelous, 'S Gershwin*. NBC.
Bob Ellison, Marty Farrell, Ken and Mitzi Welch, *Julie and Carol at Lincoln Center*. CBS.

OTHER AWARD WINNERS

OUTSTANDING MUSIC COMPOSITION
(Series program)
• Pete Rugolo, *The Lawyers, The Bold Ones*. NBC.
(Special program)
• John T. Williams, *Jane Eyre*. NBC.

OUTSTANDING MUSIC, LYRICS AND SPECIAL MATERIAL
• Ray Charles, *The Funny Side*. NBC.

OUTSTANDING MUSIC DIRECTION OF A VARIETY, MUSICAL, OR DRAMATIC PROGRAM
• Elliot Lawrence, *Jack Lemmon in 'S Wonderful, 'S Marvelous, 'S Gershwin*. NBC.

OUTSTANDING CHOREOGRAPHY
• Alan Johnson, *Jack Lemmon in 'S Wonderful, 'S Marvelous, 'S Gershwin*. NBC.

OUTSTANDING ART DIRECTION OR SCENIC DESIGN
(Series or special program)
• Jan Scott, *The Scarecrow, Hollywood Television Theatre*. PBS.
(Musical or variety program)
• E. Jay Krause, *Diana!* ABC.

OUTSTANDING COSTUME DESIGN
• Elizabeth Waller, *Elizabeth R, Masterpiece Theatre*. PBS.

OUTSTANDING MAKEUP
• Frank Westmore, *Kung Fu, ABC Movie of the Week*. ABC.

OUTSTANDING CINEMATOGRAPHY
(Series program)
• Lloyd Ahern, *Blue Print for Murder, Columbo, NBC Mystery Movie*. NBC.
(Special/ Feature-length TV program)
• Joseph Biroc, *Brian's Song, ABC Movie of the Week*. ABC.

OUTSTANDING TECHNICAL DIRECTION AND ELECTRONIC CAMERAWORK
• Heino Ripp, technical director, Albert Camoin, Frank Gaeta, Gene Martin, Donald Mulvaney, cameramen, *Jack Lemmon in 'S Wonderful, 'S Marvelous, 'S Gershwin*. NBC.

OUTSTANDING FILM EDITING
(Series program)
• Edward M. Abroms, *Columbo, NBC Mystery Movie*. NBC.
(Special or feature-length program)
• Bud S. Isaacs, *Brian's Song, Movie of the Week*. ABC.

OUTSTANDING VIDEO-TAPE EDITING
• Pat McKenna, *Hogan's Goat*. PBS.

OUTSTANDING FILM SOUND EDITING
• Jerry Christian, James Troutman, Ronald LaVine, Sidney Lubow, Richard Raderman, Dale Johnston, Sam Caylor, John Stacy, Jack Kirschner, *Duel, ABC Movie of the Weekend*. ABC.

OUTSTANDING FILM SOUND MIXING
• Theodore Soderberg, Richard Overton, *Fireball Forward, ABC Sunday Night Movie*. ABC.

OUTSTANDING LIVE OR TAPE SOUND MIXING
• Norman H. Dewes, *All in the Family*. CBS.

OUTSTANDING LIGHTING DIRECTION
• John Freschi, *Gideon, Hallmark Hall of Fame*. NBC.

THE AREAS

Each area has the possibility of multiple award winners, one winner, or no winner. Winners are listed.

OUTSTANDING ACHIEVEMENT IN DAYTIME DRAMA
(Programs)
• *The Doctors*. Allen Potter, producer. NBC.

OUTSTANDING ACHIEVEMENT IN CHILDREN'S PROGRAMMING
(Programs)
• *Sesame Street*. David D. Connell, executive producer. Jon Stone, producer. PBS.

Outstanding Achievement in Sports Programming
(Programs)
• *ABC's Wide World of Sports.* Roone Arledge, executive producer. ABC.
(Individuals)
• William P. Kelley, technical director. Jim Culley, Jack Bennett, Buddy Joseph, Mario Ciarlo, Frank Manfredi, Corey Leible, Gene Martin, Cal Shadwell, Billy Barnes, Ron Charbonneau, cameramen, *AFC Championship Game.* NBC.

Outstanding Achievement in Religious Programming
(Individuals)
• Alfredo Antonini, music director, *And David Wept.* CBS.
• Lon Stucky, lighting director, "A City of the King," *Contact.* Syndicated.

Special Classification of Outstanding Program and Individual Achievement
(General programming)
• "The Pentagon Papers," *PBS Special.* David Prowitt, executive producer. Martin Clancy, producer. PBS.
(Docu-drama)
• *The Search for the Nile.* Christopher Ralling, producer. NBC.
(Individuals)
• Michael Hastings, Derek Marlow, writers, *The Search for the Nile.* NBC.

Outstanding Achievement in Any Area of Creative Technical Crafts
• Pierre Goupil, Michel Deloire, Yves Omer, underwater cameramen, *The Undersea World of Jacques Cousteau.* ABC.

(No winners of awards for daytime programming, religious programs, or for individual achievement in children's programming or daytime drama.)

NEWS & DOCUMENTARY AWARD WINNERS
Outstanding Achievement Within Regularly Scheduled News Programs
(Programs)
• "Defeat of Dacca," *NBC Nightly News.* Wallace Westfeldt, executive producer. Robert Mulholland, David Teitelbaum, producers. NBC.
(Individuals)
• Phil Brady, reporter, "Defeat of Dacca," *NBC Nightly News.* NBC.

• Bod Schieffer, Phil Jones, Don Webster and Bill Plante, correspondents, "The Air War," *CBS Evening News with Walter Cronkite.* CBS.

Outstanding Achievement for Regularly Scheduled Magazine-Type Programs
(Programs)
• *Chronolog.* Eliot Frankel, executive producer. NBC.
• *The Great American Dream Machine.* A.H. Perlmutter, executive producer. PBS.
(Individuals)
• Mike Wallace, correspondent, *60 Minutes.* CBS.

Outstanding Achievement in Coverage of Special Events
(Programs)
• *The China Trip.* Av Westin, Wally Pfister, executive producers. Bill Lord, producer. ABC.
• *June 30, 1971, A Day for History: The Supreme Court and the Pentagon Papers.* Lawrence E. Spivak, executive producer. NBC.
• *A Ride on the Moon: The Flight of Apollo XV.* Robert Wussler, executive producer. Joan Richman, producer. CBS.

Outstanding Documentary Program Achievement
(Programs of current significance)
• "A Night in Jail, A Day in Court," *CBS Reports.* Burton Benjamin, executive producer. John Sharnik, producer. CBS.
• *This Child is Rated X: An NBC White Paper on Juvenile Justice.* Martin Carr, producer. NBC.
(Cultural programs)
• "Hollywood: The Dream Factory," *The Monday Night Special.* Nicolas Noxon, executive producer. Irwin Rosten, Bud Friedgen, producers. ABC.
• *The Undersea World of Jacques Cousteau.* Jacques Cousteau, Marshall Flaum, executive producers. Andy White, producer. ABC.
• *The Undersea World of Jacques Cousteau.* Jacques Cousteau, Marshall Flaum, executive producers. Andy White, producer. ABC.
(Individuals)
• Louis J. Hazam, writer, "Venice Be Damned!," *NBC News Special.* NBC.
• Robert Northshield, writer, *Suffer the*

Little Children: An NBC White Paper on Northern Ireland. NBC.

(No award winner for individual achievement in special-events coverage.)

Competitive awards. Winners are listed.
OUTSTANDING ACHIEVEMENT IN CINEMATOGRAPHY
(Regular news programs/ Special events coverage)
• Peter McIntyre, Lim Youn Choul, "Defeat of Dacca," *NBC Nightly News.* NBC.
(Documentary, magazine-type or mini-documentary)
• Thomas Priestley, *Venice Be Damned! NBC News Special.* NBC,

OUTSTANDING ACHIEVEMENT IN FILM EDITING
(Regular news programs/ Special events coverage)
• Darold Murray, "War Song," *NBC Nightly News.* NBC.
(Documentary, magazine-type, or mini-documentary)
• Spencer David Saxon, "Monkeys, Apes and Man," *National Geographic Society.* CBS.

SPECIAL AWARDS
OUTSTANDING ACHIEVEMENT IN ENGINEERING DEVELOPMENT
• Lee Harrison III. For Scanimate, an electronic means of generating animation.

STATION AWARD
• *Sickle Cell Disease: Paradox of Neglect.* WZZM-TV, Grand Rapids, Michigan.

CITATIONS
• Richard E. Hill and Electronic Engineering Company of California. For the development of a time code and equipment to facilitate editing of magnetic video tape.
• National Broadcasting Company. For the development of the Hum Bucker.

TRUSTEES AWARDS
• Bill Lawrence, national affairs editor, ABC News.
• Dr. Frank Stanton, president, CBS.

Emmy Goes to Walton Mountain

As Emmy turned 25, the nation's top TV shows were more mature than the favorites of the past, but they were also considered more realistic — and shocking. In 1973, Mary Tyler Moore, who played an unmarried character on her show, didn't come home from a date until morning. The prudish Archie Bunker entertained wife-swappers on *All in the Family,* and Edith Bunker's liberal cousin Maude, in her own spinoff show, had a controversial abortion. The country and its TV critics were abuzz over the outcries these shows caused, including one over the year's most talked-about made-for-TV movie, and an early favorite to sweep the drama awards: *That Certain Summer,* the story of a father who tells his son that he's gay.

Best actress Michael Learned with best actor Richard Thomas of The Waltons, *the "inevitable" choice for outstanding drama series, critics said.*

Summer began with seven nominations, but ended up with only one award, for Scott Jacoby, the 12-year-old actor who portrayed the boy who learns of his father's secret sex life. Otherwise, the hip new hit shows at least did as well as expected. Number-one-ranked *All in the Family* was named Outstanding Comedy Series for the third year in a row. It also won a prize for its writers, although this time its major stars were passed over for the same honors they received last year. In a repeat of the 1970–71 competition, for example, Carroll O'Connor was upset by Jack Klugman of *The Odd Couple* for the best actor award.

All in the Family's Jean Stapleton had dominated the category of best comic actress over the past two years, eclipsing Mary Tyler Moore, but now at last it was Moore's turn. "The evening's most extravagant applause," noted the *L.A. Times,* "went to Miss Moore herself when she finally won as best actress in a comedy series." "Finally" referred only to the recent past — Moore had won twice before for *The Dick Van Dyke Show* in the mid-1960s — but this was the first for her own show, and her victory led a sweep for other members of her show, too. Valerie Harper won for the third year in a row as Mary's sassy best friend Rhoda. The program's constantly befuddled news announcer, Ted Knight, beat his on-air boss Ed Asner, who had won the supporting actor prize twice before. Director Jay Sandrich also took a statuette.

The Mary Tyler Moore Show costar Cloris Leachman had been nominated, too, but lost in the supporting category to Harper. She won an Emmy instead for giving the year's Outstanding Single Performance by an Actress in a Leading Role for a movie-of-the-week called A Brand New Life, about a housewife who gets pregnant at the age of 40. The Emmy for the year's leading male actor went to Laurence Olivier for a British taping of his stage performance as James Tyrone in Eugene O'Neill's Long Day's Journey Into Night. Newsweek columnist Cyclops had predicted that Long Day's Journey was also "a safe bet" for the prize of outstanding single program of the year, but that went to A War of Children in a major upset. Children was the CBS Tuesday Night Movie about a Catholic housewife-turned-rebel involved in the violent "troubles" in Northern Ireland. Accepting the statuette, producer George Schaefer said, "I couldn't be more surprised." "Neither could the audience," commented TV columnist Cecil Smith. Or Smith himself, for that matter. He had been calling for That Certain Summer to win.

Predictions by Newsweek's Cyclops weren't entirely wrong. He also wrote about a certain popular new show: "There is a quality of the inevitable

> **Director Bob Fosse is the only person in awards history to win an Emmy, Oscar, and Tony in the same year.**

about The Waltons, which has been nominated for 12 Emmys. It ... will probably win for best dramatic series."

The Waltons was an unlikely hit for its time: a fresh, wholesome family series that clearly bucked the trend for less idealized and more irreverent programs. It was set in Virginia's Blue Ridge Mountains and told the story of sizeable extended family struggling for survival during the Great Depression. As predicted, it won Outstanding Drama Series and also took a prize for its lead star Richard Thomas (as John Boy Walton) who accepted it looking a little shaken and gave an acceptance speech about his acceptance speech. He'd just had a car accident, he told the audience, while driving to the ceremonies at the new Schubert Theatre and trying to think of what to say if he won. Michael Learned claimed the trophy for best actress in a dramatic series for playing his mother, Olivia. "Grandma" Ellen Corby won best supporting actress. The Waltons also took awards for film editing and writer John McGreevey. The latter caused some slight embarrassment since McGreevey won for writing a Waltons episode that competed against one written by Earl Hamner, Jr. Hamner wrote the book that the family series was based on — about his own family.

In the variety categories, awards history was made and one amazing victory was scored. In the previous few weeks, Bob Fosse had just won the Tony Award for directing Pippin on Broadway and the Oscar for directing the film version of Cabaret starring Liza Minnelli. Now he became the first and only person in entertainment awards history to win the so-called Triple Crown in the same year — and he did it as a triple Emmy winner. Fosse won one Emmy for directing Liza in Singer Presents Liza with a "Z," a second one for choreographing, and a third award for producing the special that was named outstanding single variety program of the year.

Emmy history was also made by *The Julie Andrews Hour*, which featured a broad range of guest stars appearing with the popular British performer who often sang a few of her favorite things from *The Sound of Music*, *My Fair Lady*, and *Mary Poppins*. The show lasted only one season before it was canceled by ABC, but it ended up being vastly more popular with Emmy voters. *The Julie Andrews Hour* won more Emmys than any other series had ever scored in a single season — seven, a record that would stand until 1981 when *Hill Street Blues* topped it by nabbing eight Emmys, enough to help convince NBC to keep the rookie, low-rated cop series on the air. The *Andrews Hour* wins included one for best variety series and others for its director, art director, costume designer, lighting director, video tape editor, and one award for its technical director and cameramen. Last year's victorious variety series, *The Carol Burnett Show*, won Emmys this year for its writers, director, and supporting star Tim Conway.

Changes in the award rules included outlawing single episodes of a show from competing against one-shot specials. *Broadcasting* explained: "A *Carol Burnett* [series] segment, for example, will not compete with a musical special." Another change no longer allowed limited series like last year's *Elizabeth R* to compete against regular series like *Mannix*. The winner of the new Outstanding Drama/Comedy — Limited Episode category was *Tom Brown's Schooldays* on *Masterpiece Theatre*, which also won a leading actor's award for its star Anthony Murphy. (Two-time Emmy winner Susan Hampshire won a third Emmy for her performance on *Masterpiece Theatre*'s production of *Vanity Fair*.) Other award changes included the elimination of a separate category for talk shows (they now had to compete in the

variety program category) and the creation of competitive categories for daytime dramas (winner, *The Edge of Night*) and non-dramas (winner, *Dinah's Place*, starring old Emmy favorite Dinah Shore). Individual performers like Mary Fickett of *All My Children* were still honored in the area awards.

Writing prizes went to Renee Taylor and Joseph Bologna for their special *Acts of Love — and Other Comedies* starring Marlo Thomas. For dramatic writing, actress Jean Simmons accepted the statuette for Eleanor Perry, who adapted *The House Without a Christmas Tree* for CBS. Abby Mann won for *The Marcus-Nelson Murders*, a TV film about the killing of two young career women in New York City that served as the pilot for the *Kojak* series. For Abby Mann, one of Hollywood's most respected scriptwriters, it was a long overdue first Emmy. Among his masterworks of the past that failed to win him a television award was *Judgment at Nuremberg*, which Mann wrote originally for *Playhouse 90*. (It did earn him an Oscar, though, when he adapted it for the 1961 film directed by Stanley Kramer.)

PBS swept the children's programming category with *Zoom*, *The Electric Company,* and, for the fourth year in a row, *Sesame Street*. ABC claimed all the sports prizes for its *Wide World of Sports* program and coverage of the 1972 Munich Olympic games. Two-time past winner of Outstanding Individual Achievement in Sports Programming, Jim McKay, was at the games and won a special news award for his on-the-scenes coverage of the massacre of Israeli athletes by Arab terrorists.

NEWS & DOCUMENTARY AWARDS

Three nights after the prime-time show for entertainment awards, the news and documentary awards were bestowed in a separate telecast for the very first time. Said *The Washington Post*: "The tone of the broadcast was virtually austere compared with the glamour bash in Los Angeles on Sunday .... There was no staircase set, no blaring band and no fancy production. Winners did not make acceptance speeches: Their Emmys were brought to their tables." The event took place at the ballroom of the New York Hilton and included such prestigious presenters as Coretta Scott King, who was last on hand for an Emmys ceremony in 1969. Secretary of State Henry Kissinger was also scheduled to appear, but the member of the Watergate-battered administration canceled at the last minute.

Because the Watergate scandal figured so prominently in the news, it took a high profile at these news awards. One of the night's four hosts, past academy president Walter Cronkite, referred jokingly to the accounting firm that counted the voters' ballots as Price-Watergate. Satirist Mark Russell did a five-minute act, mostly about Watergate, in which he called the scandal "a serious staff infection" for Nixon. Robert MacNeil noted that PBS was broadcasting the complete Watergate hearings and had no soap operas to interrupt, adding, "Watergate may turn out to be the making of public television."

Cronkite ended up winning two trophies for his coverage of Watergate and the attempt to assassinate Alabama Governor George Wallace. Also included in the CBS victories were five prizes for *60 Minutes*, two of them for Mike Wallace.

ABC won four, two for *Jane Goodall and the World of Animal Behavior* and two more for sports producer Roone Arledge and sportscaster Jim McKay, who just happened to be the newsmen on the spot during the violence at the Munich Olympics. McKay would earn more than a dozen Emmys in his career, but he considered this win special since it rewarded his skill as a journalist under pressure.

NBC won for its documentaries "Blue Collar Trap," about the disillusionment of America's working class, and "One Billion Dollar Weapon," about the construction of a single aircraft carrier during peacetime.

But NBC's biggest winner of all was *America*, the 13-part series produced by the BBC that gave British journalist Alistair Cooke's "personal history" of the U.S. from the days of British colonial rule to the modern-day period of social unrest and political scandals. At the news and documentary awards presentation, *America* took a trophy for Cooke as its narrator, another for him as its writer, and a third as an Outstanding Documentary Program.

None of them, though, topped the award *America* had received just three days earlier at the nighttime Emmys. In the biggest surprise of the 1973 awards, *America* beat out such hits as *The Waltons*, *M*A*S*H* and even Norman's Lear's latest — *Maude* — to be named the Outstanding New Series of the year — even though it was "limited."

1972–73

For programs telecast between March 13, 1972, and March 18, 1973. Entertainment awards broadcast on ABC on May 20, 1973, at the Shubert Theatre in Los Angeles. News & documentary Awards broadcast on CBS on May 22, 1973, at the New York Hilton Hotel.

PRIME-TIME AND DAYTIME PROGRAM AWARDS
OUTSTANDING NEW SERIES
• *America*. Michael Gill, producer. NBC.
The Julie Andrews Hour. Nick Vanoff, producer. H. Wesley Kenny, producer. ABC.
Kung Fu. Jerry Thorpe, producer. ABC.

M*A*S*H. Gene Reynolds, producer.
CBS.
Maude. Norman Lear, executive producer.
Rod Parker, producer. CBS.
The Waltons. Lee Rich, executive producer.
Robert L. Jacks, producer. CBS.

OUTSTANDING DRAMA SERIES
• *The Waltons.* Lee Rich, executive
producer. Robert L. Jacks, producer. CBS.
Cannon. Quinn Martin, executive producer.
Harold Gast, Adrian Samish, producers.
CBS.
Columbo, NBC Sunday Mystery Movie.
Dean Hargrove, producer. NBC.
Hawaii Five-0. Leonard Freeman,
executive producer. Bob Sweeney,
William Finnegan, producers. CBS.
Kung Fu. Jerry Thorpe, producer. ABC.
Mannix. Bruce Geller, executive producer.
Ivan Goff, Ben Roberts, producers. CBS.

OUTSTANDING COMEDY SERIES
• *All in the Family.* Norman Lear,
executive producer. John Rich, producer.
CBS.
The Mary Tyler Moore Show. James L.
Brooks, Allan Burns, executive producers.
Ed. Weinberger, producer. CBS.
M*A*S*H. Gene Reynolds, producer. CBS.
Maude. Norman Lear, executive producer.
Rod Parker, producer. CBS.
Sanford and Son. Bud Yorkin, executive
producer. Aaron Ruben, producer. NBC.

OUTSTANDING DRAMA/COMEDY—
LIMITED EPISODES
• *Tom Brown's Schooldays, Masterpiece
Theatre.* John D. McRae, producer. PBS.
*The Last of the Mohicans, Masterpiece
Theatre.* John D. McRae, producer. PBS.
The Life of Leonardo Da Vinci. RAI
Radiotelevisione Italiana, executive
producer. CBS.

OUTSTANDING SINGLE PROGRAM—
DRAMA OR COMEDY
• *A War of Children, The New CBS Tuesday
Night Movies.* Roger Gimbel, executive
producer. George Schaefer, producer. CBS.
Long Day's Journey Into Night. Cecil
Clarke, executive producer. ABC.
*The Marcus-Nelson Murders, The CBS
Thursday Night Movies.* Abby Mann,
executive producer. Matthew Rapf,
producer. CBS.
The Red Pony, The Bell System Family Theatre.
Frederick W. Brogger, producer. NBC.

*That Certain Summer, Wednesday Movie
of the Week.* Richard Levinson, William
Link, producers. ABC.

OUTSTANDING VARIETY MUSICAL SERIES
• *The Julie Andrews Hour.* Nick Vanoff,
William O. Harbach, producers. Julie
Andrews, star. ABC.
The Carol Burnett Show. Joe Hamilton,
executive producer. Bill Angelos, Buz
Kohan, Arnie Rosen, producers. Carol
Burnett, star. CBS.
The Dick Cavett Show. John Gilroy,
producer. Dick Cavett, star. ABC.
The Flip Wilson Show. Monte Kay,
executive producer. Bob Henry, producer.
Flip Wilson, star. NBC.
The Sonny and Cher Comedy Hour. Allan
Blye, Chris Bearde, producers. Sonny
Bono, Cher, stars. CBS.

OUTSTANDING SINGLE PROGRAM—
VARIETY AND POPULAR MUSIC
• *Singer Presents Liza with a "Z."* Bob
Fosse, Fred Ebb, producers. Liza Minnelli,
star. NBC.
Applause. Alexander Cohen, executive
producer. Joseph Kipness, Lawrence
Kasha, Dick Rosenbloom, producers. CBS.
Once Upon a Mattress. Joe Hamilton,
producer. CBS.

OUTSTANDING SINGLE PROGRAM—
CLASSICAL MUSIC
• *Sleeping Beauty.* J.W. Barnes, Robert
Kotlowitz, executive producers. Norman
Campbell, producer. PBS.
"Bernstein in London," *Special of the
Week.* Curtis W. Davis, executive
producer. Mary Feldbauer, Brian Large,
producers. Leonard Bernstein, star. PBS.
*The Metropolitan Opera Salute to Sir
Rudolf Bing.* William Eliscu, executive
producer. Charles E. Andrews, producer.
CBS.

OUTSTANDING PROGRAM ACHIEVEMENT
IN DAYTIME DRAMA
• *The Edge of Night.* Erwin Nicholson,
producer. CBS.
Days of Our Lives. Betty Corday,
executive producer. H. Wesley Kenney,
producer. NBC.
The Doctors. Allen Potter, producer. NBC.
One Life to Live. Doris Quinlan, Agnes
Nixon, producers. ABC.

OUTSTANDING PROGRAM ACHIEVEMENT IN DAYTIME
• *Dinah's Place*. Henry Jaffe, executive producer. Fred Tatashore, producer. NBC.
The Hollywood Squares. Merrill Heatter, Robert Quigley, executive producers. Bill Armstrong, Jay Redack, producers. NBC.
Jeopardy! Robert H. Rubin, producer. NBC.
The Mike Douglas Show. Barry Sand, producer. Syndicated.
Password. Frank Wayne, executive producer. Howard Felsher, producer. ABC.

PERFORMANCE, DIRECTING, AND WRITING
OUTSTANDING CONTINUED PERFORMANCE BY AN ACTOR IN A LEADING ROLE
(Drama series—Continuing)
• Richard Thomas, *The Waltons*. CBS.
David Carradine, *Kung Fu*. ABC.
Mike Connors, *Mannix*. CBS.
William Conrad, *Cannon*. CBS.
Peter Falk, *Columbo, NBC Sunday Mystery Movie*. NBC.
(Drama/comedy—Limited episodes)
• Anthony Murphy, *Tom Brown's School-days, Masterpiece Theatre*. PBS.
John Abineri, *The Last of the Mohicans, Masterpiece Theatre*. PBS.
Philippe LeRoy, *The Life of Leonardo Da Vinci*. CBS.

OUTSTANDING CONTINUED PERFORMANCE BY AN ACTRESS IN A LEADING ROLE
(Drama series —Continuing)
• Michael Learned, *The Waltons*. CBS.
Lynda Day George, *Mission: Impossible*. CBS.
Susan Saint James, *McMillan and Wife, NBC Sunday Mystery Movie*. NBC.
(Drama/comedy—Limited episodes)
• Susan Hampshire, *Vanity Fair, Masterpiece Theatre*. PBS.
Vivien Heilbron, *The Moonstone, Masterpiece Theatre*. PBS.
Margaret Tyzack, *Cousin Bette, Masterpiece Theatre*. PBS.

OUTSTANDING LEAD ACTOR IN A COMEDY SERIES
• Jack Klugman, *The Odd Couple*. ABC.
Alan Alda, *M*A*S*H*. CBS.
Redd Foxx, *Sanford and Son*. NBC.
Carroll O'Connor, *All in the Family*. CBS.
Tony Randall, *The Odd Couple*. ABC.

OUTSTANDING LEAD ACTRESS IN A COMEDY SERIES
• Mary Tyler Moore, *The Mary Tyler Moore Show*. CBS.
Beatrice Arthur, *Maude*. CBS.
Jean Stapleton, *All in the Family*. CBS.

OUTSTANDING SINGLE PERFORMANCE BY AN ACTOR IN A LEADING ROLE
• Laurence Olivier, *Long Day's Journey Into Night*. ABC.
Henry Fonda, *The Red Pony, The Bell System Family Theatre*. NBC.
Hal Holbrook, *That Certain Summer, Wednesday Movie of the Week*. ABC.
Telly Savalas, *The Marcus-Nelson Murders, The CBS Thursday Night Movies*. CBS.

OUTSTANDING SINGLE PERFORMANCE BY AN ACTRESS IN A LEADING ROLE
• Cloris Leachman, *A Brand New Life, Tuesday Movie of the Week*. ABC.
Lauren Bacall, *Applause*. CBS.
Hope Lange, *That Certain Summer, Wednesday Movie of the Week*. ABC.

OUTSTANDING PERFORMANCE BY AN ACTOR IN A SUPPORTING ROLE IN DRAMA
• Scott Jacoby, *That Certain Summer, Wednesday Movie of the Week*. ABC.
Will Geer, *The Waltons*. CBS.
James Brolin, *Marcus Welby, M.D.* ABC.

OUTSTANDING PERFORMANCE BY AN ACTRESS IN A SUPPORTING ROLE IN DRAMA
• Ellen Corby, *The Waltons*. CBS.
Gail Fisher, *Mannix*. CBS.
Nancy Walker, *McMillan and Wife, NBC Sunday Mystery Movie*. NBC.

OUTSTANDING PERFORMANCE BY AN ACTOR IN A SUPPORTING ROLE IN COMEDY
• Ted Knight, *The Mary Tyler Moore Show*. CBS.
Edward Asner, *The Mary Tyler Moore Show*. CBS.
Gary Burghoff, *M*A*S*H*. CBS.
Rob Reiner, *All in the Family*. CBS.
McLean Stevenson, *M*A*S*H*. CBS.

Outstanding Performance by an Actress in a Supporting Role in Comedy
• Valerie Harper, *The Mary Tyler Moore Show.* CBS.
Cloris Leachman, *The Mary Tyler Moore Show.* CBS.
Sally Struthers, *All in the Family.* CBS.

Outstanding Achievement by a Supporting Performer in Music or Variety
• Tim Conway, *The Carol Burnett Show.* CBS.
Harvey Korman, *The Carol Burnett Show.* CBS.
Liza Minnelli, *A Royal Gala Variety Performance in the Presence of Her Majesty the Queen.* ABC.
Lily Tomlin, *Rowan and Martin's Laugh-In.* NBC.

Outstanding Directorial Achievement in Drama
(Series program)
• Jerry Thorpe, *Kung Fu.* ABC.
Edward M. Abroms, *Columbo, NBC Sunday Mystery Movie.* NBC.
Lee Philips, *The Waltons.* CBS.
(Single program)
• Joseph Sargent, *The Marcus-Nelson Murders, The CBS Thursday Night Movies.* CBS.
Lamont Johnson, *That Certain Summer, Wednesday Movie of the Week.* ABC.
George Schaefer, *A War of Children, The New CBS Tuesday Night Movies.* CBS.

Outstanding Directorial Achievement in Comedy
(Series program)
• Jay Sandrich, *The Mary Tyler Moore Show.* CBS.
Gene Reynolds, *M*A*S*H.* CBS.
John Rich, Bob LaHendro, *All in the Family.* CBS.

Outstanding Directorial Achievement in Comedy, Variety, or Music
(Series program)
• Bill Davis, *The Julie Andrews Hour.* ABC.
Art Fisher, *The Sonny and Cher Comedy Hour.* CBS.

Tim Kiley, *The Flip Wilson Show.* NBC.
(Special program)
• Bob Fosse, *Singer Presents Liza with a "Z."* NBC.
Martin Charnin, Dave Wilson, *Jack Lemmon – Get Happy.* NBC.
Stan Harris, *Duke Ellington ... We Love You Madly.* CBS.
Walter C. Miller, *You're a Good Man Charlie Brown, Hallmark Hall of Fame.* NBC.
Dave Powers, Ron Field, *Once Upon a Mattress.* CBS.

Outstanding Writing Achievement in Drama
(Series program)
• John McGreevey, *The Waltons.* CBS
Steven Bochco, *Columbo, NBC Sunday Mystery Movie.* NBC.
Earl Hamner, Jr., *The Waltons.* CBS.

Outstanding Writing Achievement in Comedy
(Series program)
• Michael Ross, Bernie West, Lee Kalcheim, *All in the Family.* CBS.
Allan Burns, James L. Brooks, *The Mary Tyler Moore Show.* CBS.
Larry Gelbart, *M*A*S*H.* CBS.

Outstanding Writing Achievement in Drama, Original Teleplay
(Single program)
• Abby Mann, *The Marcus-Nelson Murders, The CBS Thursday Night Movies.* CBS.
David Karp, *Hawkins on Murder, The New CBS Tuesday Night Movies.* CBS.
Richard Levinson, William Link, *That Certain Summer, Wednesday Movie of the Week.* ABC.

Outstanding Writing Achievement in Drama, Adaptation
(Series program)
• Eleanor Perry, *The House Without a Christmas Tree.* CBS.
Robert Totten, Ron Bishop, *The Red Pony, The Bell System Family Theatre.* NBC.
Ellen M. Violett, *Go Ask Alice, Wednesday Movie of the Week.* ABC.

OUTSTANDING WRITING ACHIEVEMENT IN VARIETY OR MUSIC

(Series program)
• Stan Hart, Larry Siegel, Gail Parent, Woody Kling, Roger Beatty, Tom Patchett, Jay Tarses, Robert Hilliard, Arnie Kogen, Bill Angelos, Buz Kohan, *The Carol Burnett Show*. CBS.

Herbert Baker, Mike Marmer, Stan Burns, Don Hinkley, Dick Hills, Sid Green, Paul McCauley, Peter Gallay, Flip Wilson, *The Flip Wilson Show*. NBC.

Bob Ellison, Hal Goodman, Larry Klein, Jay Burton, George Bloom, Lila Garrett, John Aylesworth, Frank Peppiatt, *The Julie Andrews Hour*. ABC.

(Special program)
• Renée Taylor, Joseph Bologna, *Acts of Love — And Other Comedies*. ABC.

Fred Ebb, *Singer Presents Liza with a "Z."* NBC.

Allan Manings, Ann Elder, Karyl Geld, Richard Pryor, John Rappaport, Jim Rusk, Lily Tomlin, Jane Wagner, Rod Warren, George Yanok, *Lily Tomlin*. CBS.

OTHER AWARD WINNERS

OUTSTANDING MUSIC COMPOSITION
(Series program)
• Charles Fox, *Love, American Style*. ABC.
(Special program)
• Jerry Goldsmith, *The Red Pony, The Bell System Family Theatre*. NBC.

OUTSTANDING MUSIC, LYRICS, AND SPECIAL MATERIAL
(Series or special program)
• Fred Ebb, John Kander, *Singer Presents Liza with a "Z."* NBC.

OUTSTANDING MUSIC DIRECTION OF A VARIETY, MUSICAL, OR DRAMATIC PROGRAM
• Peter Matz, *The Carol Burnett Show*. CBS.

OUTSTANDING CHOREOGRAPHY
• Bob Fosse, *Singer Presents Liza with a "Z."* NBC.

OUTSTANDING ART DIRECTION OR SCENIC DESIGN
(Dramatic special or series)
• Tom John, *Much Ado About Nothing*. CBS.
(Musical or variety program)
• Brian Bartholomew, Keaton S. Walker, *The Julie Andrews Hour*. ABC.

OUTSTANDING COSTUME DESIGN
• Jack Bear, *The Julie Andrews Hour*. ABC.

OUTSTANDING MAKEUP
• Del Armstrong, Ellis Burman, Stan Winston, *Gargoyles, New CBS Tuesday Night Movies*. CBS.

OUTSTANDING CINEMATOGRAPHY
(Series program)
• Jack Woolf, *Kung Fu*. ABC.
(Special or feature made for TV)
• Howard Schwartz, *Night of Terror, Tuesday Movie of the Week*. ABC.

OUTSTANDING FILM EDITING
(Series program)
• Gene Fowler, Jr., Marjorie Fowler, Anthony Wollner, *The Waltons*. CBS.
(Special or feature made for TV)
• Peter C. Johnson, Ed Spiegel, "Surrender at Appomattox," *Appointment with Destiny*. CBS.

OUTSTANDING VIDEO-TAPE EDITING
• Nick Giordano, Arthur Schneider, *The Julie Andrews Hour*. ABC.

OUTSTANDING TECHNICAL DIRECTION AND ELECTRONIC CAMERAWORK
• Ernie Buttelman, technical director. Robert A. Kemp, James Angel, James Balden, Dave Hilmer, cameramen, *The Julie Andrews Hour*. ABC.

OUTSTANDING FILM SOUND EDITING
• Ross Taylor, Fred Brown, David Marshall, *The Red Pony, The Bell System Family Theatre*. NBC.

OUTSTANDING FILM SOUND MIXING
• Richard J. Wagner, George E. Porter, Eddie J. Nelson, Fred Leroy Granville, "Surrender at Appomattox," *Appointment with Destiny*. CBS.

OUTSTANDING LIVE OR TAPE SOUND MIXING
• Al Gramaglia, Mahlon Fox, *Much Ado About Nothing*. CBS.

OUTSTANDING LIGHTING DIRECTION
(Tie)
• John Freschi, John Casagrande, *The 44th Annual Academy Awards*. NBC.
• Truck Krone, *The Julie Andrews Hour*. ABC.

Outstanding Religious Programming
• *Duty Bound.* Doris Ann, executive producer. Martin Hoade, producer. NBC.

THE AREAS
Each area has the possibility of multiple award winners, one winner, or no winner. Winners are listed.

Outstanding Achievement by Individuals in Daytime Drama
• Mary Fickett, performer, *All My Children.* ABC.

Outstanding Achievement in Children's Programming
(Entertainment—Fictional)
• *Sesame Street.* Jon Stone, executive producer. Bob Cunniff, producer. PBS.
• *Zoom.* Christopher Sarson, producer. PBS.
• Tom Whedon, John Boni, Sara Compton, Tom Dunsmuir, Thad Mumford, Jeremy Stevens, Jim Thurman, writers. *The Electric Company.* PBS.
(Informational/—Factual)
• "Last of the Curlews," *The ABC Afterschool Special.* William Hanna, Joseph Barbera, producers. ABC.
• Shari Lewis, performer. "A Picture of Us," *NBC Children's Theatre.* NBC.

Outstanding Achievement in Sports Programming
• *ABC's Wide World of Sports.* Roone Arledge, executive producer. ABC.
• *1972 Summer Olympic Games.* Roone Arledge, executive producer. ABC.
• John Croak, Charles Gardner, Jakob Hierl, Conrad Kraus, Edward McCarthy, Nick Mazur, Alex Moskovic, James Parker, Louis Rende, Ross Skipper, Robert Steinback, John DeLisa, George Boettcher, Merrit Roesser, Leo Scharf, Randy Cohen, Vito Gerardi, Harold Byers, Winfield Gross, Paul Scoskie, Peter Fritz, Leo Stephan, Gerber McBeath, Louis Torino, Michael Wenig, Tom Wight, James Kelley, video tape editors, *1972 Summer Olympic Games.* ABC.

(No winner of award for individual achievement for daytime programming.)

NEWS & DOCUMENTARY AWARD WINNERS
Outstanding Achievement Within Regularly Scheduled News Programs
(Program segments)
• "The U.S./Soviet Wheat Deal: Is There a Scandal?" *CBS Evening News with Walter Cronkite.* Paul Greenberg, Russ Bensley, executive producers. Stanhope Gould, Linda Mason, producers. CBS.
(Individuals—Program segments)
• Walter Cronkite, Dan Rather, Daniel Schorr, Joel Blocker, correspondents, "The Watergate Affair," *CBS Evening News with Walter Cronkite.* CBS.
• David Dick, Dan Rather, Roger Mudd and Walter Cronkite, correspondents, "Coverage of the Shooting of Governor Wallace," *CBS Evening News with Walter Cronkite.* CBS.
• Eric Sevareid, correspondent, "L.B.J.— The Man and the President," *CBS Evening News with Walter Cronkite.* CBS.

Outstanding Achievement for Regularly Scheduled Magazine-Type Programs
(Programs)
• "The Poppy Fields of Turkey—The Heroin Labs of Marseilles—The New York Connection," *60 Minutes.* Don Hewitt, executive producer. William McClure, John Riffin, Philip Scheffler, producers. CBS.
• "The Selling of Colonel Herbert," *60 Minutes.* Don Hewitt, executive producer. Barry Lando, producer. CBS.
• *60 Minutes.* Don Hewitt, executive producer. CBS.
(Individuals)
• Mike Wallace, correspondent, "Selling of Colonel Herbert," *60 Minutes.* CBS.
• Mike Wallace, correspondent, *60 Minutes.* CBS.

Outstanding Achievement in Coverage of Special Events
(Programs)
• "Coverage of the Munich Olympic Tragedy," *ABC Special.* Roone Arledge, executive producer. ABC.
(Individuals)
• Jim McKay, commentator, "Coverage of the Munich Olympic Tragedy," *ABC Special.* ABC.

Outstanding Documentary Program Achievement

(Current events)
• "The Blue Collar Trap," *NBC News White Paper.* Fred Freed, producer. NBC.
• "The Mexican Connection," *CBS Reports.* Burton Benjamin, executive producer. Jay McMullen, producer. CBS.
• "One Billion Dollar Weapon and Now the War is Over—The American Military in the '70s," *NBC Reports.* Fred Freed, executive producer. Craig Leake, producer. NBC.

(Artistic, historical, or cultural)
• *America.* Michael Gill, executive producer. NBC.
• *Jane Goodall and the World of Animal Behavior.* Marshall Flaum, executive producer. Hugo Van Lawick, Bill Travers, James Hill, producers. ABC.

(Individuals)
• Alistair Cooke, narrator, *America.* NBC.
• Alistair Cooke, writer, *America.* NBC.
• Hugo Van Lawick, director, *Jane Goodall and the World of Animal Behavior.* ABC.

Special Classification of Outstanding Program and Individual Achievement

• *The Advocates.* Greg Harney, executive producer. Tom Burrows, Russ Morash, Peter McGhee, producers. PBS.
• "VD Blues," *Special of the Week.* Don Fouser, producer. PBS.

Outstanding Achievement in Any Area of Creative Technical Crafts

• Donald Feldstein, Robert Fontana, Joe Zuckerman, animation layout of Da Vinci's art, *Leonardo: To Know How To See.* NBC.

Competitive awards. Winners are listed.

Outstanding Achievement in Cinematography

(Regular news programs—Coverage of special events)
• Laurens Pierce, "Coverage of the Shooting of Governor Wallace," *CBS Evening News with Walter Cronkite.* CBS.

(Documentary, magazine-type, or mini-documentary)
• Des and Jan Bartlett, *The Incredible Flight of the Snow Geese.* NBC.

Outstanding Achievement in Film Editing

(Regular news programs—Coverage of special events)
• Patrick Minerva, Martin Sheppard, George Johnson, William J. Freeda, Miguel E. Portillo, Albert J. Helias, Irwin Graf, Jean Venable, Rick Hessel, Loren Berry, Nick Wilkins, Gerry Breese, Michael Shugrue, K. Su, Edwin Einarsen, Thomas Dunphy, Russel Moore, Robert Mole, *NBC Nightly News.* NBC.

(Documentary, magazine-type, or mini-documentary)
• Les Parry, *The Incredible Flight of the Snow Geese.* NBC.

SPECIAL AWARDS

Outstanding Achievement in Engineering Development
• Sony. For the development of the Trinitron.
• CMX Systems, a CBS/Memorex company. For the development of a video tape editing system, utilizing a computer.

National Award for Community Service
• *Take Des Moines ... Please.* KDIN-TV, educational station, Des Moines, Iowa.

A Super S*M*A*S*H Night

In Hollywood, where for decades now even the loftiest stars have been eclipsed by "superstars," the idea of the "Super Emmy" was inevitable. Its proponents did have an interesting proposition: Since so many Emmys, for example, are given away each year for best actor (in comedy and drama show, limited series and for special productions), why not have them compete against each other for Actor of the Year — Series or Actor of the Year — Special? The same could occur among actresses, directors, writers, and so on — for 14 Super Emmys in prime time and 5 in daytime.

Two hundred of Hollywood's biggest stars, producers, and directors protested the plan and threatened to quit the academy if it was enacted, but N.A.T.A.S. prevailed at convincing them at least to try the experiment. "There will be so many Emmys bestowed this year that it will take three separate, nationally telecast ceremonies to distribute them," academy executive director Robert Lewine said, referring to the broadcasts for prime-time, daytime, and news & documentary awards. Because there would be fewer of the Super Emmys compared to the regular ones, he said, they might help simplify the issue of who were the most important winners of the year.

But the new Super Emmy presented some new super problems. The winners of the regular Emmys had to be announced before the show in order to reserve time for the "super" competitions. Therefore, everybody knew before the ceremony even began that Mary Tyler Moore (*The Mary Tyler Moore Show*) and Alan Alda (*M*A*S*H*) had won best actress and actor in a comedy

series. "The element of surprise, which is the strong point of any telecast, is missing," *The Hollywood Reporter* complained. The results were also embarrassing since Moore and Alda were among those who threatened to resign from the academy if the Super Emmy was enacted. Now they were up for it. Worse, both of them won.

Moore beat out Michael Learned, who had previously been named Best Lead Actress in a Drama Series for *The Waltons*. As she accepted the trophy, Moore said, remorsefully, "I would like to see them do away with the 'super' structure — the award I have just won. I

Alan Alda and Wayne Rogers proved war could sometimes be wacky fun in the offbeat best humor series M*A*S*H.

TWENTIETH TELEVISION CORPORATION

don't think it's fair to compare a dramatic actress and a comedic actress. It's apples and oranges." Moore's costar Cloris Leachman was named best supporting actress in a comedy series, but failed to win in her own "super" compe-

Nominee Jean Marsh in the year's best drama series Upstairs, Downstairs *about the foibles of the British aristocracy.*

tition. *MTM*'s Treva Silverman won an award for writing — and was also named Writer of the Year – Series.

When accepting his Super Emmy for playing the wisecracking, martini-swilling Captain "Hawkeye" Pierce, Alan Alda said that he was elated to receive it, but agreed with Moore, adding that the award actually compared "apples and oranges and Volkswagens." He was up against Telly Savalas of *Kojak*, a match-up he called another "odd combination of competitors," but one Alda was not expected to win. His victory ended up causing "a few gasps from a generally reserved audience," noted *The Chicago Tribune*.

"*M*A*S*H* was a S*M*A*S*H*," said the lead sentence in the *Tribune*'s coverage the next day. The new, offbeat show about the 4077 Mobile Army Surgical Hospital in the Korean war ended up ambushing the longstanding champ *All in the Family* for the metal as Outstanding Comedy Series. It also won a (regular)

Emmy for Jackie Cooper for directing.

*M*A*S*H* was based on the hit 1970 Robert Altman movie of the same name. Within a year of its premiere as a television series, it was ranked fourth in the Nielsen ratings. Co-executive producer Larry Gelbart called the program "a labor of love" as he accepted the award for best comedy series. Indicating his Emmy, he added, "It's nice not to see that love go unrequited."

The trophy for Outstanding Drama Series was expected to go to *The Waltons* or *Kojak*, but it ended up going to another surprise winner among new shows. *Upstairs, Downstairs* was what *The New York Times* called "a *Masterpiece Theatre* import from Britain that portrays the trials and tribulations of a household in Edwardian England" — namely, the fictitious Bellamy family and their servants.

As expected, *Columbo* ended up taking Outstanding Limited Series and *The Carol Burnett Show* Outstanding Music-Variety Series. Before the telecast, the Burnett program had been tied with *M*A*S*H* for having the most series nominations — 10 — and came away with statuettes for its director, writers, and supporting actor Harvey Korman. Upon accepting the series prize, Burnett mentioned that she grew up just a few blocks away from where the ceremony was being held, which was the Pacific's Pantages Theatre, a 44-year-old Art Deco building on Hollywood Boulevard that was once the site of the Oscars ceremony. Burnett then said hello to the "kids" who grew up nearby and encouraged them to get in touch.

The Autobiography of Miss Jane Pittman had the most nominations among individual programs (12) and claimed 9 prizes in all. ("Achievements of *Jane Pittman* overshadowed everything else in the annual event," said *Variety*.) The fictitious story of a 110-

year-old ex-slave who recounts her life from the 1860s Civil War era to the 1960s fight for civil rights was named the Outstanding Special of the year and won honors for Cicely Tyson as Best Lead Actress in a Drama, beating out a real super-star of the film world — Katharine Hepburn, who had played Amanda in David Susskind's production of Tennessee Williams's *The Glass Menagerie*. Tyson then won the actual Super Emmy race against Mildred Natwick, Best Lead Actress in a Limited Series for *The Snoop Sisters* (which co-starred Helen Hayes in the story of two mystery writer-sisters who solved real-life puzzlers). Tyson was the offspring of Caribbean immigrants who had always warned her against a career in show business because of its degenerate lifestyle. As she accepted the trophy for Actress of the Year, Tyson sighed and said, "Now I can breathe!" and added, addressing her parents at home: "Mom, this wasn't a den of iniquity, after all!"

Jane Pittman also won awards for its writing (Tracy Keenan Wynn), direction, music, costume design, make-up, and hair styling.

A problem with the new Super Emmy kept cropping up all night and was observed by the *Hollywood Reporter*: "Each time a series came up against a special, the special won." The best example was in the fight over Actor of the Year in a Special. William Holden had been named Best Lead Actor in a Limited Series for his role in *The Blue Knight*, a miniseries about an old-style L.A. cop who still walked the beat through his seedy, inner-city territory. He was up against Hal Holbrook in *Pueblo*, the *ABC Theatre* recreation of the 1968 capture of the U.S. Navy ship by the North Koreans.

Holbrook won for the *Pueblo* special. He accepted the statuette by lambasting it. "Who knows out of two or three or four people who's the best?" he asked. "It's silly."

Lily Tomlin, featuring the famed *Laugh-In* star, was named Outstanding Comedy or Variety Special, a victory that introduced one of the funniest acceptance speeches of the night. Tomlin told the audience as she grasped her Emmy: "This is not the greatest moment in my life because on Friday I had a really great baked potato at Niblick's on Wilshire."

Another special that scored big was *Barbra Streisand ... and Other Musical Instruments*, which won five awards, including two for its director Dwight Hemion. *The New York Times* was outraged that Hemion was up for Director of the Year for what it called "one of his least successful efforts" and dismissed as "an absurdity" the fact that he was competing for the Super Emmy against *Jane Pittman* director John Korty. "Even

The Autobiography of Miss Jane Pittman *overshadowed all other shows, winning nine Emmys, including one for best actress Cicely Tyson* .

more absurdly," the *Times* added, "Hemion won."

Sports awards went to *ABC's Wide World of Sports* producer Roone Arledge and host Jim McKay. They were bestowed by baseball legend Willie Mays who had retired from the National Pastime the previous year and ended up getting the only standing ovation on Emmys night when he was introduced as a presenter. The Outstanding Children's Special went to *Marlo Thomas and Friends in Free to Be ... You and Me!* and was presented by swimmer Mark Spitz and his wife, "perhaps because of the their glowing youth," opined the *L.A. Times.*

The prime-time Emmys ended up setting a new record for the most awards ever won by a single network when CBS claimed 44 of them. Johnny Carson was "a wonderful host," said *The Hollywood Reporter,* "and his quote 'the balloting structure was devised by Ronald McDonald' summed up the evening." The Super Emmys were being ridiculed almost universally, even by *The New York Times,* which called them "ridiculous" and "the biggest mistake" the academy ever made. Soon after the broadcast, they were dropped, so the academy said, forever.

DAYTIME AWARDS

For the first time in Emmy history, the daytime awards were given their own separate broadcast. NBC vice president Lin Bolen told the *Washington Post,* "We want the 42 million people who watch daytime TV to be able to see the programs and performers they love finally get their proper reward."

For the first time ever, the daytime awards were given their own broadcast.

The afternoon ceremony was staged in the plaza in front of Rockefeller Center in New York City with the nominees arriving by horse-drawn carriages. John Cannon, then chairman-elect of the academy's national board, told the sun-drenched group that daytime TV had progressed considerably in recent years and had ultimately "brought forth bolder themes." Presenters and participants included Garry Moore, who paid tribute to daytime TV, which he called "the province of the working actor." Other celebrities involved were actress Arlene Francis, comedian Soupy Sales, and *All My Children*'s Mary Fickett, who became the first daytime performer ever to win an Emmy when she was cited for Outstanding Achievement by an Individual in Daytime Drama in 1973.

"ABC's daytime specials under the name of *Afternoon Playbreak* and *Matinee Today* won 13 Emmys," said *The Hollywood Reporter.* Big winners included *ABC Matinee Today*'s "The Other Woman," which was named Outstanding Drama Special. It also earned acting honors — including Daytime Actor of the Year — for Pat O'Brien, who had been acting professionally for 52 years, but had never before won a major award. He told the crowd at Rockefeller Plaza: "My heart's still pounding. I'm thrilled!"

The first daytime drama to ever win an Emmy as best series, *The Doctors* (in 1971–72), came back this year as Outstanding Drama Series. The show, which centered on fictitious Hope Memorial Hospital and also took a prize for its Dr. Althea Davis character, Elizabeth Hubbard, who was named best actress. *Days of Our Lives* earned three awards: for actor Macdonald Carey, for its director, and for its sound mixer.

The Merv Griffin Show took three major prizes, including one for being the outstanding talk show series, another for its director, and the third for its writers, which included Griffin. *Password* was named Outstanding Game Show, but *The Hollywood Squares* won the most Emmys among its kind, including two for Peter Marshall, one as Daytime Host of the Year. Coincidentally, he was also one of the hosts, along with Barbara Walters, of the Daytime Emmy Awards.

"They did a superb job," said *The Hollywood Reporter*, sizing up Marshall's and Walters's performances, and then added, "The Daytime Emmy Awards show is deserving of an award for one of the most well-done awards shows ever. It was dignified, spirited, fast-moving, and professional."

NEWS & DOCUMENTARY AWARDS

As 750 news professionals gathered in the ballroom of the New York Hilton Hotel, *The New York Times* noted that host Dick Cavett was "at his curious worst," while the show itself, broadcast nationally on ABC, proceeded slowly and, some said, dully, too.

Watergate caused a virtual flood of news awards, including ones for *Watergate: The White House Transcripts* on CBS, *CBS News Special Report: The Senate and the Watergate Affair*, and *Watergate Coverage* on PBS, which was produced by the National Public Affairs Center for Television. Fueling the old suspicion that members of the press were biased against former President Richard Nixon, America's television news leaders actually cheered a clip of his resignation speech when it appeared in a montage of the year's news highlights, much of the footage being nominated material.

Bill Moyers, who had recently resigned from PBS, won honors as outstanding news broadcaster (along with Harry Reasoner of ABC) and also nabbed an Emmy for his "Essay on Watergate." Reasoner was acknowledged for his work as coanchor (with Howard K. Smith) of the *ABC Evening News*.

CBS received the most awards for regularly scheduled news programs. It won prizes for "The Agnew Resigna- tion," "The Key Biscayne Bank Charter Struggle," and "Coverage of the October War from Israel's Northern Front."

Two Emmys each went to the Jane Goodall special "The Baboons of Gombe," the critically acclaimed *Close- up* on "Fire!," and *The Undersea World of Jacques Cousteau*. (All ABC.)

The results of the awards — and even the nominations — were considered controversial from the outset. NBC executive Richard Wald was upset that a three-hour documentary on the nation's energy crisis failed to get nominated at the blue-ribbon panel proceedings that took place in Chicago, "in spite of unanimous rave reviews," said the *L.A. Times*. Wald complained to the *Times*: "There had to be something wrong with a system that could ignore such a program. When I asked what had happened, someone told me that it had probably 'just fallen through the cracks.' That's like losing a whale in a home aquarium."

Other complaints about "behind the scenes chaos" in Chicago caused other network executives like CBS News president Richard Salant to voice additional criticism. "And nobody was mollified by the awards program itself," the *L.A. Times* continued, calling them "a slow-moving and generally witless 90 minutes on ABC which sent viewers to other channels in record numbers."

Problems with the awards in 1974 soon ended in them being scrapped altogether. "In 1975 it was CBS's turn in the Emmy barrel and that network flatly refused air time to another separate news and documentary awards show under the existing structure," the *Times* added. "Without the money from a network show, the academy was unwilling to undertake the expense of selecting and giving out news and documentary awards on its own, so the 1975 Emmy awards whizzed into history without them."

For prime-time and daytime entertainment programs telecast between March 19, 1973, and March 17, 1974. Prime-time awards broadcast on NBC on May 28, 1974, from Pacific's Pantages Theatre in Hollywood. The first daytime awards were broadcast on NBC on May 28 from Rockefeller Plaza in New York City. News & documentary prizes were broadcast on ABC on September 4, 1974, from the New York Hilton Hotel for the program eligibility period of March 19, 1973, to June 30, 1974.

PRIME-TIME PROGRAM AWARDS
OUTSTANDING DRAMA SERIES
• *Upstairs, Downstairs, Masterpiece Theatre.* Rex Firkin, executive producer. John Hawkesworth, producer. PBS.
Kojak. Abby Mann, Matthew Rapf, executive producers. James McAdams, producer. CBS.
Police Story. David Gerber, executive producer. Stanley Kallis, producer. NBC.
The Streets of San Francisco. Quinn Martin, executive producer. John Wilder, producer. ABC.
The Waltons. Lee Rich, executive producer. Robert L. Jacks, producer. CBS.

OUTSTANDING COMEDY SERIES
• *M*A*S*H.* Gene Reynolds, Larry Gelbart, producers. CBS.
All in the Family. Norman Lear, executive producer. John Rich, producer. CBS.
The Mary Tyler Moore Show. James Brooks, Allan Burns, executive producers. Ed. Weinberger, producer. CBS.
The Odd Couple. Garry Marshall, Harvey Miller, executive producers. Tony Marshall, producer. ABC.

OUTSTANDING LIMITED SERIES
• *Columbo, NBC Sunday Mystery Movie.* Dean Hargrove, Roland Kibbee, executive producers. Douglas Benton, Robert F. O'Neill, Edward K. Dodds, producers. NBC.
McCloud, NBC Sunday Mystery Movie. Glen Larson, executive producer. Michael Gleason, producer. NBC.
The Blue Knight. Lee Rich, executive producer. Walter Coblenz, producer. NBC.

OUTSTANDING SPECIAL—COMEDY OR DRAMA
• *The Autobiography of Miss Jane Pittman.* Robert Christiansen, Rick Rosenberg, producers. CBS.
The Migrants, Playhouse 90. Tom Gries, producer. CBS.
The Execution of Private Slovik, NBC Wednesday Night at the Movies. Richard Levinson, William Link, executive producer. Richard Dubelman, producer. NBC.
Steambath, Hollywood Television Theatre. Norman Lloyd, executive producer. PBS.
6 Rms Riv Vu. Joe Hamilton, producer. CBS.

OUTSTANDING MUSIC-VARIETY SERIES
• *The Carol Burnett Show.* Joe Hamilton, executive producer. Ed Simmons, producer. Carol Burnett, star. CBS.
The Sonny and Cher Comedy Hour. Allan Blye, Chris Bearde, producers. Sonny Bono, Cher, stars. CBS.
The Tonight Show Starring Johnny Carson. Fred DeCordova, producer. Johnny Carson, star. NBC.

OUTSTANDING COMEDY-VARIETY, VARIETY OR MUSIC SPECIAL
• *Lily Tomlin.* Irene Pinn, executive producer. Herb Sargent, Jerry McPhie, producers. Lily Tomlin, star. CBS.
Barbra Streisand ... and Other Musical Instruments. Martin Erlichman, executive producer. Gary Smith, Dwight Hemion, Joe Layton, producers. Barbra Streisand, star. CBS.
Magnavox Presents Frank Sinatra. Howard K. Koch, producer. Frank Sinatra, star. NBC.
The John Denver Show. Jerry Weintraub, executive producer. Rich Eustis, Al Rogers, producers. John Denver, star. ABC.

OUTSTANDING CHILDREN'S SPECIAL (Winner)
• *Marlo Thomas and Friends in Free To Be ... You and Me.* Marlo Thomas, Carole Hart, producers. Marlo Thomas, star. ABC.

PERFORMANCE, DIRECTING, AND WRITING

BEST LEAD ACTOR IN A DRAMA SERIES
• Telly Savalas, *Kojak*. CBS.
William Conrad, *Cannon*. CBS.
Karl Malden, *The Streets of San Francisco*. ABC.
Richard Thomas, *The Waltons*. CBS.

BEST LEAD ACTRESS IN A DRAMA SERIES
• Michael Learned, *The Waltons*. CBS.
Jean Marsh, *Upstairs, Downstairs, Masterpiece Theatre*. PBS.
Jeanette Nolan, *Dirty Sally*. CBS.

BEST LEAD ACTOR IN A COMEDY SERIES
• Alan Alda, *M*A*S*H*. CBS.
Redd Foxx, *Sanford and Son*. NBC.
Jack Klugman, *The Odd Couple*. ABC.
Carroll O'Connor, *All in the Family*. CBS.
Tony Randall, *The Odd Couple*. ABC.

BEST LEAD ACTRESS IN A COMEDY SERIES
• Mary Tyler Moore, *The Mary Tyler Moore Show*. CBS.
Beatrice Arthur, *Maude*. CBS.
Jean Stapleton, *All in the Family*. CBS.

BEST LEAD ACTOR IN A LIMITED SERIES
• William Holden, *The Blue Knight*. NBC.
Peter Falk, *Columbo, NBC Sunday Mystery Movie*. NBC.
Dennis Weaver, *McCloud, NBC Sunday Mystery Movie*. NBC.

BEST LEAD ACTRESS IN A LIMITED SERIES
• Mildred Natwick, *The Snoop Sisters, NBC Wednesday Movie*. NBC.
Lee Remick, *The Blue Knight*. NBC.
Helen Hayes, *The Snoop Sisters, NBC Wednesday Movie*. NBC.

BEST LEAD ACTOR IN A DRAMA
• Hal Holbrook, *Pueblo, ABC Theatre*. ABC.
Alan Alda, *6 Rms Riv Vu*. CBS.
Laurence Olivier, *The Merchant of Venice, ABC Theatre*. ABC.
Martin Sheen, *The Execution of Private Slovik, NBC Wednesday Night at the Movies*. NBC.
Dick Van Dyke, *The Morning After, Wednesday Movie of the Week*. ABC.

BEST LEAD ACTRESS IN A DRAMA
• Cicely Tyson, *The Autobiography of Miss Jane Pittman*. CBS.
Carol Burnett, *6 Rms Riv Vu*. CBS.
Katharine Hepburn, *The Glass Menagerie*. ABC.

Cloris Leachman, *The Migrants, CBS Playhouse 90*. CBS.
Elizabeth Montgomery, *A Case of Rape, NBC Wednesday Night at the Movies*. NBC.

ACTOR OF THE YEAR—SERIES
• Alan Alda, *M*A*S*H*. CBS.

ACTRESS OF THE YEAR—SERIES
• Mary Tyler Moore, *The Mary Tyler Moore Show*. CBS.

ACTOR OF THE YEAR—SPECIAL
• Hal Holbrook, *Pueblo, ABC Theatre*. ABC.

ACTRESS OF THE YEAR—SPECIAL
• Cicely Tyson, *The Autobiography of Miss Jane Pittman*. CBS.

BEST SUPPORTING ACTOR IN DRAMA
• Michael Moriarty, *The Glass Menagerie*. ABC.
Michael Douglas, *The Streets of San Francisco*. ABC.
Will Geer, *The Waltons*. CBS.
Sam Waterston, *The Glass Menagerie*. ABC.

BEST SUPPORTING ACTRESS IN DRAMA
• Joanna Miles, *The Glass Menagerie*. ABC.
Ellen Corby, *The Waltons*. CBS.
Nancy Walker, *McMillan and Wife, NBC Sunday Mystery Movie*. NBC.

BEST SUPPORTING ACTOR IN COMEDY
• Rob Reiner, *All in the Family*. CBS.
Edward Asner, *The Mary Tyler Moore Show*. CBS.
Gary Burghoff, *M*A*S*H*. CBS.
Ted Knight, *The Mary Tyler Moore Show*. CBS.
McLean Stevenson, *M*A*S*H*. CBS.

BEST SUPPORTING ACTRESS IN COMEDY
• Cloris Leachman, *The Mary Tyler Moore Show*. CBS.
Valerie Harper, *The Mary Tyler Moore Show*. CBS.
Sally Struthers, *All in the Family*. CBS.
Loretta Swit, *M*A*S*H*. CBS.

SUPPORTING ACTOR OF THE YEAR
• Michael Moriarty, *The Glass Menagerie*. ABC.

SUPPORTING ACTRESS OF THE YEAR
• Joanna Miles, *The Glass Menagerie*. ABC.

BEST SUPPORTING ACTOR IN COMEDY-VARIETY, VARIETY, OR MUSIC
• Harvey Korman, *The Carol Burnett Show*. CBS.
Foster Brooks, *The Dean Martin Comedy Hour*. NBC.
Tim Conway, *The Carol Burnett Show*. CBS.

BEST SUPPORTING ACTRESS IN COMEDY-VARIETY, VARIETY, OR MUSIC
• Brenda Vaccaro, *The Shape of Things*. NBC.
Ruth Buzzi, *The Dean Martin Comedy Hour*. NBC.
Lee Grant, *The Shape of Things*. NBC.
Vicki Lawrence, *The Carol Burnett Show*. CBS.

BEST DIRECTING IN DRAMA
(Series program)
• Robert Butler, *The Blue Knight*. NBC.
Harry Harris, *The Waltons*. CBS.
Philip Leacock, *The Waltons*. CBS.
(Single comedy or drama program)
• John Korty, *The Autobiography of Miss Jane Pittman*. CBS.
Tom Gries, *The Migrants, Playhouse 90*. CBS.
Lamont Johnson, *The Execution of Private Slovik, NBC Wednesday Night at the Movies*. NBC.
Anthony Page, *Pueblo, ABC Theatre*. ABC.
Boris Sagal, *A Case of Rape, NBC Wednesday Night at the Movies*. NBC.

BEST DIRECTING IN COMEDY
(Series program)
• Jackie Cooper, *M*A*S*H*. CBS.
Gene Reynolds, *M*A*S*H*. CBS.
Jay Sandrich, *The Mary Tyler Moore Show*. CBS.

BEST DIRECTING IN VARIETY OR MUSIC
(Series program)
• Dave Powers, *The Carol Burnett Show*. CBS.
Art Fisher, *The Sonny and Cher Comedy Hour*. CBS.
Joshua White, "In Concert," *ABC Wide World of Entertainment*. ABC.

BEST DIRECTING IN COMEDY-VARIETY OR MUSIC
(Special program)
• Dwight Hemion, *Barbra Streisand ... and Other Musical Instruments*. CBS.
Marty Pasetta, *Magnavox Presents Frank Sinatra*. NBC.
Tony Charmoli, *Mitzi ... A Tribute to the American Housewife*. CBS.
Sterling Johnson, "Peggy Fleming Visits the Soviet Union," *The Bell System Family Theatre*. NBC.

DIRECTOR OF THE YEAR—SERIES
• Robert Butler, *The Blue Knight*. NBC.

DIRECTOR OF THE YEAR—SPECIAL
• Dwight Hemion, *Barbra Streisand ... and Other Musical Instruments*. CBS.

BEST WRITING IN DRAMA
(Series program)
• Joanna Lee, *The Waltons*. CBS.
Gene R. Kearney, *Kojak*. CBS.
John McGreevey, *The Waltons*. CBS.

BEST WRITING IN COMEDY
(Series program)
• Treva Silverman, *The Mary Tyler Moore Show*. CBS.
Linda Bloodworth, Mary Kay Place, *M*A*S*H*. CBS.
McLean Stevenson, *M*A*S*H*. CBS.

BEST WRITING IN DRAMA, ORIGINAL TELEPLAY
• Fay Kanin, *Tell Me Where It Hurts, GE Theater*. CBS.
Will Lorin, *Cry Rape!, New CBS Tuesday Night Movies*. CBS.
Lanford Wilson, *The Migrants, Playhouse 90*. CBS.

BEST WRITING IN DRAMA, ADAPTATION
• Tracy Keenan Wynn, *The Autobiography of Miss Jane Pittman*. CBS.
Bruce Jay Friedman, *Steambath, Hollywood Television Theatre*. PBS.
Richard Levinson, William Link, *The Execution of Private Slovik, NBC Wednesday Night at the Movies*. NBC.

BEST WRITING IN VARIETY OR MUSIC
(Series program)
• Ed Simmons, Gary Belkin, Roger Beatty, Arnie Kogen, Bill Richmond, Gene Perret, Rudy De Luca, Barry Levinson, Dick Clair, Jenna McMahon, Barry Harman,

The Carol Burnett Show. CBS.
Chris Bearde, Allan Blye, Bob Arnott,
George Burditt, Bob Einstein, Phil Hahn,
Coslough Johnson, Jim Mulligan, Paul
Wayne, *The Sonny and Cher Comedy
Hour.* CBS.
Stan Hart, Larry Siegel, Gail Parent,
Woody Kling, Roger Beatty, Tom
Patchett, Jay Tarses, Robert Hilliard, Arnie
Kogen, Buz Kohan, Bill Angelos, *The
Carol Burnett Show.* CBS.

BEST WRITING IN COMEDY-VARIETY
OR MUSIC
(Special program)
• Herb Sargent, Rosalyn Drexler, Lorne
Michaels, Richard Pryor, Jim Rusk, James
R. Stein, Robert Illes, Lily Tomlin, George
Yanok, Jane Wagner, Rod Warren, Ann
Elder, Karyl Geld, *Lily Tomlin.* CBS.
Larry Gelbart, Mitzie Welch, Ken Welch,
*Barbra Streisand ... and Other Musical
Instruments.* CBS.
Renée Taylor, Joseph Bologna, *Paradise.*
CBS.

WRITER OF THE YEAR—SERIES
• Treva Silverman, *The Mary Tyler Moore
Show.* CBS.

WRITER OF THE YEAR—SPECIAL
• Fay Kanin, *Tell Me Where It Hurts, GE
Theater.* CBS.

OTHER AWARD WINNERS
BEST MUSIC COMPOSITION
(Series program)
• Morton Stevens, *Hawaii Five-0.* CBS.
(Special program)
• Fred Karlin, *The Autobiography of Miss
Jane Pittman.* CBS.

BEST SONG OR THEME
• Mary and David Paich, "Light the Way,"
Ironside. NBC.

BEST MUSIC DIRECTION OF A VARIETY,
MUSICAL OR DRAMATIC PROGRAM
• Jack Parnell, Ken Welch, Mitzie Welch,
*Barbra Streisand ... and Other Musical
Instruments.* CBS.

MUSICIAN OF THE YEAR
• Jack Parnell, Ken Welch, Mitzie Welch,
*Barbra Streisand ... and Other Musical
Instruments.* CBS.

OUTSTANDING CHOREOGRAPHY
• Tony Charmoli, *Mitzi ... A Tribute to the
American Housewife.* CBS.

BEST ART DIRECTION OR SCENIC DESIGN
(Dramatic program)
• Jan Scott, art director. Charles Kreiner,
set decorator, *The Lie, Playhouse 90.* CBS.
(Musical or variety program)
• Brian C. Bartholomew, *Barbra Streisand
... and Other Musical Instruments.* CBS.

ART DIRECTOR AND SET DECORATOR
OF THE YEAR
• Jan Scott, art director. Charles Kreiner,
set director, *The Lie, Playhouse 90.* CBS.

OUTSTANDING COSTUME DESIGN
• Bruce Walkup, Sandy Stewart, *The Autobiography of Miss Jane Pittman.* CBS.

OUTSTANDING MAKEUP
• Stan Winston, Rick Baker, *The Autobiography of Miss Jane Pittman.* CBS.

BEST CINEMATOGRAPHY
FOR ENTERTAINMENT PROGRAMMING
(Series program)
• Harry Wolf, *Columbo, NBC Sunday
Mystery Movie.* NBC.
(Special or feature)
• Ted Voigtlander, *It's Good to Be Alive,
G.E. Theater.* CBS.

CINEMATOGRAPHER OF THE YEAR
• Ted Voigtlander, *It's Good to Be Alive,
G.E. Theater.* CBS.

OUTSTANDING TECHNICAL DIRECTION
AND ELECTRONIC CAMERAWORK
• Gerry Bucci, technical director, Kenneth
Tamburri, Dave Hilmer, Dave Smith, Jim
Balden, Ron Brooks, cameramen. "In
Concert," *ABC Wide World of
Entertainment.* ABC.

BEST FILM EDITING FOR ENTERTAINMENT
PROGRAMMING
(Series program)
• Gene Fowler, Jr., Marjorie Fowler,
Samuel E. Beetley, *The Blue Knight.* NBC.
(Special or feature)
• Frank Morriss, *The Execution of Private
Slovik, NBC Wednesday Night at the
Movies.* NBC.

FILM EDITOR OF THE YEAR
• Frank Morriss, *The Execution of Private Slovik, NBC Wednesday Night at the Movies.* NBC.

OUTSTANDING VIDEO-TAPE EDITING
• Alfred Muller, *Pueblo, ABC Theatre.* ABC.

OUTSTANDING FILM SOUND EDITING
• Bud Nolan, *Pueblo, ABC Theatre.* ABC.

OUTSTANDING FILM OR TAPE SOUND MIXING
• Albert A. Gramaglia, Michael Shindler, *Pueblo, ABC Theatre.* ABC.

OUTSTANDING LIGHTING DIRECTION
• William M. Klages, *The Lie, Playhouse 90.* CBS.

THE AREAS
Each area has the possibility of multiple award winners, one winner, or none. Winners are listed.

OUTSTANDING INDIVIDUAL ACHIEVEMENT IN CHILDREN'S PROGRAMMING
• Charles M. Schulz, writer, *A Charlie Brown Thanksgiving.* CBS.
• William Zaharuk, art director, Peter Razmofski, set decorator, *The Borrowers, Hallmark Hall of Fame.* NBC.

OUTSTANDING SPORTS PROGRAMMING
• *ABC's Wide World of Sports.* Roone Arledge, executive producer. Dennis Lewin, producer. ABC.
• Jim McKay, host. *ABC's Wide World of Sports.* ABC.

SPECIAL CLASSIFICATION OF OUTSTANDING PROGRAM AND INDIVIDUAL ACHIEVEMENT
• *The Dick Cavett Show.* John Gilroy, producer. Dick Cavett, star. ABC.
• Tom Snyder, host, *Tomorrow.* NBC.

OUTSTANDING ACHIEVEMENTS IN ANY AREA OF CREATIVE TECHNICAL CRAFTS
• Lynda Gurasich, hair stylist, *The Autobiography of Miss Jane Pittman.* CBS.

DAYTIME AWARDS
OUTSTANDING DRAMA SERIES
• *The Doctors.* Joseph Stuart, producer. NBC.
Days of Our Lives. Betty Corday, executive producer. Ted Corday, Irna Phillips, Allan Chase, creators. H. Wesley Kenney, producer. NBC.
General Hospital. Jim Young, producer. Frank and Doris Hursley, creators. ABC.

OUTSTANDING DRAMA SPECIAL
• "The Other Woman," *ABC Matinee Today.* John Conboy, producer. ABC.
"A Special Act of Love," *ABC Afternoon Playbreak.* John Choy, producer. ABC.
"Tiger on a Chain," *CBS Daytime 90.* Tony Converse, Darryl Hickman, executive producers. Linda Fidler Wendell, producer. CBS.

BEST ACTOR IN DAYTIME DRAMA
(Series program)
• Macdonald Carey, *Days of Our Lives.* NBC.
John Beradino, *General Hospital.* ABC.
Peter Hansen, *General Hospital.* ABC.
(Special program)
• Pat O'Brien, "The Other Woman," *ABC Matinee Today.* ABC.
Peter Coffield, "Legacy of Fear," *CBS Daytime 90.* CBS.
Don Porter, "Mother of the Bride," *ABC Afternoon Playbreak.* ABC.

DAYTIME ACTOR OF THE YEAR
• Pat O'Brien, "The Other Woman," *ABC Matinee Today.* ABC.

BEST ACTRESS IN DAYTIME DRAMA
(Series program)
• Elizabeth Hubbard, *The Doctors.* NBC.
Rachel Ames, *General Hospital.* ABC.
Mary Fickett, *All My Children.* ABC.
Mary Stuart, *Search for Tomorrow.* CBS.
(Special program)
• Cathleen Nesbit, "The Mask of Love," *ABC Matinee Today.* ABC.
Eve Arden, "Mother of the Bride," *ABC Afternoon Playbreak.* ABC.
Constance Towers, "Once in Her Life," *CBS Daytime 90.* CBS.

DAYTIME ACTRESS OF THE YEAR
• Cathleen Nesbit, "The Mask of Love," *ABC Matinee Today.* ABC.

BEST INDIVIDUAL DIRECTOR FOR A DRAMA SERIES
• H. Wesley Kenney, *Days of Our Lives*. NBC.
Norman Hall, *The Doctors*. NBC.
Hugh McPhillips, *The Doctors*. NBC.

BEST INDIVIDUAL DIRECTOR FOR A SPECIAL PROGRAM
• H. Wesley Kenney, "Miss Kline, We Love You," *ABC Afternoon Playbreak*. ABC.
Burt Brinkerhoff, "The Mask of Love," *ABC Matinee Today*. ABC.
Peter Levin, "The Other Woman," *ABC Matinee Today*. ABC.
Lela Swift, "The Gift of Terror," *ABC Afternoon Playbreak*. ABC.

DAYTIME DIRECTOR OF THE YEAR
• H. Wesley Kenney, "Miss Kline, We Love You," *ABC Afternoon Playbreak*. ABC.

BEST WRITING FOR A DRAMA SERIES
• Henry Slesar, *The Edge of Night*. CBS.
Eileen and Robert Mason Pollock, James Lipton, *The Doctors*. NBC.
Frank and Doris Hursley, Bridget Dobson, Deborah Hardy, *General Hospital*. ABC.

BEST WRITING FOR A SPECIAL PROGRAM
• Lila Garrett, Sandy Krinski, "Mother of the Bride," *ABC Afternoon Playbreak*. ABC.
Robert Shaw, "Once in Her Life," *CBS Daytime 90*. CBS.
Art Wallace, "Alone with Terror," *ABC Matinee Today*. ABC.

DAYTIME WRITER OF THE YEAR
• Lila Garrett, Sandy Krinski, "Mother of the Bride," *ABC Afternoon Playbreak*. ABC.

OTHER DAYTIME AWARD WINNERS
OUTSTANDING GAME SHOW
• *Password*. Frank Wayne, executive producer. Howard Felsher, producer. ABC.

OUTSTANDING TALK, SERVICE, OR VARIETY SERIES
• *The Merv Griffin Show*. Bob Murphy, producer. Syndicated.

OUTSTANDING ENTERTAINMENT CHILDREN'S SERIES
• *Zoom*. Jim Crum, Christopher Sarson, producers. PBS.

OUTSTANDING ENTERTAINMENT CHILDREN'S SPECIAL
• "Rookie of the Year," *ABC Afterschool Special*. Dan Wilson, producer. ABC.

OUTSTANDING INFORMATIONAL CHILDREN'S SERIES
• *Make a Wish*. Lester Cooper, executive producer. Tom Bywaters, producer. ABC.

OUTSTANDING INFORMATIONAL CHILDREN'S SPECIAL
• *The Runaways*. Joseph Barbera, William Hanna, executive producers. Bill Schwartz producer. ABC.

OUTSTANDING INSTRUCTIONAL CHILDREN'S PROGRAMMING
• *Inside/Out*. Larry Walcoff, executive producer. Syndicated.

BEST HOST OR HOSTESS IN A GAME SHOW
• Peter Marshall, *The Hollywood Squares*. NBC.

BEST HOST OR HOSTESS IN A TALK, SERVICE, OR VARIETY SERIES
• Dinah Shore, *Dinah's Place*. NBC.

DAYTIME HOST OF THE YEAR
• Peter Marshall, *The Hollywood Squares*. NBC.

BEST INDIVIDUAL DIRECTOR FOR A GAME SHOW
• Mike Gargiulo, *Jackpot*. NBC.

BEST INDIVIDUAL DIRECTOR FOR A TALK, SERVICE, OR VARIETY PROGRAM
• Dick Carson, *The Merv Griffin Show*. Syndicated.

BEST WRITING FOR A GAME SHOW
• Jay Redack, Harry Friedman, Harold Schneider, Gary Johnson, Steve Levitch, Rich Kellard, Rowby Goren, *The Hollywood Squares*. NBC.

BEST WRITING FOR A TALK, SERVICE, OR VARIETY PROGRAM
• Tony Garafalo, Bob Murphy, Merv Griffin, *The Merv Griffin Show*. Syndicated.

OUTSTANDING MUSICAL DIRECTION
• Richard Clements, "A Special Act of Love," *ABC Afternoon Playbreak*. ABC.

Outstanding Art Direction or Scenic Design
• Tom Trimble, art director. Brock Broughton, set decorator. *The Young and the Restless.* CBS.

Outstanding Costume Design
• Bill Jobe, "The Mask of Love," *ABC Matinee Today.* ABC.

Outstanding Makeup
• Douglas D. Kelly, "The Mask of Love," *ABC Matinee Today.* ABC.

Outstanding Technical Direction and Electronic Camerawork
• Lou Marchand, technical director, Gerald M. Dowd, Frank Melchiorre, John Morris, cameramen, *One Life to Live.* ABC.

Outstanding Editing
• Gary Anderson, "Miss Kline, We Love You," *ABC Afternoon Playbreak.* ABC.

Outstanding Sound Mixing
• Ernest Dellutri, *Days of Our Lives.* NBC.

Outstanding Lighting Direction
• Richard Holbrook, *The Young and the Restless.* CBS.

Outstanding Individual Achievement in Children's Programming
• Ronald Baldwin, art director. Nat Mongioi, set decorator. *The Electric Company.* PBS.
• The Muppets: Jim Henson, Frank Oz, Carroll Spinney, Jerry Nelson, Richard Hunt, Fran Brill, performers, *Sesame Street.* PBS.
• Jon Stone, Joseph A. Bailey, Jerry Juhl, Emily Perl Kingsley, Jeffrey Moss, Ray Sipherd, Norman Stiles, writers, *Sesame Street.* PBS.

NEWS & DOCUMENTARY AWARD WINNERS
Outstanding Achievement Within Regularly Scheduled News Programs
• "Coverage of the October War from Israel's Northern Front," *CBS Evening News with Walter Cronkite.* John Laurence, correspondent. CBS.
• "The Agnew Resignation," *CBS Evening News with Walter Cronkite.* Paul Greenberg, executive producer. Ron Bonn, Ed Fouhy, John Lane, Don Bowers, John Armstrong, Robert Mean, producers. Walter Cronkite, Robewrt Schakne, Fred Graham, Robert Pierpoint, Roger Mudd,

Dan Rather, John Hart, Eric Sevareid, correspondents. CBS.
• "The Key Biscayne Bank Charter Struggle," *CBS Evening News with Walter Cronkite.* Ed Fouhy, producer. Robert Pierpont, correspondent. CBS.
• "Reports on World Hunger," *NBC Nightly News.* Lester N. Crystal, executive producer. Richard Fisher, Joseph Angotti, producers. Tom Streithorst, Phil Brady, John Palmer, Liz Trotta, correspondents. NBC.

Outstanding Achievement for Regularly Scheduled Magazine-Type Programs
• "America's Nerve Gas Arsenal," *First Tuesday.* Eliot Frankel, executive producer. William B. Hill, Anthony Potter, producers. Tom Pettit, correspondent. NBC.
• "The Adversaries," *Behind the Lines.* Carey Winfrey, executive producer. Peter Forbth, producer/reporter. Brendan Gill, host/moderator. PBS.
• "A Question of Impeachment," *Bill Moyers' Journal.* Jerome Toobin, executive producer. Martin Clancy, producer. Bill Moyers, broadcaster. PBS.

Outstanding Achievement in Coverage of Special Events
• *Watergate: The White House Transcripts.* Russ Bensley, executive producer. Sylvia Westerman, Barry Jagoda, Mark Harrington, Jack Kelly, producers. Walter Cronkite, Dan Rather, Barry Serafin, Bob Schieffer, Daniel Schorr, Nelson Benton, Bruce Morton, Roger Mudd, Fred Graham, correspondents. CBS.
• *Watergate Coverage.* Martin Clancy, executive producer. The NPACT staff, producers. Jim Lehrer, Peter Kaye, Robert MacNeil, reporters. PBS.

Outstanding Documentary Program Achievements
(Current events)
• "Fire!" *ABC News Closeup.* Pamela Hill, producer. Jules Bergman, correspondent/narrator. ABC.
• *CBS News Special Report: The Senate and the Watergate Affair.* Leslie Midgley, executive producer. Hal Haley, Bernard Birnbaum, David Browning, producers. Dan Rather, Roger Mudd, Daniel Schorr, Fred Graham, correspondents. CBS.

Outstanding Documentary Program Achievements

(Artistic, historical, or cultural)
• "Journey to the Outer Limits," *National Geographic Society.* Nicholas Clapp, Dennis Kane, executive producers. Alex Grasshoff, producer. ABC.
• *The World at War.* Jeremy Isaacs, producer. Syndicated.
• *CBS Reports: The Rockefellers.* Burton Benjamin, executive producer. Howard Stringer, producer. Walter Cronkite, correspondent. CBS.

Outstanding Interview Program
• "Solzhenitsyn," *CBS News Special.* Burton Benjamin, producer. Walter Cronkite, correspondent. CBS.
• "Henry Steele Commager," *Bill Moyers' Journal.* Jerome Toobin, executive producer. Martin Clancy, producer. PBS.

Outstanding Television News Broadcaster
• Harry Reasoner, *ABC News.* ABC.
• Bill Moyers, "Essay On Watergate," *Bill Moyers' Journal.* PBS.

Outstanding Achievement in News and Documentary Directing
• Pamela Hill, "Fire!" *ABC News Closeup.* ABC.

Best Music Composition
• Walter Scharf, *The Undersea World of Jacques Cousteau.* ABC.

Best Art Direction or Scenic Design
• William Sunshine, *60 Minutes.* CBS.

Best Cinematography
(Regular news programs—Special events coverage)
• Delos Hall, "Clanking Savannah Blacksmith: On the Road with Charles Kuralt," *CBS Evening News with Walter Cronkite.* CBS.
(Documentary, magazine-type, or mini-documentary)
• Walter Dombrow, "Ballerina," *60 Minutes.* CBS.

Outstanding Achievement in Any Area of Creative Technical Crafts
• Philippe Cousteau, under-ice photography. *The Undersea World of Jacques Cousteau.* ABC.
• John Chambers and Tom Burman, make-up, "Struggle for Survival," *Primal Man.* ABC.
• Aggie Whelan, courtroom drawings. "The Mitchell-Stans Trial," *CBS Evening News with Walter Cronkite.* CBS.

Best Film Editing
(Regular news programs—Special events coverage)
• William J. Freeda, "Profile of Poverty in Appalachia," *NBC Nightly News.* NBC.
(Documentary, magazine-type, or mini-documentary)
• Ann Chegwidden, "The Baboons of Gombe," *Jane Goodall and the World of Animal Behavior.* ABC.

Best Video-Tape Editing
• Gary Anderson, *Paramount Presents ... ABC Wide World of Entertainment.* ABC.

Best Technical Direction and Electronic Camerawork
• Carl Schutzman, technical director. Joseph Schwartz, William Bell, cameramen, *60 Minutes.* CBS.

Best Film or Tape Sound Mixing
• Peter Pilafian, George E. Porter, Eddie J. Nelson, Robert L. Harman, "Journey to the Outer Limits," *National Geographic Society.* ABC.

Best Film Sound Editing
• Charles L. Campbell, Robert Cornett, Larry Carow, Larry Kaufman, Cohn Mouat, Don Warne, Frank R. White, "The Baboons of Gombe," *Jane Goodall and the World of Animal Behavior.* ABC.

Outstanding Achievement in Religious Programming
• Ken Lamkin, technical director, and Sam Drummy, Gary Stanton, Robert Haffield, cameramen. "Gift of Tears," *This is the Life.* Syndicated.

(There was no winner in news and documentary writing.)

INTERNATIONAL AWARD WINNERS
Non-fiction
• *Horizon: The Making of a Natural History Film.* British Broadcasting Corporation, London.

FICTION
• *La Cabina*. Television Espanola, Madrid.

INTERNATIONAL DIRECTORATE AWARD
• Charles Curran, president, European Broadcasting Union, Director-General, British Broadcasting Corporation.

SPECIAL AWARDS
OUTSTANDING ACHIEVEMENT IN ENGINEERING DEVELOPMENT
• Consolidated Video Systems, Inc. For the application of digital video technique to the Time Base Corrector.

• RCA. For its leading role in the development of the quadraplex video-tape cartridge equipment.
• John D. Silva for conceiving the telecopter. Golden West Broadcaster for realizing the telecopter.

NATIONAL AWARD FOR COMMUNITY SERVICE
• *Through the Looking Glass Darkly*, WKY-TV, Oklahoma City.

Mary Tyler Moore, Quite Contrary

The suspense of the 1975 Emmy telecast revolved around the final award to be given away — for best comedy series — and whether or not a longstanding injustice would at last be redressed when the winner was announced. Tension was even greater as the two legendary presenters needed time to compensate for the frailties of age in order to perform their duties. Groucho Marx was 95, ailing, and needed help getting to the podium. Once there, Lucille Ball, age 64, took over, but suddenly realized she had forgotten her eyeglasses and muttered to the audience, "I'm really in trouble." Within minutes, though, the good news was finally delivered to the thousands crowding the Hollywood Palladium and the millions watching at home: The winner was the longtime losing nominee *The Mary Tyler Moore Show*.

The Mary Tyler Moore Show had reaped numerous awards in the past, but it failed to win the top comedy show prize in the five years it was on the air. It was eclipsed time and again by *All in the Family* (which it had helped get on the CBS schedule by proving that the new form of realistic comedy shows could be popular) and then by the starkly funny *M*A*S*H* in 1974. But *MTM*'s victory was resounding this time around: Not only did it finally hold the top series award, the show now had a total of 21 Emmy Awards in all — the most of any series in prime-time history.

Its other awards went to the program's film editors and, like last year, to its writers and supporting star Cloris Leachman (who tied this time with Zohra Lampert of *Kojak* for giving the best single performance by a supporting actress in a

Ironically, Mary Tyler Moore lost the best actress prize to MTM Show *alum Valerie Harper for spinoff show* Rhoda.

comedy or drama series; Leachman also won a supporting performance prize for her work on *Cher*). Other *MTM* cast members Ed Asner and Betty White were honored for giving the best continuing performances by a supporting actor and actress and were so overjoyed that they showered each other with enough congratulatory kisses to cause *The New York Daily News* to wisecrack, "If we didn't know that both Ed and Betty are married [to other people], we'd say there was a romance in progress."

Of its nine nominations, *MTM* ended up with a total of seven prizes, but one of its two losses left a tarnish on the trophies it did take away. Worse, it was a loss that mirrored the show's sad fate when it was first up for Emmys after its premiere season. As *The New York Times* said in 1971, "Everyone on *The Mary Tyler Moore Show* seemed to win an award except Mary Tyler Moore." Moore lost that year and the following to *All in the Family*'s Jean Stapleton, then rallied to claim the prize over the next two years even though the second award also led to her winning the experimental "Super Emmy," which she opposed vehemently before it was introduced. (It was dropped after that year.) Now she was a loser again on her show's triumphant evening. Her consolation: The best actress statuette went to Valerie Harper, an alumna of her program who now had her own hit spin-off series, *Rhoda*. Upon accepting the award, Harper acknowledged Moore gratefully and "felt compelled to thank everybody profusely," noted the *L.A. Times*, including her analyst. "Another Emmy first," the *Times* noted.

MTM's sweep was so vast that it nearly shut out last year's comedy show winner *M*A*S*H*, which began the night with 11 nominations (compared to nine for *MTM*) and ended up with only one award — for director Gene

nations of the night was *QB VII*, a dramatization of the Leon Uris bestseller about the prosecution of Nazi war criminals that started out with 13 nods and ended up with six trophies, including ones for supporting stars Anthony Quayle and Juliet Mills.

Over the five years that *The Odd Couple* was on the air, Tony Randall lost the prize for best actor twice to costar Jack Klugman. This year the show was being shelved and Randall finally took the honors. "I sure am glad I won," he told the Palladium audience with a relieved grin, adding, "Now if I only had a job!"

Among limited series, *Columbo*'s Peter Falk was competing for best actor against only one other nominee — Dennis Weaver of *McCloud*. Falk was seated directly behind Weaver at the ceremony when his name was announced as the winner. He then leaned forward, tapped Weaver on the shoulder, and said, "Dennis, it came out heads."

In the drama category, Robert Blake was "a surprise winner," said *The Washington Post*, for his role as the maverick policeman *Baretta*. *The New York Daily News*, noted that Blake "laughed heartily when he won for his performance." Commenting on his thank-you remarks that followed, the *Post* added: "Blake's rambling speech ... seemed to be an admission that he is, as television producers know, a difficult actor."

Comedian Flip Wilson (center, as Geraldine) with best actress Valerie Harper of Rhoda *and best actor Tony Randall of* The Odd Couple.

Reynolds. The CBS movie *Queen of the Stardust Ballroom* had scored big in the TV ratings the previous February and tied *MTM* with nine Emmy nominations, but its only major award went to lead actress Maureen Stapleton, who portrayed a lonely widow who discovers romance, reluctantly, a second time around. The show with the most nomi-

Upstairs, Downstairs came back again as Outstanding Drama Series and also took awards for director Bill Bain and lead actress Jean Marsh, who played a downstairs maid in the ongoing saga of an uppercrust household in Edwardian England. The triumph of *Benjamin Franklin* as Outstanding Limited Series "restored some sanity by winning the Emmy ... over those overstuffed and undernourished *NBC Mystery Movies*," said *L.A. Times* columnist Dick Adler in a disparaging reference to *Columbo*. The Outstanding Special — Comedy or Drama turned out to be *The Law*, a documentary-style drama that was originally planned as a series but prevailed as an *NBC World Premiere Movie* about a public defender involved in the case of a football player tortured to death.

Love Among the Ruins had been written by James Costigan as a vehicle for veteran Broadway stars Alfred Lunt and Lynn Fontanne, but it was cast for television with Laurence Olivier and Katharine Hepburn when the Lunts grew frail in their later years. *Ruins* was a charming costume drama about an aging and eccentric British actress and the barrister, once her lover, who comes to her rescue in a lawsuit. Both past Oscar winners won Emmys for their effort, as did Costigan, director George Cukor, the film's costume designer, and art and set decorators. "How seriously the crew from *Love Among the Ruins* took producer Paul Keyes' admonition to keep all acceptance speeches down to 30 seconds," Adler wrote in the *Times*. "Hepburn, Olivier, Costigan, and Cukor even failed to show up to say anything."

Also noticeably missing on Emmys night was Johnny Carson, whose *Tonight Show* had been on the air since 1962, but failed ever to take a top trophy. Most awards-watchers agreed that the program was perennially placed in the wrong voting category, but its producers continued to submit it for the same award. This year it was again nominated as a variety or music series and an irate Carson pulled it from competition before the final Emmy ballot stage. The prize went instead to last year's victor, *The Carol Burnett Show*, which also won trophies for writing and direction.

ABC THEATRE

Katharine Hepburn and Sir Laurence Olivier stood in for Lynn Fontanne and Alfred Lunt in Love Among the Ruins.

The series award was accepted by Burnett's producer/husband Joe Hamilton who acknowledged the controversy and admonished the Palladium audience of TV leaders, saying, "Johnny Carson deserves an Emmy sometime."

DAYTIME AWARDS

"It was a stroke of pure genius," said *The New York Daily News*, to hold the daytime awards ceremony on a Hudson River Dayliner boat off Manhattan. The fete was broadcast nationally by ABC while "viewers were treated to some great shots of our skyline" and "winners and losers alike were literally up the river," added the *News*.

A new show that premiered just two years earlier as an alternative soap for younger viewers, *The Young and the Restless,* was named Outstanding Daytime Drama Series and also earned gold for its director Richard Dunlap. Both top acting honors went elsewhere, however — to *Days of Our Lives* stars Macdonald Carey, who played Dr. Tom Horton, the head of internal medicine at the show's town hospital, and Susan Flannery as his daughter-in-law (psychiatrist Laura Spencer). It was Carey's second Emmy in as many years.

Again the bulk of the prizes for dramas went to a segment of *ABC Afternoon Playbreak*. "The

The Tonight Show Starring Johnny Carson *had been on the air since 1962, but still hadn't won an Emmy.*

Girl Who Couldn't Lose," which starred Julie Kavner (Valerie Harper's sister on *Rhoda*) as a game show contestant who falls in love with one of her competitors, was named Outstanding Daytime Drama and won an Emmy for its director. *Playbreak*'s "Heart in Hiding" took two prizes — for star Kay Lenz and the show's writer.

All-time Emmys champ among performers, Dinah Shore, won five of her eventual eight awards for her variety shows in the 1950s. In 1974, she was up for another as host of a new 90-minute interview program that featured the amiable singer and her guests in an intimate living room setting. The host's award ended up going to Barbara Walters of *Today*, but *Dinah!* was nonetheless named best talk show. Also back on the air was the 1960s science fiction cult favorite *Star Trek*, which returned in the mid-1970s as a half-hour Saturday morning cartoon series incorporating the voices of the show's original stars. It was hailed as the Outstanding Children's Entertainment Series.

The big news in the game show competition surrounded *The Hollywood Squares*, which would dominate its category in future years. The hit NBC program based on the age-old game of tic-tac-toe had been on the air since 1966 but failed to win a program prize, despite nominations in 1969, 1972, and 1974. Host Peter Marshall was named best quiz show host in 1974, but it was one more year before the series itself would win the Emmy game. And in 1975, Marshall won, too.

NEWS & DOCUMENTARY AWARDS

After two promising years during which the news and documentary awards were given their own prime-time telecast, they were dropped entirely both on and off the air. CBS was scheduled to broadcast them this year, but refused to do so following complaints about a dull program in 1974 and suggestions that the nomination system had been in a state of "chaos."

L.A. Times columnist Cecil Smith mourned the loss, writing, "The Emmy competition seems to me meaningless without [the news and documentary awards] ... I'll always remember that when Seymour Berns was academy president in 1969, he felt the central focus of any Emmy telecast should be on those things television is proudest of — its window on the real world .... [Without them] it is, in Edwin Arlington Robinson's phrase, celebrating the flicker, not the flame."

1974–75

For prime-time and daytime entertainment programs telecast between March 18, 1974, and March 10, 1975. Prime-time awards broadcast on CBS on May 19, 1975, from the Hollywood Palladium. The second annual daytime awards were broadcast on ABC on May 15, 1975, from the decks of the Hudson River

Dayliner ship in New York Harbor. There were no news & documentary awards bestowed.

PRIME-TIME PROGRAM AWARDS
Outstanding Drama Series
• *Upstairs, Downstairs, Masterpiece Theatre.* Rex Firkin, executive producer.

John Hawkesworth, producer. PBS.
Kojak. Matthew Rapf, executive producer.
Jack Laird, James McAdams, producers.
CBS.
Police Story. Stanley Kallis, David Gerber,
executive producers. Chris Morgan,
producer. NBC.
The Streets of San Francisco. Quinn
Martin, executive producer. John Wilder,
William Robert Yates, producers. ABC.
The Waltons. Lee Rich, executive producer.
Robert L. Jacks, producer. CBS.

OUTSTANDING COMEDY SERIES
• *The Mary Tyler Moore Show*. James L.
Brooks, Allan Burns, executive producers.
Ed. Weinberger, Stan Daniels, producers.
CBS.
All in the Family. Don Nicholl, executive
producer. Michael Ross, Bernie West,
producers. CBS.
*M*A*S*H*. Gene Reynolds, Larry Gelbart,
producers. CBS.
Rhoda. James L. Brooks, Allan Burns,
executive producers. David Davis, Lorenzo
Music, producers. CBS.

OUTSTANDING LIMITED SERIES
• *Benjamin Franklin*. Lewis Freedman,
executive producer. George Lefferts,
Glenn Jordan, producers. CBS.
Columbo, NBC Sunday Mystery Movie.
Roland Kibbee, Dean Hargrove, executive
producers. Everett Chambers, Edward K.
Dodds, producers. NBC.
McCloud, NBC Sunday Mystery Movie.
Glen A. Larson, executive producer.
Michael Gleason, Ronald Satlof, producers.
NBC.

OUTSTANDING SPECIAL—DRAMA OR COMEDY
• *The Law, NBC World Premiere Movie*.
William Sackheim, producer. NBC.
Love Among the Ruins, ABC Theatre.
Allan Davis, producer. ABC.
The Missiles of October, ABC Theatre. Irv
Wilson, executive producer. Herbert
Brodkin, Buzz Berger, producers. ABC.
QB VII, ABC Theatre. Douglas S. Cramer,
producer. ABC.
Queen of the Stardust Ballroom. Robert W.
Christiansen, Rick Rosenberg, producers.
CBS.

OUTSTANDING SPECIAL— COMEDY-VARIETY OR MUSIC
• *An Evening with John Denver*. Jerry
Weintraub, executive producer. Al Rogers,
Rich Eustis, producers. John Denver, star.
ABC.
Lily. Irene Pinn, executive producer. Jane
Wagner, Lorne Michaels, producers. Lily
Tomlin, star. ABC.
*Shirley MacLaine: If They Could See Me
Now*. Bob Wells, producer. Shirley
MacLaine, star. CBS.

OUTSTANDING COMEDY-VARIETY OR MUSIC SERIES
• *The Carol Burnett Show*. Joe Hamilton,
executive producer. Ed Simmons,
producer. Carol Burnett, star. CBS.
Cher. George Schlatter, producer. Cher,
star. CBS.

OUTSTANDING CLASSICAL MUSIC PROGRAM
(Winner)
• "Profile in Music: Beverly Sills,"
Festival '75. Patricia Foy, producer.
Beverly Sills, star. PBS.

OUTSTANDING CHILDREN'S SPECIAL
(Winner)
• *Yes, Virginia, There is a Santa Claus*.
Burt Rosen, executive producer. Bill
Melendez, Mort Green, producers. ABC.

PERFORMANCE, DIRECTING, AND WRITING
OUTSTANDING LEAD ACTOR IN A DRAMA SERIES
• Robert Blake, *Baretta*. ABC.
Karl Malden, *The Streets of San
Francisco*. ABC.
Barry Newman, *Petrocelli*. NBC.
Telly Savalas, *Kojak*. CBS.

OUTSTANDING LEAD ACTRESS IN A DRAMA SERIES
• Jean Marsh, *Upstairs, Downstairs*,
Masterpiece Theatre. PBS.
Angie Dickinson, *Police Woman*. NBC.
Michael Learned, *The Waltons*. CBS.

OUTSTANDING LEAD ACTOR IN A COMEDY SERIES
• Tony Randall, *The Odd Couple*. ABC.
Alan Alda, *M*A*S*H*. CBS.
Jack Albertson, *Chico and the Man*. NBC.
Jack Klugman, *The Odd Couple*. ABC.
Carroll O'Connor, *All in the Family*. CBS.

Outstanding Lead Actress in a Comedy Series
• Valerie Harper, *Rhoda*. CBS.
Mary Tyler Moore, *The Mary Tyler Moore Show*. CBS.
Jean Stapleton, *All in the Family*. CBS.

Outstanding Lead Actor in a Limited Series
• Peter Falk, *Columbo, NBC Sunday Mystery Movie*. NBC.
Dennis Weaver, *McCloud, NBC Sunday Mystery Movie*. NBC.

Outstanding Lead Actress in a Limited Series
• Jessica Walter, *Amy Prentiss, NBC Sunday Mystery Movie*. NBC.
Susan Saint James, *McMillan and Wife, NBC Sunday Mystery Movie*. NBC.

Outstanding Lead Actor in a Special Program—Drama or Comedy
• Laurence Olivier, *Love Among the Ruins, ABC Theatre*. ABC.
Richard Chamberlain, *The Count of Monte Cristo, Bell System Family Theatre*. NBC.
William Devane, *The Missiles of October, ABC Theatre*. ABC.
Charles Durning, *Queen of the Stardust Ballroom*. CBS.
Henry Fonda, *IBM Presents Clarence Darrow*. NBC.

Outstanding Lead Actress in a Special Program—Drama or Comedy
• Katharine Hepburn, *Love Among the Ruins, ABC Theatre*. ABC.
Jill Clayburgh, *Hustling, ABC Saturday Night Movie*. ABC.
Elizabeth Montgomery, *The Legend of Lizzie Borden, Special World Premiere ABC Monday Night Movie*. ABC.
Diana Rigg, *In This House of Brede, General Electric Theater*. CBS.
Maureen Stapleton, *Queen of the Stardust Ballroom*. CBS.

Outstanding Supporting Actor in a Drama Series
• Will Geer, *The Waltons*. CBS.
J.D. Cannon, *McCloud, NBC Sunday Mystery Movie*. NBC.
Michael Douglas, *The Streets of San Francisco*. ABC.

Outstanding Supporting Actress in a Drama Series
• Ellen Corby, *The Waltons*. CBS.
Nancy Walker, *McMillan and Wife, NBC Sunday Mystery Movie*. NBC.
Angela Baddeley, *Upstairs, Downstairs, Masterpiece Theatre*. PBS.

Betty White and Ed Asner "showered each other with kisses" when they won.

Outstanding Supporting Actor in a Comedy Series
• Edward Asner, *The Mary Tyler Moore Show*. CBS.
Rob Reiner, *All in the Family*. CBS.
Ted Knight, *The Mary Tyler Moore Show*. CBS.
Gary Burghoff, *M*A*S*H*. CBS.
McLean Stevenson, *M*A*S*H*. CBS.

Outstanding Supporting Actress in a Comedy Series
• Betty White, *The Mary Tyler Moore Show*. CBS.
Julie Kavner, *Rhoda*. CBS.
Nancy Walker, *Rhoda*. CBS.
Loretta Swit, *M*A*S*H*. CBS.

Outstanding Single Performance by a Supporting Actor in a Comedy or Drama Series
• Patrick McGoohan, *Columbo, NBC Sunday Mystery Movie*. NBC.
Lew Ayres, *Kung Fu*. ABC.
Harold Gould, *Police Story*. NBC.
Harry Morgan, *M*A*S*H*. CBS.

Outstanding Single Performance by a Supporting Actress in a Comedy or Drama Series
(Tie)
• Cloris Leachman, *The Mary Tyler Moore Show*. CBS.
• Zohra Lampert, *Kojak*. CBS.
Shelley Winters, *McCloud, NBC Sunday Mystery Movie*. NBC.

Outstanding Single Performance by a Supporting Actor in a Comedy or Drama Special
• Anthony Quayle, *QB VII, ABC Theatre*. ABC.
Ralph Bellamy, *The Missiles of October, ABC Theatre*. ABC.
Jack Hawkins, *QB VII, ABC Theatre*. ABC.
Trevor Howard, *The Count of Monte Cristo, Bell System Family Theatre*. NBC.

Outstanding Single Performance by a Supporting Actress in a Comedy or Drama Special
• Juliet Mills, *QB VII, ABC Theatre*. ABC.
Eileen Heckart, *Wedding Band, ABC Theatre*. ABC.
Charlotte Rae, *Queen of the Stardust Ballroom*. CBS.
Lee Remick, *QB VII, ABC Theatre*. ABC.

Outstanding Continuing or Single Performance by a Supporting Actor in Variety or Music
• Jack Albertson, *Cher*. CBS.
Tim Conway, *The Carol Burnett Show*. CBS.
John Denver, *Doris Day Today*. CBS.

Outstanding Continuing or Single Performance by a Supporting Actress in Variety or Music
• Cloris Leachman, *Cher*. CBS.
Vicki Lawrence, *The Carol Burnett Show*. CBS.
Rita Moreno, *Out to Lunch*. ABC.

Outstanding Directing in a Drama Series
• Bill Bain, *Upstairs, Downstairs, Masterpiece Theatre*. PBS.
Harry Falk, *The Streets of San Francisco*. ABC.
David Friedkin, *Kojak*. CBS.
Glenn Jordan, *Benjamin Franklin*. CBS.
Telly Savalas, *Kojak*. CBS.

Outstanding Directing in a Comedy Series
• Gene Reynolds, *M*A*S*H*. CBS.
Alan Alda, *M*A*S*H*. CBS.
Hy Averback, *M*A*S*H*. CBS.

Outstanding Directing in a Special Program—Drama or Comedy
• George Cukor, *Love Among the Ruins, ABC Theatre*. ABC.
John Badham, *The Law, NBC World Premiere Movie*. NBC.
Sam O'Steen, *Queen of the Stardust Ballroom*. CBS.
Tom Gries, *QB VII, ABC Theatre*. ABC.
Anthony Page, *The Missiles of October, ABC Theatre*. ABC.

Outstanding Directing in a Comedy-Variety or Music Series
• Dave Powers, *The Carol Burnett Show*. CBS.
Art Fisher, *Cher*. CBS.

Outstanding Directing in a Comedy-Variety or Music Special
• Bill Davis, *An Evening with John Denver*. ABC.
Robert Scheerer, *Shirley MacLaine: If They Could See Me Now*. CBS.
Dwight Hemion, *Ann-Margret Olsson*. NBC.

Outstanding Writing in a Drama Series
• Howard Fast, *Benjamin Franklin*. CBS.
Robert Collins, *Police Story*. NBC.
Alfred Shaughnessy, *Upstairs, Downstairs, Masterpiece Theatre*. PBS.
Loring Mandel, *Benjamin Franklin*. CBS.
John Hawkesworth, *Upstairs, Downstairs, Masterpiece Theatre*. PBS.

Outstanding Writing in a Comedy Series
• Ed. Weinberger, Stan Daniels, *The Mary Tyler Moore Show*. CBS.
David Lloyd, *The Mary Tyler Moore Show*. CBS.
Norman Barasch, Carroll Moore, David Lloyd, Lorenzo Music, Allan Burns, James L. Brooks, David Davis, *Rhoda*. CBS.

OUTSTANDING WRITING IN A SPECIAL PROGRAM—DRAMA OR COMEDY—ORIGINAL TELEPLAY
• James Costigan, *Love Among the Ruins, ABC Theatre.* ABC.
Jerome Kass, *Queen of the Stardust Ballroom.* CBS.
Stanley R. Greenberg, *The Missiles of October, ABC Theatre.* ABC.
Fay Kanin, *Hustling, ABC Saturday Night Movie.* ABC.
Joel Oliansky, *The Law, NBC World Premiere Movie.* NBC.

OUTSTANDING WRITING IN A SPECIAL PROGRAM—DRAMA OR COMEDY—ADAPTATION
• David W. Rintels, *IBM Presents Clarence Darrow.* NBC.
Edward Anhalt, *QB VII, ABC Theatre.* ABC.

OUTSTANDING WRITING IN A COMEDY-VARIETY OR MUSIC SPECIAL
• Bob Wells, John Bradford, Cy Coleman, *Shirley MacLaine: If They Could See Me Now.* CBS.
Sybil Adelman, Barbara Gallagher, Gloria Banta, Pat Nardo, Stuart Birnbaum, Matt Neuman, Lorne Michaels, Marilyn Miller, Earl Pomerantz, Rosie Ruthchild, Lily Tomlin, Jane Wagner, *Lily.* ABC.

OUTSTANDING WRITING IN A COMEDY-VARIETY OR MUSIC SERIES
• Ed Simmons, Gary Belkin, Roger Beatty, Arnie Kogen, Bill Richmond, Gene Perret, Rudy DeLuca, Barry Levinson, Dick Clair, Jenna McMahon, *The Carol Burnett Show.* CBS.
Digby Wolfe, Don Reo, Alan Katz, Iris Rainer, David Panich, Ron Pearlman, Nick Arnold, John Boni, Ray Taylor, George Schlatter, *Cher.* CBS.

OTHER AWARD WINNERS
OUTSTANDING MUSIC COMPOSITION FOR A SERIES
(Dramatic underscore/Series program)
• Billy Goldenberg, *Benjamin Franklin.* CBS.

OUTSTANDING MUSIC COMPOSITION FOR A SPECIAL
(Dramatic underscore)
• Jerry Goldsmith, *QB VII, ABC Movie Special.* ABC.

OUTSTANDING ACHIEVEMENT IN CHOREOGRAPHY
• Marge Champion, *Queen of the Stardust Ballroom.* CBS.

OUTSTANDING ACHIEVEMENT IN ART DIRECTION OR SCENIC DESIGN
(Comedy, drama, or limited series)
• Charles Lisanby, art director. Robert Checchi, set director, *Benjamin Franklin.* CBS.

OUTSTANDING ART DIRECTION OR SCENIC DESIGN
(Comedy-variety series or special)
• Robert Kelly, art director. Robert Checchi, set decorator, *Cher.* CBS.

OUTSTANDING ART DIRECTION OR SCENIC DESIGN
(Dramatic feature/Made-for-TV film)
• Carmen Dillon, art director. Tessa Davies, set decorator, *Love Among the Ruins, ABC Theatre.* ABC.

OUTSTANDING GRAPHIC DESIGN AND TITLE SEQUENCES
• Phill Norman, *QB VII, ABC Theatre.* ABC.

OUTSTANDING CINEMATOGRAPHY FOR A SERIES
• Richard C. Glouner, *Columbo, NBC Sunday Mystery Movie.* NBC.

OUTSTANDING CINEMATOGRAPHY FOR A SPECIAL
• David M. Walsh, *Queen of the Stardust Ballroom.* CBS.

OUTSTANDING TECHNICAL DIRECTION AND ELECTRONIC CAMERA WORK
• Ernie Buttelman, technical director. Jim Angel, Jim Balden, Ron Brooks, Art LaCombe, cameramen, *The Missiles of October, ABC Theatre.* ABC.

OUTSTANDING FILM EDITING FOR A SERIES
(Comedy series)
• Douglas Hines, *The Mary Tyler Moore Show.* CBS.

OUTSTANDING FILM EDITING
(Dramatic feature/Made-for-TV film)
• John A. Martinelli, *The Legend of Lizzie Borden, ABC Monday Night Movie.* ABC.

Outstanding Video-Tape Editing
• Gary Anderson, Jim McElroy, *Judgment: The Court-Martial of Lieutenant William Calley, ABC Theatre.* ABC.

Outstanding Film Sound Editing
• Marvin I. Kosberg, Richard Burrow, Milton C. Burrow, Jack Milner, Ronald Ashcroft, James Ballas, Josef Von Stroheim, Jerry Rosenthal, William Andrews, Edward Sandlin, David Horton, Alvin Kajita, Tony Garber, Jeremy Hoenack, *QB VII, ABC Theatre.* ABC.

Outstanding Film or Tape Sound Mixing
• Marshall King, *The American Film Institute Salute to James Cagney.* CBS.

Outstanding Achievement in Lighting Direction
• John Freschi, *The Perry Como Christmas Show.* CBS.

THE AREAS
Each area has the possibility of multiple award winners, one winner, or none. Winners are listed.

Special Classification of Outstanding Program and Individual Achievement
• *The American Film Institute Salute to James Cagney.* George Stevens, Jr., executive producer. Paul W. Keyes, producer. CBS.
• Alistair Cooke, host, *Masterpiece Theatre.* PBS.

Outstanding Costume Design
• Guy Verhille, *The Legend of Lizzie Borden, ABC Monday Night Movie.* ABC.
Margaret Furse, *Love Among the Ruins, ABC Theatre.* ABC.

Outstanding Any Area of Creative Technical Crafts
• Edie Panda, hairstylist. *Benjamin Franklin.* CBS.
• Doug Nelson, Norm Schwartz, double system sound editing and synchronization for stereophonic broadcasting of television programs. *Wide World in Concert.* ABC.

(There were no winners in the fields of achievement in make-up or special musical material.)

DAYTIME AWARDS

Outstanding Daytime Drama Series
• *The Young and the Restless.* John J. Conboy, producer. William J. Bell, Lee Phillip Bell, creators. CBS.
Days of Our Lives. Betty Corday, executive producer. Ted Corday, Irna Phillips, Allan Chase, creators. Jack Herzberg, producer. NBC.
Another World. Paul Rauch, executive producer. Joe Rothenberger, Mary Bonner, producers. Irna Phillips, William J. Bell, creators. NBC.

Outstanding Daytime Drama Special
• "The Girl Who Couldn't Lose," *ABC Afternoon Playbreak.* Ira Barmak, executive producer. Lila Garrett, producer. ABC.
"The Last Bride of Salem," *ABC Afternoon Playbreak.* Robert Michael Lewis, executive producer. George Paris, producer. ABC.

Outstanding Actor in a Daytime Drama Series
• Macdonald Carey, *Days of Our Lives.* NBC.
John Beradino, *General Hospital.* ABC.
Bill Hayes, *Days of Our Lives.* NBC.

Outstanding Actress in a Daytime Drama Series
• Susan Flannery, *Days of Our Lives.* NBC.
Rachel Ames, *General Hospital.* ABC.
Susan Seaforth, *Days of Our Lives.* NBC.
Ruth Warrick, *All My Children.* ABC.

Outstanding Actor in a Daytime Drama Special
• Bradford Dillman, "The Last Bride of Salem," *ABC Afternoon Playbreak.* ABC.
Jack Carter, "The Girl Who Couldn't Lose," *ABC Afternoon Playbreak.* ABC.
Bert Convy, "Oh! Baby, Baby, Baby ..." *ABC Afternoon Playbreak.* ABC.

Outstanding Actress in a Daytime Drama Special
• Kay Lenz, "Heart in Hiding," *ABC Afternoon Playbreak.* ABC.
Diane Baker," Can I Save My Children?" *ABC Afternoon Playbreak.* ABC.
Julie Kavner, "The Girl Who Couldn't Lose," *ABC Afternoon Playbreak.* ABC.
Lois Nettleton, "The Last Bride of Salem," *ABC Afternoon Playbreak.* ABC.

NBC/GLOBE PHOTO

Days of Our Lives *champs Susan Flannery and Macdonald Carey at the boatride ceremony in New York Harbor.*

OUTSTANDING INDIVIDUAL DIRECTOR FOR A DAYTIME DRAMA SERIES
• Richard Dunlap, *The Young and the Restless.* CBS.
Ira Cirker, *Another World.* NBC.
Joseph Behar, *Days of Our Lives.* NBC.

OUTSTANDING INDIVIDUAL DIRECTOR FOR A DAYTIME SPECIAL PROGRAM
• Mort Lachman, "The Girl Who Couldn't Lose," *ABC Afternoon Playbreak.* ABC.
Walter C. Miller, "Can I Save My Children?" *ABC Afternoon Playbreak.* ABC.

OUTSTANDING WRITING FOR A DAYTIME DRAMA SERIES
• Harding Lemay, Tom King, Charles Kozloff, Jan Merlin, Douglas Marland, *Another World.* NBC.
William J. Bell, *The Young and the Restless.* CBS.
William J. Bell, Pat Falken Smith, Bill Rega, *Days of Our Lives.* NBC.

OUTSTANDING WRITING FOR A DAYTIME SPECIAL PROGRAM
• Audrey Davis Levin, "Heart in Hiding," *ABC Afternoon Playbreak.* ABC.
Ruth Brooks Flippen, "Oh! Baby, Baby, Baby ..." *ABC Afternoon Playbreak.* ABC.
Lila Garrett, Sanford Krinski, "The Girl Who Couldn't Lose," *ABC Afternoon Playbreak.* ABC.

OTHER DAYTIME AWARD WINNERS
OUTSTANDING GAME OR AUDIENCE PARTICIPATION SHOW
• *The Hollywood Squares.* Merrill Heatter, Bob Quigley, executive producers. Jay Redack, producer. NBC.

OUTSTANDING TALK, SERVICE, OR VARIETY SERIES
• *Dinah!* Henry Jaffe, Carolyn Raskin, executive producers. Fred Tatashore, producer. Syndicated.

OUTSTANDING ENTERTAINMENT CHILDREN'S SPECIAL
• *Harlequin, The CBS Festival of Lively Arts For Young People.* Edward Villella, executive producer. Gardner Compton, producer. CBS.

OUTSTANDING ENTERTAINMENT CHILDREN'S SERIES
• *Star Trek.* Lou Scheimer, Norm Prescott, producers. NBC.

OUTSTANDING HOST IN A GAME OR AUDIENCE PARTICIPATION SHOW
• Peter Marshall, *The Hollywood Squares.* NBC.

OUTSTANDING HOST OR HOSTESS IN A TALK, SERVICE, OR VARIETY SERIES
• Barbara Walters, *Today.* NBC.

OUTSTANDING INDIVIDUAL DIRECTOR FOR A GAME OR AUDIENCE PARTICIPATION SHOW
• Jerome Shaw, *The Hollywood Squares.* NBC.

OUTSTANDING INDIVIDUAL DIRECTOR FOR A DAYTIME VARIETY PROGRAM
• Glen Swanson, *Dinah!* Syndicated.

OUTSTANDING INDIVIDUAL ACHIEVEMENT IN CHILDREN'S PROGRAMMING (Area award)
• Elinor Bunin, graphic design and title sequences, *Funshine Saturday & Sunday.* ABC.

(There was no award in the area of outstanding individual achievement in daytime programming.)

SPORTS AWARD WINNERS
OUTSTANDING SPORTS PROGRAM
• *ABC's Wide World of Sports.* Roone Arledge, executive producer. Doug Wilson, Ned Steckel, Dennis Lewin, John Martin, Chet Forte, producers. ABC.

OUTSTANDING SPORTS EVENT
• *Jimmy Connors vs. Rod Laver Tennis Challenge.* Frank Chirkinian, executive producer. CBS.

OUTSTANDING SPORTS BROADCASTER
• Jim McKay, *ABC's Wide World of Sports.* ABC.

OUTSTANDING INDIVIDUAL ACHIEVEMENT IN SPORTS PROGRAMMING
• Gene Schwartz, technical director, *1974 World Series.* NBC.
• Herb Altman, film editor, *The Baseball World of Joe Garagiola.* NBC.
• Corey Leible, Len Basile, Jack Bennett, Lou Gerard, Ray Figelski, electronic cameramen, *1974 Stanley Cup Playoffs.* NBC.
• John Pumo, Charles D'Onofrio, Frank Florio, technical directors. George Klimcsak, Robert Kania, Harold Hoffmann, Herman Lang, George Drago, Walt Deniear, Stan Gould, Al Diamond, Charles Armstrong, Al Brantley, Sig Meyers, Frank McSpedon, George F. Naeder, James Murphy, James McCarthy, Vern Surphlis, Al Loreto, Gordon Sweeney, Jo Sidlo, William Hathaway, Gene Pescalek, Curly Fonorow, cameramen, *Masters Tournament.* CBS.

INTERNATIONAL AWARD WINNERS
FICTION
• *Mr. Axelford's Angel,* Yorkshire Television Limited, London.

NON-FICTION
• *Aquarius: Hello Dali!* London Weekend Television, London.

INTERNATIONAL DIRECTORATE AWARD
• Dr. Joseph Charyk, president, Communications Satellite Corporation

SPECIAL AWARDS
OUTSTANDING ACHIEVEMENT IN ENGINEERING DEVELOPMENT
• CBS. For spearheading the development and realization of the Electronic News Gathering System.
• Nippon Electric Co. For development of digital television Frame Synchronizers. **(Citation)**
• Society of Motion Picture and Television Engineers for the technical development of the Universal Tape Time Code.

NATIONAL AWARD FOR COMMUNITY SERVICE
• *The Willowbrook Case: The People vs. the State of New York.* WABC-TV, New York.

TRUSTEES AWARDS
• Elmer Lower, vice president, corporate affairs, ABC, Inc.
• Dr. Peter Goldman, president, Goldmark Laboratories, Stamford, Connecticut.

Sweet Mary's Revenge
(Or, Gremlins in the Mailroom)

Revenge may be sweet, as the phrase goes, but the sweet also get their revenge. Mary Tyler Moore proved the point this year when she finally pulled off a total sweep at the Emmys. In past years, she had won the best comic actress prize and her show had won best comedy series, but never in the same year. Now she had it all at once — and "ironically" so, noted *The Washington Post*, since "the producers of *The Mary Tyler Moore Show* have announced that the coming season will be its last on the air."

It was the second year in a row that *MTM* was named best comedy series, and this year the

MTM Show *cast members (clockwise from top left): Ted Knight, Ed Asner, Gavin MacLeod, Cloris Leachman, Moore, and Valerie Harper.*

prize was bestowed by, of all people, Dick Van Dyke, Moore's costar from the 1960s. Accepting the award, *MTM* producer and writer Allan Burns said, "I'd like to thank a lot of people at CBS, but unfortunately they're not there anymore."

It turned out to be Moore's night in every respect. In addition to being the evening's comedy awards champ, she presided regally over the Emmycast proceedings at the Shubert Theatre in Los Angeles alongside her cohost, country-pop singer John Denver (who was reprimanded in the press the next day for saying "Far out!" far too often). When Moore was revealed as the winner of the best actress prize, she seemed genuinely surprised and said in her acceptance remarks, "This is like a pat on the back or a kiss on the cheek. The unusual thing about winning is that the more Emmys I have, the more important they become.

You might think I would become careless, but that's not true. I keep thinking I've done it all, and then suddenly there's another Emmy. Then I think I've got to do better and set my sights higher. It's a circle that makes you work harder instead of less."

Costar Ted Knight won the supporting actor's trophy and also seemed surprised. He told the audience, "I didn't expect to win. I came for the show." Betty White reprised her victory of last year and managed, noted *The New York Times*, to avoid "the usual monotony of thanking mom, dad and the family dog" by being "absolutely adorable as she sweetly thanked the 'evil, wonderful, nasty' business of television."

The writing honors went to David Lloyd for penning what may be the show's single most famous episode, "Chuckles Bites the Dust." At Minneapolis's fictitious WJM-TV station, where Moore and costars were employed on *MTM*, Chuckles was the station's kiddie-show clown who one day, dressed as a peanut, was shucked to death by an elephant.

MTM performed so well in part because of what *The Chicago Tribune* called "a procedural foul-up" with the mail that involved some of the show's longtime competitors. More than 50 potential nominees, including past acting winners Carroll O'Connor, Jean Stapleton, and Robert Blake, weren't nominated this year because their ballots didn't reach the academy by the March 19th deadline. Instead, they arrived six weeks late, stamped "Found in Supposedly Empty Equipment," and were therefore not eligible to be considered in the voting tally. The ballots had been posted in the mailroom at L.A. TV station KTTV, where Norman Lear also had his production offices, but they were put in a mailbox that was never fully emptied.

MTM costar Ed Asner lost this year in the supporting category to Ted Knight, but he took home a statuette for what the *L.A. Times* called his "powerful portrayal" of a tyrannical father in *Rich Man, Poor Man*, the 12-hour, eight-part, $6-million TV adaptation of the best-selling novel by Irwin Shaw about the contrasting fortunes of Asner's two on-screen sons. Asner is famous for being a tough character off screen and for playing a crusty one on *MTM*, so he said jokingly in his acceptance speech, "It didn't take much acting to play that part" and then thanked "the U.S. Postal Service for possibly eliminating other competition."

"The mini-series has arrived!" *The New York Daily News* proclaimed when *Rich Man, Poor Man* headed into the Emmy Awards with a record 23 nods, or, as the *News* said, wryly, "nominations for everybody but the guy who swept the set." *Rich Man* ended up a rel-atively poor winner, though, with only four golden trophies at night's end — Asner's, and awards for its director, its music composer, and supporting actress Fionnula Flanagan. "Miss Flanagan brought her Irish beauty to the stage in eloquent thanks," said the *L.A. Times*, and used her allotted acceptance time to correct an earlier mispronunciation of her first name. It's "Fionnula," she told the audience, "as in 'vanilla.'"

Rich Man was upstaged by *Upstairs, Downstairs* in the category of best limited series, a source of major controversy. Some thought it was deserving; others whined. *The New York Times* insisted, "*Upstairs, Downstairs* is a good series, but the third set of 13 installments of the British production did not really deserve any major awards." It ended up with only one other — for supporting actor Gordon Jackson's performance as "the perfect butler," according to the *L.A. Times*.

Upstairs, Downstairs was also controversial because it was a victim of what the *L.A. Times* called an act of category gerrymandering. TV columnist Cecil Smith wrote: "Ah, the backstage maneuvering that must have gone on to move *Upstairs, Downstairs* from best drama series, where it belongs, to best limited series, where it doesn't. Meanwhile *Columbo* was being shifted from best limited series, where it belongs, to best drama series, where it doesn't. You see, *Upstairs, Downstairs* has won the best drama series Emmy for the last two years and we can't have that now, can we? Emmys going to Britain!"

> **Dozens of people weren't nominated because of a "procedural foul-up" with the mail.**

Edward Herrmann and Jane Alexander in Eleanor and Franklin, *the made-for-TV movie with most awards: eleven.*

Columbo didn't win best drama series, but it did earn a fourth Emmy for actor Peter Falk, his third as the proud owner of the world's most famous wrinkled trench coat. The drama series award ended up going to what the *L.A. Times* called "the most consistently high-quality weekly program on the air," adding, "the victory of *Police Story* as outstanding drama series almost justified the arbitrary relegation of *Upstairs, Downstairs* to its limited category." *Police Story* competed against three other cop shows (*Columbo, Baretta*, and *The Streets of San Francisco*) but pulled rank because of its daring realism in portraying the jobs of L.A. law enforcement, as perceived — and experienced — by cop-turned-best-selling-novelist Joseph Wambaugh.

History was made at the Emmy's show with a second sweep victory of the night, one surpassing even the impressive romp of *MTM*. The David Susskind production of *Eleanor and Franklin* was a two-part, four-hour ABC special based on the Pulitzer Prize–winning biography of the Roosevelts by Joseph Lash. It began the night with 16 nominations and ended up with 11 awards, a record for the most Emmys won by a movie-of-the-week.

Eleanor and Franklin was named Outstanding Special — Drama or Comedy and also earned statuettes for its screenwriter James Costigan (who won an Emmy last year for *Love Among the Ruins)* and for director Daniel Petrie, "long overdue but nonetheless welcome honors," said the *L.A. Times*. Other prizes were bestowed for its costume design, make-up, cinematography, film editing, sound mixing, hair styling, and its art direction/set decoration. Its only acting trophy went to supporting actress Rosemary Murphy for her portrayal of Sara Delano Roosevelt.

The *L.A. Times* had warned before the Emmycast began, "The acting competitions should be a bear this year." The paper was proved right when both early favorites to win (Edward Herrmann as Franklin Roosevelt and Jane Alexander as Eleanor) were dealt upsets.

The best acting laurels for a drama or comedy special went instead to Anthony Hopkins for his performance as convicted child-napper Bruno Hauptmann in *The Lindbergh Kidnapping Case* and to Susan Clark as superstar athlete Babe Didrikson Zaharias in *Babe. The New York Daily News* was among those who cried foul: "Both men [Herrman and Hopkins] are deserving, but Herrmann, a Tony winner for *Miss Warren's Profession*, was so outstanding as FDR we don't see how he could possibly be overlooked ... [and] nobody can come close to Miss Alexander's magnificent portrait of Eleanor Roosevelt."

Other top acting awards went to Hal Holbrook for playing the lead in the six-part series *Sandburg's Lincoln* ("the first surprise of the night," said the *L.A. Times*) and to Rosemary Harris for portraying the French female novelist George Sand in *Notorious Woman* on *Masterpiece Theatre*.

Michael Learned won her third and last prize for best actress in a drama series for playing the mother on *The Waltons*, and last year's Emmy-winner for the *Cher* show, Jack Albertson, returned to be named best actor in a comedy series for *Chico and the Man* in which he played the curmudgeonly "Man" (named Ed Brown) to Freddie Prinze's "Chico" Rodriguez, both of whom worked in a auto-repair garage owned by Brown Albertson accepted the statuette saying, "It's fitting that I should win this, because I've been doing straight lines for a 21-year-old Puerto Rican kid for two years and I ought to get something for that." Their association would end tragically less than one year later when Prinze, who had been battling Quaalude addiction in private life, committed suicide with a pistol. Albertson read the eulogy at his funeral.

"*Saturday Night* won the big money," reported the *L.A. Times*, "as best variety show of the year, presented by Milton Berle." "It was the winners from this series that added the only real comedy touch to the telecast," added *The New York Daily News*. "Producer Lorne Michaels thanked New York 'for providing the rejection and alienation that keeps the comedy spirit alive.'"

NBC's Saturday Night took four awards in all, including one for director Dave Wilson and another for its writing team. "Not since the days of *Laugh-In* was there such a stampede of writers" storming the stage, noted the *L.A. Times*, "including one lass who said, 'I think my deodorant just failed.'" Also among the writers was program star Chevy Chase, who won a second trophy for appearing in such supporting roles as the show's irreverent newscaster. When accepting his acting prize, Chase took one of his signature pratfalls, thanked the late Ernie Kovacs for inspiration, and added, "This is totally expected on my part."

"Vicki Lawrence broke the *Saturday Night* hold on the awards with a win for her work on *The Carol Burnett Show*," the *L.A. Times* said. *Burnett* also won prizes for writing and music. "The awards for the best comedy variety special were spread around," the *L.A. Times* added. "Shirley MacLaine's *Gypsy in My Soul* won the award for the show, but the writers of the Lily Tomlin special won the writing award and director Dwight Hemion took the directing award for the Steve Lawrence-Eydie Gorme special." Tomlin was among the victorious writers of her own show and accepted her third Emmy by offering a whimsical insight: "Winning is much higher than losing is low."

Last year Johnny Carson withdrew his *Tonight Show* from competition as best variety series after suffering a long run of embarrassing losses. The problem, many Emmy watchers said, was that it had been competing in the wrong category and was not really a variety program. This year it was placed in the area of Special Classification of Outstanding Program Achievement and at last it took high honors. "Long overdue!" cried the *L.A. Times*. *Bicentennial Minutes*, commercial-length shorts celebrating the nation's 200-year history, and the pilot show of the soap opera spoof *Mary Hartman, Mary Hartman* were likewise acknowledged.

Again this year, there were no news and documentary awards.

DAYTIME AWARDS

It was the third year that the daytime awards had their own separate ceremony, which was broadcast on CBS from the Vivian Beaumont Theater at Lincoln Center in New York, with Bob Barker presiding as host. *Another World*, TV's second-highest-rated soap opera, was named Outstanding Daytime Drama Series. The soap was once described by its creator Irna Phillips as actually an exploration of two worlds, "the world of events we live in and the world of feelings and dreams that we strive for," the program was a pioneer of its genre for being the first to expand to a full, one-hour broadcast in 1975. Soon afterward, its competition followed suit.

The other prizes for drama were spread around among its daytime rivals: directing honors went to *One Life to Live* and the award for writing to *Days of Our Lives*. The actor's trophy went to Larry Haines who joined *Search for Tomorrow* as the character Stu Bergman soon after it went on the air in the early 1950s. He eventually became the show's second-longest-running continuous player, after actress Mary Stuart. As Maeve Ryan, mistress of the Manhattan tavern *Ryan's Hope*, Helen Gallagher took her first of two Emmys in a row as best actress.

> *"If Dinah Shore wins any more Emmys, her house will sink."*

The NBC series *First Ladies' Diaries,* which dramatized the private lives of the wives of America's presidents, swept the ceremony with seven statuettes, including one as Outstanding Daytime Drama Special for its episode on Edith Wilson, who made many of the nation's executive decisions after her husband, Woodrow, fell ill during his second term. The same segment took laurels for its director Nicholas Havings, writer Audrey Davis Levine, and star Elizabeth Hubbard, who had won an Emmy two years earlier as best actress in *The Doctors.* In a tie vote, the series also won two awards for best actor: Gerald Gordon for his portrayal of Andrew Jackson in the Rachel Jackson episode and James Luisi as George Washington in the Martha Washington segment. Due to a miscue backstage at the telecast, however, only Gordon received his statuette on the air.

Dinah! returned as the best talk show, although this time, unlike last year, with accompanying honors for hostess Dinah Shore as well as trophies for its director (who did win last year) and its art director and set decorator (who didn't). The *L.A. Times* noted, "It was once said that if [Shore] wins any more Emmys her house will sink." Now her latest win brought her career total to eight — the most won by any performer in Emmy Awards history.

Sesame Street's Muppets were singled out for Outstanding Individual Achievement. Game show prizes went to *The $20,000 Pyramid*, which was named Outstanding Daytime Game or Audience Participation Show and won a statuette for direction, too; *Password* emcee Allen Ludden snagged the best host honor. *Password* had just been dropped by ABC, but would reappear in 1979 on NBC.

The Outstanding Daytime Informational Children's Special award went, strangely, to a program that had been aired in prime time: *Happy Anniversary, Charlie Brown* was a poignant tribute to the Peanuts gang on their 25th birthday. NBC's *Go,* earlier winner of the year's Peabody Award, was named Outstanding Informational Children's Series, while other honors went to *Grammar Rock, Big Blue Marble,* and *Danny Kaye's Look-In at the Metropolitan Opera.*

SPORTS AWARDS

NBC's coverage of the 1975 World Series was named best live sports special while virtually all other trophies went to ABC: for *NFL Monday Night Football* (Outstanding Live Sports

Series), *ABC's Wide World of Sports* (best edited sports series), and four statuettes for its presentation of *The XII Winter Olympics*, which tied with *Triumph and Tragedy ... The Olympic Experience* for best edited sports special. The *L.A. Herald Examiner* described their producer, "Redheaded Roone" Arledge, as "perspiring profusely" when he accepted the gold, calling special attention to his team's Olympics work: "We all work so hard to win and I feel like a father figure to all that gang who helps. We've created personalities and made a supershow of the Olympics. We developed it when no one else wanted it and now that it is popular, everybody else wants it. I'm proud of our work."

ABC's Jim McKay was named outstanding personality (his fifth sports Emmy) and said that he felt all the awards to ABC sports were "richly deserved."

"Sports have been a regular part of the Emmy derby for only nine years," wrote *Sports Illustrated*. "With some overhauling they could help elevate Emmy's overall prestige." The sports presentation was elaborate this year and included a documentary wrapup, narrated by O.J. Simpson, of some of the year's most dramatic footage. But *SI* wanted still more. It now joined the *L.A. Times* and other Emmy watchers in calling for a separate sports awards program, preferably aired on TV.

WITHIN THE ACADEMY: "THE WAR" BEGINS

The inner politics of the academy became a serious issue this year when the decades-old rivalry between New York and Los Angeles heated up, ultimately tearing the academy in two.

By 1976, Hollywood clearly emerged over New York as capital of the country's entertainment industry and the members of its local TV academy chapter resented the fact that N.A.T.A.S. members in other chapters less involved in national programming had an equal vote in determining Emmy winners. "We felt here in Hollywood that these people in Dayton and other cities were not in our business," says Larry Stewart, former president of the Hollywood chapter. "They were in the broadcasting business, yes, but not in the manufacture of television programs on a national scale."

In the meantime, a separate battle was being waged over the election of the academy's president, a position due to be filled soon after the 1976 prime-time awards ceremony. Electioneering began early with the Hollywood contingent backing incumbent executive director (and past president) Robert Lewine, who had been on the job since the early 1970s when he was virtually drafted to rescue the academy at a time of fiscal and other crises. Lewine succeeded brilliantly at his task, but dealt a humiliating blow to New Yorkers when he closed the academy's national office in Manhattan while he was busy shoring up other N.A.T.A.S. business. New Yorkers and members of the academy's other non-Hollywood chapters formed a coalition and decided to fight back by calling for N.A.T.A.S. chairman and former New York chapter president John Cannon to become the academy's leader. In late 1975, the board of trustees refused to renew Lewine's contract and what's now become known in Emmy circles as "the war" had officially begun.

On May 18, 1976, one day after the prime-time broadcast, the Hollywood chapter filed a lawsuit demanding the dissolution of the TV academy and announced its intention to form a new, separate, national organization. Its differences with N.A.T.A.S., it said, were "irreconcilable."

For prime-time and daytime entertainment programs telecast between March 11, 1975, and March 15, 1976. Prime-time awards broadcast on ABC on May 17, 1976, from the Shubert Theater in Los Angeles. The creative arts awards were given out on May 15 at Los Angeles's Beverly Wilshire Hotel. The third annual daytime awards were broadcast on CBS from the Vivian Beaumont Theater at Lincoln Center in New York on May 11, 1976. There were no news & documentary awards bestowed again this year.

PRIME-TIME PROGRAM AWARDS

OUTSTANDING DRAMA SERIES

• *Police Story*. David Gerber, Stanley Kallis, executive producers. Liam O'Brien, Carl Pingitore, producers. NBC.
Baretta. Bernard L. Kowalski, executive producer. Jo Swerling, Jr., Robert Harris, Howie Horwitz, Robert Lewine, producers. ABC.
Columbo, NBC Sunday Mystery Movie. Everett Chambers, producer. NBC.
The Streets of San Francisco. Quinn Martin, executive producer. William Robert Yates, producer. ABC.

OUTSTANDING COMEDY SERIES

• *The Mary Tyler Moore Show*. James L. Brooks, Allan Burns, executive producers. Ed. Weinberger, Stan Daniels, producers. CBS.
All in the Family. Hal Kanter, Norman Lear, Woody Kling, executive producers. Lou Derman, Bill Davenport, producers. CBS.
*M*A*S*H*. Gene Reynolds, Larry Gelbart, producers. CBS.
Welcome Back, Kotter. James Komack, executive producer. Alan Sacks, George Yanok, Eric Cohen, producers. ABC.
Barney Miller. Danny Arnold, executive producer. Chris Hayward, Arne Sultan, producers. ABC.

OUTSTANDING LIMITED SERIES

• *Upstairs, Downstairs, Masterpiece Theatre*. Rex Firkin, executive producer. John Hawkesworth, producer. PBS.
Jennie: Lady Randolph Churchill, Great Performances. Stella Richman, executive producer. Andrew Brown, producer. PBS.
Rich Man, Poor Man. Harve Bennett, executive producer. Jon Epstein, producer. ABC.
The Adams Chronicles. Jac Venza, executive producer. Virginia Kassel, series producer. Paul Bogart, Robert Costello, James Cellan-Jones, Fred Coe, producers. PBS.
The Law. William Sackheim, producer. NBC.

OUTSTANDING SPECIAL— DRAMA OR COMEDY

• *Eleanor and Franklin, ABC Theatre*. David Susskind, executive producer. Harry Sherman, Audrey Maas, producers. ABC.
Babe. Norman Felton, Stanley Rubin, producers. CBS.
A Moon for the Misbegotten, ABC Theatre. David Susskind, Audrey Maas, producers. ABC.
Fear on Trial. Alan Landsburg, Larry Savadove, executive producers. Stanley Chase, producer. CBS.
The Lindbergh Kidnapping Case, NBC Thursday Night at the Movies. David Gerber, executive producer. Buzz Kulik, producer. NBC.

OUTSTANDING COMEDY-VARIETY OR MUSIC SERIES

• *NBC's Saturday Night*. Lorne Michaels, producer. NBC.
The Carol Burnett Show. Joe Hamilton, executive producer. Ed Simmons, producer. Carol Burnett, star. CBS.

OUTSTANDING COMEDY-VARIETY OR MUSIC SPECIAL

• *Gypsy in My Soul*. William O. Harback executive producer. Cy Coleman, Fred Ebb, producers. Shirley MacLaine, star. CBS.
The Monty Python Show, Wide World: Special. Ian McNaughton, producer. ABC.
John Denver Rocky Mountain Christmas. Jerry Weintraub, executive producer. Al Rogers, Rich Eustis, producers. John Denver, star. ABC.
Steve and Eydie: Our Love is Here to Stay. Gary Smith, executive producer. Dwight Hemion, producer. Steve Lawrence, Eydie Gorme, stars. CBS.
Lily Tomlin. Irene Pinn, executive producer. Jane Wagner, Lorne Michaels, producers. Lily Tomlin, star. ABC.

Outstanding Classical Music Program
(Winner)
• "Bernstein and the New York Philharmonic," *Great Performances*. Klaus Hallig, Harry Kraut, executive producers. David Griffiths, producer. Leonard Bernstein, star. PBS.

Outstanding Children's Special
(Winner)
• *Huckleberry Finn*. Steven North, producer. ABC.

PERFORMANCE, DIRECTING, AND WRITING
Outstanding Lead Actor
in a Drama Series
• Peter Falk, *Columbo, NBC Sunday Mystery Movie*. NBC.
James Garner, *The Rockford Files*. NBC.
Karl Malden, *The Streets of San Francisco*. ABC.

Outstanding Lead Actress
in a Drama Series
• Michael Learned, *The Waltons*. CBS.
Angie Dickinson, *Police Woman*. NBC.
Anne Meara, *Kate McShane*. CBS.
Brenda Vaccaro, *Sara*. CBS.

Outstanding Lead Actor
in a Comedy Series
• Jack Albertson, *Chico and the Man*. NBC.
Alan Alda, *M*A*S*H*. CBS.
Hal Linden, *Barney Miller*. ABC.
Henry Winkler, *Happy Days*. ABC.

Outstanding Lead Actress
in a Comedy Series
• Mary Tyler Moore, *The Mary Tyler Moore Show*. CBS.
Beatrice Arthur, *Maude*. CBS.
Lee Grant, *Fay*. NBC.
Valerie Harper, *Rhoda*. CBS.
Cloris Leachman, *Phyllis*. CBS.

Outstanding Lead Actor for a
Single Appearance
in a Drama or Comedy Series
• Edward Asner, *Rich Man, Poor Man*. ABC.
Bill Bixby, *The Streets of San Francisco*. ABC.
Tony Musante, *Medical Story*. NBC.
Robert Reed, *Medical Center*. CBS.

Outstanding Lead Actress
for a Single Appearance
in a Drama or Comedy Series
• Kathryn Walker, *The Adams Chronicles*. PBS.
Helen Hayes, *Hawaii Five-0*. CBS.
Sheree North, *Marcus Welby, M.D.* ABC.
Pamela Payton-Wright, *The Adams Chronicles*. PBS.
Martha Raye, *McMillan and Wife, NBC Sunday Mystery Movie*. NBC.

Outstanding Lead Actor
in a Limited Series
• Hal Holbrook, *Sandburg's Lincoln*. NBC.
George Grizzard, *The Adams Chronicles*. PBS.
Nick Nolte, *Rich Man, Poor Man*. ABC.
Peter Strauss, *Rich Man, Poor Man*. ABC.

Outstanding Lead Actress
in a Limited Series
• Rosemary Harris, *Notorious Woman, Masterpiece Theatre*. PBS.
Lee Remick, *Jennie: Lady Randolph Churchill, Great Performances*. PBS.
Susan Blakely, *Rich Man, Poor Man*. ABC.
Jean Marsh, *Upstairs, Downstairs, Masterpiece Theatre*. PBS.

Outstanding Lead Actor
in a Drama or Comedy Special
• Anthony Hopkins, *The Lindbergh Kidnapping Case, NBC Thursday Night at the Movies*. NBC.
William Devane, *Fear on Trial*. CBS.
Edward Herrmann, *Eleanor and Franklin, ABC Theatre*. ABC.
Jack Lemmon, *The Entertainer*. NBC.
Jason Robards, *A Moon for the Misbegotten, ABC Theatre*. ABC.

Outstanding Lead Actress
in a Drama or Comedy Special
• Susan Clark, *Babe*. CBS.
Jane Alexander, *Eleanor and Franklin, ABC Theatre*. ABC.
Colleen Dewhurst, *A Moon for the Misbegotten, ABC Theatre*. ABC.
Sada Thompson, *The Entertainer*. NBC.

Outstanding Supporting Actor
in a Drama Series
• Anthony Zerbe, *Harry O*. ABC.
Michael Douglas, *The Streets of San Francisco*. ABC.
Will Geer, *The Waltons*. CBS.

Ray Milland, *Rich Man, Poor Man.* ABC.
Robert Reed, *Rich Man, Poor Man.* ABC.

**OUTSTANDING SUPPORTING ACTRESS
IN A DRAMA SERIES**
• Ellen Corby, *The Waltons.* CBS.
Angela Baddeley, *Upstairs, Downstairs, Masterpiece Theatre.* PBS.
Susan Howard, *Petrocelli.* NBC.
Dorothy McGuire, *Rich Man, Poor Man.* ABC.
Sada Thompson, *Sandburg's Lincoln.* NBC.

**OUTSTANDING SUPPORTING ACTOR
IN A COMEDY SERIES**
• Ted Knight, *The Mary Tyler Moore Show.* CBS.
Edward Asner, *The Mary Tyler Moore Show.* CBS.
Gary R. Burghoff, *M*A*S*H.* CBS.
Harry Morgan, *M*A*S*H.* CBS.
Abe Vigoda, *Barney Miller.* ABC.

**OUTSTANDING SUPPORTING ACTRESS
IN A COMEDY SERIES**
• Betty White, *The Mary Tyler Moore Show.* CBS.
Georgia Engel, *The Mary Tyler Moore Show.* CBS.
Julie Kavner, *Rhoda.* CBS.
Loretta Swit, *M*A*S*H.* CBS.
Nancy Walker, *Rhoda.* CBS.

**OUTSTANDING SINGLE PERFORMANCE
BY A SUPPORTING ACTOR IN A COMEDY
OR DRAMA SERIES**
• Gordon Jackson, *Upstairs, Downstairs, Masterpiece Theatre.* PBS.
Bill Bixby, *Rich Man, Poor Man.* ABC.
Roscoe Lee Browne, *Barney Miller.* ABC.
Norman Fell, *Rich Man, Poor Man.* ABC.
Van Johnson, *Rich Man, Poor Man.* ABC.

**OUTSTANDING SINGLE PERFORMANCE
BY A SUPPORTING ACTRESS IN A COMEDY
OR DRAMA SERIES**
• Fionnula Flanagan, *Rich Man, Poor Man.* ABC.
Kim Darby, *Rich Man, Poor Man.* ABC.
Ruth Gordon, *Rhoda.* CBS.
Eileen Heckart, *The Mary Tyler Moore Show.* CBS.
Kay Lenz, *Rich Man, Poor Man.* ABC.

**OUTSTANDING SINGLE PERFORMANCE
BY A SUPPORTING ACTOR IN A COMEDY
OR DRAMA SPECIAL**
• Ed Flanders, *A Moon for the*

Misbegotten, ABC Theatre. ABC.
Ray Bolger, *The Entertainer.* NBC.
Art Carney, *Katherine, ABC Sunday Night Movie.* ABC.

**OUTSTANDING SINGLE PERFORMANCE
BY A SUPPORTING ACTRESS IN A COMEDY
OR DRAMA SPECIAL**
• Rosemary Murphy, *Eleanor and Franklin, ABC Theatre.* ABC.
Lois Nettleton, *Fear on Trial.* CBS.
Lilia Skala, *Eleanor and Franklin, ABC Theatre.* ABC
Irene Tedrow, *Eleanor and Franklin, ABC Theatre.* ABC.

Saturday Night *winner Chevy Chase: "This is totally expected on my part."*

**OUTSTANDING CONTINUING OR SINGLE
PERFORMANCE BY A SUPPORTING ACTOR
IN VARIETY OR MUSIC**
• Chevy Chase, *NBC's Saturday Night.* NBC.
Tim Conway, *The Carol Burnett Show.* CBS.
Harvey Korman, *The Carol Burnett Show.* CBS.

**OUTSTANDING CONTINUING OR SINGLE
PERFORMANCE BY A SUPPORTING
ACTRESS IN VARIETY OR MUSIC**
• Vicki Lawrence, *The Carol Burnett Show.* CBS.
Cloris Leachman, *Telly ... Who Loves Ya, Baby?* CBS.

**OUTSTANDING DIRECTING
IN A DRAMA SERIES**
• David Greene, *Rich Man, Poor Man.* ABC.

1975–76

Fielder Cook, *Beacon Hill*. CBS.
Christopher Hodson, *Upstairs,*
Downstairs, Masterpiece Theatre. PBS.
James Cellan Jones, *Jennie: Lady Randolph*
Churchill, Great Performances. PBS.
Boris Sagal, *Rich Man, Poor Man*. ABC.
George Schaefer, *Sandburg's Lincoln*.
NBC.

OUTSTANDING DIRECTING
IN A COMEDY SERIES
• Gene Reynolds, *M*A*S*H*. CBS.
Alan Alda, *M*A*S*H*. CBS.
Hal Cooper, *Maude*. CBS.
Joan Darling, *The Mary Tyler Moore*
Show. CBS.

OUTSTANDING DIRECTING
IN A SPECIAL PROGRAM—
DRAMA OR COMEDY
• Daniel Petrie, *Eleanor and Franklin*,
ABC Theatre. ABC.
Lamont Johnson, *Fear on Trial*. CBS.
Buzz Kulik, *Babe*. CBS.
Jose Quintero, Gordon Rigsby, *A Moon for*
the Misbegotten, ABC Theatre. ABC.

OUTSTANDING DIRECTING
IN A COMEDY-VARIETY OR MUSIC SERIES
• Dave Wilson, *NBC's Saturday Night*.
NBC.
Tim Kiley, *The Sonny and Cher Show*.
CBS.
Dave Powers, *The Carol Burnett Show*.
CBS.

OUTSTANDING DIRECTING IN A COMEDY-
VARIETY OR MUSIC SPECIAL
• Dwight Hemion, *Steve and Eydie:*
Our Love is Here to Stay. CBS.
Tony Charmoli, *Mitzi ... Roarin' in*
the '20s. CBS.
Bill Davis, *John Denver Rocky Mountain*
Christmas. ABC.

OUTSTANDING WRITING
IN A DRAMA SERIES
• Sherman Yellen, *The Adams Chronicles*.
PBS.
Dean Riesner, *Rich Man, Poor Man*. ABC.
Julian Mitchell, *Jennie: Lady Randolph*
Churchill, Great Performances. PBS.
Joel Oliansky, *The Law*. NBC.
Alfred Shaughnessy, *Upstairs, Downstairs*,
Masterpiece Theatre. PBS.

OUTSTANDING WRITING
IN A COMEDY SERIES
• David Lloyd, *The Mary Tyler Moore*
Show. CBS.
Danny Arnold, Chris Hayward, *Barney*
Miller. ABC.
Jay Folb, *Maude*. CBS.
Larry Gelbart, Simon Muntner, *M*A*S*H*.
CBS.
Larry Gelbart, Gene Reynolds, *M*A*S*H*.
CBS.

OUTSTANDING WRITING IN A SPECIAL
PROGRAM—DRAMA OR COMEDY—
ORIGINAL TELEPLAY
• James Costigan, *Eleanor and Franklin*,
ABC Theatre. ABC.
Joanna Lee, *Babe*. CBS.
J.P. Miller, *The Lindbergh Kidnapping*
Case, NBC Thursday Night at the Movies.
NBC.
Nicholas Meyer, Anthony Wilson, *The*
Night That Panicked America, ABC Friday
Night Movie. ABC.
Jeb Rosebrook, Theodore Strauss, *I Will*
Fight No More Forever, ABC Theatre.
ABC.

OUTSTANDING WRITING IN A SPECIAL
PROGRAM—DRAMA OR COMEDY—
ADAPTATION
• David W. Rintels, *Fear on Trial*. CBS.
Jeanne Wakatsuki, James D. Houston,
John Korty, *Farewell to Manzanar, NBC*
World Premiere Movie. NBC.
Elliott Baker, *The Entertainer*. NBC.

OUTSTANDING WRITING IN A COMEDY-
VARIETY OR MUSIC SERIES
• Anne Beatts, Chevy Chase, Al Franken,
Tom Davis, Lorne Michaels, Marilyn
Suzanne Miller, Michael O'Donoghue,
Herb Sargent, Tom Schiller, Rosie Shuster,
Alan Zweibel, *NBC's Saturday Night*.
NBC.
Ed Simmons, Gary Belkin, Roger Beatty,
Bill Richmond, Gene Perret, Arnie Kogen,
Ray Jessel, Rudy DeLuca, Barry Levinson,
Dick Clair, Jenna McMahon, *The Carol*
Burnett Show. CBS.
Phil Hahn, Bob Arnott, Jeanine Burnier,
Coslough Johnson, Iris Rainer, Stuart
Gillard, Frank Peppiatt, John Aylesworth,
Ted Zeigler, *The Sonny and Cher Show*.
CBS.

OUTSTANDING WRITING IN A COMEDY-VARIETY OR MUSIC SPECIAL
• Jane Wagner, Lorne Michaels, Ann Elder, Christopher Guest, Earl Pomerantz, Jim Rusk, Lily Tomlin, Rod Warren, George Yanok, *Lily Tomlin*. ABC.
Fred Ebb, *Gypsy in My Soul*. CBS.
Dick Van Dyke, Allan Blye, Bob Einstein, James Stein, George Burditt, Robert Illes, Steve Martin, Jack Mendelsohn, Rick Mittleman, *Van Dyke and Company*. NBC.
Jerry Mayer, *Mitzi ... Roarin' in the '20s*. CBS.

OTHER AWARD WINNERS

OUTSTANDING MUSIC COMPOSITION
(Dramatic underscore, series program)
• Alex North, *Rich Man, Poor Man*. ABC.
(Dramatic underscore, special program)
• Jerry Goldsmith, *Babe*. CBS.

OUTSTANDING MUSIC DIRECTION
• Seiji Ozawa, *Central Park in the Dark/A Hero's Life, Evening at Symphony*. PBS.

OUTSTANDING CHOREOGRAPHY
• Tony Charmoli, *Gypsy in My Soul*. CBS.

OUTSTANDING ART DIRECTION OR SCENIC DESIGN
(Series program)
• Tom John, art director. John Wendell, Wes Laws, set decorators, *Beacon Hill*. CBS.
(Comedy-variety special or series program)
• Raymond Klausen, art director. Robert Checchi, set decorator, *Cher*. CBS.

OUTSTANDING ACHIEVEMENT IN ART DIRECTION OR SCENIC DESIGN
(Special program)
• Jan Scott, art director. Anthony Mondello, set decorator, *Eleanor and Franklin, ABC Theatre*. ABC.

OUTSTANDING COSTUME DESIGN FOR A DRAMA SPECIAL
• Joe I. Tompkins, *Eleanor and Franklin, ABC Theatre*. ABC.

OUTSTANDING COSTUME DESIGN FOR MUSIC–VARIETY
• Bob Mackie, *Mitzi ... Roarin' in the '20s*. CBS.

OUTSTANDING ACHIEVEMENT IN COSTUME DESIGN FOR A DRAMA OR COMEDY SERIES
• Jane Robinson, *Jennie: Lady Randolph Churchill, Great Performances*. PBS.

OUTSTANDING ACHIEVEMENT IN MAKEUP
• Del Armstrong, Mike Westmore, *Eleanor and Franklin, ABC Theatre*. ABC.

OUTSTANDING CINEMATOGRAPHY
(Series)
• Harry L. Wolf, *Baretta*. ABC.
(Special or feature)
• Paul Lohmann, Edward R. Brown, Sr., *Eleanor and Franklin, ABC Theatre*. ABC.

OUTSTANDING TECHNICAL DIRECTION AND ELECTRONIC CAMERAWORK
• Leonard Chumbley, technical director. Walter Edel, John Feher, Steve Zink, cameramen, *The Adams Chronicles*. PBS.

OUTSTANDING FILM EDITING FOR A DRAMA SERIES
• Samuel E. Beetley, Ken Zemke, *Medical Story*. NBC.

OUTSTANDING FILM EDITING FOR A COMEDY SERIES
• Stanford Tischler, Fred W. Berger, *M*A*S*H*. CBS.

OUTSTANDING FILM EDITING
(Special or feature)
• Michael Kahn, *Eleanor and Franklin, ABC Theatre*. ABC.

OUTSTANDING VIDEO-TAPE EDITING
(Series program)
• Girish Bhargava and Manford Schorn, *The Adams Chronicles*. PBS.
(Special program)
• Nick V. Giordano, "Alice Cooper—The Nightmare," *Wide World: In Concert*. ABC.

OUTSTANDING FILM SOUND EDITING
(Series program)
• Douglas H. Grindstaff, Al Kajita, Marvin Kosberg, Hans Newman, Leon Selditz, Dick Friedman, Stan Gilbert, Hank Salerno, Larry Singer, William Andrews, *Medical Story*. NBC.

(Special or feature)
• Charles L. Campbell, Larry Neiman, Colin Mouat, Larry Carow, Don Warner, John Singleton, Tom McMullen, Joseph DiVitale, Carl Kress, John Kline and John Hanley, *The Night That Panicked America, The ABC Friday Night Movie.* ABC.

OUTSTANDING FILM SOUND MIXING
• Don Bassmann, Don Johnson, *Eleanor and Franklin, ABC Theatre.* ABC.

OUTSTANDING TAPE SOUND MIXING
• Dave Williams, *The Tonight Show Starring Johnny Carson.* NBC.

OUTSTANDING LIGHTING DIRECTION
• William Klages, Lon Stucky, *Mitzi and a Hundred Guys.* CBS.
John Freschi, *Mitzi ... Roarin' in the '20s.* CBS.

THE AREAS
Each area has the possibility of multiple award winners, one winner, or none. Winners are listed.

SPECIAL CLASSIFICATION OF OUTSTANDING PROGRAM AND INDIVIDUAL ACHIEVEMENT
• *Bicentennial Minutes.* Bob Markell, executive producer. Gareth Davies, Paul Waigner, producers. CBS.
• *The Tonight Show Starring Johnny Carson.* Fred DeCordova, producer. Johnny Carson, star. NBC.
• Ann Marcus, Jerry Adelman, Daniel Gregory Browne, writers. *Mary Hartman, Mary Hartman.* Syndicated.

OUTSTANDING INDIVIDUAL ACHIEVEMENT IN SPORTS PROGRAMMING
• Andy Sidaris, Don Ohlmeyer, Roger Goodman, Larry Kamm, Ronnie Hawkins, Ralph Mellanby, directors. *XII Winter Olympic Games.* ABC.

OUTSTANDING ACHIEVEMENT IN SPECIAL MUSICAL MATERIAL
• Ken Welch, Mitzie Welch, Artie Maivin, *The Carol Burnett Show.* CBS.

OUTSTANDING ACHIEVEMENT IN ANY AREA OF CREATIVE TECHNICAL CRAFTS
• Jean Burt Reilly, Billie Laughridge, hairstylists, *Eleanor and Franklin.* ABC.
• Donald Sahlin, Kermit Love, Caroly

Wilcox, John Lovelady, Rollie Krewson, costumes and props for the Muppets, *Sesame Street.* PBS.

OUTSTANDING INDIVIDUAL ACHIEVEMENT IN DAYTIME PROGRAMMING
• Rene Lagier, art director. Richard Harvey, set decorator, *Dinah!* Syndicated.

OUTSTANDING INDIVIDUAL ACHIEVEMENT IN CHILDREN'S PROGRAMMING
• Bud Nolan, Jim Cookman, film sound editors, *Bound for Freedom.* NBC.

OUTSTANDING ACHIEVEMENT IN RELIGIOUS PROGRAMMING
• Joseph J. H. Vadala, cinematographer, *A Determining Force.* NBC.

(There were no winners in the area of outstanding achievement in graphic design and title.)

SPORTS AWARD WINNERS
OUTSTANDING LIVE SPORTS SERIES
• *NFL Monday Night Football.* Roone Arledge, executive producer. Don Ohlmeyer, producer. ABC.

OUTSTANDING EDITED SPORTS SERIES
• *ABC's Wide World of Sports.* Roone Arledge, executive producer. Doug Wilson, Chet Forte, Ned Steckel, Brice Weisman, Terry Jastrow, Bob Goodrich, John Martin, Dennis Lewin, Chuck Howard, Don Ohlmeyer, producers. ABC.

OUTSTANDING LIVE SPORTS SPECIAL
• *1975 World Series.* Scotty Connal, executive producer. Roy Hammerman, producer. NBC.

OUTSTANDING EDITED SPORTS SPECIAL
• *XII Winter Olympic Games.* Roone Arledge, executive producer. Chuck Howard, Don Ohlmeyer, Geoff Mason, Chet Forte, Bob Goodrich, Ellie Riger, Brice Weisman, Doug Wilson, John Wilcox, producers. ABC.
• *Triumph and Tragedy ... The Olympic Experience.* Roone Arledge, executive producer. Don Ohlmeyer, producer. ABC.

OUTSTANDING SPORTS PERSONALITY
• Jim McKay, *ABC's Wide World of Sports, XII Winter Olympic Games.* ABC.

Outstanding Individual Achievement in Sports Programming

• John Cohan, Joe Aceti, John Delisa, Lou Frederick, Jack Gallivan, Jim Jennett, Carol Lehti, Howard Shapiro, Katsumi Aseada, John Fernandez, Peter Fritz, Eddie C. Joseph, Ken Klingbeil, Leo Stephan, Ted Summers, Michael Wenig, Ron Ackerman, Michael Bonifazio, Barbara Bowman, Charlie Burnham, John Croak, Charles Gardner, Marvin Gench, Victor Gonzales, Jakob Hierl, Nick Mazur, Ed McCarthy, Alex Moskovic, Arthur Nace, Lour Rende, Erskin Roberts, Merritt Roesser, Arthur Volk, Roger Haeneit, Curt Brand, Phil Monica, George Boettcher, Herb Ohlandt, video tape editors, *XII Winter Olympic Games.* ABC.
Dick Roes, Jack Kelly, Bill Sandreuter, Frank Bailey, Jack Kestenbaum, tape sound mixers, *XII Winter Olympic Games.* ABC.

DAYTIME AWARDS

Outstanding Daytime Drama Series

• *Another World.* Paul Rauch, executive producer. Joe Rothenberger, Mary S. Boinner, producers. NBC.
Days of Our Lives. Betty Corday, executive producer. Jack Herzberg, Al Rabin, producers. NBC.
The Young and the Restless. John J. Conboy, executive producer. Patricia Wenig, producer. CBS.
All My Children. Bud Kloss, producer. ABC.

Outstanding Daytime Drama Special

• *First Ladies' Diaries: Edith Wilson.* Jeff Young, producer. NBC.
First Ladies' Diaries: Rachel Jackson. Paul Rauch, producer. NBC.
First Ladies' Diaries: Martha Washington. Linda Wendell, producer. NBC.

Outstanding Actor in a Daytime Drama Series

• Larry Haines, *Search for Tomorrow.* CBS.
John Beradino, *General Hospital.* ABC.
Macdonald Carey, *Days of Our Lives.* NBC.
Bill Hayes, *Days of Our Lives.* NBC.
Michael Nouri, *Search for Tomorrow.* CBS.
Shepperd Strudwick, *One Life to Live.* ABC.

Outstanding Actress in a Daytime Drama Series

• Helen Gallagher, *Ryan's Hope.* ABC.
Denise Alexander, *General Hospital.* ABC.
Susan Seaforth Hayes, *Days of Our Lives.* NBC.
Frances Heflin, *All My Children.* ABC.
Mary Stuart, *Search for Tomorrow.* CBS.

Outstanding Individual Director for a Drama Series

• David Pressman, *One Life to Live.* ABC.
Richard Dunlap, *The Young and the Restless.* CBS.
Hugh McPhillips, *The Doctors.* NBC.

Outstanding Writing for a Drama Series

• William J. Bell, Kay Lenard, Pat Falken Smith, Bill Rega, Margaret Stewart, Sheri Anderson, Wanda Coleman, *Days of Our Lives.* NBC.
Henry Slesar, *The Edge of Night.* ABC.
Jerome Dobson, Bridget Dobson, Jean Rouverol, *The Guiding Light.* CBS.
William J. Bell, Kay Alden, *The Young and the Restless.* CBS.
Agnes Nixon, *All My Children.* ABC.

OTHER DAYTIME AWARD WINNERS

Outstanding Actor in a Daytime Drama Special
(Tie)

• Gerald Gordon, *First Ladies' Diaries: Rachel Jackson.* NBC.
• James Luisi, *First Ladies' Diaries: Martha Washington.* NBC.

Outstanding Actress in a Daytime Drama Special

• Elizabeth Hubbard, *First Ladies' Diaries: Edith Wilson.* NBC.

Outstanding Daytime Game or Audience Participation Show

• *The $20,000 Pyramid.* Bob Stewart, executive producer. Anne Marie Schmitt, prodcuer. ABC.

Outstanding Daytime Talk, Service, or Variety Series

• *Dinah!* Henry Jaffe, Carolyn Raskin, executive producers. Fred Tatashore, producer. Syndicated.

OUTSTANDING ENTERTAINMENT CHILDREN'S SERIES
• *Big Blue Marble*. Henry Fownes, producer. Syndicated.

OUTSTANDING ENTERTAINMENT CHILDREN'S SPECIAL
• *Danny Kaye's Look-In at the Metropolitan Opera, The CBS Festival of Lively Arts for Young People*. Sylvia Fine, executive producer. Bernard Rothman, Jack Wohl, Herbert Bonis, producers. CBS.

OUTSTANDING INFORMATIONAL CHILDREN'S SERIES
• *Go*. George A. Heinemann, executive producer. Rift Fournier, J. Philip Miller, William W. Lewis, Joan Bender, producers. NBC.

OUTSTANDING INFORMATIONAL CHILDREN'S SPECIAL
• *Happy Anniversary, Charlie Brown*. Lee Mendelson, Warren Lockhart, producers. CBS.

OUTSTANDING INSTRUCTIONAL CHILDREN'S PROGRAMMING
• *Grammar Rock*. Thomas G. Yohe, executive producer. Radford Stone, producer. ABC.

OUTSTANDING HOST OR HOSTESS IN A GAME OR AUDIENCE PARTICIPATION SHOW
• Allen Ludden, *Password*. ABC.

OUTSTANDING HOST OR HOSTESS IN A TALK, SERVICE, OR VARIETY SERIES
• Dinah Shore, *Dinah!* Syndicated.

OUTSTANDING INDIVIDUAL DIRECTOR FOR A SPECIAL PROGRAM
• Nicholas Havinga, *First Ladies' Diaries: Edith Wilson*. NBC.

OUTSTANDING INDIVIDUAL DIRECTOR FOR A GAME OR AUDIENCE PARTICIPATION SHOW
• Mike Gargiulo, *The $20,000 Pyramid*. ABC.

OUTSTANDING INDIVIDUAL DIRECTOR FOR A VARIETY PROGRAM
• Glen Swanson, *Dinah!* Syndicated.

OUTSTANDING WRITING FOR A SPECIAL PROGRAM
• Audrey Davis Levin, *First Ladies' Diaries: Edith Wilson*. NBC.

OUTSTANDING INDIVIDUAL ACHIEVEMENT IN CHILDREN'S PROGRAMMING (Area award)
• Jim Henson, Frank Oz, Jerry Nelson, Carroll Spinney, Richard Hunt. performers, *Sesame Street*. PBS.

(There was no winner in the area of individual achievement in daytime programming.)

INTERNATIONAL AWARD WINNERS
FICTION
• *The Evacuees*, British Broadcasting Corporation, U.K.

NON-FICTION
• *Inside Story: Marek*, British Broadcasting Corporation, U.K.

INTERNATIONAL DIRECTORATE AWARD
• Mr. Junzo Imamichi, chairman of the board, Tokyo Broadcasting Corp.

SPECIAL AWARDS
SPECIAL AWARDS OUTSTANDING ACHIEVEMENT IN ENGINEERING DEVELOPMENT
• Sony Corp. for the U-matic video cassette concept.
• Eastman Kodak for the development of Eastman Ektachrome Video News Film. **(Citation)**
• Tektronix for developing equipment for verifying TV transmission performance in the vertical interval.

NATIONAL AWARD FOR COMMUNITY SERVICE
• *Forgotten Children*. WBBM-TV, Chicago, Illinois.

"Little Orphan Emmy"
Pulls for *Roots*

The most-watched program in the history of television set another record on Emmys night: *Roots* received more awards than any other miniseries ever has — a total of nine. "*Roots* had a rout," is how *The New York Daily News* sized up its success. *Roots*'s winners included actors Louis Gossett, Jr., as the character Fiddler, Edward Asner as a slave ship captain, and Olivia Cole as the wife of Chicken George. It also won Outstanding Limited Series of the year.

ABC's 12-hour adaptation of Alex Haley's book tracing his African-American ancestry established an Emmy precedent earlier in the year, too, when it received a record 37 nods. But many of the miniseries's nominees were pitted against each other in the same categories, restricting its chances for an even bigger romp. The entire category of Outstanding Lead Actor for a Single Performance in a Drama or Comedy Series was made up of members of the *Roots* cast, for example. Prior to the Emmys show, John Amos, LeVar Burton, Louis Gossett, Jr., and Ben Vereen took out an ad jointly in the Hollywood trade papers announcing that, regardless of who eventually won the award, they considered it a victory shared by all. When Gossett ended up claiming the statuette, he broadened the circle of people he considered it a triumph for, saying, "*Roots* was the most positive thing that has happened for equal rights since Martin Luther King."

Olivia Cole's win as best supporting actress was the most surprising of the lot (she was up against two other actresses from *Roots*, including Cicely Tyson, who was favored), while Ed Asner (up against three other *Roots* contenders)

Roots*'s nine-award "rout" included one for best supporting actress Olivia Cole, given to her by costar Louis Gossett, Jr.*

was considered the likely winner of the supporting actor trophy from the start, having proven his ballot power with Emmy voters four times in the past, including last year for *Rich Man, Poor Man*. In his acceptance remarks for *Roots*, Asner echoed Gossett's belief that they were all involved in a higher cause, saying, "There was power and glory being in such an important project."

Another member of the *Rich Man* team to return was last year's best director, David Greene, who won this year for crafting part one of *Roots*. The miniseries also reaped awards for writing, film editing, film sound editing, and music composition.

Last year's Emmy-winning director in the category of Outstanding Special — Drama or Comedy also came back victorious. Daniel Petrie not only was rewarded for directing David Susskind's production of *Eleanor and Franklin: The White House Years* (sequel to last year's best drama special), *The White House Years* was named best special this year — tying with *Sybil*, also directed by Petrie. Appropriately enough, the program award (which had never involved a tie before) was bestowed by the master of mysterious phenomena, Alfred Hitchcock.

Like last year's *Eleanor and Franklin, Eleanor and Franklin: The White House Years* was based on Joseph Lash's Pulitzer Prize–winning writings about the Roosevelts and again starred Edward Herrmann and Jane Alexander as the presidential pair. Last year's production had set the record for most prizes won by a movie of the week (11). The sequel performed well, too, reaping an impressive 7, including statuettes for its costume design, film editing, make-up, hair stylists, and art director/set decorator.

But just like last year, neither of the film's lead stars won an acting award. The honors went instead to Ed Flanders, who performed, according to the *L.A. Times*, "a one-man tour de force" in *Harry S. Truman: Plain Speaking,* and *Sybil*'s Sally Field, who beat out costar Joanne Woodward and Jane Alexander as Eleanor Roosevelt.

Because *Sybil* was based on a real-life case of multiple personality, it offered its star the challenge of playing 16 different roles in one. At last TV's former *Gidget* and *Flying Nun* proved once and for all in *Sybil* that she was capable of serious dramatic range, although not everyone was glad she won the trophy in acknowledgment. "Forgive us for being a Monday morning quarterback," complained the TV critic for *The New York Daily News* again this year, "but we still can't believe Jane Alexander didn't win an Emmy .... It was a superior acting job and while we're not taking anything away from Sally Field for *Sybil*, recreat-

ing a character as closely as Jane did Eleanor was a real acting task."

After seven trailblazing, turbulent, and hilarious years, *The Mary Tyler Moore Show* broadcast its final episode just one week before Emmys night, a right-to-die decision made by Moore and her co-workers instead of the network. At the awards ceremony, the *L.A. Herald Examiner* noted that the group sat "together in a section of the audience for perhaps their last on-camera appearance as a television family. Moore, Ed Asner, Ted Knight, and Georgia Engel beamed and blew kisses at each other." With 12 nominations among them and their co-workers, the group silently hoped for a second *Roots*-like "rout" — just like the one they pulled off the previous year.

It didn't happen. The top acting honors went instead to members of producer Norman Lear's shows who weren't nominated last year because of a snafu in the production company's mailroom when

Roots *received more awards than any other miniseries ever has.*

Emmy ballots weren't sent out in time. Carroll O'Connor won his second statuette for *All in the Family*; spinoff show *Maude* took the best comic actress prize for a shocked Beatrice Arthur, who, like everyone else, must have thought that Mary Tyler Moore, in her final season, was an unstoppable, sentimental favorite.

The Mary Tyler Moore Show ended up with three awards, including one for film editing and another for the writing of "The Last Show," which pulled one the largest rating shares in TV history. "We kept putting off writing that last show," remembered writer/producer Allan Burns as he accepted the prize. "We frankly didn't want to have to do it. I think the show said what we wanted it

"Long overdue!" the critics cried when producer Fred DeCordova finally picked up an honor for The Tonight Show.

to say. It was poignant, and I think *MTM* was important, in the long run, for many women." The program also received Emmy's notorious "black kiss after death" — a top series award bestowed after cancellation — winning Outstanding Comedy Series for the third time in its seven-year run. Its total tally of Emmy awards stood at 29 — the most in prime-time history.

Moore's 1960s costar Dick Van Dyke led a poignant tribute to *MTM* at the Pasadena Civic Auditorium ceremonies that included clips from various episodes and "drew a standing ovation which rocked the venerable auditorium," reported the *L.A. Times*. Van Dyke received his own "black kiss" on Emmys night, too. His variety series *Van Dyke and Company* ("a flop show loved only by the critics," said the *L.A. Times*) had been dropped by NBC only 11 weeks after it went on the air, but now it was the recipient of the award for Outstanding Comedy-Variety or Music Series. "'I would like to take this and show it to NBC, hold it up and say, 'See?'" Van Dyke said, grinning. Referring then to the abrupt shelving of his variety show the previous fall, he added "Nothing can make that experience nice, but this a good try."

"This was a lousy year for variety specials," commented the *L.A. Times*, "but there was a corker, a marvel in concept and execution [that] ... astonishingly was not nominated for the variety special of the year." *America Salutes Richard Rodgers: The Sound of His Music* still took five statuettes, for its director Dwight Hemion, writers, art director, music director, and choreographer while the best-program prize went to *The Barry Manilow Special*.

After being "gerrymandered" to the category of best limited series, which it won last year, *Upstairs, Downstairs* was now placed back in competition with other regular drama series and again it won the category for a third time. Its victory, said the *L.A.Times*, "gave the academy the touch of class it needed."

The *Herald Examiner* noted last year that the nominee for best actor in a drama series, James Garner, "the grinning gumshoe of *The Rockford Files*, summed up his loss with a shrug. 'Who cares?' he yelled as he made a bee-line for the door. He departed before the dinner gala." This year he walked off again — but, triumphantly, with the statuette in hand — even though the *Herald-Examiner* had previously asserted: "He's never really cared much about bright lights or awards."

The most unexpected winner of the night was Lindsay Wagner, who was declared best actress in a drama series "to ringing boos in the press room," noted the *L.A. Times*. The *Herald Examiner* insisted that the star of *The Bionic Woman* must have "won by a bionic vote." The reason: Wagner was widely considered a dramatic lightweight compared to her competition, which included Tony Award-winner Sada Thompson of *Family* and stage veteran and three-time Emmy winner Michael Learned of *The Waltons*. "Lindsay Wagner did have a tour-de-force episode in which she played twins" that she submitted for

Emmy consideration," remembers A.T.A.S. president Larry Stewart. (Soon after the Emmycast, he would also become a director of *Bionic Woman* episodes.) "But we never thought that a show of that genre would have a prayer against any show." Wagner's chances were bolstered, Stewart says, by weak episodes submitted to the blue-ribbon panels by the other nominees as examples of their best work. Sada Thompson's was an especially poor choice, he says.

Two younger members of the *Family* series, Gary Frank and Kristy McNichol, ended up with the drama series supporting awards. "McNichol was so moved by the Emmy," noted the *Herald Examiner*, "that she broke down on the dais and, in between sobbing and laughing, expressed her thanks to numerous people." A standing ovation greeted the 85-year-old character actress Beulah Bondi as she ambled slowly up to the podium to claim the statuette for best actress in a single performance of a drama or comedy series for her guest appearance on *The Waltons*. "This is truly a bonus," she said about the Emmy in reference to her career and she thanked everyone for giving it to her while she was still alive.

Other acting honors for series work went to Tim Conway for *The Carol Burnett Show* and to Conway's former secretary in real life, Mary Kay Place, who now, in her latest job as an actress, won a supporting acting award for *Mary Hartman, Mary Hartman*. When asked how he felt about his one-time secretary winning an acting prize, Conway said, "I was more excited about that one than mine. She's a wonderful talent. If she could only type ...."

The 29th annual Emmy ceremony "ran for an eye-glazing three-and-a-half hours," said *The New York Times*, but "turned out to be one of the best award shows of the year." About its cohosts, the *Times* said Angie Dickinson was "gracious and quick-witted" but dismissed Robert Blake as "tedious." In addition to the tribute to *The Mary Tyler Moore Show*, the ceremonies also saluted Johnny Carson's *Tonight Show,* which again won a special classification award for program achievement, and two other prizes that had special meaning. They honored last year's Emmy Awards ceremony with statuettes for director John C. Moffitt and the program's two art directors.

The most dramatic award of the night, however, was presented to someone who wasn't a winner. In "a very moving and touching moment," said *The New York Daily News*, John Travolta accepted the supporting actress statuette on behalf of Diana Hyland, his costar from *The Boy in the Plastic Bubble,* who had recently died of cancer. With tears in his eyes, he thrust her Emmy heavenward, leapt up as if to pass it to her, clicked his heels, and shouted, "I love you, baby!"

DAYTIME AWARDS

In an open celebration of one of daytime's obvious advantages over night, the awards ceremony was held outdoors — in New York's sunny Central Park. "It was one of those brilliant, white days," N.A.T.A.S. president John Cannon remembers fondly today. The 90-minute show was telecast by NBC and was dominated, in terms of winners, by ABC and PBS. ABC took 10 prizes. PBS won 3, one in each category in which it was nominated.

Shortly before the ceremony, ABC withdrew *Good Morning America* as a nominee for Outstanding Daytime Talk, Service, or Variety Series. A network executive told the *L.A. Times*, "It is inappropriate to place a news, information, and public affairs series such as *Good Morning America* in competition with such pure entertainment programs as *The Gong Show, Dinah!, The Merv*

Griffin Show, and *The Mike Douglas Show.*" Coincidentally, *Good Morning America*'s host David Hartman was also host of the daytime Emmys show, over which he continued to preside despite pulling his own nomination for best host of the talk, service, and variety series programs. The series award ended up going to *The Merv Griffin Show*; Phil Donahue won the accolade for hosting.

Ryan's Hope swept the daytime drama category with awards for best series, writing, directing, and, for the second year in a row, best actress Helen Gallagher. Val Dufour was named best actor for his role as attorney John Wyatt on *Search for Tomorrow.*

The game show awards were split: *The Family Feud* was named best show; *The $20,000 Pyramid* the best directed; *Tattletales*'s Bert Convy was best host.

SPORTS AWARDS

NFL football and the Olympic games in Montreal again dominated the sports program. CBS took the category of live sports series for its *NFL Today*, while ABC's *Monday Night Football* was acknowledged for its director Chet Forte. Frank Gifford was named sports personality of the year.

ABC producer Roone Arledge's crew again helped to turn the Olympics into a TV event and they were rewarded with trophies for live sports special and in three technical craft categories. An ABC Olympics preview special took an additional award. PBS's *The Olympiad* was designated best edited sports series.

"THE WAR" ENDS

"Little Orphan Emmy" read the banner headline in *Variety* as it chronicled the intensifying battle between the academy's Hollywood chapter and the rest of its national membership. By 1977, Hollywood produced the vast majority of the entertainment programs shown on TV and

its academy chapter wanted more control over the awards that went primarily to the shows they made. Other N.A.T.A.S. chapters believed strongly in the organization as a national body and fought back, bolstered by support from N.A.T.A.S.'s powerful New York chapter.

In an effort to prove its strength — and its point — Hollywood sued for the dissolution of the national academy one day after the Emmy broadcast of 1976. The New York chapter countered by trying to revoke Hollywood's charter. Meanwhile, in a vote of questionable legality, New York–backed John Cannon was elected academy president over Robert Lewine, who had been endorsed by the Hollywood chapter. Cannon's victory was considered questionable because Hollywood's trustees had boycotted the election meeting and therefore claimed no quorum existed.

As the May 15th date for the 1977 Emmys broadcast date approached, more than a hundred members of the Hollywood chapter threatened to boycott the ceremonies unless their demands were met. Among the notables were Norman Lear, Grant Tinker, Mary Tyler Moore, James Garner, Carroll O'Connor, Jean Stapleton, Richard Thomas, and Buddy Ebsen. The Emmys show was postponed. "No stars, no Emmys," commented *American Film* magazine.

But the postponement caused new problems. As an alternative to the honors, different TV prizes were presented on the air for the first time that spring and threatened Emmy's preeminence. The Television Critics Awards, hosted by Beverly Sills and Steve Lawrence, were broadcast on April 11 and involved the input of 200 TV critics in 100 cities voting on nominees in 19 categories.

By September, the Emmys war was over and the show was ready to go back on the air. The rift was settled by the establishment of a new national organization based in Hollywood — the Academy of Television Arts and Sciences — that would award the statuettes for prime-time entertainment shows from now on. Meanwhile, the National Academy of Television Arts and Sciences, based in New York, would continue to supervise daytime, sports, and news and documentary prizes in addition to organizing the national network of academy chapters that bestowed local Emmy awards.

One of "the war's" more interesting developments was the eventual issuance of two sets of prime-time nominations, one pooled for the aborted May broadcast and one compiled later on for the successful September awards show.

How did they differ? Some nominations stayed pretty much the same. The lineup for best drama series, for example, included only one change: *The Waltons* was replaced by *Police Story*. In the race for best comedy series, only *All in the Family* was on both lists. The May lineup also included *Happy Days*, *Laverne & Shirley*, and *Welcome Back, Kotter*.

The nominees for best lead actress in comedy series were completely different in May and September. May's contenders Bonnie Franklin (*One Day at a Time*), Linda Lavin (*Alice*), Penny Marshall (*Laverne & Shirley*), and Nancy Walker (*Blansky's Beauties*) were supplanted by Beatrice Arthur (*Maude*), Valerie Harper (*Rhoda*), Mary Tyler Moore (*The Mary Tyler Moore Show*), Suzanne Pleshette (*The Bob Newhart Show*), and Jean Stapleton (*All in the Family*).

In the categories of lead actor in a comedy and drama series, eventual winners Carroll O'Connor and James Garner weren't even nominated the first time around. The nominees for best actress in a drama series stayed the same, but took on two additional names in September: Michael Learned for *The Waltons* and Emmycast cohost Angie Dickinson for *Police Woman*.

NEWS & DOCUMENTARY AWARDS

Having omitted presentations for news and documentary awards for two years, the Emmy Awards made an effort to keep the category alive this year while it settled other issues at stake in its "war."

After 1977, the awards category would become the sole responsibility of the National Academy of Television Arts and Sciences, but in the meantime the new Academy of Television Arts and Sciences tried to acknowledge leadership in the field with plaques bestowed by a special committee headed by independent producer David Wolper. According to the peace settlement between the two academies, A.T.A.S. could not give out actual Emmy trophies for news programs. The plaques given out instead were called Achievement in Broadcast Journalism Awards and were presented off the air at the creative arts luncheon at the Beverly Wilshire Hotel. Winners were Eric Sevareid, the League of Women Voters, *60 Minutes,* and *The MacNeil-Lehrer Report.*

Don Hewitt, executive producer of *60 Minutes*, refused to accept what he called "an ersatz Emmy," adding: "If Laverne and Shirley and the Fonz get legitimate Emmys during the telecast on the air, I have no intention of having Mike Wallace, Morley Safer, and Dan Rather sit in the back of the bus and get plaques instead of Emmys."

Sevareid was also not at the luncheon, but did telegram his regrets and sent his son to accept the award on his behalf.

Robert MacNeil was the most gracious of the winners who did attend. Acknowledging the crafts people with whom he shared the luncheon, he said that "journalism is a craft like yours." He said he didn't care if the award came from "upstairs or downstairs." He only cared, he said, "about the company I'm in."

For prime-time entertainment programs telecast between March 16, 1976, and March 13, 1977. Prime-time awards broadcast on NBC on September 11, 1977, from the Pasadena Civic Auditorium in California. The fourth annual daytime awards were broadcast on NBC from Central Park in New York on May 12, 1977. The news & documentary awards were bestowed with the creative arts honors on September 10 at the Beverly Wilshire Hotel in L.A. The sports awards were bestowed on November 6, 1977.

PRIME-TIME PROGRAM AWARDS
OUTSTANDING DRAMA SERIES
• *Upstairs, Downstairs, Masterpiece Theatre.* John Hawkesworth, Joan Sullivan, producers. PBS.
Baretta. Anthony Spinner, Bernard Kowalski, Leigh Vance, executive producers. Charles E. Dismukes, producer. ABC.
Columbo, NBC Sunday Mystery Movie. Everett Chambers, producer. NBC.
Family. Aaron Spelling, Leonard Goldberg, Mike Nichols, executive producers. Nigel McKeand, producer. ABC.
Police Story. David Gerber, executive producer. Liam O'Brien, producer. Mel Swope, coproducer. NBC.

OUTSTANDING COMEDY SERIES
• *The Mary Tyler Moore Show.* Allan Burns, James L. Brooks, executive producers. Ed. Weinberger, Stan Daniels, producers. CBS.
All in the Family. Mort Lachman, executive producer. Milt Josefsberg, producer. CBS.
Barney Miller. Danny Arnold, executive producer. Roland Kibbee, Danny Arnold, producers. ABC.
The Bob Newhart Show. Tom Patchett, Jay Tarses, executive producers. Michael Zinberg, Gordon Farr, Lynne Farr, producers. CBS.
*M*A*S*H.* Gene Reynolds, executive producer. Allan Katz, Don Reo, Burt Metcalfe, producers. CBS.

OUTSTANDING LIMITED SERIES
• *Roots.* David L. Wolper, executive producer. Stan Margulies, producer. ABC.
The Adams Chronicles. Jac Venza, executive producer. Virginia Kassel, series producer. Robert Costello, coordinating producer. Fred Coe, James Cellan-Jones, producers. PBS.
Captains and the Kings, Best Sellers. Roy Huggins, executive producer. Jo Swerling, Jr., producer. NBC.
Madame Bovary, Masterpiece Theatre. Richard Beynon, producer. PBS.
The Moneychangers, The Big Event. Ross Hunter, Jacque Mapes, producers. NBC.

OUTSTANDING SPECIAL—
DRAMA OR COMEDY
• *Eleanor and Franklin: The White House Years, ABC Theatre.* David Susskind, executive producer. Harry R. Sherman, producer. ABC.
Sybil, The Big Event. Peter Dunne, Philip Capice, executive producers. Jacqueline Babbin, producer. NBC.
Harry S. Truman: Plain Speaking. David Susskind, producer. PBS.
Raid on Entebbe, The Big Event. Edgar J. Scherick, Daniel H. Blatt, executive producers. NBC.
21 Hours at Munich. Edward S. Feldman, executive producer. Frank von Zerneck, Robert Greenwald, producers. ABC.

OUTSTANDING COMEDY-VARIETY
OR MUSIC SERIES
• *Van Dyke and Company.* Byron Paul, executive producer. Allan Blye, Bob Einstein, producers. Dick Van Dyke, star. NBC.
The Carol Burnett Show. Joe Hamilton, executive producer. Ed Simmons, producer. Carol Burnett, star. CBS.
Evening at Pops. William Cosel, producer. Arthur Fiedler, star. PBS.
The Muppet Show. Jim Henson, David Lazar, executive producers. Jack Burns, producer. The Muppets (Frank Oz, Richard Hunt, Dave Goelz, Eren Ozker, John Lovelady, Jerry Nelson), stars. Syndicated.
NBC's Saturday Night. Lorne Michaels, producer. NBC.

OUTSTANDING SPECIAL—
COMEDY-VARIETY OR MUSIC
• *The Barry Manilow Special.* Miles Lourie, executive producer. Steve Binder, producer. Barry Manilow, star. ABC.

Doug Henning's World of Magic. Jerry Goldstein, executive producer. Walter C. Miller, producer. Doug Henning, star. NBC.

The Neil Diamond Special. Jerry Weintraub, executive producer. Gary Smith, Dwight Hemion, producers. Neil Diamond, star. NBC.

The Shirley MacLaine Special:. Where Do We Go From Here? George Schlatter, producer, Shirley MacLaine, star. CBS.

Sills and Burnett at the Met. Joe Hamilton, producer, Beverly Sills, Carol Burnett, stars. CBS.

OUTSTANDING CLASSICAL PROGRAM IN THE PERFORMING ARTS
(Winner)
• "American Ballet Theatre: Swan Lake," *Live From Lincoln Center, Great Performances.* John Goberman, producer. PBS.

OUTSTANDING CHILDREN'S SPECIAL
(Winner)
• "Ballet Shoes" *Piccadilly Circus.* John McRae, Joan Sullivan, producers. PBS.

SPECIAL CLASSIFICATION OF OUTSTANDING PROGRAM ACHIEVEMENT
(Winner—Area award)
• *The Tonight Show Starring Johnny Carson.* Fred DeCordova, producer. Johnny Carson, star. NBC.

PERFORMANCE, DIRECTING, AND WRITING
OUTSTANDING LEAD ACTOR IN A DRAMA SERIES
• James Garner, *The Rockford Files.* NBC.
Robert Blake, *Baretta.* ABC.
Peter Falk, *Columbo, NBC Sunday Mystery Movie.* NBC.
Jack Klugman, *Quincy.* NBC.
Karl Malden, *The Streets of San Francisco.* ABC.

OUTSTANDING LEAD ACTRESS IN A DRAMA SERIES
• Lindsay Wagner, *The Bionic Woman.* ABC.
Angie Dickinson, *Police Woman.* NBC.
Kate Jackson, *Charlie's Angels.* ABC.
Michael Learned, *The Waltons.* CBS.
Sada Thompson, *Family.* ABC.

OUTSTANDING LEAD ACTOR IN A COMEDY SERIES
• Carroll O'Connor, *All in the Family.* CBS.
Jack Albertson, *Chico and the Man.* NBC.
Alan Alda, *M*A*S*H.* CBS.
Hal Linden, *Barney Miller.* ABC.
Henry Winkler, *Happy Days.* ABC.

OUTSTANDING LEAD ACTRESS IN A COMEDY SERIES
• Beatrice Arthur, *Maude.* CBS.
Valerie Harper, *Rhoda.* CBS.
Mary Tyler Moore, *The Mary Tyler Moore Show.* CBS.
Suzanne Pleshette, *The Bob Newhart Show.* CBS.
Jean Stapleton, *All in the Family.* CBS.

OUTSTANDING LEAD ACTOR FOR A SINGLE PERFORMANCE IN A DRAMA OR COMEDY SERIES
• Louis Gossett, Jr., *Roots.* ABC.
John Amos, *Roots.* ABC.
LeVar Burton, *Roots.* ABC.
Ben Vereen, *Roots.* ABC.

OUTSTANDING LEAD ACTRESS FOR A SINGLE PERFORMANCE IN A DRAMA OR COMEDY SERIES
• Beulah Bondi, *The Waltons.* CBS.
Susan Blakely, *Rich Man, Poor Man— Book II.* ABC.
Madge Sinclair, *Roots.* ABC.
Leslie Uggams, *Roots.* ABC.
Jessica Walter, *The Streets of San Francisco.* ABC.

OUTSTANDING LEAD ACTOR IN A LIMITED SERIES
• Christopher Plummer, *The Moneychangers, The Big Event.* NBC.
Stanley Baker, *How Green was my Valley, Masterpiece Theatre.* PBS.
Richard Jordan, *Captains and the Kings, Best Sellers.* NBC.
Steven Keats, *Seventh Avenue, Best Sellers.* NBC.

OUTSTANDING LEAD ACTRESS IN A LIMITED SERIES
• Patty Duke Astin, *Captains and the Kings, Best Sellers.* NBC.
Susan Flannery, *The Moneychangers, The Big Event.* NBC.
Dori Brenner, *Seventh Avenue, Best Sellers.* NBC.

Eva Marie Saint, *How the West was Won.*
ABC.
Jane Seymour, *Captains and the Kings,*
Best Sellers. NBC.

• Ed Flanders, *Harry S. Truman: Plain*
Speaking. PBS.
Peter Boyle, *Tail Gunner Joe, The Big*
Event. NBC.
Peter Finch, *Raid on Entebbe, The Big*
Event. NBC.
Edward Herrmann, *Eleanor and Franklin:*
The White House Years, ABC Theatre.
ABC.
George C. Scott, *Beauty and the Beast,*
Hallmark Hall of Fame. NBC.

OUTSTANDING LEAD ACTRESS
IN A DRAMA OR COMEDY SPECIAL
• Sally Field, *Sybil, The Big Event.* NBC.
Jane Alexander, *Eleanor and Franklin:*
The White House Years, ABC Theatre.
ABC.
Susan Clark, *Amelia Earhart, NBC*
Monday Night at the Movies. NBC.
Julie Harris, *The Last of Mrs. Lincoln,*
Hollywood Television Theatre. PBS.
Joanne Woodward, *Sybil, The Big Event.*
NBC.

OUTSTANDING CONTINUING
PERFORMANCE BY A SUPPORTING ACTOR
IN A DRAMA SERIES
• Gary Frank, *Family.* ABC.
Noah Beery, *The Rockford Files.* NBC.
David Doyle, *Charlie's Angels.* ABC.
Tom Ewell, *Baretta.* ABC.
Will Geer, *The Waltons.* CBS.

OUTSTANDING CONTINUING
PERFORMANCE BY A SUPPORTING
ACTRESS IN A DRAMA SERIES
• Kristy McNichol, *Family.* ABC.
Meredith Baxter Birney, *Family.* ABC.
Ellen Corby, *The Waltons.* CBS.
Lee Meriwether, *Barnaby Jones.* CBS.
Jacqueline Tong, *Upstairs, Downstairs,*
Masterpiece Theatre. PBS.

OUTSTANDING CONTINUING
PERFORMANCE BY A SUPPORTING ACTOR
IN A COMEDY SERIES
• Gary Burghoff, *M*A*S*H.* CBS.
Edward Asner, *The Mary Tyler Moore*
Show. CBS.

Ted Knight, *The Mary Tyler Moore Show.*
CBS.
Harry Morgan, *M*A*S*H.* CBS.
Abe Vigoda, *Barney Miller.* ABC.

OUTSTANDING CONTINUING
PERFORMANCE BY A SUPPORTING
ACTRESS IN A COMEDY SERIES
• Mary Kay Place, *Mary Hartman, Mary*
Hartman. Syndicated.
Georgia Engel, *The Mary Tyler Moore*
Show. CBS.
Julie Kavner, *Rhoda.* CBS.
Loretta Swit, *M*A*S*H.* CBS.
Betty White, *The Mary Tyler Moore Show.*
CBS.

OUTSTANDING SINGLE PERFORMANCE
BY A SUPPORTING ACTOR
IN A COMEDY OR DRAMA SERIES
• Edward Asner, *Roots.* ABC.
Charles Durning, *Captains and the Kings,*
Best Sellers. NBC.
Moses Gunn, *Roots.* ABC.
Robert Reed, *Roots.* ABC.
Ralph Waite, *Roots.* ABC.

OUTSTANDING SINGLE PERFORMANCE
BY A SUPPORTING ACTRESS
IN A COMEDY OR DRAMA SERIES
• Olivia Cole, *Roots.* ABC.
Sandy Duncan, *Roots.* ABC.
Eileen Heckart, *The Mary Tyler Moore*
Show. CBS.
Cicely Tyson, *Roots.* ABC.
Nancy Walker, *Rhoda.* CBS.

OUTSTANDING PERFORMANCE
BY A SUPPORTING ACTOR IN A COMEDY
OR DRAMA SPECIAL
• Burgess Meredith, *Tail Gunner Joe, The*
Big Event. NBC.
Martin Balsam, *Raid on Entebbe, The Big*
Event. NBC.
Mark Harmon, *Eleanor and Franklin: The*
White House Years, ABC Theatre. ABC.
Yaphet Kotto, *Raid on Entebbe, The Big*
Event. NBC.
Walter McGinn, *Eleanor and Franklin:*
The White House Years, ABC Theatre.
ABC.

OUTSTANDING PERFORMANCE
BY A SUPPORTING ACTRESS IN A COMEDY
OR DRAMA SPECIAL
• Diana Hyland, *The Boy in the Plastic*
Bubble, ABC Friday Night Movie. ABC.

Ruth Gordon, *The Great Houdinis, ABC Friday Night Movie*. ABC.
Rosemary Murphy, *Eleanor and Franklin: The White House Years, ABC Theatre*. ABC.
Patricia Neal, *Tail Gunner Joe, The Big Event*. NBC.
Susan Oliver, *Amelia Earhart, NBC Monday Night at the Movies*. NBC.

OUTSTANDING CONTINUING OR SINGLE PERFORMANCE BY A SUPPORTING ACTOR IN VARIETY OR MUSIC
• Tim Conway, *The Carol Burnett Show*. CBS.
John Belushi, *NBC's Saturday Night*. NBC.
Chevy Chase, *NBC's Saturday Night*. NBC.
Harvey Korman, *The Carol Burnett Show*. CBS.
Ben Vereen, *The Bell Telephone Jubilee*. NBC.

OUTSTANDING CONTINUING OR SINGLE PERFORMANCE BY A SUPPORTING ACTRESS IN VARIETY OR MUSIC
• Rita Moreno, *The Muppet Show*. Syndicated.
Vicki Lawrence, *The Carol Burnett Show*. CBS.
Gilda Radner, *NBC's Saturday Night*. NBC.

OUTSTANDING DIRECTING IN A DRAMA SERIES
• David Greene, *Roots*. ABC.
Marvin Chomsky, *Roots*. ABC.
Fred Coe, *The Adams Chronicles*. PBS.
John Erman, *Roots*. ABC.
Gilbert Moses, *Roots*. ABC.

OUTSTANDING DIRECTING IN A COMEDY SERIES
• Alan Alda, *M*A*S*H*. CBS.
Paul Bogart, *All in the Family*. CBS.
Joan Darling, *M*A*S*H*. CBS.
Alan Rafkin, *M*A*S*H*. CBS.
Jay Sandrich, *The Mary Tyler Moore Show*. CBS.

OUTSTANDING DIRECTING IN A SPECIAL PROGRAM—DRAMA OR COMEDY
• Daniel Petrie, *Eleanor and Franklin: The White House Years, ABC Theatre*. ABC.
Fielder Cook, *Judge Horton and the Scottsboro Boys, NBC World Premiere Movie*. NBC.

Tom Gries, *Helter Skelter*. CBS.
Irvin Kershner, *Raid on Entebbe, The Big Event*. NBC.
Jud Taylor, *Tail Gunner Joe, The Big Event*. NBC.

OUTSTANDING DIRECTING IN A COMEDY-VARIETY OR MUSIC SERIES
• Dave Powers, *The Carol Burnett Show*. CBS.
John C. Moffitt, *Van Dyke and Company*. NBC.
Dave Wilson, *NBC's Saturday Night*. NBC.

OUTSTANDING DIRECTING IN A COMEDY-VARIETY OR MUSIC SPECIAL
• Dwight Hemion, *America Salutes Richard Rodgers: The Sound of His Music*. CBS.
Steve Binder, *The Barry Manilow Special*. ABC.
Tony Charmoli, *The Shirley MacLaine Special: Where Do We Go From Here?* CBS.
Walter C. Miller, *Doug Henning's World of Magic*. NBC.
David Powers, *Sills and Burnett at the Met*. CBS.

OUTSTANDING WRITING IN A DRAMA SERIES
• Ernest Kinoy, William Blinn, *Roots*. ABC.
James Lee, *Roots*. ABC.
Roger O. Hirson, *The Adams Chronicles*. PBS.
M. Charles Cohen, *Roots*. ABC.
Tad Mosel, *The Adams Chronicles*. PBS.

OUTSTANDING WRITING IN A COMEDY SERIES
• Allan Burns, James L. Brooks, Ed. Weinberger, Stan Daniels, David Lloyd, Bob Ellison, *The Mary Tyler Moore Show*. CBS.
Alan Alda, *M*A*S*H*. CBS.
Danny Arnold, Tony Sheehan, *Barney Miller*. ABC.
David Lloyd, *The Mary Tyler Moore Show*. CBS.
Earl Pomerantz, *The Mary Tyler Moore Show*. CBS.

OUTSTANDING WRITING, SPECIAL PROGRAM—DRAMA OR COMEDY—ORIGINAL TELEPLAY
• Lane Slate, *Tail Gunner Joe, The Big Event*. NBC.

Best actor winner Louis Gossett, Jr., called Roots *a victory for equal rights.*

Barry Beckerman, *Raid on Entebbe, The Big Event.* NBC.
James Costigan, *Eleanor and Franklin: The White House Years, ABC Theatre.* ABC.
Ernest Kinoy, *Victory at Entebbe.* ABC.
Douglas Day Stewart, teleplay. Joe Morgenstern, Douglas Day Stewart, story. *The Boy in the Plastic Bubble, The ABC Friday Night Movie.* ABC.

OUTSTANDING WRITING IN A SPECIAL PROGRAM—DRAMA OR COMEDY—ADAPTATION
• Stewart Stern, *Sybil, The Big Event.* NBC.
William Bast, "The Man in the Iron Mask," *The Bell System Presents.* NBC.
John McGreevey, *Judge Horton and the Scottsboro Boys, NBC World Premiere Movie.* NBC.
Carol Sobieski, *Harry S. Truman: Plain Speaking.* PBS.
Steven Gethers, *A Circle of Children.* CBS.

OUTSTANDING WRITING IN A COMEDY-VARIETY OR MUSIC SERIES
• Anne Beatts, Dan Aykroyd, Al Franken, Tom Davis, James Downey, Lorne Michaels, Marilyn Suzanne Miller, Michael O'Donoghue, Herb Sargent, Tom Schiller, Rosie Shuster, Alan Zweibel,

John Belushi, Bill Murray, *NBC's Saturday Night.* NBC.
Jim Henson, Jack Burns, Marc London, Jerry Juhl, *The Muppet Show.* Syndicated.
Anne Beatts, Chevy Chase, Al Franken, Tom Davis, Lorne Michaels, Marilyn Suzanne Miller, Michael O'Donoghue, Herb Sargent, Tom Schiller, Rosie Shuster, Alan Zweibel, *NBC's Saturday Night.* NBC.
Ed Simmons, Roger Beatty, Elias Davis, David Pollock, Rick Hawkins, Liz Sage, Adele Styler, Burt Styler, Tim Conway, Bill Richmond, Gene Perret, Dick Clair, Jenna McMahon, *The Carol Burnett Show.* CBS.
Bob Einstein, Allan Blye, George Burditt, Garry Ferrier, Ken Finkelman, Mitch Markowitz, Tommy McLoughlin, Don Novello, Pat Proft, Leonard Ripps, Mickey Rose, Aubrey Tadman, Dick Van Dyke, Paul Wayne, *Van Dyke and Company.* NBC.

OUTSTANDING WRITING IN A COMEDY-VARIETY OR MUSIC SPECIAL
• Alan Buz Kohan, Ted Strauss, *America Salutes Richard Rodgers: The Sound of His Music.* CBS.
Alan Thicke, Don Clark, Susan Clark, Ronny Pearlman, Steve Binder, Barry Manilow, Bruce Vilanch, *The Barry Manilow Special.* ABC.
Bill Dyer, Ntozake Shange, *An Evening with Diana Ross, The Big Event.* NBC.
Ken Welch, Mitzie Welch, Kenny Solms, Gail Parent, *Sills and Burnett at the Met.* CBS.
Digby Wolfe, George Schlatter, *John Denver and Friend.* ABC.

OTHER AWARD WINNERS
OUTSTANDING COVERAGE OF SPECIAL EVENTS—INDIVIDUALS
• John C. Moffitt, director, *The 28th Annual Emmy Awards.* ABC.

OUTSTANDING MUSIC COMPOSITION—SERIES
(Dramatic underscore)
• Quincy Jones, Gerald Fried. *Roots.* ABC.

OUTSTANDING MUSIC COMPOSITION—SPECIAL
(Dramatic underscore)
• Leonard Rosenman, Alan Bergman, Marilyn Bergman, *Sybil, The Big Event.* NBC.

OUTSTANDING MUSIC DIRECTION
• Ian Fraser, *America Salutes Richard Rodgers: The Sound of His Music*. CBS.

OUTSTANDING CHOREOGRAPHY
• Ron Field, *America Salutes Richard Rodgers: The Sound of His Music*. CBS.

OUTSTANDING ART DIRECTION OR SCENIC DESIGN FOR A DRAMA SERIES
• Tim Harvey, scenic designer, *The Pallisers*. PBS.

OUTSTANDING ART DIRECTION OR SCENIC DESIGN FOR A COMEDY SERIES
• Thomas E. Azzari, art director, *Fish*. ABC.

OUTSTANDING ART DIRECTION OR SCENIC DESIGN FOR A COMEDY-VARIETY OR MUSIC SERIES
• Romain Johnston, art director, *The Mac Davis Show*. NBC.

OUTSTANDING ART DIRECTION OR SCENIC DESIGN FOR A DRAMATIC SPECIAL
• Jan Scott, art director. Anne D. McCulley, set decorator, *Eleanor and Franklin: The White House Years, ABC Theatre*. ABC.

OUTSTANDING ART DIRECTION OR SCENIC DESIGN FOR A COMEDY-VARIETY OR MUSIC SPECIAL
• Robert Kelly, art director, *America Salutes Richard Rodgers: The Sound of His Music*. CBS.

OUTSTANDING COSTUME DESIGN FOR A DRAMA OR COMEDY SERIES
• Raymond Hughes, *The Pallisers*. PBS.

OUTSTANDING COSTUME DESIGN FOR MUSIC-VARIETY
• Jan Skalicky, "The Barber of Seville," *Live From Lincoln Center, Great Performances*. PBS.

OUTSTANDING COSTUME DESIGN FOR A DRAMA SPECIAL
• Joe I. Tompkins, *Eleanor and Franklin: The White House Years, ABC Theatre*. ABC.

OUTSTANDING CINEMATOGRAPHY IN ENTERTAINMENT PROGRAMMING FOR A SERIES
• Ric Waite, *Captains and the Kings, Best Sellers*. NBC.

OUTSTANDING CINEMATOGRAPHY IN ENTERTAINMENT PROGRAMMING FOR A SPECIAL
• Wilmer C. Butler, *Raid on Entebbe, The Big Event*. NBC.

OUTSTANDING TECHNICAL DIRECTION AND ELECTRONIC CAMERAWORK
• Karl Messerschmidt, technical director. Jon Olson, Bruce Gray, John Gutierrez, Jim Dodge, Wayne McDonald, cameramen, *Doug Henning's World of Magic*. NBC.

OUTSTANDING FILM EDITING IN A COMEDY SERIES
• Douglas Hines, *The Mary Tyler Moore Show*. CBS.

OUTSTANDING FILM EDITING IN A DRAMA SERIES
• Neil Travis, *Roots*. ABC.

OUTSTANDING FILM EDITING FOR A SPECIAL
• Rita Roland, Michael S. McLean, *Eleanor and Franklin: The White House Years, ABC Theatre*. ABC.

OUTSTANDING VIDEO-TAPE EDITING FOR A SERIES
• Roy Stewart, *The War Widow, Visions*. PBS.

OUTSTANDING VIDEO-TAPE EDITING FOR A SPECIAL
• Gary H. Anderson, *American Bandstand's 25th Anniversary*. ABC.

OUTSTANDING FILM SOUND EDITING FOR A SERIES
• Larry Carow, Larry Neiman, Don Warner, Colin Mouat, George Fredrick, Dave Pettijohn, Paul Bruce Richardson, *Roots*. ABC.

OUTSTANDING FILM SOUND EDITING FOR A SPECIAL
• Bernard F. Pincus, Milton C. Burrow, Gene Eliot, Don Ernst, Tony Garber, Don V. Isaacs, Larry Kaufman,William L. Manger, A. David Marshall, Richard Oswald, Edward L.Sandlin, Russ Tinsley, *Raid on Entebbe, The Big Event*. NBC.

Outstanding Film Sound Mixing
• Alan Bernard, George E. Porter, Eddie J. Nelson, Robert L. Harman, *The Savage Bees, NBC Monday Night at the Movies.* NBC.

Outstanding Graphic Design and Title Sequences
• Eytan Keller, Stu Bernstein, *The Bell Telephone Jubilee.* NBC.

Outstanding Lighting Direction
• William M. Klages, Peter Edwards, *The Dorothy Hamill Special.* ABC.

Outstanding Makeup
• Ken Chase, makeup design. Joe Dibella, makeup artist. *Eleanor and Franklin: The White House Years, ABC Theatre.* ABC.

Outstanding Tape Sound Mixing
• Doug Nelson, *John Denver and Friend.* ABC.

Outstanding Individual Achievement in Any Area of Creative Technical Crafts
• Emma di Vittorio, Vivienne Walker, hairstylists, *Eleanor and Franklin: The White House Years, ABC Theatre.* ABC.

Special Classification of Outstanding Individual Achievement
• Allen Brewster, Bob Roethle, William Lorenz, Manuel Martinez, Ron Fleury, Mike Welch, Jerry Burling, Walter Balderson, Chuck Droege, video tape editing, *The First Fifty Years, The Big Event.* NBC.

Outstanding Individual Achievement in Children's Programming
• Jean De Joux, Elizabeth Savel, video animation. *Peter Pan, Hallmark Hall of Fame, The Big Event.* NBC.
• Bill Hargate, costume designer, *Pinocchio.* CBS.
• Jerry Greene, video tape editor, *Pinocchio.* CBS.

Outstanding Coverage of Special Events—Individuals
• Brian C. Bartholomew, Keaton S. Walker, art directors, *The 28th Annual Emmy Awards.* ABC.

(No awards for outstanding coverage of special events—programs or special musical material.)

DAYTIME AWARDS
Outstanding Daytime Drama Series
• *Ryan's Hope.* Paul Avila Mayer, Claire Labine, executive producers. Robert Costello, producer. ABC.
All My Children. Bud Kloss, Agnes Nixon, producers. ABC.
Another World. Paul Rauch, executive producer. Mary S. Bonner, Joseph H. Rothenberger. producers. NBC.
Days of Our Lives. Betty Corday, executive producer. H. Wesley Kenny, Jack Herzberg, producers. NBC.
The Edge of Night. Erwin Nicholson, producer. ABC.

Outstanding Actor in a Daytime Drama Series
• Val Dufour, *Search for Tomorrow.* CBS.
Farley Granger, *One Life to Live.* ABC.
Larry Haines, *Search for Tomorrow.* CBS.
Lawrence Keith, *All My Children.* ABC.
James Pritchett, *The Doctors.* NBC.

Outstanding Actress in a Daytime Drama Series
• Helen Gallagher, *Ryan's Hope.* ABC.
Nancy Addison, *Ryan's Hope.* ABC.
Beverlee McKinsey, *Another World.* NBC.
Mary Stuart, *Search for Tomorrow.* CBS.
Ruth Warrick, *All My Children.* ABC.

Outstanding Individual Director for a Daytime Drama Series
• Lela Swift, *Ryan's Hope.* ABC.
Joseph Behar, *Days of Our Lives.* NBC.
Ira Cirker, *Another World.* NBC.
Paul E. Davis, Leonard Valenta, *As the World Turns.* CBS.
Al Rabin, *Days of Our Lives.* NBC.
John Sedwick, *The Edge of Night.* ABC.

Outstanding Writing for a Daytime Drama Series
• Claire Labine, Paul Avila Mayer, Mary Munisteri, *Ryan's Hope.* ABC.
William J. Bell, Pat Falken Smith, William Rega, Kay Lenard, Margaret Stewart, *Days of Our Lives.* NBC.
Harding Lemay, Tom King, Peter Swet, Barry Berg, Jan Merlin, Arthur Giron, Kathy Callaway, *Another World.* NBC.
Agnes Nixon, Wisner Washam, Kathryn McCabe, Mary K. Wells, Jack Wood, *All My Children.* ABC.
Robert Soderberg, Edith Sommer, Ralph Ellis, Eugenie Hunt, Theodore Apstain, Gillian Spencer, *As the World Turns.* CBS.

OTHER DAYTIME AWARD WINNERS
OUTSTANDING ACHIEVEMENT
IN DAYTIME DRAMA SPECIALS
• *The American Woman: Portraits of Courage.* Gaby Monet, producer. Lois Nettleton, performer. Gaby Monet, Anne Grant, writers. ABC.

OUTSTANDING DAYTIME TALK, SERVICE, OR VARIETY SERIES
• *The Merv Griffin Show.* Bob Murphy, producer. Syndicated.

OUTSTANDING HOST OR HOSTESS
IN A TALK, SERVICE, OR VARIETY SERIES
• Phil Donahue, *Donahue.* Syndicated.

OUTSTANDING GAME OR AUDIENCE
PARTICIPATION SHOW
(Daytime or nighttime programs)
• *Family Feud.* Howard Felsher, producer. ABC.

OUTSTANDING HOST OR HOSTESS
IN A GAME OR AUDIENCE
PARTICIPATION SHOW
(Daytime or nighttime programs)
• Bert Convy, *Tattletales.* CBS.

OUTSTANDING INDIVIDUAL DIRECTOR
FOR A GAME OR AUDIENCE
PARTICIPATION SHOW
(Daytime and night series)
• Mike Gargiulo, *The $20,000 Pyramid.* ABC.

OUTSTANDING INDIVIDUAL DIRECTOR
FOR A DAYTIME VARIETY PROGRAM
(Single episode)
• Donald R. King, *The Mike Douglas Show.* Syndicated.

OUTSTANDING CHILDREN'S SERIES
ENTERTAINMENT
• *Zoom.* Cheryl Susheel Bibbs, executive producer. Monia Joblin, Mary Benjamin, producers.

OUTSTANDING CHILDREN'S SPECIAL
ENTERTAINMENT
• "Big Henry and the Polka Dot Kid," *Special Treat.* Linda Gottlieb, producer. NBC.

OUTSTANDING CHILDREN'S
INFORMATIONAL SERIES
• *The Electric Company,* Samuel Y. Gibbon, Jr., executive producer. PBS.

OUTSTANDING CHILDREN'S
INFORMATIONAL SPECIAL
• "My Mom's Having a Baby," *ABC Afterschool Special.* David H. DePatie, Friz Freleng, executive producers. Bob Chenault, producer. ABC.

OUTSTANDING CHILDREN'S
INSTRUCTIONAL PROGRAMMING—
SERIES AND SPECIALS
• *Sesame Street,* Jon Stone, executive producer. Dulcy Singer, producer. PBS.

SPORTS AWARD WINNERS
OUTSTANDING LIVE SPORT SERIES
• *The NFL Today/ NFL Football on CBS.* Michael Pearl, Hal Classon, Sid Kaufman, producers. CBS.

OUTSTANDING EDITED SPORTS SERIES
• *The Olympiad.* Cappy Petrash Greenspan, executive producer. Bud Greenspan, producer. PBS.

OUTSTANDING LIVE SPORTS SPECIAL
• *1976 Olympic Games,* Montreal, Canada. Roone Arledge. executive producer. Chuck Howard, Don Ohlmeyer, Chet Forte, Dennis Lewin, Bob Goodrich, Geoffrey Mason, Terry Jastrow, Eleanor Riger, Ned Steckel, Brice Weisman, John Wilcox, Doug Wilson, producers. ABC.

OUTSTANDING EDITED SPORTS SPECIAL
• *A Special Preview of the 1976 Olympic Games from Montreal, Canada.* Roone Arledge, executive producer. Chuck Howard, Don Ohlmeyer, Chet Forte, Dennis Lewin, Bob Goodrich, Geoffrey Mason, Terry Jastrow, Eleanor Riger, Nid Steckel, Brice Weisman, John Wilcox and Doug Wilson, producers. ABC.

OUTSTANDING SPORTS PERSONALITY
• Frank Gifford. ABC.

OUTSTANDING DIRECTING IN SPORTS
PROGRAMMING
• Chet Forte, *ABC NFL Monday Night Football.* ABC.

OUTSTANDING INDIVIDUAL ACHIEVEMENT
IN SPORTS PROGRAMMING
(Cinematography — Area award)
• Peter Henning, Harvey Harrison, Harry Hart, D'Arcy March, Don Shapiro, Don Shoemaker, Joe Valentine, *1976 Olympic Games.* ABC.

(Film editing— Area award)
• John Petersen, Angelo Bernaducci, Irwin Krechaf, Margaret Murphy, Vincent Reda, Anthony Zaccaro, *1976 Olympic Games*. ABC.

(No awards were bestowed in the areas of tape sound mixing or graphic design.)

INTERNATIONAL AWARD WINNERS
DIRECTOR AWARD
• Talbot Duckmanton, chairman, and Sir Charles Moses, secretary-general, Asian Broadcasting Union.

SPECIAL DIRECTORATE AWARD CITATIONS
• Howard Thomas, chairman of Thames Television, Ltd. and Dr. Roberto Marinho, president, TV-Globo Network of Brazil.

FICTION AWARD
• *The Naked Civil Servant*. Thames Television Limited, London, U.K.

NON-FICTION AWARD
• *Reach for Tomorrow*, Nippon Television Network, Tokyo, Japan.

SPECIAL AWARDS
OUTSTANDING ACHIEVEMENT IN BROADCAST JOURNALISM
• *The MacNeil-Lehrer Report*
• Eric Sevareid
• League of Women Voters
• *60 Minutes*

OUTSTANDING ENGINEERING DEVELOPMENT
• ABC, for leadership in establishing Circularly Polarized Transmission to improve television reception.
(Citation)
Varian Associates.

OUTSTANDING ENGINEERING OR TECHNICAL ACHIEVEMENT
• General Electric Company

NATIONAL AWARD FOR COMMUNITY SERVICE
• *Rape: A Woman's Special*. WGBH-TV, Boston, Massachusetts.

Peace and Prejudice

It was an impressive night for messages about racial and religious bigotry. The show that debated both topics on a weekly basis, *All in the Family,* swept the comedy awards, the miniseries *Holocaust* took the bulk of drama prizes, and President Jimmy Carter interrupted the Emmy-cast with the dramatic real-life news of a sudden peace breakthrough between Arabs and Jews in the Middle East.

Midway through the Emmys' 30th anniversary party at the Pasadena Civic Auditorium, Carter preempted programming on all major networks for nearly 30 minutes to make the historic announcement. The interruption came live from the president's Camp David retreat in Maryland where a grinning Carter was shown flanked by Egyptian President Anwar Sadat and Israeli Prime Minister Menachem Begin. Together they endorsed a new treaty they hoped would be the first step in preventing another Arab-Israeli war. "It was television's finest moment," said the *L.A. Herald Examiner*, "and it seemed appropriate it should come in the middle of the CBS telecast of the traditional Emmy show."

A previous, private war against the Jews was the subject of a major Emmy contender: the four-part, 9 1/2-hour-long miniseries that was nominated for 16 awards. *Holocaust*, the story of a Jewish family named Weiss living in Nazi-terrorized Berlin, ended up with eight prizes in all, including Outstanding Limited Series and honors for its director, writer, costume designer, and film editor. Performance laurels went to Michael Moriarty as best lead actor in a limited series for playing the ambitious Nazi

One of Holocaust's *eight awards was for best actress Meryl Streep, who played the Christian wife of a Jew in Nazi Germany.*

major Eric Dorf. Meryl Streep was hailed as best actress for her portrayal of Inga, a Christian who married into the doomed Weiss brood. Best supporting actress honors went to the performer who played Anna, the Weiss family's only daughter, Blanche Baker, who, ironically, was the daughter of a real-life Dachau concentration camp survivor.

All in the Family was back dominating the comedy series awards now that its longtime nemesis *The Mary Tyler Moore Show* was off the air, taking six out of the seven categories in which it was nominated. As the *L.A. Times* noted reference to the sole category it lost — best supporting actress: "Only Sally Struthers struck out."

For a historic fourth time, *All in the Family* was voted Outstanding Comedy Series, which tied it with *The Dick Van Dyke Show*'s record of having the most best-series victories. *All in the Family* also garnered awards for its writing and directing as well a third trophy each for stars Carroll O'Connor and Jean Stapleton. Stapleton thanked her producers and the network for their "artistic freedom from the day one." (Carroll O'Connor had a nosebleed and couldn't thank anyone.) Rob Reiner was named best supporting actor for a second time and noted in his acceptance remarks that the cast was heading to Washington, D.C., the following weekend for a important presentation. The show's centerpiece easy chairs — the middle-class thrones occupied each week by lead characters Archie and Edith Bunker — were being donated to the Smithsonian Institution.

Rockford Files

pulled an upset

as best drama

series; **All in**

the Family *won*

best comedy

program for a

fourth time.

The drama series awards were split among a number of shows. *The Rockford Files*, which followed the exploits of an ex-con-turned-private-eye, pulled an upset in the category of best series over *Lou Grant*, a new program spun off from the now-defunct *Mary Tyler Moore Show*. *Grant* gave a startlingly realistic portrayal of the goings-on at a big city newspaper — the fictitious *Los Angeles Tribune* — and took three awards in all: for supporting actress Nancy Marchand, who played the paper's imperial publisher; for recent Tony award-winner Barnard Hughes, who guest-starred in an episode called "Judge"; and for star Ed Asner, who thus became the first actor in Emmy history to win awards for playing the same part in two different series. *Rhoda*, another *MTM* spin-off, won supporting actress honors for Julie Kavner, and Sada Thompson of *Family* made up for her loss last year to *The Bionic Woman*'s Lindsay Wagner by being named best actress in a drama series — this time,after submitting a much more impressive example of her work to the judging panelists.

A Family Upside Down was a TV film with an extraordinary cast, four of whom were up for acting statuettes: Fred Astaire, Helen Hayes, Patty Duke Astin, and Efrem Zimbalist, Jr. Only Astaire prevailed, but his victory helped settle an old score that started with the "Astaire Affair" of 1959. The veteran Hollywood star won an acting award that year for one of his variety specials, and he quietly suffered the ridicule from critics who may have valued him as a showman but dismissed his "acting" on the program. Astaire won a second, far less controversial acting award in 1961, one designated specifically for a variety show performance, but now he was being honored for his serious dramatic skills again, and specifically how he demonstrated them opposite costar Helen Hayes as they played elderly parents who become burdens on their children.

"My gosh, I never dreamed of this," a humble Astaire told the roomful of admirers who stood up to honor him with an ovation described by *The Washington Post* as "the biggest applause of the night." "I'm absolutely delighted with this," Astaire responded, clutching his third Emmy. He then added, coyly: "I'm going to get off while I'm still ahead."

The award for Outstanding Lead Actress in a Special went to Joanne Woodward for playing a middle-aged housewife who attempts the Boston Marathon in *See How She Runs*. The one-time Oscar winner for *The Three Faces of Eve* said, "This is such a nice way to come back to television. I started out here 25 years ago."

Winner of the year's trophy for Outstanding Special — Drama or Comedy ("the most prestigious of the Emmy Awards," the *L.A. Times* told its readers) was *The Gathering*, a powerful drama about a dying father (played by Ed Asner) who calls his family together for one last Christmas reunion. Maureen Stapleton portrayed Asner's long-suffering satellite wife and handled it so compellingly that many Emmy watchers expected her to beat Woodward for best actress.

When *The Muppet Show* was created as a half-hour variety program based on some of the riotous *Sesame Street* characters, all three networks turned it down because they believed adults would never tune in. *The Muppet Show* went on to became the most popular first-run syndicated series in TV history. At the Emmys, it was again underestimated. Its victory as Outstanding Comedy-Variety or Music Series was a major upset.

The sentimental favorite to win had been *The Carol Burnett Show*, which was the all-time Emmys champ in its series category, having triumphed as best program three times in the past. But this year it was competing for the last time. The second-longest-running prime-time series (after *Walt Disney*) was going off the air after 11 years, and the Emmycast presented what the *L.A. Times* called a "hilarious tribute [that] was a highlight of the program." *Burnett* was up for eight awards in all and, while it failed to win the series trophy, it did end up with five others: for actor Tim Conway, its director, video tape editor, music composers, and writers, the latter described by the *Herald Examiner* as "a small army which includ-ed Tim Conway." In all, the show had 22 Emmys when it went off the air, making it the second most honored program in prime-time history (after *The Mary Tyler Moore Show*). Burnett herself possessed five awards, three of them as a result of her variety series.

In the category of variety specials, *The Sentry Collection Presents Ben Vereen — His Roots* won six statuettes (director, art director, music director, music composers, cameramen, and video tape editor), while the trophy for best special of the year went to *Bette Midler — Ol' Red Hair is Back*. Other top program winners included *American Ballet Theatre's "Giselle"* as best classical program, Dr. Seuss's *Halloween is Grinch Night* as best children's special, *The Body Human* as the best informational series, and *National Geographic*'s "The Great Whales" as top informational special.

The 30th annual prime-time Emmy Awards made for a good show, but a ponderously long one. It established an Emmycast record of three hours and 35 minutes, which did not include the 28 minutes for the Carter-Sadat-Begin interruption. Opposite the CBS-broadcast ceremony, NBC had scheduled the concluding segment of an epic movie remake and ABC showed a premiere of what *The Washington Post* called its "expensively explosive *Battlestar Galactica*," the network's most bally-hooed new series ever. *All in the Family* producer Norman Lear chastised both networks when he took his turn at the podium on Emmys night, saying: "So proud are ABC and NBC of their very own shows and stars who win Emmys on CBS tonight that they have scheduled against us a three-hour debut of the most expensive new series ever made and the conclusion of [the 1976 film version of] *King Kong*." It was the equivalent, he added, of "Dracula biting his own neck."

SPORTS AWARDS

For the first time since their inception, the sports awards were not bestowed on the air and ABC, which had traditionally dominated the competition, took the slight as occasion to pull out of the race altogether. That suddenly left the field wide open to other contenders who had been overlooked in the past, particularly CBS sportscaster Jack Whitaker who, argued *Sports Illustrated*, should have won the sports personality Emmy long ago.

CBS ended up dominating the sports trophies this time (which were handed out at ceremonies held in New York) with its coverage of ballooning, NFL football, and the first heavyweight championship bout between Muhammad Ali and Leon Spinks that saw Spinks nail Ali in 15 rounds. No single show won more than one or two awards.

The regrouping that followed the split of the TV academies caused the 1977–78 sports awards to be given late, on February 13, 1979. The eligibility period was extended to cover more than a year.

DAYTIME AWARDS

ABC may have boycotted the sports competition, but it joined in, and even broadcast, the daytime honors — and it was well rewarded. "ABC, which also does well after dark," noted *The New York Times*, "led the list of the Fifth Annual Emmy Awards for Daytime Television, which were presented in televised ceremonies at the New York Hilton." Celebrity presenters included Rita Moreno, Cheryl Tiegs, and Susan Lucci.

ABC scored big among the children's program prizes, especially with its *After-school Specials*: "Hewitt's Just Different," the story of a boy who befriends a retarded child who lives next door, was judged best entertainment special; and "Very Good Friends," about the death of an 11-year-old boy, was voted best informational special.

In a coincidence that would be repeated often in the future, the host of the daytime Emmys ceremony was also cited for his skills as host of a nominated show — in this case Richard Dawson of *The Family Feud*. It was the first time Dawson had even been nominated. As he held the statuette, he joked, "It's nice, but I was hoping for a Longines." *Feud* was also up for the director's award, which it lost to *The $20,000 Pyramid*, and for the best game show prize. When the top program award went to 1975's winner *The Hollywood Squares*, the stage microphone caught Dawson whispering, "Well, one out of three isn't bad." Also returning this year was Phil Donahue as best talk show host. His show won the program award, too.

Among soap operas, no show won more than one award. Last year's sweepstakes winner *Ryan's Hope* reprised only its writing prize while the series laurels went to *Days of Our Lives*, which, *The New York Times* noted, "is now in its 13th year of spinning its daytime yarns about Dr. Tom Hays and his friends and relatives." While accepting the trophy, producer Jack Herzberg also noted that the show had been on the air for some time, but had never won the top series award. Looking at the Emmy approvingly, he now said, "We've been here so many times I'm glad we're finally going to get married!"

Acting prizes went to *Another World*'s Laurie Heinemann (as the character Sharlene Watts Matthews) who accepted the statuette saying, "Oh, this is amazing!" and to James Pritchett for his role as Dr. Matt Powers on *The Doctors*. Pritchett thanked "everybody who had anything to do with this moment" and added, "I don't care if it was inadvertent or illegal." Richard Dunlap of *The Young and the Restless* won the director's honors and thanked his mother and the show's whole crew.

The most dramatic development at this year's ceremonies surrounded CBS's *Captain Kangaroo*. The show had been on the air since 1955 and "has won all sorts of other honors," noted *The New York Times*, but never the Emmy. When it was named best children's entertainment series this year, its grateful producer Jim Hirschfeld said, "It's been 23 years we've been waiting for this — and we finally made it!"

NEWS & DOCUMENTARY AWARDS
The networks' news divisions were reluctant to participate in the Emmys until a full program for news and documentary prizes could be reinstated following the creation of two TV academies. Meanwhile, the Academy of Television Arts and Sciences tried to keep the category alive by continuing to give away plaques for Achievement in Broadcast Journalism.

Of the four honors bestowed at the creative arts luncheon at the Beverly Wilshire Hotel in Los Angeles, only Sylvia Chase, producer of *20/20*, showed up to accept one. Missing were CBS reporters Charles Kuralt and Bill Moyers as well as the producers of *CBS Reports'* "The Fire Next Door."

1977–78

For prime-time programs telecast between March 14, 1977, and June 30, 1978. The prime-time awards ceremony was broadcast on CBS on Sept. 17, 1978, from the Pasadena Civic Auditorium. The news plaques were bestowed at the creative arts awards banquet on September 9, 1978. The daytime awards ceremony was broadcast on ABC on June 7, 1978, and involved programs aired between March, 1977, and March, 1978. The first annual sports awards were held on Feb. 13, 1979, for programs telecast from March 14, 1976, to June 15, 1978.

PRIME-TIME PROGRAM AWARDS
OUTSTANDING DRAMA SERIES
• *The Rockford Files*. Meta Rosenberg, executive producer. Stephen J. Cannell, supervising producer. David Chase, Chas. Floyd Johnson, producers. NBC.
Columbo, NBC Sunday Mystery Movie. Richard Alan Simmons, producer. NBC.
Family. Aaron Spelling, Leonard Goldberg, executive producers. Nigel McKeand, producer. ABC.
Lou Grant. James L. Brooks, Allan Burns, Gene Reynolds, executive producers. Gene Reynolds, producer. CBS.
Quincy. Glen A. Larson, Jud Kinberg, Richard Irving, executive producers. B.W. Sandefur, supervising producer. Chris Morgan, Peter J. Thompson, Edward J. Montagne, Robert F. O'Neill, producers.

Michael Sloan, associate executive producer. NBC.

OUTSTANDING COMEDY SERIES
• *All in the Family*. Mort Lachman, executive producer. Milt Josefsberg, producer. CBS.
Barney Miller. Danny Arnold, executive producer. Tony Sheehan, producer. ABC.
*M*A*S*H*. Burt Metcalfe, producer. CBS.
Soap. Paul Junger Witt, Tony Thomas, executive producers. Susan Harris, producer. ABC.
Three's Company. Don Nicholl, Michael Ross, Bernie West, producers. ABC.

OUTSTANDING LIMITED SERIES
• *Holocaust, The Big Event*. Herbert Brodkin, executive producer. Robert Berger, producer. NBC.
King. Edward S. Feldman, executive producer. Paul Maslansky, producer. William Finnegan, supervising producer. NBC.
Washington: Behind Closed Doors. Stanley Kallis, executive producer. Eric Bercovici, David W. Rintels, supervising producers. Norman Powell, producer. ABC.
Anna Karenina, Masterpiece Theatre. Ken Riddington, executive producer. Donald Wilson, producer. Joan Sullivan, series producer. PBS.

I, Claudius, Masterpiece Theatre. Martin Lisemore, producer. Joan Sullivan, series producer. PBS.

OUTSTANDING SPECIAL— DRAMA OR COMEDY
• *The Gathering.* Joseph Barbera, executive producer. Harry R. Sherman, producer. ABC.
A Death in Canaan. Robert W. Christiansen, Rick Rosenberg, producers. CBS.
Jesus of Nazareth. Bernard J. Kingham, executive producer. Vincenzo Labella, producer. NBC.
Our Town, The Bell System Special. Saul Jaffe, executive producer. George Schaefer, producer. NBC.
Young Joe, The Forgotten Kennedy. William McCutchen, producer. ABC.

OUTSTANDING COMEDY-VARIETY OR MUSIC SERIES
• *The Muppet Show.* David Lazer, executive producer. Jim Henson, producer. Frank Oz, Jerry Nelson, Richard Hunt, Dave Goelz, Jim Henson, stars. Syndicated.
America 2Night. Alan Thicke, producer. Syndicated.
The Carol Burnett Show. Joe Hamilton, executive producer. Edward Simmons, producer. Carol Burnett, star. CBS.
Evening at Pops. Bill Cosel, producer. Arthur Fiedler, star. PBS.
NBC's Saturday Night Live. Lorne Michaels, producer. NBC.

OUTSTANDING SPECIAL— COMEDY-VARIETY OR MUSIC
• *Bette Midler — Ol' Red Hair is Back.* Aaron Russo, executive producer. Gary Smith, Dwight Hemion, producers. Bette Midler, star. NBC.
Doug Henning's World of Magic. Jerry Goldstein, executive producer. Walter C. Miller, producer. Doug Henning, star. NBC.
The George Burns One-Man Show. Irving Fein, executive producer. Stan Harris, producer. George Burns, star. CBS.
Neil Diamond: I'm Glad You're Here With Me Tonight. Jerry Weintraub, executive producer. Art Fisher, producer. Neil Diamond, star. NBC.
The Second Barry Manilow Special. Miles J. Lourie, executive producer. Ernest Chambers, Barry Manilow, producers. Barry Manilow, star. ABC.

OUTSTANDING CLASSICAL PROGRAM IN THE PERFORMING ARTS
(Winner)
• American Ballet Theatre's "Giselle," *Live from Lincoln Center.* John Goberman, producer. PBS.

OUTSTANDING CHILDREN'S SPECIAL
(Winner)
• *Halloween is Grinch Night.* David H. DePatie, Friz Freleng, executive producers. Ted Geisel, producer. ABC.

OUTSTANDING INFORMATIONAL SERIES
(Winner)
• *The Body Human.* Thomas W. Moore, executive producer. Alfred R. Kelman, producer. CBS.

OUTSTANDING INFORMATIONAL SPECIAL
(Winner)
• "The Great Whales," *National Geographic Specials.* Thomas Skinner, Dennis B. Kane, executive producers. Nicolas Noxon, producer. PBS.

SPECIAL CLASSIFICATION OF OUTSTANDING PROGRAM ACHIEVEMENT
(Winner)
• *The Tonight Show Starring Johnny Carson.* Fred DeCordova, producer. Johnny Carson, star. NBC.

PERFORMANCE, DIRECTING, AND WRITING
OUTSTANDING LEAD ACTOR IN A DRAMA SERIES
• Edward Asner, *Lou Grant.* CBS.
James Broderick, *Family.* ABC.
Peter Falk, *Columbo, NBC Sunday Mystery Movie.* NBC.
James Garner, *The Rockford Files.* NBC.
Jack Klugman, *Quincy.* NBC.
Ralph Waite, *The Waltons.* CBS.

OUTSTANDING LEAD ACTRESS IN A DRAMA SERIES
• Sada Thompson, *Family.* ABC.
Melissa Sue Anderson, *Little House on the Prairie.* NBC.
Fionnula Flanagan, *How the West Was Won.* ABC.
Kate Jackson, *Charlie's Angels.* ABC.
Michael Learned, *The Waltons.* CBS.
Susan Sullivan, *Julie Farr, M.D.* ABC.

Outstanding Lead Actor in a Comedy Series
• Carroll O'Connor, *All in the Family*. CBS.
Alan Alda, *M*A*S*H*. CBS.
Hal Linden, *Barney Miller*. ABC.
John Ritter, *Three's Company*. ABC.
Henry Winkler, *Happy Days*. ABC.

Outstanding Lead Actress in a Comedy Series
• Jean Stapleton, *All in the Family*. CBS.
Beatrice Arthur, *Maude*. CBS.
Cathryn Damon, *Soap*. ABC.
Valerie Harper, *Rhoda*. CBS.
Katherine Helmond, *Soap*. ABC.
Suzanne Pleshette, *The Bob Newhart Show*. CBS.

Outstanding Lead Actor in a Limited Series
• Michael Moriarty, *Holocaust, The Big Event*. NBC.
Hal Holbrook, *The Awakening Land*. NBC.
Jason Robards, Jr., *Washington: Behind Closed Doors*. ABC.
Fritz Weaver, *Holocaust, The Big Event*. NBC.
Paul Winfield, *King*. NBC.

Outstanding Lead Actress in a Limited Series
• Meryl Streep, *Holocaust, The Big Event*. NBC.
Rosemary Harris, *Holocaust, The Big Event*. NBC.
Elizabeth Montgomery, *The Awakening Land*. NBC.
Lee Remick, *Wheels*. NBC.
Cicely Tyson, *King*. NBC.

Outstanding Lead Actor for a Single Appearance in a Drama or Comedy Series
• Barnard Hughes, *Lou Grant*. CBS.
David Cassidy, *Police Story*. NBC.
Will Geer, *The Love Boat*. ABC.
Judd Hirsch, *Rhoda*. CBS.
John Rubinstein, *Family*. ABC.
Keenan Wynn, *Police Woman*. NBC.

Outstanding Lead Actress for a Single Appearance in a Drama or Comedy Series
• Rita Moreno, *The Rockford Files*. NBC.
Patty Duke Astin, *Having Babies*. ABC.

Kate Jackson, *James at 15/16*. NBC.
Jayne Meadows, *Meeting of Minds*. PBS.
Irene Tedrow, *James at 15/16*. NBC.

Outstanding Lead Actor in a Drama or Comedy Special
• Fred Astaire, *A Family Upside Down*. NBC.
Alan Alda, *Kill Me If You Can*. NBC.
Hal Holbrook, *Our Town, The Bell System Special*. NBC.
Martin Sheen, *Taxi!!, Hallmark Hall of Fame*. NBC.
James Stacy, *Just a Little Inconvenience*. NBC.

Outstanding Lead Actress in a Drama or Comedy Special
• Joanne Woodward, *See How She Runs, G.E. Theatre*. CBS.
Helen Hayes, *A Family Upside Down*. NBC.
Eva Marie Saint, *Taxi!!, Hallmark Hall of Fame*. NBC.
Maureen Stapleton, *The Gathering*. ABC.
Sada Thompson, *Our Town, The Bell System Special*. NBC.

Outstanding Supporting Actor in a Drama Series
• Robert Vaughn, *Washington: Behind Closed Doors*. ABC.
Ossie Davis, *King*. NBC.
Will Geer, *The Waltons*. CBS.
Sam Wanamaker, *Holocaust, The Big Event*. NBC.
David Warner, *Holocaust, The Big Event*. NBC.

Outstanding Supporting Actress in a Drama Series
• Nancy Marchand, *Lou Grant*. CBS.
Meredith Baxter Birney, *Family*. ABC.
Tovah Feldshuh, *Holocaust, The Big Event*. NBC.
Linda Kelsey, *Lou Grant*. CBS.
Kristy McNichol, *Family*. ABC.

Outstanding Supporting Actor in a Comedy Series
• Rob Reiner, *All in the Family*. CBS.
Tom Bosley, *Happy Days*. ABC.
Gary Burghoff, *M*A*S*H*. CBS.
Harry Morgan, *M*A*S*H*. CBS.
Vic Tayback, *Alice*. CBS.

OUTSTANDING SUPPORTING ACTRESS IN A COMEDY SERIES
• Julie Kavner, *Rhoda*. CBS.
Polly Holliday, *Alice*. CBS.
Sally Struthers, *All in the Family*. CBS.
Loretta Swit, *M*A*S*H*. CBS.
Nancy Walker, *Rhoda*. CBS.

OUTSTANDING SINGLE PERFORMANCE BY A SUPPORTING ACTOR IN A COMEDY OR DRAMA SERIES
• Ricardo Montalban, *How the West was Won*. ABC.
Will Geer, *Eight is Enough*. ABC.
Larry Gelman, *Barney Miller*. ABC.
Harold Gould, *Rhoda*. CBS.
Abe Vigoda, *Barney Miller*. ABC.

OUTSTANDING SINGLE PERFORMANCE BY A SUPPORTING ACTRESS IN A COMEDY OR DRAMA SERIES
• Blanche Baker, *Holocaust, The Big Event*. NBC.
Ellen Corby, *The Waltons*. CBS.
Jeanette Nolan, *The Awakening Land*. NBC.
Beulah Quo, *Meeting of Minds*. PBS.
Beatrice Straight, *The Dain Curse*. CBS.

OUTSTANDING PERFORMANCE BY A SUPPORTING ACTOR IN A COMEDY OR DRAMA SPECIAL
• Howard Da Silva, *Verna: USO Girl*, *Great Performances*. PBS.
James Farentino, *Jesus of Nazareth*. NBC.
Burgess Meredith, *The Last Hurrah*, *Hallmark Hall of Fame*. NBC.
Donald Pleasence, *The Defection of Simas Kudirka*. CBS.
Efrem Zimbalist, Jr., *A Family Upside Down*. NBC.

OUTSTANDING PERFORMANCE BY A SUPPORTING ACTRESS IN A DRAMA OR COMEDY SPECIAL
• Eva Le Gallienne, *The Royal Family*. PBS.
Patty Duke Astin, *A Family Upside Down*. NBC.
Tyne Daly, *Intimate Strangers*. ABC.
Mariette Hartley, *The Last Hurrah*, *Hallmark Hall of Fame*. NBC.
Cloris Leachman, *It Happened One Christmas*. ABC.
Viveca Lindfors, *A Question of Guilt*. CBS.

OUTSTANDING CONTINUING OR SINGLE PERFORMANCE BY A SUPPORTING ACTOR IN VARIETY OR MUSIC
• Tim Conway, *The Carol Burnett Show*. CBS.
Dan Aykroyd, *NBC's Saturday Night Live*. NBC.
John Belushi, *NBC's Saturday Night Live*. NBC.
Louis Gossett, Jr., *The Sentry Collection Presents Ben Vereen — His Roots*. ABC.
Peter Sellers, *The Muppet Show*. Syndicated.

OUTSTANDING CONTINUING OR SINGLE PERFORMANCE BY A SUPPORTING ACTRESS IN VARIETY OR MUSIC
• Gilda Radner, *NBC's Saturday Night Live*. NBC.
Beatrice Arthur, *Laugh-In*. NBC.
Jane Curtin, *NBC's Saturday Night Live*. NBC.
Dolly Parton, *Cher... Special*. ABC.
Bernadette Peters, *The Muppet Show*. Syndicated.

OUTSTANDING DIRECTING IN A DRAMA SERIES
• Marvin J. Chomsky, *Holocaust, The Big Event*. NBC.
Abby Mann, *King*. NBC.
Gary Nelson, *Washington: Behind Closed Doors*. ABC.
E. W. Swackhamer, *The Dain Curse*. CBS.
Herbert Wise, *I, Claudius*, *Masterpiece Theatre*. PBS.

OUTSTANDING DIRECTING IN A COMEDY SERIES
• Paul Bogart, *All in the Family*. CBS.
Hal Cooper, *Maude*. CBS.
Burt Metcalfe, Alan Alda, *M*A*S*H*. CBS.
Jerry Paris, *Happy Days*. ABC.
Jay Sandrich, *Soap*. ABC.

OUTSTANDING DIRECTING IN A SPECIAL PROGRAM—DRAMA OR COMEDY
• David Lowell Rich, *The Defection of Simas Kudirka*. CBS.
Lou Antonio, *Something for Joey*. CBS.
Randal Kleiser, *The Gathering*. ABC.
Delbert Mann, *Breaking Up*. ABC.
Ronald Maxwell, *Verna: USO Girl*, *Great Performances*. PBS.
George Schaefer, *Our Town*, *The Bell System Special*. NBC.

**OUTSTANDING DIRECTING
IN A COMEDY-VARIETY OR MUSIC SERIES**
• Dave Powers, *The Carol Burnett Show*.
CBS.
Steve Binder, *Shields and Yarnell*. CBS.
Peter Harris, *The Muppet Show*. Syndicated.
John C. Moffitt, *The Richard Pryor Show*.
NBC.
Dave Wilson, *NBC's Saturday Night Live*.
NBC.

**OUTSTANDING DIRECTING IN A COMEDY-
VARIETY OR MUSIC SPECIAL**
• Dwight Hemion, *The Sentry Collection
Presents Ben Vereen — His Roots*. ABC.
Tony Charmoli, *Mitzi ... Zings Into Spring*.
CBS.
Walter C. Miller, *Doug Henning's World
of Magic*. NBC.
George Schaefer, *The Second Barry
Manilow Special*. ABC.
Dave Wilson, *The Paul Simon Special*.
NBC.

**OUTSTANDING WRITING
IN A DRAMA SERIES**
• Gerald Green, *Holocaust, The Big Event*.
NBC.
Steve Allen, *Meeting of Minds*. PBS.
Alan Ayckbourn, *The Norman Conquests*.
PBS.
Robert W. Lenski, *The Dain Curse*. CBS.
Abby Mann, *King*. NBC.

**OUTSTANDING WRITING
IN A COMEDY SERIES**
• Bob Weiskopf, Bob Schiller, teleplay.
Barry Harman, Harve Brosten, story, *All in
the Family*. CBS.
Alan Alda, *M*A*S*H*. CBS.
Mel Tolkin, Larry Rhine, teleplay. Erik
Tarloff, story, *All in the Family*. CBS.
Bob Weiskopf, Bob Schiller, *All in the
Family*. CBS.

**OUTSTANDING WRITING IN A SPECIAL
PROGRAM—DRAMA OR COMEDY—
ORIGINAL TELEPLAY**
• George Rubino, *The Last Tenant*. ABC.
Bruce Feldman, *The Defection of Simas
Kudirka*. CBS.
Richard Levinson, William Link, *The
Storyteller*. NBC.
Loring Mandel, *Breaking Up*. ABC.
Jerry McNeely, *Something for Joey*. CBS.
James Poe, *The Gathering*. ABC.

**OUTSTANDING WRITING
IN A SPECIAL PROGRAM—DRAMA OR
COMEDY—ADAPTATION**
• Caryl Lender, *Mary White*. ABC.
Blanche Hanalis, *A Love Affair — The
Eleanor and Lou Gehrig Story*. NBC.
Albert Innaurato, *Verna: USO Girl, Great
Performances*. PBS.
Jerome Lawrence, Robert E. Lee, *Actor,
Hollywood Television Theatre*. PBS.
Barbara Turner, *The War Between the
Tates*. NBC.

**OUTSTANDING WRITING IN A COMEDY-
VARIETY OR MUSIC SERIES**
• Ed Simmons, Roger Beatty, Rick
Hawkins, Liz Sage, Robert Illes,
James Stein, Franelle Silver, Larry Siegel,
Tim Conway, Bill Richmond, Gene Perret,
Dick Clair, Jenna McMahon, *The Carol
Burnett Show*. CBS.
Ed Simmons, Roger Beatty, Elias David,
David Pollock, Rick Hawkins, Liz Sage,
Adele Styler, Burt Styler, Tim Conway,
Bill Richmond, Gene Perret, Dick Clair,
Jenna McMahon, *The Carol Burnett Show*.
CBS.
Jerry Juhl, Don Hinkley, Joseph Bailey,
Jim Henson, *The Muppet Show*.
Syndicated.
Alan Thicke, John Boni, Norman Stiles,
Jeremy Stevens, Tom Moore, Robert Illes,
James Stein, Harry Shearer, Tom
Dunsmuir and Dan Wilcox, *America
2Night*. Syndicated.
Dan Aykroyd, Anne Beatts, Tom Davis,
James Downey, Brian Doyle-Murray, Al
Franken, Lorne Michaels, Marilyn
Suzanne Miller, Don Novello, Michael
O'Donoghue, Herb Sargent, Tom Schiller,
Rosie Shuster, Alan Zweibel, *NBC's
Saturday Night Live* (with Steve Martin).
NBC.

**OUTSTANDING WRITING IN A COMEDY-
VARIETY OR MUSIC SPECIAL**
• Lorne Michaels, Paul Simon, Chevy
Chase, Tom Davis, Al Franken, Charles
Grodin, Lily Tomlin, Alan Zweibel, *The
Paul Simon Special*. NBC.
Alan Buz Kohan, Rod Warren, Pat
McCormick, Tom Eyen, Jerry Blatt, Bette
Midler, Bruce Vilanch, *Bette Midler — Ol'
Red Hair is Back*. NBC.
Elon Packard, Fred Fox, Seaman Jacobs,
The George Burns One-Man Show. CBS.
Ernest Chambers, Barry Manilow, *The*

Second Barry Manilow Special. ABC. Michael H. Kagan, *The Sentry Collection Presents Ben Vereen — His Roots.* ABC.

OTHER AWARD WINNERS

OUTSTANDING MUSIC COMPOSITION FOR A SERIES
(Dramatic underscore)
• Billy Goldenberg, *King.* NBC.

OUTSTANDING MUSIC COMPOSITION FOR A SPECIAL-DRAMATIC UNDERSCORE
• Jimmie Haskell, *See How She Runs, G.E. Theatre.* CBS.

OUTSTANDING MUSIC DIRECTION
• Ian Fraser, *The Sentry Collection Presents Ben Vereen — His Roots.* ABC.

OUTSTANDING SPECIAL MUSICAL MATERIAL
(Tie)
• Stan Freeman, Arthur Malvin, music and lyrics, *The Carol Burnett Show.* CBS.
• Mitzie Welch, Ken Welch, music and lyrics, *The Sentry Collection Presents Ben Vereen — His Roots.* ABC.

OUTSTANDING CHOREOGRAPHY
• Ron Field, *The Sentry Collection Presents Ben Vereen — His Roots.* ABC.

OUTSTANDING COSTUME DESIGN FOR A DRAMA OR COMEDY SERIES
• Peggy Farrell, Edith Almoslino, *Holocaust, The Big Event.* NBC.

OUTSTANDING COSTUME DESIGN FOR MUSIC-VARIETY
• Bob Mackie, Ret Turner, *Mitzi ... Zings Into Spring.* CBS.

OUTSTANDING COSTUME DESIGN FOR A DRAMA SPECIAL
• Noel Taylor, *Actor, Hollywood Television Theatre.* PBS.

OUTSTANDING ART DIRECTION FOR A DRAMA SERIES
• Tim Harvey, art director, *I, Claudius, Masterpiece Theatre.* PBS.

OUTSTANDING ART DIRECTION FOR A COMEDY SERIES
• Edward Stephenson, production designer. Robert Checchi, set decorator, *Soap.* ABC.

OUTSTANDING ART DIRECTION FOR A DRAMATIC SPECIAL
• John De Cuir, production designer. Richard C. Goddard, set decorator, *Ziegfeld — The Man and His Women.* NBC.

OUTSTANDING ART DIRECTION FOR A COMEDY-VARIETY OR MUSIC SERIES
• Roy Christopher, *The Richard Pryor Show.* NBC.

OUTSTANDING ART DIRECTION FOR A COMEDY-VARIETY OR MUSIC SPECIAL
• Romain Johnston, art director. Kerry Joyce, set decorator, *The Sentry Collection Presents Ben Vereen — His Roots.* ABC.

OUTSTANDING MAKEUP
• Richard Cobos, Walter Schenck, *How the West was Won.* ABC.

OUTSTANDING GRAPHIC DESIGN AND TITLE SEQUENCES
• Bill Davis, *NBC: The First Fifty Years — A Closer Look.* NBC.

OUTSTANDING CINEMATOGRAPHY IN ENTERTAINMENT PROGRAMMING FOR A SERIES
• Ted Voigtlander, *Little House on the Prairie.* NBC.

OUTSTANDING CINEMATOGRAPHY IN ENTERTAINMENT PROGRAMMING FOR A SPECIAL
• Gerald Perry Finnerman, *Ziegfeld — The Man and His Women.* NBC.

OUTSTANDING IN TECHNICAL DIRECTION AND ELECTRONIC CAMERAWORK
• Gene Crowe, technical director. Wayne Orr, Larry Heider, Dave Hilmer, Bob Keys, cameramen, *The Sentry Collection Presents Ben Vereen — His Roots.* ABC.

OUTSTANDING FILM EDITING IN A DRAMA SERIES
• Stephen A. Rotter, Robert M. Reitano, Craig McKay, Alan Heim, Brian Smedley-Aston, *Holocaust, The Big Event.* NBC.

OUTSTANDING FILM EDITING IN A COMEDY SERIES
• Ed Cotter, *Happy Days.* ABC.

**OUTSTANDING FILM EDITING
FOR A SPECIAL**
• John A. Martinelli, *The Defection of
Simas Kudirka.* CBS.

**OUTSTANDING VIDEO-TAPE EDITING
FOR A SERIES**
• Tucker Wiard, *The Carol Burnett Show.*
CBS.

**OUTSTANDING VIDEO-TAPE EDITING
FOR A SPECIAL**
• Pam Marshall, Andy Zall, *The Sentry
Collection Presents Ben Vereen — His
Roots.* ABC.

OUTSTANDING FILM SOUND MIXING
• William Teague, George E. Porter, Eddie
J. Nelson, Robert L. Harman, *Young Joe,
The Forgotten Kennedy.* ABC.

**OUTSTANDING FILM SOUND EDITING
FOR A SERIES**
• Douglas H. Grindstaff, Hank Salerno,
Larry Singer, Christopher Chulack,
Richard Raderman, Don Crosby, H. Lee
Chaney, Mark Dennis, Don V. Isaacs,
Steve Olson, Al Kajita, *Police Story.* NBC.

**OUTSTANDING FILM SOUND EDITING
FOR A SPECIAL**
• Jerry Rosenthal, Michael Corrigan, Jerry
Pirozzi, William Jackson, James Yant,
Richard LeGrand, Donald Higgins, John
Strauss, John Kline, *The Amazing Howard
Hughes.* CBS.

OUTSTANDING TAPE SOUND MIXING
• Thomas J. Huth, Edward J. Greene and
Ron Bryan, *Bette Midler — Ol' Red Hair
is Back.* NBC.

OUTSTANDING LIGHTING DIRECTION
• Greg Brunton, *Cher ... Special.* ABC.

**OUTSTANDING INDIVIDUAL
ACHIEVEMENT IN ANY AREA OF
CREATIVE TECHNICAL CRAFTS
(Area award)**
• William F. Bronwell, John H. Kantrowe,
Jr., sound effects, *Our Town, The Bell
System Special.* NBC.

**SPECIAL CLASSIFICATION
OF OUTSTANDING INDIVIDUAL
ACHIEVEMENT
(Area award)**
• William Pitkin. costume design, *Romeo
and Juliet.* PBS.

**OUTSTANDING INDIVIDUAL ACHIEVEMENT
IN CHILDREN'S PROGRAMMING
(Area award)**
• Ken Johnson, art director. Robert Chec-
chi, set decorator, *Once Upon a Brothers
Grimm.* CBS.
• Bill Hargate, costume designer, *Once
Upon a Brothers Grimm.* CBS.

DAYTIME AWARDS
OUTSTANDING DAYTIME DRAMA SERIES
• *Days of Our Lives.* Betty Corday, H.
Wesley Kenny, executive producers. Jack
Herzberg, producer. NBC.
All My Children. Bud Kloss, Agnes Nixon,
producers. ABC.
Ryan's Hope. Claire Labine, Paul Avila
Mayer, executive producers. Robert
Costello, producer. ABC.
The Young and the Restless. John Conboy,
executive producer. Patricia Wenig,
producer. CBS.

**OUTSTANDING ACTOR IN A DAYTIME
DRAMA SERIES**
• James Pritchett, *The Doctors.* NBC
Matthew Cowles, *All My Children.* ABC.
Larry Keith, *All My Children.* ABC.
Michael Levin, *Ryan's Hope.* ABC.
Andrew Robinson, *Ryan's Hope.* ABC.
Michael Storm, *One Life to Live.* ABC.

**OUTSTANDING ACTRESS
IN A DAYTIME SERIES**
• Laurie Heinemann, *Another World.* NBC.
Mary Fickett, *All My Children.* ABC.
Susan Seaforth Hayes, *Days of Our Lives.*
NBC.
Jennifer Harmon, *One Life to Live.* ABC.
Susan Lucci, *All My Children.* ABC.
Beverlee McKinsey, *Another World.* NBC.
Victoria Wyndham, *Another World.* NBC.

**OUTSTANDING INDIVIDUAL DIRECTOR
FOR A DAYTIME DRAMA SERIES**
• Richard Dunlap, *The Young and the
Restless.* CBS.
Ira Cirker, *Another World.* NBC.
Richard T. McCue, *As the World Turns.*
CBS.

Daytime drama's best actor and actress: Laurie Heinemann of Another World *and James Prichett of* The Doctors.

Robert Myhrum, *Love of Life.* CBS.
Al Rabin, *Days of Our Lives.* NBC.
Lela Swift, *Ryan's Hope.* ABC.

OUTSTANDING WRITING
FOR A DAYTIME DRAMA SERIES
• Claire Labine, Paul Avila Mayer, Mary Munisteri, Allan Leicht, Judith Pinsker, *Ryan's Hope.* ABC.
William J. Bell, Kay Lenard, Bill Rega, Pat Falken Smith, Margaret Stewart, *Days of Our Lives.* NBC.
Jerome and Bridget Dobson, Nancy Ford, Jean Ruverol, Robert and Phyllis White, *The Guiding Light.* CBS.
Agnes Nixon, Cathy Chicos, Doris Franker, Ken Harvey, Kathryn McCabe, Wisner Washam, Mary K. Wells, Jack Wood, *All My Children.* ABC.
Ann Marcus, Ray Goldstone, Joyce Perry, Michael Robert David, Laura Olsher, Rocci Chaffield, Elizabeth Harrower, *Days of Our Lives.* NBC.

OTHER DAYTIME AWARD WINNERS
OUTSTANDING GAME OR AUDIENCE
PARTICIPATION SHOW
• *The Hollywood Squares.* Merrill Heatter, Bob Quigley, executive producers. Jay Redack, producer. NBC.

OUTSTANDING TALK, SERVICE,
OR VARIETY SERIES
• *Donahue.* Richard Mincer, executive producer. Patricia McMillen, producer. Syndicated.

OUTSTANDING HOST OR HOSTESS
IN A GAME OR AUDIENCE
PARTICIPATION SHOW
• Richard Dawson, *The Family Feud.* ABC.

OUTSTANDING HOST OR HOSTESS
IN A TALK, SERVICE, OR VARIETY SERIES
• Phil Donahue, *Donahue.* Syndicated.

OUTSTANDING INDIVIDUAL DIRECTOR
FOR A DAYTIME GAME OR AUDIENCE
PARTICIPATION SHOW
• Mike Gargiulo, *The $20,000 Pyramid.* ABC.

OUTSTANDING INDIVIDUAL DIRECTOR
FOR A VARIETY PROGRAM
• Martin Haig Mackey, *Over Easy.* PBS.

OUTSTANDING CHILDREN'S
ENTERTAINMENT SPECIAL
• "Hewitt's Just Different," *ABC Afterschool Special.* Daniel Wilson, executive producer. Fran Sears, producer. ABC.

OUTSTANDING CHILDREN'S
ENTERTAINMENT SERIES
• *Captain Kangaroo.* Jim Hirschfeld, producer. CBS.

OUTSTANDING CHILDREN'S
INFORMATIONAL SERIES
• *Animals Animals Animals.* Lester Cooper, executive producer. Peter Weinberg, producer. ABC.

OUTSTANDING CHILDREN'S
INFORMATIONAL SPECIAL
• "Very Good Friends," *ABC Afterschool Special,* Martin Tahse, producer. ABC.

OUTSTANDING CHILDREN'S
INSTRUCTIONAL SERIES
• *Schoolhouse Rock.* Tom Yohe, executive producer. Radford Stone, George Newall, producers. ABC.

SPECIAL CLASSIFICATION
OF OUTSTANDING PROGRAM ACHIEVEMENT
(Area award)
• "Recital of Tenor Luciano Pavarotti from the Met," *Live from Lincoln Center.* John Goberman, executive producer. PBS.

OUTSTANDING ACHIEVEMENT IN COVERAGE OF SPECIAL EVENTS
(Area award)
• *The Great English Garden Party — Peter Ustinov Looks at 100 Years of Wimbledon.* Ken Ashton, Allison Hawkes, Pamela Moncur, producers. NBC.

OUTSTANDING INDIVIDUAL ACHIEVEMENT IN CHILDREN'S PROGRAMMING
(Area award)
• Tom Aldredge, performer, "Henry Winkler Meets William Shakespeare," *CBS Festival of Lively Arts for Young People.* CBS.
• Jan Hartman, writer, "Hewitt's Just Different," *ABC Weekend Specials.* ABC.
• David Wolf, writer, "The Magic Hat," *Unicorn Tales.* Syndicated.
• Tony Di Girolamo, lighting director, "Henry Winkler Meets William Shakespeare," *CBS Festival of Lively Arts for Young People.* CBS.
• Bonnie Karrin, film editor, "Big Apple Birthday," *Unicorn Tales.* Syndicated.
• Brianne Murphy, cinematographer, "Five Finger Discount," *Special Treat.* NBC.
• Ken Johnson, art director. Robert Checchi, set decorator, *Once Upon a Brothers Grimm.* CBS.
• Bill Hargate, costume designer, *Once Upon a Brothers Grimm.* CBS.

OUTSTANDING INDIVIDUAL ACHIEVEMENT IN DAYTIME PROGRAMMING
(Area award)
• Connie Wexter, costume design, *Search for Tomorrow.* CBS.
• Steve Cunningham, technical director. Hector Ramirez, Sheldon Mooney, Martin Wagner, Dave Finch, cameramen, *After Hours: Singin', Swingin' & All That Jazz.* CBS.
• Steve Cunningham, technical director. Fred Gough, Mike Stitch, Joe Vicens, cameramen, *The Young and the Restless.* CBS.
• David M. Clark, lighting director, *The Mike Douglas Show.* Syndicated.
• Joyce Tamara Grossman, video-tape editing, *The Family Feud.* ABC.

OUTSTANDING RELIGIOUS PROGRAMMING
• *Woman of Valor.* Doris Ann, executive producer. Martin Hoade, producer. NBC.

OUTSTANDING INDIVIDUAL ACHIEVEMENT IN RELIGIOUS PROGRAMMING
(Area award)
• Carolee Campbell, performer, *This is My Son.* NBC.
• Douglass Watson, performer, *Continuing Creation.* NBC.
• Joseph Vadala, cinematographer, *Continuing Creation.* NBC.

(There were no winners in the following categories: special classification of outstanding individual achievement or outstanding achievement in coverage of special events—programs.)

SPORTS AWARD WINNERS
OUTSTANDING LIVE SPORTS SERIES
• *The NFL Today/NFL Football on CBS.* Michael Pearl, producer. CBS.

OUTSTANDING EDITED SPORTS SERIES
• *The Way It Was.* Gerry Gross, executive producer. Gary Brown, Dick Enberg, producers. Syndicated.

OUTSTANDING LIVE SPORTS SPECIALS
• *World Championship Boxing: Ali/Spinks,* Frank Chirkinian, producer. CBS.

OUTSTANDING EDITED SPORTS SPECIAL
• *The Impossible Dream: Ballooning Across the Atlantic.* Ed Goren, producer. CBS.

OUTSTANDING SPORTS PERSONALITY
• Jack Whitaker. CBS.

OUTSTANDING DIRECTING IN SPORTS PROGRAMMING
• Ted Nathanson, *AFC Championship Football.* NBC.

SPORTS AREA AWARDS
Each area has the possibility of multiple winners, one winner, or none. Winners are listed.

OUTSTANDING INDIVIDUAL ACHIEVEMENT IN SPORTS PROGRAMMING
(Writing)
• Steve Sabol, "Joe and the Magic Bean: The Story of Superbowl III," *NFL Today.* CBS.

(Cinematography)
• Steve Sabol, "Skateboard Fever," *Sportsworld*. NBC.
(Film editing)
• Steve Sabol, "Skateboard Fever," *Sportsworld*. NBC.
(Engineering supervision/technical direction /Electronic camerawork)
• Arthur Tinn, engineering supervisor, *The Superbowl Today/Superbowl* XII. CBS.
(Video-tape editing and associate directors)
• Bob Levy, associate director. Jerome Haggart, Richard Leible, Charles Liotta and John Olszewski, video-tape editors, *Sportsworld*. NBC.

INTERNATIONAL AWARD WINNERS
DIRECTORATE AWARD
• Alphonse Ouiment, chairman of the board, Telesat, Canada.

FICTION AWARD
• *The Collection*, Granada Television Ltd., Manchester, U.K.

NON-FICTION
• *Henry Ford's America*, Canadian Broadcasting Corp., Toronto, Canada.

SPECIAL AWARDS
OUTSTANDING ACHIEVEMENT IN BROADCAST JOURNALISM
• Charles Kuralt, "On the Road," *CBS News*,.Bill Moyers, *CBS Reports*. CBS.

• "The Fire Next Door," *CBS Reports*, Howard Stringer, executive producer. CBS.
"Exploding Gas Tanks," *20/20*, Sylvia Chase, correspondent. Stanhope Gould, producer. ABC.

OUTSTANDING ACHIEVEMENT IN THE SCIENCE OF TELEVISION ENGINEERING
• CBS, Inc.
• PBS Engineering
• Thomson-CSF Laboratories

OUTSTANDING ACHIEVEMENT IN ENGINEERING DEVELOPMENT
• Petro Vlahos of Vlahos-Gottschalk Research Corporation.
(Citation)
Society of Motion Picture and Television Engineers.

NATIONAL AWARD FOR COMMUNITY SERVICE
• *Water*. KOOL-TV, Phoenix, Arizona.

GOVERNORS AWARDS
• William S. Paley, Chairman of the Board, CBS.
• Larry Stewart, president of A.T.A.S., 1975–1977.
• Frederick Wolcott, Governors Medallion recipient for his 30 years of service on the A.T.A.S. Engineering Awards Panel.

A Slim, Trim Emmy
Takes a *Taxi* Ride

Following last year's longest Emmys show in history, an effort was made to streamline the ceremony by trimming the number of prime-time awards — drastically. A.T.A.S. slashed them by almost 30 percent, from 75 to 56, with trophies presented on the air cut from 42 to 32. "A distinct improvement," commented *American Film*. The *L.A. Times* wanted even more cuts, insisting, "They should be sent back to a fat farm because there's an awful lot of reducing yet to do."

In its first season Taxi *began a three-year joyride through the comedy category, eventually reaping honors for Judd Hirsch and Danny DeVito, too.*

The *Herald Examiner* complained that the streamlining "resulted in a cutback on recognition for specials" when the acting, directing, and writing awards for specials were combined with those of limited series, while similar economizing was also done by grouping the nominees for comedy and variety series.

Henry Winkler and Cheryl Ladd were hosts at the Pasadena Civic Auditorium where the crowd literally sweated out the night's suspense because of problems with the air conditioning. The suspense would be considerable, too, thanks to an abundance of upsets in the works.

Special Emmys went to such industry luminaries as Walter Cronkite, who accepted a Governors Award by assessing that he and his colleagues in TV news had done "a pretty fair job, but not good enough." (He also confessed, in a flip aside, "I always wanted to be a song and dance man.") Veteran gagster and 1949 Emmy-winner Milton Berle was given a special presentation acknowledging him as "Mr. Television," but he said he had only one one-liner to use on this occasion: "I can't tell you what this means to me."

"This year's Emmys looked like a repeat," observed the *Herald Examiner* because of the reappearance of President Jimmy Carter, who interrupted the broadcast this time to pay tribute to three newsmen who were killed while on assignment: NBC cameramen Don Harris and Robert Brown, who died outside the Jonestown religious cult compound in Guyana during the attack on Congressman Leo Ryan, and Bill Stewart of ABC, who was slain while covering the Nicaraguan civil war. "They died in the service of a free press," Carter said. "They died in the service of us all." The widows of all three newsmen were in the audience and were given a standing ovation.

The night also seemed familiar because the miniseries *Roots* was again up for Emmys, but this time for its 12-hour sequel, *The Next Generations*, which was named Outstanding Limited

Bette Davis (with Gena Rowlands, left, in Strangers) *beat out old foe Katharine Hepburn to be named TV's best actress.*

Series. As the *L.A. Times* noted, the sequel was "generally praised by TV critics as artistically superior to the first," although those who didn't think so claimed that the new material lacked heart. Either way, it didn't disappoint its fans. Each of its 7 episodes ended up in the weekly Nielsen's top 11 as the continuing saga of author Alex Haley's ancestry was traced from 1882 to 1967 and again offered a star cast that included James Earl Jones, Paul Winfield, Ruby Dee, Henry Fonda, Olivia de Havilland — and Emmy's best supporting actor choice, Marlon Brando.

It was Brando's first dramatic TV appearance in 30 years. "His portrayal of American Nazi leader George Lincoln Rockwell was mesmerizing," said the *Herald Examiner*, "and it was not entirely unexpected that he walked off with the prize." But the notoriously aloof Brando actually didn't walk off with anything. The absent star's Emmy was accepted by presenter John Ritter, who said, wryly, "I'm sure if Marlon Brando

were here, he would want to thank the academy. Perhaps not."

Another dramatic special that did well was *Friendly Fire*, which was named Outstanding Drama Special and also won honors for its director, film sound editor, and music composer. The controversial three-hour ABC film told the story of an Iowa couple investigating the death of their son, who was accidentally killed by American artillery in the Vietnam War. Carol Burnett and Ned Beatty gave powerful performances as the parents and were considered the front-runners to be named best actor and actress.

Instead, Bette Davis ended up with the actress statuette in a contest that looked more like one of her old Oscar bouts with Katharine Hepburn than the typical Emmys match-up. Hepburn was also up for the award, and most ironically, for a made-for-TV remake, directed by George Cukor, of a Bette Davis classic from the 1940s, *The Corn is Green*. But Davis got the prize for initiating a new role in *Strangers: The Story of a Mother and Daughter*, about a widow visited by her estranged daughter (Gena Rowlands) after 20 years of separation.

Peter Strauss was acclaimed best actor for *The Jericho Mile*, about a prison inmate who struggles to become an Olympic runner. Jail rehabilitation was also the focus of this year's Outstanding Informational Special *Scared Straight!*, an Oscar-winning documentary about convicts trying to dissuade young offenders from a life of crime. The Oscars figured so prominently in these TV awards that last year's 51st Annual Academy Awards ceremony even ended up with an Emmy for Outstanding Program Achievement — beating the Tonys.

As it had in the past, *All in the Family*, with seven nominations, was expected to go all the way again. It came through with trophies for Carroll O'Connor as Archie Bunker and Sally

Struthers as his daughter, Gloria (settling an old score — Struthers was the only principal cast member not to win an Emmy in 1978). But it lost the top series award in a startling upset.

The year's Outstanding Comedy Series, *Taxi*, was a new show created by four alumni of *The Mary Tyler Moore Show* (producers and writers James L. Brooks, Stan Daniels, David Davis, and Ed. Weinberger) who used a broad ensemble cast to explore the comic possibilities of life in a big city taxi garage. The result was an instant hit. *Taxi* was in the Nielsen top ten during its premiere season and would remain Emmy's comedy series champ for three years in a row. This year actress Ruth Gordon also won a top prize, for a guest appearance in an episode called "Sugar Mama."

Lou Grant entered the evening with the most series nominations — 14 — and was expected to dominate the drama prizes after its surprising loss last year to

The Oscars won an Emmy when the 51st annual ceremony (featuring Olivia Newton-John singing, above) was hailed for program achievement.

The Rockford Files. Star Ed Asner told the *Herald-Examiner*, "I would hope we win in the dramatic category because it helps to legitimize, gain respect, and bring much-needed prestige to a show." Asner summed up the results as "compromising": *Lou Grant* was voted Outstanding Drama Series, but it took only one other award — for writing. Asner had mixed emotions about the outcome, particularly since he lost the best actor honors to Ron Leibman of the canceled series *Kaz*. At the Governors' Ball after the ceremony, Asner was asked how he thought he fared overall. He told the *Herald Examiner*: "Losing never feels right. So now I'll just try to find my wife — and drink my compromising vodka."

The rest of the drama series awards were scattered: Mariette Hartley was named best actress for being the credible wife of *The Incredible Hulk*; Kristy McNichol of *Family* was voted best supporting actress for the second time in three years; Stuart Margolin became best supporting actor for the shady character Angel Martin on *The Rockford Files*.

Two men known primarily for their acting abilities won trophies for other talents. Jackie Cooper, who had won an Emmy in 1974 for directing an episode of *M*A*S*H*, was given the same accolade this year for crafting a segment of *The White Shadow*. Actor Alan Alda, noted the *L.A. Herald-Express*, "drew a roar from the crowd" when he did a cartwheel down the aisle on his way to receive a writing award for *M*A*S*H*.

DAYTIME AWARDS

Televised by CBS from the Vivian Beaumont Theater at New York's Lincoln Center, the daytime race was the focus of a minor, preshow controversy when Bob Barker of *The Price is Right* was disqualified as a contender for outstanding host of a game show. His producers accidentally sent Emmy judges examples of Barker's work that did not fit into the eligibility period of March 22, 1978 to March 5, 1979. The award ended up going to Dick Clark of *The $20,000 Pyramid*, but Barker was so gracious about his defeat that he continued as planned to be the ceremony host at Lincoln Center.

"For the first time in 22 years of working in daytime TV, I was nominated for an Emmy," Barker told the audience, "but I was disqualified. You can imagine how I felt. I have not known such agony, anguish, and despair since the last time I saw *Love of Life*."

Al Freeman, Jr., lost for Roots II, but won for One Life to Live.

The ceremony brought back a number of old favorites. For a third year in a row, Phil Donahue was named outstanding talk show host, and it was the second successive year for his program to be named the choice chat series. The *Herald Examiner* obviously approved, saying, "The best thing in television today is Donahue. He has real people talking about real issues on his show." Donahue was away on assignment last year and couldn't accept his award in person, but this year he was present and expressed his appreciation, saying, "When this all began for us 12 years ago in Dayton, Ohio, we never thought that this would happen to us. I'm a very lucky guy."

The Hollywood Squares came back as outstanding game show, the third time it took the top honors. Coincidentally, the award was bestowed by Paul Lynde, the program's outrageous center-square gagster.

Last year's best written soap, *Ryan's Hope*, took the same laurels this year, in addition to winning the director's award and being named daytime series

of the year — a sweep identical to its 1977 romp, except for one prize. This time the actress trophy went to Irene Dailey of *Another World*, who was one of four actresses who had played the character Liz Matthews since the show premiered in 1964.

Al Freeman, Jr., who distinguished himself this year as a prime-time nominee for *Roots: The Next Generations*, lost the supporting acting award to Marlon Brando, but was hailed as daytime's best actor for playing Lieutenant Ed Hall on *One Life to Live*, which just last year had expanded its air time to a full hour. Since Freeman didn't have the chance to say anything at the prime-time broadcast, he was eager to speak up at the daytime show, but as soon as he arrived at the podium to deliver his thank-you remarks, he was flagged by the program's director. "Wouldn't you know it?" Freeman griped jokingly. "After 24 years of being an actor, they tell me we're jammed for time."

The award for daytime's best supporting actor went to Peter Hansen of *General Hospital*, who joined the show as attorney Lee Baldwin just two years after its inception in 1963, replacing actor Ross Elliott, and continued in the role for 16 years. He accepted his trophy saying, "When I was in the elevator the other day, I heard someone say about me, 'He's a late bloomer,' but better late than never!" Suzanne Rogers of *Days of Our Lives* accepted her award as best supporting actress, saying, "It's very difficult being in a category and wanting everyone to win, but I'm so glad I did!" Rogers suffered in real life from the muscle disease myasthenia gravis, an infirmity that was incorporated into her TV role as Maggie Simmons.

ABC dominated the awards for children's series, both instructional and entertainment, for *Science Rock* and *Kids Are People Too*. CBS's *Razzmatazz* was voted best informational special for children, and NBC's *The Tap Dance Kid* was youngsters' entertainment special of the year.

SPORTS AWARDS

After boycotting the sports awards last year because they weren't included in the traditional evening broadcast, ABC rejoined the competition, which was held at the legendary Rainbow Room, where Curt Gowdy and Lindsey Nelson hosted. The network was coincidentally rewarded with a slew of them, including trophies for best live sports series (*Monday Night Football*), best edited sports series (*The American Sportsman*), best edited sports special (*Spirit of '78: The Flight of the Double Eagle II*), and sports personality Jim McKay (who was honored for the sixth time). NBC won best live sports special for its airing of Superbowl XIII, which saw the Pittsburgh Steelers beat the Dallas Cowboys 35–31.

NEWS & DOCUMENTARY AWARDS

It was another big year for CBS when the Emmys were staged at New York's Sheraton Centre Hotel. The network's documentary division *CBS Reports* had four winning programs: "Showdown in Iran," "The Boat People," "Anyplace But Here," and "The Boston Goes to China." It also had award-winning specials on incest and the state of American education.

60 Minutes won program trophies for profiles on the Boston Pops, dancer Mikhail Baryshnikov, TV ratings, and the mayor of Jerusalem. CBS took all of this year's writing awards, too, including one for *60 Minutes* essayist Andy Rooney, in addition to sweeping the categories of cinematography, film editing, and — with one exception — directing.

The exception was for ABC's Tom Priestly, who directed *The Killing Ground*, which also won a program prize and dealt with the controversies surrounding disposal of hazardous chemical waste. Other program winners included *ABC News Closeup*'s "The Police Tapes," which followed the routine of police officers on duty in the South Bronx in New York City, and "Mission: Mind Control," which explored the legality of mind-control experiments by U.S. intelligence agencies.

NBC scored with its "Migrants" segment on *NBC Nightly News* and "Children of Hope" and "A Very Special Place" on *Weekend*.

1978–79

For prime-time programs telecast July 1, 1978, through June 30, 1979. The prime-time ceremony was broadcast on ABC from the Pasadena Civic Auditorium on September 9, 1979. Creative arts banquet held on September 8, 1979. Daytime awards presented May 17, 1979, for programs aired between March 22, 1978, and March 5, 1979. The news & documentary awards were given away on February 11, 1980, for programs aired between July 1, 1978, and May 31, 1979. Sports awards presented March 4, 1980, for programming from June 16, 1978, to July 18, 1979.

PRIME-TIME PROGRAM AWARDS
OUTSTANDING DRAMA SERIES
• *Lou Grant*. Gene Reynolds, executive producer. Seth Freeman, Gary David Goldberg, producers. CBS.
The Paper Chase. Robert C. Thompson, executive producer. Robert Lewin, Albert Aley, producers. CBS.
The Rockford Files. Meta Rosenberg, executive producer. Stephen J. Cannell, supervising producer. Chas. Floyd Johnson, David Chase, Juanita Bartlett, producers. NBC.

Outstanding Comedy Series

• *Taxi.* James L. Brooks, Stan Daniels, David Davis, Ed. Weinberger, executive producers. Glen Charles, Les Charles, producers. ABC.
All in the Family. Mort Lachman, executive producer. Milt Josefsberg, producer. CBS.
Barney Miller. Danny Arnold, executive producer. Tony Sheehan, Reinhold Weege, coproducers. ABC.
*M*A*S*H.* Burt Metcalfe, producer. CBS.
Mork & Mindy. Garry Marshall, Tony Marshall, executive producers. Dale McRaven, Bruce Johnson, producers. ABC.

Outstanding Limited Series

• *Roots: The Next Generations.* David L. Wolper, executive producer. Stan Margulies, producer. ABC.
Backstairs at the White House. Ed Friendly, executive producer. Ed Friendly, Michael O'Herlihy, producers. NBC.
Blind Ambition. David Susskind, executive producer. George Schaefer, Renée Valente, producers. CBS.

Outstanding Drama
or Comedy Special

• *Friendly Fire, ABC Theatre.* Martin Starger, executive producer. Philip Barry, producer. Fay Kanin, coproducer. ABC.
Dummy. Frank Konigsberg, executive producer. Sam Manners, Ernest Tidyman, producers. CBS.
First You Cry. Phillip Barry, producer. CBS.
The Jericho Mile. Tim Zinnemann, producer. ABC.
Summer of My German Soldier. Linda Gottlieb, producer. NBC.

Outstanding Comedy-Variety
or Music Program

• *Steve & Eydie Celebrate Irving Berlin.* Steve Lawrence, Gary Smith, executive producers. Gary Smith, Dwight Hemion, producers. Steve Lawrence, Eydie Gormé, stars. NBC.
Arthur Fiedler: Just Call Me Maestro. William Cosel, producer. Arthur Fiedler, star. PBS.
The Muppet Show. David Lazer, executive producer. Jim Henson, producer. The Muppets: Frank Oz, Jerry Nelson, Richard Hunt, Dave Goelz, Jim Henson, stars. Syndicated.

NBC's Saturday Night Live. Lorne Michaels, producer. Dan Aykroyd, John Belushi, Jane Curtin, Garrett Morris, Bill Murray, Laraine Newman, Gilda Radner, stars. NBC.
Shirley MacLaine at the Lido. Gary Smith, Dwight Hemion, producers. Shirley MacLaine, star. CBS.

Outstanding Informational Program
(Winner)

• *Scared Straight!* Arnold Schapiro, producer. Syndicated.

Outstanding Classical Program
in the Performing Arts
(Winner)

• "Balanchine IV," *Dance in America, Great Performances.* Jac Venza, executive producer. Merrill Brockway, series producer. Emile Ardolino, series coordinating producer. Judy Kinberg, producer. PBS.

Outstanding Animated Program
(Winner—Area award)

• *The Lion, The Witch and the Wardrobe.* David Connell, executive producer. Steve Melendez, producer. CBS.

Outstanding Children's Program
(Winner—Area award)

• *Christmas Eve on Sesame Street.* Jon Stone, executive producer. Dulcy Singer, producer. PBS.

Outstanding Program Achievement—
Special Events
(Winner—Area award)

• *The 51st Annual Awards Presentation of the Academy of Motion Picture Arts and Sciences.* Jack Haley, Jr., producer. ABC.

Outstanding Program Achievement—
Special Class
(Winners—Area award)

• *The Tonight Show Starring Johnny Carson.* Fred DeCordova, producer. Johnny Carson, star. NBC.
• *Lifeline.* Thomas W. Moore, Robert E. Fuisz, M.D., executive producers. Alfred Kelman, producer. Geof Bartz, coproducer. NBC.

PERFORMANCE, DIRECTING, AND WRITING
OUTSTANDING LEAD ACTOR
IN A DRAMA SERIES
• Ron Leibman, *Kaz.* CBS.
Edward Asner, *Lou Grant.* CBS.
James Garner, *The Rockford Files.* NBC.
Jack Klugman, *Quincy.* NBC.

OUTSTANDING LEAD ACTRESS
IN A DRAMA SERIES
• Mariette Hartley, *The Incredible Hulk.*
CBS.
Barbara Bel Geddes, *Dallas.* CBS.
Rita Moreno, *The Rockford Files.* NBC.
Sada Thompson, *Family.* ABC.

OUTSTANDING LEAD ACTOR
IN A COMEDY SERIES
• Carroll O'Connor, *All in the Family.*
CBS.
Alan Alda, *M*A*S*H.* CBS.
Judd Hirsch, *Taxi.* ABC.
Hal Linden, *Barney Miller.* ABC.
Robin Williams, *Mork & Mindy.* ABC.

OUTSTANDING LEAD ACTRESS
IN A COMEDY SERIES
• Ruth Gordon, *Taxi.* ABC.
Katherine Helmond, *Soap.* ABC.
Linda Lavin, *Alice.* CBS.
Isabel Sanford, *The Jeffersons.* CBS.
Jean Stapleton, *All in the Family.* CBS.

OUTSTANDING LEAD ACTOR
IN A LIMITED SERIES OR A SPECIAL
• Peter Strauss, *The Jericho Mile.* ABC.
Ned Beatty, *Friendly Fire, ABC Theatre.*
ABC.
Louis Gossett, Jr., *Backstairs at the White
House.* NBC.
Kurt Russell, *Elvis.* ABC.

OUTSTANDING LEAD ACTRESS
IN A LIMITED SERIES OR A SPECIAL
• Bette Davis, *Strangers: The Story of a
Mother and Daughter.* CBS.
Carol Burnett, *Friendly Fire, ABC
Theatre.* ABC.
Olivia Cole, *Backstairs at the White
House.* NBC.
Katharine Hepburn, *The Corn is Green.*
CBS.
Mary Tyler Moore, *First You Cry.* CBS.

OUTSTANDING SUPPORTING ACTOR
IN A COMEDY OR COMEDY-VARIETY
OR MUSIC SERIES
• Robert Guillaume, *Soap.* ABC.
Gary Burghoff, *M*A*S*H.* CBS.
Danny DeVito, *Taxi.* ABC.
Max Gail, *Barney Miller.* ABC.
Harry Morgan, *M*A*S*H.* CBS.

OUTSTANDING SUPPORTING ACTRESS
IN A COMEDY OR COMEDY-VARIETY OR
MUSIC SERIES
• Sally Struthers, *All in the Family.* CBS.
Polly Holliday, *Alice.* CBS.
Marion Ross, *Happy Days.* ABC.
Loretta Swit, *M*A*S*H.* CBS.

OUTSTANDING SUPPORTING ACTOR
IN A DRAMA SERIES
• Stuart Margolin, *The Rockford Files.*
NBC.
Mason Adams, *Lou Grant.* CBS.
Noah Beery, *The Rockford Files.* NBC.
Joe Santos, *The Rockford Files.* NBC.
Robert Walden, *Lou Grant.* CBS.

OUTSTANDING SUPPORTING ACTRESS
IN A DRAMA SERIES
• Kristy McNichol, *Family.* ABC.
Linda Kelsey, *Lou Grant.* CBS.
Nancy Marchand, *Lou Grant.* CBS.

OUTSTANDING SUPPORTING ACTOR
IN A LIMITED SERIES OR A SPECIAL
• Marlon Brando, *Roots: The Next
Generations.* ABC.
Ed Flanders, *Backstairs at the White
House.* NBC.
Al Freeman, Jr., *Roots: The Next
Generations.* ABC.
Robert Vaughn, *Backstairs at the White
House* NBC.
Paul Winfield, *Roots: The Next
Generations.* ABC.

OUTSTANDING SUPPORTING ACTRESS
IN A LIMITED SERIES OR A SPECIAL
• Esther Rolle, *Summer of My German
Soldier.* NBC.
Ruby Dee, *Roots: The Next Generations.*
ABC.
Colleen Dewhurst, *Silent Victory: The
Kitty O'Neil Story.* CBS.
Eileen Heckart, *Backstairs at the White
House.* NBC.
Celeste Holm, *Backstairs at the White
House.* NBC.

**OUTSTANDING DIRECTING
IN A DRAMA SERIES**
• Jackie Cooper, *The White Shadow*. CBS.
Burt Brinckerhoff, *Lou Grant*. CBS.
Mel Damski, *Lou Grant*. CBS.
Gene Reynolds, *Lou Grant*. CBS.

**OUTSTANDING DIRECTING IN A COMEDY
OR COMEDY-VARIETY OR MUSIC SERIES**
• Noam Pitlik, *Barney Miller*. ABC.
Alan Alda, *M*A*S*H*. CBS.
Paul Bogart, *All in the Family*. CBS.
Charles Dubin, *M*A*S*H*. CBS.
Jay Sandrich, *Soap*. ABC.

**OUTSTANDING DIRECTING
IN A LIMITED SERIES OR A SPECIAL**
• David Greene, *Friendly Fire,
ABC Theatre*. ABC.
Lou Antonio, *Silent Victory: The Kitty
O'Neil Story*. CBS.
Glenn Jordan, *Les Miserables*. CBS.

**OUTSTANDING WRITING
IN A DRAMA SERIES**
• Michele Gallery, *Lou Grant*. CBS.
Jim Bridges, *The Paper Chase*. CBS.
Gene Reynolds, *Lou Grant*. CBS.
Leon Tokatyan, *Lou Grant*. CBS.

**OUTSTANDING WRITING
IN A LIMITED SERIES OR A SPECIAL**
• Patrick Nolan, Michael Mann, *The
Jericho Mile*. ABC.
Gwen Bagni, Paul Dubov, *Backstairs at
the White House*. NBC.
Jane Howard Hammerstein, *Summer of My
German Soldier*. NBC.
Fay Kanin, *Friendly Fire, ABC Theatre*.
ABC.
Ernest Kinoy, *Roots: The Next
Generations*. ABC.

**OUTSTANDING WRITING IN A COMEDY
OR COMEDY-VARIETY OR MUSIC SERIES**
• Alan Alda, *M*A*S*H*. CBS.
Dan Aykroyd, Anne Beatts, Tom Davis,
James Downey, Brain Doyle-Murry, Al
Franken, Brian McConnachie, Lorne
Michaels, Don Novello, Herb Sargent,
Tom Schiller, Rosie Shuster, Walter
Williams, Alan Zweibel, *NBC's Saturday
Night Live*. NBC.
Milt Josefsberg, Phil Sharp, Bob Schiller,
Bob Weiskopf, *All in the Family*. CBS.
Michael Leeson, *Taxi*. ABC.
Ken Levine, David Isaacs, *M*A*S*H*. CBS.

**OUTSTANDING INDIVIDUAL
ACHIEVEMENT—
INFORMATIONAL PROGRAM
(Winner—Area award)**
• John Korty, director, *Who Are the
DeBolts – and Where Did They Get
19 Kids?* ABC.

**OUTSTANDING INDIVIDUAL
ACHIEVEMENT—SPECIAL EVENTS
(Winner—Area award)**
• Mikhail Baryshnikov, *Baryshnikov at the
White House*. PBS.

(There was no winner in the area of individual
achievement in animated programs.)

CREATIVE ARTS AWARD WINNERS
**OUTSTANDING MUSIC
COMPOSITION FOR A SERIES**
• David Rose, *Little House on the Prairie*.
NBC.

**OUTSTANDING MUSIC COMPOSITION
FOR A LIMITED SERIES OR A SPECIAL**
• Leonard Rosenman, *Friendly Fire, ABC
Theatre*. ABC.

OUTSTANDING CHOREOGRAPHY
• Kevin Carlisle, *The 3rd Barry Manilow
Special*. ABC.

**OUTSTANDING COSTUME DESIGN
FOR A SERIES**
• Jean-Pierre Dorleac, *Battlestar
Galactica*. ABC.

**OUTSTANDING COSTUME DESIGN
FOR A LIMITED SERIES OR A SPECIAL**
• Ann Hollowood, Sue Le Cash, Christine
Wilson, *Edward the King*. Syndicated.

OUTSTANDING MAKEUP
• Tommy Cole, Mark Bussan, Ron Walters, *Backstairs at the White House*. NBC.

OUTSTANDING HAIRSTYLING
• Janice D. Brandow, *The Triangle
Factory Fire Scandal*. NBC.

**OUTSTANDING ART DIRECTION
FOR A SERIES**
• Howard E. Johnson, art director. Richard
B. Goddard, set decorator, *Little Women*.
NBC.

OUTSTANDING ART DIRECTION FOR A LIMITED SERIES OR A SPECIAL
• Jan Scott, art director and production designer. Bill Harp, set decorator, *Studs Lonigan, NBC Novels for Television*. NBC.

OUTSTANDING GRAPHIC DESIGN AND TITLE AND TITLE SEQUENCES
• Stu Bernstein, Eytan Keller, *Cinderella at the Palace*. CBS.

OUTSTANDING CINEMATOGRAPHY FOR A SERIES
• Ted Voigtlander, *Little House on the Prairie*. NBC.

OUTSTANDING CINEMATOGRAPHY FOR A LIMITED SERIES OR A SPECIAL
• Howard Schwartz, *Rainbow*. NBC.

OUTSTANDING TECHNICAL DIRECTION AND ELECTRONIC CAMERAWORK
• Jerry Weiss, technical director. Don Barker, Peggy Mahoney, Reed Howard, Kurt Tonnessen, William Landers, Louis Cywinski, George Loomis, Brian Sherriffe, camerapersons, *Dick Clark's Live Wednesday*. NBC.

OUTSTANDING FILM EDITING FOR A SERIES
• M. Pam Blumenthal, *Taxi*. ABC.

OUTSTANDING FILM EDITING FOR A LIMITED SERIES OR A SPECIAL
• Arthur Schmidt, *The Jericho Mile*. ABC.

OUTSTANDING VIDEO-TAPE EDITING FOR A SERIES
• Andy Zall, *Stockard Channing in Just Friends*. CBS.

OUTSTANDING VIDEO-TAPE EDITING FOR A LIMITED SERIES OR A SPECIAL
• Ken Denisoff, Tucker Wiard, Janet McFadden, *The Scarlet Letter*. PBS.

OUTSTANDING FILM SOUND EDITING
• William H. Wistrom, *Friendly Fire, ABC Theatre*. ABC.

OUTSTANDING FILM SOUND MIXING
• Bill Teague, George E. Porter, Eddie J. Nelson, Ray West, *The Winds of Kitty Hawk*. NBC.

OUTSTANDING TAPE SOUND MIXING
Ed Greene, Phillip J. Seretti, Dennis S. Sands, Garry Ulmer, *Steve & Eydie Celebrate Irving Berlin*. NBC.

OUTSTANDING INDIVIDUAL ACHIEVEMENT—CREATIVE TECHNICAL CRAFTS
• John Dykstra, special effects coordinator. Richard Edlund, director of miniature photography. Joseph Goss, mechanical special effects, *Battlestar Galactica*. ABC.
• Tom Ancell, live stereo sound mixing, *Giulini's Beethoven's 9th Live — A Gift from Los Angeles*. PBS.

OUTSTANDING ACHIEVEMENT IN LIGHTING DIRECTION (Electronic)
• George Riesenberger, lighting consultant and designer. Roy A. Barnett, director of photography, "E," *You Can't Take It with You*. CBS.

OUTSTANDING INDIVIDUAL ACHIEVEMENT—INFORMATION PROGRAM
• Robert Niemack, film editor, *Scared Straight!* Syndicated.

(There were no winners in the areas of individual achievement in animation, children's program, special class, or special events.)

DAYTIME AWARDS

OUTSTANDING DAYTIME DRAMA SERIES
• *Ryan's Hope,* Claire Labine, Paul Avila Mayer, executive producers. Ellen Barrett, Robert Costello, producers. ABC.
All My Children, Agnes Nixon, executive producer. Bud Kloss, producer. ABC.
Days of Our Lives, Betty Corday, H. Wesley Kenney, executive producers. Jack Herzberg, producer. NBC.
The Young and the Restless, John Conboy, executive producer. Ed Scott, producer. CBS.

OUTSTANDING ACTOR IN A DAYTIME DRAMA SERIES
• Al Freeman, Jr., *One Life to Live*. ABC.
Jed Allan, *Days of Our Lives*. NBC.
Nicholas Benedict, *All My Children*. ABC.
John Clarke, *Days of Our Lives*. NBC.
Joel Crothers, *The Edge of Night*. ABC.
Michael Levin, *Ryan's Hope*. ABC.

OUTSTANDING ACTRESS IN A DAYTIME DRAMA SERIES
• Irene Dailey, *Another World*. NBC.
Nancy Addison, *Ryan's Hope*. ABC.

Helen Gallagher, *Ryan's Hope*. ABC.
Beverlee McKinsey, *Another World*. NBC.
Susan Seaforth Hayes, *Days of Our Lives*. NBC.
Victoria Wyndham, *Another World*. NBC.

OUTSTANDING SUPPORTING ACTOR IN A DAYTIME DRAMA SERIES
• Peter Hansen, *General Hospital*. ABC.
Lewis Arlt, *Search for Tomorrow*. CBS.
Bernard Barrow, *Ryan's Hope*. ABC.
Joe Gallison, *Days of Our Lives*. NBC.
Ron Hale, *Ryan's Hope*. ABC.
Mandel Kramer, *The Edge of Night*. ABC.

OUTSTANDING SUPPORTING ACTRESS IN A DAYTIME DRAMA SERIES
• Suzanne Rogers, *Days of Our Lives*. NBC.
Rachel Ames, *General Hospital*. ABC.
Susan Brown, *General Hospital*. ABC.
Lois Kibbee, *The Edge of Night*. ABC.
Frances Reid, *Days of Our Lives*. NBC.

OUTSTANDING DIRECTION FOR A DAYTIME DRAMA SERIES
• Jerry Evans, Lela Swift, *Ryan's Hope*. ABC.
Ira Cirker, Melvin Bernhardt, Paul Lammers, Robert Calhoun, *Another World*. NBC.
Jack Coffey, Del Hughes, Henry Kaplan, *All My Children*. ABC.
Richard Dunlap, Bill Glenn, *The Young and the Restless*. CBS.
Al Rabin, Joe Behar, Frank Pacelli, *Days of Our Lives*. NBC.
John Sedwick, Richard Pepperman, *The Edge of Night*. ABC.

OUTSTANDING WRITING FOR A DAYTIME DRAMA SERIES
• Claire Labine, Paul Avila Mayer, Mary Munisteri, Judith Pinsker, Jeffrey Lane, *Ryan's Hope*. ABC.
William J. Bell, Kay Alden, Elizabeth Harrower, *The Young and the Restless*. CBS.
Ann Marcus, Michael Robert David, Raymond E. Goldstone, Joyce Perry, Elizabeth Harrower, Rocci Chatfield, Laura Olsher, *Days of Our Lives*. NBC.
Agnes Nixon, Wisner Washam, Jack Wood, Mary K. Wells, Kenneth Harvey, Cathy Chicos, Caroline Franz, Doris Frankel, William Delligan, *All My Children*. ABC.

Phil Donahue with the Emmys for him and his show. The Herald Examiner *said Donahue is "the best thing in TV today."*

OTHER DAYTIME AWARD WINNERS

OUTSTANDING GAME OR AUDIENCE PARTICIPATION SHOW
• *The Hollywood Squares*. Merrill Heatter, Bob Quigley, executive producers. Jay Redack, producer. NBC.

OUTSTANDING HOST OR HOSTESS IN A GAME OR AUDIENCE PARTICIPATION SHOW
• Dick Clark, *The $20,000 Pyramid*. ABC.

OUTSTANDING INDIVIDUAL DIRECTION FOR A GAME OR AUDIENCE PARTICIPATION SHOW
• Jerome Shaw, *The Hollywood Squares*. NBC.

OUTSTANDING TALK, SERVICE, OR VARIETY SERIES
• *Donahue,* Richard Mincer, executive producer. Patricia McMillen, producer. Syndicated.

OUTSTANDING HOST OR HOSTESS IN A TALK, SERVICE, OR VARIETY SHOW
• Phil Donahue, *Donahue*. Syndicated.

**OUTSTANDING INDIVIDUAL DIRECTION
FOR A VARIETY PROGRAM**
• Rob Wiener, *Donahue.* Syndicated.

**OUTSTANDING CHILDREN'S
ENTERTAINMENT SERIES**
• *Kids Are People Too.* Lawrence Einhorn,
executive producer. Laura Schrock,
producer. Noreen Conlin, coproducer.
ABC.

**OUTSTANDING CHILDREN'S
ENTERTAINMENT SPECIAL**
• *The Tap Dance Kid.* Linda Gottlieb,
executive producer. Evelyn Barron,
producer. NBC.

**OUTSTANDING CHILDREN'S
INFORMATIONAL SERIES**
• *Big Blue Marble.* Robert Wiemer,
executive producer. Richard Berman,
producer. Syndicated.

**OUTSTANDING CHILDREN'S
INFORMATIONAL SPECIAL**
• *Razzmatazz.* Joel Heller, executive
producer. Vern Diamond, producer. CBS.

**OUTSTANDING CHILDREN'S
INSTRUCTIONAL SERIES**
• *Science Rock.* Tom Yohe, executive
producer. George Newall, Radford Stone,
producers. ABC.

**OUTSTANDING ACHIEVEMENT
IN TECHNICAL EXCELLENCE
FOR A DAYTIME DRAMA SERIES**
• *The Edge of Night.* William Edwards,
technical director. Joanne Goodhart,
associate director. Paul York, video.
Edward R. Atchison, audio. William
Hughes, Arie Hefter, Jay Millard,
camerapersons. Music by Elliot Lawrence
Productions. Barbara Miller, music
coordinator. Robert Saxon, sound effects
technician. Roman Spinner, teleprompter.
ABC.

**OUTSTANDING ACHIEVEMENT
IN DESIGN EXCELLENCE
FOR A DAYTIME DRAMA SERIES**
• *Love of Life.* Lloyd R. Evans, scenic
designer. Wesley Laws, set decorator.
Dean Nelson, lighting director. Bob Anton,
costume designer. Lee Halls, makeup
designer. Phyllis Sagnei, hairdresser. Lou
Dorfsman, graphic design/title sequence.
CBS

DAYTIME AREA AWARDS
*Each area has the possibility of multiple
winners, one winner, or none. Winners
are listed.*

**OUTSTANDING INDIVIDUAL ACHIEVEMENT
IN CHILDREN'S PROGRAMMING**
• Geraldine Fitzgerald, performer, *Special
Treat.* NBC.
• Jack Gilford, performer, *Big Blue
Marble.* Syndicated
• Jim Henson, Frank Oz, Carroll Spinney,
Jerry Nelson, Richard Hunt, performers,
Sesame Street. PBS.
• Larry Elikann, director, *ABC Afterschool
Special.* ABC.
• Charles Gross, composer, *Special Treat.*
NBC.
• John Morris, composer, *Special Treat.* NBC.
• Dick Maitland, Roy Carch, sound effects,
Sesame Street. PBS.
• Gene Piotrowsky, tape sound mixer, *CBS
Festival of Lively Arts for Young
People.* CBS.
• Michael Baugh, art director, *Villa Alegre.*
PBS.
• Dorothy Weaver, costume designer,
Special Treat. NBC.
• Rene Verzier, cinematographer, *Big Blue
Marble.* Syndicated
• Dick Young, cinematographer, *Big Blue
Marble.* Syndicated
• Norman Gay, film editor, *The Tap Dance
Kid.* NBC.
• Vince Humphrey, film editor, *Gaucho.*
ABC.
• Ian Maitland, cinematographer, *Special
Treat.* NBC.
• Michael Baugh, graphic designer/titles,
Villa Alegre. PBS.
• Jack Regas, Harvey Berger, Ron Hays,
graphic designers/titles, *Kraft Superstar
Hour.* NBC.
• Harvey Berger, video-tape editor, *Kraft
Superstar Hour.* NBC.
• Ken Gutstein, video-tape editor, *Festival
of Lively Arts for Young People.* CBS.
• Roy Stewart, video-tape editor,
Freestyle! PBS.

**OUTSTANDING INDIVIDUAL ACHIEVEMENT
IN RELIGIOUS PROGRAMMING**
• Rolanda Mendels, performer,
Interrogation in Budapest. NBC.
• Martin Hoad, director, *Interrogation in
Budapest.* NBC.
• Joseph J.H. Vadala, cinematographer,
This Other Eden. NBC.

SPORTS AWARD WINNERS
OUTSTANDING LIVE SPORTS SERIES
• *ABC's NFL Monday Night Football.*
Roone Arledge, executive producer.
Dennis Lewin, producer. ABC.

OUTSTANDING EDITED SPORTS SERIES
• *The American Sportsman.* Roone Arledge,
executive producer. John Wilcox, producer.
ABC.

OUTSTANDING LIVE SPORTS SPECIAL
• *Super Bowl XIII,* Don Ohlmeyer, executive producer. George Finkel, Michael
Weisman, producers. NBC.

OUTSTANDING EDITED SPORTS SPECIAL
• *Spirit of '78 — The Flight of Double
Eagle II,* Roone Arledge, executive producer. John Wilcox, producer. ABC.

OUTSTANDING DIRECTING SPORTS PROGRAMMING
• Harry Coyle, *1978 World Series.* NBC.

OUTSTANDING CINEMATOGRAPHY
• Bob Angelo, Ernie Ernst, Jay Gerber,
Stan Leshner, Hank McElwee, Howard
Neef, Jack Newman, Steve Sabol, Bob
Smith, Art Spieler, Phil Tuckett,
cinematographers, *NFL Game of the Week.*
Syndicated.

TECHNICAL DIRECTION/ENGINEERING SUPERVISION/ELECTRONIC CAMERAWORK
• Sandy Bell, Bob Brown, technical
directors. Ralph Savignano, Art Tinn,
engineering supervisors. Barry Drago, Jim
McCarthy, Joe Sokota, George Rothweiler,
George Naeder, John Lincoln, Tom
McCarthy, Hans Singer, Keith Lawrence,
Jim Murphy, Neil McCaffrey, Herman
Lang, Frank McSpedon, electronic
camerapersons. Anthony Hlavaty, Wayne
Wright, Johnny Morris, Ed Ambrosini,
Frank Florio, Tom Spalding, electronic
camerapersons for Minicam and Microwave
Systems, *Daytona 500.* CBS.
• Horace Ruiz, technical director. Joe
Commare, Bob McKernin, Jack Bennet,
engineering supervisors. George Loomis,
Rodger Harbaugh, William W.Landers,
Michael C. Stramisky, Roy V. Ratliff,
Leonard Basile, Mario J. Ciarlo, Tom C.
Dezondorf, Steve Cimino, William Goetz,
Louis Gerard, Len Stucker, Steven H, Gonzales, Jim Johnson, Cory Lieble, Don Mulvaney, Al Rice, Jr., Russ K. Ross, electronic
camerapersons, *Superbowl Xlll.* NBC.
• Horace Ruiz, Dick Roecker, Ray
Figelski, technical directors. Robert
McKearnin, Jack Bennett, Ernest Thiel,
Jerry Ireland, Bob Brown, engineering
supervisors. Leonard G. Basile, Mario J.
Ciarlo, Roy Ratliff, George Loomis,
Bernard Joseph, Louis Gerard, Steve Cimino, Mike Stramisky, Rodger Harbaugh, Al
Rice Jr., William M. Goetz, Jim Johnson,
Brian Cherriffe, Phil Cantrell, Steven H.
Gonzales, Russ K. Ross, Art Parker, Bill
Landers, Jim Bragg, James Culley, Cory
Liebele, Len Stucker, electronic
camerapersons, *1978 World Series.* NBC.

GRAPHIC DESIGN/TITLE SEQUENCES
• James W. Grau, graphic designer/titles,
all CBS sports programs. CBS.

OUTSTANDING SPORTS PERSONALITY
• Jim McKay. ABC.

(There were no winners in the areas of sports
writing, music composition, or associate
direction/video-tape editing.)

NEWS & DOCUMENTARY AWARD WINNERS
PROGRAMS AND PROGRAM SEGMENTS
• "Showdown in Iran," *CBS Reports.*
Leslie Midgley, executive producer. CBS.
• "The Boat People," *CBS Report.,*
Andrew Lack, producer. CBS.
• "Anyplace But Here," *CBS Report.,* Tom
Spain, producer. CBS.
• "Is Anyone Out There Learning?," *CBS
Report Card on American Education.* Jane
Bartels, Bernard Birnbaum, Hal Haley,
producers. CBS.
• "The Police Tapes," *ABC News Closeup.*
Alan Raymond, Susan Raymond,
producers. ABC.
• "The Rating Game," *60 Minutes.* Marion
Goldin, producer. CBS.
• "Migrants," *NBC Nightly News.* Brian
Ross, Janet Pearce, coproducers. NBC.
• "Children of Hope," *NBC Weekend.*
Christine Huneke, producer. NBC.
• "Erasing Vietnam," *NBC Nightly News.*
John Hart, producer/correspondent. NBC.
Mission: Mind Control. Paul Altmeyer,
producer. ABC.
• *The Killing Ground.* Steve Singer,
producer. ABC.
• *Paul Jacobs and the Nuclear Gang.* Jack
Willis, producer. PBS.
• "Misha," *60 Minutes.* David Lowe, Jr.,
producer. Mike Wallace, interviewer. CBS.

Producers Stan Margulies (center) and David Wolper (left) claimed the top trophy for Roots: The Next Generations.

• "Teddy Kolleck's Jerusalem," *60 Minutes.* Joseph Wershba, producer. Morley Safer, interviewer. CBS.
• "Incest: The Best Kept Secret," *CBS March Magazine.* Jo Ann Caplin, producer. Sharon Lovejoy, interviewer. CBS.
• "Pops," *60 Minutes.* Mary Drayne, producer. Morley Safer, interviewer. CBS.
• *Palestine.* Mike Wooller, executive producer. PBS.
• *1968 — CBS News Special.* Shareen Blair Brysac, producer. CBS.
• "The Boston Goes To China," *CBS Reports.* Howard Stringer, executive producer. CBS.
• *A Very, Very Special Place — NBC Weekend.* Craig Leake, Producer. Janet

Janjigian, associate producer. NBC.
• "Noah," *60 Minutes.* Imre Horvath, producer. CBS.

INTERNTIONAL AWARD WINNERS
FICTION
• *The Fly.* Televisie Radio Omroep Stichting, the Netherlands.

NON-FICTION
• *Four Women.* Canadian Broadcasting Corporation, Canada.

SPECIAL AWARDS
ACHIEVEMENT IN ENGINEERING DEVELOPMENT
• Sony Video Products Company
• The Panasonic Company

NATIONAL AWARD FOR COMMUNITY SERVICE
• *Old Age: Do Not Go Gentle,* KGO-TV, San Francisco.

ACADEMY TRIBUTE
• Don Harris, Robert Brown, Bill Stewart, news broadcasters who lost their lives in Guyana and Nicaragua.

SPECIAL PRESENTATION
• Milton Berle, "Mr. Television."

A.T.A.S. GOVERNORS AWARD
• Walter Cronkite

N.A.T.A.S. TRUSTEES AWARD
• William S. Paley

"The Night the Stars Didn't Shine"

What if you had an Emmycast and nobody came? It virtually happened in 1980 when Hollywood actors boycotted the awards ceremony in order to increase pressure on the television networks to settle a seven-week-old strike staged by the Screen Actors Guild and the American Federation of Television and Radio Artists.

"It was a bitter time," remembers Ed Asner, who was the strike's unofficial street spokesman. "We all suffered."

The boycott was announced at the last minute, causing serious organizational problems for the Emmys show. Bob Newhart, Michael Landon, and Lee Remick all canceled as emcees. "The day before the show we got a call from Steve Allen volunteering to be there to do whatever we wanted, so he immediately became the host," remembers then-president of A.T.A.S. Hank Rieger. "The same day we got a call from Dick Clark who also offered his help, so we took Dick and decided to use him as cohost. Then, of all things, we got a call from the Smothers Brothers and they were our entertainment." Tom and Dick Smothers said that they had been asked to be on the show back in June, but then said that nobody called them about the boycott.

But could the show still go on? Before the boycott, the theme planned for the broadcast, ironically, was a celebration of television as one big "show biz family." Scheduled entertainment included showing lots of classic TV footage, but as soon as the boycott was under way, A.F.T.R.A. refused to grant permission for its use. Suddenly, in addition to new hosts, the show needed a

Dick Clark stood in as cohost when scores of Hollywood actors boycotted the Emmys as part of their network strike.

new focus, too, particularly if few celebrities were going to show up. (With only one exception, all 52 nominated actors and actresses refused to attend.) The new theme decided upon: all the noncelebrities in the show biz family. The Emmycast would honor the people who work behind the scenes in the creative arts.

"For years winners have been talking about all the people behind the scenes they owed their Emmys to," Rieger told *The Washington Post*. "Well, this year, viewers will get the chance to meet them." The evening's entertainment included what *Variety* described as "a number of prefilmed segments used to provide a little insight into lesser-known crafts that are part of the creative process. These segments worked rather well."

It was "The Night the Stars Didn't Shine," according to the banner headline in the *L.A. Herald Examiner* the next day. But to Hollywood insiders, the night actually had a refreshing sense of renewed priority about it. In accepting his award as Outstanding Director in a Dramatic Series for *Lou Grant*, Roger Young expressed the sentiment of many when he looked out over the sea of unknown faces in the audience, which was made up mostly of crafts workers, and said, "A lot of the stars of television are here tonight."

One acting star was, too.

The one nominee who decided not to shun the ceremony ended up winning in his category. The award presenters, who were mostly producers and network executives, weren't expecting it, however, since all night long they routinely accepted each trophy on behalf of the absent star, smiled nervously and then slipped off the stage. Brandon Stoddard, an ABC vice president, ended up having a different experience when he bestowed the prize for best lead actor in a limited series or a special.

"It was incredible," Stoddard said in the press room after the show. "We'd been told no one would be there, so we were looking to make a quick exit off stage. All of a sudden I looked up and said, 'My God, there's Jim Jones coming toward us!'"

It was really 31-year-old actor Powers Boothe, who portrayed the lead character in *Guyana Tragedy: The Story of Jim Jones*. Jones was the fanatic minister who had recently led his parishioners in a fantastic exodus — from the U.S. to the South American country where he then led them in a massive suicide rite to take them from this life to the next.

Boothe's unexpected appearance "was the moment of the show," Emmy-cast producer Ken Ehrlich told the *L.A. Times*. "On other award shows you try to build in those moments, but with this one we just closed our eyes and hoped."

Boothe accepted the statuette saying, "This is either the most courageous moment of my career or the stupidest." He also said he'd thought "long and hard" about whether or not to come to the ceremony, but finally decided to do it "because this is America and one has to do what one believes. I believe in the academy. I also believe in my fellow actors in their stand." The audience at the Pasadena Civic Auditorium rose to its feet and cheered.

The oft-cynical *Washington Post* noted, "Boothe got a standing ovation, literally, just for showing up." But the young star was also acknowledged for beating such formidable competition as Henry Fonda, Jason Robards, and Tony Curtis.

Boothe's upset was one of the few big surprises of the night in terms of the award

"It was a bitter time," Ed Asner said about the actors' boycott.

results. The prizes for best comedy and drama series went to the same winners as last year — *Taxi* and *Lou Grant* — so they hardly seemed shocking. But still, *Taxi*'s victory was not the cinch that *Lou Grant*'s was.

Taxi had been in a dead-heat contest with *M*A*S*H* from the moment the nominations were announced, although *M*A*S*H* had an obvious advantage: 11 nods compared to *Taxi*'s 5. Actor Judd Hirsch of *Taxi* was apparently so jealous that he was heard grousing at the nomination ceremony, "If you're not on *Lou Grant* or *M*A*S*H*, you don't get nominated!" But that wasn't so. Hirsch himself was nominated for best actor on *Taxi*, although he lost to Richard Mulligan of *Soap*. (*Soap* had a clean sweep of the lead acting honors in comedy when Cathryn Damon was named best

The only actor to defy the Emmy boycott was Powers Booth of Guyana Tragedy, *who ended up being voted best actor.*

actress.) *Taxi* took only two other awards: for its director and film editor. *M*A*S*H* ended up with two in all: for supporting performers Harry Morgan and Loretta Swit.

Lou Grant began the contest with the most nominations of all series — a whopping sum of 15 — and ended up the biggest champ on the Emmys night. "It's an ironic win," noted *Variety*, "since its star, Ed Asner, is one of the leaders of the boycott."

"I'd give anything to be there" at the ceremony, Asner had told the *L.A. Times* during the festivities. "It's a red-letter day for *Lou Grant*." *Grant* ended up with six awards (one short of the record for a series): for Outstanding Drama Series, for Asner as best actor, for its director, writers, music composer, and supporting actress Nancy Marchand, who had also won two years earlier.

Edward & Mrs. Simpson was voted best limited series, but, surprisingly, it took no other awards. The six-part special dramatized the historic love affair between Britain's King Edward VIII, played by Edward Fox, and the Ameri-

can divorcée Wallis Simpson, portrayed by Cynthia Harris. Neither performer was nominated for an acting prize, although both received favorable critical notices when the series was first aired in syndication. Instead, the acting honors went to Patty Duke Astin for best actress for a remake of *The Miracle Worker*, the classic drama about the deaf-and-blind Helen Keller who learned to speak thanks to her inspirational teacher. Duke had won an Oscar for starring in the original 1962 film version as the young Keller, but this time, in an act of inspired casting, she played Keller's mentor Anne Sullivan, a role that also once earned an Oscar for film costar Anne Bancroft. *The Miracle Worker* began the night with five nominations, and ended up with three prizes, including the biggest one: Outstanding Drama Special.

Dancing dominated the variety category as *Baryshnikov on Broadway* swept up four prizes, including Outstanding Variety or Music Program, directing honors for Dwight Hemion, and laurels for its art and music direction. The choreography award went to *Shirley MacLaine ... "Every Little Movement,"* which also won the writing prize. A third high-stepping special, *Fred Astaire: Change Partners and Dance*, was cited for Outstanding Program Achievement — Special Class.

Despite the absence of victorious celebrities gushing with colorful thank-you comments, the Emmys show, in the opinion of *Variety*, was a "smooth" telecast that "reflected the professional excellence that the awards themselves were supposed to be celebrating." *Variety* called Steve Allen "the top winner of the night" because he "distinguished himself by being witty on his feet for the entire show." Dick Clark was cool and "able," said the critics, while the one-time "bad boys of network TV" — the

Smothers Brothers, who had been seen only infrequently since their controversial variety series was canceled in 1970 — got mixed reviews. The *L. A. Times* said they were "a decided asset," while others considered them a decided embarrassment. When *Baryshnikov on Broadway* producer Gary Smith took his time

Lou Grant's Ed Asner, an unofficial leader of the boycott, ironically missed out on "a red letter day" for his show.

expressing appreciation for the variety program award, for example, Tom Smothers could be overheard gasping, "Get off!" Smith cut his comments short and slunk off the stage. Deftly, Steve Allen rescued the awkward moment that followed by saying, "Thank you very much, Tom Smothers. We'll see you in another 12 years."

Because of the shortage of star power, A.T.A.S. president Rieger had made a risky prediction before the Emmycast began. "I can promise one thing," he told *The Washington Post*. "For once, we'll finish the show on time." It was an overly optimistic call. Once "the program yawned beyond 11:30," noted the *Post*, it was already past its allotted two-and-a-

half hour schedule. At midnight, just before it was finally about to blink off the airwaves, a naughty Steve Allen teased the gathered crowd, "For all you hostages in the audience, you are now in hour three of your captivity."

The 32nd Annual Emmy Awards ended up 32nd in the weekly Nielsens.

DAYTIME AWARDS

"Phil Donahue had another big day," noted the *L.A. Times*, reporting the results of the daytime Emmys, which were telecast by NBC from the network's Studio 811 in New York. For the fourth consecutive year, Donahue was named outstanding talk show host while his controversial program — which routinely explored some of the hottest topics seldom discussed so openly on TV, such as abortion rights and discrimination against heterosexual cross dressing — was voted best talk show series for the third straight year.

In a tie with the *The $20,000 Pyramid*, *The Hollywood Squares* came back for a third time in a row, too, as best game show. Also awarded were the program's host Peter Marshall and its director.

Guiding Light, which dramatized the intrigues of the German-American Bauer family, was named outstanding daytime drama for the first time in its long history. Originally launched in 1937 as a radio series, it was created by "Queen of the Soaps" writer Irna Phillips who also developed such other successful sudsers as *Another World*, *As the World Turns*, and *Days of Our Lives*. *Guiding Light* was then the second longest-running daytime drama on the tube, after *Search for Tomorrow*. ("The" was dropped officially from the show's title in 1978.)

The best actor honors went to that other Irna Phillips soap, *Another World*, for actor Douglass Watson as the character Mackenzie Cory. Named

1979–80   253

Douglass Watson of Another World *and Judith Light of* One Life to Live *were the jubilant winners of the acting trophies.*

best actress was *One Life to Live*'s Judith Light, who portrayed nurse Karen Martin (and who would eventually go on to shine in prime time, too, as a star of *Who's the Boss?*). *Ryan's Hope* took the trophies for directing and writing while *All My Children* took virtually all the other awards: two for technical crafts and two more for supporting performers Warren Burton and Francesca James.

Sesame Street won a children's program award (for the sixth time in its venerable history), as did the entertainment series *Hot Hero Sandwich*, which had recently been dropped by NBC. The children's entertainment special of the year was one of *ABC Afterschool Special*'s most talked-about productions — "The Late Great Me: Story of a Teenage Alcoholic," which dramatized the plight of a 15-year-old girl who developed trouble with liquor after befriending a heavy drinker at school. In addition to the program award, it also won four more Emmys — for its writer, director, film editor, and the individual achievement of its lead performer, Maia Danziger.

In the area of individual achievement for special events coverage, the PBS production of *La Gioconda*, an opera by Amilcare Ponchielli, won eight prizes, including ones for its star performers Luciano Pavarotti and Renata Scotto.

SPORTS AWARDS

ABC once again swept the sports competition, picking up six trophies for its coverage of the 1980 Olympic Winter Games at Lake Placid, New York (including one to Chuck Mangione for the theme music "Give It All You Got"); the Live Sports Series prize for its coverage of NCAA football; and the designation of sports personality of the year for Jim McKay, who now had seven sports Emmys.

Super Bowl XIV, pitting the Los Angeles Rams against the victorious Pittsburgh Steelers, earned CBS a directing award. The widely syndicated *NFL Game of the Week* won two awards — for sports series editing and its cinematographers.

NEWS & DOCUMENTARY AWARDS

At ceremonies staged at the landmark Rainbow Room atop Rockefeller Center in New York City, *CBS Reports* and ABC's *20/20* tied for the most program awards, with four each.

CBS Reports's winning programs included *Miami: The Trial That Sparked the Riots, What Shall We Do About Mother?, On the Road* (with Charles Kuralt), and *Teddy* (Kennedy). CBS's other awards went to *60 Minutes* segments "Onward Christian Voters," "Bette Davis," and "Here's Johnny!" (Carson).

20/20's top shows were "George Burns: An Update," "Arson for Profit — Parts I & II," "VW Beetle: The Hidden Danger," and "Nicaragua." ABC also earned a program statuette for "Post Election Special Edition."

National Geographic took two program awards — for *Mysteries of the Mind* and *The Invisible World*, both aired on PBS.

For prime-time programs telecast between July 1, 1979, and June 30, 1980. The prime-time ceremony was broadcast on NBC from the Pasadena Civic Auditorium on September 7, 1980. Creative arts banquet held on September 6, 1980. Daytime awards presented on June 2 and 4, 1980, for programs aired between March 6, 1979, to March 5, 1980. News & documentary awards presented April 13, 1981, for programs aired between June 1, 1979, and Nov. 14, 1980. The third annual sports awards were presented December 10, 1980, for programs aired between July 19, 1979, and July 15, 1980.

PRIME-TIME PROGRAM AWARDS

OUTSTANDING DRAMA SERIES
• *Lou Grant*. Gene Reynolds, executive producer. Seth Freeman, producer. CBS.
Dallas. Philip Capice, Lee Rich, executive producers. Leonard Katzman, producer. CBS.
Family. Aaron Spelling, Leonard Goldberg, executive producers. Edward Zwick, producer. ABC.
The Rockford Files. Meta Rosenberg, executive producer. Stephen J. Cannell, supervising producer. David Chase, Chas. Floyd Johnson, Juanita Bartlett, producers. NBC.
The White Shadow. Bruce Paltrow, executive producer. Mark Tinker, producer. CBS.

OUTSTANDING COMEDY SERIES
• *Taxi*. James L. Brooks, Stan Daniels, Ed. Weinberger, executive producers. Glen Charles, Les Charles, producers. ABC.
Barney Miller. Danny Arnold, executive producer. Tony Sheehan, Noam Pitlik, producers. Gary Shaw, coproducer. ABC.
*M*A*S*H*. Burt Metcalfe, executive producer. Jim Mulligan, John Rappaport, producers. CBS.
Soap. Paul Junger Witt, Tony Thomas, executive producers. Susan Harris, producer. ABC.
WKRP in Cincinnati. Hugh Wilson, executive producer. Rod Daniel, producer. CBS.

OUTSTANDING LIMITED SERIES
• *Edward & Mrs. Simpson*. Andrew Brown, producer. Syndicated.

Disraeli, Portrait of a Romantic, *Masterpiece Theatre*. Joan Wilson, series producer. Cecil Clarke, producer. PBS.
The Duchess of Duke Street, *Masterpiece Theatre*. Joan Wilson, series producer. John Hawkesworth, producer. PBS.
Moviola. David L. Wolper, executive producer. Stan Margulies, producer. NBC.

OUTSTANDING VARIETY OR MUSIC PROGRAM
• *Baryshnikov on Broadway*. Herman Krawitz, executive producer. Gary Smith, Dwight Hemion, producers. Mikhail Baryshnikov, star. ABC.
The Benny Hill Show. Philip Jones, executive producer. Keith Beckett, David Bell, Ronald Fouracre, Peter Frazer Jones, Dennis Kirkland, John Robbins, Mark Stuart, producers. Benny Hill, star. Syndicated.
Goldie and Liza Together. George Schlatter, executive producer. Don Mischer, Fred Ebb, producers. Goldie Hawn, Liza Minnelli, stars. CBS.
The Muppet Show. David Lazer, executive producer. Jim Henson, producer. Dave Goelz, Louise Gold, Jim Henson, Richard Hunt, Kathryn Mullen, Jerry Nelson, Frank Oz, Steve Whitmire, stars. Syndicated.
Shirley MacLaine ... "Every Little Movement." Gary Smith, Dwight Hemion, producers. Shirley MacLaine, star. CBS.

OUTSTANDING DRAMA OR COMEDY SPECIAL
• *The Miracle Worker, NBC Theatre*. Raymond Katz, Sandy Gallin, executive producers. Fred Coe, producer. NBC.
All Quiet on the Western Front, Hallmark Hall of Fame. Martin Starger, executive producer. Norman Rosemont, producer. CBS.
Amber Waves. Philip Mandelker, executive producer. Stanley Kallis, producer. ABC.
Gideon's Trumpet, Hallmark Hall of Fame. John Houseman, executive producer. David W. Rintels, producer. CBS.
Guyana Tragedy: The Story of Jim Jones. Frank Konigsberg, executive producer. Ernest Tidyman, Sam Manners, producers. CBS.

OUTSTANDING CLASSICAL PROGRAM IN THE PERFORMING ARTS
(Winner)
• *Live from Studio 8H: A Tribute to Toscanini.* Alvin Cooperman, Judith De Paul, producers. NBC.

OUTSTANDING INFORMATIONAL PROGRAM
• *The Body Human: The Magic Sense.* Thomas W. Moore, executive producer. Alfred R. Kelman, Robert E. Fuisz, M.D., producers. Charles A. Bangert, Vivian R. Moss, coproducers. CBS.

OUTSTANDING PROGRAM ACHIEVEMENT— SPECIAL EVENTS
(Winner—Area award)
• *The 34th Annual Tony Awards.* Alexander H. Cohen, executive producer. Hildy Parks, producer. Roy A. Somiyo, coproducer. CBS.

OUTSTANDING PROGRAM ACHIEVEMENT— SPECIAL CLASS
(Winner)
• *Fred Astaire: Change Partners and Dance.* George Page, Jac Venza, executive producers. David Heeley, producer. PBS.

OUTSTANDING ANIMATED PROGRAM
(Winner—Area award)
• *Carlton Your Doorman.* Lorenzo Music, Barton Dean, producers. CBS.

(No award was given for Outstanding Children's Program.)

PERFORMANCE, DIRECTING, AND WRITING
OUTSTANDING LEAD ACTOR IN A DRAMA SERIES
• Edward Asner, *Lou Grant.* CBS.
James Garner, *The Rockford Files.* NBC.
Larry Hagman, *Dallas.* CBS.
Jack Klugman, *Quincy.* NBC.

OUTSTANDING LEAD ACTRESS IN A DRAMA SERIES
• Barbara Bel Geddes, *Dallas.* CBS.
Lauren Bacall, *The Rockford Files.* NBC.
Mariette Hartley, *The Rockford Files.* NBC.
Kristy McNichol, *Family.* ABC.
Sada Thompson, *Family.* ABC.

OUTSTANDING LEAD ACTOR IN A COMEDY SERIES
• Richard Mulligan, *Soap.* ABC.
Alan Alda, *M*A*S*H.* CBS.

Robert Guillaume, *Benson.* ABC.
Judd Hirsch, *Taxi.* ABC.
Hal Linden, *Barney Miller.* ABC.

OUTSTANDING LEAD ACTRESS IN A COMEDY SERIES
• Cathryn Damon, *Soap.* ABC.
Katherine Helmond, *Soap.* ABC.
Polly Holliday, *Flo.* CBS.
Sheree North, *Archie Bunker's Place.* CBS.
Isabel Sanford, *The Jeffersons.* CBS.

OUTSTANDING LEAD ACTOR IN A LIMITED SERIES OR A SPECIAL
• Powers Boothe, *Guyana Tragedy: The Story of Jim Jones.* CBS.
Tony Curtis, *Moviola: The Scarlett O'Hara War.* NBC.
Henry Fonda, *Gideon's Trumpet, Hallmark Hall of Fame.* CBS.
Jason Robards, *F.D.R.: The Last Year.* NBC.

OUTSTANDING LEAD ACTRESS IN A LIMITED SERIES OR A SPECIAL
• Patty Duke Astin, *The Miracle Worker, NBC Theatre.* NBC.
Bette Davis, *White Mama.* CBS.
Melissa Gilbert, *The Miracle Worker, NBC Theatre.* NBC.
Lee Remick, *Haywire.* CBS.

OUTSTANDING SUPPORTING ACTOR IN A DRAMA SERIES
• Stuart Margolin, *The Rockford Files.* NBC.
Mason Adams, *Lou Grant.* CBS.
Noah Beery, *The Rockford Files.* NBC.
Robert Walden, *Lou Grant.* CBS.

OUTSTANDING SUPPORTING ACTRESS IN A DRAMA SERIES
• Nancy Marchand, *Lou Grant.* CBS.
Nina Foch, *Lou Grant.* CBS.
Linda Kelsey, *Lou Grant.* CBS.
Jessica Walter, *Trapper John, M.D.* CBS.

OUTSTANDING SUPPORTING ACTOR IN A LIMITED SERIES OR A SPECIAL
• George Grizzard, *The Oldest Living Graduate.* NBC.
Ernest Borgnine, *All Quiet on the Western Front, Hallmark Hall of Fame.* CBS.
John Cassavetes, *Flesh and Blood.* CBS.
Charles Durning, *Attica.* ABC.
Harold Gould, *Moviola.* NBC.

OUTSTANDING SUPPORTING ACTRESS IN A LIMITED SERIES OR A SPECIAL
• Mare Winningham, *Amber Waves*. ABC.
Eileen Heckart, *F.D.R.: The Last Year*. NBC.
Patricia Neal, *All Quiet on the Western Front, Hallmark Hall of Fame*. CBS.
Carrie Nye, *Moviola: The Scarlett O'Hara War*. NBC.

OUTSTANDING SUPPORTING ACTOR IN A COMEDY, VARIETY, OR MUSIC SERIES
• Harry Morgan, *M*A*S*H*. CBS.
Mike Farrell, *M*A*S*H*. CBS.
Max Gail, *Barney Miller*. ABC.
Howard Hesseman, *WKRP in Cincinnati*. CBS.
Steve Landesberg, *Barney Miller*. ABC.

OUTSTANDING SUPPORTING ACTRESS IN A COMEDY OR VARIETY OR MUSIC SERIES
• Loretta Swit, *M*A*S*H*. CBS.
Loni Anderson, *WKRP in Cincinnati*. CBS.
Polly Holliday, *Alice*. CBS.
Inga Swenson, *Benson*. ABC.

OUTSTANDING DIRECTING IN A DRAMA SERIES
• Roger Young, *Lou Grant*. CBS.
Burt Brinckerhoff, *Lou Grant*. CBS.
Peter Levin, *Lou Grant*. CBS.
Frank Perry, *Skag*. NBC.
Gene Reynolds, *Lou Grant*. CBS.

OUTSTANDING DIRECTING IN A COMEDY SERIES
• James Burrows, *Taxi*. ABC.
Alan Alda, *M*A*S*H*. CBS.
Charles Dubin, *M*A*S*H*. CBS.
Burt Metcalfe, *M*A*S*H*. CBS.
Harry Morgan, *M*A*S*H*. CBS.

OUTSTANDING DIRECTING IN A VARIETY OR MUSIC PROGRAM
• Dwight Hemion, *Baryshnikov on Broadway*. ABC.
Steve Binder, *The Big Show*. NBC.
Tony Charmoli, *John Denver and the Muppets: A Christmas Together*. ABC.
Peter Harris, *The Muppet Show*. Syndicated.

OUTSTANDING DIRECTING IN A LIMITED SERIES OR A SPECIAL
• Marvin J. Chomsky, *Attica*. ABC.
John Erman, *Moviola: The Scarlett O'Hara War*. NBC.
William A. Graham, *Guyana Tragedy: The Story of Jim Jones*. CBS.
Delbert Mann, *All Quiet on the Western Front, Hallmark Hall of Fame*. CBS.
Joseph Sargent, *Amber Waves*. ABC.

OUTSTANDING WRITING IN A COMEDY SERIES
• Bob Colleary, *Barney Miller*. ABC.
Glen Charles, Les Charles, *Taxi*. ABC.
Stan Daniels, Ed. Weinberger, *The Associates*. ABC.
David Isaacs, Ken Levine, *M*A*S*H*. CBS.
Michael Leeson, teleplay. Charlie Hauck, story. *The Associates*. ABC.

OUTSTANDING WRITING IN A DRAMA SERIES
• Seth Freeman, *Lou Grant*. CBS.
Allan Burns, Gene Reynolds, *Lou Grant*. CBS.
Stephen J. Cannell, *Tenspeed and Brown Shoe*. ABC.
Michele Gallery, *Lou Grant*. CBS.
Abby Mann, *Skag*. NBC.

OUTSTANDING WRITING IN A VARIETY OR MUSIC PROGRAM
• Buz Kohan, *Shirley MacLaine ... "Every Little Movement."* CBS.
Peter Aykroyd, Anne Beatts, Tom Davis, James Downey, Brian Doyle-Murray, Al Franken, Tom Gammill, Lorne Michaels, Matt Neuman, Don Novello, Sarah Paley, Max Pross, Herb Sargent, Tom Schiller, Harry Shearer, Rosie Shuster, Alan Zweibel, *Saturday Night Live*. NBC.
Fred Ebb, *Goldie and Liza Together*. CBS.
Jim Henson, Don Hinkley, Jerry Juhl, David Odell, *The Muppet Show*. Syndicated.
Bob Arnott, Roger Beatty, Dick Clair, Tim Conway, Ann Elder, Arnie Kogen, Buz Kohan, Jenna McMahon, Kenny Solms, *Carol Burnett & Company*. ABC.

OUTSTANDING WRITING
IN A LIMITED SERIES OR A SPECIAL
• David Chase, *Off the Minnesota Strip.* ABC.
James S. Henerson, *Attica.* ABC.
James Lee, *Moviola: This Year's Blonde.* NBC.
David W. Rintels, *Gideon's Trumpet, Hallmark Hall of Fame.* CBS.
Ken Trevey, *Amber Waves.* ABC.

OTHER AWARD WINNERS
OUTSTANDING MUSIC COMPOSITION
FOR A SERIES
(Dramatic underscore)
• Patrick Williams, *Lou Grant.* CBS.

OUTSTANDING MUSIC COMPOSITION
FOR A LIMITED SERIES OR A SPECIAL
(Dramatic underscore)
• Jerry Fielding, *High Midnight.* CBS.

OUTSTANDING MUSIC DIRECTION
• Ian Fraser, music director. Ralph Burns, Billy Byers, principal arrangers, *Baryshnikov on Broadway.* ABC.

OUTSTANDING ACHIEVEMENT
IN CHOREOGRAPHY
• Alan Johnson, *Shirley MacLaine... "Every Little Movement."* CBS.

OUTSTANDING ART DIRECTION
FOR A SERIES
• James D. Bissell, art director. William Webb, set decorator, *Palmerstown, U.S.A.* CBS.

OUTSTANDING ART DIRECTION
FOR A LIMITED SERIES OR A SPECIAL
• Wilfred Shingleton, production designer. Julian Sacks, Jean Taillandier, art directors. Cheryal Kearney, Robert Christides, set decorators, *Gauguin the Savage.* CBS.

OUTSTANDING ART DIRECTION
FOR A VARIETY OR MUSIC PROGRAM
• Charles Lisanby, art director. Dwight Jackson, set decorator, *Baryshnikov on Broadway.* ABC.

OUTSTANDING COSTUME DESIGN
FOR A SERIES
• Pete Menefee, *The Big Show.* NBC.

OUTSTANDING COSTUME DESIGN
FOR A LIMITED SERIES OR A SPECIAL
• Travilla, *Moviola: The Scarlett O'Hara War.* NBC.

OUTSTANDING MAKEUP
• Richard Blair, *Moviola: The Scarlett O'Hara War.* NBC.

OUTSTANDING HAIRSTYLING
• Larry Germain, Donna Gilbert, *The Miracle Worker, NBC Theatre.* NBC.

OUTSTANDING GRAPHIC DESIGN
AND TITLE SEQUENCES
• Phill Norman, *The French Atlantic Affair.* ABC.

OUTSTANDING CINEMATOGRAPHY
FOR A SERIES
• Enzo A. Martinelli, *The Contender.* CBS.

OUTSTANDING CINEMATOGRAPHY
FOR A LIMITED SERIES OR A SPECIAL
• Gayne Rescher, *Moviola: The Silent Lovers.* NBC.

OUTSTANDING FILM EDITING FOR A SERIES
• M. Pam Blumenthal, *Taxi.* ABC.

OUTSTANDING FILM EDITING
FOR A LIMITED SERIES OR A SPECIAL
• Bill Blunden, Alan Pattillo, *All Quiet on the Western Front, Hallmark Hall of Fame.* CBS.

OUTSTANDING VIDEO-TAPE EDITING
FOR A SERIES
• John Hawkins, *The Muppet Show.* Syndicated.

OUTSTANDING VIDEO-TAPE EDITING
FOR A LIMITED SERIES OR A SPECIAL
• Danny White, *Olivia Newton-John: Hollywood Nights.* ABC.

OUTSTANDING FILM SOUND EDITING
• Don Crosby, Mark Dennis, Tony Garber, Doug Grindstaff, Don V. Isaacs, Hank Salerno, Larry Singer, *Power.* NBC.

OUTSTANDING FILM SOUND MIXING
• Ray Barons, David Campbell, Bob Pettis, John Reitz, *The Ordeal of Dr. Mudd.* CBS.

OUTSTANDING TAPE SOUND MIXING
• Bruce Burns, Jerry Clemans, *Sinatra: The First 40 Years.* NBC.

Outstanding Technical Direction and Electronic Camerawork
• Wayne Parsons, technical director. Tom Geren, Dean Hall, Bob Highton, William Landers, Ron Sheldon, camerapersons, *The Oldest Living Graduate.* NBC.

Outstanding Lighting Direction (Electronic)
• Peter G. Edwards, William Knight, Peter S. Passas, *F.D.R.: The Last Year.* NBC.

Outstanding Individual Achievement—Informational Program
(Area awards)
• Bryan Anderson, Bob Elfstrom, Al Gaddings, cinematographers, *Mysteries of the Sea.* ABC.
• David Clark, Joel Fein, Robert L. Harman, George E. Porler, film sound mixers, "Dive to the Edge of Creation," *National Geographic Special.* PBS.
• Robert Eisenhardt, Hank O'Karma, Jane Kurson, film editors, *The Body Human: The Body Beautiful.* CBS.

Oustanding Individual Achievement—Special Class
(Area award)
• Geof Bartz, film editor, *Operation Lifeline.* NBC.

Outstanding Individual Achievement—Children's Program
(Area award)
• Bob O'Bradovich, makeup, *The Halloween that Almost Wasn't.* ABC.

Outstanding Individual Achievement Creative Technical Crafts
• Scott Schachter, live audio mixing, *Live from Studio 8H: A Tribute to Toscanini.* NBC.
• Mark Schubin, live stereo simulcast, "Luciano Pavarotti and the New York Philharmonic," *Live from Lincoln Center.* PBS.

(There was no award in the area of individual achievement in animation programs or special events.)

DAYTIME AWARDS
Outstanding Daytime Drama Series
• *Guiding Light.* Allen M. Potter, executive producer. Leslie Kwartin, Joe Willmore, producers. CBS.
All My Children. Agnes Nixon, executive producer. Jorn Winther, producer. ABC.
Another World. Paul Rauch, executive producer. Mary S. Bonner, Robert Costello, producers. NBC.

Outstanding Actor in a Daytime Drama Series
• Douglass Watson, *Another World.* NBC.
John Gabriel, *Ryan's Hope.* ABC.
Michael Levin, *Ryan's Hope.* ABC.
Franc Luz, *The Doctors.* NBC.
James Mitchell, *All My Children.* ABC.
William Mooney, *All My Children.* ABC.

Outstanding Actress in a Daytime Drama Series
• Judith Light, *One Life to Live.* ABC.
Julia Barr, *All My Children.* ABC.
Leslie Charleson, *General Hospital.* ABC.
Kim Hunter, *The Edge of Night.* ABC.
Beverlee McKinsey, *Another World.* NBC.
Kathleen Noone, *All My Children.* ABC.

Outstanding Performance by an Actor in a Supporting Role for a Daytime Drama Series
• Warren Burton, *All My Children.* ABC.
Vasili Bogazianos, *The Edge of Night.* ABC.
Larry Haines, *Search for Tomorrow.* CBS.
Ron Hale, *Ryan's Hope.* ABC.
Julius LaRosa, *Another World.* NBC.
Shepperd Strudwick, *Love of Life.* CBS.

Outstanding Performance by an Actress in a Supporting Role for a Daytime Drama Series
• Francesca James, *All My Children.* ABC.
Deidre Hall, *Days of Our Lives.* NBC.
Lois Kibbee, *The Edge of Night.* ABC.
Elaine Lee, *The Doctors.* NBC.
Valerie Mahaffey, *The Doctors.* NBC.
Louise Shaffer, *Ryan's Hope.* ABC.

Outstanding Direction for a Daytime Drama Series
• Lela Swift, Jerry Evans, *Ryan's Hope.* ABC.
Henry Kaplan, Jack Coffey, Sherrell Hoffman, Jorn Winther, *All My Children.* ABC.

Ira Cirker, Melvin Bernhardt, Robert Calhoun, Barnet Kellman, Jack Hofsiss, Andrew Weyman, *Another World*. NBC.
John Sedwick, Richard Pepperman, *The Edge of Night*. ABC.
Marlena Laird, Alan Pultz, Phil Sogard, *General Hospital*. ABC.
Larry Auerbach, Robert Scinto, *Love of Life*. CBS.

OUTSTANDING WRITING
FOR A DAYTIME DRAMA SERIES
• Claire Labine, Paul Avila Mayer, Mary Munisteri, Judith Pinsker, Jeffrey Lane, *Ryan's Hope*. ABC.
Agnes Nixon, Wisner Washam, Jack Wood, Caroline Franz, Mary K. Wells, Cathy Chicos, Clarice Blackburn, Anita Jaffe, Ken Harvey, *All My Children*. ABC.
Henry Slesar, Steve Lehrman, *The Edge of Night*. ABC.
Gordon Russell, Sam Hall, Peggy O'Shea, Don Wallace, Lanie Bertram, Cynthia Benjamin, Marisa Gioffre, *One Life to Live*. ABC.

OTHER DAYTIME AWARD WINNERS
OUTSTANDING TECHNICAL EXCELLENCE
FOR A DAYTIME DRAMA SERIES
• Joseph Solomito, Howard Zweig, technical directors. Lawrence Hammond, Robert Ambrico, Dianne Cates-Cantrell, Christopher N. Mauro, Larry Strack, Vincent Senatore, electronic camerapersons. Albin S. Lemanski, audio engineer. Len Walas, video engineer. Diana Wenman, Jean Dadaho, associate directors. Roger Haeneit, John L. Grella, video-tape editors. Irving Robbin, Jim Reichert, music composers. Ted Smith, music director, *All My Children*. ABC.

OUTSTANDING DESIGN EXCELLENCE
FOR A DAYTIME DRAMA SERIES
• William Mickley, scenic designer. William Itkin, Donna Larson, Mel Handelsman, lighting directors. Carol Luiken, costume designer. Sylvia Lawrence, makeup designer. Michael Huddle, hair designer. Hy Bley, graphic designer, *All My Children*. ABC.

OUTSTANDING GUEST/CAMEO
APPEARANCE IN A DAYTIME DRAMA
SERIES
• Hugh McPhillips, *Days of Our Lives*. NBC.

OUTSTANDING GAME OR AUDIENCE
PARTICIPATION SHOW
(Tie)
• *The Hollywood Squares,* Merrill Heatter, Robert Quigley, executive producers. Jay Redack, producer. NBC.
• *The $20,000 Pyramid*. Bob Stewart, executive producer. Anne Marie Schmitt, Jane Rothchild, producers. ABC.

OUTSTANDING HOST OR HOSTESS
IN A GAME OR AUDIENCE
PARTICIPATION SHOW
• Peter Marshall, *The Hollywood Squares*. NBC.

OUTSTANDING INDIVIDUAL DIRECTION
FOR A GAME OR AUDIENCE
PARTICIPATION SHOW
• Jerome Shaw, *The Hollywood Squares*. NBC.

OUTSTANDING TALK, SERVICE,
OR VARIETY SERIES
• *Donahue*. Richard Mincer, executive producer. Patricia McMillen, senior producer. Darlene Hayes, Sheri Singer, producers. Syndicated.

OUTSTANDING HOST OR HOSTESS
IN A TALK, SERVICE, OR VARIETY SERIES
• Phil Donahue, *Donahue*. Syndicated.

OUTSTANDING INDIVIDUAL
DIRECTION FOR A TALK, SERVICE,
OR VARIETY SERIES
• Duke Struck, *Good Morning America*. ABC.

OUTSTANDING CHILDREN'S
ENTERTAINMENT SPECIAL
• "The Late Great Me: Story of a Teenage Alcoholic," *ABC Afterschool Special*. Daniel Wilson, executive producer. Linda Marmelstein, producer. ABC

OUTSTANDING CHILDREN'S
ENTERTAINMENT SERIES
• *Hot Hero Sandwich*. Bruce Hart, Carole Hart, executive producers. Howard G. Malley, producer. NBC.

OUTSTANDING CHILDREN'S
ANTHOLOGY/DRAMATIC PROGRAMMING
• "Animal Talk," *CBS Library*. Diane Asselin, executive producer. Paul Asselin, producer. CBS.

• "The Gold Bug," *ABC Weekend Special.* Linda Gottlieb, executive produer. Doro Backrach, producer. ABC.
• "Leatherstocking Tales," *Once Upon a Classic.* Jay Rayvid, executive producer. Bob Walsh, producer. PBS.
• "Once Upon a Midnight Dreary," *CBS Library.* Diane Asselin, Paul Asselin, producers. CBS.

OUTSTANDING CHILDREN'S INFORMATIONAL INSTRUCTIONAL SERIES/SPECIALS
• *Sesame Street.* Al Hyslop, executive producer. Dave Freyss, producer. PBS.
• *30 Minutes.* Joel Heller, executive producer. Allan Ducovny, Madeline Amgott, Diego Echevarria, Horace Jenkens, Elizabeth Lawrence, Patti Obrow White, Robert Rubin, Susan Mills, Catherine Olian, Virginia Gray, producers. CBS.
• "Why a Conductor?" *CBS Festival of Lively Arts for Young People.* Kirk Browning, executive producer. CBS.

OUTSTANDING CHILDREN'S INFORMATIONAL/INSTRUCTIONAL PROGRAMMING—SHORT FORMAT
• *Schoolhouse Rock.* Thomas Yohe, executive producer. George Newall, Radford Stone, producers. ABC.
• "Help!!!" *Dr. Henry's Emergency Lessons for People.* Ken Greengrass, Phil Lawrence, executive producers. Lynn Ahrens, producer. ABC.
• *In the News.* Joel Heller, executive producer. Walter Lister, producer. CBS.

OUTSTANDING INDIVIDUAL ACHIEVEMENT IN CHILDREN'S PROGRAMMING (Winners—Area awards)
• Melissa Sue Anderson, performer, "Which Mother is Mine?," *ABC Afterschool Special.* ABC.
• Maia Danziger, performer, "The Late Great Me: Story of a Teenage Alcoholic," *ABC Afterschool Special.* ABC.
• Butterfly McQueen, performer, "The Seven Wishes of a Rich Kid," *ABC Afterschool Special.* ABC.
• Fred Rogers, performer. *Mister Rogers' Neighborhood.* PBS.
• David Axelrod, Joseph A. Bailey, Andy Breckman, Richard Camp, Sherry Coben, Bruce Hart, Carole Hart , Marianne Meyer, writers, *Hot Hero Sandwich.* NBC.
• Jan Hartman, writer, "The Late Great

Me: Story of a Teenage Alcoholic," *ABC Afterschool Special.* ABC.
• Anthony Lover, director, "The Late Great Me: Story of a Teenage Alcoholic," *ABC Afterschool Special.* ABC.
• Arthur Allen Seidelman, director, "Which Mother is Mine?" *ABC Afterschool Special.* ABC.
• Steven Zink, director of photography (tape) single camera; film style, *Sesame Street.* PBS.
• George Alch, audio engineer, "A Special Gift," *ABC Afterschool Special.* ABC. Lee Dichter, film sound mixer, *Big Blue Marble.* Syndicated.
• Robert Collins, cinematographer, "Heartbreak Winner," *ABC Afterschool Special.* ABC.
• David Sanderson, cinematographer, "Once upon a Midnight Dreary," *CBS Library.* CBS.
• Alex Thompson, cinematographer, "The Gold Bug," *ABC Weekend Special.* ABC.
• Jack Sholder, film editor, *3-2-1 Contact.* PBS.
• Vincent Sklena, film editor, "The Late Great Me: Story of a Teenage Alcoholic," *ABC Afterschool Special.* ABC.
• Merle Worth, film editor, *3-2-1 Contact.* PBS.
• Ronald Baldwin, art director, *3-2-1 Contact.* PBS.
• Nat Mongioi, set decorator, *3-2-1 Contact.* PBS.
• Steven Atha, makeup and hair designer. "The Gold Bug," *ABC Weekend Special.* ABC.
• Michael Baugh, graphic designer, *Villa Alegre.* PBS.

OUTSTANDING RELIGIOUS PROGRAMMING—SERIES/SPECIALS
• *Directions.* Sid Darion, executive producer. ABC.
• *For Our Times.* Pamela Iiott, executive producer. Joseph Clement, Chalmers Dale, Marlene DiDonato, Ted Holmes, producers. CBS.

OUTSTANDING INDIVIDUAL ACHIEVEMENT IN RELIGIOUS PROGRAMMING (Area award)
• Dean Jagger, performer, "Independence and 76," *This is the Life.* Syndicated.
• Richard F. Morean, writer, "If No Birds Sang," *This is the Life,* Syndicated.
• Justus Taylor, sound recordist, "Seeds of Revolution," *Directions.* ABC.

• John Duffy, music composer/director, *A Talent for Life: Jews of the Italian Renaissance.* NBC.
• Thomas E. Azzari, art director, "Stable Boy's Christmas," *This is the Life.* Syndicated.

OUTSTANDING ACHIEVEMENT IN COVERAGE OF SPECIAL EVENTS
• *La Gioconda.* Jeanne Mulcahy, executive producer. John Goberman, producer; for KCET Los Angeles. PBS.
• *Macy's 53rd Annual Thanksgiving Day Parade.* Dick Schneider, producer. NBC.

SPECIAL CLASSIFICATION OF OUTSTANDING PROGRAM ACHIEVEMENT (Area award)
• *FYI.* Yanna Kroyt Brandt, producer. ABC.

SPECIAL CLASSIFICATION OF OUTSTANDING INDIVIDUAL ACHIEVEMENT (Area award)
• Danny Seagren, "Puppet Design and Construction, Miss Peach of the Kelly School," *The Annual Thanksgiving Turkey Day Rattle.* Syndicated.

OUTSTANDING INDIVIDUAL ACHIEVEMENT IN COVERAGE OF SPECIAL EVENTS (Area awards)
• Luciano Pavarotti, performer, *La Gioconda.* PBS.
• Renata Scotto, performer, *La Gioconda.* PBS.
• Kirk Browning, director, *La Gioconda.* PBS.
• Ron Graft, technical director. Kenneth Patterson, Gary Emrick, Luis A. Fuerte, Daniel J. Webb, Jack Reader, Thomas Tucker, William Kelsey, electronic camerapersons, *La Gioconda.* PBS.
• Greg Harms, video engineer, *La Gioconda.* PBS.
• Tom Ancell, audio mixer, *La Gioconda.* PBS.
• Zack Brown, scenic designer/set decorator, *La Gioconda.* PBS.
• Ken Dettling, lighting director, *La Gioconda.* PBS.
• Zack Brown, costume designer, *La Gioconda.* PBS.

(No award was bestowed in the category of individual achievement in any area of creative technical crafts.)

NEWS & DOCUMENTARY AWARD WINNERS
PROGRAMS AND PROGRAM SEGMENTS
• *Pope John Paul II in Poland,* Helen Marmor, producer. Philip Scharper, correspondent. NBC.
• "Post Election Special Edition," *ABC News Nightline.* Jeff Gralnick, William Lord, producers. Ted Koppel, Frank Reynolds, Barbara Walters, Max Robinson, Lynn Sherr, correspondents. ABC.
• "A Fishing Boat Sinks," *NBC Nightly News.* Nancy Fernandez, Jeff Weinstock, producers. Lee McCarthy, correspondent. NBC.
• "Murder of a Correspondent," *ABC World News Tonight.* Ken Luckoff, producer. Al Dale, correspondent. ABC.
• *CBS Reports: Miami — The Trial That Sparked the Riots.* Eric F. Saltzman, producer. Ed Bradley, correspondent. CBS.
• "Lights, Cameras ... Politics," *ABC News Closeup.* Ann G. Black, Tom Priestley, producers. Richard Reeves, correspondent. ABC.
• "Nicaragua," *20/20.* Lowell Bergman, Neil Cunningham, producers. Dave Marash, correspondent. ABC.
• "Onward Christian Voters," *60 Minutes.* Joel Bernstein, producer. Dan Rather, correspondent. CBS.
• "Too Little, Too Late?" *CBS News: Magazine.* Janet Roach, producer. Ed Bradley, correspondent. CBS.
• "Hot Shells: U.S. Arms for South Africa," *World.* William Cran, producer. PBS.
• "Who Killed Georgi Markov?" *World.* Phil Harding, producer. Michael Cockerrell, correspondent. PBS.
• "Arson for Profit," *20/20.* Peter Lance, producer. Geraldo Rivera, correspondent. ABC.
• "Urethane," *Prime Time Saturday.* Peter Jeffries, producer. John Dancy, correspondent. NBC.
• "VW Beetle: The Hidden Danger," *20/20.* Jeff Diamond, producer. Sylvia Chase, correspondent. ABC.
• *CBS Reports: Teddy.* Andrew Lack, producer. Roger Mudd, interviewer. CBS.
• "Bette Davis," *60 Minutes.* Nancy Lea, producer. Mike Wallace, interviewer. CBS.
• "Here's Johnny!" *60 Minutes.* David Lowe Jr., producer. Mike Wallace, interviewer. CBS.

1979–80

• *CBS Reports: On the Road.* Bernard Birnbaum, Charles Kuralt, producers. Charles Kuralt, correspondent. CBS.
• "The Invisible World," *National Geographic Special.* Alex Pomasanoff, producer. PBS.
• "Mysteries of the Mind," *National Geographic Special.* Irwin Rosten, producer. PBS.
• "George Burns: An Update," *20/20.* Betsy Osha, producer. Bob Brown, correspondent. ABC.
• "Heart Transplant," *Prime Time Sunday.* Robert Eaton, George Lewis, Arthur Lord, producers. Jack Perkins, correspondent. NBC.

OUTSTANDING INDIVIDUAL ACHIEVEMENT IN NEWS AND DOCUMENTARY PROGRAMMING
(Writing)
• Bill Moyers, "Our Times," *Bill Moyers' Journal.* PBS.
• Irwin Rosten, "Mysteries of the Mind," *National Geographic Special.* PBS.
• Marlene Sanders, Judy Towers Reemtsma, *CBS Reports: What Shall We Do About Mother?* CBS.
• Morton Silverstein, Chris Wallace, *NBC Reports: The Migrants, 1980.* NBC.
• Perry Wolff, "American Dream, American Nightmare," *CBS News Special Report.* CBS.
(Direction)
• Patrick M. Cook, "Death in a Southwest Prison," *ABC News Closeup.* ABC.
• Ray Lockhart, *NBC White Paper — If Japan Can, Why Can't We?* NBC.
• Roger Phenix, *NBC Reports: To Be a Doctor.* NBC.
• Morton Silverstein, *NBC Reports: The Migrants, 1980.* NBC.
(Technical direction/Electronic camera)
• Jon Alpert, camera. *Third Avenue: Only the Strong Survive.* PBS.
• Jack Clark, camera. "Shooting of Bill Stuart—Nicaragua," *ABC World News Tonight.* ABC.
(Cinematography)
• Mike Edwards, "Inside Afghanistan," *60 Minutes.* CBS.
• Alan Raymond, "To Die for Ireland," *ABC News Closeup.* ABC.
(Associate direction and/or video-tape editing)
• John Godfrey, Jon Alpert and Keiko Tsuno, video-tape editors. *Third Avenue: Only the Strong Survive.* PBS.

• Ruth Neuwald, video-tape editor. *CBS Reports: Miami—The Trial That Sparked the Riots.* CBS.
(Film editing)
• Maurice Murad, *CBS Reports: The Saudis.* CBS.
• Steve Sheppard, "Inside Afghanistan," *60 Minutes.* CBS.
• Kenneth E. Werner, Nils Rassmussen, "Death in a Southwest Prison," *ABC News Closeup.* ABC.
(Audio)
• Jim Cefalo, sound recordist, "Shooting of Bill Stuart—Nicaragua," *ABC World News Tonight.* ABC.
• Robert Rogow, location sound recordist. Joel Dulberg, rerecording mixer, "Pavarotti," *60 Minutes.* CBS.
(Music direction)
• Lionel Hampton, *No Maps on My Taps.* PBS.

(No awards were bestowed in the areas of lighting direction, graphic design, music direction, or music scenic/set design.)

SPORTS AWARD WINNERS
OUTSTANDING LIVE SPORTS SERIES
• *NCAA College Football,* Roone Arledge, executive producer. Chuck Howard, senior producer. Bob Goodrich, Eleanor Riger, Curt Gowdy, Jr., Dick Buffinton, Chris Carmody, Ned Steckel, Doug Wilson, Terry O'Neil, producers. ABC.

OUTSTANDING EDITED SPORTS SERIES
• *NFL Game of the Week,* Ed Sabol, executive producer. Steve Sabol, producer. Syndicated.

OUTSTANDING LIVE SPORTS SPECIAL
• *1980 Winter Olympic Games.* Roone Arledge, executive producer. Chuck Howard, Chet Forte and Dennis Lewin, senior producers. Bob Goodrich, Curt Gowdy Jr., Terry Jastrow, Terry O'Neil, Eleanor Riger, Ned Steckel and Doug Wilson, producers. Jeff Rune, coordinating producer. Bruce Weisman, producer, "Up Close and Personals." Robert Riger and Bud Greenspan, special projects producers. ABC.

OUTSTANDING EDITED SPORTS SPECIAL
• *Gossamer Albatross — Flight of Imagination.* Eddie Einhorn, executive producer. Joseph A. Thompson, producer. CBS.

Curt Gowdy (right) presented the Outstanding Sports Personality award to six-time past Emmy winner Jim McKay.

OUTSTANDING DIRECTING IN SPORTS PROGRAMMING
• Sandy Grossman, *Super Bowl XIV.* CBS.

OUTSTANDING INDIVIDUAL ACHIEVEMENT IN SPORTS PROGRAMMING
(Cinematography)
• Bob Angelo, Ernie Ernst, Jay Gerber, Stan Leshner, Don Marx, Hank McElwee, Howard Neef, Jack Newman, Steve Sabol, Bob Smith, Art Spieller, Phil Tucker, cinematographers, *NFL Game of the Week.* Syndicated.
• Harvey Harrison, Harry Hart and Don Shapiro, cinematographers, "Up Close and Personals," *1980 Winter Olympic Games.* ABC.
(Associate direction/Video-tape editing)
• Barbara Bowman, Paul Fanelli, Charles Gardner, Marvin Gench, Roger Haenelt, Conrad Kraus, Alex Moscovic, Lou Rende, Nathan Rogers, Erskin Roberts, Mario Schencman, Ann Stone, Arthur Volk, Francis Giugliano, Ronald Ackerman, Michael Altieri, Tom Capace, John Croak, Jack Hierl, Tony Jutchenko, Hector Kicelian, Ken Klingbeil, Pete Murphy, Hiorshi Nakamoto, Carl Pollack, Merrit Roesser, Winston Sadoo, Fausto Sanchez, Rene Sanchez, Leo Stephen, Richard Velasco, Ed Zlotnick, vide-otape editors, *1980 Winter Olympic Games,* ABC.

(Film editing)
• Angelo Bernarducci, Jon Day, Sam Fine, John Petersen, Vincent Reda, Anthony Scandiffio, Wayne Weiss and Ted Winterburn, film editors, "Up Close and Personals," *1980 Winter Olympic Games.* ABC.
(Audio)
• Trevor Carless, George Hause, Jim Lynch, Dennis Fierman and Jan Schulte, location sound mixers, "Up Close and Personals," *1980 Winter Olympic Games.* ABC.
(Music composition/Direction)
• Chuck Mangione, music composer/director, *1980 Winter Olympic Games,* including original theme, "Give It All You Got." ABC.
(Engineering supervision/Technical direction/Electronic camerawork)
• Julius Barnathan, Joseph DeBonis, Bill Stone, Joseph A. Maltz, David E. Eschelbacher, Charles Baidour, David Linick, Eric Rosenthal, Abdeinour Tadros, Tony Uyttendaele, engineering supervisors. Dick Horan, Robert Armbruster, Bill Blumel, Loren Coltran, Geoffrey Felger, Mike Jochim, Jacques Lesgards, Bill Maier, Gary Larkins, Joseph Polito, Elliott R. Reed, Martin Sandberg, Tony Versley, Mike Fisher, Joseph Kresnicka (Chicago), Bud Untiedt (West Coast), technical managers. Les Weiss, Werner Gunther, Chester Mazurek, William Morris, Joseph Schiavo, Joe Nesi (West Coast), Ernie Buftleman, J. Allen, Gerry Bucci, H. Falk, David Smith, technical directors. Dianne Cates-Cantrell, Gary Donatelli, Danny LaMothe, Charles Mitchell, Steve Nikifor, William Sullivan, Don Farnham (Chicago). Rick Knipe, Morton Lipow, Joseph Montesano (minicam), electronic camerapersons, *1980 Winter Olympic Games.* ABC.

SPECIAL CLASSIFICATION OF OUTSTANDING PROGRAM AND INDIVIDUAL ACHIEVEMENT
(Individual achievement)
• Jerry P. Caruso, Harry Smith, creators/developers of Radio Frequency Golf Cup Mic, *Bob Hope Golf Classic.* NBC.

OUTSTANDING SPORTS PERSONALITY
• Jim McKay. ABC.

(No awards were given in the areas
of graphic design, lighting direction,
or associate direction.)

INTERNATIONAL AWARD WINNERS
DOCUMENTARY
• *The Secret Hospital,* Part 1, Rampton,
Yorkshire, Television, Ltd., United
Kingdom.

PERFORMING ARTS
• *Elegies for the Deaths of Three Spanish
Poets,* Allegro Films, United Kingdom.

DRAMA
• *On Giants' Shoulders,* British
Broadcasting Corporation, U.K.

SPECIAL AWARDS
**OUTSTANDING ENGINEERING
DEVELOPMENT**
• National Bureau of Standards, Public
Broadcasting Service, and American
Broadcasting Company for their
development of the Closed Captioning
for the Deaf system.

(Citations)
• David Bargen
• Vital Industries
• Convergence Corporation.

**OUTSTANDING ACHIEVEMENT
IN THE SCIENCE OF ENGINEERING**
• RCA
• CCLD
• Video Systems
• Quantel Limited
• Ikegami Electronics
• Vital Industries

**NATIONAL AWARD
FOR COMMUNITY SERVICE**
• *Agent Orange, The Human Harvest,*
WBBM-TV, Chicago, Illinois.

A.T.A.S GOVERNORS AWARD
• Johnny Carson

N.A.T.A.S. TRUSTEES AWARD
• Leonard H. Goldenson, for his role in
forming the American Broadcasting
Corporation and guiding its growth.

No More Blues
on *Hill Street*

It was the greatest and most dramatic victory in the history of the Emmys.

When *Hill Street Blues* first entered the awards contest, it was also involved in a much larger struggle for survival. The show once described by the *L.A. Times* as a "series about an unlikely group of compassionate cops vaguely trying to cope with urban crime" was universally hailed by the critics, but it ranked only a dismal 87th among the 96 series in prime time. NBC agreed to try it out for one more year, but only with enormous reluctance: *HSB* thus became the lowest-rated series ever renewed by the network. Something dramatic was needed if the program was eventually going to find its audience. Then the Emmy nominations came out.

Hill Street set off an avalanche: Its 21 nods not only represented the most nominations in a season ever heaped upon a new series, it was the most ever heaped upon any series. Then, on Emmys night, *HSB* established the record of the most awards ever won in a season by a prime-time show: eight.

"*Hill Street Blues* won in every major category it was entered in," noted *Variety*, "except best supporting actress, where its two nominees in that category may well have countermanded each other." The show was named Outstanding Drama Series, won trophies for three of its actors, and also reaped honors for writing, directing, cinematography, and film sound editing. Ironically, another award it didn't get, in addition to best supporting actress, was the prize for its innovative intro music. *HSB* may have been wallowing at the bottom of the television ratings heap, but its theme

Best actor in a drama series Daniel J. Travanti was "ecstatic" about Hill Street Blues*'s avalanche of awards.*

music was so popular on radio and in record stores that it was in *Billboard*'s Top Ten. "With that kind of theme, I'd be hooked on *Dukes of Hazzard*," said a smitten writer for the *L.A. Times*.

"Perhaps the best indication of the academy voters' enthusiasm for the series was the victory of Barbara Babcock as outstanding lead actress in a drama series," *Variety* wrote, "as Babcock had appeared in only a few episodes, as a recurring guest star in which she was hardly the lead actress. When you're hot, you're hot, however, and no one is likely to quibble over Babcock's triumph." Babcock wept as she accepted her award and said, "I certainly feel as if I paid my dues. I worked for 20 years."

The other two performance trophies went to Daniel J. Travanti (best lead actor), who accepted his Emmy shouting, "Oh, boy!" and Michael Conrad (best supporting actor), who roared, "Wow!" Back in the press room later on, while trying to describe the effect that the awards sweep was having on cast and crew, Travanti was a little more wordy: "We've been ecstatic, passionate, and demonstrative," he told reporters.

The show's writers and creators, however, were more succinct when they accepted their awards. Michael Kozoll said he hoped and believed that *HSB*'s success at the Emmys would boost its popularity. Steven Bochco took the time to settle an old score by thanking Fred Silverman ("wherever you are"), the former NBC chairman who originally commissioned the show. Silverman had been replaced by Grant Tinker, former head of MTM Enterprises, which produced *HSB*. Bochco thanked him, too.

The drama series winner of the past two years, *Lou Grant*, began the evening with 13 nominations, but thanks to the near shutout by *HSB*, ended up with only one award — in a single category that *HSB* failed to sweep. As a result, Nancy Marchand was named best supporting actress for a third time.

Unlike *Lou Grant*, the other series winner of the past two years, *Taxi*, did make an impressive return trip this year. Of its nine nominations, *Taxi* took six awards: for Outstanding Comedy Series, directing, writing, film editing, and for two of its actors who had never won before, despite the show's popularity with Emmy voters. Danny DeVito, who played the taxi garage's tyrannical dispatcher, was named best supporting actor and Judd Hirsch was voted best lead actor for his role as a career cabbie,

the show's single level-headed character. To Hirsch, doing the show was not only a labor of love, it was hard labor, in a sense, served to offset his past reputation for being difficult to work with. He told the *L.A. Herald Examiner*: "I'm gonna do *Taxi* for as long as they can stand me. I want to erase the nemesis I had before."

Honors for Outstanding Lead Actress in a Comedy Series went to Isabel Sanford, who was more than a little surprised by her success. The 10-year veteran of *All in the Family* and *The Jeffersons* was backstage chewing on a piece of cheese when her name was announced. She raced to the podium."I've waited so long for this," she said upon accepting the Emmy, still chewing the cheese, "my humility is all gone." She then gulped hard and went on to thank God and producer Norman Lear. "That's a remarkable thing to say in a town that usually places those two names in reverse order," commented the *Herald Examiner*. The supporting actress award in comedy went to Eileen Brennan of *Private Benjamin*. Earlier in the year, Brennan had been Oscar-nominated for playing the same role in the movie, but lost.

It was no surprise when *Shogun* was voted best limited series. The 12-hour saga of an English sea pilot who becomes a samurai after being shipwrecked in feudal Japan kept America spellbound in front of its TV sets for five days the previous September. But the miniseries, based on the James Clavell bestseller, began the Emmy race with 14 nominations and was expected to do better than it did. *Shogun* ended up with only two other awards: for graphic

Hill Street Blues set the new record for most Emmys won by a prime-time show in a year.

design and its lavish costumes. Most noticeable was the loss suffered by its star, Richard Chamberlain, who had been considered a shoo-in for best actor — if he wasn't overtaken, that is, by Peter O'Toole of *Masada*, which he wasn't. Instead, they both lost in a huge upset to Anthony Hopkins who gave a "chilling" portrayal, said the *L.A.Times*, of Adolph Hitler during his final hours in *The Bunker*.

Nazi Germany was also the setting of the year's Outstanding Drama Special, playwright Arthur Miller's haunting study of a women's orchestra at Auschwitz that was literally *Playing for Time* while other inmates marched by en route to their deaths. In a controversial bit of casting, pro-Palestinian advocate Vanessa Redgrave played the Jewish lead character Fania Fenelon and was named best actress of the year. ("She deserves the Emmy," the *L.A. Times* insisted, defending her.) Jane Alexander may have been wronged in the past for not winning either of the two Emmys she probably deserved for playing Mrs. Roosevelt in the two *Eleanor and Franklin* TV films, but this time she took one home as best supporting actress for what the *L.A.Times* called her "gleaming work" as the prison camp's daring orchestra leader.

The prime-time ceremony again took place at the Pasadena Civic Auditorium, with Shirley MacLaine and Ed Asner as hosts. "More than one spectator commented on Asner's active part in the show this year compared to his very vocal role in last year's Emmy boycott," commented the *Herald Examiner*. "'I think it's ironic,' said one observer. 'Last year he was talking to everyone by phone from his living room in West L.A.'"

After the acrimony of the boycott last year, this show had the theme of "One Big Happy Family" that actually turned into one big happy family reunion. The program was deftly handled by the producing/directing team of Gary Smith and Dwight Hemion, both multiple Emmy winners, and included heart-warming tributes to writer Paddy Chayefsky, band leader Lawrence Welk, and, on the occasion of her 30th year in television, comedienne Lucille Ball. The Ball tribute was followed by a standing ovation and the presentation of a special plaque. MacLaine told the Queen of Comedy as she passed Lucy the prize: "You're just a human national treasure."

"Last night's Emmys were rich in class and dignity," said the *Herald Examiner*. The *L.A Times* called it "the best show in recent memory."

DAYTIME AWARDS

The $20,000 Pyramid host Dick Clark was also the host for the Eighth Annual Daytime Emmy Awards and opened the ceremonies noting that "daytime TV produces about twice as many hours of programming as nighttime, so that means there's twice as much competition for those Emmys." He also commented on the sudden popularity of prime-time soaps such as *Dallas*, saying, "You know, the nighttime people used to laugh at the daytime dramas, but now they're copying them. Imitation is the sincerest form of flattery, but they've got to learn how to make a three-minute, torrid phone call last for two weeks over the rating period."

Never before had the *L.A. Times* been so bold as to try to predict the outcome of the daytime awards. For instance, it summed up the race for Outstanding Daytime Series thus: "Since the eligibility period for Emmy consideration is from March 6, 1980, to March 5, 1981, *General Hospital* should win in this category by a landslide. Although the program has dragged its story feet since the end of '80, it was the most innovatively produced program last year. *All My*

Children was steady and reliable, but also predictable. It didn't have the gumption to take the spectacular and often gloriously effective risks that *General Hospital* managed. *Ryan's Hope* had a rather lackluster 'off' year and it's surprising that this show was nominated instead of the more varied and adventuresome *One Life to Live*."

The *Times* turned out to be right. Not only did *General Hospital* take the series prize, the number-one-rated soap also won awards for the show's director, who made a special point of crediting her producer, saying, "Thanks to her vision and her wanting to take a chance, Gloria Monty has changed the look of daytime drama." *General Hospital* also took laurels for supporting actress Jane Elliot who accepted the honor, saying, "I won a little portable TV set in a raffle when I was 13 years old. It really doesn't prepare you at all for this."

For best actor, the paper failed to be so accurate. It was rooting for Anthony Geary (Luke Spencer on *General Hospital*) who was "the golden boy of soaps," said the *Times*, "having changed the scope of serial acting with a finesse and range of improvisational-like skill that is awesomely spellbinding." The prize went instead to "long shot" Douglass Watson of *Another World*, who won the statuette last year. In accepting his latest Emmy, Watson noted that, after "40 years of acting, nothing is dearer to me than the approval of my work by my peers in my profession, of which I am very proud."

The *Times* continued: "Among the lead actress nominees for drama is Judith Light (Karen Martin on *One Life to Live*), who won last year and seems an outsider this go-around since she wasn't called upon to further enhance her character .... The most worthy choice would be Robin Strasser (Dorian Callison on *One Life to Live*), who was a veritable fireworks display in a role that

ranged from the childishly giddy to the mordantly vengeful." But Light struck again — to make it two in a row, too.

The *Times* did predict correctly that *Guiding Light* would win the writing award ("Its writing," the paper said, "was the most complex and ingratiating of the lot"), and that *General Hospital* would nab the director's prize.

The *Times* didn't venture any guesses about the supporting awards, but the prize for supporting actor went to the best actor winner of 1975–76, Larry Haines of *Search for Tomorrow*, who was hilarious when he accepted this statuette saying, "I'd like to dedicate this to my wife, Trudy, who I've been supporting for 38 years." He also noted that *Search for Tomorrow* was celebrating its 30th year on the air.

It was a big year for repeat daytime winners — and game show losers, too. Peter

"Daytime TV produces about twice as many hours of programming as nighttime."

Marshall of *The Hollywood Squares* returned this year as best game show host, but noted that the show was soon due to go off the air. "This is our last year," he told the audience. "It's a bye-bye in September, but, boy, has it been fun!" (Although the show had been canceled by NBC, it would return in syndication in 1986 with John Davidson replacing Peter Marshall as host.)

Squares was voted best quiz show last year in a tie with *The $20,000 Pyramid*, but *Pyramid* pulled ahead this year in a hollow victory of sorts. ABC had just canceled the program. Ironically, it had been dropped once before — by CBS — just before it won its first award as outstanding game show in 1976. Producer Bob Stewart accepted this accolade, noting, "This is the second time we've won since we've been canceled. We've won more awards for being off the air than being on the air and that says something." *Pyramid* also reaped directing honors for Mike Gargiulo who addressed *Pyramid* and Emmycast host Dick Clark personally, saying, "I'm sorry, Dick, that we went off the air due to reruns of *Love Boat,* but maybe someday great shows like *Pyramid* will come back." It did — in syndication the next year.

Phil Donahue pulled even with his show when *Donahue* was named Outstanding Talk or Service Series (host Donahue had won four Emmys in the past, while his show had named been best talk series only three times). Hugh Downs of *Over Easy* nabbed the award for best talk show host. The prize for variety series was also split, with the program statuette going to *The Merv Griffin Show* and awards for hosting and writing both going to *The David Letterman Show,* which was aired as unsuccessfully in daytime for four months in 1980. (It would return to TV as *Late Night with David Letterman* in 1982.) Letterman was typically flip as he accepted his host's trophy, saying, "Obviously, there's been some kind of mixup here. All I did is pretty much show up in a clean suit every day."

In the children's category, the trophy for entertainment series went to the 1977-78 champ *Captain Kangaroo* (host Dick Clark joked that while the show had been on the air for more than 20 years, the poor captain had never been promoted). *ABC Afterschool Specials* again swept the drama awards with "A Matter of Time" (about a family trying to cope with its mother's terminal illness) voted Outstanding Entertainment Special, "Stoned" (which featured Scott Baio as a marijuana abuser) cited for directing, and "Family of Strangers" acclaimed for the perfor-

"Now you know what it feels like to win the World Series," Johnny Bench told NBC sportcaster Dick Enberg (above).

mance by Danny Aiello and the work of its costume designer.

On CBS, *The Body Human* had been named Outstanding Informational Series at the prime-time awards. Now the children's daytime version, *The Body Human* (with separate segments for boys and girls) won a number of prizes, too: for performers Ken Howard and Marlo Thomas in addition to its cinematographers and writers. The network's version of *60 Minutes* for young people — *30 Minutes* — returned from last year as the best informational series for kids, and *Big Blue Marble* took four crafts awards.

SPORTS AWARDS

Nearly 700 sports enthusiasts gathered at the Sheraton Centre's Imperial Ballroom in New York City for the Fourth Annual Sports Awards ceremony. Cohosts included baseball legend Johnny Bench, ABC's Jim McKay, and Pat Summerall of CBS. Reported the N.A.T.A.S. newsletter: "A record number of people attending the ceremony enjoyed the finest food and drink, an illustrious line-up of professionals, and a finely tuned production that included video highlights of the last year's most memorable moments in sports on television."

The top awards for sports personalities went to NBC's Dick Enberg and ABC's Dick Button. Enberg won in the play-by-play category and was so overwhelmed that he lingered a while backstage after winning, feeling stunned. Johnny Bench walked up to him, put his arm around him and said, "Now you know what it feels like to win the World Series."

As usual, ABC producer Roone Arledge took the bulk of the top program awards, with trophies going to *The American Sportsman*, coverage of the Kentucky Derby, and a 20th anniversary remembrance of *ABC's Wide World of Sports*. The *PGA Tour on CBS* was voted best live sports series.

NEWS & DOCUMENTARY AWARDS
A record was set in the news and documentary category when nearly 800 entries were submitted for Emmy consideration. From that, 105 nominees were chosen — 60 for programs and 45 for individuals — resulting in 53 winners. They were bestowed at the Grand Hyatt Hotel in New York by an array of

notable newsmakers that included Kitty Carlisle Hart, senator Christopher Dodd of Connecticut, and Governor Thomas Kean of New Jersey.

ABC won the most statuettes, with 11 of its 22 total going to the news magazine show *20/20*. Eight were for program segments on subjects such as the Berlin Wall, singer Ray Charles, and an examination of "Unnecessary Surgery." The network's evening news broadcast was cited for program segments on Libya, the recent Italian earthquake, and the bells of London's famed St. Paul's Church. *ABC News Nightline* was awarded its first Emmy, which recognized its episode focusing on containing the worldwide opium traffic.

CBS's news magazine *60 Minutes* took four program awards for segments on topics including auto safety and mafia leader Jimmy Fratianno. Satirist Andy Rooney was also honored for his fussy "Few Minutes" that concluded each program with an appropriately sassy finish. The network's other statuettes were mostly for *CBS Reports* on teenage murder and for its five-part study of American defense policies, "The Defense of the United States," which won eight awards.

1980–81

For prime-time programs telecast between July 1, 1980, and June 30, 1981. The prime-time ceremony was broadcast on CBS from the Pasadena Civic Auditorium on September 13, 1981. Creative arts banquet held on September 12, 1981. Daytime awards presented on May 19 and 21, 1980, for programs aired between March 6, 1980, to March 5, 1981. News & documentary awards presented April 12, 1982, for programs aired between November 15, 1980, and November 14, 1981. The sports awards were presented December 15, 1981, for programs aired between July 16, 1980, and July 15, 1981.

PRIME-TIME PROGRAM AWARDS
OUTSTANDING DRAMA SERIES
• *Hill Street Blues*. Steven Bochco, Michael Kozoll, executive producers. Gregory Hoblit, producer. NBC.
Dallas. Philip Capice, executive producer. Leonard Katzman, producer. CBS.
Lou Grant. Gene Reynolds, executive producer. Seth Freeman, producer. CBS.
Quincy. David Moessinger, executive producer. William O. Cairncross, Lester William Berke, supervising producers. Sam Egan, producer. NBC.
The White Shadow. Bruce Paltrow, executive producer. Mark Tinker, producer. John Masius, coordinating producer. CBS.

Outstanding Comedy Series
• *Taxi*. James L. Brooks, Stan Daniels, Ed. Weinberger, executive producers. Glen Charles, Les Charles, producers. ABC.
Barney Miller. Danny Arnold, executive producer. Tony Sheehan, Noam Pitlik, producers. Gary Shaw, coproducer. ABC.
*M*A*S*H*. Burt Metcalfe, executive producer. John Rappaport, producer. CBS.
Soap. Paul Junger Witt, Tony Thomas, Susan Harris, executive producers. Stu Silver, Dick Clair, Jenna McMahon, producers. ABC.
WKRP in Cincinnati. Hugh Wilson, executive producer. Rod Daniel, supervising producer. Blake Hunter, Steven Kampmann, Peter Torokvei, producers. CBS.

Outstanding Limited Series
• *Shogun*. James Clavell, executive producer. Eric Bercovici, producer. NBC.
East of Eden. Mace Neufeld, executive producer. Barney Rosenzweig, producer. Ken Wales, coproducer. ABC.
Masada. George Eckstein, producer. ABC.
Rumpole of the Bailey, Mystery! Joan Wilson, series producer. Jacqueline Davis, producer. PBS.
Tinker, Tailor, Soldier, Spy, Great Performances. Jac Venza, executive producer. Jonathan Powell, producer. Samuel J. Paul, III, series producer. PBS.

Outstanding Variety, Music, or Comedy Program
• *Lily: Sold Out*. Lily Tomlin, Jane Wagner, executive producers. Rocco Urbisci, producer. Lily Tomlin, star. CBS.
The American Film Institute Salute to Fred Astaire. George Stevens, Jr., producer. CBS.
The Benny Hill Show. John Robins, Dennis Kirkland, Mark Stuart, Keith Beckett, producers. Benny Hill, star. Syndicated.
The Muppet Show. David Lazer, executive producer. Jim Henson, producer. Frank Oz, Jerry Nelson, Richard Hunt, Dave Goelz, Louise Gold, Steve Whitmire, Kathryn Mullen, Brian Muehl, Karen Prell, Jim Henson, stars. Syndicated.
The Tonight Show Starring Johnny Carson. Fred DeCordova, producer. Peter Lassally, coproducer. Johnny Carson, star. NBC.

Outstanding Drama Special
• *Playing for Time*. Linda Yellen, executive producer and producer. John E. Quill, coproducer. CBS.
Evita Peron. Harry Evans Sloan, Lawrence L. Kuppin, Selma Jaffe, executive producers. Fred Baum, supervising producer. Marvin Chomsky, producer. David R. Ames, coproducer. NBC.
Fallen Angel. Jim Green, Allen Epstein, executive producers. Lew Hunter, Audrey Blasdel-Goddard, producers. CBS.
The Shadow Box. Jill Marti, Susan Kendall Newman, producers. ABC.
The Women's Room. Philip Mandelker, executive producer. Glenn Jordan, supervising producer. Kip Gowans, Anna Cottle, producers. ABC.

Outstanding Classical Program in the Performing Arts
(Winner)
• *Live from Studio 8H: An Evening of Jerome Robbins' Ballets with Members of the New York City Ballet*. Alvin Cooperman, Judith DePaul, producers. NBC.

Outstanding Informational Series
(Winner)
• *Meeting of Minds*. Loring d'Usseau, producer. PBS.

Outstanding Informational Special
(Winner)
• *The Body Human: The Bionic Breakthrough*. Thomas W. Moore, executive producer. Alfred R. Kelman, Robert E. Fuisz, M.D., producers. Charles A. Bangert, Nancy Smith, coproducers. CBS.

Outstanding Children's Program
(Winner)
• *Donahue and Kids*. Walter Bartlett, executive producer. Don Mischer, producer. Jan Cornell, coproducer. NBC.

Outstanding Animated Program
(Winner)
• *Life is a Circus, Charlie Brown*. Lee Mendelson, executive producer. Bill Melendez, producer. CBS.

PERFORMANCE, DIRECTING, AND WRITING

**OUTSTANDING LEAD ACTOR
IN A DRAMA SERIES**
• Daniel J. Travanti, *Hill Street Blues*. NBC.
Edward Asner, *Lou Grant*. CBS.
Jim Davis, *Dallas*. CBS.
Louis Gossett, Jr., *Palmerstown, U.S.A.* CBS.
Larry Hagman, *Dallas*. CBS.
Pernell Roberts, *Trapper John, M.D.* CBS.

**OUTSTANDING LEAD ACTRESS
IN A DRAMA SERIES**
• Barbara Babcock, *Hill Street Blues*. NBC.
Barbara Bel Geddes, *Dallas*. CBS.
Linda Gray, *Dallas*. CBS.
Veronica Hamel, *Hill Street Blues*. NBC.
Michael Learned, *Nurse*. CBS.
Stefanie Powers, *Hart to Hart*. ABC.

**OUTSTANDING LEAD ACTOR
IN A COMEDY SERIES**
• Judd Hirsch, *Taxi*. ABC.
Alan Alda, *M*A*S*H*. CBS.
Hal Linden, *Barney Miller*. ABC.
Richard Mulligan, *Soap*. ABC.
John Ritter, *Three's Company*. ABC.

**OUTSTANDING LEAD ACTRESS
IN A COMEDY SERIES**
• Isabel Sanford, *The Jeffersons*. CBS.
Eileen Brennan, *Taxi*. ABC.
Cathryn Damon, *Soap*. ABC.
Katherine Helmond, *Soap*. ABC.
Lynn Redgrave, *House Calls*. CBS.

**OUTSTANDING LEAD ACTOR IN A LIMITED
SERIES OR A SPECIAL**
• Anthony Hopkins, *The Bunker*. CBS.
Richard Chamberlain, *Shogun*. NBC.
Toshiro Mifune, *Shogun*. NBC.
Peter O'Toole, *Masada*. ABC.
Peter Strauss, *Masada*. ABC.

**OUTSTANDING LEAD ACTRESS
IN A LIMITED SERIES OR A SPECIAL**
• Vanessa Redgrave, *Playing for Time*. CBS.
Ellen Burstyn, *The People vs. Jean Harris*. NBC.
Catherine Hicks, *Marilyn: The Untold Story*. ABC.
Yoko Shimada, *Shogun*. NBC.
Joanne Woodward, *Crisis at Central High*. CBS.

**OUTSTANDING SUPPORTING ACTOR
IN A DRAMA SERIES**
• Michael Conrad, *Hill Street Blues*. NBC.
Mason Adams, *Lou Grant*. CBS.
Charles Haid, *Hill Street Blues*. NBC.
Robert Walden, *Lou Grant*. CBS.
Bruce Weitz, *Hill Street Blues*. NBC.

**OUTSTANDING SUPPORTING ACTRESS
IN A DRAMA SERIES**
• Nancy Marchand, *Lou Grant*. CBS.
Barbara Barrie, *Breaking Away*. ABC.
Barbara Bosson, *Hill Street Blues*. NBC.
Linda Kelsey, *Lou Grant*. CBS.
Betty Thomas, *Hill Street Blues*. NBC.

**OUTSTANDING SUPPORTING ACTOR
IN A COMEDY OR VARIETY OR MUSIC
SERIES**
• Danny DeVito, *Taxi*. ABC.
Howard Hesseman, *WKRP in Cincinnati*. CBS.
Steve Landesberg, *Barney Miller*. ABC.
Harry Morgan, *M*A*S*H*. CBS.
David Ogden Stiers, *M*A*S*H*. CBS.

**OUTSTANDING SUPPORTING ACTRESS
IN A COMEDY OR VARIETY OR MUSIC
SERIES**
• Eileen Brennan, *Private Benjamin*. CBS.
Loni Anderson, *WKRP in Cincinnati*. CBS.
Marla Gibbs, *The Jeffersons*. CBS.
Anne Meara, *Archie Bunker's Place*. CBS.
Loretta Swit, *M*A*S*H*. CBS.

**OUTSTANDING SUPPORTING ACTOR
IN A LIMITED SERIES OR A SPECIAL**
• David Warner, *Masada*. ABC.
Andy Griffith, *Murder in Texas*. NBC.
Yuki Meguro, *Shogun*. NBC.
Anthony Quayle, *Masada*. ABC.
John Rhys-Davies, *Shogun*. NBC.

**OUTSTANDING SUPPORTING ACTRESS
IN A LIMITED SERIES OR A SPECIAL**
• Jane Alexander, *Playing for Time*. CBS.
Patty Duke Astin, *The Women's Room*. ABC.
Colleen Dewhurst, *The Women's Room*. ABC.
Shirley Knight, *Playing for Time*. CBS.
Piper Laurie, *The Bunker*. CBS.

Outstanding Directing in a Drama Series
• Robert Butler, *Hill Street Blues*. NBC.
Corey Allen, *Hill Street Blues*. NBC.
Burt Brinckerhoff, *Lou Grant*. CBS.
Georg Stanford Brown, *Hill Street Blues*. NBC.
Mel Damski, *American Dream*. ABC.
Gene Reynolds, *Lou Grant*. CBS.

Outstanding Directing in a Comedy Series
• James Burrows, *Taxi*. ABC.
Alan Alda, *M*A*S*H*. CBS.
Rod Daniel, *WKRP in Cincinnati*. CBS.
Linda Day, *Archie Bunker's Place*. CBS.
Burt Metcalfe, *M*A*S*H*. CBS.
Jerry Paris, *Happy Days*. ABC.
Noam Pitlik, *Barney Miller*. ABC.

Outstanding Directing in a Variety, Music, or Comedy Program
• Don Mischer, *The Kennedy Center Honors: A National Celebration of the Performing Arts*. CBS.
Emile Ardolino, "Nureyev and the Joffrey Ballet/ In Tribute to Nijinsky," *Dance in America*. PBS.
Tony Charmoli, *Sylvia Fine Kaye's Musical Comedy Tonight*. PBS.
Dwight Hemion, *Linda in Wonderland*. CBS.
Bob Henry, *Barbara Mandrell & the Mandrell Sisters*. NBC.
Marty Pasetta, *The 53rd Annual Academy Awards*. ABC.

Outstanding Directing in a Limited Series or a Special
• James Goldstone, *Kent State*. NBC.
Jerry London, *Shogun*. NBC.
Paul Newman, *The Shadow Box*. ABC.
Boris Sagal, *Masada*. ABC.
Roger Young, *Bitter Harvest*. NBC.

Outstanding Writing in a Drama Series
• Michael Kozoll, Steven Bochco, *Hill Street Blues*. NBC.
Michael Kozoll, Steven Bochco, Anthony Yerkovich, *Hill Street Blues*. NBC.
Ronald M. Cohen, Barbara Corday, Ken Hecht, *American Dream*. ABC.
Seth Freeman, *Lou Grant*. CBS.
April Smith, *Lou Grant*. CBS.

Outstanding Writing in a Comedy Series
• Michael Leeson, *Taxi*. ABC.
David Lloyd, *Taxi*. ABC.
Stephen J. Cannell, *The Greatest American Hero*. ABC.
Glen Charles, Les Charles, *Taxi*. ABC.
Mike Farrell, John Rappaport, Dennis Koenig, teleplay. Thad Mumford, Dan Wilcox, Burt Metcalfe, story. *M*A*S*H*. CBS.

Outstanding Writing in a Limited Series or a Special
• Arthur Miller, *Playing for Time*. CBS.
Eric Bercovici, *Shogun*. NBC.
Michael Cristofer, *The Shadow Box*. ABC.
Richard Friedenberg, *Bitter Harvest*. NBC.
Joel Oliansky, *Masada*. ABC.

Outstanding Writing in a Variety, Music, or Comedy Program
• Jerry Juhl, David Odell, Chris Langham, *The Muppet Show*. Syndicated.
Nancy Audley, Ann Elder, Irene Mecchi, Elaine Pope, Ziggy Steinberg, Rocco Urbisci, Jane Wagner, Rod Warren, *Lily: Sold Out*. CBS.
Sylvia Fine Kaye, *Sylvia Fine Kaye's Musical Comedy Tonight*. PBS.
Raymond Siller, Hal Goodman, Larry Klein, Michael Barrie, Jim Mulholland, Kevin Mulholland, Robert Smith, Gary Murphy, Greg Fields, Pat McCormick, *The Tonight Show Starring Johnny Carson 18th Anniversary Show*. NBC.
George Stevens Jr., Joseph Mc Bride, *The American Film Institute Salute to Fred Astaire*. CBS.

OTHER AWARD WINNERS
Outstanding Cinematography for a Series
• William H. Cronjager, *Hill Street Blues*. NBC.

Outstanding Cinematography For a Limited Series or a Special
• Arthur F. Ibbetson, *Little Lord Fauntleroy*. CBS.

Outstanding Art Direction for a Series
• Howard E. Johnson, production designer. John M. Dwyer, Robert George Freer, set decorators, *The Gangster Chronicles*. NBC.

OUTSTANDING ART DIRECTION FOR A LIMITED SERIES OR A SPECIAL
• Ray Storey, art director. Dennis Peeples, David Love, set decorators, *East of Eden*. ABC.

OUTSTANDING ART DIRECTION FOR A VARIETY OR A MUSIC PROGRAM
• Roy Christopher, art director, *The 53rd Annual Academy Awards*. ABC.

OUTSTANDING CHOREOGRAPHY
• Walter Painter, *Lynda Carter's Celebration*. CBS.

**OUTSTANDING MUSIC COMPOSITION FOR A SERIES
(Dramatic underscore)**
• Bruce Broughton, *Buck Rogers in the 25th Century*. NBC.

**OUTSTANDING MUSIC COMPOSITION FOR A LIMITED SERIES OR A SPECIAL
(Dramatic underscore)**
• Jerry Goldsmith, *Masada*. ABC.

OUTSTANDING MUSIC AND LYRICS
• Ken Welch, composer. Mitzie Welch, lyricist, *Linda in Wonderland*. Song: "This is My Night." CBS.

OUTSTANDING MUSIC DIRECTION
• Ian Fraser, music director. Billy Byers, Chris Boardman, Bob Florence, arrangers, *Linda in Wonderland*. CBS.

OUTSTANDING COSTUME DESIGN FOR A SERIES
• Shin Nishida, *Shogun*. NBC.

OUTSTANDING COSTUME DESIGN FOR A SPECIAL
• Willa Kim, "The Tempest, Live with the San Francisco Ballet," *Dance in America*. PBS.

OUTSTANDING MAKEUP
• Albert Paul Jeyte, James Kail, *Peter and Paul*. CBS.

OUTSTANDING HAIRSTYLING
• Shirley Padgett, *Madame X*. NBC.

OUTSTANDING GRAPHIC DESIGN AND TITLE SEQUENCES
• Phill Norman, *Shogun*. NBC.

OUTSTANDING FILM EDITING FOR A SERIES
• M. Pam Blumenthal, Jack Michon, *Taxi*. ABC.

OUTSTANDING FILM EDITING FOR A LIMITED SERIES OR A SPECIAL
• John A. Martinelli, *Murder in Texas*. NBC.

OUTSTANDING FILM SOUND EDITING
• Samuel Horta, supervising editor. Robert Cornet, Denise Horta, Eileen Horta, editors, *Hill Street Blues*. NBC.

OUTSTANDING VIDEO-TAPE EDITING FOR A SERIES
• Andy Ackerman, *WKRP in Cincinnati*. CBS.

OUTSTANDING VIDEO-TAPE EDITING FOR A LIMITED SERIES OR A SPECIAL
• Marco Zappia, video-tape editor. Branda S. Miller, film editor, *Perry Como's Christmas in the Holy Land*. ABC.

OUTSTANDING FILM SOUND MIXING
• William R. Teague, production mixer. Robert L. Harman, William L. McCaughey, Howard Wollman, rerecording mixers, *Evita Peron*. NBC.

OUTSTANDING TAPE SOUND MIXING
• Jerry Clemans, Doug Nelson, Donald Worsham, *John Denver with His Special Guest George Burns: Two of a Kind*. ABC.

OUTSTANDING TECHNICAL DIRECTION AND ELECTRONIC CAMERA WORK
• Heino Ripp, technical director. Peter Basil, Al Camoin, Tom Dezendorf, Vince DiPietro, Gene Martin, camerapersons, *Live from Studio 8H: An Evening of Jerome Robbins' Ballets with Members of the New York City Ballet*. NBC.

OUTSTANDING LIGHTING DIRECTION
• Ralph Holmes, "Nureyev and the Joffrey Ballet/ In Tribute to Nijinsky," *Dance in America*. PBS.

THE AREAS

Each area has the possibility of multiple winners, one winner, or none. Winners are listed.

OUTSTANDING INDIVIDUAL ACHIEVEMENT—SPECIAL CLASS
• Sarah Vaughan, performer, *Rhapsody and Song — A Tribute to George Gershwin*. PBS.

OUTSTANDING INDIVIDUAL ACHIEVEMENT—CREATIVE TECHNICAL CRAFTS
• John Allison, Adolf Schauer, Don Davis, Rick Sternbach, John Lomberg, Brown, Anne Norcia, Ernie Norcia, astronomical artists, *Cosmos*. PBS.
• Carey Melcher, technical designer. Bob Buckner, Steve Burum, Jim Dow, John Gale, Larry Heider, Mike Johnson, Robert C. King, Cleve Landsberg, Joseph Matza, George C. Reilly, Joe Wolcott, magicam crew, *Cosmos*. PBS.

OUTSTANDING INDIVIDUAL ACHIEVEMENT—INFORMATIONAL PROGRAMMING
• Kent Gibson, Gerald Zelinger, tape sound mixers, *Cosmos*. PBS.
Dick Rector, production mixer. Gary Bourgeois, Dave Dockendorf, John Mack, rerecording mixers, "Gorilla," *National Geographic Special*. PBS.

(There were no winners in the areas of individual achievement in animated or children's programming.)

DAYTIME AWARDS

OUTSTANDING DAYTIME DRAMA SERIES
• *General Hospital*. Gloria Monty, producer. ABC.
All My Children. Agnes Nixon, executive producer. Jorn Winther, producer. ABC.
Ryan's Hope. Paul Avila Mayer, Claire Labine, executive producers. Ellen Barrett, producer. ABC.

OUTSTANDING ACTOR IN A DAYTIME DRAMA SERIES
• Douglass Watson, *Another World*. NBC.
James Mitchell, *All My Children*. ABC.
Larry Bryggman, *As the World Turns*. CBS.
Henderson Forsythe, *As the World Turns*. CBS.
Anthony Geary, *General Hospital*. ABC.

Best game show host Peter Marshall of The Hollywood Squares*: "It's bye-bye in September, but, boy, has it been fun!"*

OUTSTANDING ACTRESS IN A DAYTIME DRAMA SERIES
• Judith Light, *One Life to Live*. ABC.
Julia Barr, *All My Children*. ABC.
Helen Gallagher, *Ryan's Hope*. ABC.
Susan Lucci, *All My Children*. ABC.
Robin Strasser, *One Life to Live*. ABC.

OUTSTANDING ACTOR IN A SUPPORTING ROLE FOR A DAYTIME DRAMA SERIES
• Larry Haines, *Search for Tomorrow*. CBS.
Richard Backus, *Ryan's Hope*. ABC.
Matthew Cowles, *All My Children*. ABC.
Justin Deas, *As the World Turns*. CBS.
William Mooney, *All My Children*. ABC.

OUTSTANDING ACTRESS IN A SUPPORTING ROLE FOR A DAYTIME DRAMA SERIES
• Jane Elliot, *General Hospital*. ABC.
Randall Edwards, *The Edge of Night*. ABC.
Lois Kibbee, *The Edge of Night*. ABC.
Elizabeth Lawrence, *All My Children*. ABC.
Jacklyn Zeman, *General Hospital*. ABC.

OUTSTANDING DIRECTION FOR A DAYTIME DRAMA SERIES
• Marlena Laird, Alan Pultz, Phillip Sogard, *General Hospital*. ABC.
Larry Auerbach, Jack Coffey, Sherrell Hoffman, Jorn Winther, *All My Children*. ABC.

David Pressman, Peter Miner, Norman Hall, *One Life to Live*. ABC.

OUTSTANDING WRITING FOR A DAYTIME DRAMA SERIES
• Douglas Marland, Robert Dwyer, Nancy Franklin, Harding Lemay, *Guiding Light*. CBS.
Agnes Nixon, Wisner Washam, Jack Wood, Mary K. Wells, Clarice Blackburn, Caroline Franz, Cathy Chicos, Cynthia Benjamin, *All My Children*. ABC.
Pat Falken Smith, Margaret DePriest, Sheri Anderson, Frank Salisbury, Margaret Stewart, *General Hospital*. ABC.
Sam Hall, Peggy O'Shea, Don Wallace, Lanie Bertram, Gordon Russell, Fred Corke, *One Life to Live*. ABC.

OTHER DAYTIME AWARD WINNERS
OUTSTANDING GAME OR AUDIENCE PARTICIPATION SHOW
• *The $20,000 Pyramid*. Bob Stewart, executive producer. Anne Marie Schmitt, Jane Rothchild, producers. ABC.

OUTSTANDING HOST/HOSTESS IN A GAME OR AUDIENCE PARTICIPATION SHOW
• Peter Marshall, *The Hollywood Squares*. NBC.

OUTSTANDING INDIVIDUAL DIRECTION FOR A GAME OR AUDIENCE PARTICIPATION SHOW
• Mike Gargiulo, *The $20,000 Pyramid*. ABC.

OUTSTANDING TALK/SERVICE SERIES
• *Donahue*. Richard Mincer, executive producer. Patricia McMillen, senior producer. Darlene Hayes, Sheri Singer, producers. Syndicated.

OUTSTANDING HOST/HOSTESS IN A TALK/SERVICE SERIES
• Hugh Downs, *Over Easy*. PBS.

OUTSTANDING INDIVIDUAL DIRECTION FOR A TALK/SERVICE SERIES
• Jerry Kupcinet, *The Richard Simmons Show*. Syndicated.

OUTSTANDING VARIETY SERIES
• *The Merv Griffin Show*. Peter Barsocchini, producer. Syndicated.

OUTSTANDING HOST/HOSTESS IN A VARIETY SERIES
• David Letterman, *The David Letterman Show*. NBC.

OUTSTANDING INDIVIDUAL DIRECTION FOR A VARIETY SERIES
• Sterling Johnson, *Dinah and Friends in Israel*. Syndicated.

OUTSTANDING CHILDREN'S ENTERTAINMENT SERIES (Tie)
• *Captain Kangaroo*. Robert Keeshan, executive producer. Joel Kosofsky, producer. CBS.
• "A Tale of Two Cities," *Once Upon a Classic*, Jay Rayvid, executive producer. James A. DeVinney, Barry Letts, producers. Christine Ochtun, coproducer. PBS.

OUTSTANDING CHILDREN'S ENTERTAINMENT SPECIAL
• "A Matter of Time," *ABC Afterschool Special*. Martin Tashe, executive producer/producer. ABC.

OUTSTANDING CHILDREN'S INFORMATIONAL/INSTRUCTIONAL SERIES
• *30 Minutes*. Joel Heller, executive producer. Madeline Amgott, Vern Diamond, Allen Ducovny, Diego Echeverria, Virginia Gray, Susan Mills, Patti Obrow White, Catherine Olian, Robert Rubin, Martin Smith, producers. CBS.

OUTSTANDING CHILDREN'S INFORMATIONAL/INSTRUCTIONAL SPECIAL
• "Julie Andrews' Invitation to the Dance with Rudolf Nureyev," *The CBS Festival of Lively Arts for Young People*. Jack Wohl, Bernard Rothman, producers. CBS.

(No award was bestowed in the area of Outstanding Children's Informational/ Instructional Programming—Short Form.)

OUTSTANDING ACHIEVEMENT IN TECHNICAL EXCELLENCE FOR A DAYTIME DRAMA SERIES

• Joseph Solomito, Howard Zweig, technical directors. Lawrence Hammond, Dianne Cates-Cantrell, Robert Ambrico, Christopher Mauro, Larry Strack, Salvatore Augugliaro, Vincent Senatore, Thomas McGrath. electronic camera. Len Walas, senior video engineer. Albin S. Lemanski, Peter Bohm, Charles Eisen, senior audio engineers. Barbara Wood, sound effects engineer. Diana Wenman, Jean Dadario, associate directors. Roger Haenelt, video-tape editor, *All My Children.* ABC.

OUTSTANDING ACHIEVEMENT IN DESIGN EXCELLENCE FOR A DAYTIME DRAMA SERIES

• *Ryan's Hope,* Sy Tomashoff, scenic designer. John Connolly, lighting director. David Murin, Michele Reish, costume designers. James Cola, makeup designer. John K. Quinn, hair designer. Sybil Weinberger, music supervisor. ABC.

OUTSTANDING INDIVIDUAL ACHIEVEMENT IN CHILDREN'S PROGRAMMING

(Performers)
• Bill Cosby, *The New Fat Albert Show.* CBS.
• Ken Howard, *The Body Human: Facts for Boys.* CBS.
• Marlo Thomas, *The Body Human: Facts for Girls.* CBS.
• Danny Aiello, "Family of Strangers," *ABC Afterschool Special.* ABC.

(Directors)
• John Herzfeld, "Stoned," *ABC Afterschool Special.* ABC.

(Writers)
• Blossom Elfman, "I Think I'm Having a Baby," *CBS Afternoon Playhouse.* CBS.
• Robert E. Fuisz, M.D., *The Body Human: Facts for Girls.* CBS.
• Mary Munisteri, "Mandy's Grandmother," *Young People's Special.* Syndicated.

(Cinematographers)
• Joe Consentino, *Big Blue Marble.* Syndicated.
• Robert Elfstrom, *The Body Human: Facts for Boys.* CBS.
• Eric Van Heren Noman, *Big Blue Marble.* Syndicated.

(Film editors)
• Peter Hammer, *Big Blue Marble.* Syndicated.
• Allen Kirkpatrick, *Big Blue Marble.* Syndicated.

(Lighting directors)
• Dave Clark, William Knight, *Sesame Street.* PBS.

(Audio)
• Dick Maitland, sound effects engineer, *Sesame Street.* PBS.

(Music composers and/or directors)
• Dick Hyman, composer, "Sunshine's on the Way," *NBC Special Treat.* NBC.

(Costume designers)
• Dorothy Weaver, "Family of Strangers," *ABC Afterschool Special.* ABC.

(Makeup and hair designers)
• Steve Atha, "Sunshine's on the Way," *NBC Special Treat.* NBC.

(Graphics and animation designers)
• Lewis Gifford, Paul Kim, Tom Yohe, animation layout designers, *Drawing Power.* NBC.

SPECIAL CLASSIFICATION OF OUTSTANDING PROGRAM ACHIEVEMENT

• *F.Y.I.* Yanna Kroyt Brandt, producer. Mary Ann Donahue, coordinating producer. ABC.

SPECIAL CLASSIFICATION OF OUTSTANDING INDIVIDUAL ACHIEVEMENT

(Writers)
• Merrill Markoe, Rich Hall, David Letterman, Gerard Mulligan, Paul Raley, Ron Richards, *The David Letterman Show.* NBC.

(Puppet design, construction, and costuming)
• Caroly Wilcox, Cheryl Blalock, Edward G. Christie, *Sesame Street.* PBS.

OUTSTANDING INDIVIDUAL ACHIEVEMENT IN ANY AREA OF CREATIVE TECHNICAL CRAFTS

(Technical director/Electronic camera)
• Robert Hoffman, technical director. Anthony Gambino, Lawrence Hammond, electronic camera. Remote: Savannah, *All My Children.* ABC.

(Costume designer)
• Dayton Anderson, *The Mike Douglas Show.* Syndicated.

(Graphic and animation designers)
• Michael Gass, graphic designer, *Good Morning America*. ABC.
• Donald Spagnolia, graphic designer—Opening Logo. Thomas Burton, Claudia Zeitlin Burton, animation designers—Opening, *The John Davidson Show*. Syndicated.

OUTSTANDING ACHIEVEMENT IN RELIGIOUS PROGRAMMING
• *Directions*. Sid Darion, producer. ABC.
• *Insight*. Ellwood E. Kieser, C.S.P., executive producer. Mike Rhodes, producer. Syndicated.

OUTSTANDING INDIVIDUAL ACHIEVEMENT IN RELIGIOUS PROGRAMMING
(Performer)
• Martin Sheen, *Insight*. Syndicated.
(Cinematographer)
• Joseph J.H. Vadala, *Work and Worship: The Legacy of St. Benedict*. NBC.
(Art directors/Set decorator)
• C. Murawski, Dahl Delu, art directors. Scott Heineman, set decorator, *Insight*. Syndicated.

(No awards were bestowed in the area of Outstanding Individual Achievement in the Coverage of Special Events.)

SPORTS AWARD WINNERS
OUTSTANDING LIVE SPORTS SERIES
• *PGA Tour on CBS*. Frank Chirkinian, executive producer. Bob Bailey, Frank Chirkinian, directors. Series. CBS.

OUTSTANDING LIVE SPORTS SPECIAL
• *1981 Kentucky Derby*. Roone Arledge, executive producer. Chuck Howard, producer. Chet Forte, director. ABC.

OUTSTANDING EDITED SPORTS SERIES
• *The American Sportsman*. Roone Arledge, executive producer. John Wilcox, series producer. Chris Carmody, coordinating producer. Robert Nixon, Curt Gowdy, producers. John Wilcox, Bob Nixon, directors. ABC.

OUTSTANDING EDITED SPORTS SPECIAL
• *ABC's Wide World of Sports 20th Anniversary Show*. Roone Arledge, executive producer. Dennis Lewin, Doug Wilson, producers. Larry Kamm, director. ABC.

SPORTS PERSONALITY — HOST
(Play by play)
• Dick Enberg, NBC.

SPORTS PERSONALITY — ANALYST
(Commentary)
• Dick Button, ABC.

OUTSTANDING INDIVIDUAL ACHIEVEMENT IN SPORTS PROGRAMMING
(Cinematography)
• Edgar Boyles, David Conley, Jon Hammond, Peter Henning, Mike Hoover, D'Arcy Marsh, Dan Merkel, Stanton Waterman, Steve Petropoulos, Roger Brown, cinematographers, *The American Sportsman*. ABC.
(Associate direction/Video-tape editing)
• Rob Beiner, Dick Buffinton, Jeff Cohan, Kathy Cook, Vince Dedario, John Delisa, Joel Feld, Ben Harvey, Bob Hersh, Jack Graham, Bob Lanning, Peter Lasser, Carol Lehti, Brian McCullough, Dennis Mazzocco, Bob Rosburg, Norm Samet, Ned Simon, Toni Slotkin, Larry Cavolina and Bob Dekas, associate directors, *ABC's Wide World of Sports*. ABC.
• Tony Tocci, Ken Browne, Gary Bradley, video-tape editors, *The Baseball Bunch*. Syndicated.
• Matthew McCarthy, associate director. Mark Kankeloff, Richard Leible, Jim McQueen, Jeff U'Ren, video-tape editors, *NBC Sportsworld*. NBC.
• Cathy Barreto, associate director. Joel Aronowitz, Jack Black, Bob Coffey, Joe D'Ornellas, Stanley Faer, Bob Halper, Beth Hermelin, Howard N. Miller, Gady Reinhold, Roni Scherman, Steve Dellapietra, Barry Hicks, associate directors–Highlights and coords. George Palmisano, John Wells, senior video operator. Jim Alkins, Curtis Campbell, Bob Clark, Ted Demers, Joe Drake, Tom Durkin, Bob Foster, Harve Gilman, Al Golly, Sig Gordon, Elliott Greenblatt, Bob Hickson, Frank Hodnett, George Joanitis, Andy Klein, Gary Kozak, Ed Knudholt, Pete Lacorte, Marvin Lee, George Magee, Mario Marino, Walter Matwichuk, John Mayer, Henry Menusan, Jesse Michnick, Jeff Ringel, Charlotte Robinson, Allan Segal, Bill Vandenort, Irv Villafana, Hank Wolf, Bill Zizza, video-tape editors, *NFL Today*. CBS.

(Film editing)
• Angelo Bernarducci, Vincent Reda, Richard Rossi, Anthony Scandiffio, Norman Smith, Chris Riger, Ted Winterburn, Anthony Zaccaro, film editors, *The American Sportsman*. ABC.
• Mike Adams, Bob Ryan, Phil Tucker, film editors, *NFL Symfunny*. Syndicated.
(Audio)
• Jack Newman, Dave Paul, Don Paravati, Bill Gray, location sound recordists, *Saviors, Saints and Sinners*. NBC.
(Engineering supervision, technical managers)
• Ray Savignano, Jesse Rineer, engineering supervisors, *1981 Daytona 500*. CBS. Louis Scannapieco, Arthur Tinn, engineering supervisors, *1981 Masters.Golf Tournament*. CBS.
• Walter Pile, engineering supervisor, *NFC Championship Game*. CBS.
(Technical direction/Senior video operators/Electronic camerawork)
• Sandy Bell, Robert Brown, technical directors. Edward Ambrosini, Robert Squittieri and Ronald Resch, senior video operators. James Murphy, Neil McCaffrey, Herman Lang, Frank McSpedon, Thomas McCarthy, Barry Drago, Joseph Sokota, Stephen Gorsuch, George Rothweiler, George Naeder, David Graham, Jeffrey Pollack, James McCarthy, Hans Singer, Sigmund Meyers, electronic camerapersons, *1981 Daytona 500*. CBS.
• Charles D'Onofrio, Sandy Bell, technical directors. Robert Hanford, Edward Ambrosini, Robert Pieringer , Frank Florio, senior video operators. Robert Squittieri, Louis Ledger, Daniel Chan, William Berridge, Thomas Delilla, video operators. Rick Blane. George Klimcsak, George Naeder, James McCarthy, George Rothweiler, Al Loreto, Herman Lang, Hans Singer, Nicholas Lauria, James Murphy, Harry Haigood, Michael English, John Lincoln, Frank McSpedon, Stan Gould, Dennis McBride, Joseph Sokota, Barry Drago, Neil McCaffrey, David Graham, Walter Soucy, Robert Welch, David Finch, Richard E. Kearney, Joseph Sidio, W. Haigood, electronic camerapersons, *1981 Masters Golf Tournament*. CBS.
• Robert Brown, Edward Kushner, technical directors. Robert Hanford, Frank Florio, senior video operators. Rick Blane, Stan Gould, Stephen Gorsuch, John Lincoln, George Klimcsak, Robert Jamieson, David Graham, James Murphy, Frank McSpedon, Jeffrey Pollack, Joseph Vincens, David Finch, electronic camerapersons, *NFC Championship Game*. CBS.
• Joe Schiavo, technical director. Joseph Lee, senior video operator. Drew Derosa, Jim Heneghan, Andrew Armentani, Gary Donatelli, Jack Dorfman, Jesse Kohn, Jack Savoy, Tom O'Connell, Steve Nikifor, Joe Cotugno, Roy Hutchings, electronic camerapersons, *NFL Football Sunday Night*. ABC.
• Gilbert A. Miller, technical director. Ronald Resch and Emanuel Kaufman. senior video operators. John Curtin, Thomas McCarthy, James McCarthy, Neil McCallrey, Stephen Gorsuch, Michael English, electronic camerapersons, *NFL Today*. CBS.

PRIMARY GRAPHIC DESIGNERS
• James W. Grau, *NBA on CBS*. CBS.
• James W. Grau, *U.S. Open*. CBS.

**SPECIAL CLASSIFICATION OF OUTSTANDING PROGRAM AND INDIVIDUAL ACHIEVEMENT
(Program)**
• *The Baseball Bunch*. Larry Parker, executive producer. Jody Shapiro, producer. Syndicated.
• "The Arlberg Kandahar Downhill from St. Anton," *NBC Sportsworld*. Don Ohlmeyer, executive producer. Linda Jonsson. coordinating producer. Terry Ewert, Geoff Mason, producers. Bob Levy. coordinating director/director. NBC.
(Individual)
• Don Ohlmeyer, Ted Nathanson, producers. Louma Camera Crane. *Friday Night Fights*. NBC.
• Steve Gonzalez, electronic camera, *Super Bowl XV*. NBC.

NEWS & DOCUMENTARY AWARD WINNERS
PROGRAMS AND PROGRAM SEGMENTS
• "Inside Awacs," *Magazine with David Brinkley*. Sid Feders, producer. Garrick Utley, correspondent. NBC.
• "Italian Earthquake," *ABC World News Tonight*. Dean Johnson, producer. Gregg Dobbs, Bill Blakemore, correspondents. ABC.
• "Moment of Crisis — Hyatt Disaster," *20/20*. Stanhope Gould, Peter W. Kunhardt, producers. Tom Jarriel, correspondent. ABC.

• *CBS Reports: Murder Teenage Style.* Irina Posner, producer. Ed Bradley, correspondent. CBS.
• "Soldiers of the Twilight," *ABC News Closeup.* Malcolm Clarke, producer. Marshall Frady, correspondent. ABC.
• "Death in the Fast Lane," *20/20.* Danny Schechter, producer. Catherine Mackin, correspondent. ABC.
• "Ghost Town," *20/20.* Pete Simmons, Ellen Rossen, producers. John Laurence, correspondent. ABC.
• "... 'Grain' a Few Minutes with Andy Rooney," *60 Minutes.* Andrew A. Rooney, producer/reporter. CBS.
• "Libya," *ABC World News Tonight.* Liz Colton, Denise Schreiner, producers. Lou Cioffi, correspondent. ABC.
• "The War on Opium," *ABC News Nightline.* Tom Yellin, producer. Mark Litke, correspondent. ABC.
• *CBS Reports: The Defense of the United States: Nuclear Battlefield.* Judy Crichton, producer. Harry Reasoner, correspondent. CBS.
• *CBS Reports: The Defense of the United States: The War Machine.* Craig Leake, producer. Richard Threlkeld, correspondent. CBS.
• *The Hunter and the Hunted.* Thomas F. Madigan, executive producer. John Oakley, Lisa Cantini-Sequin, Bill Bemister, producers. Bill Bemister, correspondent. PBS.
• "Near Armageddon: The Spread of Nuclear Weapons in the Middle East," *ABC News Closeup.* Christopher Isham, producer. Marshall Frady, William Sherman, correspondents. ABC.
• "The Middle East," *ABC News Closeup.* Christopher Isham, producer. Marshall Frady, William Sherman, correspondents. ABC.
• "Why America Burns," *Nova.* Brian Kaufman, producer. PBS.
• "Formula for Disaster," *20/20.* John Fager, producer. Geraldo Rivera, correspondent. ABC.
• "Killer Wheels," *60 Minutes.* Allan Maraynes, producer. Mike Wallace, correspondent. CBS.
• "Rockets for Sale," *Magazine with David Brinkley,* Tony Van Witsen, producer. Garrick Utley, correspondent. NBC.
• "Teen Models," *Magazine with David Brinkley.* Beth Polson, producer. Jack Perkins, correspondent. NBC.
• "Unnecessary Surgery," *20/20.* Peter

Lance, Janice Tomlin, producers. Peter Lance, correspondent. ABC.
• "Clark Clifford on Presidents and Power," *Bill Moyers' Journal.* Douglas Lutz, producer. Bill Moyers, interviewer. PBS.
• "George Steiner on Literature, Language & Culture," *Bill Moyers' Journal.* Douglas Lutz, producer. Bill Moyers, interviewer. PBS.
• "The Last Mafioso: Jimmy Fratianno," *60 Minutes.* Marion F. Goldin, producer. Mike Wallace, interviewer. CBS.
• "Wanted: Terpil/Korkala Interview," *60 Minutes.* Barry Lando, producer. Mike Wallace, interviewer. CBS.
• *Close Harmony.* Nigel Noble, producer. PBS.
• "The Colonel Comes to Japan," *Enterprise,* John Nathan, producer. PBS.
• "Louis is 13," *Sunday Morning.* Lee Reichenthal, producer. Morton Dean, correspondent. CBS.
• "Moment of Crisis: Berlin Wall," *20/20,* Richard O'Regan, Rolfe Tessem, producers. Tom Jarriel, correspondent. ABC.
• "Moment of Crisis: Vietnam Withdrawal," *20/20,* Peter W. Kunhardt, producer. Tom Jarriel, correspondent. ABC.
• "Ray Charles," *20/20.* Betsy Osha, producer. Bob Brown, correspondent. ABC.
• "St. Paul's Bells," *ABC World News Tonight.* Phil Bergman, producer. Hughes Rudd, correspondent. ABC.

OUTSTANDING INDIVIDUAL ACHIEVEMENT IN NEWS AND DOCUMENTARY PROGRAMMING
(Writers)
• Philip Buton Jr., Larry L. King, *CBS Reports: The Best Little Statehouse in Texas.* CBS.
• Walter Pincus, Andrew Lack, Howard Stringer, Bob Schieffer, *CBS Reports: The Defense of the United States: Ground Zero.* CBS.
• Judy Crichton, Howard Stringer, Leslie Cockburn, *CBS Reports: The Defense of the United States: Nuclear Battlefield.* CBS.
• Judy Towers Reemtsma, Marlene Sanders, *CBS Reports: Nurse, Where Are You?* CBS.
• Perry Wolff, "Inside Hollywood: The Movie Business," *CBS News Special.* CBS.

(Directors)
• Craig Leake, *CBS Reports: The Defense of the United States: The War Machine.* CBS.

(Technical direction/Electronic camera)
• Richard Jeffreys, electronic camera, "The Assassination of Anwar Sadat," *CBS Evening News with Dan Rather.* CBS.
• Tom Woods, electronic camera, "Inside Afghanistan," *Magazine with David Brinkley.* NBC.
• Rupen Vosgimorukian, Barry Fox, electronic camera, "Italian Earthquake," *ABC World News Tonight.* ABC.
• Stephen N. Stanford, electronic camera, "Monarch Butterflies," *20/20.* ABC.
• Sheldon Fielman, electronic camera, "President Reagan Shooting," *NBC News Special Report.* NBC.

(Cinematography)
• Billy Wagner, Jan Morgan, John Boulter, John Peters, cinematographers, *CBS Reports: The Defense of the United States: Nuclear Battlefield.* CBS.

(Film editing)
• John J. Martin, film editor, "An American Adventure: The Rocket Pilots," *NBC News Special.* NBC.
• Mili Bonsignori, film editor, *CBS Reports: The Defense of the United States: Call to Arms.* CBS.
• Ara Chekmayan, Christopher Dalrymple, film editors, *CBS Reports: The Defense of the United States: The War Machine.* CBS.
• David R. Ward, film editor, "Jackie Gleason: How Sweet It Is," *20/20.* ABC.

(Audio)
• Ed Jennings, tape sound editor, "Carter's Final Hours," *ABC News Nightline.* ABC.

(Associate direction and/or video-tape editing)
• Neil Philpson, senior associate director — post production. Jerry Chernak, associate director — post production. Ed Buda, Thomas R. Gubar, senior video-tape editors. Sam Hadley, Robert Brandt, Alan Campbell, Henriette Huehne, David Harten, Robert Kerr, Vicki Papazian, Dave Rummel, Donna Rowlinson, video-tape editors. Harvey Beal, Eileen Clancy, John Croak, Dean Irwin, Catherine Isabella, Conrad Kraus, Mike Mazella, Tom Miller, Peter Murphy, Erskin Roberts, Mario Schencman, Mike Siegel, Barry Spitzer, Chris Von Benge, video-tape editors — post production, "America Held Hostage: The Secret Negotiations," *ABC News Special.* ABC.
• David G. Rummel Jr., video-tape editor, "Monarch Butterflies," *20/20.* ABC.

(Graphic design)
• Freida Reiter, graphic artist/illustrator, • "America Held Hostage: The Secret Negotiations," *ABC News Special.* ABC.
• Gerry Andrea, graphic designer/illustrator, "Shooting of Pope John Paul II," *ABC World News Tonight.* ABC.

INTERNATIONAL AWARD WINNERS
DOCUMENTARY
• *Fighting Back*, Canadian Broadcasting Corporation, Canada.

PERFORMING ARTS
• *L'Oiseau de Feu (The Firebird)*, Société Radio, Canada.

DRAMA
• *A Rod of Iron*, Yorkshire Television Limited, U.K..

SPECIAL AWARDS
OUTSTANDING ACHIEVEMENT IN THE SCIENCE OF TELEVISION ENGINEERING
• CBS

OUTSTANDING ACHIEVEMENT IN ENGINEERING DEVELOPMENT
• *Rank Precision Industries Ltd.* for the design and development of the Rank Cintel Mark III Flying Spot Telecine, which converts film to video.

NATIONAL AWARD FOR COMMUNITY SERVICE
• *Minneapolis Housing Inspectors*, WCCO-TV, Minneapolis, Minnesota.

A.T.A.S. GOVERNORS AWARD
• Elton H. Rule

N.A.T.A.S. TRUSTEES AWARD
• Agnes E. Nixon, for her distinguished creative contributions to daytime television.

Cops on Top

Despite the odds and old maxims that say it just can't happen, lightning struck twice at the Emmy Awards when *Hill Street Blues* received 21 nominations in 1982 — the exact same number it garnered last year when it set the record. But this time the program was not facing the same uphill battle it did before. One of the first great cop shows that was actually more about cops than crime had climbed significantly in the ratings over the past twelve months and was now, said the *Herald Examiner*, "fly-

The *"popular knockabout police station sitcom"* Barney Miller *had lost the best comedy prize six times in the past, but finally got the last laugh.*

ing high." The same could not be said of the other winners. "It was less an awards show than a memorial service," suggested *The Washington Post.* "At the 34th annual Emmy Awards, telecast live from Pasadena by ABC, the honorees included the late Ingrid Bergman, the departed comedy series *Barney Miller*, the canceled *Lou Grant*, the soon-to-expire *M*A*S*H* and the axed — but then reprieved — *Taxi.*"

HSB took only six trophies compared to its previous, precedent-setting eight, but again it was named Outstanding Drama Series and repeated wins for its lead actor Daniel J. Travanti ("To have you give me this is almost too much," he said, clutching his award, "but I'll take it!") and supporting actor Michael Conrad. The *Herald Examiner* had noted when the nominations came out, "So complete was the *Hill Street Blues* triumph that, in a stunning Emmy occurrence, it swept all five nominations in the best supporting actor category."

Conrad had not been considered a front runner since he'd missed the first four shows of the season due to illness, but when he ended up surpassing his fellow cast members, he claimed the statuette again saying "Wow!" and added, "It's very awkward when your competitors are all your friends who are on the same show." *HSB* had also taken four out of the five nods for writing and ended up reprising its win in that category, too. It scored two new triumphs with the awards for film editing and film sound mixing.

Cops were considered in a much lighter vein on *Barney Miller*, what the *Post* called, "the popular knockabout, police station sitcom which ended its seven-year run on ABC this year." Over those seven years it had been nominated for Outstanding Comedy Series seven times, but this year it finally got the last laugh, while also bringing to a screeching halt *Taxi*'s three-year roll over the category. *Taxi* had faced even more bad news recently: It had been canceled by

ABC, but was then suddenly hailed by NBC, which agreed to give it a test ride in the same time slot it had fared so poorly in on Thursday nights on ABC. ("Same time, better station!" its commercials insisted.) NBC then, in midseason, switched the series to Saturday nights and then to Wednesday nights before dropping it entirely at the end of the year.

But the show was still popular with Emmy voters. Of its eight nominations, *Taxi* picked up three awards: for writing, best actress Carol Kane (who played Simka, wife of the archetypal, semi-intelligible immigrant Latka Gravas), and supporting actor Christopher Lloyd (as "Reverend Jim," the "drug-bedeviled driver," according to *The New York Times*.)

Other past Emmy champs were also reaching the end of the road. *Lou Grant* had been dropped by CBS, but not before salvaging a final bow to Nancy Marchand, her fourth Emmy and third in a row as best supporting actress in a drama series. She thanked her show's cast, which "was not a family," she said. "It was a group of real craftsmen."

M*A*S*H would soon be ending its ten years on the tube with a two-hour farewell planned for midseason, but in the meantime it won honors for Alan Alda as best actor (who ended his acceptance remarks with an impassioned "God bless America!") and Loretta Swit as supporting actress. "Oh my, oh my, oh, oh," Swit said at the podium. "I'm overwhelmed. I've been an actress for 15 years and I've never been so unprepared on a stage in my life." She had also won an Emmy two years before, but wouldn't defy the Emmy boycott to accept it in person.

> Ingrid Bergman died of cancer just prior to her victory for Golda.

Another past Emmy winner, Michael Learned of *The Waltons*, returned this year to be named best actress in a drama series for reprising the strong performance she gave in the 1980 made-for-TV movie *Nurse*, which had become a short-lived CBS series about a widow who returns to work at a metropolitan hospital soon after the death of her husband. "I'm so stunned," Learned said, accepting the statuette, "I swallowed my chewing gum."

Fame was another new series based on a popular film, a feature-release hit about the talented students at New York's High School for the Performing Arts. It began the night with 12 nominations and ended up with a respectable four prizes (for direction, cinematography, art direction, and choreographer Debbie Allen). But it was not the same *HSB*-type sweep of 1981 — or even of 1982 — that many critics were expecting. *Fame* was one of those high-quality, low-rated programs that NBC was nonetheless bravely sticking by in the hope that it would find a wider audience in time. But time was running out. After its moderate success at the 1982 Emmys, NBC remained loyal only one more year before finally letting *Fame* slip into possible obscurity. It was ultimately saved, however, by its courageous producers who saw to it that the show-biz show would, in fact, go on — in syndication.

That syndicated programs could compete successfully for Emmys was proved best this year by *A Woman Called Golda*, a two-part docu-drama on the career of Israeli prime minister Golda Meir that became the first syndicated television film ever to be voted Outstanding Drama Special. Golda Meir was played by three-time Oscar winner Ingrid Bergman, who also won an Emmy 22 years earlier for portraying the governess in *The Turn of the Screw*. Bergman continued the rigors of starring in *Golda* despite suffering a battle with cancer that she would finally lose just weeks after Emmy's blue-ribbon panels secretly voted her the year's best actress. "I think she showed the same courage and determination and dignity Golda did," said her daughter, arts critic Pia Lindstrom, as she accepted the award on her mother's behalf. "I really do think she deserved this award, not only for her performance on camera, but for her performance off camera. She will live in my heart forever." Interestingly, Bergman was competing against four other actresses who portrayed famous women, including Jean Stapleton as Eleanor Roosevelt, Glenda Jackson as actress Patricia Neal, Ann Jillian as actress Mae West, and Cicely Tyson as the noted Chicago schoolteacher Marva Collins. *Golda* also won an award for film editing.

Mickey Rooney was voted best actor for playing the lead in *Bill*, the true story of a mentally retarded man's struggle to live in the real world after spending 46 years in a mental institution. Like Bergman, Rooney also triumphed over formidable competition, which included Anthony Hopkins in *The Hunchback of Notre Dame* and the two popular young actors (Jeremy Irons and Anthony Andrews) from the hugely successful PBS miniseries *Brideshead Revisited*. *Brideshead* was based on the Evelyn Waugh classic about the decline of the British aristocracy and had America's intelligentsia revisiting their boob tubes over 11 nights in early 1982 to keep tuned into one of the most widely discussed and critically acclaimed mini-series ever. Laurence Olivier won his fourth Emmy when he was named best supporting actor for playing Irons's dying father, Lord Marchmain. It was the only award that *Brideshead* eventually claimed despite 11 nominations.

Brideshead had been considered a shoo-in for Outstanding Limited Series, but was upset by *Marco Polo*, what *The Washington Post* called "NBC's lavish, costly and snail's paced dramatic travelogue" that ended up with only one other award — for costume design.

The year's best variety program, ABC's *Night of 100 Stars*, showcased the likes of Elizabeth Taylor, James Cagney, and Miss Piggy in a 100th anniversary celebration of the Actor's Fund of America. Director's honors went to Dwight Hemion, who earned his 14th career Emmy for *Goldie and Kids ... Listen to Us*, featuring Goldie Hawn in a CBS special that did poorly in the ratings.

The prime-time Emmy ceremony was ably handled by hosts John Forsythe and Marlo Thomas and included tributes to news pioneer Edward R. Murrow (who died in 1965), original *Today* show host Dave Garroway (who died the previous July), and Bob Hope, who was still going strong at age 79. The evergreen comedian joked that he was now so old that the NBC's trademark peacock "was hatched from an egg I laid."

The *L.A. Times* noted that NBC's "peacock had plenty to be proud of" when a tally was made of the night's winners. The network had been called "the perennial doormat" by *Variety* because it had been in last place for seven years, but now it was trying to upgrade its ratings by championing prestige programming. The *Herald Examiner* insisted that the single best night of prime-time entertainment was the network's Thursday evening lineup, which included *Hill Street Blues*, *Fame*, and *Taxi*. "There will be a fourth Thursday series on NBC this fall," the paper then added, "a new comedy called *Cheers*." The paper noted that Emmy award voters seemed to like shows that have "a touch of grit" and added, "Whether *Cheers* will also fit into this category remains to be seen."

DAYTIME AWARDS

The date of the broadcast was not just any other day in New York, a town where 10 of TV's 14 daytime dramas were taped. In honor of the Emmy awards ceremony, Mayor Ed Koch officially declared it Soap Opera Day.

The last time accomplished game show host Bob Barker hosted the daytime Emmys, in 1979, he was disqualified as a nominee because his producers submitted a wrong episode of *The Price is Right* for consideration. That was the first time Barker had even been nominated in his 22-year career, but this year he was back as both host and nominee again — and won.

The 90-minute ceremony (held in the ballroom of New York's Waldorf-Astoria Hotel and broadcast by CBS, which received its highest ratings in daytime TV ever) was a homecoming for other talent, too, particularly for the 1980 best drama series *Guiding Light*, which won writing honors last year and now was back reaping both awards. The *L.A. Times* apparently disagreed with the outcome. *Guiding Light*'s success "wasn't surprising," the paper said. "It's a fine serial. But once again the academy bypassed the exemplary *All My Children*, which should have won for either writing or series." The rest of the winners, the paper opined, "were, by and large, deserved."

> **Best actor**
> **Anthony Geary**
> **(Luke Spencer)**
> **was General**
> **Hospital's**
> **"golden boy."**

Last year the *L.A. Times* predicted that the top acting honors would surely go to Anthony Geary, the "golden boy of soaps" who played *General Hospital*'s Luke Spencer (whom Geary once described as the perfect "antihero"), and

Robin Strasser, who gave a "veritable fireworks display" of a performance as Dorian Callison on *One Life to Life*. Both calls were wrong last year, but eerily came to pass in 1982. Geary was largely responsible for *General Hospital*'s continued status as the number one soap in America thanks to his character's on-again, off-again romance with Laura (played by Genie Francis) that finally resulted in their hugely hyped marriage. When the event aired in November, 1981, it brought the highest ratings ever received by a daytime drama.

If home viewers had their pick for best actress, it probably would have gone to Susan Lucci, who played the manipulative, sassy, self-absorbed vixen Erica Kane on the number two–rated *All My Children*. *People* magazine once called her "one of the most enduring, high-camp video bitches this side of Joan Collins" (in a comparative reference to prime-time *Dynasty*'s equivalent). "Every weekday nine million Erica watchers tune in to witness the havoc she is wreaking in Pine Valley, U.S.A." After losing the prize last year, Lucci was getting anxious to win, but when Robin Strasser's name was announced, "she pounded the table in rage," *People* reported.

General Hospital won three additional awards — a design trophy, a prize for its direction, and another for supporting actor David Lewis (as Edward Quartermaine). *All My Children* came in second place with a total of three awards, including two for technical achievement and one for supporting actress Dorothy Lyman (as Opal Gardner), who had starred in five different soaps throughout her career but had never before won an Emmy. "It's the most exciting day of my life," she told *People*.

Losing nominee James Mitchell of *All My Children* also spoke to *People* and said, "I think the Emmy belongs to all of us. We all worked our asses off." In order to relax and also to celebrate Soap Opera Day after the Emmy ceremony, soap casts and crews ended up dancing off those same body parts at the fashionable dance club Magique where acting winners Geary and Strasser were photographed giving each other a passionate victory kiss and other winners kidded and clowned around.

Two new shows ended up with top series prizes in other categories. NBC had only premiered *The Regis Philbin Show* the previous November, but the program featuring the former sidekick of comedian Joey Bishop was already declared best variety series. Exercise guru Richard Simmons's show won three statuettes: for being the best talk or service series, for its art direction, and for its costume design. After his four-year winning streak was broken by Hugh Downs last year, talk show host Phil Donahue returned to take the Emmy again. *Password Plus* had succeeded *Password* and *Password Allstars* in 1979 and now, following the death of longtime host Allen Ludden, was hosted by Tom Kennedy. In its revamped format, it was named Outstanding Game Show.

In the children's category, *Captain Kangaroo* returned as Outstanding Children's Entertainment Series and also finally won a performance award for its star, "captain" Bob Keeshan. Four *ABC Afterschool Specials* swept a large number of the other prizes, including Outstanding Children's Entertainment Special, which was awarded to "She Drinks a Little," about a girl trying to cope with her mother's alcoholism.

SPORTS AWARDS

It was "the biggest night of the year for sports recognition," according to a press account published by N.A.T.A.S., but the evening was seriously marred by NBC's refusal to participate. Former NBC executive Bud Rukeyser says, "We had become convinced that there was an inability on the part of N.A.T.A.S. to administer awards in a proper way."

N.A.T.A.S. accommodated the calls for change by making some alterations in the awards procedure that the networks had been seeking for some time, such as allowing network staffers to sit on the Emmy judging panels if they could prove no conflicts of interest. But NBC wasn't placated. The network had suspicions of frequent mistakes being made in the balloting procedure and of bloc voting by another network. It not only refused to participate in the sports contest, it withdrew from the news and documentary awards. In each case the action was considering nonbinding on network employees: NBC, as a corporate entity, declined to participate, although its individual employees could — and would — continue to submit their own work for consideration. None, however, won.

The sports ceremony was held in the Imperial Ballroom of the Sheraton Centre in New York and was hosted in part by Jim McKay, who won an Emmy for Outstanding Sports Personality—Host, bringing his career total to nine (eight for sports, one for news coverage). John Madden was named Outstanding Sports Personality—Analyst.

Independently produced syndicated shows ended up winning sports Emmys for the first time in history, including Special Classification program trophies for *Reggie Jackson* and *The Baseball Bunch* and an award for the cinematographers of *Sports Illustrated: A Series for Television*.

CBS and ABC each ended up with 10 statuettes, with CBS dominating the live program categories when *NFL Football* was named outstanding series and *NCAA Basketball Championship Final* was voted best special. ABC swept the edited program categories with best series *The American Sports-man* and coverage of the *1982 Indi-anapolis 500* being named best special. The Indy 500 also won prizes for its associate directors, technical editors, and video-tape and film editors.

NEWS & DOCUMENTARY AWARDS

CBS may have ended up in last place at the prime-time Emmys, but it led the two other major networks by claiming an impressive total of 17 news and docu-mentary prizes. ABC originally led in the number of nominations, but ended up in second place with 13 awards, com-pared to 12 earned by PBS. NBC boy-cotted the competition, just as it did this

The Outstanding Interview news award went to ABC News Nightline *for Ted Koppel's conversations with Yasser Arafat in "Palestinian Viewpoint."*

which won seven awards for segments such as its famous interview with singer Lena Horne, an investigation into Nazi-ism, and the whimsical analysis of world events by in-house curmudgeon Andy Rooney. *The CBS Evening News with Dan Rather* reaped four awards (for pro-files on subjects such as domestic unem-ployment) while *CBS Reports* was hon-ored for a documentary on the political and military problems of Guatemala, and *Sunday Morning* for its profile of songmaster Quincy Jones.

ABC's *20/20* originally outscored *60 Minutes* in nominations, but ended up with only one trophy — for an interview with past Emmy winner Sid Caesar. It was *ABC News Nightline* that led the network's win-ning shows with three prizes, including one for coverage of the recent air-line crash on the Potomac River and another for its interviews with Palestinian leaders on Midwest ten-sions. The ABC documen-tary *Vietnam Requiem* won two awards, one for out-standing program achieve-ment and another for its directors.

PBS's statuettes were bestowed for feature foot-age on Nicaragua, Chrysler, and the Taj Mahal. NBC won for its *Nightly News* program and for the documentaries *Along Route 30* and *The Man Who Shot the Pope: A Study in Terrorism.*

Entertainment Tonight cameras were among those on hand to catch "a rousing comment by Dan Rather of CBS," said the N.A.T.A.S. newsletter, "who expressed on behalf of his colleagues the importance of having an evening to gather together and celebrate excellence in broadcast journalism."

year's sports event, because of objec-tions to the process of winner selection, but it ended up with three statuettes as a result of permitting employees to contin-ue to participate independently.

The dinner ceremony was held in the grand ballroom of the Grand Hyatt Hotel in New York City and included such presenters as Notre Dame president Theodore Hesburgh and a then relatively obscure congresswoman from Queens, N.Y., named Geraldine Ferraro. The night's biggest winner was *60 Minutes*,

For prime-time programs telecast between July 1, 1981, and June 30, 1982. The prime-time ceremony was broadcast on ABC from the Pasadena Civic Auditorium on September 19, 1982. Creative arts banquet held on September 12, 1982. Daytime awards broadcast on CBS on June 8, 1982, for programs aired between March 6, 1981, to March 5, 1982. News & documentary awards presented October 17, 1983, for programs aired between November 15, 1981, and December 31, 1982. The sports awards were presented March 1, 1983, for programs aired between July 16, 1981 and July 15, 1982.

PRIME-TIME PROGRAM AWARDS
OUTSTANDING DRAMA SERIES
• *Hill Street Blues.* Steven Bochco, executive producer. Gregory Hoblit, supervising producer. David Anspaugh, Anthony Yerkovich, producers. NBC.
Dynasty. Aaron Spelling, Douglas S. Cramer, executive producers. E. Duke Vincent, supervising producer. Ed Ledding, Elaine Rich, producers. ABC.
Lou Grant. Gene Reynolds, executive producer. Seth Freeman, producer. CBS.
Magnum, P.I. Donald P. Bellisario, executive producer. Douglas Green, Andrew Schneider, Rick Weaver, producers. CBS.
Fame. William Blinn, Gerald I. Isenberg, executive producers. Stan Rogow, Mel Swope, producers. NBC.

OUTSTANDING COMEDY SERIES
• *Barney Miller.* Danny Arnold, Roland Kibbee, executive producers. Frank Dungan, Jeff Stein, producers. Gary Shaw, coproducer. ABC.
Love, Sidney. George Eckstein, executive producer. Ernest Chambers, Bob Brunner, Ken Hecht, supervising producers. April Kelly, Mel Tolkin, Jim Parker, producers. NBC.
*M*A*S*H.* Burt Metcalfe, executive producer. John Rappaport, supervising producer. Thad Mumford, Dan Wilcox, Dennis Koenig, producers. CBS.
Taxi. James L. Brooks, Stan Daniels, Ed. Weinberger, executive producers. Glen Charles, Les Charles, supervising producers. Ken Estin, Howard Gewirtz, Ian Praiser, producers. Richard Sakai,

coproducer. ABC.
WKRP in Cincinnati. Hugh Wilson, executive producer. Blake Hunter, Peter Torokvei, Dan Guntzelman, Steve Marshall, producers. CBS.

OUTSTANDING LIMITED SERIES
• *Marco Polo.* Vincenzo LaBella, producer. NBC.
Brideshead Revisited, Great Performances. Jac Venza, Robert Kotlowitz, executive producers. Sam Paul, series producer. Derek Granger, producer. PBS.
Flickers, Masterpiece Theatre. Joan Wilson, executive producer. Joan Brown, producer. PBS.
Oppenheimer, American Playhouse. Peter Goodchild, producer. Lindsay Law, coordinating producer. PBS.
A Town Like Alice, Masterpiece Theatre. Joan Wilson, executive producer. Henry Crawford, producer. PBS.

OUTSTANDING DRAMA SPECIAL
• *A Woman Called Golda.* Harve Bennett, executive producer. Gene Corman, producer. Syndicated.
Bill. Alan Landsburg, executive producer. Mel Stuart, producer. CBS.
The Elephant Man. Martin Starger, executive producer. Richmond Crinkley, producer. ABC.
Inside the Third Reich. E. Jack Neuman, producer. ABC.
Skokie. Herbert Brodkin, executive producer. Robert Berger, producer. CBS.

OUTSTANDING VARIETY, MUSIC, OR COMEDY PROGRAM
• *Night of 100 Stars.* Alexander H. Cohen, executive producer. Hildy Parks, producer. Roy A. Somlyo, coproducer. ABC.
Ain't Misbehavin'. Alvin Cooperman, executive producer. Alvin Cooperman, Buddy Bregman, producers. NBC.
American Film Institute Salute to Frank Capra. George Stevens, Jr., producer. CBS.
Baryshnikov in Hollywood, Herman E. Krawitz, executive producer. Don Mischer, producer. Mikhail Baryshnikov, star. CBS.
SCTV Comedy Network. Andrew Alexander, Doug Holtby, Len Stuart, Jack

Rhodes, executive producers. Patrick Whitley, supervising producer. Barry Sand, Don Novello, producers. Nicolas Wry, coproducer. NBC.

OUTSTANDING CLASSICAL PROGRAM IN THE PERFORMING ARTS (Winner)
• *La Bohème, Live from the Met.* Michael Bronson, executive producer. Clemente D'Alessio, producer. PBS.

OUTSTANDING INFORMATIONAL SERIES (Winner)
• *Creativity with Bill Moyers.* Merton Koplin, Charles Grinker, Bill Moyers, executive producers. Betsy McCarthy, coordinating producer. PBS.

OUTSTANDING INFORMATIONAL SPECIAL (Winner)
• *Making of "Raiders of the Lost Ark."* Sidney Ganis, executive producer. Howard Kazanjian, producer. PBS.

OUTSTANDING CHILDREN'S PROGRAM (Winner)
• *The Wave.* Virginia L. Carter, executive producer. Fern Field, producer. ABC.

OUTSTANDING ANIMATED PROGRAM (Winner)
• *The Grinch Grinches the Cat in the Hat.* David H. DePatie, executive producer. Ted Geisel, Friz Freleng, producers. ABC.

PERFORMANCE, DIRECTING, AND WRITING
OUTSTANDING LEAD ACTOR IN A DRAMA SERIES
• Daniel J. Travanti, *Hill Street Blues.* NBC.
Edward Asner, *Lou Grant.* CBS.
John Forsythe, *Dynasty.* ABC.
James Garner, *Bret Maverick.* NBC.
Tom Selleck, *Magnum, P.I.* CBS.

OUTSTANDING LEAD ACTRESS IN A DRAMA SERIES
• Michael Learned, *Nurse.* CBS.
Debbie Allen, *Fame.* NBC.
Veronica Hamel, *Hill Street Blues.* NBC.
Michele Lee, *Knots Landing.* CBS.
Stefanie Powers, *Hart to Hart.* ABC.

OUTSTANDING LEAD ACTOR IN A COMEDY SERIES
• Alan Alda, *M*A*S*H.* CBS.
Robert Guillaume, *Benson.* ABC.

Judd Hirsch, *Taxi.* ABC.
Hal Linden, *Barney Miller.* ABC.
Leslie Nielsen, *Police Squad!* ABC.

OUTSTANDING LEAD ACTRESS IN A COMEDY SERIES
• Carol Kane, *Taxi.* ABC.
Nell Carter, *Gimme a Break.* NBC.
Bonnie Franklin, *One Day at a Time.* CBS.
Swoosie Kurtz, *Love, Sidney.* NBC.
Charlotte Rae, *The Facts of Life.* NBC.
Isabel Sanford, *The Jeffersons.* CBS.

OUTSTANDING LEAD ACTOR IN A LIMITED SERIES OR A SPECIAL
• Mickey Rooney, *Bill.* CBS.
Anthony Andrews, *Brideshead Revisited, Great Performances.* PBS.
Philip Anglim, *The Elephant Man.* ABC.
Anthony Hopkins, *The Hunchback of Notre Dame, Hallmark Hall of Fame.* CBS.
Jeremy Irons, *Brideshead Revisited, Great Performances.* PBS.

OUTSTANDING LEAD ACTRESS IN A LIMITED SERIES OR A SPECIAL
• Ingrid Bergman, *A Woman Called Golda.* Syndicated.
Glenda Jackson, *The Patricia Neal Story.* CBS.
Ann Jillian, *Mae West.* ABC.
Jean Stapleton, *Eleanor, First Lady of the World.* CBS.
Cicely Tyson, *The Marva Collins Story, Hallmark Hall of Fame.* CBS.

OUTSTANDING SUPPORTING ACTOR IN A DRAMA SERIES
• Michael Conrad, *Hill Street Blues.* NBC.
Taurean Blacque, *Hill Street Blues.* NBC.
Charles Haid, *Hill Street Blues.* NBC.
Michael Warren, *Hill Street Blues.* NBC.
Bruce Weitz, *Hill Street Blues.* NBC.

OUTSTANDING SUPPORTING ACTRESS IN A DRAMA SERIES
• Nancy Marchand, *Lou Grant.* CBS.
Barbara Bosson, *Hill Street Blues.* NBC.
Julie Harris, *Knots Landing.* CBS.
Linda Kelsey, *Lou Grant.* CBS.
Betty Thomas, *Hill Street Blues.* NBC.

OUTSTANDING SUPPORTING ACTOR IN A COMEDY, VARIETY, OR MUSIC SERIES
• Christopher Lloyd, *Taxi.* ABC.
Danny DeVito, *Taxi.* ABC.

Ron Glass, *Barney Miller*. ABC.
Steve Landesberg, *Barney Miller*. ABC.
Harry Morgan, *M*A*S*H*. CBS.
David Ogden Stiers, *M*A*S*H*. CBS.

**OUTSTANDING SUPPORTING ACTRESS
IN A COMEDY, VARIETY OR MUSIC SERIES**
• Loretta Swit, *M*A*S*H*. CBS.
Eileen Brennan, *Private Benjamin*. CBS.
Marla Gibbs, *The Jeffersons*. CBS.
Andrea Martin, *SCTV Comedy Network*.
NBC.
Anne Meara, *Archie Bunker's Place*. CBS.
Inga Swenson, *Benson*. ABC.

**OUTSTANDING SUPPORTING ACTOR
IN A LIMITED SERIES OR A SPECIAL**
• Laurence Olivier, *Brideshead Revisited,
Great Performances*. PBS.
Jack Albertson, *My Body, My Child*. ABC.
John Gielgud, *Brideshead Revisited, Great
Performances*. PBS.
Derek Jacobi, *Inside the Third Reich*.
ABC.
Leonard Nimoy, *A Woman Called Golda*.
Syndicated.

**OUTSTANDING SUPPORTING ACTRESS
IN A LIMITED SERIES OR A SPECIAL**
• Penny Fuller, *The Elephant Man*. ABC.
Claire Bloom, *Brideshead Revisited, Great
Performances*. PBS.
Judy Davis, *A Woman Called Golda*.
Syndicated.
Vicki Lawrence, *Eunice*. CBS.
Rita Moreno, *Portrait of a Showgirl*. CBS.

**OUTSTANDING DIRECTING
IN A DRAMA SERIES**
• Harry Harris, *Fame*. NBC.
Jeff Bleckner, *Hill Street Blues*. NBC.
Robert Butler, *Hill Street Blues*. NBC.
Gene Reynolds, *Lou Grant*. CBS.
Robert Scheerer, *Fame*. NBC.

**OUTSTANDING DIRECTING
IN A COMEDY SERIES**
• Alan Rafkin, *One Day at a Time*. CBS.
Alan Alda, *M*A*S*H*. CBS.
Hy Averback, *M*A*S*H*. CBS.
James Burrows, *Taxi*. ABC.
Charles S. Dubin, *M*A*S*H*. CBS.
Burt Metcalfe, *M*A*S*H*. CBS.

**OUTSTANDING DIRECTING
IN A LIMITED SERIES OR A SPECIAL**
• Marvin J. Chomsky, *Inside the Third
Reich*. ABC.

Lee Philips, *Mae West*. ABC.
Charles Sturridge, Michael Lindsay-Hogg,
*Brideshead Revisited, Great
Performances*. PBS.
Herbert Wise, *Skokie*. CBS.

**OUTSTANDING DIRECTING
IN A VARIETY OR MUSIC PROGRAM**
• Dwight Hemion, *Goldie and Kids ...
Listen to Us*. ABC.
Clark Jones, *Night of 100 Stars*. ABC.
Don Mischer, *Baryshnikov in Hollywood*.
CBS.
Marty Pasetta, *The 54th Annual Academy
Awards*. ABC.
Robert Scheerer, "An Evening with Danny
Kaye and the New York Philharmonic,"
Live from Lincoln Center. PBS.

**OUTSTANDING WRITING
IN A DRAMA SERIES**
• Steven Bochco, Anthony Yerkovich,
Jeffrey Lewis, Michael Wagner, teleplay.
Michael Kozoll, Steven Bochco, story, *Hill
Street Blues*. NBC.
Steven Bochco, Anthony Yerkovich,
Robert Crais, teleplay. Michael Kozoll,
Steven Bochco, Anthony Yerkovich, story,
Hill Street Blues. NBC.
Steven Bochco, Anthony Yerkovich,
Jeffrey Lewis, Michael Wagner, *Hill Street
Blues*. NBC.
Seth Freeman, *Lou Grant*. CBS.
Michael Wagner, *Hill Street Blues*. NBC.

**OUTSTANDING WRITING
IN A COMEDY SERIES**
• Ken Estin, *Taxi*. ABC.
Alan Alda, *M*A*S*H*. CBS.
Frank Dungan, Jeff Stein, Tony Sheehan,
Barney Miller. ABC.
Barry Kemp, teleplay. Holly Holmberg
Brooks, story, *Taxi*. ABC.
David Zucker, Jim Abrahams, Jerry
Zucker, *Police Squad!* ABC.

**OUTSTANDING WRITING
IN A LIMITED SERIES OR A SPECIAL**
• Corey Blechman, teleplay. Barry
Morrow, story, *Bill*. CBS.
Oliver Hailey, *Sidney Shorr*. NBC.
Ernest Kinoy, *Skokie*. CBS.
John Mortimer, *Brideshead Revisited,
Great Performances*. PBS.
Peter Prince, *Oppenheimer*, *American
Playhouse*. PBS.

1981–82   291

Best comedy series actor Alan Alda of M*A*S*H *backstage with best supporting actress Carol Kane of* Taxi.

OUTSTANDING WRITING IN A VARIETY OR MUSIC PROGRAM
• John Candy, Joe Flaherty, Eugene Levy, Andrea Martin, Rick Moranis, Catherine O'Hara, Dave Thomas, Dick Blasucci, Paul Flaherty, Bob Dolman, John McAndrew, Doug Steckler, Mert Rich, Jeffrey Barron, Michael Short, Chris Cluess, Stuart Kreisman, Brian McConnachie, *SCTV Comedy Network*. NBC.
Richard Alfieri, Rita Mae Brown, Rick Mitz, Arthur Alan Seidelman, Norman Lear, *I Love Liberty*. ABC.
John Candy, Joe Flaherty, Eugene Levy, Andrea Martin, Rick Moranis, Catherine O'Hara, Dave Thomas, Dick Blasucci, Paul Flaherty, Bob Dolman, John McAndrew, Doug Steckler, Jeffrey Barron, *SCTV Comedy Network*. NBC.
John Candy, Joe Flaherty, Eugene Levy, Andrea Martin, Rick Moranis, Catherine O'Hara, Dave Thomas, Dick Blasucci, Paul Flaherty, Bob Dolman, John McAndrew, Doug Steckler, Michael Short, Tom Couch, Eddie Gorodetsky, Don Novello, *SCTV Comedy Network*. NBC.
John Candy, Joe Flaherty, Eugene Levy, Andrea Martin, Rick Moranis, Catherine O'Hara, Dave Thomas, Dick Blasucci, Paul Flaherty, Bob Dolman, John McAndrew, Doug Steckler, Mert Rich, Jeffrey Barron, *SCTV Comedy Network*. NBC.

OTHER AWARD WINNERS

OUTSTANDING CINEMATOGRAPHY FOR A SERIES
William W. Spencer, *Fame*. NBC.

OUTSTANDING CINEMATOGRAPHY FOR A LIMITED SERIES OR A SPECIAL
James Crabe, *The Letter*. ABC.

OUTSTANDING ART DIRECTION FOR A SERIES
Ira Diamond, art director. Joseph Stone, set decorator, *Fame*. NBC.

OUTSTANDING ART DIRECTION FOR A LIMITED SERIES OR A SPECIAL
James Hulsey, art director, Jerry Adams, set decorator, *The Letter*. ABC.

OUTSTANDING ART DIRECTION FOR A VARIETY OR MUSIC PROGRAM
Ray Klausen, art director, *The 54th Annual Academy Awards*. ABC.

OUTSTANDING MUSIC COMPOSITION FOR A SERIES (Dramatic underscore)
David Rose, *Little House on the Prairie*. NBC.

OUTSTANDING MUSIC COMPOSITION FOR A LIMITED SERIES OR SPECIAL (Dramatic underscore)
Patrick Williams, *The Princess and the Cabbie*. CBS.

OUTSTANDING MUSIC DIRECTION
Elliot Lawrence, music director. Bill Elton, Tommy Newsom, Torrie Zito, Lanny Meyers, Jonathan Tunick, principal arrangers, *Night of 100 Stars*. ABC.

OUTSTANDING MUSIC AND LYRICS
Larry Grossman, composer. Alan Buz Kohan, lyricist, *Shirley MacLaine ... Illusions*. Song: "On the Outside Looking In." CBS.

OUTSTANDING CHOREOGRAPHY
Debbie Allen, *Fame*. NBC.

OUTSTANDING COSTUME DESIGN FOR A REGULAR OR LIMITED SERIES
Enrico Sabbatini, *Marco Polo*. NBC.

**OUTSTANDING COSTUME DESIGN
FOR A SPECIAL**
• Donald Brooks, *The Letter.* ABC.

OUTSTANDING MAKEUP
• Paul Stanhope, *World War* III. NBC.

OUTSTANDING HAIRSTYLING
• Hazel Catmull, *Eleanor, First Lady of the World.* CBS.

OUTSTANDING FILM EDITING FOR A SERIES
• Andrew Chulack, *Hill Street Blues.* NBC.

**OUTSTANDING FILM EDITING
FOR A LIMITED SERIES OR A SPECIAL**
• Robert F. Shugrue, *A Woman Called Golda.* Syndicated.

OUTSTANDING FILM SOUND EDITING
• William H. Wistrom, Russ Tinsley, supervising film sound editors. Peter Bond, Tom Cornwell, David Elliott, Tony Garber, Peter Harrison, Charles W. McMann, Joseph Mayer, Joseph Melody, R. William A. Thiederman, Rusty Tinsley, editors, *Inside the Third Reich,* ABC.

OUTSTANDING FILM SOUND MIXING
• William Marky, production mixer. Robert W. Glass, Jr., William M. Nicholson, Howard Wilmarth, rerecording mixers, *Hill Street Blues.* NBC.

OUTSTANDING TAPE SOUND MIXING
• Christopher L. Haire, Richard J. Masci, Doug Nelson, *Perry Como's Easter in Guadalajara.* ABC.

**OUTSTANDING VIDEO-TAPE EDITING
FOR A SERIES**
• Ken Denisoff, *Barbara Mandrell & the Mandrell Sisters.* NBC.

**OUTSTANDING VIDEO-TAPE EDITING
FOR A LIMITED SERIES OR A SPECIAL**
• William H. Breshears, Sr., Pam Marshall, Tucker Wiard, *American Bandstand's 30th Anniversary Special.* ABC.

**OUTSTANDING TECHNICAL DIRECTION
AND ELECTRONIC CAMERAWORK**
• Jerry Weiss, technical director. Bruce Bottone, Ken Dahlquist, Dean Hall, James Herring, Royden Holm, Tom Munshower, Wayne Nostaja, David Nowell, camerapersons, *The Magic of David Copperfield.* CBS.

**OUTSTANDING LIGHTING DIRECTION
(Electronic)**
• George W. Riesenberger, lighting designer. Ken Dettling, lighting director, *Working, American Playhouse.* PBS.

**OUTSTANDING INDIVIDUAL
ACHIEVEMENT—SPECIAL CLASS
(Area award)**
• Nell Carter, performer, *Ain't Misbehavin'.* NBC.
• Andre DeShields, performer, *Ain't Misbehavin'.* NBC.
• Marilyn Matthews, costume supervisor, *Fame.* NBC.

**OUTSTANDING INDIVIDUAL
ACHIEVEMENT—CREATIVE
SPECIAL ACHIEVEMENT
(Area award)**
• Andy Zall, video-tape editor, *Shirley MacLaine ... Illusions.* CBS.

**OUTSTANDING INDIVIDUAL
ACHIEVEMENT—ANIMATED
PROGRAMMING
(Area award)**
• Bill Perez, director, *The Grinch Grinches the Cat in the Hat.* ABC.

**OUTSTANDING INDIVIDUAL
ACHIEVEMENT—CHILDREN'S
PROGRAMMING
(Area award)**
• Ralph Holmes, lighting designer, "Alice at the Palace," *Project Peacock.* NBC.

(No awards were bestowed in the areas of individual achievement in informational programming, art direction, costume design, graphic design and title sequences, film editing, or film sound mixing.)

DAYTIME AWARDS
OUTSTANDING DAYTIME DRAMA SERIES
• *Guiding Light.* Allen Potter, executive producer. Joe Willmore, Leslie Kwartin, producers. CBS.
All My Children. Jorn Winther, producer. ABC.
General Hospital. Gloria Monty, producer. ABC.
Ryan's Hope. Ellen Barrett, producer. ABC.

OUTSTANDING ACTOR
IN A DAYTIME DRAMA SERIES
• Anthony Geary, *General Hospital*. ABC.
James Mitchell, *All My Children*. ABC.
Richard Shoberg, *All My Children*. ABC.
Larry Bryggman, *As the World Turns*.
CBS.
Stuart Damon, *General Hospital*. ABC.

OUTSTANDING ACTRESS
IN A DAYTIME DRAMA SERIES
• Robin Strasser, *One Life to Live*. ABC.
Susan Lucci, *All My Children*. ABC.
Ann Flood, *The Edge of Night*. ABC.
Sharon Gabet, *The Edge of Night*. ABC.
Leslie Charleson, *General Hospital*. ABC.

OUTSTANDING ACTOR IN A SUPPORTING
ROLE IN A DAYTIME DRAMA SERIES
• David Lewis, *General Hospital*. ABC.
Darnell Williams, *All My Children*. ABC.
Doug Sheehan, *General Hospital*. ABC.
Gerald Anthony, *One Life to Live*. ABC.

OUTSTANDING ACTRESS IN A SUPPORTING
ROLE IN A DAYTIME DRAMA SERIES
• Dorothy Lyman, *All My Children*. ABC.
Elizabeth Lawrence, *All My Children*.
ABC.
Meg Mundy, *The Doctors*. NBC.
Louise Shaffer, *Ryan's Hope*. ABC.

OUTSTANDING DIRECTION
FOR A DAYTIME DRAMA SERIES
• Marlena Laird, Alan Pultz, Phillip
Sogard, *General Hospital*. ABC.
Larry Auerbach, Jack Coffey, Sherrell
Hoffman, Jorn Winther, *All My Children*.
ABC.
Richard Pepperman, John Sedwick, *The
Edge of Night*. ABC.
Norman Hall, Peter Miner, David
Pressman, *One Life to Live*. ABC.

OUTSTANDING WRITING
FOR A DAYTIME DRAMA SERIES
• Patricia Mulcahey, Gene Palumbo, Frank
Salisbury, *Guiding Light*. CBS.
Agnes Nixon, Wisner Washam, Jack
Wood, Mary K. Wells, Clarice Blackburn,
Lorraine Broderick, Cynthia Benjamin,
John Saffron, Elizabeth Wallace, *All My
Children*. ABC.
Henry Slesar, Lois Kibbee, *The Edge of
Night*. ABC.
Douglas Marland, Nancy Franklin, Sam
Hall, Peggy O'Shea, Don Wallace, Lanie

Bertram, Fred Corke, S. Michael
Schnessel, *One Life to Live*. ABC.

OTHER DAYTIME AWARD WINNERS
OUTSTANDING GAME OR AUDIENCE
PARTICIPATION SHOW
• *Password Plus*. Robert Sherman,
producer. NBC.

OUTSTANDING HOST OR HOSTESS
IN A GAME OR AUDIENCE
PARTICIPATION SHOW
• Bob Barker, *The Price is Right*. CBS.

OUTSTANDING INDIVIDUAL DIRECTION
FOR A GAME OR AUDIENCE
PARTICIPATION SHOW
• Paul Alter, *The Family Feud*. ABC.

OUTSTANDING VARIETY SERIES
• *The Regis Philbin Show*. E.V. DiMassa,
Jr., Fred Tatashore, producers. NBC.

OUTSTANDING HOST OR HOSTESS
IN A VARIETY SERIES
• Merv Griffin, *The Merv Griffin Show*.
Syndicated.

OUTSTANDING INDIVIDUAL DIRECTION
FOR A VARIETY SERIES
• Barry Glazer, *American Bandstand*.
ABC.

OUTSTANDING TALK OR SERVICE SERIES
• *The Richard Simmons Show*. Woody
Fraser, executive producer. Nora Fraser,
producer. Syndicated.

OUTSTANDING HOST OR HOSTESS
IN A TALK OR SERVICE SERIES
• Phil Donahue, *Donahue*. Syndicated.

OUTSTANDING INDIVIDUAL DIRECTION
FOR A TALK OR SERVICE SERIES
• Ron Weiner, *Donahue*. Syndicated.

OUTSTANDING CHILDREN'S
ENTERTAINMENT SERIES
• *Captain Kangaroo*. Bob Keeshan,
executive producer. Joel Kosofsky,
producer. CBS.

OUTSTANDING CHILDREN'S
ENTERTAINMENT SPECIAL
• "Starstruck," *ABC Afterschool Special*.
Paul Freeman, producer. ABC.

**Outstanding Performer
in Children's Programming**
• Bob Keeshan, *Captain Kangaroo*. CBS.

**Outstanding Individual Direction
in Children's Programming**
• Arthur Allan Seidelman, "She Drinks a Little," *ABC Afterschool Special*. ABC.

**Outstanding Writing
for Children's Programming**
• Paul W. Cooper, "She Drinks a Little," *ABC Afterschool Special*. ABC.

**Outstanding Children's
Informational/Instructional Series**
• *30 Minutes*. Joel Heller, executive producer. Madeline Amgott, John Block, Jo Ann Caplin, Vern Diamond, Nancy Dutty, Carolyn Kreskey, Irene Moinar, Susan Mills, Robert Rubin, Martin Smith, Patti Obrow White, producers. CBS.

**Outstanding Informational/
Instructional Programming—
Short Format**
• *In the News*. Joel Heller, executive producer. Walter Lister, producer. CBS.

**Outstanding Children's
Informational/Instructional Special**
• *Kathy*. Kier Cline, Barry Teacher, producers. PBS.

**Outstanding Music
Composition/Direction in Children's
Programming**
• Elliot Lawrence, composer/director, "The Unforgivable Secret," *ABC Afterschool Special*. ABC.

**Outstanding Cinematography
in Children's Programming**
• Tom Hurwitz, *Big Blue Marble*. Syndicated.

**Outstanding Technical Excellence
for a Daytime Drama Series**
• Joseph Solomito, Howard Zweig, technical directors. Diana Wenman, Jean Dedario, Barbara Martin Simmons, associate directors. Lawrence Hammond, Robert Ambrico, Larry Strack, Vincent Senatore, Jay Kenn, Trevor Thompson, electronic cameramen. Len Walas, senior video engineer. Ai Lemanski, Charles Eisen, audio engineers. Roger Haeneit, video-tape editor. Barbara Wood, sound effects engineer, *All My Children*. ABC.

**Outstanding Design Excellence
for a Daytime Drama Series**
• James Ellingwood, art director. Mercer Barrows, set decorator. Grant Velie, Thomas Markle, John Zak, lighting directors. Jim O'Daniel, costume designer. P.K. Cole, Vikki McCarter, Diane Lewis, makeup designers. Katherine Kotarakos, Debbie Holmes, hair designers. Dominic Missinger, Jill Farren Phelps, music directors. Charles Paul, music composer, *General Hospital*. ABC.

THE AREAS
Each area has the possibility of one award winner, multiple winner, or none. Winners are listed.

**Outstanding Coverage
of Special Events
(Writing)**
• Bernard N. Eisman, *The Body Human: The Loving Process—Women*. CBS.

**Special Classification
of Outstanding Program
Achievement**
• *FYI*. Yanna Kroyt Brandt, producer. Mary Ann Donahue, coproducer. ABC.

**Special Classification
of Outstanding Individual
Achievement
(Writing)**
• Elaine Meryl Brown, Betty Cornfeld, Mary Ann Donahue, Joe Gustaitis, Robin Westen, *FYI*. ABC.
(Directing)
• Alfred R. Kelman, *The Body Human: The Loving Process—Women*. CBS.

**Outstanding Individual
Achievement in any Area
of Creative Technical Crafts
(Technical direction/ Electronic camerawork)**
• Sanford Bell, Hal Classon, technical directors. Remote: Kent Falls State Park, Danbury, Connecticut. *Guiding Light*. CBS.
• Lawrence Hammond, Nicholas Hutak, Thomas Woods, electronic camera, *All My Children*. ABC.
(Art direction/Scenic design/Set decoration)
• Bob Keene, Graff Lambert, art directors, *The Richard Simmons Show*. Syndicated.
(Lighting direction)
• Everett Melosh, *One Life to Live*. ABC.

(Costume design)
• Nancy Simmons, *The Richard Simmons Show*. Syndicated.

OUTSTANDING INDIVIDUAL ACHIEVEMENT IN CHILDREN'S PROGRAMMING
(Film editing)
• Peter Hammer, Allen Kirkpatrick, *Big Blue Marble*. Syndicated.
(Art direction/Scenic design/ Set decoration)
• Claude Bonniere, art director, "My Mother Was Never a Kid," *ABC Afterschool Special*. ABC.
(Audio)
• Steven J. Palecek, tape sound recordist, "An Orchestra Is a Team, Too!" *CBS Festival of the Lively Arts for Young People*. CBS.
(Makeup and hair design)
• Judi Cooper Sealy, hair designer, "My Mother Was Never a Kid," *ABC Afterschool Special*. ABC.
(Graphic design)
• Ray Favata, Michael J. Smollin, graphic designers, opening animation, *The Great Space Coaster*. Syndicated.

OUTSTANDING RELIGIOUS PROGRAMMING
(Series)
• *Insight*. Ellwood E. Kieser, executive producer. Mike Rhodes and Terry Sweeney, producers. Syndicated.

(No awards were given in the areas of directing, music, technical direction/electronic camerawork, lighting direction, art direction, costume design, film editing, technical director/electronic camera, performers— special classification of outstanding individual achievement, or religious programming for outstanding special or performers.)

SPORTS AWARD WINNERS
OUTSTANDING LIVE SPORTS SERIES
• *NFL Football*. Terry O'Neil, executive producer. Charles H. Milton Ill, senior producer. Michael Burks, David Dinkins, Jr., Sherman Eagan, John Faratis, Ed Goren, Bob Rowe, Perry Smith, Jim Silman, Robert D. Stenner and David Winner, producers. Peter Bleckner, Larry Cavolina, Joe Carolie, Bob Dailey, Bob Dunphy, Robert Fishman, Sandy Grossman, Andy Kindle, John McDonough, Jim Silman and Tony Verna, directors. CBS.

OUTSTANDING LIVE SPORTS SPECIAL
• *NCAA Basketball Championship Final*. Kevin O'Malley, executive producer. Rick Sharp, producer. Robert Fishman, director. CBS.

OUTSTANDING EDITED SPORTS SERIES/ANTHOLOGIES
• *ABC's Wide World of Sports*. Roone Arledge, executive producer. Dennis Lewin, coordinating producer. Chuck Howard, Mike Pearl, Jeff Rube, Brice Weisman, Doug Wilson, Eleanor Sanger Riger, Ken Wolfe, Bob Goodrich, Curt Gowdy, Jr., and Carol Lehti, producers. Craig Janoff, Larry Kamm, Ralph Abraham, Jim Jennett, Joe Aceti, Roger Goodman, Ken Fouts, Chet Forte, Andy Sidaris, directors. ABC.

OUTSTANDING EDITED SPORTS SPECIAL
• *1982 Indianapolis 500*. Roone Arledge, executive producer. Mike Pearl, Bob Goodrich, producers. Chuck Howard, coordinating producer. Larry Kamm, Roger Goodman, directors. ABC.

OUTSTANDING INDIVIDUAL ACHIEVEMENT IN SPORTS PROGRAMMING
(Associate directors)
• Jeff Cohan, Bob Lanning and Ned Simon, *1982 Indianapolis 500*. ABC.
(Writing)
• Steve Roffeld, "The Legend of Jackie Robinson," *Greatest Sports Legends*. Syndicated.
(Cinematographers)
• Ernie Ernst, Hand McElwee, Howard Neef, Steve Sabol, Phil Tuckett, *Sports Illustrated: A Series for Television*. Syndicated.
(Video-tape/Film editors)
• Steve Purcell, *Reggie Jackson*. CBS. Martin Bell, Joe Clark, Finbar Collins, Ron Feszchur, Chuck Gardner, Bruce Giaraffe, Clare Gilmour, Hector Kicilian, M. Schencman, Mike Seigel, Mike Wenig, Tom White, *1982 Indianapolis 500*. ABC.
(Technical/Engineering supervisors)
• James Patterson, Jesse Rineer, Louis Scanna, Arthur Tinn, Philip Wilson, *Super Bowl XVI*. CBS.
(Technical directors/Electronic camerapersons/Senior video operators)
• Sanford Bell, Robert Brown, Anthony Hlavaty, technical directors. Anthony Filippi, Robert Pieringer, Robert Squittieri, senior video operators. James Murphy,

Neil McCaffrey, Steve Gorsuch, Herman Lang, Barry Drago, Joseph Sokota, Frank McSpedon, George Rothweiler, Jeffrey Pollack, George Naeder, George Graffeo, Thomas McCarthy, Sigmund Meyers, Sol Bress, James McCarthy, Hans Singer, Walter Soucy, electronic camerapersons, *1982 Daytona 500.* CBS.
• John Allen, technical director. Mike Michales, senior video operator. John Morreale, Frank Melchiore, Diane Cates, John Dukewich, Evan Baker, Mike Freedman, Sal Folino, Warren Cress, Dan Langford, Dale Welsh, electronic camerapersons, *Sugar Bowl.* ABC.
Gene Affrunti, John Figer, Rich Gelber, Wink Gunther, technical directors. John Monteleone, senior video operator. Mort Levin, F. Merklein, J. Sapienza, A. Best, John Cordone, D. Spanos, George Montanez, D. Lamothe, Jack Cronin, J. Woodle, A. Demamos, R. Westline, J. Schafer, Tony Gambino, Kenneth Sanborn, R. Wolff, Phil Fontana, A. Petter, R. Hammond, T. Mortellaro, Serf Menduina, W. Sullivan, R. Bernstein, S. Madjanski, J. Stefanoni, electronic camerapersons, *New York Marathon.* ABC.
• Wink Gunther, Chet Mazurek, technical directors. Cyril Tywang, Ken Amow, senior video operators. A. Petter, W. Sullivan, Steve Nikifor, J. Morreale, R. Hammond, A. DeRosa, Joe Cotugno, Jesse Kohn, Andy Armentani, Jack Savoy, Gene Wood, Jack Dorfman, Tom O'Connell, Joe Stefanoni, Frank Melchiorre, Mort Levin, Joe Sapienza, Serf Menduina, Gary Donatelli, Steve Wolff, electronic camerapersons. *1982 Indianapolis 500.* ABC.
(Senior audio engineers)
• Jack Brandes, Jim Davis, Jack Hughes, Norm Kiernan, Morley Lang, *U.S. Open.* ABC.
(Graphics)
• Peggy Hughes, *NCAA College Football.* ABC.
• James W. Grau, *Super Bowl XVI Show Opening Title Sequences.* CBS.

OUTSTANDING SPORTS PERSONALITY— ANALYST
• John Madden. CBS.

OUTSTANDING SPORTS PERSONALITY—HOST
• Jim McKay. ABC.

SPECIAL CLASSIFICATION OF OUTSTANDING PROGRAM (Programs)
• *Reggie Jackson.* CBS.
• *The Baseball Bunch.* Larry Parker, executive producer. Jody Shapiro, Gary Cohen, producers. Syndicated.
• *ABC Sportsbeat.* (No individuals noted.) ABC.

SPECIAL CLASSIFICATION FOR INDIVIDUAL ACHIEVEMENT (Individuals)
• *Racecam at the Daytona 500.* Jim Harrington, executive producer. Robert D. Stenner, producer. Robert Fishman, director. Walter Pile, field technical manager. John Porter, Peter Larsson, David Curtis. engineers. George Graffeo, cameraman. CBS.

NEWS & DOCUMENTARY AWARD WINNERS
OUTSTANDING COVERAGE OF A SINGLE BREAKING NEWS STORY
• "Disaster on the Potomac," *ABC News Nightline.* William Lord, executive producer. Stuart Schwartz, senior producer. Ted Koppel, anchorman. ABC.
• "New Mexico's Yates Oil Company," *CBS Evening News with Dan Rather.* Steve Kroft, producer. Steve Kroft, reporter/correspondent. CBS.
• "Personal Note/Beirut," *ABC World News Tonight.* John Boylan, producer. Peter Jennings, reporter/correspondent. ABC.
• "Linda Down's Marathon," *ABC's World News This Morning.* Peter Heller, producer. Fred Wymore, reporter/correspondent. ABC.

OUTSTANDING COVERAGE OF A CONTINUING NEWS STORY
• *The Paterson Project,* Howard Husock, producer. Scott Simon, reporter/correspondent. PBS.
• "Coverage of American Unemployment," *CBS Evening News with Dan Rather.* Rita Braver, David Browning, Quentin Neufeld, Terry Martin, David Gelber, producers. Bruce Morton, Jerry Bowen, Terry Drinkwater, Ed Rabel, Ray Brady, correspondents. CBS.

Outstanding Background/Analysis of a Single Current Story
(Programs)

• *Chrysler: Once upon a Time ... and Now.* Shelby Newhouse, producer. Andrew Kokas, reporter/correspondent. PBS.
From the Ashes ... Nicaragua Today. Helena Solberg Ladd, Glen Silber, producers. PBS.
"Guatemala," *CBS Reports.* Martin Smith, producer. Ed Rabel, reporter/correspondent. CBS.
• "College Sports, The Money Game," *NBC Nightly News.* M.L. Flynn, Paul Hazzard, Barry Hohlfelder, producers. Bob Jamieson, coproducer. Bob Jamieson, reporter/correspondent. NBC.
• "'Tanks' — A Few Minutes with Andy Rooney," *60 Minutes.* Jane Bradford, producer. Andrew A. Rooney, reporter/correspondent. CBS.
• "Welcome to Palermo," *60 Minutes.* William McClure, producer. Harry Reasoner, reporter/ correspondent. CBS.

Outstanding Interview/Interviewer(s)

• "The Palestinian Viewpoint," *ABC News Nightline.* Bob Jordan, producer. Ted Koppel, interviewer. ABC.
• *The Barbara Walters Special.* Beth Poison, producer. Barbara Walters, interviewer. ABC.
• "In the Belly of the Beast," *60 Minutes.* Monika Jensen, producer. Ed Bradley, interviewer. CBS.

Special Classification for Outstanding Program Achievement

• *Vietnam Requiem.* Jonas McCord, William Couturie, producers. ABC.
• "It Didn't Have to Happen," *60 Minutes.* Norman Gorin, producer. Morley Safer, correspondent. CBS.

Outstanding Informational, Cultural, or Historical Programming

• *Here's Looking at You, Kid.* Andrew McGuire, producer. PBS.
• *The Taj Mahal.* James M. Messenger, Stuart Sillery, producers. PBS.
• "Eclectic: a Profile of Quincy Jones," *Sunday Morning.* Brett Alexander, producer. Billy Taylor, reporter/ correspondent. CBS.
• "Lena," *60 Minutes.* Jeanne Solomon, producer. Ed Bradley, reporter/

correspondent. CBS.
• "Sid Caesar," *20/20.* Betsy Osha, producer. Dick Schaap, reporter/correspondent. ABC.

Outstanding Investigative Journalism
(Programs)

• *Frank Terpil: Confessions of a Dangerous Man.* David Fanning, producer. Antony Thomas, reporter/correspondent. PBS.

Outstanding Investigative Journalism
(Segments)

• "The Nazi Connection," *60 Minutes.* Ira Rosen, producer. Mike Wallace, reporter/correspondent. CBS.
• "Air Force Surgeon," *60 Minutes.* Tom Bettag, producer. Morley Safer, reporter/correspondent. CBS.

Outstanding Individual Achievement in News and Documentary Programming
(Writers)

• Sharon Blair Brysac, Perry Wolff, *Juilliard and Beyond: A Life in Music.* CBS.
• Charles Kuralt, "Cicada Invasion," *CBS Evening News with Dan Rather.* CBS.
(Directors)
• Jonas McCord, William Couturie, *Vietnam Requiem.* ABC.
• Bill Jersey, *Children of Violence.* PBS.
(Cinematographers)
• Norris Brock, "Egypt: Quest for Eternity," *National Geographic Special.* PBS.
• Arnie Serlin, *The Taj Mahai.* PBS.
• James Deckard, James Lipscomb, "Polar Bear Alert," *National Geographic Special.* PBS.
(Electronic camerapersons: Videographers)
• David Green, cameraperson, "Guerillas in Usulatan," *CBS Evening News with Dan Rather.* CBS.
• George Fridrick, electronic camera, *Along Route 30.* NBC.
(Sound)
• Simon Jones, Mike Lonsdale, David Moshlak, Kim Ornitz, film recordists. Rudy Boyer, Ken Blaylock, Jack Gray, Bill Barry, Jeffrey Cree, video recordists. Jonathan M. Lory, Tom Glazner, Kathleen Jalbert, Morley Lang, Don V. Scholtes, Hesh Q. Yarmark, audio post production.

Roy Carch, Al James, post production —
sound effects. Alan Berliner, Seymour
Hymowitz, Frank Martinez, Robert
Sandbo, sound editors. Tom Fleischman,
rerecording mixer, *FDR*. ABC.
• Tom Cohen, sound recordist, *The
Campaign*. PBS.
**(Video-tape editors, video-tape post
production editors)**
• Thomas Micklas, video-tape editor, "Ice
Sculptor," *CBS Evening News with Dan
Rather*. CBS.
• Anthony Ciccimarro, Kathy Hardigan,
Don Orrico, Matty Powers, video-tape edi-
tors, *The Man Who Shot the Pope: A Study
in Terrorism*. NBC.
**(Film editors and film post production
editors)**
• James Flanagan, Nils Rasmussen,
William Longo, Walter Essenfeld, film
editors, *FDR*. ABC.
• Nobuko Oganesoff, film editor, *Juilliard
and Beyond: A Life in Music*. CBS.
• Bob Brady, film editor, *The Campaign*.
PBS.
**(Graphic designers, electronic graphics,
graphic illustrators, electronic and film
animation)**
• David Millman, graphic artist illustrator,
"The Cuban Missile Crisis," *ABC News
Nightline*. ABC.
• Rebecca Allen, graphic designer, *Walter
Cronkite's Universe*. CBS.
(Music composers)
• James G. Pirie, music composer/
conductor, *Alaska: Story of a Dream*.
Syndicated.

INTERNATIONAL AWARD WINNERS
DOCUMENTARY
• *Charters Pour L'Enfer (Charters to
Hell)*, Societe National de Television
Francaise – 1, France.

PERFORMING ARTS
• *Sweeney Todd: Scenes from the Making
of a Musical*, London Weekend
Television, United Kingdom.

POPULAR ARTS
• *Vinicius Para Criancas or Carca de Noe
(Noah's Ark)*, Teve Globo, Ltds., Brazil.

DRAMA
• *A Town Like Alice*, Mariner Films and
Channel 7, Australia.

FOUNDER'S AWARD
• Michael Landon

SPECIAL AWARDS
**OUTSTANDING ACHIEVEMENT
IN THE SCIENCE OF TELEVISION
ENGINEERING**
• Bosch Fernseh
• British Broadcasting Corporation,
Research Department
• Arthur C. Clarke
• Eastman Kodak Company
• Fuji Photo Film Co., Ltd.
• Rank Cintel Limited

**OUTSTANDING ACHIEVEMENT
IN ENGINEERING DEVELOPMENT**
• Hal Collins for his contributions to the
art and development of video-tape editing.
• *Dubner Computer Systems, Inc.* and *ABC*
for the Dubner CBG-2 electronic character
and background generator.
(Citation)
• *Chapman Studio Equipment* for the
development of crane systems.

**N.A.T.A.S. NATIONAL AWARD
FOR COMMUNITY SERVICE**
• *The Klan*, WTHR-TV, Indianapolis,
Indiana.

A.T.A.S. GOVERNORS AWARD
• Hallmark Cards, Inc., for the Hallmark
Hall of Fame.

N.A.T.A.S. TRUSTEES AWARD
• Walter Cronkite

An X-Rated but *Cheers*-ful Event

Cheers, in its first season, may have been ranked a lowly 74th in the list of 98 shows in prime time, but it had high hopes for the Emmys. The NBC sitcom about a Boston bar run by a former Red Sox pitcher and recovering alcoholic scored 13 nominations at the outset. But how good was it really in terms of being able to take on such established champs as *Taxi* and *M*A*S*H*? *Cheers*, in the opinion of the *L.A. Times,* was "the finest comedy on TV ... a perfect blend of cast and material in a half-hour destined to be recalled as one of TV's best ever."

At the awards ceremony, *Cheers* scored a grand slam plus one when it claimed five trophies, including Outstanding Comedy Series and statuettes for its graphic design, writing, director James Burrows, and best actress Shelley Long. Long is an alumna of Chicago's Second City improvisational theater where she cultivated her performance skills while still in her mid-20s. Now, at age 33, she played *Cheers*'s brainy but bubble-headed waitress whose frustrating love-hate, platonic-romantic relationship with the pub's owner (portrayed by Ted Danson) was one of the most seductive aspects of the show.

While up at the podium, accepting her statuette, Long deferred to costar Danson, a losing nominee, thoughtfully, saying, "No actress could ask for a better partner."

NBC's *Hill Street Blues* received 17 nominations, four less than its record-setting number of the previous two years, but again it won six awards, including Outstanding Drama Series and trophies for its director, film editor, film sound editor, and film sound mixer. The

Shelley Long was hailed as best actress for Cheers, *the new Outstanding Comedy Series called "one of TV's best ever."*

sixth award went to first-time scriptwriter David Milch, a former creative writing professor at Yale University. Milch's victory was especially impressive since the category was comprised exclusively of such veteran *HSB* writers as creator Steven Bochco.

NBC had been in last place among the Big Three for eight years in a row. But now Emmys night was suddenly proving to be an NBC romp, thus vindicating the network for its stubborn commitment to quality programming as part of a long-term strategy to pick up ratings points.

Another NBC series in its freshman season, *St. Elsewhere* (described by the *L.A. Times* as a "not unflawed medical drama of rare intelligence and humanity") was ranked a lowly 88th in the Nielsens, but was potentially a big Emmy winner, having started out with 10 nominations. It did not do as well as expected, but it at least took three awards, including one for lead actor Ed Flanders as the hospital chief. The other two went to supporting guest stars James Coco and Doris Roberts, who worked together years earlier on Broadway in *The Last of the Red Hot Lovers* and now were cast opposite each other, noted the *L.A. Times*, "as an impoverished couple whose love and need for one another took precedence over an operation that would have meant separation."

Accepting her award, Roberts said, "Oh, I'm so glad I had my nails done!" Suddenly, then, she became serious, her voice quivered, and she mentioned her husband, William, who had died only a few weeks earlier. "It's for him and everybody else who believed," she said, holding up her trophy triumphantly. Coco's acceptance was much less dramatic by comparison. "I'm so glad we both won," he said.

NBC was not quite so loyal to all its lower-rated shows, particularly one that wasn't its offspring originally. "If NBC was bolstered by its landslide of Emmy wins," wrote *The Washington Post*, "it was humiliated by the three Emmy awards that went to *Taxi*, which the network canceled after a four-year, multi-Emmy-winning run." *Taxi* had actually been on NBC for only a year — its previous three seasons were on ABC — so when the show failed after both networks gave it a try, arguably the wrong one took the heat, which came from cast member Judd Hirsch.

Hirsch was one of three *Taxi* actors honored this year with performance awards, the other two being supporting stars Christopher Lloyd and Carol Kane, both repeat winners from last year. Hirsch made a reference to his own previous win when he picked up his new one for best actor, and said, "I'd like to take this thing and shove it right alongside the one I won in 1981!"

Instead of giving an acceptance speech ("There are people I don't wish to thank at all tonight," Hirsch said), he publicly petitioned NBC to extend *Taxi*'s ride even longer. "When a show like this is so honored," he said, "if you can't get it out of your minds ... and you got to keep giving some kind of laurels to us ... then you should really put us back on the air." He addressed his next remarks personally to NBC president Grant Tinker, who was seated in the audience. "We're ready, Grant," Hirsch said. "We'll come back anytime you ask." The ploy failed. NBC chose not to renew the series and *Taxi* came to the end of the road.

NBC's sweep was so complete that it ended up taking 21 of the 29 Emmys bestowed on the air, virtually shutting out number one-ranked CBS, which took only one. The *L.A. Herald Examiner* noted: "To compound CBS's humiliation, the single award that it won before the TV audience was for Tyne Daly as best leading actress in a drama series — *Cagney & Lacey* — which was canceled by the network in May."

Cohosts were Joan Rivers and Eddie Murphy: "What shocker would they utter next?"

Unlike *Taxi*, there was some hope for *Cagney & Lacey*, however, since the network was still negotiating with its stars about the possibility of trying out seven more episodes the following season. Since nothing was definite yet, Daly chose not to say anything in her own acceptance speech and instead only thanked CBS "for having us on the network." Ultimately, it was her award that helped convince the network that the unconventional show about two sensi-

Former acting partners Doris Roberts and James Coco reunited for their prize-winning guest roles on St. Elsewhere.

tive female cops must go on. Two years later CBS was well rewarded when *Cagney & Lacey* was voted Outstanding Drama Series, finally toppling *Hill Street Blues* from its four-year, king-of-the-hill reign over the category.

The year's Outstanding Variety or Music Program was *Motown 25: Yesterday, Today, Forever*, a surprise choice that so overwhelmed coexecutive producer Suzanne de Passe that she playfully told reporters backstage, "I'm having a heart attack!" The writing award went to *SCTV Network*, which was canceled by NBC, but subsequently picked up by the premium cable channel Cinemax. The *L.A. Times* called the Second City troupe's irreverent and innovative comedy series "often brilliant and miles above the crowd. Well, most of the crowd, but not *Motown 25*."

NBC was also lauded for one of its most unusual programs, *Special Bulletin*, which was declared Outstanding Drama Special. Coproducer and cowriter Edward Zwick accepted the statuette saying that his victory underscored the TV academy's commitment to programs that can be "unconventional, uncompromising, and even political." *Special Bulletin* was certainly unconven-

tional. It starred *St. Elsewhere*'s Emmy-winner Ed Flanders in a brilliant and horrifying drama about a fictitious nuclear disaster in Charleston, S.C., as viewed through the lens of television news show. The program had such a realistic look and feel to it that NBC, fearing a *War of the Worlds*-like panic, weakened its full dramatic impact by running frequent, intrusive reminders that it was only a drama. *Special Bulletin* won four Emmys in all, including honors for its writing, video-tape editing, and camerawork. Said its executive producer Don Ohlmeyer as he accepted the prize for drama special: "This is the first time *Special Bulletin* has been on television without a disclaimer."

ABC dominated the miniseries competition with two strong entries — *The Winds of War* and *The Thorn Birds*. *Winds* was the favorite, with 13 nominations, but, as the *Herald Examiner* noted, Emmy "viewers saw a total shutout in the major awards for the most-touted show of last season." The $40-million, 18-hour drama based on the Herman Wouk bestseller about the tempest building up to World War II ended up with only three awards — for cinematography, costumes, and art direction.

The Thorn Birds was a four-night, 10-hour adaptation of the Colleen McCullough bestseller set in the Australian outback that featured Richard Chamberlain in the controversial role of a priest torn between his religious vow of celibacy and his forbidden love for a woman. After *Roots*, *The Thorn Birds* was the highest-rated miniseries ever aired and received six Emmys in all, including ones for its art director, makeup artists, film editors, and the two supporting stars, Jean Simmons and Richard Kiley, who played the married owners of a sheep station. Chamberlain was favored to be named best actor. Not only was his performance considered first rate, but there was a old injustice to redress this year: He had been passed over once before, in 1981, when it was expected he'd take the best actor accolade for *Shogun*. In a major upset, however, Chamberlain lost again, this time to Tommy Lee Jones, who played death row convict Gary Gilmore in the dramatization of Norman Mailer's best-seller *The Executioner's Song*.

Ann-Margret had been considered a shoo-in for best actress in *Who Will Love My Children?*, a made-for-TV film based on the real story of a terminally ill Iowa farm wife who tries to find homes for her ten children before she dies. But another upset was in the making. The trophy went instead to 76-year-old screen icon Barbara Stanwyck for her portrayal of a wealthy matriarch in *The Thorn Birds*. The past Emmy winner was responsible for what the *L.A. Times* called "the evening's most touching moment" when she deferred to Ann-Margret in her acceptance speech. "She gave us a film last season in which she gave one of the finest, most beautiful performances I have ever seen," Stanwyck said up at the podium, then added, "Ann-Margret, you were superb." Out in the audience, the losing nominee buried her head in the shoulder of husband Roger Smith and cried.

Of all the upsets in the category, none was greater than that scored by *Nicholas Nickleby*, the Royal Shakespeare Company's four-part adaptation of the Charles Dickens classic about a young man's struggles to protect his family. *Nickleby* won only one award, but it was the category clincher — best limited series — that no doubt made all three major networks regret they had turned the program down. The *L.A. Times* was among those that had been rooting for the syndicated drama to take the top prize all along, not only because of its artistic value but "because its slow evo-lution across four nights was so demanding of audiences accustomed to entertainment in jabs and spurts."

All the surprises of the Emmy Awards night were surpassed by the performances of those in charge. The *Herald Examiner* noted: "The program hosts, Eddie Murphy and Joan Rivers, recovered from a shaky beginning to create a certain suspense: What shocker would they utter next?"

Rivers was the more outlandish of the duo. She changed clothes nine times throughout the broadcast, each time revealing a gown more outrageous than the one before. "Like this?" she asked the audience at one point, modeling one of them. "I just got it off the rack, which is what Joan Crawford used to say about her daughter."

Over the course of the night, Rivers uttered such forbidden prime-time phrases as "God damn" and made fun of herpes, gays, hookers, her own sexual ability, and U.S. Secretary of the Interior James Watt. ("Is he an idiot?" she howled about Watt to Murphy.) At her bawdiest, she struck out at *Dynasty* star Joan Collins, saying that the TV vixen "has had more hands up her dress than the Muppets." Offstage, in the meantime, her humor was lighting up broadcaster NBC's switchboards across America.

After the ceremony, reporters ambushed Grant Tinker for his reaction to Rivers's performance. "I don't think the world will stop," he said, calmly. "As some wise man once said, 'It's only television.'"

It may have been an evening full of irreverent remarks, but more reverent ones were also spoken — in honor of Lucille Ball, Milton Berle, screenwriter Paddy Chayefsky, producer Norman Lear, journalist Edward R. Murrow, CBS founder William S. Paley, and NBC founder David Sarnoff. They had the honor of becoming the first inductees into the new A.T.A.S. Hall of Fame, which would be the subject of a separate broadcast to be aired in spring 1984.

DAYTIME AWARDS

On the occasion of their 10th anniversary, the daytime awards were given an empty present. For the first time since their inception, the festivities would not be televised. NBC, which last year boycotted N.A.T.A.S.'s sports and news & documentary awards, declined to air the daytime show this year, said the *L.A. Times*, "apparently as part of an ongoing dispute with the academy over how it administers the awards."

It was the daytime ratings leader of the past five years, ABC, that won the most nominations and prizes. The network's soap opera *All My Children* started out with 15 nods and won four trophies, including laurels for supporting actor Darnell Williams (who played Jessie Hubbard), as well as its technical and design teams. Dorothy Lyman as *All My Children*'s "tacky" Opal Gardner and Susan Lucci as the bitchy temptress Erica Kane whom soap opera lovers loved to hate were locked in a heated contest for the the fourth prize — best actress. Lucci pounded her fist on the table in rage last year when she lost for the third time. This year when the award went to Lyman, "she stormed from the room in tears," *People* reported, describing a performance eerily similar to one of Lucci's famous on-screen tantrums.

In its latest incarnation, Pyramid came back again triumphant.

One Life to Live had the second most nominations — 14 — but ended up with only two statuettes — for best actor Robert Woods (who played Bo Buchanan) and the show's director.

Ryan's Hope won the prize for writing and supporting actress Louise Shaffer (as Rae Woodard).

CBS's 1975 winner of the best daytime drama series award — *The Young and the Restless* — finally reclaimed that distinction this year.

After spending a few years in syndication, *The $20,000 Pyramid* was picked up by CBS as *The New $25,000 Pyramid* and featured Dick Clark as its latest host, replacing Bill Cullen. Soon afterward, *Pyramid* was again named best game show, the first time it held the title since it was canceled by ABC in 1980. CBS had aired — and axed — the show once before, in 1976, the same year it won the top program Emmy for the first time.

The PBS series on home renovations, *This Old House,* was declared Outstanding Talk or Service Series. Phil Donahue started yet another winning streak in the host category by repeating his win of last year. Other hosting honors went to Betty White for the game show *Just Men!* and to Leslie Uggams for overseeing the "variety series" *Fantasy* (which was actually a game show showering contestants with prizes that made their fantasies come true). The talk/variety series award went to *The Merv Griffin Show*.

In the competition for children's programming, the series prizes went to *Sesame Street* (best informational/instructional show) and the *Smurfs* (best entertainment series) while *ABC Afterschool Specials* "Sometimes I Don't Love My Mother" and the highly acclaimed, "The Woman Who Willed a Miracle" swept the categories for specials. "Miracle," which dealt with the story of a severely retarded boy who suddenly demonstrates hidden intelligence, also won a Peabody Award and was named Emmy's Outstanding Entertainment Special. It also earned two other prizes — performance honors for star Cloris Leachman and a writing award.

Because of NBC's refusal to air the ceremony, the daytime event, staged at the Imperial Ballroom of New York's Sheraton Center, was held in the evening for the very first time.

SPORTS AWARDS

Responding to NBC's boycott of the competition last year, the N.A.T.A.S. sports awards committee refined the screening and voting procedure, which satisfied the network enough to rejoin the competition. The overhaul was followed by what committee chairman Dick Auerbach called "a record number of entries by all three networks and independents."

The ceremony was held on November 30, 1983, at the Sheraton Centre Hotel in New York. NBC won both awards for sports specials, with its World Series broadcasts prevailing in the live category and its coverage of Wimbledon tennis taking the honors for best edited special. Among the series awards, the NFL games on CBS won for live coverage while *The American Sportsman* was named the best edited series.

The American Sportsman had a sweep this year, claiming five additional awards, including a writing prize for a segment on actor William Holden's work to save the vanishing species of Africa and three more for its breakthrough microwave transmission from atop Mt. Everest.

The N.A.T.A.S. newsletter identified "this year's big winner" as NBC's Outstanding Personality/ Host Dick Enberg, who was presented the prize by longtime friend Curt Gowdy. John Madden was named best sports analyst for the second year in a row.

NEWS & DOCUMENTARY AWARDS

Between 1981 and 1983, the news awards switched over gradually to a calendar year eligiblity period, causing a ceremony to be skipped.

1982–83

For prime-time programs telecast between July 1, 1982, and June 30, 1983. The prime-time ceremony was broadcast on NBC from the Pasadena Civic Auditorium on September 25, 1983. Creative arts banquet held on September 13, 1983. Daytime awards were bestowed on June 6 1983, for programs aired between March 6, 1982, to March 5, 1983. News & documentary awards for 1983 were presented on August 30, 1984. The sports awards were presented November 30, 1983, for programs aired between July 16, 1982, and July 15, 1983.

PRIME-TIME PROGRAM AWARDS
OUTSTANDING DRAMA SERIES
• *Hill Street Blues.* Steven Bochco, executive producer. Gregory Hoblit, co-executive producer. Anthony Yerkovich, supervising producer. David Anspaugh, Scott Brazil, producers. NBC.
Cagney & Lacey. Barney Rosenzweig, executive producer. Harry R. Sherman, Richard M. Rosenbloom, supervising producers. April Smith, Joseph Stern, Terry Louise Fisher, Steve Brown, producers. CBS.
Fame. William Blinn, executive producer. Mel Swope, producer. NBC.
Magnum, P.I. Donald P. Bellisario, executive producer. Douglas Green, Joel Rogosin, supervising producers. Chas. Floyd Johnson, supervising producers. Rick Weaver, Reuben Leder, coproducers. CBS.
St. Elsewhere. Bruce Paltrow, executive producer. Mark Tinker, John Masius, John Falsey, Joshua Brand, producers. NBC.

OUTSTANDING COMEDY SERIES
• *Cheers.* James Burrows, Glen Charles, Les Charles, executive producers. Ken Levine, David Isaacs, coproducers. NBC.
Buffalo Bill. Bernie Brillstein, Tom Patchett, Jay Tarses, executive producers. Dennis Klein, Carol Gary, producers. NBC.
*M*A*S*H.* Burt Metcalfe, executive producer. John Rappaport, supervising producer. Dan Wilcox, Thad Mumford, producers. CBS.

Newhart. Barry Kemp, executive producer. Sheldon Bull, producer. CBS.
Taxi. James L. Brooks, Stan Daniels, Ed. Weinberger, executive producers. Ken Estin, Sam Simon, Richard Sakai, producers. NBC.

Outstanding Limited Series
• *Nicholas Nickleby.* Colin Callender, producer. Syndicated.
Smiley's People. Jonathan Powell, producer. Syndicated.
The Thorn Birds. David L. Wolper, Edward Lewis, executive producers. Stan Margulies, producer. ABC.
To Serve Them All My Days, Masterpiece Theatre. Ken Riddington, producer. PBS.
The Winds of War. Dan Curtis, producer. ABC.

Outstanding Drama Special
• *Special Bulletin.* Don Ohlmeyer, executive producer. Marshall Herskovitz, Edward Zwick, producers. NBC.
Little Gloria ... Happy at Last. Edgar J. Scherick, Scott Rudin, executive producers. David Nicksay, Justine Heroux, producers. NBC.
M.A.D.D.: Mothers Against Drunk Drivers. David Moessinger, executive producer. Douglas Benton, supervising producer. Michael Braverman, producer. NBC.
The Scarlet Pimpernel. Mark Shelmerdine, executive producer. David Conroy, producer. CBS.
Who Will Love My Children? Paula Levenback, Wendy Riche, producers. ABC.

Outstanding Variety, Music, or Comedy Program
• *Motown 25: Yesterday, Today, Forever.* Suzanne de Passe, executive producer. Don Mischer, Buz Kohan, producers. Suzanne Coston, producer for Motown. NBC.
Kennedy Center Honors: A Celebration of the Performing Arts. George Stevens, Jr., Nick Vanoff, producers. CBS.
SCTV Network. Andrew Alexander, senior executive producer. Andrew Alexander, Len Stuart, Jack E. Rhodes, Doug Holtby, executive producers. Patrick Whitley, supervising producer. Patrick Whitley, Nancy Geller, Don Novello, producers. NBC.
The Tonight Show Starring Johnny Carson. Fred DeCordova, producer. Peter Lassally, coproducer. Johnny Carson, host. NBC.
37th Annual Tony Awards. Alexander H. Cohen, executive producer. Hildy Parks, producer. Roy A. Somlyo, coproducer. CBS.

Outstanding Classical Program in the Performing Arts
(Winner)
• *Pavarotti in Philadelphia: La Boheme.* Margarett Anne Everitt, executive producer. Clemente D'Alessio, producer. Luciano Pavarotti, star. PBS.

Outstanding Informational Series
(Winner)
• *The Barbara Walters Specials.* Beth Polson, producer. Barbara Walters, host. ABC.

Outstanding Informational Special
(Winner)
• *The Body Human: The Living Code.* Thomas W. Moore, executive producer. Robert E. Fuisz, M.D., Alfred R. Kelman, producers. Charles A. Bangert, Franklin Getchell, Nancy Smith, coproducers. CBS.

Outstanding Animated Program
(Winner)
• *Ziggy's Gift.* Lena Tabori, executive producer. Richard Williams, Tom Wilson, Lena Tabori, producers. ABC.

Outstanding Children's Program
(Winner)
• *Big Bird in China.* Jon Stone, executive producer. David Liu, Kuo Bao-Xiang, Xu Ja-Cha, producers. NBC.

PERFORMANCE, DIRECTING, AND WRITING
Outstanding Lead Actor in a Drama Series
• Ed Flanders, *St. Elsewhere.* NBC.
William Daniels, *St. Elsewhere.* NBC.
John Forsythe, *Dynasty.* ABC.
Tom Selleck, *Magnum, P.I.* CBS.
Daniel J. Travanti, *Hill Street Blues.* NBC.

Outstanding Lead Actress in a Drama Series
• Tyne Daly, *Cagney & Lacey.* CBS.
Debbie Allen, *Fame.* NBC.
Linda Evans, *Dynasty.* ABC.
Sharon Gless, *Cagney & Lacey.* CBS.
Veronica Hamel, *Hill Street Blues.* NBC.

OUTSTANDING LEAD ACTOR IN A COMEDY SERIES
• Judd Hirsch, *Taxi*. NBC.
Alan Alda, *M*A*S*H*. CBS.
Dabney Coleman, *Buffalo Bill*. NBC.
Ted Danson, *Cheers*. NBC.
Robert Guillaume, *Benson*. ABC.

OUTSTANDING LEAD ACTRESS IN A COMEDY SERIES
• Shelley Long, *Cheers*. NBC.
Nell Carter, *Gimme a Break!* NBC.
Mariette Hartley, *Goodnight, Beantown*. CBS.
Swoosie Kurtz, *Love, Sidney*. NBC.
Rita Moreno, *9 to 5*. ABC.
Isabel Sanford, *The Jeffersons*. CBS.

OUTSTANDING LEAD ACTOR IN A LIMITED SERIES OR A SPECIAL
• Tommy Lee Jones, *The Executioner's Song*. NBC.
Robert Blake, *Blood Feud*. Syndicated.
Richard Chamberlain, *The Thorn Birds*. ABC.
Sir Alec Guinness, *Smiley's People*. Syndicated.
Roger Rees, *Nicholas Nickleby*. Syndicated.

OUTSTANDING LEAD ACTRESS IN A LIMITED SERIES OR A SPECIAL
• Barbara Stanwyck, *The Thorn Birds*. ABC.
Ann-Margret, *Who Will Love My Children?* ABC.
Rosanna Arquette, *The Executioner's Song*. NBC.
Mariette Hartley, *M.A.D.D.: Mothers Against Drunk Drivers*. NBC.
Angela Lansbury, *Little Gloria ... Happy at Last*. NBC.

OUTSTANDING SUPPORTING ACTOR IN A DRAMA SERIES
• James Coco, *St. Elsewhere*. NBC.
Ed Begley, Jr., *St. Elsewhere*. NBC.
Michael Conrad, *Hill Street Blues*. NBC.
Joe Spano, *Hill Street Blues*. NBC.
Bruce Weitz, *Hill Street Blues*. NBC.

OUTSTANDING SUPPORTING ACTRESS IN A DRAMA SERIES
• Doris Roberts, *St. Elsewhere*. NBC.
Barbara Bosson, *Hill Street Blues*. NBC.
Christina Pickles, *St. Elsewhere*. NBC.
Madge Sinclair, *Trapper John, M.D.* CBS.
Betty Thomas, *Hill Street Blues*. NBC.

OUTSTANDING SUPPORTING ACTOR IN A COMEDY, VARIETY, OR MUSIC SERIES
• Christopher Lloyd, *Taxi*. NBC.
Nicholas Colasanto, *Cheers*. NBC.
Danny DeVito, *Taxi*. NBC.
Harry Morgan, *M*A*S*H*. CBS.
Eddie Murphy, *Saturday Night Live*. NBC.

OUTSTANDING SUPPORTING ACTRESS IN A COMEDY, VARIETY, OR MUSIC SERIES
• Carol Kane, *Taxi*. NBC.
Eileen Brennan, *Private Benjamin*. CBS.
Marla Gibbs, *The Jeffersons*. CBS.
Rhea Perlman, *Cheers*. NBC.
Loretta Swit, *M*A*S*H*. CBS.

OUTSTANDING SUPPORTING ACTOR IN A LIMITED SERIES OR A SPECIAL
• Richard Kiley, *The Thorn Birds*. ABC.
Ralph Bellamy, *The Winds of War*. ABC.
Bryan Brown, *The Thorn Birds*. ABC.
Christopher Plummer, *The Thorn Birds*. ABC.
David Threlfall, *Nicholas Nickleby*. Syndicated.

OUTSTANDING SUPPORTING ACTRESS IN A LIMITED SERIES OR A SPECIAL
• Jean Simmons, *The Thorn Birds*. ABC.
Dame Judith Anderson, *Medea, Kennedy Center Tonight*. PBS.
Polly Bergen, *The Winds of War*. ABC.
Bette Davis, *Little Gloria ... Happy at Last*. NBC.
Piper Laurie, *The Thorn Birds*. ABC.

OUTSTANDING INDIVIDUAL PERFORMANCE IN A VARIETY OR MUSIC PROGRAM
• Leontyne Price, "Leontyne Price, Zubin Mehta and the New York Philharmonic," *Live from Lincoln Center*. PBS.
Carol Burnett, *Texaco Star Theater*. NBC.
Michael Jackson, *Motown 25: Yesterday, Today, Forever*. NBC.
Luciano Pavarotti, "Luciano Pavarotti and the New York Philharmonic," *Live from Lincoln Center*. PBS.
Richard Pryor, *Motown 25: Yesterday, Today, Forever*. NBC.

OUTSTANDING DIRECTING IN A DRAMA SERIES
• Jeff Bleckner, *Hill Street Blues*. NBC.
Marc Daniels, *Fame*. NBC.
Leo Penn, *The Mississippi*. CBS.
Robert Scheerer, *Fame*. NBC.

Outstanding Directing
in a Limited Series or a Special
• John Erman, *Who Will Love My Children?* ABC.
Dan Curtis, *The Winds of War*. ABC.
Daryl Duke, *The Thorn Birds*. ABC.
Simon Langton, *Smiley's People*. Syndicated.
Edward Zwick, *Special Bulletin*. NBC.

Outstanding Directing
in a Comedy Series
• James Burrows, *Cheers*. NBC.
Alan Alda, *M*A*S*H*. CBS.
Jim Drake, *Buffalo Bill*. NBC.
Burt Metcalfe, *M*A*S*H*. CBS.
Tom Patchett, *Buffalo Bill*. NBC.
Bob Sweeney, *The Love Boat*. ABC.

Outstanding Directing
in a Variety or Music Program
• Dwight Hemion, *Sheena Easton ... Act One*. NBC.
Emile Ardolino, "Stravinsky and Balanchine—Genius Has a Birthday!" *Lincoln Center Special*. PBS.
John Blanchard, John Bell, *SCTV Network*. NBC.
Kirk Browning, "Zubin Mehta Conducts Beethoven's Ninth with the New York Philharmonic," *Live from Lincoln Center*. PBS.
Don Mischer, *Motown 25: Yesterday, Today, Forever*. NBC.
Marty Pasetta, *The 55th Annual Academy Awards*. ABC.

Outstanding Writing
in a Drama Series
• David Milch, *Hill Street Blues*. NBC.
Steven Bochco, Anthony Yerkovich, Jeffrey Lewis, *Hill Street Blues*. NBC.
Karen Hall, *Hill Street Blues*. NBC.
Michael Wagner, David Milch, teleplay. Steven Bochco, Anthony Yerkovich, Jeffrey Lewis, story, *Hill Street Blues*. NBC.
Anthony Yerkovich, David Milch, Karen Hall, teleplay. Steven Bochco, Anthony Yerkovich, Jeffrey Lewis, story, *Hill Street Blues*. NBC.

Outstanding Writing
in a Comedy Series
• Glen Charles, Les Charles, *Cheers*. NBC.
Ken Estin, *Taxi*. NBC.
Ken Levine, David Isaacs, *Cheers*. NBC.
David Lloyd, *Cheers*. NBC.
Tom Patchett, Jay Tarses, *Buffalo Bill*. NBC.

Outstanding Writing
in a Limited Series or a Special
• Marshall Herskovitz, teleplay. Edward Zwick, Marshall Herskovitz, story, *Special Bulletin*. NBC.
Michael Bortman, *Who Will Love My Children?* ABC.
David Edgar, *Nicholas Nickleby*. Syndicated.
William Hanley, *Little Gloria ... Happy at Last*. NBC.
Norman Mailer, *The Executioner's Song*. NBC.

Outstanding Writing
in a Variety or Music Program
• John Candy, Joe Flaherty, Eugene Levy, Andrea Martin, Martin Short, Dick Blasucci, Paul Flaherty, John McAndrew, Doug Steckler, Bob Dolman, Michael Short, Mary Charlotte Wilcox, *SCTV Network*. NBC.
John Candy, Joe Flaherty, Eugene Levy, Andrea Martin, Martin Short, Dick Blasucci, Paul Flaherty, John McAndrew, Doug Steckler, Bob Dolman, Michael Short, Jeffrey Barron, Mary Charlotte Wilcox, John Hemphill, *SCTV Network*. NBC.
John Candy, Joe Flaherty, Eugene Levy, Andrea Martin, Martin Short, Dick Blasucci, Paul Flaherty, John McAndrew, Doug Steckler, Bob Dolman, Michael Short, Jeffrey Barron, Mary Charlotte Wilcox, Dave Thomas, *SCTV Network*. NBC.
John Candy, Joe Flaherty, Eugene Levy, Andrea Martin, Martin Short, Dick Blasucci, Paul Flaherty, John McAndrew, Doug Steckler, Bob Dolman, Michael Short, Jeffrey Barron, Mary Charlotte Wilcox, *SCTV Network*. NBC.
John Candy, Joe Flaherty, Eugene Levy, Andrea Martin, Catherine O'Hara, Martin Short, Dick Blasucci, Paul Flaherty, John McAndrew, Doug Steckler, Bob Dolman, Michael Short, Mary Charlotte Wilcox, *SCTV Network*. NBC.

OTHER AWARD WINNERS
Outstanding Music Composition
for a Series
(Dramatic underscore)
• Bruce Broughton, *Dallas*. CBS.

**OUTSTANDING MUSIC COMPOSITION
FOR A LIMITED SERIES OR A SPECIAL
(Dramatic underscore)**
• Billy Goldenberg, *Rage of Angels*. NBC.

OUTSTANDING MUSIC DIRECTION
• Dick Hyman, music director and principal arranger, *Eubie Blake: A Century of Music, Kennedy Center Tonight*. PBS.

OUTSTANDING MUSIC AND LYRICS
• James Di Pasquale, composer. Dory Previn, lyricist, *Two of a Kind, General Electric Theater*. Song: "We'll Win This World." CBS.

OUTSTANDING CHOREOGRAPHY
• Debbie Allen, *Fame*. NBC.

**OUTSTANDING ART DIRECTION
FOR A SERIES**
• John W. Corso, production designer. Frank Grieco, Jr., art director. Robert George Freer, set decorator, *Tales of the Gold Monkey*. ABC.

**OUTSTANDING ART DIRECTION
FOR A LIMITED SERIES OR A SPECIAL**
• Robert MacKichan, art director. Jerry Adams, set decorator, *The Thorn Birds*. ABC.

**OUTSTANDING ART DIRECTION
FOR A VARIETY OR MUSIC PROGRAM**
• Ray Klausen, art director. Michael Corenblith, set decorator, *The 55th Annual Academy Awards*. ABC.

**OUTSTANDING COSTUME DESIGN
FOR A SERIES**
• Theadora Van Runkle, *Wizards and Warriors*. CBS.

**OUTSTANDING COSTUME DESIGN
FOR A LIMITED SERIES OR A SPECIAL**
• Phyllis Dalton, *The Scarlet Pimpernel*. CBS.

OUTSTANDING MAKEUP
• Del Acevedo, *The Thorn Birds*. ABC.

OUTSTANDING HAIRSTYLING
• Edie Panda, *Rosie: The Rosemary Clooney Story*. CBS.

**OUTSTANDING CINEMATOGRAPHY
FOR A SERIES**
• Joseph Biroc, *Casablanca*. NBC.

**OUTSTANDING CINEMATOGRAPHY
FOR A LIMITED SERIES OR A SPECIAL**
• Charles Correll, Stevan Larner, *The Winds of War*. ABC.

**OUTSTANDING TECHNICAL DIRECTION
AND ELECTRONIC CAMERAWORK
FOR A SERIES**
• Heino Ripp, technical director. Mike Bennett, Al Camoin, Jan Kasoff, John Pinto, Maurey Vershore, camerapersons, *Saturday Night Live*. NBC.

**OUTSTANDING TECHNICAL DIRECTION
AND ELECTRONIC CAMERAWORK
FOR A LIMITED SERIES OR A SPECIAL**
• Hank Geving, cameraperson, *Special Bulletin*. NBC.

**OUTSTANDING FILM EDITING
FOR A SERIES**
• Ray Daniels, *Hill Street Blues*. NBC.

**OUTSTANDING FILM EDITING
FOR A LIMITED SERIES OR A SPECIAL**
• C. Timothy O'Meara, *The Thorn Birds*. ABC.

**OUTSTANDING FILM SOUND EDITING
FOR A SERIES**
• Sam Horta, supervising editor. Don Ernst, Avram Gold, Eileen Horta, Constance A. Kazmer, Gary Krivacek, editors, *Hill Street Blues*. NBC.

**OUTSTANDING FILM SOUND EDITING
FOR A LIMITED SERIES OR A SPECIAL**
• Jim Troutman, supervising editor. Dave Caldwell, Paul Clay, Paul Laune, Tony Magro, Richard Raderman, Karen Rasch, Jeff Sandler, William Shenberg, Dan Thomas, Ascher Yates, editors, *The Executioner's Song*. NBC.

**OUTSTANDING FILM SOUND MIXING
FOR A SERIES**
• William B. Marky, production mixer. John B. Asman, William Nicholson, Ken S. Polk, rerecording mixers, *Hill Street Blues*. NBC.

**OUTSTANDING FILM SOUND MIXING
FOR A LIMITED SERIES OR A SPECIAL**
• John Mitchell, production mixer. Gordon L. Day, Stanley A. Wetzel, Howard Wilmarth, rerecording mixers, *The Scarlet and the Black*. CBS.

Susan Lucci (center) in All My Children: *Her frustrating quest for the best actress Emmy became a soap opera all its own.*

OUTSTANDING VIDEO-TAPE EDITING FOR A SERIES
• Larry M. Harris, *The Jeffersons*. CBS.

OUTSTANDING VIDEO-TAPE EDITING FOR A LIMITED SERIES OR A SPECIAL
• Arden Rynew, *Special Bulletin*. NBC.

OUTSTANDING TAPE SOUND MIXING FOR A SERIES
• Frank Kulaga, production. Ken Hahn, postproduction, *The Magic Flute, Dance in America*. PBS.

OUTSTANDING TAPE SOUND MIXING FOR LIMITED SERIES OR A SPECIAL
• Edward J. Greene, preproduction. Ron Estes, production. Carroll Pratt, postproduction, *Sheena Easton ... Act One*. NBC.

OUTSTANDING LIGHTING DIRECTION (ELECTRONIC) FOR A SERIES
• Robert A. Dickinson, lighting consultant. C. Frank Olivas, lighting director, *Solid Gold*. Syndicated.

OUTSTANDING LIGHTING DIRECTION (ELECTRONIC) FOR A LIMITED SERIES OR SPECIAL
• John Rook, lighting designer. Ken Wilcox, Bob Pohle, lighting directors, *Sheena Easton ... Act One*. NBC.

OUTSTANDING INDIVIDUAL ACHIEVEMENT (Costumers)
• Tommy Welsh, costume supervisor. John Napolitano, Paul Vachon, Johannes Nikerk, wardrobe, *The Winds of War*. ABC.
(Graphic design and title sequences)
• James Castle, Bruce Bryant, *Cheers*. NBC.
(Special visual effects)
• Gene Warren Jr., Peter Kleinow, Leslie Huntley, special visual effects. Jackson De Govia, production designer. Michael Minor, art director, *The Winds of War*. ABC.

OUTSTANDING INDIVIDUAL ACHIEVEMENT—INFORMATIONAL PROGRAMMING
• Alfred R. Kelman, Charles Bangert, directors, *The Body Human: The Living Code*. CBS.
• Louis H. Gorfain, Robert E. Fuisz, M.D., writers, *The Body Human: The Living Code*. CBS.

DAYTIME AWARDS

OUTSTANDING DAYTIME DRAMA SERIES
• *The Young and the Restless*. William J. Bell, executive producer. H. Wesley Kenney, executive producer. Edward Scott, producer. CBS.
All My Children. Jacqueline Babbin, producer. ABC.
Days of Our Lives. Betty Corday, executive producer. Al Rabin, supervising executive producer. Patricia Wenig, supervising producer. Ken Corday, producer. NBC.
General Hospital. Gloria Monty, producer. ABC.
One Life to Live. Joseph Stuart, producer. ABC.

OUTSTANDING ACTOR IN A DAYTIME DRAMA SERIES
• Robert Woods, *One Life to Live*. ABC.
Peter Bergman, *All My Children*. ABC.
Stuart Damon, *General Hospital*. ABC.
Anthony Geary, *General Hospital*. ABC.
James Mitchell, *All My Children*. ABC.

OUTSTANDING ACTRESS IN A DAYTIME DRAMA SERIES
• Dorothy Lyman, *All My Children.* ABC.
Leslie Charleson, *General Hospital.* ABC.
Susan Lucci, *All My Children.* ABC.
Erika Slezak, *One Life to Live.* ABC.
Robin Strasser, *One Life to Live.* ABC.

OUTSTANDING ACTOR IN A SUPPORTING ROLE IN A DAYTIME DRAMA SERIES
• Darnell Williams, *All My Children.* ABC.
Anthony Call, *One Life to Live.* ABC.
Al Freeman, Jr., *One Life to Live.* ABC.
David Lewis, *General Hospital.* ABC.
Howard E. Rollins, Jr., *Another World.* NBC.
John Stamos, *General Hospital.* ABC.

OUTSTANDING ACTRESS IN A SUPPORTING ROLE IN A DAYTIME DRAMA SERIES
• Louise Shaffer, *Ryan's Hope.* ABC.
Kim Delaney, *All My Children.* ABC.
Eileen Herlie, *All My Children.* ABC.
Robin Mattson, *General Hospital.* ABC.
Brynn Thayer, *One Life to Live.* ABC.
Marcy Walker, *All My Children.* ABC.

OUTSTANDING DIRECTION FOR A DAYTIME DRAMA SERIES
• Allen Fristoe, Norman Hall, Peter Miner, David Pressman, *One Life to Live.* ABC.
Lawrence Auerbach, Jack Coffey, Sherrel Hoffman, Francesca James, *All My Children.* ABC.
Marlena Laird, Alan Pultz, Phillip Sogard. *General Hospital.* ABC.

OUTSTANDING WRITING FOR A DAYTIME DRAMA SERIES
• Claire Labine, Paul Avila Mayer, Mary Ryan Munisteri, Eugene Price, Judith Pinsker, Nancy Ford, B.K. Perlman, Rory Metcalf, Trent Jones, *Ryan's Hope.* ABC.
Agnes Nixon, Wisner Washam, Lorraine Broderick, Jack Wood, Mary K. Wells, Clarice Blackburn, Carolyn Franz, Elizabeth Wallace, John Saffron, *All My Children.* ABC.
Anne Howard Bailey, A.J. Russell, Leah Laiman, Thom Racina, Jack Turley, Jeanne Glynn, Robert Guza, Jr., Charles Pratt, Jr., Robert Shaw, *General Hospital.* ABC.
Sam Hall, Peggy O'Shea, S. Michael Schnessel, Victor Miller, Don Wallace,

Lanie Bertram, Fred Corke, Craig Carlson, *One Life to Live.* ABC.

OTHER DAYTIME AWARD WINNERS
OUTSTANDING GAME OR AUDIENCE PARTICIPATION SHOW
• *The New $25,000 Pyramid.* Bob Stewart, executive producer. Anne Marie Schmitt, Sande Stewart, producers. CBS.

OUTSTANDING HOST/HOSTESS IN A GAME OR AUDIENCE PARTICIPATION SHOW
• Betty White, *Just Men!* NBC.

OUTSTANDING INDIVIDUAL DIRECTION FOR A GAME OR AUDIENCE PARTICIPATION SHOW
• Mark Breslow, *The Price is Right.* CBS.

OUTSTANDING TALK/SERVICE SERIES
• *This Old House.* Russell Morash, producer. PBS.

OUTSTANDING HOST/HOSTESS IN A TALK/SERVICE SERIES
• Phil Donahue, *Donahue.* Syndicated.

OUTSTANDING INDIVIDUAL DIRECTION FOR A TALK/SERVICE SERIES
• Glen Swanson, *Hour Magazine.* Syndicated.

OUTSTANDING VARIETY SERIES
• *The Merv Griffin Show.* Peter Barsocchini, producer. Syndicated.

OUTSTANDING HOST/HOSTESS IN A VARIETY SERIES
• Leslie Uggams, *Fantasy.* NBC.

OUTSTANDING INDIVIDUAL DIRECTION FOR A VARIETY SERIES
• Dick Carson, *The Merv Griffin Show.* Syndicated.

OUTSTANDING CHILDREN'S ENTERTAINMENT SERIES
• *Smurfs.* William Hanna, Joseph Barbera, executive producers. Gerard Baldwin, producer. NBC.

OUTSTANDING CHILDREN'S ENTERTAINMENT SPECIAL
• "The Woman Who Willed a Miracle," *ABC Afterschool Special.* Dick Clark, Preston Fischer, executive producers. Joanne A. Curley, Sharon Miller, producers. ABC.

**OUTSTANDING CHILDREN'S
INFORMATIONAL/INSTRUCTIONAL SERIES**
• *Sesame Street.* Dulcy Singer, executive
producer. Lisa Simon, producer. PBS.

**OUTSTANDING CHILDREN'S
INFORMATIONAL/INSTRUCTIONAL SPECIAL**
• *Winners.* Tom Robertson, producer.
Syndicated.

**OUTSTANDING INFORMATIONAL/
INSTRUCTIONAL PROGRAMMING
(Short form)**
• *In the News.* Joel Heller, executive
producer. Walter Lister, producer. CBS.

**OUTSTANDING PERFORMER
IN CHILDREN'S PROGRAMMING**
• Cloris Leachman, "The Woman Who
Willed a Miracle," *ABC Afterschool
Special.* ABC.

**ACHIEVEMENT IN CHILDREN'S
PROGRAMMING FOR DIRECTING**
• Sharon Miller, "The Woman Who Willed
a Miracle," *ABC Afterschool Special.* ABC.

**OUTSTANDING INDIVIDUAL ACHIEVEMENT
IN CHILDREN'S PROGRAMMING
FOR WRITING**
• Arthur Heinemann, "The Woman Who
Willed a Miracle," *ABC Afterschool
Special.* ABC.

**OUTSTANDING MUSIC COMPOSITION/
DIRECTION IN CHILDREN'S PROGRAMMING**
• Elliot Lawrence, music director,
"Sometimes I Don't Love My Mother,"
ABC Afterschool Special. ABC.

**OUTSTANDING CINEMATOGRAPHY
IN CHILDREN'S PROGRAMMING**
• Terry Meade, "The Shooting," *CBS
Afternoon Playhouse.* CBS.

**OUTSTANDING FILM EDITING
IN CHILDREN'S PROGRAMMING**
• Scott McKinsey, "The Shooting," CBS
Afternoon Playhouse. CBS.

**OUTSTANDING INDIVIDUAL ACHIEVEMENT
IN CHILDREN'S PROGRAMMING
(Associate direction/Video-tape editing)**
• Ilie Agopian, video-tape editor, *Young
People's Specials.* Syndicated.
(Art direction/ Scenic design/Set decoration)
• Victor DiNapoli, art director, *Sesame
Street.* PBS.

(Graphic design)
• Gerri Brioso, *Sesame Street.* PBS.

**OUTSTANDING TECHNICAL EXCELLENCE
FOR A DAYTIME DRAMA SERIES**
• Howard Zweig, Henry Enrico Ferro,
technical directors. Diana Wenman, Jean
Dadario, associate directors. Lawrence
Hammond, Robert Ambrico, Trevor
Thompson, Vincent Senatore, Robert
Ballairs, Thomas French, Richard
Westlein, electronic camera. Len Walas,
senior video engineer. Fran Gertler,
Kathryn Tucker-Bacheider, audio
engineers. Roger Haeneit, video tape
editor. Barbara Woods, sound effects
engineer, *All My Children.*
ABC.

**OUTSTANDING DESIGN EXCELLENCE
FOR A DAYTIME DRAMA SERIES**
• William Mickley, scenic designer.
William Itkin, Donna Larson, Donald
Gavitt, Robert Griffin, lighting directors.
Carol Luiken, costume designer. Sylvia
Lawrence, makeup. Scott Hersh, makeup
designer. Richard Greene, hair. Robert
Chui, hair designer. Teri Smith, music
director. Sid Ramin, music composer,
All My Children. ABC.

**SPECIAL CLASSIFICATION
OF OUTSTANDING PROGRAM
ACHIEVEMENT**
• *American Bandstand.* Dick Clark,
executive producer. Larry Klein, producer.
Barry Glazer, coproducer.
ABC.

**OUTSTANDING COVERAGE OF SPECIAL
EVENTS**
• *Macy's Thanksgiving Day Parade.* Dick
Schneider, producer. NBC.

**OUTSTANDING PROGRAM ACHIEVEMENT
IN THE PERFORMING ARTS**
• "Hansel and Gretel," *Live from the Met.*
Michael Bronson, executive producer.
Clemente D'Alessio, producer. PBS.
Zubin and the I.P.O. Samuel Elfert,
producer. NBC.

**OUTSTANDING INDIVIDUAL ACHIEVEMENT
IN THE PERFORMING ARTS
(Audio)**
• Jay David Saks, audio director. "Hansel
and Gretel," *Live from the Met.* PBS.

(Performers)
• Zubin Mehta, *Zubin and the I.P.O.* NBC.

SPECIAL CLASSIFICATION
OF OUTSTANDING INDIVIDUAL
ACHIEVEMENT—PERFORMERS
• Hal Linden, *FYI.* ABC.

OUTSTANDING INDIVIDUAL ACHIEVEMENT
IN THE COVERAGE OF SPECIAL EVENTS
(Technical direction/Electronic camerawork)
• Terry Rohnke, technical director. Mike
Bennett, Carl Eckett, Eric Eisenstein,
Barry Frischer, Bill Goetz, Steve
Gonzalez, Dave Hagen, John Hillyer, Gene
Martin, Don Mulvaney, John Pinto,
electronic camera, *Macy's Thanksgiving
Day Parade.* NBC.

OUTSTANDING ACHIEVEMENT
IN ANY AREA OF CREATIVE TECHNICAL
CRAFTS
(Cinematography)
• Robert Ryan, *Lorne Greene's New
Wilderness.* Syndicated.
(Film editing)
• Les Brown, *Lorne Greene's New
Wilderness.* Syndicated.
(Audio)
• John N. Castaldo, audio engineer,
Donahue. Syndicated.
(Composition/Direction)
• Jack Urbont, composer/director, *Lorne
Greene's New Wilderness.* Syndicated.
(Lighting direction)
• Nicholas Hutak, *Guiding Light.* Remote:
Franconia Notch. CBS.

OUTSTANDING ACHIEVEMENT
IN RELIGIOUS PROGRAMMING—SERIES
• *Insight.* Ellwood E. Kieser,
executive producer. Mike Rhodes, Terry
Sweeney, producers. Syndicated.

OUTSTANDING ACHIEVEMENT
IN RELIGIOUS PROGRAMMING—SPECIALS
• *The Juggler of Notre Dame.* Ellwood E.
Kieser, executive producer. Mike Rhodes,
Terry Sweeney, producers. Syndicated.
• *Land of Fear, Land of Courage.* Helen
Marmor, executive producer. NBC.

OUTSTANDING INDIVIDUAL ACHIEVEMENT
IN RELIGIOUS PROGRAMMING—
PERFORMERS
• Lois Nettleton, *Insight.* Syndicated.
Edwin Newman, *Kids, Drugs and Alcohol.*
NBC.

OUTSTANDING INDIVIDUAL ACHIEVEMENT
IN RELIGIOUS PROGRAMMING
(Film editing)
• Scott McKinsey, *Insight.* Syndicated.
• Ed Williams, *Land of Fear, Land of
Courage.* NBC.

SPORTS AWARD WINNERS
OUTSTANDING LIVE SPORTS SERIES
• *CBS Sports Presents the National
Football League.* Terry O'Neil, executive
producer. Charles Milton, Michael Burks,
Bob Stenner, David Dinkins, John
Faratzis, Ed Goren, David Michaels, Jim
Silman, David Winner, producers. Sandy
Grossman, Andrew Kindle, Joe Aceti, Bob
Dunphy, John McDonough, Peter
Bleckner, Bob Dailey, Larry Cavolina,
directors. CBS.

OUTSTANDING LIVE SPORTS SPECIAL
• *The 79th World Series.* Michael
Weisman, George Finkel, producers. Harry
Coyle, Andy Rosenberg, directors. NBC.

OUTSTANDING EDITED SPORTS
SERIES/ANTHOLOGIES
• *The American Sportsman.* Roone
Arledge, executive producer. John Wilcox,
senior producer. Chris Carmody,
coordinating producer. Bob Nixon, Curt
Gowdy, producers. ABC.

OUTSTANDING EDITED SPORTS SPECIAL
• *Wimbledon '83.* Michael Weisman,
executive producer. Ted Nathanson,
coordinating producer. Geoffrey Mason,
producer. Ted Nathanson, Bob Levy,
directors. Richard Cline, producer/director.
Terry Ewert, video-tape producer. NBC.

OUTSTANDING INDIVIDUAL ACHIEVEMENT
IN SPORTS PROGRAMMING
(Associate directors)
• *The American Sportsman.* Angelo
Bernaducci, Jean MacLean. ABC.
(Graphic designers)
• Douglas E. Towey, Bill Feigenbaum,
NBA World Championship Series. CBS.
(Film editors)
• Yale Nelson, *The 79th World Series.*
NBC.
(Music composers, music directors)
• John Tesh, *World University Games.*
CBS.
(Writing)
• George Bell, Jr., *The American
Sportsman.* ABC.

• Steve Sabol, Phil Tuckett, *Wake Up the Echoes: The History of Notre Dame Football.* Independent.
(Engineering/Technical supervisors)
• *Daytona 500.* Walter Pile, John Pumo. CBS.
(Lighting directors)
• *NCAA Football on CBS.* Joe Crookham. CBS.
(Cinematographers)
• *The American Sportsman.* Kurt Diemburger, David Breashears. ABC.
• *The Iditarod Sled Dog Race.* Peter Henning, Bill Philbin. CBS.
(Technical directors/Electronic camerapersons/Senior video operators/Senior audio engineers—Technical team)
• *Daytona 500.* Sandy Bell, Bob Brown, Anthony Filippi, technical directors. Bob Siderman, Tom Jimenez, audio. Robert Pieringer, Tom Delilla, Bill Berridge, Ron Rasch, video. Jim Murphy, Neil McCaffrey, Tom McCarthy, Herman Lang, Barry Drago, Joe Sokota, Jim McCarthy, Jeff Pollack, Frank McSpedon, George Rothweiler, George Neader, George Graffeo, Ray Chiste, Hans Sincer, Sig Meyer, Walt Soucy, camera. Walter Pile, John Pumo, electronic camera. CBS.
(Video-tape editors)
• *Closing Segment — NCAA Basketball Championship Game.* Bob Hickson, George Joanitis, Lito Magpayo. CBS.
• *1982 World Series Pre-Game Show.* Mike Kostel, Rick Reed, Rich Domich, John Servideo. NBC.

SPECIAL CLASSIFICATION OF OUTSTANDING ACHIEVEMENT
(Innovative technical achievement)
• Microwave transmission from the summit of Mt. Everest, *The American Sportsman.* David Breashears, Randy Hermes, Allan Weschsler, John Wilcox, Nick Pantelakis, Peter Pilafian, Steve Marts. ABC.
(Sports journalism)
• *ABC Sports Beat.* Michael Marley, Ed Silverman, producing managing editor. Howard Cosell, Sr. producer. Maury Rubin, Noubar Stone, Rob Beiner, directors. ABC.

OUTSTANDING SPORTS PERSONALITY—ANALYST
• John Madden. CBS.

OUTSTANDING SPORTS PERSONALITY—HOST
• Dick Enberg. NBC.

COMMENTARY
• John Madden. CBS.

OUTSTANDING ACHIEVEMENT— PROGRAM ACHIEVEMENT
• *ABC's Wide World of Sports.* Roone Arledge, executive producer. Dennis Lewin, coordinating producer. Larry Kamm, producer. Peter Lasser, Larry Kamm, directors. ABC.
• *Football in America.* Robert Carmichael, producer. PBS.
• *The American Sportsman.* John Wilcox, producer/director. ABC.

INTERNATIONAL AWARD WINNERS
OUTSTANDING DOCUMENTARY
• *Is There One Who Understands Me? The World of James Joyce.* Radio Telefis Eireann, Ireland.

OUTSTANDING DRAMA
• *A Voyage 'Round My Father.* Thames Television Ltd., United Kingdom.

PERFORMING ARTS
• *A Lot of Happiness.* Granada Television Ltd., United Kingdom.

POPULAR ARTS
• *Death and Life Severinian.* TV Globo Ltda., Brazil.

DIRECTORATE AWARD
• Akio Morita

SPECIAL AWARDS
OUTSTANDING ACHIEVEMENT IN THE SCIENCE OF TELEVISION ENGINEERING
• The Ampex Corporation
• The International Radio Consultative Committee of the International Telecommunication Union (CCIR)
• The European Broadcasting Union
• RCA CCSD Video Systems
• SMPTE
• 3M Corporation
• Xerox Corporation
• Mel Slater
• Richard Shoup

**OUTSTANDING ACHIEVEMENT
IN ENGINEERING DEVELOPMENT**
• Eastman Kodak Co. for the development of a color negative film with improved picture quality under low light levels.
(Citations)
• Ikegami Electronics and CBS for an electronic cinematography camera; and Ampex Corp. for a digital effects unit with improved picture quality.

**NATIONAL AWARD
FOR COMMUNITY SERVICE**
• *Sexual Abuse of Children*, WCCO-TV, Minneapolis, Minnesota.

A.T.A.S. GOVERNORS AWARD
• Sylvester L. "Pat" Weaver Jr.

N.A.T.A.S. TRUSTEES AWARD
• Bob Short

Hill Street's Summit

Excitement ran high over *Hill Street Blues* even before the Emmycast began. The big question was: Could the show tie the record held by *The Dick Van Dyke Show* and *All in the Family* for being voted best series the most times (four)?

Hill Street Blues had a total of 20 Emmys, the third most of any series and the most ever awarded to a drama program. Having 18 nominations this year, it was possible that it could even win enough new awards to surpass *The Mary Tyler Moore Show*'s record of the most total Emmys — 29. With five statuettes, it could at least beat out number-two ranked *The Carol Burnett Show*.

Hill Street Blues did reach its peak in 1984 by winning the program prize for a historic fourth time and an additional four honors that established it as the second most awarded series in Emmy history. Producer Steven Bochco was asked at a press conference back stage: How long could the show keep up this amazing winning streak? "We feel like kids in an egg toss," he answered. "Every year we take one step further back. We know the egg is going to splat sooner or later."

The gritty, realistic cop show once described by Associated Press as "a drama with overtones of black comedy about a police precinct in a slum" was also honored for its directing and film sound mixing, in addition to the work of two supporting performers — Bruce Weitz, who played the disgruntled detective Mike Belker, and guest star Alfre Woodard, who portrayed the mother of a boy who is killed accidentally in a police shooting. The tough Weitz turned out to be a softie up on stage when he thanked his mom. Woodard

MTM ENTERPRISES

After picking up five more statuettes, Hill Street Blues *became the second biggest series winner in Emmy history.*

wore a strapless gown and noted, "I almost lost my clothes coming up here."

In the comedy category, *Cheers* once again heard the roar of the academy crowd when it was acclaimed Outstanding Comedy Series and earned three additional awards: for writing, film editing, and supporting actress Rhea Perlman, who played the sassiest waitress at Boston's most hopping bar. Star Ted Danson was nominated again for *Cheers* as well as for being the star of the TV film *Something About Amelia*, but he lost both prizes.

Cheers beat out one of the most popular and critically acclaimed new series, *Kate & Allie*, which centered on the exploits of two former school chums who adjust to their recent divorces by moving in with each other and their children. The show starred Susan Saint James as Kate and former *Saturday Night Live* comedienne Jane Curtin as Allie and was such an instant hit that it landed in the Nielsen top 10 while still in its first season. Emmys went to the show's director and to Curtin as best actress.

The year's outstanding comic actor was *Three's Company*'s John Ritter, who had been nominated once before, in 1978, and was the son of late country singer Tex. Ritter said in his acceptance speech: "I wish my dad were here tonight so I could show off."

The choice of best dramatic actor was a popular one with TV viewers, but less so with TV critics. *Magnum, P.I.*'s Tom Selleck "was named best actor in a 'dramatic' series for baring his chest weekly," reported the oft-wry *Washington Post*. But Selleck had cause for such casual approach to his character: He played a private investigator who lives in Hawaii where the climate invites such open communion with nature. *Magnum, P.I.* was ranked sixth in the Nielsens and Selleck himself was such a popular TV star that he was asked to co-host the Emmys. He obviously didn't expect any further honors, though, particularly since he had been nominated twice before and lost. This year he was so shocked to hear his name announced as the winner that he arrived at the podium stunned, merely said "thank you," and then jogged across the stage to the opposite podium where he resumed his duties as master of ceremonies.

Tyne Daly of *Cagney & Lacey* was named best actress for a second year in a row. "Too much, too much," she said when she arrived on stage, nearly breathless. ("The Emmys are like a horse race," she'd told the *L.A. Herald Examiner* earlier. "It's fun for the spectators. It's not so fun for the horses.") But now with the waiting and running behind her, Daly was obviously having a good time. Beaming up on stage, she said the prize demonstrated that TV need not be about women who go to the beauty parlor five or six time a week, but about "women who have beautiful souls."

The most breathless winner of the night turned out to be Jane Fonda, who was voted best actress in a limited series or a special for *The Dollmaker*, the story of an impoverished Kentucky mountain woman who moves to Detroit with her family during World War II. "Oh, my heart!" Fonda gasped as she accepted the prize for her TV film debut. Her victory was a heart-stopper to more than just Fonda: Ann-Margret was favored to win for *A Streetcar Named Desire*, but was now getting numb to upsets. Another film veteran, Barbara Stanwyck, did the same thing to her the previous year.

Another reason Fonda was so excited was because *The Dollmaker* was a production that took her 12 years to bring to the air. "This project was very special to me and it means more than almost anything that's happened in my career," she said. "I was never nervous about the Oscars like this."

> **Jane Fonda said, "I was never nervous about the Oscars like this."**

Sir Laurence Olivier received the fifth Emmy of his career for starring in his own production of Shakespeare's *King Lear*, which was ultimately shown in syndication after all three networks turned it down. Obviously, the networks preferred more contemporary fare such as the most hotly debated TV film of the 1980s, ABC's *The Day After*, about the aftermath of a nuclear bomb's devastation of Lawrence, Kansas. Tied with *Cheers* for having the second most nominations of the night — 12 — *The Day After* was the favorite to sweep the category of drama/comedy specials. It ended up with only two technical awards. The top program prize went instead to *Something About Amelia*, a chilling exploration of father-daughter incest that ended up with additional trophies for its writer and for supporting actress Roxana Zal, who played the abused 14-year-old girl. *Concealed Enemies*, a PBS *American Playhouse* drama based on the Alger Hiss spy case, was declared best limited series. It also won a director's statuette for Jeff Bleckner, an Emmy winner from last year for *Hill Street Blues*.

The Kennedy Center Honors, which pays tribute to legends of the entertainment world, was voted best variety show and also won a lighting award. Producer George Stevens, Jr., picked up the program trophy and used his time in front of the TV cameras to tell his children in Georgetown to go to bed. Emmy collector Dwight Hemion added one more to his formidable stash (no individual has more prime-time Emmys than Hemion) for directing *Here's Television Entertainment*. Cloris Leachman gave the best performance in a variety show by acting out the various stages in an actress's life in *The Screen Actors Guild 50th Anniversary Celebration*, which also won for music direction. Leachman triumphed over Lily Tomlin (nominated for her special *Live ... and in Person*), who was shown on camera in the audience pretending to sob hysterically into a handkerchief as the winner mounted the stage. But Leachman certainly knew what losing what like. She'd just experienced it with a nomination for her portrayal of Ernie Kovac's mother in a film bio of the late comedy giant in a category she lost to *Amelia*'s Roxana Zal. Accepting the Emmy she did win, Leachman said, "Not many people get to lose and win in the same night."

The Emmycast began 34 minutes past its scheduled 8:30 p.m. starting time in the East because it followed a late-running Dallas-Green Bay NFL game. Even

The surprise choice of best drama series actor was Emmy cohost Tom Selleck of the number six-ranked Magnum P.I.

with being up against obvious pressures to cut the program short as a result, it ran a total of three hours and 36 minutes — the longest show ever, beating out the 1978 broadcast by one minute.

DAYTIME AWARDS

While NBC continued its boycott, the daytime awards ceremony was again not televised, but went on as scheduled at New York's Sheraton Center. "This left the kissy-kissy trauma of winning and losing to be shared among the more than 600 people on hand for the ceremony," *People* magazine noted wryly.

ABC began with the most nominations — 80 — and ended up with the most prizes, foremost among them Outstanding Daytime Drama Series for its still number one-rated soap (and 1980-81 Emmy winner) *General Hospital*, which, strangely, took no other prizes. Another oddity in the category was that last year's winner *The Young and the Restless* wasn't even nominated this year.

CBS finally pulled ahead of ABC as the number-one ranked network in daytime and reaped the bulk of the performance awards. *As the World Turns*'s Larry Bryggman (Dr. John Dixon on the show) was named best actor and costar Justin Deas (who played Tom Hughes) was voted supporting actor of the year. Judi Evans (Beth Raines on *Guiding Light*) was selected best supporting actress. Erika Slezak (as the character Victoria Lord Buchanan) was outstanding actress for ABC's *One Life to Live*.

Last year the then four-time nominee Susan Lucci of *All My Children* stormed out of the awards ceremony when she failed to win the actress trophy, but this year was more composed as she watched it go to Slezak, a friend of hers. "I wanted to win," Lucci said to Slezak's husband after the announcement, as reported in *People* magazine, "but if I had to lose, I wanted to lose to her."

It's possible that the blow was softened for her by knowing ahead of time who won. Many of the contestants did, thanks to *The New York Post*, which obtained a press release of the winners before the event and printed their names in an edition that was seen by some of the nominees before the victors were officially announced. *People* noted, "The tip-off put *All My Children* actor Bob Gentry in the embarrassing spot of sitting near his competing friends, Lucci and Slezak, fully aware of who had won. 'I couldn't look either of them in the eye,' Gentry said."

The syndicated *Merv Griffin Show* and CBS's *The $25,000 Pyramid* repeated their wins of last year, with Griffin also winning as host. *Woman to Woman*, a new program that tackled key women's issues in an intelligent discussion format, was named best talk/service series, but it failed to win a strong enough audience in syndication and was canceled after its first year on the air.

The *ABC Afterschool Special* "Andrea's Story: A Hitchhiking Tragedy" (about a girl who is raped while thumbing a ride) swept the field of children's specials, pulling five awards, including best director. But it failed to take the top award for best special, which went to another *ABC Afterschool Special* "The Great Love Experiment," the story of an unpopular high school girl whose classmates try to make her hip and cool.

For the first time ever there was a tie in the category of outstanding children's entertainment series. NBC's *Smurfs* pulled even with *Captain Kangaroo*, which was the last weekday network show for kids. *Kangaroo* was then being bounced around in early morning time slots by CBS until the longest-running network program for children, which was first aired in 1955, was dropped by the end of 1984.

SPORTS AWARDS

The usual sports awards "fell apart," reported *The Washington Post*, "when NBC Sports, complaining of the method for choosing winners, boycotted the awards and CBS in turn expressed its concern." The prizes would next be presented in August, 1986 for the period spanning 1984–85.

NEWS & DOCUMENTARY AWARDS

"PBS Dominates News Awards" said the headlines the next day, a phenomenon that would be repeated often in years to come. But it was a first in 1983. PBS won 19 honors compared to 11 for ABC, 10 for CBS, and 6 for NBC. The last numbers were impressive considering NBC was continuing its boycott of the recent past, although the network still allowed employees to submit their own work separately for consideration.

All six nominated episodes of *Vietnam: A Television History* ended up with statuettes. The 13-part PBS special documentary series was a critically acclaimed chronicle of the conflict in Southeast Asia from the days of French occupation through the toppling of Saigon by the North Vietnamese. PBS also garnered two awards for segments of its *MacNeil-Lehrer Newshour* and three others for its half-hour *Inside Story* series hosted by Hodding Carter III.

Robert MacNeil and Jim Lehrer were honored with a news award for coverage of the U.S. military action in Grenada.

> *Henry Kissinger said he was the bull handing an award to the matador.*

The three commercial networks shared the laurels for investigative journalism for segments of news shows: ABC for "Growing Up in Smoke" on *20/20*, CBS for "Lenell Geters in Jail" on *60 Minutes,* and NBC for "Poison on Your Plate," about potentially harmful food additives, on *First Camera*. ABC won a total of four trophies for *20/20*, including ones for profiles of jazz singer Mel Tormé and the parents of attempted presidential assassin John W. Hinckley.

The bulk of CBS's awards went to the evening news report with Dan Rather, which won five statuettes for segments on such diverse subjects as cancer, computers, and the Beirut bombing that killed more than 200 U.S. servicemen.

Celebrity presenters at the awards ceremony included Henry Kissinger, Donald Trump, and New York Archbishop John J. O'Connor. O'Connor said he was "delighted, honored, flattered, but I don't know why I'm here."

Kissinger countered during his time at the podium: "Unlike His Grace, the Archbishop, I know why I'm here," he said. "I'm here to make history. It's the first time the bull has had the opportunity to hand an award to the matador."

1983–84

For prime-time programs telecast between July 1, 1983, and June 30, 1984. The prime-time ceremony was broadcast on CBS from the Pasadena Civic Auditorium on Setpember 23, 1984. Creative arts banquet held on September 16, 1984. Daytime awards presented June 27, 1984, for programs aired between March 6, 1983, and March 5, 1984. News & documentary awards for 1983 were bestowed on August 30, 1984. No sports awards were presented.

PRIME-TIME PROGRAM AWARDS
OUTSTANDING DRAMA SERIES
• *Hill Street Blues.* Steven Bochco, executive producer. Gregory Hoblit, co-executive producer. Scott Brazil, supervising producer. Jeffrey Lewis, Sascha Schneider, producers. David Latt, coproducer. NBC.
Cagney & Lacey. Barney Rosenzweig, executive producer. Peter Lefcourt, producer. CBS.
Fame. William Blinn, executive producer. Ken Ehrlich, producer. Syndicated.
Magnum, P.I. Donald P. Bellisario, executive producer. Douglas Benton,

supervising producer in Hollywood. Chas. Floyd Johnson, supervising producer in Hawaii. Reuben Leder, producer. Rick Weaver, Nick Thiel, coproducers. CBS.
St. Elsewhere. Bruce Paltrow, executive producer. Mark Tinker, supervising producer. John Masius, Tom Fontana, producers. Abby Singer, coordinating producer. NBC.

OUTSTANDING COMEDY SERIES
• *Cheers.* James Burrows, Glen Charles, Les Charles, producers. NBC.
Buffalo Bill. Bernie Brillstein, Tom Patchett, Jay Tarses, executive producers. Dennis Klein, Carol Gary, producers. NBC.
Family Ties. Gary David Goldberg, Lloyd Garver, executive producers. Lloyd Garver, Michael J. Weithorn, producers. Carol Himes, coproducer. NBC.
Kate & Allie. Mort Lachman, Merrill Grant, executive producers. Bill Persky, Bob Randall, producers. George Barimo, coordinating producer. CBS.
Newhart. Barry Kemp, executive producer. Sheldon Bull, producer. CBS.

OUTSTANDING LIMITED SERIES
• *Concealed Enemies, American Playhouse.* Lindsay Law, David Elstein, executive producers. Peter Cook, producer. PBS.
Chiefs. Martin Manulis, executive producer. Jerry London, supervising producer. John E. Quill, producer. CBS.
George Washington. David Gerber, executive producer. Buzz Kulik, supervising producer. Richard Fielder, producer. CBS.
Nancy Astor, Masterpiece Theatre. Philip Hinchcliffe, producer. PBS.
Reilly: Ace of Spies, Mystery! Verity Lambert, executive producer. C.J. Burt, producer. PBS.

OUTSTANDING VARIETY, MUSIC, OR COMEDY PROGRAM
• *The 6th Annual Kennedy Center Honors: A Celebration of the Performing Arts.* Nick Vanoff, George Stevens, Jr., producers. CBS.
The American Film Institute Salute to Lillian Gish. Georges Stevens, Jr., producer. CBS.
Late Night with David Letterman. Jack Rollins, executive producer. Barry Sand, producer. David Letterman, host. NBC.

The Tonight Show Starring Johnny Carson. Fred DeCordova, executive producer. Peter Lassaly, producer. Johnny Carson, host. NBC.
The 1984 Tony Awards. Alexander H. Cohen, executive producer. Hildy Parks, producer. Martha Mason, coproducer. CBS.

OUTSTANDING DRAMA/COMEDY SPECIAL
• *Something About Amelia, ABC Theatre.* Leonard Goldberg, executive producer. Michele Rappaport, producer. ABC.
Adam. Alan Landsburg, Joan Barnett, executive producers. Linda Otto, producer. NBC.
The Day After, ABC Theatre. Robert A. Papazian, producer. ABC.
The Dollmaker, ABC Theatre. Bruce Gilbert, executive producer. Bill Finnegan, producer. ABC.
A Streetcar Named Desire, ABC Theatre. Keith Barish, Craig Baumgarten, executive producers. Marc Trabulus, producer. ABC.

OUTSTANDING CLASSICAL PROGRAM IN THE PERFORMING ARTS
(Winner)
• "Placido Domingo Celebrates Seville," *Great Performances.* Horant H. Hohlfeld, executive producer. David Griffiths, producer. Placido Domingo, host. PBS.

OUTSTANDING INFORMATIONAL SPECIAL
(Winner)
• *America Remembers John F. Kennedy.* Thomas F. Horton, producer. Syndicated.

OUTSTANDING INFORMATIONAL SERIES
(Winner)
• *A Walk Through the 20th Century with Bill Moyers.* Merton Y. Koplin, senior executive producer. Charles Grinker, Sanford H. Fisher, executive producers. Betsy McCarthy, coordinating producer. David Grubin, Ronald Blumer, producers. Bill Moyers, host. PBS.

OUTSTANDING ANIMATED PROGRAM
(Winner)
• *Garfield on the Town.* Jay Poynor, executive producer. Lee Mendelson, Bill Melendez, producers. CBS.

Best supporting actress Rhea Perlman won for playing the brazen, smart-talking waitress on best comedy series Cheers.

OUTSTANDING CHILDREN'S PROGRAM (Winner)
• *He Makes Me Feel Like Dancin'*. Edgar J. Scherick, Scott Rudin, executive producers. Emile Ardolino, producer. Judy Kinberg, coproducer. NBC.

PERFORMANCE, DIRECTING, AND WRITING

OUTSTANDING LEAD ACTOR IN A DRAMA SERIES
• Tom Selleck, *Magnum, P.I.* CBS.
William Daniels, *St. Elsewhere.* NBC.
John Forsythe, *Dynasty.* ABC.
Daniel J. Travanti, *Hill Street Blues.* NBC.

OUTSTANDING LEAD ACTRESS IN A DRAMA SERIES
• Tyne Daly, *Cagney & Lacey.* CBS.
Debbie Allen, *Fame.* Syndicated.
Joan Collins, *Dynasty.* ABC.
Sharon Gless, *Cagney & Lacey.* CBS.
Veronica Hamel, *Hill Street Blues.* NBC.

OUTSTANDING LEAD ACTOR IN A COMEDY SERIES
• John Ritter, *Three's Company.* ABC.
Dabney Coleman, *Buffalo Bill.* NBC.
Ted Danson, *Cheers.* NBC.
Robert Guillaume, *Benson.* ABC.
Sherman Hemsley, *The Jeffersons.* CBS.

OUTSTANDING LEAD ACTRESS IN A COMEDY SERIES
• Jane Curtin, *Kate & Allie.* CBS.
Joanna Cassidy, *Buffalo Bill.* NBC.
Shelley Long, *Cheers.* NBC.

Susan Saint James, *Kate & Allie.* CBS.
Isabel Sanford, *The Jeffersons.* CBS.

OUTSTANDING LEAD ACTOR IN A LIMITED SERIES OR A SPECIAL
• Laurence Olivier, *King Lear.* Syndicated.
Ted Danson, *Something About Amelia, ABC Theatre.* ABC.
Louis Gossett, Jr., *Sadat.* Syndicated.
Mickey Rooney, *Bill: On His Own.* CBS.
Daniel J. Travanti, *Adam.* NBC.

OUTSTANDING LEAD ACTRESS IN A LIMITED SERIES OR A SPECIAL
• Jane Fonda, *The Dollmaker, ABC Theatre.* ABC.
Jane Alexander, *Calamity Jane.* CBS.
Ann-Margret, *A Streetcar Named Desire, ABC Theatre.* ABC.
Glenn Close, *Something About Amelia, ABC Theatre.* ABC.
JoBeth Williams, *Adam.* NBC.

OUTSTANDING SUPPORTING ACTOR IN A DRAMA SERIES
• Bruce Weitz, *Hill Street Blues.* NBC.
Ed Begley, Jr., *St. Elsewhere.* NBC.
Michael Conrad, *Hill Street Blues.* NBC.
John Hillerman, *Magnum, P.I.* CBS.
James B. Sikking, *Hill Street Blues.* NBC.

OUTSTANDING SUPPORTING ACTRESS IN A DRAMA SERIES
• Alfre Woodard, *Hill Street Blues.* NBC.
Barbara Bosson, *Hill Street Blues.* NBC.
Piper Laurie, *St. Elsewhere.* NBC.
Madge Sinclair, *Trapper John, M.D.* CBS.
Betty Thomas, *Hill Street Blues.* NBC.

OUTSTANDING SUPPORTING ACTOR IN A COMEDY SERIES
• Pat Harrington, *One Day at a Time.* CBS.
Rene Auberjonois, *Benson.* ABC.
Nicholas Colasanto, *Cheers.* NBC.
Tom Poston, *Newhart.* CBS.
George Wendt, *Cheers.* NBC.

OUTSTANDING SUPPORTING ACTRESS IN A COMEDY SERIES
• Rhea Perlman, *Cheers.* NBC.
Julia Duffy, *Newhart.* CBS.
Marla Gibbs, *The Jeffersons.* CBS.
Paula Kelly, *Night Court.* NBC.
Marion Ross, *Happy Days.* ABC.

OUTSTANDING SUPPORTING ACTOR IN A LIMITED SERIES OR A SPECIAL

• Art Carney, *Terrible Joe Moran, ITT Theatre*. CBS.
Keith Carradine, *Chiefs*. CBS.
John Gielgud, *The Master of Ballantrae, Hallmark Hall of Fame*. CBS.
John Lithgow, *The Day After, ABC Theatre*. ABC.
Randy Quaid, *A Streetcar Named Desire, ABC Theatre*. ABC.
David Ogden Stiers, *The First Olympics—Athens 1896*. NBC.

OUTSTANDING SUPPORTING ACTRESS IN A LIMITED SERIES OR A SPECIAL

• Roxana Zal, *Something About Amelia, ABC Theatre*. ABC.
Patty Duke Astin, *George Washington*. CBS.
Beverly D'Angelo, *A Streetcar Named Desire, ABC Theatre*. ABC.
Cloris Leachman, *Ernie Kovacs: Between the Laughter*. ABC.
Tuesday Weld, *The Winter of Our Discontent, Hallmark Hall of Fame*. CBS.

OUTSTANDING INDIVIDUAL PERFORMANCE IN A VARIETY OR MUSIC PROGRAM

• Cloris Leachman, *Screen Actors Guild 50th Anniversary Celebration*. CBS.
Debbie Allen, *Live ... and in Person*. NBC.
George Burns, *George Burns Celebrates 80 Years in Show Business*. NBC.
Eddie Murphy, *Saturday Night Live*. NBC.
Joe Piscopo, *Saturday Night Live*. NBC.
Lily Tomlin, *Live ... and in Person*. NBC.

OUTSTANDING DIRECTING IN A DRAMA SERIES

• Corey Allen, *Hill Street Blues*. NBC.
Thomas Carter, *Hill Street Blues*. NBC.
Robert Scheerer, *Fame*. Syndicated.
Arthur Alan Seidelman, *Hill Street Blues*. NBC.

OUTSTANDING DIRECTING IN A COMEDY SERIES

• Bill Persky, *Kate & Allie*. CBS.
James Burrows, *Cheers*. NBC.
Ellen Chaset Falcon, *Buffalo Bill*. NBC.
Larry Gelbart, *AfterM*A*S*H*. CBS.

OUTSTANDING DIRECTING IN A LIMITED SERIES OR A SPECIAL

• Jeff Bleckner, *Concealed Enemies, American Playhouse*. PBS.
John Erman, *A Streetcar Named Desire, ABC Theatre*. ABC.
Randa Haines, *Something About Amelia, ABC Theatre*. ABC.
Lamont Johnson, *Ernie Kovacs: Between the Laughter*. ABC.
Nicholas Meyer, *The Day After, ABC Theatre*. ABC.

OUTSTANDING DIRECTING IN A VARIETY OR MUSIC PROGRAM

• Dwight Hemion, *Here's Television Entertainment*. NBC.
Clark Jones, *The 1984 Tony Awards*. CBS.
Don Mischer, *The 6th Annual Kennedy Center Honors: A Celebration of the Performing Arts*. CBS.
Marty Pasetta, *Burnett "Discovers" Domingo*. CBS.

OUTSTANDING WRITING IN A DRAMA SERIES

• John Ford Noonan, teleplay. John Masius, Tom Fontana, story, *St. Elsewhere*. NBC.
Tom Fontana, John Masius, *St. Elsewhere*. NBC.
Jeffrey Lewis, Michael Wagner, Karen Hall, Mark Frost, teleplay. Steven Bochco, Jeffrey Lewis, David Milch, story, *Hill Street Blues*. NBC.
John Masius, Tom Fontana, Garn Stephens, Emilie R. Small, *St. Elsewhere*. NBC.
Peter Silverman, teleplay. Steven Bochco, Jeffrey Lewis, David Milch, story, *Hill Street Blues*. NBC.
Mark Tinker, John Tinker, teleplay. John Masius, Tom Fontana, story, *St. Elsewhere*. NBC.

OUTSTANDING WRITING IN A COMEDY SERIES

• David Angel, *Cheers*. NBC.
Glen Charles, Les Charles, *Cheers*, NBC.
David Lloyd, *Cheers*. NBC.
Tom Patchett, *Buffalo Bill*. NBC.
Jay Tarses, *Buffalo Bill*. NBC.

OUTSTANDING WRITING IN A LIMITED SERIES OR A SPECIAL

• William Hanley, *Something About Amelia, ABC Theatre*. ABC.
Susan Cooper, Hume Cronyn, *The Dollmaker, ABC Theatre*. ABC.
Edward Hume, *The Day After, ABC Theatre*. ABC.
Alan Leicht, *Adam*. NBC.
April Smith, *Ernie Kovacs: Between the Laughter*. ABC.

Outstanding Writing in a Variety or Music Program

• Steve O'Donnell, Gerard Mulligan, Sanford Frank, Joseph E. Toplyn, Christopher Elliott, Matt Wickline, Jeff Martin, Ted Greenberg, David Yazbek, Merrill Markoe, David Letterman, *Late Night with David Letterman*. NBC.

James Downey, Gerard Mulligan, George Meyer, Steve O'Donnell, Sanford Frank, Joseph E. Toplyn, Christopher Elliott, Matt Wickline, Merrill Markoe, Tom Gammill, Max Pross, David Letterman, *Late Night with David Letterman*. NBC.

James Downey, Gerard Mulligan, Andy Breckman, George Meyer, Steve O'Donnell, Sanford Frank, Merrill Markoe, David Letterman, *Late Night with David Letterman*. NBC.

Hildy Parks, *The 1984 Tony Awards*. CBS.

Andrew Smith, Jim Belushi, Andy Breckerman, Robin Duke, Adam Green, Mary Gross, Nate Herman, Tim Kazurinsky, Kevin Kelton, Andrew Kurtzman, Michael McCarthy, Eddie Murphy, Pamela Norris, Margaret Oberman, Joe Piscopo, Herb Sargent, Bob Tischler, Eliot Wald, *Saturday Night Live*. NBC.

George Stevens, Jr., Joseph McBride, *The American Film Institute Salute to Lillian Gish*. CBS.

George Stevens Jr., L.T. Ilehart, Jr., Sara Lukinson, Marc London, *"A Celebration of the Performing Arts,"The 6th Annual Kennedy Center Honors*. CBS.

OTHER AWARD WINNERS

Outstanding Choreography

• Michael Smuin, "A Song for Dead Warriors, San Francisco Ballet," *Dance in America*. PBS.

Outstanding Cinematography
for a Series

• James Crabe, *Mickey Spillane's Mike Hammer*. CBS.

Outstanding Cinematography
for a Limited Series or a Special

• Bill Butler, *A Streetcar Named Desire, ABC Theatre*. ABC.

Outstanding Art Direction
for a Series

• James Hulsey, art director. Bruce Kay, set decorator, *The Duck Factory*. NBC.

Outstanding Art Direction
for a Limited Series or a Special

• James Hulsey, production designer. George R. Nelson, set decorator, *A Streetcar Named Desire, ABC Theatre*. ABC.

Outstanding Art Direction
for a Variety or Music Program

• Roy Christopher, art director, *The 56th Annual Academy Awards*. ABC.

Outstanding Music Composition
for a Series
(Dramatic underscore)

• Bruce Broughton, *Dallas*. CBS.

Outstanding Music Composition
for a Limited Series or a Special
(Dramatic underscore)

• Bruce Broughton, *The First Olympics — Athens 1896*. NBC.

Outstanding Music Direction

• Ian Fraser, music director. Billy Byers, Chris Boardman, J. Hill, Lenny Stack, principal arrangers, *The Screen Actors Guild 50th Anniversary Celebration*. CBS.

Outstanding Music and Lyrics

• Larry Grossman, composer. Buz Kohan, lyricist, *Here's Television Entertainment*. Song: "Gone Too Soon." NBC.

Outstanding Costume Design
for a Series
(Tie)

• Bob Mackie, original costume concept. Ret Turner, costumes, *Mama's Family*. CBS.

• Nolan Miller, *Dynasty*. ABC.

Outstanding Costume Design
for a Limited Series or a Special

• Julie Weiss, *The Dollmaker, ABC Theatre*. ABC.

Outstanding Makeup

• Michael Westmore, special makeup, *Why Me?* ABC.

Outstanding Hairstyling

• Dino Ganziano, *The Mystic Warrior*. ABC.

Outstanding Film Editing
for a Series

• Andrew Chulack, *Cheers*. NBC.

Outstanding Film Editing for a Limited Series or a Special
• Jerrold L. Ludwig, *A Streetcar Named Desire, ABC Theatre.* ABC.

Outstanding Film Sound Editing for a Series
• Sam Shaw, supervising editor. Michael Ford, Don-Lee Jorgensen, Mark Roberts, Breck Warwick, Bob Weatherford, Michael Wilhoit, editors. Nicholas Korda, ADR editor. Gene Gillette, music editor, *Airwolf.* CBS.

Outstanding Film Sound Editing for a Limited Series or a Special
• Christopher T. Welch, supervising editor. Brian Courcier, Greg Dillon, David R. Elliott, Michael Hilkene, Fred Judkins, Carl Mahakian, Joseph Mayer, Joseph Melody, Catherine Shorr, Richard Shorr, editors. Jill Taggart, ADR editor. Roy Prendergast, music editor, *The Day After, ABC Theatre.* ABC.

Outstanding Film Sound Mixing for a Series
• David Schneiderman, production mixer. John B. Asman, William M. Nicholson, Ken S. Polk, rerecording sound mixers, *Hill Street Blues.* NBC.

Outstanding Film Sound Mixing for a Limited Series or a Special
• Richard Raguse, production mixer. William L. McCaughey, Mel Metcalfe, Terry Porter, rerecording mixers, *A Streetcar Named Desire, ABC Theatre.* ABC.

Outstanding Live and Tape Sound Mixing and Sound Effects for a Series
• Mark Hanes, production. Stu Fox, preproduction. Dean Okrand, postproduction. Ed Suski, sound effects, *Real People.* NBC.

Outstanding Live and Tape Sound Mixing and Sound Effects for a Limited Series or a Special
• Edward J. Greene, production. Carroll Pratt, sound effects, *Anne Murray's Winter Carnival ... from Quebec.* CBS.

Outstanding Technical Direction/Camerawork/Video for a Series
• Gene Crowe, technical director. Sam Drummy, Larry Heider, Dave Levisohn, Wayne Orr, Ron Sheldon, camerapersons. Mark Sanford, senior video control, *On Stage America.* Syndicated.

Outstanding Technical Direction/Camerawork/Video for a Limited Series or a Special
• Lou Fusari, technical director. Les Atkinson, Bruce Bottone, George Falardeau, Dean Hall, Dave Hilmer, Roy Holm, David Nowell, camerapersons. Jerry R. Smith, senior video control, *The Magic of David Copperfield.* CBS.

Outstanding Video-Tape Editing for a Series
• Howard Brock, *Fame.* Syndicated.

Outstanding Video-Tape Editing for a Limited Series or a Special
• Jim McQueen, video-tape editor. Catherine Shields, film editor, *American Film Institute Salute to Lillian Gish.* CBS.

Outstanding Lighting Direction (Electronic) for a Series
• Robert A. Dickinson, lighting consultant. C. Frank Olivas, lighting director, *Solid Gold.* Syndicated.

Outstanding Lighting Direction (Electronic) for a Limited Series or a Special
• William M. Klages, *The 6th Annual Kennedy Center Honors: A Celebration of the Performing Arts.* CBS.

Outstanding Individual Achievement—Animated Programming
• R. O. Blechman, director, *The Soldier's Tale.* PBS.

Outstanding Individual Achievement—Special Visual Effects
(Tie)
• William M. Klages, lighting director, *The 26th Annual Grammy Awards.* CBS.
• Robert Balack, Nancy Rushlow, Dan Pinkham, Chris Regan, Larry Stevens, Dan Nosenchuck, Chris Dierdorf, graphic artists, *The Day After, ABC Theatre.* ABC

OUTSTANDING INDIVIDUAL ACHIEVEMENT—GRAPHIC DESIGN AND TITLE SEQUENCES
• Ted Woolery, Gerry Woolery, *The Duck Factory*. NBC.

OUTSTANDING INDIVIDUAL ACHIEVEMENT—CLASSICAL MUSIC/DANCE PROGRAMMING
• Merrill Brockway, director, "A Song for Dead Warriors, San Francisco Ballet," *Dance in America*. PBS.
James Levine, performer, *Live from the Met*. PBS.
• Leontyne Price, performer, *In Performance at the White House: An Evening of Spirituals and Gospel Music*. PBS.

OUTSTANDING INDIVIDUAL ACHIEVEMENT—INFORMATIONAL PROGRAMMING
• Emile Ardolino, director, *He Makes Me Feel Like Dancin'*. NBC.
• Bill Moyers, writer, *Marshall, Texas*. PBS.

(There were no winners in Outstanding Individual Achievement—Costumers or Special Sound Achievement.)

DAYTIME AWARDS

OUTSTANDING DAYTIME DRAMA SERIES
• *General Hospital*. Gloria Monty, producer. ABC.
All My Children. Jacqueline Babbin, producer. ABC.
Days of Our Lives. Betty Corday, executive producer. Al Rabin, supervising executive producer. Ken Corday, producer. Shelley Curtis, producer. NBC.

OUTSTANDING ACTOR IN A DAYTIME DRAMA SERIES
• Larry Bryggman, *As the World Turns*. CBS.
James Mitchell, *All My Children*. ABC.
Joel Crothers, *The Edge of Night*. ABC.
Larkin Malloy, *The Edge of Night*. ABC.
Stuart Damon, *General Hospital*. ABC.
Terry Lester, *The Young and the Restless*. CBS.

OUTSTANDING ACTRESS IN A DAYTIME DRAMA SERIES
• Erika Slezak, *One Life to Live*. ABC.
Susan Lucci, *All My Children*. ABC.
Deidre Hall, *Days of Our Lives*. NBC.

Erika Slezak was named best daytime actress for playing the character Victoria Lord Buchanan on One Life to Live *.*

Ann Flood, *The Edge of Night*. ABC.
Sharon Gabet, *The Edge of Night*. ABC.

OUTSTANDING ACTOR IN A SUPPORTING ROLE IN A DAYTIME DRAMA SERIES
• Justin Deas, *As the World Turns*. CBS.
Louis Edmonds, *All My Children*. ABC.
Paul Stevens, *Another World*. NBC.
David Lewis, *General Hospital*. ABC.
Anthony Call, *One Life to Live*. ABC.

OUTSTANDING ACTRESS IN A SUPPORTING ROLE IN A DAYTIME DRAMA SERIES
• Judi Evans, *Guiding Light*. CBS.
Eileen Herlie, *All My Children*. ABC.
Marcy Walker, *All My Children*. ABC.
Lois Kibbee, *The Edge of Night*. ABC.
Loanne Bishop, *General Hospital*. ABC.
Christine Ebersole, *One Life to Live*. ABC.

OUTSTANDING DIRECTION FOR A DAYTIME DRAMA SERIES
• Larry Auerbach, George Keathley, Peter Miner, David Pressman, *One Life to Live*. ABC.
Jack Coffey, Sherrell Hoffman, Henry Kaplan, Francesca James. *All My Children*. ABC.

OUTSTANDING WRITING FOR A DAYTIME DRAMA SERIES
• Claire Labine, Paul Avila Mayer, Mary Ryan Munisteri, Judith Pinsker, Nancy Ford, B.K. Perlman, *Ryan's Hope*. ABC.
Agnes Nixon, Wisner Washam, Lorraine Broderick, Dani Morris, Jack Wood, Mary K. Wells, Clarice Blackburn, Elizabeth Wallace, Roni Dengel, Susan Kirshenbaum, Carolina Della Pietra, *All My Children*. ABC.
Margaret De Priest, Sheri Anderson, Maralyn Thoma, Michael Robert David, Susan Goldberg, Bob Hansen, Leah Markus, Dana Soloff, *Days of Our Lives*. NBC.
Anne Howard Bailey, A.J. Russell, Leah Laiman, Norma Monty, Thom Racina, Doris Silverton, Robert Guza, Jr., Charles Pratt, Jr., Peggy Schibi, Robert Shaw, *General Hospital*. ABC.

OTHER DAYTIME AWARD WINNERS
OUTSTANDING GAME OR AUDIENCE PARTICIPATION SHOW
• *The $25,000 Pyramid*. Bob Stewart, executive producer. CBS.

OUTSTANDING HOST/HOSTESS IN A GAME OR AUDIENCE PARTICIPATION SHOW
• Bob Barker, *The Price is Right*. CBS.

OUTSTANDING INDIVIDUAL DIRECTION FOR A GAME OR AUDIENCE PARTICIPATION SHOW
• Marc Breslow, *The Price is Right*. CBS.

OUTSTANDING TALK/SERVICE SERIES
• *Woman to Woman*. Mary Muldoon, producer. Syndicated.

OUTSTANDING HOST/HOSTESS IN A TALK/SERVICE SERIES
• Gary Collins, *Hour Magazine*. Syndicated.

OUTSTANDING INDIVIDUAL DIRECTION FOR A TALK/SERVICE SERIES
• Ron Weiner, *Donahue*. Syndicated.

OUTSTANDING VARIETY SERIES
• *The Merv Griffin Show*. Bob Murphy, executive producer. Peter Barsocchini, producer. Syndicated.

OUTSTANDING HOST/HOSTESS IN A VARIETY SERIES
• Merv Griffin, *The Merv Griffin Show*. Syndicated.

OUTSTANDING CHILDREN'S ENTERTAINMENT SERIES
• *Captain Kangaroo*. Bob Keeshan, Jim Hirschfeld, executive producers. Bette Chichon, Ruth Manecke, producers. CBS.

OUTSTANDING CHILDREN'S ENTERTAINMENT SPECIALS
• "The Great Love Experiment," *ABC Afterschool Special*. Jane Startz, executive producer. Doro Bachrach, producer. ABC.

OUTSTANDING CHILDREN'S INFORMATIONAL/INSTRUCTIONAL SPECIAL
• *Dead Wrong: The John Evans Story*. S. Bryan Hickox, Jay Daniel, executive producers. CBS.

OUTSTANDING CHILDREN'S INFORMATIONAL/INSTRUCTIONAL PROGRAMMING—SHORT FORM
• *Just Another Stupid Kid*. Tom Robertson, producer. Syndicated.

OUTSTANDING CHILDREN'S INFORMATIONAL/INSTRUCTIONAL PROGRAMMING
• *The ABC Weekend Special*. ABC.

OUTSTANDING PERFORMER IN CHILDREN'S PROGRAMMING
• Dick Van Dyke, *The Wrong Way Kid*, *CBS Library*. CBS.

OUTSTANDING INDIVIDUAL ACHIEVEMENT IN CHILDREN'S PROGRAMMING—DIRECTING
• Robert Mandel, "Andrea's Story: A Hitchhiking Tragedy," *ABC Afterschool Special*. ABC.

OUTSTANDING INDIVIDUAL ACHIEVEMENT IN CHILDREN'S PROGRAMMING—WRITING
• Norman Stiles, Gary Belkin, Sara Compton, Tom Dunsmuir, Judy Freudberg, Tony Geiss, Emily P. Kingsley, David Korr, Sonia Manzano, Jeff Moss, Luis Santeiro, *Sesame Street*. PBS.

OUTSTANDING TECHNICAL EXCELLENCE FOR A DAYTIME DRAMA SERIES
• Martin Gavrin, Louis Marchand, technical director. Charlie Henry, John Morris, Rich Schiaffro, Frank Schiraidi, Wallace Hewitt, Howie Zeidman, electronic camerapersons. Herb Segall, Frank Bailey, Marianne Malitz, senior video engineer. Susan Pomerantz, Stuart Silver, associate directors. Al Forman, Leona K. Zeira, video-tape editors, *One Life to Live*. ABC.

OUTSTANDING DESIGN EXCELLENCE FOR A DAYTIME DRAMA SERIES
• Richard Hankins, Harry Miller, art directors. Paul Hickey, Wes Laws, set decorators. Ralph Holmes, Lincoln Stulik, lighting directors. Robert Anton, David Dangle, costume designers. Joseph Cola, Susan Saccavino, makeup. Linda Williams, Alba Samperisi, hair designers. Barbara Miller, music supervisor, *Guiding Light*. CBS.

OUTSTANDING CINEMATOGRAPHY IN CHILDREN'S PROGRAMMING
• Hanania Baer, cinematographer, "Andrea's Story: A Hitchhiking Tragedy," *ABC Afterschool Special*. ABC.

OUTSTANDING FILM EDITING IN CHILDREN'S PROGRAMMING
• Thomas Haneke, Charlotte Grossman, film editors, *He Makes Me Feel Like Dancin'*. NBC.

OUTSTANDING MUSIC COMPOSITION IN CHILDREN'S PROGRAMMING
• Misha Segal, composer, "Andrea's Story: A Hitchhiking Tragedy," *ABC Afterschool Special*. ABC.

THE AREAS
Each area has the possibility of one award winner, multiple winners, or none. Winners are listed.

SPECIAL CLASSIFICATION OF OUTSTANDING PROGRAM ACHIEVEMENT
• *FYI*. Yanna Kroyt Brandt, producer. Mary Ann Donahue, coordinating producer. ABC.

OUTSTANDING INDIVIDUAL ACHIEVEMENT IN THE COVERAGE OF SPECIAL EVENTS
(Directors)
• Dick Schneider, *Macy's Thanksgiving Day Parade*. NBC.
(Technical direction/Electronic camerawork)
• Terry Rohnke, technical director. Bill Goetz, John Hillyer, Steve Gonzales, Barry Fisher, John Pinto, Don Mulvaney, Michael Bennett, Gene Martin, Karl Eckett, electronic camera. *Macy's Thanksgiving Day Parade*. NBC.

OUTSTANDING PROGRAM ACHIEVEMENT IN THE PERFORMING ARTS
• *Live from the Met*. Michael Bronson, executive producer. Clemente D'Allessio, producer. PBS.

OUTSTANDING INDIVIDUAL ACHIEVEMENT IN THE PERFORMING ARTS
(Host/Hostess)
• Dorothy Hamill, *Romeo & Juliet on Ice*. CBS.
(Directing)
• Rob Iscove, *Romeo & Juliet on Ice*. CBS.
(Audio)
• Jay David Saks, audio mixer, "Metropolitan Opera Centennial Gala," *Live from the Met*, PBS.
(Music)
• James Levine, music director/conductor, *Live from the Met*. PBS.

SPECIAL CLASSIFICATION OF OUTSTANDING INDIVIDUAL ACHIEVEMENT
(Performers)
• Carol Spinney. Role: Big Bird, Oscar, puppeteer. *Sesame Street*. PBS.
(Directing)
• Mike Gargiulo, *FYI*. ABC.
(Host/Hostess)
• Hal Linden, *FYI*. ABC.
(Audio)
• Paul Colten, Jack Hughes, audio mixers. *All My Children*, Remote: air plane crash. ABC.

OUTSTANDING ACHIEVEMENT IN RELIGIOUS PROGRAMMING—SERIES
(Tie)
• *Directions*. Sid Darion, executive producer. ABC.
• *Insight*. Ellwood E. Kieser, executive producer. Mike Rhodes, Terry Sweeney, producers. Syndicated.

OUTSTANDING INDIVIDUAL ACHIEVEMENT IN RELIGIOUS PROGRAMMING DIRECTING
• Jay Sandrich, *Insight.* Syndicated.

OUTSTANDING ACHIEVEMENT IN ANY AREA OF CREATIVE TECHNICAL CRAFTS
(Electronic camera)
• William J. Millard III, *The Edge of Night,* Remote: Gateway National Park. ABC.
(Art direction)
• Val Strazovec, scenic designer, *Romeo & Juliet on Ice.* CBS.

OUTSTANDING INDIVIDUAL ACHIEVEMENT IN CHILDREN'S PROGRAMMING
(Lighting direction)
• Randy Nodstrom, *Sesame Street.* PBS.
(Art direction)
• Cary White, "Andrea's Story: A Hitchhiking Tragedy," *ABC Afterschool Special.* ABC.

OUTSTANDING INDIVIDUAL ACHIEVEMENT IN TECHNICAL CRAFTS IN CHILDREN'S PROGRAMMING
(Technical direction)
• Ralph Mensch, *Sesame Street.* PBS.
(Audio)
• Blake Norton, *Sesame Street.* PBS.
(Video-tape editing)
• Arthur Schneider, "Andrea's Story: A Hitchhiking Tragedy," *ABC Afterschool Special.* ABC.
• Marie-Ange Ripka. "The Great Love Experiment," *ABC Afterschool Special.* ABC.

(No awards were bestowed in the areas of host/hostess and music in special events; costume design in the performing arts; writing and music in special classification; performers, sound editors, or mixers in religious programming; and graphic and costume designs in children's programming.)

NEWS & DOCUMENTARY AWARD WINNERS
OUTSTANDING COVERAGE OF A SINGLE BREAKING NEWS STORY (SEGMENTS)
• "The Assassination of Benigno Aquino," *ABC News,* William Stewart, producer. Jim Laurie, correspondent. ABC.
• "The Grenada Coverage," *The MacNeil-Lehrer Newshour,* Lester M. Crystal, executive producer. Dan Werner, senior producer. Robert MacNeil, Jim Lehrer, Charlayne Hunter-Gault, correspondents. PBS.
• "The Beirut Bombing," *The CBS Evening News with Dan Rather,* Howard Stringer, executive producer. Lane Venardos, senior producer. Harry Radliffe, Roxanne Russell, Al Ortiz, Susan Zirinsky, Phil O'Connor, Marquita Pool, producers. Tom Fenton, Bruce Morton, David Martin, Alan Pizzey, Bruce Hall, Leslie Stahl, reporter/correspondents. CBS.

BACKGROUND ANALYSIS, SINGLE CURRENT STORY
• *A Doomsday Scenario: Banking at the Brink.* Stephen D. Atlas, executive producer. Glenda Baugh Manzi, producer. Paul Solman, correspondent. PBS.
• "Abortion Clinic," *Frontline.* Mark Obenhaus, producer. Rita Stern, Michael Schwarz, coproducers. Jessica Savitch, reporter/ correspondent. PBS.
• "Nicaragua: A House Divided," *Inside Story.* Christopher Koch, executive producer. Hodding Carter III, correspondent. PBS.
• *Crime in America: Myth and Reality.* Paul Friedman, Bob Roy, executive producers. Charles C. Stuart, producer. Richard Threlkeld, reporter/correspondent. ABC.

OUTSTANDING BACKGROUND ANALYSIS OF A SINGLE CURRENT STORY (SEGMENTS)
• "U.S./U.S.S.R.: A Balance of Powers," *ABC World News Tonight.* Robert E. Frye, executive producer. David Guilbault, coordinating producer. Bob Aglow, Amy Entelis, Sally Holm, Steve Jacobs, David Kaplan, John Lower, Charles Stuart, Jonathan Talmadge, producers. Peter Jennings, John McWethy, Bob Zelnick, Sam Donaldson, Pierre Salinger, Richard Threlkeld, Rick Inderfurth, Dan Cordtz, correspondents. ABC.
• "The Countdown Against Cancer," *The CBS Evening News with Dan Rather.* Howard Stringer, executive producer. Linda Mason, senior producer. David Browning, producer. Terry Drinkwater, reporter/correspondent. CBS.
• "The Computers are Coming," *The CBS Evening News with Dan Rather.* Howard Stringer, executive producer. Linda Mason, senior producer. David Browning, producer. Dan Rather, reporter/ correspondent. CBS.
• "Marines in Beirut," *The MacNeil-Lehrer Newshour.* Michael Joseloff, producer. Jim Webb, correspondent. PBS.

• "Quest for Justice," *20/20.* Janice Tomlin, producer. Tom Jarriel, reporter/correspondent. ABC.

OUTSTANDING INVESTIGATIVE JOURNALISM
(Programs)
• "Uncounted Enemy, Unproven Conspiracy," *Inside Story.* Rose Economou, Joseph Russin, producers. Hodding Carter III, correspondent. PBS.

OUTSTANDING INVESTIGATIVE JOURNALISM
(Segments)
• "Growing Up in Smoke," *20/20.* Alice Irene Pifer, producer. John Stossel, correspondent. ABC.
• "Lenell Geters in Jail," *60 Minutes.* Suzanne St. Pierre, producer. Morley Safer, reporter/correspondent. CBS.
• "Poison on Your Plate," *First Camera.* Chuck Collins, Brian McTigue, producers. Mark Nykanen, correspondent. NBC.

OUTSTANDING INTERVIEW/INTERVIEWER(S)
(Programs)
• "The Day After," *Viewpoint.* William Lord, executive producer. George Watson, William Moore, Stuart Schwartz, Robert Jordan, senior producers. Carla De Landri, producer. Ted Koppel, reporter/correspondent. ABC.

OUTSTANDING INTERVIEW/INTERVIEWER(S)
(Segments)
• "Larry," *60 Minutes.* Jean Solomon, producer. Ed Bradley, reporter/correspondent. CBS.
• "Michael Doyle's Camden," *60 Minutes.* Elliot Bernstein, producer. Harry Reasoner, correspondent. CBS.
• "There But for the Grace of God: The Parents of John W. Hinckley, Jr.," *20/20.* Marion Goldin, producer. Barbara Walters, correspondent. ABC.

OUTSTANDING COVERAGE OF A CONTINUING NEWS STORY
(Programs)
• "Dateline: Moscow/Inside the USSR," *Inside Story.* Ned Schnurman, executive producer. Philip Burton, Christopher Koch Joseph Russin, producers. Hodding Carter III, correspondent. PBS.

OUTSTANDING COVERAGE OF A CONTINUING NEWS STORY
(Segments)
• "After the Parades," *Sunday Morning.* Kathy Sulkes, producer. David Culhane, reporter/correspondent. CBS.
• "Nicaragua 1983," *Today.* Jon Alpert, producer and reporter/ correspondent. NBC.

OUTSTANDING INFORMATIONAL, CULTURAL, OR HISTORICAL PROGRAMS
• "Rain Forest," *National Geographic Special.* David Hughes, Carol Hughes, producers. PBS.
• "America Takes Charge," *Vietnam: A Television History.* Richard Ellison, executive producer. Stanley Karnow, chief correspondent. .Andrew Pearson, producer. PBS.
• "LBJ Goes to War," *Vietnam: A Television History.* Richard Ellison, executive producer. Stanley Karnow, chief correspondent, Austin Hoyt, producers. PBS.
• "Peace is at Hand," *Vietnam: A Television History.* Richard Ellison, executive producer. Stanley Karnow, chief correspondent. Martin Smith, producer. PBS.
• "Legacies," *Vietnam: A Television History.* Richard Ellison, executive producer/producer. Stanley Karnow, chief correspondent. PBS.
• "Roots of a War," *Vietnam: A Television History.* Richard Ellison, executive producer. Stanley Karnow, chief correspondent. Judith Vecchione, producer. PBS.
• "The End of the Tunnel," *Vietnam: A Television History."* Richard Ellison, executive producer. Stanley Karnow, chief correspondent. Elizabeth Deane, producer. PBS.

OUTSTANDING INFORMATIONAL, CULTURAL, OR HISTORICAL SEGMENTS
• "Holocaust Remembrance," *ABC News Nightline.* Pamela Kahn, producer. ABC.
• "Aging," *Sunday Morning.* James Houtrides, producer. Bruce Morton, reporter/correspondent. CBS.

OUTSTANDING INFORMATIONAL, CULTURAL, OR HISTORICAL SEGMENTS
• "Black Family," *The CBS Evening News with Dan Rather.* Howard Stringer, executive producer. Marquita Pool, Chris Welcher, producers. Lem Tucker, reporter/

correspondent. CBS.
• "Mel Torme," *20/20.* Joe Pfifferling, producer. Bob Brown, reporter/correspondent. ABC.
• "The Mien People," *The CBS Evening News with Dan Rather.* Brian Healy, senior producer. Beth Pearlman, Charles Wolfson, producers. Bruce Morton, reporter/correspondent. CBS.

SPECIAL CLASSIFICATION
OF OUTSTANDING PROGRAM
ACHIEVEMENT
• "The Crisis Game," *ABC News Nightline.* William Lord, executive producer. William Moore, senior producer. Ted Koppel, reporter/correspondent. ABC.
• *The Miracle of Life.* John Mansfield, executive producer. Bo G. Erikson, Carl O. Lofman, producers and reporter/correspondents. PBS.
(Segments)
• "A Stranger in the Home," *Monitor.* Christine Huneke, producer. Rebecca Sobel, reporter/ correspondent. NBC.

OUTSTANDING INDIVIDUAL ACHIEVEMENT
(Writers)
• Judy Crichton, Andrew Schlesinger, Steve Singer, Bill Redeker, Pamela Hill, Richard Richter, *Oh, Tell the World What Happened.* ABC.
(Directors)
• Paul Fine, Holly Fine, *The Plane that Fell from the Sky.* CBS.
Jim Brown, *The Weavers: Wasn't That a Time.* PBS.
(Cinematographers)
• Gregory Andracke, *American Journey.* PBS.
(Camerapersons: Videographers)
• George J. Fridrich, "Repeat Offenders Segment," *First Camera.* NBC.
(Sound)
• David Clark, "Save the Panda," *National Geographic Special.* PBS.
(Tape editors)
• John J. Godfrey, Jon Alpert, John Custodio, "Nicaragua 1983," *Today.* NBC. Wayne Dennis, "Repeat Offenders Segment," *First Camera.* NBC.
(Film editors)
• Kris Liem, James Flanagan, Ara Chekmayan, Patrick M. Cook, John Martin, Bernard Stone, "JFK," *ABC News Special.* ABC.

(Scenic designers)
• Francis Mahard, "Crisis in Zimbabwe," *Frontline.* PBS.

INTERNATIONAL AWARD WINNERS
DOCUMENTARY
• *The Miracle of Life,* Swedish Television, SVT, Sweden.

PERFORMING ARTS
• *Dangerous Music,* HTV Ltd., Wales, U.K.

POPULAR ARTS
• *The Black Adder: The Archbishop*, BBC, U.K.

DRAMA
• *King Lear,* Granada Television Ltd., U.K.

CHILDREN'S PROGRAMMING
• *Fraggle Rock*, Canadian Broadcasting Corporation Corp., Canada.

SPECIAL AWARDS
OUTSTANDING ACHIEVEMENT
IN THE SCIENCE OF TELEVISION
ENGINEERING
• Ampex Corporation
• Kudelski, SA (Nagra)
• Lexicon, Inc.
• Sony Broadcast, Inc.
• Tektronic Inc.
• RCA Corp.

OUTSTANDING ACHIEVEMENT
IN ENGINEERING DEVELOPMENT
• Corporate Communications Consultants, Inc., for a color correction system that improves broadcast quality of film on television

NATIONAL AWARD FOR COMMUNITY
SERVICE
• *Priority One*, WNEV-TV, Boston.

A.T.A.S. GOVERNORS AWARD
• Bob Hope

SPECIAL RECOGNITION
• David L. Wolper

N.A.T.A.S. TRUSTEES AWARD
• Vladimir Zworykin

Male Hoaxer Crashes "Ladies' Night"

Everyone expected what the *L.A. Times* flagged in its headline — a "Cop Show Shoot-Out" — when the Emmys arrived to decide the contest of cops and robbers played by some of prime time's leading men and women. But few predicted correctly who the victors would be.

Hill Street Blues was aiming to nab the most best series awards of any show, after having tied *The Dick Van Dyke Show* and *All in the Family*'s record last year. *Cagney & Lacey*'s ratings were still in the basement, but its producers and many critics still hoped that the obvious quality of this unconventional program about two intelligent female cops might appeal to enlightened Emmy panel judges. However, both shows were up against a formidable adversary. *Miami Vice* was TV's latest megahit, a slick, postmodern detective series featuring hot fashions, cool pastel-colored scenes, and a catchy rock 'n' roll score. The *L.A. Herald Examiner* sized up the showdown as "the gritty slice-of-life realism of *Hill Street* against the flashy, stylish new look — and new sound — of *Miami Vice. Vice* ... would appear to have a good chance of dethroning the champion."

"Yes, it will be *Hill Street Blues* vs. *Miami Vice* as the main attraction," the *L.A. Times* agreed.

Once the awards match-up was under way, however, and the smoke started to clear, the *Herald Examiner* revealed the shocking results: "Throughout the night, favorites fell by the wayside. None was more deflated than *Miami Vice*, which led the Emmy nominations with 15, but ended up with only four awards .... Voters apparently

ORION

Sharon Gless and three-time best actress winner Tyne Daly of the twice-canceled and now triumphant Cagney & Lacey.

felt reluctant to give numerous awards to a show that is heavy on hedonism, violence, drugs and sexual flavor."

Vice's prizes were for cinematography, art direction, film sound editing, and supporting actor Edward James Olmos, who played the series' mysterious police lieutenant. Referring to the recent earthquake south of the border in which hundreds died, Olmos said, "I'm torn, torn between the catastrophe in Mexico City and this honor right now."

Vice star Don Johnson was favored to win best actor, but the honor ended up going to William Daniels, who portrayed a heart surgeon on *St. Elsewhere*, the stark, dark hospital series that had a loyal following among the country's cognoscenti. The veteran Broadway actor said, "I don't for a moment imagine that this award belongs solely to me.

It belongs to *St. Elsewhere*."

HSB entered the night's "shoot-out" with 11 nominations and was only five awards shy of topping *The Mary Tyler Moore Show*'s record of having the most Emmys. Assuming a poor showing by *Miami Vice*, it was the clear front runner, although, as *Variety* reported, "Not all of the night went off according to plan."

HSB's sole honor went to supporting actress Betty Thomas, whose trophy was accepted by a tuxedo-clad man who said he was standing in for the winner and then thanked, of all people, sportscaster Dick Schaap. "The audience murmured in astonishment," the *Herald Examiner* reported. "The bewildered Thomas then came on stage for her award, ABC cut to a commercial and viewers were still confused when she returned after the break with her acceptance speech."

The hoaxer was Barry Bremen, who was known in the athletic world as "the sports imposter" for often pretending to be a professional athlete. (On two occasions, he succeeded in warming up with pro baseball and basketball teams before All-Star games.) Once offstage, Bremen was arrested by Pasadena police, not for impersonating an Emmy winner, but for grand theft, because, said the local sergeant, "I guess those statuettes are worth more than $400." (They're not; each one costs roughly $150 to make.) *The Washington Post* described Bremen's ploy as "the most dramatic such interruption of a live awards show since 1974 when a streaker dashed across the stage at the Academy Awards telecast to the seeming surprise of actor David Niven then at the podium."

The ceremony just wasn't turning out to be the typical male-dominated event of years past, as evidenced by the eventual shoot-out victor. *Cagney & Lacey*, "twice bounced off CBS because of poor ratings," noted *Variety*, "only to bounce right back and become a winner," ended up with the most trophies of any program. It took six honors in all, for best drama series, directing, writing, film editing, film sound mixing, and, for a third year in a row, best actress Tyne Daly. "I'm the luckiest lady alive," said the pregnant Daly, one week overdue. When accepting the series award, producer Terry Louis Fisher referred to the producers of the other nominated series and said, "I'm the only one on the list without a Y chromosome. Ladies, we did it! It's our year!"

In the comedy runoff, Jane Curtin of *Kate & Allie* returned as best actress, as did supporting actress Rhea Perlman of *Cheers*. *Cheers* started out with 12 nods, including one for each of the six regular series actors, but like its cowinner of Emmys past, *Hill Street Blues*, it took only one prize this time. Perlman said," Twice is really a lot to be up here. I really feel I should thank everyone and I'm going to." After completing her roll call, she addressed her husband, *Taxi* star and past Emmy winner Danny DeVito, saying, "Danny, I love you. I got two. You only got one. Ha-ha!" John Larroquette of *Night Court* was named best supporting actor.

When *The Cosby Show* was hailed as best comedy series, it was "no surprise," noted *Variety*, "for the sitcom that has won both ratings and applause since it debuted." It was also acclaimed for its writing and direction. Producer Marcy Carsey accepted the series prize saying, "We thank Bill Cosby, who is the heart and soul of our show and who gives us pleasure every working day."

The Cosby Show was such a popular success that it was already in the

Did hedonism, violence, drugs, and sex make **Miami Vice** *lose so badly?*

David Letterman kept his thank-you remarks short "so we can save time for other impersonators in the audience."

Nielsen's top five after its premiere season and was largely responsible for pulling NBC up from its long-standing third-place rank. The series depicted an ordinary professional family, the Huxtables, headed by Cosby as a Brooklyn obstetrician and Phylicia Ayers-Allen as his attorney wife. And it was a big brood. In an interesting parallel, Cosby had four daughters and a son both on and off the screen.

Cosby surely would have been nominated for, and probably would have won, best actor, but he refused to run this year. The five-time past Emmy champ issued a statement before the initial voting, saying, "I welcome nominations for other members of the cast, but I personally choose not to participate." Cosby no longer believed in competing against fellow actors and wanted to give others a chance for the honor.

It went to Robert Guillaume, who created his role of the butler on *Soap* and then got his own show, *Benson*, in which he was eventually promoted to — that is, voted — his state's lieutenant governor. Guillaume had been nominated for an Emmy six times in the past, but now, finally a winner, said, "I'd like to thank Bill Cosby for not being here."

"In a sane world, *The Jewel in the Crown* would be the hands-down winner for outstanding limited series," wrote the *Herald Examiner*. The Emmys night could easily have turned out to be crazy, thanks to the hoaxer episode, but it was judged sane after all when *Jewel* took the crowning honor of its category. The PBS miniseries about the fading days of British colonial rule in India was the fourth non-American production in a row to prevail as best limited series.

Richard Crenna was named best actor for *The Rape of Richard Beck*. "His portrayal of a macho cop who is sexually assaulted by men gains a new understanding of the humiliation suffered by women victims," wrote the *Herald Examiner*. Farrah Fawcett was expected to be named best actress for her portrayal of a battered housewife in the highest-rated TV movie of the year, *The Burning Bed*, but instead the award went to past Emmy favorite Joanne Woodward for her portrayal of a woman stricken with Alzheimer's disease in *Do You Remember Love*. It also won the scribbler's trophy for first-time screenwriter Vickie Patik.

The most awards in the limited series/special category were claimed by *Wallenberg: A Hero's Story*, a drama based on the struggle of the heroic Swedish diplomat who saved thousands of Jews during World War II. It earned a director's statuette and three more for technical achievement.

In the variety category, *Motown Returns to the Apollo* was named best program, while *Sweeney Todd* took three prizes, including one for George Hearn for his performance as the bloodthirsty British barber. The writing award went to *Late Night with David Letterman* and was accepted by its host, who said he would keep his remarks brief "so we can save plenty of time for other impersonators who may be in the audience."

DAYTIME AWARDS

The daytime awards finally returned to the airwaves for the first time since 1982 thanks to an historic agreement between N.A.T.A.S. and A.T.A.S. to share the task of staging them. It was the first time that the two TV academies joined forces since their split in 1977. The result was impressive: Nearly 10 million viewers tuned in to their afternoon gala held at the Grand Ballroom of the Waldorf-Astoria Hotel in New York where Bob Barker, host of the number one-rated game show *The Price is Right*, presided as master of ceremonies.

Broadcaster CBS took the bulk of the prizes, including five for *The Young and the Restless*, which established a new record by winning the best series award for an unprecedented third time. (Earlier wins were in 1975 and 1983.) *The Young and the Restless* was also acknowledged for makeup, its technical production staff, supporting actress Beth Maitland (who played Traci Abbott Romalotti), and "ingenue" Tracey E. Bregman (as Lauren Fenmore Williams). The Outstanding Ingenue category was new, just as its male equivalent, Outstanding Juvenile/Young Man, which went to Brian Bloom (Dustin Donovan) of CBS's *As the World Turns*. The same network's *Guiding Light* won the second most trophies — four — for directing, design excellence, supporting actor Larry Gates (H.B. Lewis), and best actress Kim Zimmer (Reva Shayne Lewis), who was so excited about winning her first Emmy that she left a shoe behind in her scramble to the podium.

Emmys emcee Barker was nominated for best game show host, but lost to Dick Clark of *The $25,000 Pyramid*, which also won the series award.

In the early days of *Donahue*'s network airing, it often reaped the honors for both best talk show and its host, but the last time it swept both categories was five years earlier. This time it was back in full force. *Donahue* himself last received the host's award in 1983, but he was obviously buoyed by winning it again, as he kissed his wife, actress Marlo Thomas, in the audience upon hearing the news and then vaulted up to the stage to collect it. Then *Donahue*, which recently had moved from Chicago to New York, took the top series honors.

Sesame Street was another old favorite that returned this year (as best children's series), while spinoff show *Jim Henson's Muppet Babies* was named best animated program. Throughout the 1980s, *ABC Afterschool Specials* virtually dominated the award for Outstanding Children's Specials, but this year it went to the *CBS Schoolbreak Special* "All the Kids Do It," which dramatized teenage alcohol abuse. It was produced by prime-time *Happy Days* star Henry Winkler, who also made his directorial debut with the drama.

The Young and the Restless *won best series for an historic third time.*

SPORTS AWARDS

The sports awards "have been in limbo since the 1982–83 awards," reported *The Washington Post*. Some network executives thought the tonic they needed was to give them their own broadcast again while others continued to voice concern over the balloting procedure. NBC was among the latter and yet again declined to participate officially.

Winners were formerly chosen by journalists and television academy members, but N.A.T.A.S. decided to accommodate the networks' requests to allow representatives of their sports departments to vote as long as they could demonstrate no conflicts of interest. "The latest method still raises questions of integrity and there have been calls for public disclosure of how each network sports department voted," the *Post* added. But still the Seventh Annual Sports Awards took place — albeit late, in August 1986 — at a champagne reception held at the Essex House along New York's Central Park.

Given that the extended eligibility period included an Olympics year, ABC swept up most of the trophies for its comprehensive coverage as it did four years earlier, reaping gold for best live sports special, for sports journalism, individual achievement, its video-tape editors, and its technical team. On the occasion of its 20th anniversary, ABC's *American Sportsman* was hailed as best edited sports series. The program, hosted by Curt Gowdy and featuring athletes and other famous folk hunting and fishing, was also given a trophy for program achievement.

A syndicated preview to the Superbowl pitting the Miami Dolphins against the eventual champion San Francisco '49ers was voted best edited sports special. NBC's George Michael was named program host of the year for *The George Michael Sports Machine*, which was produced by the NBC affiliate in Washington, D.C.

NEWS & DOCUMENTARY AWARDS

After a vigorous N.A.T.A.S. campaign to solicit more material for Emmy consideration, nomination entries increased by more than 75 percent over last year. Winners were revealed at the Grand Hyatt Hotel in New York where presenters included such notables as Harry Belafonte (who recently helped initiate the benefit recording for the USA for Africa charity campaign) and Christa McAuliffe, "the teacher with the right stuff" who would soon die in the explosion of the space shuttle Challenger when she became the first private citizen in space.

The CBS Evening News took the bulk of prizes with seven segments claiming honors, including footage on Beirut, Afghanistan, and the reelection campaign of President Reagan. The network's short-lived new series *Crossroads* was reaping low ratings opposite the popular prime-time *A-Team* series, but it nabbed an impressive two awards for segments on steeplejacks and the White House's Strategic Defense Initiative. *Crossroads* cohost Bill Moyers also won for his ambitious survey show *A Walk Through the 20th Century with Bill Moyers*. The 19-week documentary series revealing what Moyers called "the vivacity of the past" was voted Outstanding Informational Series at A.T.A.S.'s prime-time awards and now took an additional N.A.T.A.S. news trophy for its "World War II Propaganda Battle" episode.

Despite the ongoing NBC boycott, *NBC Nightly News* took three awards for such segments as profiles on the Cold War and the human brain. Its *Monitor* news series had been revamped and retitled *First Camera* in 1983 and placed opposite *60 Minutes*. It failed to dislodge its competitor, but it was appreciated enough by Emmy voters to win an investigative trophy for a segment on the antics of political cult leader Lyndon LaRouche. Also recognized for its investigative work was *Today*.

ABC won two Emmys for *20/20* and a program trophy for "Massacre in San Ysidro" on *ABC News Nightline*.

PBS, which took the most news statuettes last year, made another strong showing with an *Inside Story* piece on Jesse Jackson, two segments of *The MacNeil-Lehrer Newshour* and three programs of *Frontline*, which had been launched in January 1983, with Jessica Savitch serving as host prior to her fatal auto crash the following fall.

1984-85

The prime-time ceremony was broadcast on ABC from the Pasadena Civic Auditorium on September 22, 1985, for prime-time programs telecast between July 1, 1984, and June 30, 1985. Daytime awards broadcast on CBS from the Waldorf-Astoria Hotel on August 1, 1985, for programs aired between March 6, 1984, and March 5, 1985. News & documentary awards presented August 29, 1985, for 1984 programs. Sports awards were presented on August 12, 1986.

PRIME-TIME PROGRAM AWARDS

OUTSTANDING DRAMA SERIES
• *Cagney & Lacey.* Barney Rosenzweig, executive producer. Steve Brown, Terry Louise Fisher, Peter Lefcourt, producers. CBS.
Hill Street Blues. Steven Bochco, executive producer. Gregory Hoblit, co-executive producer. Scott Brazil, supervising producer. Jeffrey Lewis, producer. David Milch, coproducer. NBC.
Miami Vice. Michael Mann, Anthony Yerkovich, executive producers. John Nicolella, Liam O'Brien, supervising producers. John Nicolella, Mel Swope, producers. Richard Brams, George E. Crosby, coproducers. NBC.
Murder, She Wrote. Peter S. Fischer, Richard Levinson, William Link, executive producers. Robert F. O'Neill, supervising producer. Robert F. O'Neill, Douglas Benton, producers. CBS.
St. Elsewhere. Bruce Paltrow, executive producer. Mark Tinker, supervising producer. John Masius, Tom Fontana, producers. Abby Singer, coordinating producer. NBC.

OUTSTANDING COMEDY SERIES
• *The Cosby Show.* Marcy Carsey, Tom Werner, executive producers. Earl Pomerantz, Elliot Shoenman, co-executive producers. John Markus, supervising producer. Caryn Sneider, producer. Jerry

Ross, Michael Loman, coproducers. NBC.
Cheers. James Burrows, Glen Charles, Les Charles, executive producers. Ken Estin, Sam Simon, producers. NBC.
Family Ties. Gary David Goldberg, Lloyd Garver, executive producers. Michael J. Weithorn, supervising producer. Ruth Bennett, Alan Uger, producers. Carol Himes, line producer. NBC.
Kate & Allie. Mort Lachman, Merrill Grant, executive producers. Bill Persky, Bob Randall, producers. Allan Leicht, coproducer. George Barimo, coordinating producer. CBS.
Night Court. Reinhold Weege, executive producer. Jeffrey Melman, producer. NBC.

OUTSTANDING LIMITED SERIES
• *The Jewel in the Crown, Masterpiece Theatre.* Denis Forman, executive producer. Christopher Morahan, producer. PBS.
Barbara Taylor Bradford's "A Woman of Substance." Ian Warren, Tom Donald, executive producers. Diane Baker, producer. Syndicated.
Ellis Island. Gabriel Katzka, Frank Konigsberg, executive producers. Jerry London, supervising producer. Nick Gillot, producer. CBS.
Robert Kennedy and His Times. Rick Rosenberg, Bob Christiansen, producers. CBS.
Space. Dick Berg, executive producer. Martin Manulis, producer. Allan J. Marcil, coproducer. Jack Clements, Robert Birnbaum, coordinating producers. CBS.

OUTSTANDING DRAMA/COMEDY SPECIAL
• *Do You Remember Love.* Dave Bell, executive producer. Marilyn Hall, co-executive producer. Wayne Threm, James E. Thompson, producers. Walter Halsey Davis, coproducer. CBS.
The Burning Bed. Jon Avent, Steve Tisch, executive producers. Carol Schreder,

producer. Rose Leiman Goldemberg, coproducer. NBC.
Fatal Vision. Mike Rosenfeld, Daniel Wigutow, executive producers. Richard L. O'Connor, producer. NBC.
Heartsounds, ABC Theatre. Norman Lear, executive producer. Fay Kanin, Fern Field, producers. ABC.
Wallenberg: A Hero's Story. Dick Berg, executive producer. Richard Irving, producer. Lamont Johnson, Phillip I. Levitan, coproducers. NBC.

Outstanding Variety, Music, or Comedy Program
• *Motown Returns to the Apollo*. Suzanne de Passe, executive producer. Don Mischer, producer. Suzanne Coston, Michael L. Weisbarth, coproducers. NBC.
The American Film Institute Salute to Gene Kelly. George Stevens, Jr., producer. CBS.
Late Night with David Letterman. Jack Rollins, executive producer. Barry Sand, producer. David Letterman, host. NBC.
Lena Horne: The Lady and Her Music, Great Performances. Robert Manby, executive producer. Diane M. Gioia, supervising producer. Sherman Sneed, producer. Bill Siegler, coordinating producer. Lena Horne, host. PBS.
The Tonight Show Starring Johnny Carson. Fred DeCordova, executive producer. Peter Lassally, producer. Johnny Carson, host. NBC.

Outstanding Classical Program in the Performing Arts
(Winner)
• "Tosca," *Live From the Met*. Michael Bronson, executive producer. Samuel J. Paul, producer. PBS.

Outstanding Informational Series
(Winner)
• *The Living Planet: A Portrait of the Earth*. Richard Brock, executive producer. Adrian Warren, Ned Kelly, Andrew Neal, Richard Brock, producers. PBS.

Outstanding Informational Special
(Winner)
• *Cousteau: Mississippi*. Jacques-Yves Cousteau, Jean-Michel Cousteau, executive producers. Andrew Solt, producer. Jacques-Yves Cousteau, host. Syndicated.

Outstanding Animated Program
(Winner)
• *Garfield in the Rough*. Jay Poynor, executive producer. Phil Roman, producer. Jim Davis, writer. Phil Roman, director. CBS.

Outstanding Children's Program
(Winner)
• *Displaced Person, American Playhouse*. Allison Maher, Barry Solomon, Rick Traum, Patrick Lynch, executive producers. Patrick Dromgoole, supervising executive producer. Barry Levinson, producer. PBS.

PERFORMANCE, DIRECTING, AND WRITING
Outstanding Lead Actor in a Drama Series
• William Daniels, *St. Elsewhere*. NBC.
Ed Flanders, *St. Elsewhere*. NBC.
Don Johnson, *Miami Vice*. NBC.
Tom Selleck, *Magnum, P.I.* CBS.
Daniel J. Travanti, *Hill Street Blues*. NBC.

Outstanding Lead Actress in a Drama Series
• Tyne Daly, *Cagney & Lacey*. CBS.
Debbie Allen, *Fame*. Syndicated.
Sharon Gless, *Cagney & Lacey*. CBS.
Veronica Hamel, *Hill Street Blues*. NBC.
Angela Lansbury, *Murder, She Wrote*. CBS.

Outstanding Lead Actor in a Comedy Series
• Robert Guillaume, *Benson*. ABC.
Harry Anderson, *Night Court*. NBC.
Ted Danson, *Cheers*. NBC.
Bob Newhart, *Newhart*. CBS.
Jack Warden, *Crazy Like a Fox*. CBS.

Outstanding Lead Actress in a Comedy Series
• Jane Curtin, *Kate & Allie*. CBS.
Phylicia Ayers-Allen, *The Cosby Show*. NBC.
Shelley Long, *Cheers*. NBC.
Susan Saint James, *Kate & Allie*. CBS.
Isabel Sanford, *The Jeffersons*. CBS.

Outstanding Lead Actor in a Limited Series or Special
• Richard Crenna, *The Rape of Richard Beck, ABC Theatre*. ABC.
Richard Chamberlain, *Wallenberg: A Hero's Story*. NBC.
James Garner, *Heartsounds, ABC Theatre*. ABC.

Richard Kiley, *Do You Remember Love.*
CBS.
George C. Scott, *A Christmas Carol.*
CBS.

**OUTSTANDING LEAD ACTRESS
IN A LIMITED SERIES OR SPECIAL**
• Joanne Woodward, *Do You Remember
Love.* CBS.
Jane Alexander, *Malice in Wonderland.*
CBS.
Peggy Ashcroft, *The Jewel in the Crown,
Masterpiece Theatre.* PBS.
Farrah Fawcett, *The Burning Bed.* NBC.
Mary Tyler Moore, *Heartsounds, ABC
Theatre.* ABC.

**OUTSTANDING SUPPORTING ACTOR
IN A DRAMA SERIES**
• Edward James Olmos, *Miami Vice.* NBC.
Ed Begley, Jr., *St. Elsewhere.* NBC.
John Hillerman, *Magnum, P.I.* CBS.
John Karlen, *Cagney & Lacey.* CBS.
Bruce Weitz, *Hill Street Blues.* NBC.

**OUTSTANDING SUPPORTING ACTRESS
IN A DRAMA SERIES**
• Betty Thomas, *Hill Street Blues.* NBC.
Barbara Bosson, *Hill Street Blues.* NBC.
Christina Pickles, *St. Elsewhere.* NBC.
Doris Roberts, *Remington Steele.* NBC.
Madge Sinclair, *Trapper John, M.D.* CBS.

**OUTSTANDING SUPPORTING ACTOR
IN A COMEDY SERIES**
• John Larroquette, *Night Court.* NBC
Nicholas Colasanto, *Cheers.* NBC.
Michael J. Fox, *Family Ties.* NBC.
John Ratzenberger, *Cheers.* NBC.
George Wendt, *Cheers.* NBC.

**OUTSTANDING SUPPORTING ACTRESS
IN A COMEDY SERIES**
• Rhea Perlman, *Cheers.* NBC.
Selma Diamond, *Night Court.* NBC.
Julia Duffy, *Newhart.* CBS.
Marla Gibbs, *The Jeffersons.* CBS.
Inga Swenson, *Benson.* ABC.

**OUTSTANDING SUPPORTING ACTOR
IN A LIMITED SERIES OR SPECIAL**
• Karl Malden, *Fatal Vision.* NBC.
Richard Burton, *Ellis Island.* CBS
Sir John Gielgud, *Romance on the Orient
Express.* NBC.
Richard Masur, *The Burning Bed.* NBC.
Rip Torn, *The Atlanta Child Murders.*
CBS.

**OUTSTANDING SUPPORTING ACTRESS
IN A LIMITED SERIES OR SPECIAL**
• Kim Stanley, *Cat on a Hot Tin Roof,
American Playhouse.* PBS.
Penny Fuller, *Cat on a Hot Tin Roof,
American Playhouse.* PBS.
Ann Jillian, *Ellis Island.* CBS.
Deborah Kerr, *Barbara Taylor Bradford's
"A Woman of Substance."* Syndicated.
Alfre Woodard, "Words By Heart,"
Wonderworks. PBS.

**OUTSTANDING INDIVIDUAL PERFORMANCE
IN A VARIETY OR MUSIC PROGRAM**
• George Hearn, *Sweeney Todd, Great
Performances.* PBS.
Billy Crystal, *Saturday Night Live.* NBC.
Gregory Hines, *Motown Returns to the
Apollo.* NBC.
Patti La Belle, *Motown Returns to the
Apollo.* NBC.
Angela Lansbury, *Sweeney Todd, Great
Performances.* NBC.

**OUTSTANDING DIRECTING
IN A DRAMA SERIES**
• Karen Arthur, *Cagney & Lacey.* CBS.
Georg Stanford Brown, *Hill Street Blues.*
NBC.
Thomas Carter, *Hill Street Blues.* NBC.
Paul Michael Glaser, *Miami Vice.* NBC.
Lee H. Katzin, *Miami Vice.* NBC.

**OUTSTANDING DIRECTING
IN A COMEDY SERIES**
• Jay Sandrich, *The Cosby Show.* NBC.
James Burrows, *Cheers.* NBC.
Robert Butler, *Moonlighting.* ABC.
Marc Daniels, *Alice.* CBS.
Bill Persky, *Kate & Allie.* CBS.

**OUTSTANDING DIRECTING
IN A LIMITED SERIES OR SPECIAL**
• Lamont Johnson, *Wallenberg: A Hero's
Story.* NBC.
Jeff Bleckner, *Do You Remember Love.*
CBS.
Gilbert Cates, *Consenting Adult, ABC
Theater.* ABC.
David Greene, *Fatal Vision.*
NBC.
Robert Greenwald, *The Burning Bed.*
NBC.
Christopher Morahan, Jim O'Brien, *The
Jewel in the Crown, Masterpiece Theatre.*
PBS.

**OUTSTANDING DIRECTING
IN A VARIETY OR MUSIC PROGRAM**
• Terry Hughes, *Sweeney Todd, Great Performances*. PBS.
Hal Burnee, *Late Night with David Letterman—3rd Anniversary Special*. NBC.
Clark Jones, *Night of 100 Stars II*. ABC.
Don Mischer, *Motown Returns to the Apollo*. NBC.

**OUTSTANDING WRITING
IN A DRAMA SERIES**
• Patricia Green, *Cagney & Lacey*. CBS.
Deborah Arakelian, *Cagney & Lacey*. CBS.
Jacob Epstein, teleplay. Michael Wagner, story, *Hill Street Blues*. NBC.
Tom Fontana, John Masius, Steve Bello, *St. Elsewhere*. NBC.
John Masius, Tom Fontana, *St. Elsewhere*. NBC.
Anthony Yerkovich, *Miami Vice*. NBC.

**OUTSTANDING WRITING
IN A COMEDY SERIES**
• Ed. Weinberger, Michael Leeson, *The Cosby Show*. NBC.
Peter Casey, David Lee, *Cheers*. NBC.
Glen Charles, Les Charles, *Cheers*. NBC.
David Lloyd, *Cheers*, NBC.
Earl Pomerantz, *The Cosby Show*. NBC.

**OUTSTANDING WRITING
IN A VARIETY OR MUSIC PROGRAM**
• Gerard Mulligan, Sandy Frank, Joe Toplyn, Chris Elliott, Matt Wickline, Jeff Martin, Eddie Gorodetsky, Randy Cohen, Larry Jacobson, Kevin Curran, Fred Graver, Merrill Markoe, David Letterman, *Late Night with David Letterman*. NBC.
Buz Kohan, Peter Elbling, Samm-Art Williams, *Motown Returns to the Apollo*. NBC.
Steve O'Donnell, Sandy Frank, Joe Toplyn, Chris Elliott, Matt Wickline, Jeff Martin, Gerard Mulligan, Randy Cohen, Larry Jacobson, Kevin Curran, Fred Graver, David Letterman, *Late Night with David Letterman*. NBC.
Steve O'Donnell, Sandy Frank, Joe Toplyn, Chris Elliott, Matt Wickline, Jeff Martin, Gerard Mulligan, Randy Cohen, Larry Jacobson, Kevin Curran, Fred Graver, Merrill Markoe, David Letterman, *Late Night with David Letterman*. NBC.
George Stevens, Jr., Lane Jeffrey. *The American Film Institute Salute to Gene Kelly*. CBS.

**OUTSTANDING WRITING
IN A LIMITED SERIES OR SPECIAL**
• Vickie Patik, *Do You Remember Love*. CBS.
John Gay, *Fatal Vision*. NBC.
Rose Leiman Goldemberg, *The Burning Bed*. NBC.
Gerald Green, *Wallenberg: A Hero's Story*. NBC.
Ken Taylor, *The Jewel in the Crown, Masterpiece Theatre*. PBS.

A.T.A.S.

Best lead actor in a comedy series Robert Guillaume of Benson thanked Bill Cosby "for not being here."

OTHER AWARD WINNERS
**OUTSTANDING ART DIRECTION
FOR A SERIES**
• Jeffrey Howard, art director. Robert Lacey, Jr., set decorator, *Miami Vice*. NBC.

**OUTSTANDING ART DIRECTION
FOR A LIMITED SERIES OR A SPECIAL**
• Jan Scott, production designer. Charles C. Bennett, David Davis, art directors. Robert Lee Drumheller, Jacques Bradette, set decorators, *Evergreen*. NBC.

**OUTSTANDING ART DIRECTION
FOR A VARIETY OR MUSIC PROGRAM**
• Rene Lagler, production designer. Jeremy Railton, art director, *The 57th Annual Academy Awards*. ABC.

**OUTSTANDING MUSIC COMPOSITION
FOR A SERIES
(Dramatic underscore)**
• John Addison, *Murder, She Wrote*. CBS.

**OUTSTANDING MUSIC COMPOSITION
FOR A LIMITED SERIES OR A SPECIAL
(Dramatic underscore)**
• Allyn Ferguson, *Camille*, *Hallmark Hall
of Fame*. CBS.

OUTSTANDING MUSIC DIRECTION
• Ian Fraser, music director. Ian Fraser,
Bill Byers, Angela Morley, principal
arrangers, *Christmas in Washington*. NBC.

OUTSTANDING MUSIC AND LYRICS
• James DiPasquale, composer. Douglas
Brayfield, lyricist, *Love Lives On*. ABC.

OUTSTANDING CHOREOGRAPHY
• Twyla Tharp, "Baryshnikov by Tharp
with American Ballet Theatre," *Dance in
America*. PBS.

**OUTSTANDING COSTUME DESIGN
FOR A SERIES**
• Travilla, *Dallas*. CBS.

**OUTSTANDING COSTUME DESIGN
FOR A LIMITED SERIES OR A SPECIAL**
• Barbara Lane, *Ellis Island*. CBS.

OUTSTANDING MAKEUP
• Michael G. Westmore, special makeup
designed and created by Bob Norin,
makeup supervisor. Jamie Brown, Sandy
Cooper, makeup artists, *The Three Wishes
of Billy Grier*. ABC.

OUTSTANDING HAIRSTYLING
• Robert L. Stevenson, *The Jesse Owens
Story*. Syndicated.

**OUTSTANDING CINEMATOGRAPHY
FOR A SERIES**
• Robert E. Collins, *Miami Vice*. NBC.

**OUTSTANDING CINEMATOGRAPHY
FOR A LIMITED SERIES OR SPECIAL**
• Philip Lathrop, *Malice in Wonderland*.
CBS.

**OUTSTANDING TECHNICAL
DIRECTION/ELECTRONIC CAMERAWORK/
VIDEO CONTROL FOR A SERIES**
• Herm Falk, technical director. Randall
Baer, Stephen Jones, Bill McCloud, Donna
Quante, camerapersons. Victor Bagdadi,
senior video control, *Benson*. ABC.

**OUTSTANDING TECHNICAL
DIRECTION/ELECTRONIC
CAMERAWORK/VIDEO CONTROL
FOR A LIMITED SERIES OR SPECIAL**
• Louis Fusari, technical director. Les
Atkinson, Jim Herring, Mike Higuera, Roy
Holm, Dave Levisohn, Dana Martin, Mike
Stramisky, camerapersons. Jerry Smith,
senior video control, *The Magic of David
Copperfield VII*. CBS.

**OUTSTANDING FILM EDITING
FOR A SERIES**
• Jim Gross, *Cagney & Lacey*. CBS.

**OUTSTANDING FILM EDITING
FOR A LIMITED SERIES OR A SPECIAL**
• Paul F. La Mastra, *Wallenberg: A Hero's
Story*. NBC.

**OUTSTANDING VIDEO-TAPE EDITING
FOR A SERIES**
• Jim McElroy, *Fame*. Syndicated.

**OUTSTANDING VIDEO-TAPE EDITING
FOR A LIMITED SERIES OR A SPECIAL**
• Jimmy B. Frazier, editor, *Sweeney Todd,
Great Performances*. PBS.

**OUTSTANDING FILM SOUND EDITING
FOR A SERIES**
• Chuck Moran, supervisor. Bruce Bell,
Victor B. Lackey, Ian MacGregor-Scott,
Carl Mahakian, John Oettinger, Bernie
Pincus, Warren Smith, Bruce Stambler,
Mike Wilhoit, Kyle Wright, editors. Paul
Wittenberg. Jerry Sanford Cohen, music,
Miami Vice. NBC.

**OUTSTANDING FILM SOUND EDITING –
LIMITED SERIES OR A SPECIAL**
• Jeff Clark, supervisor. Paul Carden, Nick
Eliopoulos, Jim Koford, Don Malouf, Dick
Raderman, Greg Stacy, Dan Thomas,
James Troutman, Mike Virnig, editors.
Tally Paulos, John Lasalandra, music,
Wallenberg: A Hero's Story. NBC.

**OUTSTANDING FILM SOUND MIXING
FOR A SERIES**
• Maury Harris, production. John B.
Asman, William Nicholson, Ken S. Polk,
rerecording, *Cagney & Lacey*. CBS.

OUTSTANDING FILM SOUND MIXING FOR A LIMITED SERIES OR A SPECIAL
• Clark David King, production. David J. Hudson, Mel Metcalfe, Terry Porter, rerecording, *Space*. CBS.

OUTSTANDING LIVE AND TAPE SOUND MIXING AND SOUND EFFECTS FOR A SERIES
• Douglas Gray, preproduction. Michael Ballin, production; Thomas Huth, postproduction. Sam Black, sound effects, *Cheers*. NBC.

OUTSTANDING LIVE AND TAPE SOUND MIXING AND SOUND EFFECTS FOR A LIMITED SERIES OR A SPECIAL
• Robert Liftin, preproduction. Edward J. Greene, production. Russ Terrana, postproduction. Carroll Pratt, sound effects, *Motown Returns to the Apollo*. NBC.

OUTSTANDING LIGHTING DIRECTION (ELECTRONIC) FOR A SERIES
• George Spiro Dibie, director of photography. *Mr. Belvedere*. ABC.

OUTSTANDING LIGHTING DIRECTION (ELECTRONIC) FOR A LIMITED SERIES OR A SPECIAL
• Bill Klages, Arnie Smith. "Baryshnikov by Tharp with American Ballet Theatre," *Dance in America*. PBS.

THE AREAS
Each area has the possiblity of multiple winners, one winner, or none. Winners are listed.

OUTSTANDING INDIVIDUAL ACHIEVEMENT
(Outstanding performing—Classical music/Dance programming)
• Luciano Pavarotti, "Rigoletto," *Great Performances*. PBS.
(Outstanding directing—Classical music/Dance programming)
• Don Mischer, Twyla Tharp, "Baryshnikov by Tharp with American Ballet Theatre," *Dance in America*. PBS.
• Franco Zeffirelli, "I Pagliacci," *Great Performances*. PBS.
(Outstanding writing—Informational programming)
• Howard Enders, John G. Fox, Michael Joseloff, Marc Siegel, *Heritage: Civilization and the Jews*. PBS.

Brian Winston, *Heritage: Civilization and the Jews*. PBS.
(Outstanding costuming)
• Tommy Welsh, costume supervisor, U.S.A. Bob E. Horn, costumer, U.S.A. Marko Cerovec (costumer, Yugoslavian) *Wallenberg: A Hero's Story*. NBC.
(Outstanding graphic and title design)
• John Tribe, graphic designer, *Agatha Christie's "Partners in Crime."* PBS.
• Alex Weil, Charles Levi, title sequence creators, *Saturday Night Live*. NBC.
• Rocky Morton, Annabel Jankel, title designers. Dick Ebersol, executive producer, *Friday Night Videos*. NBC.
(Outstanding special visual effects)
• Albert Whitlock, visual effects supervisor and matte artist. Syd Dutton, matte artist. Mark Whitlock, assistant matte artist. Bill Taylor, Dennis Glouner, matte photography. Lynn Ledgerwood, special rigging, *A.D.* NBC.
• John Allison, director, designer and supervisor of special visual effects, *The Brain*. PBS.
• Michael Pangrazio, visual effects supervisor. Dennis Muren, postproduction effects supervisor. Phil Tippett, stop motion supervisor. Jon Berg, creature supervisor. Harley Jessup, art director. John Ellis, optical photography supervisor. Chris Evans, matte painting supervisor, *The Ewok Adventure*. ABC.
• Bill Mesa, introvision visual effects director and director of photography. Mike Hanan, introvision art director. Tim Donahue, introvision stage-matte artist. Gene Rizzardi, model ship supervisor, *The Hugga Bunch*. Syndicated.

OUTSTANDING ACHIEVEMENT IN ENGINEERING DEVELOPMENT
• Ron and Richard Grant for the development of the Auricle Time Processor.

OUTSTANDING ENGINEERING EXCELLENCE
• RCA Corporation
• ABC

(There were no winners in the areas of outstanding performance in informational programming and outstanding writing in music and dance.)

DAYTIME AWARDS
OUTSTANDING DAYTIME DRAMA SERIES
• *The Young and the Restless*. H. Wesley Kenney, William J. Bell, executive producers. Edward Scott, producer. CBS.
All My Children. Jacqueline Babbin, producer. ABC.
Days of Our Lives. Al Rabin, Betty Corday, executive producers. Ken Corday, Shelly Curtis, producers. NBC.
General Hospital. Gloria Monty, producer. ABC.
Guiding Light. Gail Kobe, executive producer. John P. Whitesell, Robert D. Kochman, Leslie Dartwin, producers. CBS

OUTSTANDING ACTOR
• Darnell Williams, *All My Children*. ABC.
Larry Bryggman, *As the World Turns*. CBS.
David Canary, *All My Children*. ABC.
Terry Lester, *The Young and the Restless*. CBS.
James Mitchell, *All My Children*. ABC.

OUTSTANDING ACTRESS
• Kim Zimmer, *Guiding Light*. CBS.
Deidre Hall, *Days of Our Lives*. NBC.
Susan Lucci, *All My Children*. ABC.
Gillian Spencer, *All My Children*. ABC.
Robin Strasser, *One Life to Live*. ABC.

OUTSTANDING SUPPORTING ACTOR
• Larry Gates, *Guiding Light*. CBS.
Anthony Call, *One Life to Live*. ABC.
Louis Edmonds, *All My Children*. ABC.
David Lewis, *General Hospital*. ABC.
Robert Lupone, *All My Children*. ABC.

OUTSTANDING SUPPORTING ACTRESS
• Beth Maitland, *The Young and the Restless*. CBS.
Norma Connolly, *General Hospital*. ABC.
Eileen Herlie, *All My Children*. ABC.
Maeve Kinkead, *Guiding Light*. CBS.
Elizabeth Lawrence, *All My Children*. ABC.

OUTSTANDING DIRECTING
John Whitesell II, Bruce Barry, Matthew Diamond, Irene M. Pace, directors. Robert D. Kochman, Joanne Rivituso, Matthew Diamond, Joanne Sedwick, associate directors. *Guiding Light*. CBS.
Jack Coffey, Sherrell Hoffman, Henry Kaplan, James Francesca, directors. Jean Dadario Burke, Barbara Martin Simmons, associate directors, *All My Children*. ABC.

Maria Wagner. Bob Schwartz, Richard Dunlap, Paul Lammers, Richard Pepperman, directors. Portman Paget, Joel Aronowitz, associate directors, *As the World Turns*. CBS.
Al Rabin, Joseph Behar, Susan Orlikoff Simon, Stephan Wyman, Herb Stein, directors. Gay Linvill, Sheryl Harmon, Becky Greenlaw, associate directors, *Days of Our Lives*. NBC.
David Pressman, Peter Miner, Larry Auerbach, Melvin Bernhardt, John Sedwick, Ron Lagomarsino, directors. Susan Pomerantz, Stuart Silver, associate directors, *One Life to Live*. ABC.

OUTSTANDING WRITING
• Agnes Nixon, Lorraine Broderick, Victor Miller, Art Wallace, Jack Wood, Mary K. Wells, Clarice Blackburn, Susan Kirshenbaum, Elizabeth Wallace, Elizabeth Page, Carlina Della Pietra, Wisner Washam, *All My Children*. NBC.
Sheri Anderson, head writer. Leah Laiman, Margaret DePriest, Maralyn Thoma, Dana Soloff, Anne Schoettle, Michael Roger David, Leah Markus, Thom Racina, *Days of Our Lives*. NBC.
Pamela Long Hammer, Jeff Ryder, head writers. John Kuntz, Addie Walsh, Christopher Whitesell, Carolyn Demoney Culliton, Samuel D. Ratcliffe, breakdown writers. Robin Amos, Stephanie Braxton, Stephen Demorest, Trent Jones, N. Gail Lawrence, Michelle Poteet Lisanti, Megan McTavish, Pete T. Rich, Emily Squires, Edward Parone, associate writers, *Guiding Light*. CBS.
Gary Tomlin, Samuel D. Ratcliffe, Judith Donato, David Cherrill, head writers. Richard Culliton, Judith Pinsker, Francis Myers, Roger Newman, Carolyn Culliton, David Colson, Lloyd Gold, Cynthia Saltzman, *Another World*. NBC.

OTHER DAYTIME AWARD WINNERS
OUTSTANDING JUVENILE/YOUNG MAN IN A DRAMA SERIES
• Brian Bloom, *As the World Turns*. CBS.

OUTSTANDING INGENUE IN A DRAMA SERIES
• Tracey E. Bregman, *The Young and the Restless*. CBS.

The top drama series performers of the year: St. Elsewhere's William Daniels and Cagney & Lacey's Tyne Daly.

OUTSTANDING GAME/AUDIENCE PARTICIPATION SHOW
• *The $25,000 Pyramid*. Bob Stewart, executive producer. Anne Marie Schmitt, producer. CBS.

OUTSTANDING HOST IN A GAME SHOW
• Dick Clark, *The $25,000 Pyramid*. CBS.

OUTSTANDING DIRECTING IN A GAME SHOW
• Marc Breslow, *The Price is Right*. CBS.

OUTSTANDING TALK OR SERVICE SERIES
• *Donahue*. Richard Mincer and Patricia McMillen, executive producers. Darlene Hayes, senior producer. Gail Steinberg, Lorri Antosz Benson, Susan Sprecher, Marlaine Selip, producers. Syndicated.

OUTSTANDING HOST OR HOSTESS IN A TALK/SERVICE SHOW
• Phil Donahue. *Donahue*. Syndicated.

OUTSTANDING DIRECTING IN A TALK OR SERVICE SERIES
• Dick Carson. *The Merv Griffin Show*. Syndicated.

OUTSTANDING CHILDREN'S SERIES
• *Sesame Street*. Dulcy Singer, executive producer. Lisa Simon, producer. PBS.

CHILDREN'S SERIES WRITING
• Fred Rogers, *Mister Rogers' Neighborhood*. PBS.

OUTSTANDING CHILDREN'S SPECIAL
• "All the Kids Do It," *CBS Schoolbreak Special*. Roger Birnbaum, Henry Winkler, executive producers. Edna Hallinan, producer. CBS.

PERFORMER IN CHILDREN'S PROGRAMMING
• John Carradine, *Umbrella Jack*. Syndicated.

DIRECTING IN CHILDREN'S PROGRAMMING
• Joan Darling, "Mom's on Strike," *ABC Afterschool Special*. ABC.

OUTSTANDING WRITING IN A CHILDREN'S SPECIAL
• Charles Purpura. "The Day the Senior Class Got Married," *CBS Schoolbreak Special*. CBS.

OUTSTANDING ANIMATED PROGRAM
• *Jim Henson's Muppet Babies*. Margaret Loesch, Lee Gunther, Jim Henson, executive producers. Bob Richardson, producer. Hank Saroyan, John Gibbs, directors. Jeffrey Scott, writer. CBS.

SPECIAL CLASS PROGRAMS
• *To See a World (For Our Times)*. Pamela Ilott, executive producer. Chalmers Dale, producer. CBS.

OUTSTANDING MUSIC DIRECTION AND COMPOSITION
• Susan Markowitz, music director. Elliot Lawrence, composer, *The Edge of Night*. ABC.

OUTSTANDING DRAMA SERIES TECHNICAL TEAM
• Robert Schulz, Harry Tatarian, technical directors. Toby Brown, Mike Denney, Sheldon Mooney, Joe Vicens, electronic cameras. David Fisher, Scha Jani, video control. Scott Millan, Tommy Persson, production mixers. Donald Henderson, Rafael O. Valentin, postproduction mixers. Peter Roman, Larry Maggiore, sound effects. Dan Brumett, Brian Cunneen, video-tape editors, *The Young and the Restless*. CBS.

Outstanding Drama Series Design Team
• Richard C. Hankins, Harry Miller, Ron Placzek, art directors. Wesley Laws, Ron Kelson, Paul Hickey, set decorators. Ralph Holmes, Jene Youtt, Lincoln John Stulik, lighting directors. David Dangle, costume designer, *Guiding Light.* CBS.

Outstanding Art Direction
• Romaine Johnston, Debe Hale, art directors, *Pryor's Place.* CBS.

Outstanding Costume Design
• Madeline Graneto, *Pryor's Place.* CBS.

Outstanding Makeup
• Nick Schillace, Mark Landon, Ed Heim, Barry Kopper, Patti Greene, *The Young and the Restless.* CBS.

Outstanding Hairstyling
• Deborah Holmes, Katherine Kotarakos, Mary Guerrero, Catherine Marcatto. *General Hospital.* ABC.

Outstanding Graphics and Title Design
• Phill Norman, *Santa Barbara.* NBC.

Outstanding Cinematography
• Barry Sonnenfeld, *Out of Step.* ABC.

Outstanding Film Editing
• Michael Lynch, "Backwards: The Riddle of Dyslexia," *ABC Afterschool Special.* ABC.

Outstanding Technical Direction, Electronic Camera, and Video Control
• Ray Angona, technical director. Ted Morales, Keeth Lawrence, Martin Wagner, Joseph Arvizu, electronic cameras. Allen Latter, video control, *The Price is Right.* CBS.

Outstanding Video-Tape Editing
• Ted May, supervising editor. Evamarie Keller, Vincent Sims, editors, *Sesame Street.* PBS.

Outstanding Film Sound Editing
• Richard Allen, supervising music editor. Bob Gillis, supervising editor. Bruce Elliott, Michael Depatie, Michael Tomack,

Ron Fedele, sound effects editors, *Jim Henson's Muppet Babies.* CBS.

Outstanding Film Sound Mixing
• Charles "Bud" Grenzbach, Hoppy Mehterian, rerecording mixers, *Pole Position.* CBS.

Outstanding Live and Tape Sound Mixing and Sound Effects
• Joel Soifer, preproduction mixer. Mark Bovos, production mixer. Thomas J. Huth, postproduction mixer. Doug Gray, sound effects. "Contract For Life: The S.A.D.D. Story," *CBS Schoolbreak Special.* CBS.

Outstanding Lighting Direction
• Marc Palius, *Henry Hamilton, Graduate Ghost.* ABC.

Special Recognition
• Larry Haines
• Mary Stuart
• Charita Bauer.

(There were no winners in the areas of outstanding writing or directing in special class programs.)

SPORTS AWARD WINNERS
Outstanding Live Sports Special
• *Games of the XXIII Olympiad.* Roone Arledge, executive producer. Chet Forte, Chuck Howard, Dennis Lewin, senior producers. Jeff Ruhe, coordinating producer, and the producing colleagues. Roger Goodman, coordinating director, and the team of directors. ABC.

Outstanding Edited Sports Series
• *The American Sportsman.* John Wilcox, series producer. George Bell, Curt Gowdy, Chris Carmody, coordinating producers. ABC.

Outstanding Edited Sports Special
• *Road to the Superbowl '85.* Steve Sabol, producer. Syndicated.

Outstanding Sports Personality— Host
• George Michael. NBC.

Outstanding Technical Team— Remote/Studio
• *1984 Summer Olympics.* Engineering technical supervisors team, technical directing team, senior video operators

team, senior audio operators team, video-tape operators, graphics, camera operators, electronic camerapersons. ABC.

OUTSTANDING TECHNICAL TEAM—FILM CINEMATOGRAPHERS, FILM EDITORS
• *Road to the Superbowl '85*. Phil Tuckett, Hank McElwee, Howard Neef, Jack Newman, Ernie Ernst, Bob Angelo, Donald Marx, Ted Manahan, Bob Smith, Art Spieller, Dan Sheridan, Dave Paul and Dave Douglas, cinematographers. Syndicated.

OUTSTANDING ASSOCIATE DIRECTORS
• *1984 Summer Olympics*. The team of associate directors. ABC.

OUTSTANDING VIDEO-TAPE EDITORS
• *This is the USFL*. Robert Klug, Vincent Ceriale, Bill Denahy. Syndicated.
Breeders Cup. Scott L. Rader. NBC.
• *Major League Baseball: An Inside Look*. Mike Kostel, Rick Reed, Roger Drake, John Servidio. NBC.
• *Sportsworld Americana* (Special Olympics). Scott L. Rader; Jeffery Wurtz. NBC.
• *1984 Summer Olympics*. Carlo Gennarelli, Marvin Gench, Mike Siegel and colleagues. ABC.

OUTSTANDING GRAPHICS DESIGNERS (Openings)
• *Super Sports Bowl XIX*. Wendy Vanguard, Don Venhaus, Roger Goodman. ABC.

OUTSTANDING SPORTS JOURNALISM
• *Sports Features*. Dick Schaap. ABC.
CBS Sports Sunday. Joseph Valerio. CBS.
1984 Summer Olympics (segment features). Steve Skinner. ABC.
• *ABC Sportsbeat*. Howard Cosell, Ed Silverman, Noubar Stone, James Roberts, Peter Bonventre, Michael Marley. Kevin Granath. ABC.

OUTSTANDING PROGRAM ACHIEVEMENT
• *Race Across America*. Roone Arledge, Amy Sacks, Joel Field, Dennis Lewin. ABC.
• *The American Sportsman — 20th Anniversary Moment*. John Wilcox, George Bell, Curt Gowdy. ABC.

SPECIAL CLASSIFICATION— INDIVIDUAL ACHIEVEMENT
• *1984 Summer Olympics—Closing: "Ode to Joy."* Roone Arledge, Carol Lehti. ABC.
• *ABC's Wide World of Sports — 1984 Year End Show*. Roone Arledge, Jonathan Lory, Amy Sacks, Theresa Mader, Al James. ABC.
• *1984 Summer Olympics*. Marvin Bader, chief Olympic organization coordinator. ABC.

(There was no winner of Oustanding Live Sports Series.)

NEWS & DOCUMENTARY AWARD WINNERS
COVERAGE OF A SINGLE BREAKING NEWS STORY (Segments)
• "India Broadcast," *The CBS Evening News with Dan Rather*. Lane Venardos, executive producer. Andrew Heyward, Tom Bettag, senior producers. Gordon Joseloff, Peter Scheweitzer, Harry Radliffe, Kent Garrett, Jan Albert, producers. Wyatt Andrews, Tom Fenton, Steve Kroft, Bob Simon, Bill Moyers, correspondents. CBS.

COVERAGE OF A SINGLE BREAKING NEWS STORY (Programs)
• "Massacre in San Ysidro," *ABC News Nightline*. Richard Kaplan, executive producer. Robert Jordan, senior producer. Bob LeDonne, Steve Lewis, Tara Sonenshine, Heather Vincent, producers. Ted Koppel, anchor. ABC.

BACKGROUND/ ANALYSIS OF A SINGLE CURRENT STORY (Programs)
• "Living Below the Line," *Frontline*. David Fanning, executive producer. Mark Obenhaus, producer. Edward Gray, Michael Schwarz, coproducers. PBS.
• "Cry Ethiopia, Cry," *Frontline*. David Fanning, executive producer. Michael Kirk, senior producer. Nicholas Claxton, Andrew Liebman, producers. PBS.

BACKGROUND/ANALYSIS OF A SINGLE CURRENT STORY (Segments)
• "Beirut: A Retrospective," *The CBS Evening News with Dan Rather*. Lane Venardos, executive producer. Bob

Anderson, producer. Bob Simon, reporter, correspondent. CBS.
• "TV Campaigning," *The CBS Evening News with Dan Rather*. Lane Venardos, executive producer, Tom Bettag, senior producer. Richard Cohen, David Browning, producers. Bruce Morton, Bob Schieffer, correspondents. CBS.
• "Zumwalt—Agent Orange," *The MacNeil- Lehrer Newshour*. Lester M. Crystal, executive producer. Tim Smith, Maura Lerner, producers. Charlayne Hunter-Gault, correspondent. Lee Korovokis, reporter. PBS.
• "Reagan's Reelection," *The CBS Evening News with Dan Rather*. Lane Venardos, executive producer. Brian Healy, senior producer. Susan Kirinsky, Bill Skane, producers. Lesley Stahl, Bill Plante, correspondents. CBS.
• "Star Wars," *Crossroads*. Andrew Lack, senior executive producer. Elena Mannes, producer. Bill Moyers, reporter, correspondent. CBS.

INVESTIGATIVE JOURNALISM
(Programs)
• "The Silent Shame," *NBC Nightly News*. Thomas Tomizawa, executive producer. Chuck Collins, producer. Mark Myhanen, reporter/correspondent. NBC.
• "Hard Metals Disease," *Today*. Jon Alpert, Steve Friedman, producers. Jon Alpert, Karen Ranucci, reporter/correspondents. NBC.

INVESTIGATIVE JOURNALISM
(Segments)
• "General Dynamics," *The CBS Evening News with Dan Rather*. Lane Venardos, executive producer. Bill Willson, producer. Linda Mason, senior producer. Rita Braver, reporter/correspondent. CBS.
• "Leader LaRouche," *First Camera*. Sy Pearlman, executive producer. Tom Tomizawa, senior producer. Patricia Lynch, producer. Mark Nykanen, correspondent. NBC.
• "What Happened to the Children?" *20/20*. Danny Schechter, producer. Tom Jarriel, reporter/correspondent. ABC.

INTERVIEW/INTERVIEWERS
(Programs)
• "World War II Propaganda Battle," *A Walk Through the 20th Century with Bill Moyers*. Merv Koplin, executive producer. David Grubin, producer. Ronald Blumer,

coproducer. Bill Moyers, correspondent. PBS.

INTERVIEW/INTERVIEWERS
(Segments)
• "Race in America," *The CBS Evening News with Dan Rather*. Lane Venardos, executive producer. Kent Garrett, producer. Bob Faw, reporter/correspondent. CBS.

COVERAGE OF A CONTINUING NEWS STORY
(Programs)
• "Jesse Jackson and the Press," *Inside Story*. Chris Koch, executive producer. Ned Schnurman, senior executive producer. Susan Udelson, producer. Hodding Carter III, correspondent. PBS.

COVERAGE OF A CONTINUING NEWS STORY
(Segments)
• "Afghanistan," *The CBS Evening News with Dan Rather*. Lane Venardos, executive producer. Linda Mason, senior producer. Harry Radliffe, producer. Dan Rather, reporter/correspondent. CBS.
• "Wall of Tears, Wall of Hope," *20/20*. Alice Irene Pifer, producer. Bob Brown, correspondent. ABC.
• "Farm Coverage," *The MacNeil-Lehrer Newshour*. Lester M. Crystal, executive producer. Joe Quinlan, Brendan Henahan, Carol Blakeslee, producers. Marie Maclean, Kwame Holman, Elizather Bracket, reporters/correspondents. PBS.

INFORMATION, CULTURAL, OR HISTORICAL
(Programs)
• "The Mind of a Murderer, Part 1," *Frontline*. David Fanning, executive producer. michael kirk, senior producer. Michael Barnes, producer. PBS.
• "The Mind of a Murderer, Part 2," *Frontline*. David Fanning, executive producer. Michael Kirk, senior producer. Michael Barnes, producer. PBS.
• Captive in El Salvador," *Frontline*. David Fanning, executive producer. Michael Kirk, senior producer. Ofra Bikel, producer. PBS.
• "Among the Wild Chimpanzees," *National Geographic Special*. Barbara Jampeel, producer. Dennis Kane, Thomas Skinner, co-executive producers. Hugo Van Lawick, coproducer. Alexander Scourby, narrator. PBS.

INFORMATION, CULTURAL, OR HISTORICAL
(Segments)
• "B-1 Bomber," *Good Morning America.* Bille Geddie, producer. David Hartman, correspondent. ABC.
• "Anne Morrow Lindbergh," *Smithsonian World.* Margaret Murphy, producer. David McCullough, reporter/correspondent. PBS.

SPECIAL CLASSIFICATION FOR OUTSTANDING PROGRAM/ INDIVIDUAL
(Programs)
• "The Sovereign Self: Right to Live, Right to Die," *The Constitution: That Delicate Balance.* Stuart Sucherman, executive producer. Jude Dratt, producer. Arthur Miller, reporter. PBS.

SPECIAL CLASSIFICATION FOR OUTSTANDING PROGRAM/ INDIVIDUAL
(Segments)
• "The New Cold War," *NBC Nightly News.* Ron Bonn, Joseph DeCola, producers. Garrick Utley, reporter/ correspondent. NBC.
• "Steeplejacks," *Crossroads.* Andrew Lack and Russ Bensley, executive producers. Bernard Birnbaum, senior producer. Norman Morris, producer. Charles Kuralt, reporter/correspondent. CBS.
• "Three-Part Brain Series," *NBC Nightly News.* Carolyn Schatz, Robert Bazell, producers. Robert Bazell, reporter/ correspondent. NBC.

INDIVIDUAL ACHIEVEMENT
(Writers)
• Theodore H. White, Larry McCarthy, *Television and the Presidency.* Syndicated. Ron Powers, *Sunday Morning.* CBS.
• Marshall Frady, Judy Crichton, Richard Gerdau, Kathy Slobogin, Joseph Angier, Thomas Lennon, *To Save Our Schools, To Save Our Children.* ABC.
(Directors)
• Robert Eisenhardt, *Spaces: The Architecture of Paul Rudolph.* PBS. Nelson E. Breen, *Bearden Plays Bearden.* PBS.
(Cinematographers)
• Hugo van Lawick, Martin Bell, "Among the Wild Chimpanzees," *National Geographic Special.* PBS.
(Electronic camerapersons)
• Jon Alpert, "American Survival, 1984,"

Today. NBC.
(Sound)
• Stephen Powell, "On the Range," *20/20.* ABC.
(Tape editors)
• Warren Lustig, Pat Cronin, "1984 Republican Convention Coverage," *Nightwatch.* CBS.
• John Stephen Hyjek, "The North Shore," *America Today.* PBS.
(Film editors)
• Alison Ellwood, "Living Below the Line," *Frontline.* PBS.
(Scenic design)
• Clinton Heitman, *The National Science Test.* PBS.
(Music)
• John Duffy, music composer, director, and conductor, *Heritage: Civilization and the Jews.* PBS.

INTERNATIONAL AWARD WINNERS
OUTSTANDING DOCUMENTARY
• *The Heart of the Dragon: Remembering* (Episode one), Channel 4, U.K.

OUTSTANDING DRAMA
• *The Jewel in the Crown,* Granada TV, U.K.

OUTSTANDING PERFORMING ARTS
• *The Tragedy of Carmen,* Channel 4, U.K.

OUTSTANDING POPULAR ARTS
• *Fresh Fields,* Thames Television, U.K.

OUTSTANDING CHILDREN'S PROGRAM
• *Wind in the Willows,* Thames TV, U.K.

INTERNATIONAL DIRECTORATE AWARD
• Lord Sidney Bernstein, founder, Granada Television.

FOUNDERS AWARD
• David L. Wolper

SPECIAL AWARDS
OUTSTANDING ACHIEVEMENT IN THE SCIENCE OF TELEVISION ENGINEERING
• ABC
• RCA Corporation

**NATIONAL AWARD
FOR COMMUNITY SERVICE**
• *Child at Risk* (KUHT-TV) Houston,
Texas.

SPECIAL RECOGNITION
• National Endowment for the Arts

A.T.A.S. GOVERNORS AWARD
• Alistair Cooke

N.A.T.A.S. TRUSTEES AWARD
• Roone Arledge
• Julius Barnathan (ABC — for the
Olympics)

Family Ties

Last year's victorious comedy series, *The Cosby Show*, would hold onto its ranking as the number one show in the Nielsen rankings for the next four years. Heading into the 38th annual Emmy Awards show, *Cosby* also seemed destined to hold onto the comedy program prize, just as *All in the Family* had 15 years earlier, the last time a series was in the same situation.

But the series featuring the sly-but-self-effacing king of comedy was up against four clever "golden girls" who were in fact silver-haired senior citizens who shared a house in Miami where the worst vice was indulging in cheesecake at 2 a.m. *The Golden Girls* was the first hit show in TV history with an all-female cast and was also unusual for its sensitive and hilarious celebration of life after 60. In accepting the series honor, producer-writer Paul Witt paid credit to the seniors everywhere, saying, "They're our joy and inspiration."

Between the lead and supporting actress categories, all four "girls" were nominated. But it was three-time past Emmy winner Betty White who topped two of her roommates for best actress. (Estelle Getty was nominated in the supporting category.) "I'm the lucky one who gets to come up and pick up this beautiful golden girl," White said. "I want to thank the network for taking a chance on four old broads — uh, ladies." The show also won for writing and its technical craftsmen.

The lead actor prize went to Michael J. Fox of *Family Ties*, who played the bright, self-absorbed, radically conservative yuppie-in-training Alex P. Keaton. *Family Ties* was actually about an other-

A.T.A.S.

"I feel four feet tall!" the 5'4" Michael J. Fox roared. The past best supporting actor loser was suddenly victorious as best actor.

wise liberal family living with disillusionment in the prosperous Reagan era, but it sagged in the ratings until Fox became more of a central character and NBC had the shrewdness to schedule it on Thursday nights immediately after *The Cosby Show*.

The vastly popular, 5-foot, 4-inch tall, 25-year-old actor prevailed over such veteran nominees as Bob Newhart, Ted Danson, and Jack Warden (Fox's own choice) to win the performance honor and said upon accepting it, "I feel four feet tall!" Soon after the ceremony he took the statuette home, he once told E! Network, and placed it prominently on a table in the foyer of his parents' house. His mother, however, would have nothing to do with such Alex P. Keaton-like arrogance, however. She took it upstairs and put it inside a glass case next to his family members' other trophies for bowling, baseball, and bridge accomplishments. What was the difference, Fox was asked? "Mine had breasts," he told E!

The Cosby Show ended up with three awards, including ones for its directors, writers, and Roscoe Lee Browne in the newly introduced category of best guest performer. (Cosby again refused to compete against his peers in the best actor category.) *Night Court*'s John Larroquette returned as best supporting actor in a comedy series, saying, "This time it was more shocking. First time you're hoping, second time you think it's impossible." Rhea Perlman won her third as best supporting actress on *Cheers*. She thanked her "wonderful and silly" daughters and husband/actor Danny DeVito, formerly of *Taxi,* "who isn't here tonight," she said. "I guess he couldn't take it."

Celebrating actual family ties became a recurring theme throughout the Emmys ceremony. Georg Stanford Brown, the husband of last year's best drama series actress Tyne Daly of *Cagney & Lacey*, won for directing one of the show's episodes (he was nominated last year for a segment of *Hill Street Blues* but lost) while Daly's on-screen husband, John Karlen, was named best supporting actor. "I need this more than a working man needs a loaf of bread," Karlen said, accepting the statuette. For three years in a row, Sharon Gless (as Chris Cagney) lost the prize for best actress to on-air police partner Daly (as Mary Beth Lacey), but this year it was Cagney's turn. "I'm the luckiest girl in the world," Gless said, now finally clutching her own award.

Last year *Cagney & Lacey*'s victory as best drama series was called "the biggest surprise of the night" by *The Detroit News* when it overtook front-runner *Miami Vice*. This year it pulled yet another upset by eclipsing *Moonlighting*, the heavily favored hit new series that paired Cybill Shepherd as the owner of the Blue Moon Detective Agency with an amorous gumshoe employee played Bruce Willis. The show was full of inventive wisecracks and such chancy departures from normal exposition as sometimes having the characters address the camera directly. A few months after the Emmy ceremony, the characters did

Past winner Bill Cosby now refused to compete against fellow actors.

so just to complain to the viewing audience how it had fared at the awards: *Moonlighting* was shut out except for a single editing honor.

Family ties were also evidenced on *St. Elsewhere*. Noted *Broadcasting* magazine: "The show holds the distinction of having the first couple married on and off the screen, William Daniels and Bonnie Bartlett, who took the awards for best lead actor and best supporting actress in a drama series." *St. Elsewhere* also took laurels for writing, art direction, costumes, and sound mixing.

An eight-hour, four-part, $26-million miniseries chronicling the life of the western-looking Russian Tsar Peter the Great was named best miniseries. Filmed in the U.S.S.R., and with the full cooperation of the Soviet government, *Peter the Great* had a cast as regal as its title character, who was played by Maximilian Schell. Supporting performers included Vanessa Redgrave, Omar Shariff, and Laurence Olivier, but the only other awards it won, in addition to the miniseries prize, were for music composition and costume design.

Dustin Hoffman ended up with the top male acting statuette for his portrayal of American Everyman Willy Loman in a new production of Arthur Miller's classic *Death of a Salesman*. John Malkovich won in the supporting category for his role as Loman's troubled son Biff while the feature was also honored for its art direction. *The Washington Post* called *Salesman* "the most critically praised dramatic presentation of the year" and it was considered a shoo-in for best drama special, but, in another major upset, the Emmy went to *Love Is Never Silent*, a drama about the daughter of deaf parents who is torn between being their link to the hearing world and her own desire to have an independent life.

Marlo Thomas gave the performance of the year, and perhaps of her career, in *Nobody's Child,* based on the story of real-life mental patient Marie Balter, who rehabilitated herself, earned a master's degree from Harvard, and became a mental health administrator. "I found the role inspiring," Thomas said accepting the award. "It occurred to me that no matter what happened to me, if her spirit came through, then I felt that mine could remain intact, too." Keeping with the unofficial family theme of the evening, Thomas noted that her brother Tony was an Emmy winner, too, being a producer of *The Golden Girls*.

An Early Frost was considered the likely choice to take the drama special award in the event *Salesman* didn't prevail, having started out with 14 nominations. *Frost* was a controversial TV film about a gay man, played by Aidan Quinn, who tells his parents that he's dying of AIDS. It ended up with three awards — for cinematography, editing, and writing. Writer Rob Cowen thanked "those people with AIDS who gave so generously to us of their time and energy when they had very little time and energy left to give." Colleen Dewhurst was voted best supporting actress for playing an iron-willed woman who must come to terms with her daughter-in-law, played by Farrah Fawcett, in *Between Two Women*.

The night turned out to have yet another family tie involving the father of Mark Tinker, a supervising producer of the one show that won more individual awards than any other on that Emmys night — *St. Elsewhere*, which took six. His father, Grant Tinker, helped champion the amazing ratings turnaround at NBC that took it from last place to first by insisting, as network chairman, that airing premium programs would do it. He was right and was now rewarded by witnessing the highest number of trophies ever bestowed to his network (34) — including a clean sweep of all the major comedy awards. But Grant had recently resigned from NBC when its parent company, RCA, was purchased by General Electric. Emmys cohost David Letterman addressed him in audience, saying, "Your commitment to quality was an example to us all," then added facetiously, "and if you need anything to help you get back on your feet, don't be bashful."

Letterman shared the hosting honors with *Cheers* star Shelley Long. Together they presided over a telecast that received the highest ratings since 1979, another record year for Emmy viewership. All family tie-ins aside, the evening's official theme was nostalgia and included a tribute to TV's old friend Red Skelton. After accepting a Governors Award from Lucille Ball, Skelton addressed the home and auditorium audiences, saying, "For the last 16 years, I've missed you folks every Tuesday night."

DAYTIME AWARDS

The Susan Lucci cliffhanger was building dramatically from year to year. *People* magazine finally voiced the star's and her fans' exasperation in a headline published shortly before the daytime ceremony: "After Seven Years, Susan Lucci May Ask: Who Does a Soap Bitch Have to Kill to Win an Emmy?"

It was reputed that the 37-year-old Lucci was the highest paid actress on daytime TV with an annual salary estimated at more than a half million dollars for her portrayal of *All My Children*'s sexpot hellion Erica Kane (a role she'd performed for 16 years), "but The Thing She Really Wants has eluded her," *People* added. "Every year I get my hopes up," Lucci told the magazine. "I feel like a little puppy dog. I get the nomination and I'm thrilled and then I don't get the award." In the past, she banged a table with her fist when she lost and even stormed out of the ceremony. "Such dramatics hardly made her a popular favorite," *People* added, but "she has borne her more recent losses with admirable grace."

This year at the Waldorf-Astoria hotel in New York Lucci was called upon to be gracious again when the Emmy eluded her for a seventh time. Like it did two years ago, though, the award went to Lucci's personal friend Erika Slezak, who played two roles on *One Life to Live* (a decided plus in helping a daytime star win an Emmy, according to *TV Guide*) — "prim Viki Buchanan and her vampy alter ego Niki Smith," said the magazine. Lucci's costar David Canary (who also played twins: evil Adam and his good-natured brother, Stuart Chandler) was voted best actor, while the show's Michael Knight was named Outstanding Younger Leading Man.

While Lucci may have stayed calm, it was again a year for *The Young and the Restless*. Last year's best drama series returned triumphantly this year by establishing yet another new record: its fourth win as the best soap, the most held by any series. It also won statuettes for directing, sound work, and video tape editing. Since *Y&R* failed to take any performance awards, however, the five top series prizes were split evenly between five different shows. *As the World Turns*'s John Wesley Shipp (as killer Doug Cummings) was named supporting actor of the year while Leann Hunley (Anna Brady Di-Mera) of *Days of Our Lives* took the honors for supporting actress. Ellen Wheeler of *Another World* was the year's saluted ingenue. America's number one-ranked sudser *General Hospital* was shut out except for a single honor, an acknowledgment for makeup. *Guiding Light* nabbed golden statuettes for direction, hairstyling, and costume design.

"Who Does a Soap Bitch Have to Kill to Win an Emmy?" People asked.

Guiding Light also won the writing award, but because of a mistake made by the accounting firm tabulating the results, the prize was wrongly bestowed to *The Young and the Restless* at the Emmys show. Reporting the snafu, *The New York Times* wrote, "This story has two winners and no winner. It has humiliation and human error. It is the stuff of soap operas. But this is real."

The mistake occurred, added *The Times*, "when information was incorrectly transferred from a list to the card read on television — the first gaffe of its kind in Emmy history .... Only after the ceremony ended did some people notice that the news release ... named the winner as the team, headed by Pamela K. Long,

Heads above the competition: elated best ingenue Ellen Wheeler of Another World.

from another CBS show, *Guiding Light.*" About what happened afterward, N.A.T.A.S. President John Cannon says, "I arranged for a special party at the St. Regis Hotel and we gave them their award properly."

Last year's winners for best game show and host (*The $25,000 Pyramid* emceed by Dick Clark) and talk show and host (*Donahue,* featuring Phil Donahue) returned as repeat winners.

Jim Henson's Muppet Babies was voted best animated program while *Sesame Street* won four awards, including the honor for children's series. A *CBS Schoolbreak Special,* "Babies Having Babies," also won four awards — for writing, direction, video-tape editing, and sound work, while the prize for children's special went to a different segment of the same program, "The War Between the Classes." A contemporary version of the Cinderella fable — the *ABC Afterschool Special* "Cindy Eller: A Modern Fairy Tale" — won a gold trophy for Pearl Bailey, who played a bag lady who is really a fairy godmother.

The 13th Annual Daytime Emmy Awards were broadcast on NBC and received a 8.8 rating/27 share, the highest in the program's history, and ranked third among all daytime shows for the week.

SPORTS AWARDS

As the awards switched over to a calendar-year eligibility period, a ceremony was dropped to accommodate the change.

NEWS & DOCUMENTARY AWARDS

The highlight of the awards ceremony had to do not with a winner of the top news prizes, but a presenter. Eric Sevareid had been out of the public eye for the most part since he reached the mandatory retirement age of 65 at CBS in 1977. The former protégé of Edward R. Murrow did occasional news specials, but his presence at the Emmy Awards offered his peers a chance to express how much they'd missed his full involvement in their craft. As he mounted the stage, "the entire audience rose to give Mr. Sevareid a standing ovation," the N.A.T.A.S. newsletter reported.

Other notable presenters at New York's Grand Hyatt Hotel included former congresswoman Bella Abzug, Manhattan borough president and future mayor David Dinkins, New Jersey senator Frank Lautenberg, and mob-busting U.S. district attorney Rudolph Giuliani.

PBS made the strongest showing, pulling 19 awards, including three statuettes for *Frontline* episodes such as "Men Who Molest" and one segment prize. *Nova*'s examinations of AIDS and acid rain also won program trophies while *The MacNeil-Lehrer Newshour* captured two awards. The PBS documentary *The Times of Harvey Milk,* about the assassinated San Francisco supervisor and gay activist, was cited three times, including for outstanding program achievement.

CBS continued its recent domination of news awards among the commercial networks with six winning segments for the *CBS Evening News* (including coverage of the Mexico City earthquake and a look at contemporary Vietnam) and two for the *CBS Reports* episode "Whose America is It Anyway?" *60 Minutes* took four awards for segments on subjects such as Ronald Reagan's Hollywood

career and the fanciful eccentricities of the British Broadcasting Company.

ABC World News Tonight and *ABC News Nightline* each reaped three statuettes. *Nightline* was acknowledged for outstanding coverage of a single-breaking news story for "Crash of Delta" and "Columbian Volcano," while the news show was hailed for "Vietnam Remembered," "International Christian Aid Investigation," and "Children in Poverty." *20/20* won two awards.

NBC continued its refusal to participate officially in the news awards, although *NBC Nightly News* did take a prize for investigative journalism.

1985–86

The prime-time ceremony was broadcast on NBC from the Pasadena Civic Auditorium on September 21, 1986, for prime-time programs telecast between July 1, 1985, and June 30, 1986. Daytime awards broadcast on NBC from the Waldorf-Astoria Hotel on July 17, 1986, for programs aired between March 6, 1985, and March 5, 1986. The sports awards were switched over to a calendar-year eligibility period and this year's ceremony was dropped to accommodate the change. News & documentary awards presented at the Grand Hyatt Hotel in New York on August 27, 1986, for 1985 programs.

PRIME-TIME PROGRAM AWARDS
OUTSTANDING DRAMA SERIES
• *Cagney & Lacey.* Barney Rosenzweig, executive producer. Liz Coe, supervising producer. Ralph Singleton, Patricia Green, Steve Brown, producers. P.K. Knelman, coproducer. CBS.
Hill Street Blues. Jeffrey Lewis, executive producer. David Milch, co-executive producer. Scott Brazil, supervising producer. Michael Vittes, producer. Walon Green, coproducer. Penny Adams, coordinating producer. NBC.
Moonlighting. Glenn Gordon Caron, executive producer. Jay Daniel, co-executive producer. Artie Mandelberg, supervising producer. Jay Daniel, Ron Osborn, Jeff Reno, producers. ABC.
Murder, She Wrote. Peter S. Fischer,

executive producer. Robert F. O'Neill, producer. CBS.
St. Elsewhere. Bruce Paltrow, executive producer. Mark Tinker, supervising producer. John Masius, Tom Fontana, producers. Abby Singer, coordinating producer. NBC.

OUTSTANDING COMEDY SERIES
• *The Golden Girls.* Paul Junger Witt, Tony Thomas, executive producers. Paul Bogart, supervising producer. Kathy Speer, Terry Grossman, producers. Marsha Posner Williams, coproducer. NBC.
Cheers. James Burrows, Glen Charles, Les Charles, executive producers. Peter Casey, David Lee, Heide Perlman, David Angell, producers. Tim Berry, coproducer. NBC.
The Cosby Show. Marcy Carsey, Tom Werner, executive producers. John Markus, co-executive producer. Caryn Sneider Mandabach, Carmen Finestra, producers. Matt Williams, coproducer. NBC.
Family Ties. Gary David Goldberg, executive producer. Michael J. Weithorn, supervising producer. Alan Uger, Ruth Bennett, producers. Carol Himes, line producer. NBC.
Kate & Allie. Mort Lachman, Merrill Grant, executive producers. Bill Persky, Bob Randall, producers. George Barimo, coordinating producer. CBS.

Outstanding Miniseries
• *Peter the Great*. Lawrence Schiller, executive producer. Marvin J. Chomsky, producer. Konstantin Thoeren, line producer. NBC.
Dress Gray. Frank von Zerneck, executive producer. Glenn Jordan, producer. William Beaudine, Jr., coproducer. NBC.
The Long Hot Summer. Leonard Hill, John Thomas Lenox, executive producers. Ron Gilbert, supervising producer. Dori Weiss, producer. NBC.
Lord Mountbatten: The Last Viceroy, *Masterpiece Theatre*. George Walker, executive producer. Judith DePaul, producer. PBS.
On Wings of Eagles. Edgar J. Scherick, executive producer. Lynn Raynor, producer. NBC.

Outstanding Drama/Comedy Special
• *Love is Never Silent*, *Hallmark Hall of Fame*. Marian Rees, executive producer. Juliana Fjeld, co-executive producer. Dorothea G. Petrie, producer. NBC.
Amos. Peter Douglas, executive producer. Bill Finnegan, Sheldon Pinchuk, producers. CBS.
Death of a Salesman. Arthur Miller, Dustin Hoffman, executive producers. Robert F. Colesberry, producer. CBS.
An Early Frost. Perry Lafferty, producer. Arthur Seidel, coproducer. NBC.
Mrs. Delafield Wants to Marry. Merill H. Karpf, executive producer. George Schaefer, producer. James Prideaux, coproducer. CBS.

Outstanding Variety, Music, or Comedy Program
• *The Kennedy Center Honors: A Celebration of the Performing Arts*. Nick Vanoff, George Stevens, Jr., producers. CBS.
The American Film Institute Salute to Billy Wilder. George Stevens, Jr., producer. NBC.
Late Night with David Letterman. Jack Rollins, executive producer. Barry Sand, producer. David Letterman, host. NBC.
The Tonight Show Starring Johnny Carson. Fred DeCordova, executive producer. Peter Lassally, producer. Johnny Carson, host. NBC.
The 1986 Tony Awards. Alexander H. Cohen, executive producer. Hildy Parks, producer. Martha Mason, coproducer. CBS.

Outstanding Classical Program in the Performing Arts
(Winner)
• *Wolf Trap Presents the Kirov: Swan Lake*. Michael B. Styer, executive producer. Phillip Byrd, senior producer. John T. Potthast, producer. PBS.

Outstanding Informational Special
(Winner)
• *W.C. Fields Straight Up*. Robert B. Weide, executive producer. Ronald J. Fields, coproducer. PBS.

Outstanding Informational Series
(Winners—Tie)
• "Laurence Olivier—A Life," *Great Performances*. Nick Evans, Nick Elliott, executive producers. Bob Bee, producer. PBS.
• *Planet Earth*. Thomas Skinner, executive producer. Gregory Andorfer, series producer. Georgann Kane, coordinating producer. PBS.

Outstanding Animated Program
(Winner)
• *Garfield's Halloween Adventure*. Jay Poynor, executive producer. Phil Roman, producer. Jim Davis, writer. Phil Roman, director. CBS.

Outstanding Children's Program
(Winner)
• "Anne of Green Gables," *Wonderworks*. Kevin Sullivan, Lee Polk, executive producers. Kevin Sullivan, Ian McDougall, producers. PBS.

PERFORMANCE, DIRECTING, AND WRITING
Outstanding Lead Actor in a Drama Series
• William Daniels, *St. Elsewhere*. NBC.
Ed Flanders, *St. Elsewhere*. NBC.
Tom Selleck, *Magnum, P.I.* CBS.
Bruce Willis, *Moonlighting*. ABC.
Edward Woodward, *The Equalizer*. CBS.

Outstanding Lead Actress in a Drama Series
• Sharon Gless, *Cagney & Lacey*. CBS.
Tyne Daly, *Cagney & Lacey*. CBS.
Angela Lansbury, *Murder, She Wrote*. CBS.
Cybill Shepherd, *Moonlighting*. ABC.
Alfre Woodard, *St. Elsewhere*. NBC.

**OUTSTANDING LEAD ACTOR
IN A COMEDY SERIES**
• Michael J. Fox, *Family Ties*. NBC.
Harry Anderson, *Night Court*. NBC.
Ted Danson, *Cheers*. NBC.
Bob Newhart, *Newhart*. CBS.
Jack Warden, *Crazy Like a Fox*. CBS.

**OUTSTANDING LEAD ACTRESS
IN A COMEDY SERIES**
• Betty White, *The Golden Girls*. NBC.
Beatrice Arthur, *The Golden Girls*. NBC.
Shelley Long, *Cheers*. NBC.
Rue McClanahan, *The Golden Girls*. NBC.
Phylicia Rashad, *The Cosby Show*. NBC.

**OUTSTANDING LEAD ACTOR
IN A MINISERIES OR A SPECIAL**
• Dustin Hoffman, *Death of a Salesman*.
CBS.
Kirk Douglas, *Amos*. CBS.
Ben Gazzara, *An Early Frost*. NBC.
John Lithgow, *Resting Place*, *Hallmark
Hall of Fame*. CBS.
Aidan Quinn, *An Early Frost*. NBC.

**OUTSTANDING LEAD ACTRESS
IN A MINISERIES OR A SPECIAL**
• Marlo Thomas, *Nobody's Child*. CBS.
Katharine Hepburn, *Mrs. Delafield Wants
to Marry*. CBS.
Vanessa Redgrave, *Second Serve*. CBS.
Gena Rowlands, *An Early Frost*. NBC.
Mare Winningham, *Love is Never Silent*,
Hallmark Hall of Fame. NBC.

**OUTSTANDING SUPPORTING ACTOR
IN A DRAMA SERIES**
• John Karlen, *Cagney & Lacey*. CBS.
Ed Begley, Jr., *St. Elsewhere*. NBC.
John Hillerman, *Magnum, P.I.* CBS.
Edward James Olmos, *Miami Vice*. NBC.
Bruce Weitz, *Hill Street Blues*. NBC.

**OUTSTANDING SUPPORTING ACTRESS
IN A DRAMA SERIES**
• Bonnie Bartlett, *St. Elsewhere*. NBC.
Allyce Beasley, *Moonlighting*. ABC.
Christina Pickles, *St. Elsewhere*. NBC.
Betty Thomas, *Hill Street Blues*. NBC.

**OUTSTANDING SUPPORTING ACTOR
IN A COMEDY SERIES**
• John Larroquette, *Night Court*. NBC.
Tom Poston, *Newhart*. CBS.
John Ratzenberger, *Cheers*. NBC.
Malcolm-Jamal Warner, *The Cosby Show*.
NBC.

George Wendt, *Cheers*. NBC.

**OUTSTANDING SUPPORTING ACTRESS
IN A COMEDY SERIES**
• Rhea Perlman, *Cheers*. NBC.
Justine Bateman, *Family Ties*. NBC.
Lisa Bonet, *The Cosby Show*. NBC.
Julia Duffy, *Newhart*. CBS.
Estelle Getty, *The Golden Girls*. NBC.
Keshia Knight Pulliam, *The Cosby Show*.
NBC.

**OUTSTANDING SUPPORTING ACTOR
IN A MINISERIES OR A SPECIAL**
• John Malkovich, *Death of a Salesman*.
CBS.
Charles Durning, *Death of a Salesman*.
CBS.
John Glover, *An Early Frost*. NBC.
Harold Gould, *Mrs. Delafield Wants to
Marry*. CBS.
Pat Morita, *Amos*. CBS.

**OUTSTANDING SUPPORTING ACTRESS
IN A MINISERIES OR A SPECIAL**
• Colleen Dewhurst, *Between Two Women*.
ABC.
Phyllis Frelich, *Love is Never Silent*,
Hallmark Hall of Fame. NBC.
Dorothy McGuire, *Amos*. CBS.
Vanessa Redgrave, *Peter the Great*. NBC.
Sylvia Sidney, *An Early Frost*. NBC.

**OUTSTANDING INDIVIDUAL PERFORMANCE
IN A VARIETY OR MUSIC PROGRAM**
• Whitney Houston, *The 28th Annual
Grammy Awards*. CBS.
Debbie Allen, *An All Star Celebration
Honoring Martin Luther King, Jr.* NBC.
Patti LaBelle, "Sylvia Fine Kaye's Musical
Comedy Tonight III," *Great
Performances*. PBS.
Jon Lovitz, *Saturday Night Live*. NBC.
Sarah Vaughan, *The 28th Annual Grammy
Awards*. CBS.
Stevie Wonder, *An All Star Celebration
Honoring Martin Luther King, Jr.* NBC.

**OUTSTANDING GUEST PERFORMER
IN A COMEDY SERIES**
• Roscoe Lee Browne, *The Cosby Show*.
NBC.
Earle Hyman, *The Cosby Show*. NBC.
Danny Kaye, *The Cosby Show*. NBC.
Clarice Taylor, *The Cosby Show*. NBC.
Stevie Wonder, *The Cosby Show*. NBC.

OUTSTANDING GUEST PERFORMER IN A DRAMA SERIES
• John Lithgow, *Amazing Stories*. NBC.
Whoopi Goldberg, *Moonlighting*. ABC.
Edward Herrmann, *St. Elsewhere*. NBC.
Peggy McCay, *Cagney & Lacey*. CBS.
James Stacy, *Cagney & Lacey*. CBS.

OUTSTANDING DIRECTING IN A DRAMA SERIES
• Georg Stanford Brown, *Cagney & Lacey*. CBS.
Gabrielle Beaumont, *Hill Street Blues*. NBC.
Will MacKenzie, *Moonlighting*. ABC.
Steven Spielberg, *Amazing Stories*. NBC.
Peter Werner, *Moonlighting*. ABC.

OUTSTANDING DIRECTING IN A COMEDY SERIES
• Jay Sandrich, *The Cosby Show*. NBC.
James Burrows, *Cheers*. NBC.
Jim Drake, *The Golden Girls*. NBC.
Terry Hughes, *The Golden Girls*. NBC.
Bill Persky, *Kate & Allie*. CBS.

OUTSTANDING DIRECTING IN A MINISERIES OR A SPECIAL
• Joseph Sargent, *Love Is Never Silent*, *Hallmark Hall of Fame*. NBC.
John Erman, *An Early Frost*. NBC.
John Korty, *Resting Place, Hallmark Hall of Fame*. CBS.
Daniel Petrie, *The Execution of Raymond Graham, ABC Theater*. ABC.
Volker Schlordorff, *Death of a Salesman*. CBS.

OUTSTANDING DIRECTING IN A VARIETY OR MUSIC PROGRAM
• Waris Hussein, *Copacabana*. CBS.
Kirk Browning, "The Gospel at Colonus," *Great Performances*. PBS.
Dwight Hemion, *Neil Diamond ... Hello Again*. CBS.
Marty Pasetta, *The 58th Annual Academy Awards*. ABC.

OUTSTANDING WRITING IN A DRAMA SERIES
• Tom Fontana, John Tinker, John Masius, *St. Elsewhere*. NBC.
Glenn Gordon Caron, *Moonlighting*. ABC.
Charles H. Eglee, John Tinker, Channing Gibson, teleplay. John Masius, Tom Fontana, story. *St. Elsewhere*. NBC.
Debra Frank, Carl Sautter, *Moonlighting*. ABC.

Dick Wolf, *Hill Street Blues*. NBC.

OUTSTANDING WRITING IN A COMEDY SERIES
• Barry Fanaro, Mort Nathan, *The Golden Girls*. NBC.
Peter Casey, David Lee, *Cheers*. NBC.
Susan Harris, *The Golden Girls*. NBC.
John Markus, *The Cosby Show*. NBC.
Michael J. Weithorn, *Family Ties*. NBC.
Matt Williams, Carmen Finestra, John Markus, *The Cosby Show*. NBC.

OUTSTANDING WRITING IN A MINISERIES OR A SPECIAL
• Ron Cowen, Daniel Lipman, teleplay. Sherman Yellen, story, *An Early Frost*. NBC.
David Butler, *Lord Mountbatten: The Last Viceroy, Masterpiece Theatre*. PBS.
Darlene Craviotto, *Love is Never Silent, Hallmark Hall of Fame*. NBC.
Carol Evan McKeand, Nigel McKeand, *Alex: The Life of a Child*. ABC.
Kevin Sullivan, Joe Wiesenfeld, "Anne of Green Gables," *Wonderworks*. PBS.
Gore Vidal, *Dress Grey*. NBC.

OUTSTANDING WRITING IN A VARIETY OR MUSIC PROGRAM
• David Letterman, Steve O'Donnell, Sandy Frank, Joe Toplyn, Chris Elliott, Matt Wickline, Jeff Martin, Gerard Mulligan, Randy Cohen, Larry Jacobson, Kevin Curran, Fred Graver, Merrill Markoe, *Late Night with David Letterman Fourth Anniversary Special*. NBC.
Sylvia Fine Kaye, "Sylvia Fine Kaye's Musical Comedy Tonight III," *Great Performances*. PBS.
Hildy Parks, *The 1986 Tony Awards*. CBS.
Raymond Siller, Kevin M. Mulholland, Robert Keane, Hal Goodman, Andrew Nichols, Jim Mulholland, Darrell Vickers, Gary Belken, Larry Klein, Mike Barrie, *The Tonight Show Starring Johnny Carson*. NBC.
George Stevens, Jr., Jeffrey Lane, *The American Film Institute Salute to Billy Wilder*. NBC.

OTHER AWARD WINNERS
OUTSTANDING CHOREOGRAPHY
• Walter Painter, "Sylvia Fine Kaye's Musical Comedy Tonight III," *Great Performances*. PBS.

OUTSTANDING MUSIC COMPOSITION FOR A SERIES (Dramatic underscore)
• Arthur B. Rubinstein, *Scarecrow and Mrs. King*. CBS.

OUTSTANDING MUSIC COMPOSITION FOR A MINISERIES OR A SPECIAL (Dramatic underscore)
• Laurence Rosenthal, *Peter the Great*. NBC.

OUTSTANDING MUSIC DIRECTION
• Elliot Lawrence, music director. James Lawrence, Lanny Meyers, Tommy Newsome, Glen Roven, Larry Schwartz, Torrie Zito, principal arrangers, *The 1986 Tony Awards*. CBS.

OUTSTANDING MUSIC AND LYRICS
• Larry Grossman, composer. Buz Kohan, lyricist, *My Christmas Wish: Andy Williams and the NBC Kids Search for Santa*. NBC.

OUTSTANDING COSTUME DESIGN FOR A SERIES
• Alfred E. Lehman, *Murder, She Wrote*. CBS.

OUTSTANDING COSTUME DESIGN FOR A MINISERIES OR A SPECIAL
• Ella Maklakova (U.S.S.R.), Sibylle Ulsamer (Italy), *Peter the Great*. NBC.

OUTSTANDING COSTUME DESIGN FOR A VARIETY OR MUSIC PROGRAM
• Bill Hargate, "Sylvia Fine Kaye's Musical Comedy Tonight III," *Great Performances*. PBS.

OUTSTANDING COSTUMING FOR A SERIES
• Susan Smith-Nashold, costume supervisor. Robert M. Moore, costumes. Charles Drayman, Ann Winsor, Kathy O'Rear, costumers, *St. Elsewhere*. NBC.

OUTSTANDING COSTUMING FOR A MINISERIES OR A SPECIAL
• Joie Hutchinson, Vicki Sanchez, women's costume supervisors. Pat McGrath, men's costume supervisor, *North and South,* Book I. ABC.

OUTSTANDING MAKEUP FOR A SERIES
• Rod Wilson, *Airwolf*. CBS.

OUTSTANDING MAKEUP FOR A MINISERIES OR A SPECIAL
• Del Acevedo, makeup creator. Paul Stanhope, makeup artist, *Second Serve*. CBS.

OUTSTANDING HAIRSTYLING FOR A SERIES
• Bernadette (Bunny) Parker, *Amazing Stories*. NBC.

OUTSTANDING HAIRSTYLING FOR A MINISERIES, OR SPECIAL
• K.G. Ramsey, *Second Serve*. CBS.

OUTSTANDING ART DIRECTION FOR A SERIES
• Jacqueline Webber, art director. Norman Rockett, set decorator, *St. Elsewhere*. NBC.

OUTSTANDING ART DIRECTION FOR A MINISERIES OR A SPECIAL
• Tony Walton, production designer. John Kasarda, art director. Robert J. Franco, set decorator, *Death of a Salesman*. CBS.

OUTSTANDING ART DIRECTION FOR A VARIETY OR MUSIC PROGRAM
• Roy Christopher, production designer, *The 58th Annual Academy Awards*. ABC.

OUTSTANDING CINEMATOGRAPHY FOR A SERIES
• John McPherson, *Amazing Stories*. NBC.

OUTSTANDING CINEMATOGRAPHY FOR A MINISERIES OR A SPECIAL
• Sherwood Woody Omens, *An Early Frost*. NBC.

OUTSTANDING TECHNICAL DIRECTION/ELECTRONIC CAMERAWORK/VIDEO CONTROL FOR A SERIES
• Gerry Bucci, technical director. Randy Baer, Dale Carlson, Steve Jones, Donna J. Quante, camerapersons. Victor Bagdadi, senior video control, *The Golden Girls*. NBC.

OUTSTANDING TECHNICAL DIRECTION/ELECTRONIC CAMERA/VIDEO CONTROL FOR A MINISERIES OR A SPECIAL
• Gene Crowe, Harry Tatarian, technical directors. Toby Brown, Ed Chaney, Mike Denney, Larry Heider, Pat Kenney, Bob Keys, Dave Levisohn, Wayne Orr, Hector

After losing three times to Cagney & Lacey *costar Tyne Daly, Sharon Gless finally had her turn as best actress.*

Ramirez, Ron Sheldon, camerapersons. John Palacio, Keith Winikoff, senior video control, *Neil Diamond ... Hello Again.* CBS.

OUTSTANDING EDITING FOR A SERIES
(Single camera production)
• Neil Mandelberg, *Moonlighting.* ABC.
(Multicamera production)
• Henry F. Chan, *The Cosby Show.* NBC.

OUTSTANDING EDITING
FOR A MINISERIES OR A SPECIAL
(Single camera production)
• Jerrold L. Ludwig, *An Early Frost.* NBC.
(Multicamera production)
• Pam Marshall, *American Bandstand's 33-1/3 Celebration.* ABC.

OUTSTANDING SOUND EDITING
FOR A SERIES
• Richard Anderson, supervising sound editor. Wayne Alwine, James Christopher, George Frederick, John Stacy, Burton Weinstein, sound editors. Lettie Odney, Denise Whiting, ADR editors. Ken Wannberg, music editor, *Amazing Stories.* NBC.

OUTSTANDING SOUND EDITING
FOR A MINISERIES OR A SPECIAL
• David R. Elliott, supervising sound editor. Dino Di Muro, David R. Elliott, Mark Friedgen, Mike Graham, Larry Kemp, Joe Mayer, Joseph A. Melody, Stewart Nelson, Gregory Schorer, Eric Scott, Rusty Tinsley, Scot Tinsley, Bill Williams, sound editors. Russ Tinsley,

ADR editor. Daniel A. Carlin, music editor, *Under Siege.* NBC.

OUTSTANDING SOUND MIXING
FOR A DRAMA SERIES
• William Gazecki, Andy MacDonald, Bill Nicholson, Blake Wilcox, *St. Elsewhere.* NBC.

OUTSTANDING SOUND MIXING
FOR A COMEDY SERIES OR A SPECIAL
• Michael Ballin, Robert Douglas, Douglas Grey, Thomas Huth, *Cheers.* NBC.

OUTSTANDING SOUND MIXING
FOR A VARIETY OR MUSIC SERIES
OR A SPECIAL
• Tom Ancell, David E. Fluhr, *Mr. Previn Comes to Town.* PBS.

OUTSTANDING SOUND MIXING
FOR A DRAMA MINISERIES OR A SPECIAL
• David E. Campbell, John T. Reitz, Gregg C. Rudloff, Keith A. Wester, *An Early Frost.* NBC.

OUTSTANDING LIGHTING DIRECTION
(ELECTRONIC) FOR A SERIES
• Bob Dickinson, *Solid Gold.* Syndicated.

OUTSTANDING LIGHTING DIRECTION
(ELECTRONIC) FOR A MINISERIES
OR A SPECIAL
• Marilyn Lowey, John Rook, Kim Killingsworth, *Neil Diamond ... Hello Again.* CBS.

THE AREAS
Each area has the possibility of one winner, multiple winners, or none. Winners are listed.

OUTSTANDING INDIVIDUAL ACHIEVEMENT
(Classical music/Dance programming —
Directors)
• Franco Zeffirelli, "Cavalleria Rusticana," *Great Performances.* PBS.
(Informational programming — Directors)
• David Heeley, *The Spencer Tracy Legacy: A Tribute by Katharine Hepburn.* PBS.
(Writers)
• John L. Miller, *The Spencer Tracy Legacy: A Tribute by Katharine Hepburn.* PBS.
(Special visual effects)
• Phil Tipper, *Dinosaur!* CBS.
• Michael McAlister, *Ewoks: The*

Battle for Endor. ABC.
(Graphics and title design)
• Betty Green, *Stingray*. NBC.
(Engineering development)
• Stefan Kudelski for his development of the Nagra Recorder.
• CBS, Sony, and CINEDCO for the design and implementation of electronic editing systems for film programs.

(No awards were bestowed in the areas of outstanding writers or performers in classical music/dance programming or for performers in informational programming.)

DAYTIME AWARDS
OUTSTANDING DRAMA SERIES
• *The Young and the Restless*. William J. Bell, H. Wesley Kenney, executive producers. Edward Scott, Tom Langan, producers. CBS.
All My Children. Jacqueline Babbin, producer. ABC.
As the World Turns. Robert Calhoun, executive producer. Michael D. Laibson, Bonnie Bogard, Christine Banas, producers. CBS.
General Hospital. Gloria Monty, executive producer. Jerry Balme, Joseph Willmore, coordinating producers. ABC.

OUTSTANDING ACTOR
• David Canary, *All My Children*. ABC.
Scott Bryce, *As the World Turns*. CBS.
Larry Bryggman, *As the World Turns*. CBS.
Robert S. Woods, *One Life to Live*. ABC.
Nicolas Coster, *Santa Barbara*. NBC.
Terry Lester, *The Young and the Restless*. CBS.

OUTSTANDING ACTRESS
• Erika Slezak, *One Life To Live*. ABC.
Susan Lucci, *All My Children*. ABC.
Elizabeth Hubbard, *As the World Turns*. CBS.
Peggy McCay, *Days of Our Lives*. NBC.
Kim Zimmer, *Guiding Light*. CBS.

OUTSTANDING SUPPORTING ACTOR
• John Wesley Shipp, *As the World Turns*. CBS.
Louis Edmonds, *All My Children*. ABC.
Larry Gates, *Guiding Light*. CBS.
Al Freeman, Jr., *One Life to Live*. ABC.
Gregg Marx, *As the World Turns*. CBS.

OUTSTANDING SUPPORTING ACTRESS
• Leann Hunley, *Days of Our Lives*. NBC.
Judith Anderson, *Santa Barbara*. NBC.
Uta Hagen, *One Life to Live*. ABC.
Eileen Herlie, *All My Children*. ABC.
Kathleen Widdoes, *As the World Turns*. CBS.

OUTSTANDING DRAMA SERIES DIRECTING TEAM
• Dennis Steinmetz, Rudy Vejar, Frank Pacelli, directors. Randy Robbins, Betty Rothenberg, associate directors, *The Young and the Restless*. CBS.
Paul Lammers, Bob Schwarz, Richard Pepperman, Maria Wagner, directors. Joel Aronowitz, Michael Kerner, associate directors, *As the World Turns*. CBS.
Susan Orlikoff Simon, Joseph Behar, Herb Stein, Stephen Wyman, directors. Gay Linvill, Sheryl Harmon, Becky Greenlaw, associate directors, *Days of Our Lives*. NBC.
Irene Pace, Bruce Barry, Matthew Diamond, directors. Jo Anne Sedwick, Jo Ann Rivituso, associate directors, *Guiding Light*. CBS.
Larry Auerbach, Peter Miner, David Pressman, directors. Susan Pomerantz, Stuart Silver, associate directors, *One Life to Live*. ABC.

OUTSTANDING DRAMA SERIES WRITING TEAM
• Pam Long Hammer, Jeff Ryder, head writers. Addie Walsh, John Kuntz, Christopher Whitesell, breakdown writers. Megan McTavish, Stephen Demorest, Victor Gialanella, Mary Pat Gleason, Trent Jones, Pete T. Rich, Gail N. Lawrence, Nancy Curlee, associate writers, *Guiding Light*. CBS.
Douglas Marland, Susan B. Horgan, head writers. Jeanne Glynn, Garin Wolf, breakdown writers. Patti DiCenzo, M.B. Hatch, Caroline Franz, Chris Auer, Meredith Post, Jane Willis, Steve Wasserman, Emily Squires, Courtney Simon, Charles DiZenzo, Jessica Klein, writers, *As the World Turns*. CBS.
Norma Monty, Patricia Falken Smith, head writers. A.J. Russell, story consultant. James Reilly, Patrick Smith, outline writers. Robert Guza, Doris Silverton, Robert Soderberg, Maralyn Thoma, writers, *General Hospital*. ABC.
William J. Bell, head writer. Kay Alden, John F. Smith, Sally Sussman, Eric

Freiwald, John Randall Holland, Meg Bennett, Enid Powell, writers, *The Young and the Restless*. CBS.

OTHER AWARD WINNERS

OUTSTANDING YOUNGER LEADING MAN IN A DAYTIME DRAMA SERIES
• Michael E. Knight, *All My Children*. ABC.

OUTSTANDING INGENUE IN A DAYTIME DRAMA SERIES
• Ellen Wheeler, *Another World*. NBC.

OUTSTANDING GAME/AUDIENCE PARTICIPATION SHOW
• *The $25,000 Pyramid*. Bob Stewart, executive producer. Anne Marie Schmitt, producer. CBS.

OUTSTANDING GAME SHOW HOST
• Dick Clark, *The $25,000 Pyramid*. CBS.

OUTSTANDING DIRECTING IN A GAME/AUDIENCE PARTICIPATION SHOW
• Dick Carson, *Wheel of Fortune*. NBC.

OUTSTANDING TALK OR SERVICE PROGRAM
• *Donahue*. Patricia McMillen, executive producer. Gail Steinberg, senior producer. Lorri Antoszi Benson, Janet Harrell, Marlaine Selip, Susan Sprecher, producers. Syndicated.

OUTSTANDING TALK/SERVICE SHOW HOST
• Phil Donahue, *Donahue*. Syndicated.

OUTSTANDING DIRECTING IN A TALK/SERVICE PROGRAM
• Russell F. Morash, *This Old House*. PBS.

OUTSTANDING CHILDREN'S SERIES
• *Sesame Street*. Dulcy Singer, executive producer. Lisa Simon, producer. PBS.

OUTSTANDING CHILDREN'S SPECIAL
• "The War Between the Classes," *CBS Schoolbreak Special*. Frank Doelger, Mark Gordon, executive producers. Alan C. Blomquist, producer. CBS.

OUTSTANDING ANIMATED PROGRAM
• *Jim Henson's Muppet Babies*. Jim Henson, Margaret Loesch, Lee Gunther, executive producers. Bob Richardson, producer. John Gibbs, director. Jeffrey Scott, writer. CBS.

OUTSTANDING PERFORMER IN CHILDREN'S PROGRAMMING
• Pearl Bailey, "Cindy Eller: A Modern Fairy Tale," *ABC Afterschool Special*. ABC.

OUTSTANDING DIRECTING IN CHILDREN'S PROGRAMMING
• Martin Sheen, "Babies Having Babies," *CBS Schoolbreak Special*. CBS.

OUTSTANDING WRITING IN A CHILDREN'S SERIES
• Norman Stiles, Sara Compton, Tom Dunsmuir, Judy Freudberg, Tony Geiss, Emily Kingsley, David Korr, Sonia Manzano, Jeff Moss, Mark Saltzman, Nancy Sans, Luis Santeiro, Cathi Rosenberg-Turow, Gary Belkin, Ray Sipherd, *Sesame Street*. PBS.

OUTSTANDING WRITING IN A CHILDREN'S SPECIAL
• Kathryn Montgomery, Jeffrey Auerbach, "Babies Having Babies," *CBS Schoolbreak Special*. CBS.

SPECIAL CLASS WRITING AREA (Area award)
• Catherine Faulkner, *Chagall's Journey*. NBC.

OUTSTANDING MUSIC DIRECTION AND COMPOSITION FOR A DAYTIME DRAMA SERIES
• Jill Diamond, Rae Kraus, music directors. Billy Chinnock, Patricia Stotter, James Lawrence, composers, *Search for Tomorrow*. NBC.

OUTSTANDING MUSIC DIRECTION AND COMPOSITION
• Michael Franks, music director/ composer, "Are You My Mother?" *ABC Afterschool Special*. ABC.

OUTSTANDING GRAPHICS AND TITLE DESIGN
• James Castle, *New Love, American Style*. ABC.

OUTSTANDING ART DIRECTION/ SET DECORATION/SCENIC DESIGN FOR A DAYTIME DRAMA SERIES
• Sy Tomashoff, art director. Jay Garvin, set decorator, *Capitol*. CBS.

**OUTSTANDING ART DIRECTION/
SET DECORATION/SCENIC DESIGN**
• Victor DiNapoli, art director. Nat
Mongioi, set decorator, *Sesame Street.*
PBS.

**OUTSTANDING COSTUME DESIGN
FOR A DAYTIME DRAMA SERIES**
• David Dangle, Nanzi Adzima, Bud
Santora, *Guiding Light.* CBS.

OUTSTANDING COSTUME DESIGN
• Bill Kellard, live actors. Caroly Wilcox,
Richard Termine, David Valasquez,
Robert Flanagan, muppets, *Sesame Street.*
PBS.

**OUTSTANDING MAKEUP FOR A DAYTIME
DRAMA SERIES**
• Pam P.K. Cole, head makeup artist.
Diane Lewis, Donna Messina, Catherine
McCann Davison, Sundi Martino, Becky
Bowen, *General Hospital.* ABC.

**HAIRSTYLING FOR A DAYTIME
DRAMA SERIES**
• Linda Librizzi Williams, Ralph
Stanzione, *Guiding Light.* CBS.

OUTSTANDING CINEMATOGRAPHY
• Robert Elswit, "The War Between the
Classes," *CBS Schoolbreak Special.* CBS.

**OUTSTANDING TECHNICAL DIRECTION,
ELECTRONIC CAMERA & VIDEO CONTROL
FOR A DRAMA SERIES**
• Rick Labgold, Chuck Guzzi, technical
directors. Gorm Erickson, Pat Kenney,
Bob Welsh, Ted Morales, Toby Brown,
Paul Johnson, camera personnel. Roberto
Bosio, Janice Bendiksen, senior video
control. *Capitol.* CBS.

**OUTSTANDING TECHNICAL DIRECTION,
ELECTRONIC CAMERA & VIDEO CONTROL**
• Dick Holden, technical director/
electronic camera. *This Old House.* PBS.

OUTSTANDING FILM EDITING
• Harvey Greenstein, Wally Katz, Douglas
W. Smith, *3-2-1 Contact.* PBS.

**OUTSTANDING VIDEO-TAPE EDITING
FOR A DRAMA SERIES**
• Dan Brumett, *The Young and the
Restless.* CBS.

OUTSTANDING VIDEO-TAPE EDITING
• Stuart Pappe, "Babies Having Babies,"
CBS Schoolbreak Special. CBS.

OUTSTANDING FILM SOUND EDITING
• David Gelfand, supervising editor. Laura
Civiello, sound editor. David Gelfand,
supervising music editor, "Don't Touch,"
ABC Afterschool Special. ABC.

OUTSTANDING FILM SOUND MIXING
• Petur Hliddal, production mixer. Thomas
Fleischman, rerecording mixer, "Can A
Guy Say No," *ABC Afterschool Special.* ABC.

**OUTSTANDING LIVE & TAPE SOUND
MIXING & SOUND EFFECTS
FOR A DAYTIME DRAMA SERIES**
• Scott A. Millan, preproduction and
production mixer. Tommy Persson,
production mixer. Rafael O. Valentin,
Donald D. Henderson, postproduction
mixers. Larry Maggiore, Peter Romano,
sound effects technicians, *The Young and
the Restless.* CBS.

**OUTSTANDING LIVE & TAPE SOUND
MIXING & SOUND EFFECTS**
• Mark Bovos, production mixer. Tom
Huth, postproduction mixer. Mike Mitchel,
sound effects technician, "Babies Having
Babies," *CBS Schoolbreak Special.* CBS.

**OUTSTANDING LIGHTING DIRECTION
FOR A DAYTIME DRAMA SERIES**
• Frank Olson, Jene Youtt, Hal Anderson,
Lincoln John Stulik, *As the World Turns.* CBS.

OUTSTANDING LIGHTING DIRECTION
• Carl Gibson, *Kids, Incorporated.*
Syndicated.

**SPECIAL CLASS PROGRAM AREA
(Area award)**
• *Chagall's Journey.* Helen Marmor,
executive producer. Randolph Wands,
Jennie Tong, producers. NBC.
• "Chamber Music Society of Lincoln
Center with Irene Worth and Horacio
Gutierrez," *Live from Lincoln Center.* John
Goberman, producer. PBS.

OUTSTANDING HAIRSTYLING
• Sherry Baker, *Pippi Longstocking.* ABC.

(No awards were bestowed in the areas
of directors or makeup in special classification.)

NEWS & DOCUMENTARY AWARD WINNERS
OUTSTANDING COVERAGE OF A SINGLE BREAKING NEWS STORY
(Programs)
• *Mexican Earthquake.* Lane Venardos, executive producer. David Browning, Tom Bettag, senior producers. Kathy Olian, producer. Dan Rather, reporter/correspondent. CBS.
• "Crash of Delta," *ABC News Nightline.* Richard N. Kaplan, executive producer. William Moore, Robert Jordan, senior producers. Robert LeDonne, Steve Lewis, Tara Sonenshine, Heather Vincent, Kyle Gibson, producers. James Walker, Ted Koppel, reporter/correspondents. ABC.
• "Colombian Volcano," *ABC News Nightline.* Richard N. Kaplan, executive producer. William Moore, Robert Jordan, senior producers. Sergio Guerrero, Monica Harari Schnee, producers. Ted Koppel, reporter/ correspondent. ABC.

OUTSTANDING COVERAGE OF A SINGLE BREAKING NEWS STORY
(Segments)
• "In the Fire's Path," *20/20.* David Doss, producer. Ken Kashiwahara, reporter/correspondent. ABC.
"A Bank Fails," *The CBS Evening News with Dan Rather.* Lane Venardos, executive producer. Linda Mason, senior producer. Lance Heflin, producer. Jane Bryant Quinn, reporter. CBS.
• "Trojan Horse," *The CBS Evening News with Dan Rather.* Michael Gavshon, producer. Alan Pizzey, reporter. CBS.

OUTSTANDING BACKGROUND/ANALYSIS OF A SINGLE CURRENT STORY
(Programs)
• "In South Africa," *ABC News Nightline.* Richard N. Kaplan, executive producer. William Moore, Robert Jordan, Betsy West, senior producers. Lionel Chapman, Terry Irving, Steve Lewis, Tara Sonenshine, producers. Kenneth Walker, Jeff Greenfield, reporters. ABC.
• "Acid Rain — New Bad News," *Nova.* John Angier, producer/reporter. PBS.
• "Men Who Molest," *Frontline.* David Fanning, Mary Lynn Earls, executive producers. Rachel V. Lyon, producer. Bobbie Birieffi, reporter. PBS.

OUTSTANDING BACKGROUND/ANALYSIS OF A SINGLE CURRENT STORY
(Segments)
• "Schizophrenia," *60 Minutes.* Alan Maraynes, producer. Ed Bradley, reporter. CBS.
• "Farm Suicide," *The MacNeil-Lehrer Newshour.* Les Crystal, executive producer. Mike Joseloff, Jon Meyersohn, Joe Quinlan, producers. Kwame Holman, correspondent. Marie MacLean, reporter. PBS.
• "Vietnam Remembered," *ABC World News Tonight.* Sally V. Holm, producer. Richard Threlkeld, correspondent. ABC.
• "Ronald Reagan: The Movie," *60 Minutes.* Suzanne St. Pierre, producer. Morley Safer, correspondent. CBS.

OUTSTANDING INVESTIGATIVE JOURNALISM
(Programs)
• "Retreat From Beirut," *Frontline.* David Fanning, executive producer. Sherry Jones, senior producer. Nancy Sloss, producer. William Greider, correspondent. PBS.

OUTSTANDING INVESTIGATIVE JOURNALISM
(Segments)
• "Mob Gas," *NBC Nightly News.* Brian Ross, Ira Silverman, producers. Brian Ross, reporter. NBC.
• "International Christian Aid Investigation," *ABC World News Tonight.* Charles Stuart, senior producer. Tom Yellen, producer. Karen Burnes, reporter. ABC.
• *Military Medicine.* Chuck Collins, producer. Mark Nykanen, reporter. NBC.

OUTSTANDING INTERVIEW/INTERVIEWERS
(Program)
• *The Times of Harvey Milk.* David Loxton, executive producer. Robert Epstein, Richard Schmiechen, producers. Harvey Fierstein, interviewer. PBS.

OUTSTANDING INTERVIEW/INTERVIEWER(S)
(Segments)
• "Liz Carpenter: A Conversation with Bill Moyers," *Sunday Morning.* Lindsay Miller, producer. Bill Moyers, interviewer. CBS.

OUTSTANDING COVERAGE
OF A CONTINUING NEWS STORY
(Programs)
• "AIDS: Chapter One," *Nova*. Paula S. Apsell, executive producer. Thea Chalow, producer. PBS.

OUTSTANDING COVERAGE
OF A CONTINUING NEWS STORY
(Segments)
• "Children in Poverty," *ABC World News Tonight*. Richard O'Regan, Susan Aasen, producers. Karen Burnes, reporter. ABC.
• "Africa: Struggle for Survival," *The CBS Evening News with Dan Rather*. Martin Koughan, producer. Bill Moyers, reporter. CBS.
• "Vietnam Now," *The CBS Evening News with Dan Rather*. Lane Venardos, executive producer. Linda Mason, senior producer. Bob Anderson, producer. Bob Simon, reporter. CBS.

SPECIAL CLASSIFICATION
FOR OUTSTANDING PROGRAM
ACHIEVEMENT
(Programs)
• *The Skin Horse*. Ricki Green, executive producer. Nigel Evans, Sue Ducat, producers. PBS.
• *The Times of Harvey Milk*. Robert Epstein, Richard Schmiechen, producers. PBS.

SPECIAL CLASSIFICATION
FOR OUTSTANDING PROGRAM
ACHIEVEMENT
(Segments)
• "Paul Host," *America Today*. Jim Douglas, Joan Steffend, producers, reporters/correspondents. PBS.
• "Bicycle Messengers," *CBS Evening News ... On the Road*. Bernard Birnbaum, senior producer. Cathy Lewis, producer. Charles Kuralt, reporter/correspondent. CBS.

OUTSTANDING INFORMATIONAL,
CULTURAL, OR HISTORICAL
PROGRAMMING
(Programs)
• "My Heart, Your Heart," *The MacNeil-Lehrer Newshour*. Lawrence Pomeroy, producer. Jim Lehrer, reporter/correspondent. PBS.
• *Hiroshima Remembered*. Laurie Toth, producer. Gail Harris, reporter/

correspondent. Paul Frees, narrator, PBS.
"The Lifer and the Lady," *Frontline*. John Kastner, producer. PBS.
• "A Class Divided," *Frontline*. David Fanning, executive producer. William Peters, producer. Charlie Cobb, correspondent. PBS.

OUTSTANDING INFORMATIONAL,
CULTURAL OR HISTORICAL
PROGRAMMING
(Segments)
• "The Music Man," *American Almanac*. Linda Eliman, producer. Lucky Severson, correspondent. NBC.
• "The Beeb," *60 Minutes*. John Tiffin, producer. Morley Safer, reporter/correspondent. CBS.
• "Julia," *60 Minutes*. Don Hewitt, executive producer. Philip Scheffler, senior producer. Marti Galovic Palmer, producer. CBS.

THE AREAS
Each area has the possibility of one award winner, multiple winners, or none. Winners are listed.

OUTSTANDING INDIVIDUAL ACHIEVEMENT
(Writers)
• Perry Wolff, Elena Mannes. "Whose America is It?" *CBS Reports*. CBS.
• Nelson E. Breen, David Altshuler, Arnost Lustig, *The Precious Legacy*. PBS.
• Marshall Frady, Judy Crichton, John Fielding, Christopher Isham, Phil Lewis, Steve Singer, Andrew Schlesinger, Peter Bull, "The Fire Unleashed," *ABC News Closeup*. ABC.
(Directors)
• Elena Mannes, "Whose America is It?" *CBS Reports*. CBS.
• Paul Wagner, Marjorie Hunt, *The Stone Carvers*. PBS.
• Harry Rasky, *Homage to Chagall — The Colours of Love*. PBS.
(Cinematographers)
• Belinda Wright, Stanley Breeden, "Land of the Tiger," *National Geographic Special*. PBS.
(Electronic camerapersons: Videographers)
• Michael Watson, Three segments: "Desert," "Winter Calving," "Colorado Gold," *America Today*. PBS.
• Isadore Bleckman, "Bicycle Messengers," *CBS Evening News ... On the Road*. CBS.

(Sound)
• Joan Franklin, sound editor. Alan Berliner, Alsee Gordon, sound recordists, "The Slave Ships of the Sulu Sea," *20/20*. ABC.
• Belinda Wright, "Land of the Tiger," *National Geographic Special*. PBS.
(Film editors and film postproduction editors)
• Annamaria Szanto, *The Precious Legacy*. PBS.
• Deborah Hoffman, Robert Epstein, *The Times of Harvey Milk*. PBS.
(Tape editors)
• Jess Bushyhead, video-tape editor, "The Music Man," *American Almanac*. NBC.
• Jess Bushyhead, video-tape editor, "The Year 1985 in Review," *Today*. NBC.
(Title sequences)
• John Ridgway, art director. Craig Rice, Teri Freedman, Ron Clark, Harry Marks. *Entertainment This Week*. Syndicated.
(Music composers)
• Lyn Murray, Scott Harper, "Miraculous Machines," *National Geographic Special*. PBS.

INTERNATIONAL AWARD WINNERS
OUTSTANDING DOCUMENTARY
• *28 Up*. Granada Television Ltd., United Kingdom

OUTSTANDING DRAMA
• *Das Boot* (The Boat). Bavaria Atelier in association with Westdeutscher Rundfunk and Sueddeutscher Rundfunk, West Germany.

OUTSTANDING PERFORMING ARTS
• *Omnibus: The Treble*. The British Broadcasting Corporation (BBC), U.K.

OUTSTANDING POPULAR ARTS
• *Spitting Image*. Central Independent Television, U.K.

OUTSTANDING CHILDREN'S PROGRAM
• *Supergran*. Tyne Tees Television, U.K..

INTERNATIONAL DIRECTORATE AWARD
• Leonard H. Goldenson

FOUNDERS AWARD
• Sir David Attenborough

SPECIAL AWARDS
OUTSTANDING ACHIEVEMENT IN THE SCIENCE OF TELEVISION ENGINEERING
• Abekas
• Ampex
• dbx, Inc.
• Electronic Industries Association
• JVC Corporation
• M/A Communications, Inc.
• Matsushita (Panasonic)
• National Broadcasting Company
• Quantel Corporation
• RCA Corporation
• Sony Corporation
• Zenith Electronics Corp.

NATIONAL AWARD FOR COMMUNITY SERVICE
• *AIDS Lifeline Series*, KPIX-TV, San Francisco, California.

SPECIAL AWARD
• Presentation to BBC Chairman Marmaduke Hussey honoring the British Broadcasting Corporation for 50 years of television broadcasting.

A.T.A.S. GOVERNORS AWARD
• Red Skelton

Feast of the Foxes

Ever since 1955, when the Emmys were first seen by a nationwide audience, they had been telecast by one of the three major networks and followed a format that seldom varied. In the mid-1980s, however, there was a new satellite-delivered programming service for independent stations that was aiming to become a fourth national network — Fox. What made it a formidable threat was that Fox had innovative new programming, gads of money to spend, and the nerve to take on its established foes by trying to wrest the Emmys away.

The brash budding network initially outfoxed its competition by outbidding them with a total offer of $4.5 million to broadcast the prime-time ceremonies and the new annual Hall of Fame awards program over a three-year period. The Big Three networks didn't want the Hall of Fame program and would only offer $875,000 per year for the prime-time show, a bid that was nonetheless a considerable increase over last year's rate of $750,000. The Big Three also wanted to trim the number of on-air prizes from 32 to 22 in order to keep the show short. Fox wanted a full, complete show — and got both awards programs in the bargain. "I think the academy went after the bucks and that's really it," *Broadcasting* quoted an unnamed network official as saying. A.T.A.S. acknowledged the "favorable financial benefits" of the deal with Fox, but also said that the integrity of the awards was at stake in its decision.

Fox was so adamant about a complete show that it revamped the telecast with some innovative enhancements that included voiceovers to inform the viewing audience how many times a certain

Starting with a hefty 20 nominations, new series L.A. Law *won an impressive verdict: seven awards, including best drama.*

winner had been nominated and won in the past as he or she approached the stage and also by giving a recap of the night two-thirds of the way through.

Other novelties involved winners being interviewed backstage as they still maintained the rosy glow of victory, and humor spots were dropped in intermittently such as Jane Curtin's "newscast" referring to the unsuccessful Supreme Court nominee Robert Bork. She told viewers, "Judge Bork can find no mention of television in the Constitution and so watching tonight's show could be a federal offense."

Fox wanted no cap on how long thank-yous could run. "We don't want to limit television's superstars to a 30-second acceptance speech when everyone is watching the show to see them and share that special moment," executive producer Donald Ohlmeyer told the *L.A. Times*.

Rue McClanahan reaped the best actress gold for The Golden Girls, *Outstanding Comedy Series for a second year in a row.*

The newspaper countered with a warning: "The 30-second limit, like the heart, has its reasons."

Over the past few years it seemed that every time a hot new series entered the Emmys race with a bounty of nominations and an inevitable air of invincibility about it, the show ended up suffering a painful public lesson in humility. *Miami Vice* and *Moonlighting* both fared poorly after their initial success at the nomination stage in the last several years and now another new show faced the same potential fate.

L.A. Law had a shrewd battery of sun-glazed, smog-toughened attorneys behind it, though, when it started out with 20 nods, a record number second only to *Hill Street Blues*'s performance in 1981. Ironically, the two shows shared the same creator. *HSB*'s Steven Bochco developed the new series with lawyer Terry Louise Fisher, who was also a producer of *Cagney & Lacey*. *L.A. Law* shared the other series' gritty sense of realism and humor, too, along with plot lines that

sometimes continued over several episodes and had unhappy endings.

The verdict? *L.A. Law* took custody of six golden statuettes, including ones for best drama series, direction, writing (Bochco and Fisher), art direction, and sound mixing. The sixth prize went to guest performer Alfre Woodard, who played a rape victim in the program pilot. Woodard had won an Emmy once before, in 1984, for a guest role on Bochco's *Hill Street Blues*.

Moonlighting's cast might have asked that the series decision be appealed had it not been for its own sudden rise in other categories. Last year its self-assured star Bruce Willis strolled up the red carpet into the Pasadena Civic Auditorium wearing a lamb suede tuxedo (sans tie) and a confident look on his face. When he lost to *St. Elsewhere*'s William Daniels, the *L.A. Herald Examiner* said, "Too bad, since it could have been fun to see Bruce Willis reemerge in his leather-encrusted bathrobe." This year, dressed in more conformist formal black tie, Willis — "finally," said the *L.A. Times* — got the honor. But his response was hardly humble. "His Surliness," as the *Herald Examiner* called him, stuck out his tongue at the camera when he heard the news from where he sat and then somewhat redeemed himself up on stage with a gracious acceptance speech. (In his backstage commentary, he told a Fox interviewer, "Somewhere in the back of my mind, when I went into this business, this night was there.")

The stars of *Cagney & Lacey* continued to monopolize the best actress category thanks to an unusual chemistry they enjoyed on screen. "There are no women buddy pictures," *Ms.* magazine once noted. "Cagney and Lacey are buddies — they joke, they fight, both with each other and side by side, they share pizzas and gossip, but they also share the deep recesses of their hearts." Sharon

Gless ("Cagney") shared her deep recesses this time with the Emmy audience as she accepted her second statuette with heart-felt thoughts about her "reel" and "real" fathers. Supporting honors went to John Hillerman, "Higgins" of *Magnum P.I.*, and to Bonnie Bartlett once again for *St. Elsewhere*.

Proof that those silver-haired foxes sharing a single sunny den in Miami still had staying power past the age of 60, *The Golden Girls* came back again as best comedy series, the second year in a row that it surpassed the still number one-ranked 1985 Emmy champ *The Cosby Show*. Once again, too, all four stars were nominated either for best actress or best supporting actress. Betty White won last year, but this time the lead honor went to senior sexpot Rue McClanahan "who politely overlooked the fact," noted *The Washington Post*,

"His Surliness" best actor Bruce Willis: "In the back of my mind, when I went into this business, this night was there."

"that presenter Howie Mandel mispronounced her name 'McCallahan.'"

But Emmy night also marked another return, of a real Fox — Michael J. — the star of *Family Ties* who picked up his second best-actor statuette, resulting in a minor controversy over series classifications. *Broadcasting* was among those that noted that Fox won the comedy award for a tragic episode involving the death of a friend while Bruce Willis, who played a wisecracking detective on *Moonlighting*, won the drama trophy for a segment that had "many comedic elements," according the *L.A. Times*.

The fox analogy also applied to supporting actress winner Jackée Harry, who played the saucy, sex-starved role of Sandra Clark on *227* while the homecoming quality of the whole comedy category saw the return of *Night Court*'s John Larroquette. (Accepting his third Emmy in a row, Larroquette admitted to being "slightly embarrassed.") It was presented to him by Joan Rivers, who was making her first public appearance since the suicide of her husband.

The best miniseries, *A Year in the Life*, was a three-part saga about the family of a plastics manufacturer in Seattle that *TV Guide* called "remarkable television entertainment." The mother character dies in the miniseries, but enthusiastic NBC program executives still tried to keep the family drama alive by continuing *Year* as a one-hour series. Unfortunately, *Year* failed to find a faithful audience and was canceled after an eight-month run.

The mother character also died in this year's best drama special, *Promise*, the story of a carefree bachelor who suddenly faces a pledge he once made to his mother to look after his schizophrenic brother after she's gone. The bachelor was played by James Garner (1977 Emmy winner for *The Rockford Files*), who also coproduced the film. Garner "was noticeably moved as he came onstage with his producers and writers," noted *Variety*. "He observed they were grateful they could bring the disease of schizophrenia 'into the open for people to look at, to see and to feel.'" James Woods (lead actor) and Piper Laurie (supporting actress) were both honored for their performances in the program, which also won trophies for direction and writing. Woods was hailed for his portrayal of the schizophrenic brother. "His speech included a tribute to costar Garner," said *The Washington Post*, "and was uncommonly generous in sharing credit."

Emmy's new broadcaster simply outfoxed the Big Three networks.

The generous spirit that a former First Lady showed in publicly battling her addictions to booze and prescription drugs so that a nation might benefit was the focus of *The Betty Ford Story*, which earned Gena Rowlands the lead actress's statuette. Rowlands triumphed over Ann-Margret of *The Two Mrs. Grenvilles,* who twice before, in 1983 and 1984, came close to nabbing the actress's trophy but lost.

Another entertainment awards event, the Oscars, won a top program prize in 1979. This year it was the Tony Awards' turn, winning in the variety category while last year's victor, *The Kennedy Center Honors,* returned to take the writing award and *A Carol Burnett Special* won two prizes, including a performance salute to Robin Williams.

If the Emmys evening turned out to be a Night for the Hungry Foxes, it appeared that at least one of them bit off more than it could chew. Thanks to the Fox network's insistence on having a complete show, this one set a new record as the longest ever by running just 20 seconds short of four hours. It was also a ratings disaster, just as many critics had predicted, even if the same viewer numbers gave Fox its highest national exposure to date. In the past, the Big Three networks generally avoided scheduling first-run series programs opposite the Emmycast, but this time they lifted the embargo and aired original episodes of *Family Ties*, *60 Minutes,* and *Spencer: For Hire.* In 1986, on NBC, the Emmys had its highest ratings in seven years, a 36 share. This year its share was 14, the lowest in history.

Despite its drawbacks, the awards show was still "predictably glitzy and gloriously silly," said the *L.A. Times*, thanks to its insistence on a lighthearted approach. (Next year, wisecracked comedian Jay Leno, the Emmys will appear "on the Du Mont network," which had been out of business for 30 years.) The ceremony included a fond farewell to *Hill Street Blues* (which went off the air this year), Mary Tyler Moore paying tribute to the late Fred Astaire, and Audrey Meadows, seated in a reconstructed set of *The Honeymooners*, paying her last respects to recently deceased costar Jackie Gleason, who never won an Emmy.

People magazine concluded, "The baby network did OK."

DAYTIME AWARDS

"I want her to be a bitch again!" Kim Zimmer told the press backstage about her character Reva Shayne Lewis on *Guiding Light* after winning the best actress prize for the second time in three years. (Zimmer then planted an endearing kiss on best actor Larry Bryggman, the villainous Dr. John Dixon on *As the World Turns*.) Kathleen Noone (Ellen Chandler of *All My Children*) was so elated by her victory as best supporting actress that she said, "It's taken me ten years to get this. I'm going to build a mantel for it." Top ingenue Martha Byrne (as Lilly Walsh on *As the World*

Turns) piped in, "This is the biggest thing that's ever happened to me," although she then remembered, "My prom was nice."

It was dizzying day of triumph for *As the World Turns*. The sudser set in the mythical Midwestern town of Oakdale had been the number one-rated daytime drama in the 1950s and '60s when it was first introduced. It sagged for a decade after that, but now its ratings were climbing again just as it was named best drama series and also took awards for Bryggman, Byrne, and supporting actor Gregg Marx (as the amorous Tom Hughes). *As the World Turns* began the race as the early leader with 20 nominations. A video-tape prize brought the tally to five trophies, an unsurpassed number tied only by the series winner of the past two years, *The Young and the Restless*, which this year garnered four crafts awards and one for its director. *Guiding Light* came in third place with three, including the one for the freshly sweetened-up Zimmer.

A number of other daytime program winners from last year returned triumphantly, including *Sesame Street* and *The $25,000 Pyramid*, although Bob Barker of *The Price is Right* won the game show hosting honors this time instead of Dick Clark. Noticeably absent from the winner's circle were Phil Donahue and his show, which had mostly dominated the talk show category for more than a decade. His success spawned so many programs like his that he was finally — and perhaps inevitably — dislodged by one of his own imitators. *The Oprah Winfrey Show* took all three top awards, in fact — for series, host, and director. Winfrey, who was also hostess of the afternoon Emmy Awards ceremony, celebrated after the show by dancing "till the wee hours," reported *Us* magazine, "at two New York nightclubs."

Jim Henson's Muppet Babies contin-ued its reign over animated programs while ABC reclaimed the honor for Outstanding Children's Special from last year's recipient CBS. Its winning *Afterschool Special* was "Wanted: The Perfect Guy," about a boy who tries to fix his divorced mother up with a new man. Madeline Kahn won a performance prize for playing the single mom.

> *It was a dizzying day of triumph for* As the World Turns.

The ceremony was held at the Sheraton Center in New York and was not broadcast by Fox. ABC aired the festivities, which were attended by 1,100 fans and viewed by 36 percent of its daytime audience, a record.

SPORTS AWARDS

When national cable television programming won Emmys for the first time in open competition, it occurred, appropriately enough, in sports. The awards were given for the Goodwill Games staged between the U.S. and Soviet Union by media maverick Ted Turner. The Turner Broadcasting System of Atlanta broadcast the Olympics-like event and was acknowledged for its technical innovation and also won three more trophies for its crafts crew.

Emmy winner of years past John Madden of CBS was cohost for the awards ceremonies held at New York's Sheraton Center, along with ABC's Jim McKay and Dick Enberg of NBC. (NBC was no longer boycotting the event; N.A.T.A.S.'s ongoing improvements in the awards procedure had finally convinced the network to rejoin.) Madden also received a prize of his own for being acclaimed best sports analyst. The sports host prize, however, went to Brooklyn-born Al Michaels of ABC,

Sports show cohost John Madden not only presented awards, he won one for best game analysis, his fourth statuette.

who had been reporting baseball play-by-play action before he became sportscaster of *NFL Monday Night Football* in 1986.

The Emmys show included a 30-minute tape to familiarize the audience with the top nominated footage. "The film highlights added tremendous drama to the evening," reported *N.A.T.A.S. News*. Celebrity presenters included baseball's Tom Seaver, world championship runner Eamonn Coughlan, and jockey Angel Cordero.

Two of the four leading program categories went to past Emmy favorites, one to *ABC's Wide World of Sports* (best edited sports series) and the other to the show's *25th Anniversary Special*, which was voted best edited sports special. *NFL on CBS* was named best live sports series while *Daytona 500* was the year's best live sports special.

NEWS & DOCUMENTARY AWARDS

"When the final group of Emmy awards were announced," *The New York Times*

noted, "most of the 15-inch statues were toted off to places of honor in production studios in New York and Los Angeles." One, though, it added, "is deep within a prison in which the eight-pound statue would be regarded as a dangerous weapon."

Two inmates of the Taconic Correctional Facility just north of New York City occupied their time by filming "AIDS: A Bad Way to Die," which was meant to teach fellow convicts about ways to avoid getting the deadly disease. When it came to the attention of *New York Daily News* columnist Jimmy Breslin, who also had his own TV series called *Breslin's People*, the columnist/broadcaster told the *Times*, "You would have to be a moron not to put it on the air. We got it for zero dollars, cut it in two sections and ran it. It's one of the most powerful documentaries ever done." At the Emmys, the program was acknowledged for Outstanding Background and Analysis of a Single Current News Story and Breslin called its success story "a real lesson in TV," adding, "It shows, if you teach a person skills in prison and give them an opportunity, [they] can do something worthwhile."

The awards show, held at the Waldorf-Astoria Hotel, also included names more familiar to those in the news. Dan Rather, Tom Brokaw, and Connie Chung were in the audience. Presenters included Gloria Steinem (founder of *Ms.* magazine), two astronauts from the Voyager space shuttle, and Hawaiian senator Daniel Inouye, who "made a special trip from Washington just after the Iran-Contra hearing had been completed," noted the N.A.T.A.S. newsletter.

Another winner of the award for analysis of a single current story was *20/20*, which won several other awards as well, including one for its segment "By His Father's Hand: The

Zumwalts," an examination of the harmful effects of the defoliant Agent Orange on the American soldiers in Vietnam. ABC's other top prizes included an honor for investigative journalism for *MIAs — The Story That Would Not Die* and an informational program trophy for a *Good Morning America* segment on East Africa.

NBC's leading awards were for its coverage of the memorial service held for the astronauts killed in the Challenger space shuttle explosion and for its profile of the Philippines following the fall of President Ferdinand Marcos.

ABC News Nightline was also rewarded for its Philippines reporting and for covering the "Pan Am Flight 73 Hijack."

Honors for investigative journalism went to *60 Minutes* for its probe into the alleged sexual abuses at the McMartin Preschool, and to *The CBS Evening News with Dan Rather* for an exposé on "Helicopter Dangers." The evening news show was also cited for its coverage of a single breaking news story when it followed President Reagan's summit meeting in Iceland with Soviet leader Mikhail Gorbachev. *CBS News Nightwatch* won for its exclusive interview with convicted murderer Charles Manson.

PBS took the most awards of the night — 11 — for such *Frontline* programs as "Sue the Doctor?" and two for the documentary *Before Stonewall*, chronicling the early gay rights movement.

1986–87

The prime-time ceremony was broadcast on the Fox network from the Pasadena Civic Auditorium on September 20, 1987, for prime-time programs telecast between July 1, 1986, and June 30, 1987. Daytime awards broadcast on ABC from the Sheraton Center Hotel in New York on June 30, 1987, for programs aired between March 6, 1986, and March 5, 1987. News & documentary awards for 1986 were bestowed on September 8, 1987. The sports awards for 1986, were given away on September 29, 1987.

PRIME-TIME PROGRAM AWARDS
OUTSTANDING DRAMA SERIES
• *L.A. Law*. Steven Bochco, executive producer. Gregory Hoblit, co-executive producer. Terry Louise Fisher, supervising producer. Ellen S. Pressman, Scott Goldstein, producers. Phillip M. Goldfarb, coordinating producer. NBC.
Cagney & Lacey. Barney Rosenzweig, executive producer. Jonathan Estrin, Shelley List, supervising producers. Ralph Singleton, Georgia Jeffries, producers. P.K. Knelman, coproducer. CBS.
Moonlighting. Glenn Gordon Caron, executive producer. Jay Daniel, co-executive producer. Artie Mandelberg, Karen Hall, supervising producers. Ron Osborn, Jeff Reno, Roger Director,

producers. ABC.
Murder, She Wrote. Peter S. Fischer, executive producer. Robert F. O'Neill, producer. CBS.
St. Elsewhere. Bruce W. Paltrow, executive producer. Mark Tinker, supervising producer. John Masius, Tom Fontana, producers. Abby Singer, coordinating producer. NBC.

OUTSTANDING COMEDY SERIES
• *The Golden Girls*. Paul Junger Witt, Tony Thomas, Susan Harris, executive producers. Kathy Speer, Terry Grossman, producers. Mort Nathan, Barry Fanaro, Winifred Hervey, Marsha Posner Williams, coproducers. NBC.
Cheers. James Burrows, Glen Charles, Les Charles, executive producers. Peter Casey, David Lee, David Angell, producers. Tim Berry, coproducer. NBC.
The Cosby Show. Marcy Carsey, Tom Werner, executive producers. John Markus, co-executive producer. Carmen Finestra, supervising producer. Caryn Mandabach, Matt Williams, producers. Carmen Finestra, Gary Kott, coproducers. NBC.
Family Ties. Gary David Goldberg, executive producer. Alan Uger, Ruth Bennett, supervising producers. Marc Lawrence, producer. Carol Himes, line

James Garner (right) looks after his schizophrenic brother (best actor James Woods, left) in the top TV film Promise.

producer. June Galas, coproducer. NBC.
Night Court. Reinhold Weege, executive producer. Jeff Melman, supervising producer. Bob Stevens, producer. Tim Steele, coproducer. NBC.

OUTSTANDING MINISERIES
• *A Year in the Life.* Joshua Brand, John Falsey, executive producers. Stephen Cragg, producer. NBC.
Anastasia: The Mystery of Anna. Michael Lepiner, Kenneth Kaufman, executive producers. Graham Cottle, supervising producer. Marvin J. Chomsky, producer. NBC.
Nutcracker: Money, Madness, Murder. Chuck McLain, William Hanley, executive producers. William Beaudine, Jr., producer. NBC.
Out on a Limb. Stan Margulies, producer. Colin Higgins, coproducer. ABC.
The Two Mrs. Grenvilles. Susan Pollock, executive producer. John Erman, supervising producer. Preston Fischer, producer. NBC.

OUTSTANDING DRAMA/COMEDY SPECIAL
• *Promise, Hallmark Hall of Fame.* Peter K. Duchow, James Garner, executive producers. Glenn Jordan, producer. Richard Friedenberg, coproducer. CBS.
Escape from Sobibor. Martin Starger, executive producer. Dennis E. Doty, producer. Howard Alston, coproducer. CBS.

LBJ: The Early Years. Louis Rudolph, executive producer. John Brice, Sandra Saxon Brice, producers. NBC.
Pack of Lies, Hallmark Hall of Fame. Robert Halmi, Jr., executive producer. Robert Halmi, Sr., producer. CBS.
Unnatural Causes. Blue Andre, Robert M. Myman, executive producers. Blue Andre, producer. Stephen Doran, Martin M. Goldstein, coproducers. NBC.

OUTSTANDING VARIETY, MUSIC, OR COMEDY PROGRAM
• *The 1987 Tony Awards.* Don Mischer, executive producer. David J. Goldberg, producer. CBS.
Late Night with David Letterman. Jack Rollins, David Letterman, executive producers. Barry Sand, producer. David Letterman, host. NBC.
Liberty Weekend—Closing Ceremonies. David L. Wolper, executive producer. Don Mischer, producer. ABC.
The Tonight Show Starring Johnny Carson. Fred DeCordova, executive producer. Peter Lassally, producer. Johnny Carson, host. NBC.
The Tracey Ullman Show. James L. Brooks, Jerry Belson, Ken Estin, Heide Perlman, executive producers. Richard Sakai, producer. Paul Flaherty, Dick Blasucci, coproducers. Tracey Ullman, host. Fox.

OUTSTANDING CLASSICAL PROGRAM IN THE PERFORMING ARTS (Winner)
• *Vladimir Horowitz: The Last Romantic.* Peter Gelb, executive producer. Susan Froemke, producer. Vladimir Horowitz, star. PBS.

OUTSTANDING INFORMATIONAL SERIES (Winners—Tie)
• *Smithsonian World.* Adrian Malone, executive producer. David Grubin, producer. PBS.
• "Unknown Chaplin," *American Masters.* Kevin Brownlow, David Gill, producers. PBS.

OUTSTANDING INFORMATIONAL SPECIAL (Winner)
• "Dance in America: Agnes, the Indomitable De Mille," *Great Performances.* Jac Venza, executive producer. Judy Kinberg, producer. PBS.

OUTSTANDING ANIMATED PROGRAM
(Winner)
• *Cathy*. Lee Mendelson, executive producer. Bill Melendez, producer. Cathy Guisewite, writer. Evert Brown, director. CBS.

OUTSTANDING CHILDREN'S PROGRAM
(Winner)
• *Jim Henson's The Storyteller: Hans My Hedgehog*. Jim Henson, executive producer. Mark Shivas, producer. NBC.

PERFORMANCE, DIRECTING, AND WRITING
OUTSTANDING LEAD ACTOR
IN A DRAMA SERIES
• Bruce Willis, *Moonlighting*. ABC.
Corbin Bernsen, *L.A. Law*. NBC.
William Daniels, *St. Elsewhere*. NBC.
Ed Flanders, *St. Elsewhere*. NBC.
Edward Woodward, *The Equalizer*. CBS.

OUTSTANDING LEAD ACTRESS
IN A DRAMA SERIES
• Sharon Gless, *Cagney & Lacey*. CBS.
Tyne Daly, *Cagney & Lacey*. CBS.
Susan Dey, *L.A. Law*. NBC.
Jill Eikenberry, *L.A. Law*. NBC.
Angela Lansbury, *Murder, She Wrote*. CBS.

OUTSTANDING LEAD ACTOR
IN A COMEDY SERIES
• Michael J. Fox, *Family Ties*. NBC.
Harry Anderson, *Night Court*. NBC.
Ted Danson, *Cheers*. NBC.
Bob Newhart, *Newhart*. CBS.
Bronson Pinchot, *Perfect Strangers*. ABC.

OUTSTANDING LEAD ACTRESS
IN A COMEDY SERIES
• Rue McClanahan, *The Golden Girls*. NBC.
Beatrice Arthur, *The Golden Girls*. NBC.
Blair Brown, *The Days and Nights of Molly Dodd*. NBC.
Jane Curtin, *Kate & Allie*. CBS.
Betty White, *The Golden Girls*. NBC.

OUTSTANDING LEAD ACTOR
IN A MINISERIES OR A SPECIAL
• James Woods, *Promise, Hallmark Hall of Fame*. CBS.
Alan Arkin, *Escape from Sobibor*. CBS.
James Garner, *Promise, Hallmark Hall of Fame*. CBS.
Louis Gossett, Jr., *A Gathering of Old Men*. CBS.
Randy Quaid, *LBJ: The Early Years*. NBC.

OUTSTANDING LEAD ACTRESS
IN A MINISERIES OR A SPECIAL
• Gena Rowlands, *The Betty Ford Story*. ABC.
Ellen Burstyn, *Pack of Lies, Hallmark Hall of Fame*. CBS.
Ann-Margret, *The Two Mrs. Grenvilles*. NBC.
Lee Remick, *Nutcracker: Money, Madness, Murder*. NBC.
Alfre Woodard, *Unnatural Causes*. NBC.

OUTSTANDING SUPPORTING ACTOR
IN A DRAMA SERIES
• John Hillerman, *Magnum, P.I.* CBS.
Ed Begley, Jr., *St. Elsewhere*. NBC.
John Karlen, *Cagney & Lacey*. CBS.
Jimmy Smits, *L.A. Law*. NBC.
Michael Tucker, *L.A. Law*. NBC.

OUTSTANDING SUPPORTING ACTRESS
IN A DRAMA SERIES
• Bonnie Bartlett, *St. Elsewhere*. NBC.
Allyce Beasley, *Moonlighting*. ABC.
Christina Pickles, *St. Elsewhere*. NBC.
Susan Ruttan, *L.A. Law*. NBC.
Betty Thomas, *Hill Street Blues*. NBC.

OUTSTANDING SUPPORTING ACTOR
IN A COMEDY SERIES
• John Larroquette, *Night Court*. NBC.
Woody Harrelson, *Cheers*. NBC.
Tom Poston, *Newhart*. CBS.
Peter Scolari, *Newhart*. CBS.
George Wendt, *Cheers*. NBC.

OUTSTANDING SUPPORTING ACTRESS
IN A COMEDY SERIES
• Jackée Harry, *227*. NBC.
Justine Bateman, *Family Ties*. NBC.
Julia Duffy, *Newhart*. CBS.
Estelle Getty, *The Golden Girls*. NBC.
Rhea Perlman, *Cheers*. NBC.

OUTSTANDING SUPPORTING ACTOR
IN A MINISERIES OR A SPECIAL
• Dabney Coleman, *Sworn to Silence*. ABC.
Stephen Collins, *The Two Mrs. Grenvilles*. NBC.
John Glover, *Nutcracker: Money, Madness, Murder*. NBC.
Laurence Olivier, *Lost Empires, Masterpiece Theatre*. PBS.
Eli Wallach, *Something in Common*. CBS.

**OUTSTANDING SUPPORTING ACTRESS
IN A MINISERIES OR A SPECIAL**
• Piper Laurie, *Promise, Hallmark Hall of
Fame*. CBS.
Claudette Colbert, *The Two Mrs.
Grenvilles*. NBC.
Olivia de Havilland, *Anastasia: The
Mystery of Anna*. NBC.
Christine Lahti, *Amerika*. ABC.
Elizabeth Wilson, *Nutcracker: Money,
Madness, Murder*. NBC.

**OUTSTANDING INDIVIDUAL PERFORMANCE
IN A VARIETY OR MUSIC PROGRAM**
• Robin Williams, *A Carol Burnett
Special: Carol, Carl, Whoopi & Robin.*
ABC.
Billy Crystal, *The 29th Annual Grammy
Awards*. CBS.
Julie Kavner, *The Tracey Ullman Show*.
Fox.
Angela Lansbury, *The 1987 Tony Awards*.
CBS.
John Lovitz, *Saturday Night Live*. NBC.

**OUTSTANDING GUEST PERFORMER
IN A DRAMA SERIES**
• Alfre Woodard, *L.A. Law*. NBC.
Jayne Meadows Allen, *St. Elsewhere*.
NBC.
Steve Allen, *St. Elsewhere*. NBC.
Jeanne Cooper, *L.A. Law*. NBC.
Edward Herrmann, *St. Elsewhere*. NBC.

**OUTSTANDING GUEST PERFORMER
IN A COMEDY SERIES**
• John Cleese, *Cheers*. NBC.
Art Carney, *The Cavanaughs*. CBS.
Herb Edelman, *The Golden Girls*. NBC.
Lois Nettleton, *The Golden Girls*. NBC.
Nancy Walker, *The Golden Girls*. NBC.

**OUTSTANDING DIRECTING
IN A DRAMA SERIES**
• Gregory Hoblit, *L.A. Law*. NBC.
Alan Arkush, *Moonlighting*. ABC.
Will MacKenzie, *Moonlighting*. ABC.
Sharron Miller, *Cagney & Lacey*. CBS.
Donald Petrie, *L.A. Law*. NBC.

**OUTSTANDING DIRECTING
IN A COMEDY SERIES**
• Terry Hughes, *The Golden Girls*. NBC.
James Burrows, *Cheers*. NBC.
Will MacKenzie, *Family Ties*. NBC.
Jay Sandrich, *The Cosby Show*. NBC.
Jack Shea, *Designing Women*. CBS.

**OUTSTANDING DIRECTING
IN A MINISERIES OR A SPECIAL**
• Glenn Jordan, *Promise, Hallmark Hall of
Fame*. CBS.
Paul Bogart, *Nutcracker: Money,
Madness, Murder*. NBC.
Jack Gold, *Escape from Sobibor*. CBS.
Lamont Johnson, *Unnatural Causes*. NBC.
Peter Werner, *LBJ: The Early Years*. NBC.

**OUTSTANDING DIRECTING
IN A VARIETY OR MUSIC PROGRAM**
• Don Mischer, *The Kennedy Center
Honors: A Celebration of the Performing
Arts*. CBS.
Hal Gurnee, *Late Night with David
Letterman 5th Anniversary Special*. NBC.
Dwight Hemion, *Liberty Weekend—
Opening Ceremonies*. ABC.
Walter C. Miller, *The 1987 Annual Tony
Awards*. CBS.
Ted Bessell, Stuart Margolin, *The Tracey
Ullman Show*. Fox.

**OUTSTANDING WRITING
IN A DRAMA SERIES**
• Steven Bochco, Terry Louise Fisher, *L.A.
Law*. NBC.
Glenn Gordon Caron, Jeff Reno, teleplay.
Ron Osborn, Karen Hall, Roger Director,
Charles H. Eglee, story, *Moonlighting*.
ABC.
William M. Finkelstein, *L.A. Law*. NBC.
Georgia Jeffries, *Cagney & Lacey*. CBS.
Ron Osborn, Jeff Reno, *Moonlighting*.
ABC.
John Tinker, Tom Fontana, John Masius,
St. Elsewhere. NBC.
Jeffrey Lewis, David Milch, John Romano,
Hill Street Blues. NBC.

**OUTSTANDING WRITING
IN A COMEDY SERIES**
• Gary David Goldberg, Alan Uger,
Family Ties. NBC.
Jeffrey Duteil, *The Golden Girls*. NBC.
Janet Leahy, *Cheers*. NBC.
David Mirkin, *Newhart*. CBS.
Jay Tarses, *The Days and Nights of Molly
Dodd*. NBC.

**OUTSTANDING WRITING IN A VARIETY
OR MUSIC PROGRAM**
• Steve O'Donnell, Sandy Frank, Joe
Toplyn, Chris Elliott, Matt Wickline, Jeff
Martin, Gerard Mulligan, Randy Cohen,
Larry Jacobson, Kevin Curran, Fred
Graver, Adam Resnick, David Letterman,

Late Night with David Letterman 5th Anniversary Special. NBC.
Andy Breckman, A. Whitney Brown, Jean E. Carroll, James Downey, Al Franken, Eddie Gorodetsky, Phil Hartman, George Meyer, Lorne Michaels, Kevin Nealon, Margaret Oberman, Herb Sargent, Marc Shaiman, Rosie Shuster, Robert Smigel, Jon Vitti, Tom Davis, Bonnie Turner, Terry Turner, Christine Zander, *Saturday Night Live.* NBC.
James L. Brooks, Jerry Belson, Heide Perlman, Ken Estin, Paul Flaherty, Dick Blasucci, Susan Herring, Matt Groening, Kim Fuller, Sam Simon, Marc Flanagan, *The Tracey Ullman Show.* Fox.
Raymond Siller, Michael Barrie, James Mulholland, Kevin Mulholland, Bob Keane, Andrew Nicholls, Darrell Vickers, Hal Goodman, Larry Klein, Gary Belkin, *The Tonight Show Starring Johnny Carson.* NBC.
Jeffrey Lane, *The 1987 Tony Awards.* CBS.

Outstanding Writing
in a Miniseries or a Special
• Richard Friedenberg, teleplay. Kenneth Blackwell, Tennyson Flowers, Richard Friedenberg, story. *Promise, Hallmark Hall of Fame.* CBS.
Joshua Brand, John Falsey, *A Year in the Life.* NBC.
Ralph Gallup, *Pack of Lies, Hallmark Hall of Fame.* CBS.
William Hanley, *Nutcracker: Money, Madness, Murder.* NBC.
Reginald Rose, *Escape from Sobibor.* CBS.

OTHER AWARD WINNERS
Outstanding Music Composition
for a Series
(Dramatic underscore)
• Joel Rosenbaum, *Knots Landing.* CBS.

Outstanding Music Composition
for a Miniseries or a Special
(Dramatic underscore)
• Laurence Rosenthal, *Anastasia: The Mystery of Anna.* NBC.

Outstanding Music Direction
• Don Pippin, music director. Eric Stern, Buster Davis, principal arrangers, "Broadway Sings: The Music of Jule Styne," *Great Performances.* PBS.

Outstanding Music and Lyrics
• Larry Grossman, composer. Buz Kohan, lyricist. *Liberty Weekend—Opening Ceremonies.* Song: "Welcome to Liberty." ABC.

Outstanding Choreography
• Dee Dee Wood, Michael Peters, *Liberty Weekend — Closing Ceremonies.* ABC.

Outstanding Art Direction
for a Series
• Jeffrey L. Goldstein, production designer. Richard D. Kent, set decorator, *L.A. Law.* NBC.

Outstanding Art Direction
for a Miniseries or a Special
• Malcolm Middleton, production designer. Herbert Westbrook, art director. Harry Cordwell, set decorator, *The Two Mrs. Grenvilles.* NBC.

Outstanding Art Direction
in a Variety or Music Program
• Rene Lagler, production designer. *Liberty Weekend — Closing Ceremonies.* ABC.

Outstanding Costume Design
for a Series
• Robert Turturice, *Moonlighting.* ABC.

Outstanding Costume Design
for a Miniseries or a Special
• Jane Robinson, *Anastasia: The Mystery of Anna.* NBC.

Outstanding Costume Design
for a Variety or Music Program
• Ray Aghayan, Ret Turner, *Diana Ross ... Red Hot Rhythm and Blues.* ABC.

Outstanding Costuming for a Series
• Nanrose Buchman, costumer, *Fame.* Syndicated.

Outstanding Costuming
for a Miniseries or a Special
• Frances Hays, costume supervisor, *Independence.* NBC.

Outstanding Makeup for a Series
• Michael Westmore, Mark Bussan, Charles House, Zoltan Elek, Fred Blau, Jr. *Amazing Stories.* NBC.

**OUTSTANDING MAKEUP
FOR A MINISERIES OR A SPECIAL**
• Del Acevedo, Patton makeup designer.
Eddie Knight, Alan Boyle, chief makeup
artists, *The Last Days of Patton*. CBS.

OUTSTANDING HAIRSTYLING FOR A SERIES
• Kathryn Blondell, Ms. Shepherd's
hairstylist. Josee Normand, hairstylist,
Moonlighting. ABC.

**OUTSTANDING HAIRSTYLING
FOR A MINISERIES OR A SPECIAL**
• Marsha Lewis, Mike Lockey, hairstylists.
Sydney Guilaroff, hairstylist for Ann-
Margret, *The Two Mrs. Grenvilles*. NBC.

**OUTSTANDING CINEMATOGRAPHY
FOR A SERIES**
• Woody Omens, *Heart of the City*. ABC.

**OUTSTANDING CINEMATOGRAPHY
FOR A MINISERIES OR A SPECIAL**
• Philip Lathrop, *Christmas Snow*. NBC.

**OUTSTANDING TECHNICAL
DIRECTION/ELECTRONIC
CAMERAWORK/VIDEO CONTROL
FOR A SERIES**
• Parker Roe, technical director. Paul
Basta, Tom Dasbach, Richard Price, John
Repczynski, camerapersons. Eric Clay,
senior video control, *Family Ties*. NBC.

**OUTSTANDING TECHNICAL
DIRECTION/ELECTRONIC CAMERA/VIDEO
CONTROL FOR A MINISERIES
OR A SPECIAL**
• Karl Messerschmidt, technical director.
Les Atkinson, Roy Holm, Dana Martin, J.
O'Neill, camerapersons. Jerry Smith,
senior video control, *Barbara Mandrell's
Christmas: A Family Reunion*. CBS.

OUTSTANDING EDITING FOR A SERIES
(Single camera production)
• Roger Bondelli, Neil Mandelberg,
Moonlighting. ABC.
(Multicamera production)
• Jerry Davis, *Night Court*. NBC.

**OUTSTANDING EDITING FOR A MINISERIES
OR A SPECIAL**
(Single camera production)
• Steve Cohen, *LBJ: The Early Years*. NBC.
(Multicamera production)
• Kris Trexler, *Happy Birthday,
Hollywood*. ABC.

**OUTSTANDING SOUND EDITING
FOR A SERIES**
• Douglas H. Grindstaff, Richard G. Cor-
win, supervising editors. Clark Conrad,
Brad Sherman, Richard Taylor, James
Wolvington, editors. Richard G. Corwin,
Dick Bernstein, music, *Max Headroom*.
ABC.

**OUTSTANDING SOUND EDITING
FOR A MINISERIES OR A SPECIAL**
• Vince R. Gutierrez, supervising editor.
William H. Angarola, Clark Conrad,
Douglas Gray, Mace Matiosian, Anthony
Mazzei, Michael Mitchell, Matthew
Sawelson, Edward F. Suski, Jim
Wolvington, Barbara Issak, editors. John
Johnson, ADR. Dan Carlin, senior music
editor, *Unnatural Causes*. NBC.

**OUTSTANDING SOUND MIXING
FOR A COMEDY SERIES OR SPECIAL**
• Michael Ballin, Bob Douglas, Doug
Grey, Tom Huth, *Cheers*. NBC.

**OUTSTANDING SOUND MIXING
FOR A DRAMA SERIES**
• Gary Alexander, Joseph Kenworthy, Tim
Philben, R. William A. Thiederman, *Max
Headroom*. ABC.

**OUTSTANDING SOUND MIXING
FOR A VARIETY OR MUSIC SERIES
OR A SPECIAL**
• Roger Cortes, Ron Estes, Carroll Pratt,
*The Tonight Show Starring Johnny
Carson*. NBC.

**OUTSTANDING SOUND MIXING
FOR A DRAMA MINISERIES OR A SPECIAL**
• Joseph Citarella, Charles Grenzbach,
David Lee, George R. West, *Unnatural
Causes*. NBC.

**OUTSTANDING LIGHTING DIRECTION
(ELECTRONIC) FOR A SERIES**
• George Spiro Dibie, director of
photography, *Growing Pains*. ABC.

**OUTSTANDING LIGHTING DIRECTION
(ELECTRONIC) FOR A MINISERIES
OR A SPECIAL**
• Greg Brunton, *Diana Ross ... Red Hot
Rhythm and Blues*. ABC.

THE AREAS

*Each area has the possiblity of multiple
winners, one winner, or none. Winners
are listed.*

**OUTSTANDING PERFORMERS—CLASSICAL
MUSIC/DANCE PROGRAMMING**
• Leonard Bernstein, *Carnegie Hall: The
Grand Reopening.* CBS.
• Isaac Stern, *Carnegie Hall: The Grand
Reopening.* CBS.

**OUTSTANDING DIRECTING—CLASSICAL
MUSIC/DANCE PROGRAMMING**
• Kirk Browning, "Goya with Placido
Domingo," *Great Performances.* PBS.
Albert Maysles, David Maysles, *Vladimir
Horowitz: The Last Romantic.* PBS.

**OUTSTANDING WRITERS—
INFORMATIONAL PROGRAMMING**
• Robert McCrum, Robert MacNeil, *The
Story of English.* PBS.

**OUTSTANDING GRAPHICS
AND TITLE DESIGN**
• Wayne Fitzgerald, David Oliver Pfeil,
The Bronx Zoo. NBC.
• Sandy Dvore, *A Carol Burnett Special:
Carol, Carl, Whoopi & Robin.* ABC.

**OUTSTANDING ENGINEERING
DEVELOPMENT**
• Joseph J. Sayovitz, Jr., Jay D. Sherbon.

(No awards were bestowed in the areas
of outstanding directors or performers in
informational programming, or to writers of
classical music/ dance programming.)

DAYTIME AWARDS

OUTSTANDING DAYTIME DRAMA SERIES
• *As the World Turns.* Robert Calhoun,
executive producer. Ken Fitts, supervising
producer. Chris Banas, Michael Laibson,
Bonnie Bogard, Lisa Wilson, producers. CBS.
All My Children. Jacqueline Babbin, Jorn
Winther, producers. Randi Subarsky,
coordinating producer. ABC.
Santa Barbara. Bridget Dobson, Jerome
Dobson, executive producers. Mary-Ellis
Bunim, co-executive producer. Steven
Kent, Jill Farren Phelps, Leonard
Friedlander, producers. NBC.
The Young and the Restless. William J.
Bell, H. Wesley Kenney, executive
producers. Edward Scott, supervising
producer. Tom Langan, producer. CBS.

OUTSTANDING LEAD ACTOR
• Larry Bryggman, *As the World Turns.*
CBS.
Eric Braeden, *The Young and the Restless.*
CBS.
Scott Bryce, *As the World Turns.* CBS.
Terry Lester, *The Young and the Restless.*
CBS.
A Martinez, *Santa Barbara.* NBC.

OUTSTANDING LEAD ACTRESS
• Kim Zimmer, *Guiding Light.* CBS.
Elizabeth Hubbard, *As the World Turns.*
CBS.
Susan Lucci, *All My Children.* ABC.
Frances Reid, *Days of Our Lives.* NBC.
Marcy Walker, *Santa Barbara.* NBC.

OUTSTANDING SUPPORTING ACTOR
• Gregg Marx, *As the World Turns.* CBS.
Anthony Call, *One Life to Live.* ABC.
Justin Deas, *Santa Barbara.* NBC.
Richard Eden, *Santa Barbara.* NBC.
Al Freeman, Jr., *One Life to Live.* ABC.

OUTSTANDING SUPPORTING ACTRESS
• Kathleen Noone, *All My Children.* ABC.
Lisa Brown, *As the World Turns.* CBS.
Robin Mattson, *Santa Barbara.* NBC.
Peggy McCay, *Days of Our Lives.* NBC.
Kathleen Widdoes, *As the World Turns.*
CBS.

**OUTSTANDING DRAMA SERIES
DIRECTING TEAM**
• Frank Pacelli, Rudy Vejar, directors.
Betty Rothenberg, Randy Robbins,
associate directors, *The Young and the
Restless.* CBS.
Joseph Behar, Susan Orlikoff, Herb Stein,
Stephen Wyman, directors. Becky
Greenlaw, Gay Linville, Sheryl Harmon,
associate directors, *Days of Our Lives.*
NBC.
Jack Coffey, Sherrell Hoffman, Francesca
James, Henry Kaplan, directors. Jean
Dadario Burke, Barbara Martin Simmons,
Shirley Simmons, associate directors, *All
My Children.* ABC.
Paul Lammers, Bob Schwarz, Maria
Wagner, directors. Joel Aronowitz,
Michael Kerner, associate directors, *As the
World Turns.* CBS.

OUTSTANDING DRAMA SERIES WRITING TEAM

• Peggy O'Shea, head writer. S. Michael Schnessel, Craig Carlson, Lanie Bertram, Ethel M. Brez, Mel Brez, Lloyd Gold, associate head writers, *One Life to Live*. NBC.

William J. Bell, head writer. Kay Alden, John F. Smith, Sally Sussman, Eric Freidwald, Enid Powell, writers, *The Young and the Restless*. CBS.

Leah Laiman, Sheri Anderson, Thom Racina, head writers. Anne M. Schoettle, Dena Breshears, Richard J. Allen, associate head writers. M.M. Shelly Moore, Penina Spiegel, associate writers, *Days of Our Lives*. NBC.

OTHER DAYTIME AWARD WINNERS

OUTSTANDING YOUNGER LEADING MAN IN A DAYTIME DRAMA SERIES

• Michael E. Knight, *All My Children*. ABC.

OUTSTANDING INGENUE IN A DAYTIME DRAMA SERIES

• Martha Byrne, *As the World Turns*. CBS.

OUTSTANDING GUEST PERFORMER IN A DAYTIME DRAMA SERIES

• John Wesley Shipp, *Santa Barbara*. NBC.

OUTSTANDING GAME/AUDIENCE PARTICIPATION SHOW

• *The $25,000 Pyramid*. Bob Stewart, executive producer. Anne Marie Schmitt, supervising producer. David Michaels, Francine Bergman, producers. CBS.

OUTSTANDING GAME SHOW HOST

• Bob Barker, *The Price is Right*. CBS.

OUTSTANDING DIRECTING IN A GAME/AUDIENCE PARTICIPATION SHOW

• Marc Breslow, *The Price is Right*. CBS.

OUTSTANDING TALK/SERVICE SHOW

• *The Oprah Winfrey Show*. Debra DiMaio, executive producer. Mary Kay Clinton, Christine Tardio, Dianne Hudson, Ellen Rakietan, producers. Syndicated.

OUTSTANDING TALK/SERVICE SHOW HOST

• Oprah Winfrey, *The Oprah Winfrey Show*. Syndicated.

OUTSTANDING DIRECTING IN A TALK/SERVICE SHOW

• Jim McPharlin, *The Oprah Winfrey Show*. Syndicated.

OUTSTANDING ANIMATED PROGRAM

• *Jim Henson's Muppet Babies*. Margaret Loesch, Jim Henson, Lee Gunther, executive producers. Bob Richardson, producer. CBS.

OUTSTANDING CHILDREN'S SERIES

• *Sesame Street*. Dulcy Singer, executive producer. Lisa Simon, producer. PBS.

OUTSTANDING CHILDREN'S SPECIAL

• "Wanted: The Perfect Guy," *ABC Afterschool Special*. Milton Justice, executive producer. Joseph Feury, producer. ABC.

OUTSTANDING PERFORMER IN CHILDREN'S PROGRAMMING

• Madeline Kahn, "Wanted: The Perfect Guy," *ABC Afterschool Special*. ABC.

OUTSTANDING DIRECTING IN CHILDREN'S PROGRAMMING

• Dan F. Smith, *Square One TV*. PBS.

OUTSTANDING WRITING IN A CHILDREN'S SERIES

• Norman Stiles, Cathi Rosenberg-Turow, Jeffrey Moss, Sonia Manzano, Mark Saltzman, Belinda Ward, David Korr, Sara Compton, Tom Dunsmuir, Tony Geiss, Emily Perl Kingsley, Judy Freudberg, Jon Stone, Nancy Sans, Luis Santeiro, *Sesame Street*. PBS.

OUTSTANDING WRITING IN A CHILDREN'S SPECIAL

• Melvin Van Peebles, "The Day They Came to Arrest the Book," *CBS Schoolbreak Special*. CBS.

OUTSTANDING MUSIC DIRECTION AND COMPOSITION FOR A DRAMA SERIES

• Dominic Messinger, music director/composer, *Santa Barbara*. NBC.

OUTSTANDING MUSIC DIRECTION AND COMPOSITION

• Charles Bernstein, music director/composer, "Little Miss Perfect," *CBS Schoolbreak Special*. CBS.

OUTSTANDING ART DIRECTION/SET DECORATION/SCENIC DESIGN FOR A DAYTIME DRAMA SERIES
• William Hullstrom, art director. Joseph Bevacqua, Andrea Joel, Eric Fischer, set decorators, *The Young and the Restless*. CBS.

OUTSTANDING ART DIRECTION/SET DECORATION/SCENIC DESIGN
• Gary Panter, production designer. Sidney J. Bartholomew, Jr., art director. Nancy Greenstein, set decorator. Wayne Wilkes White, Ric Heitzman, co-production designers, *Pee-Wee's Playhouse*. CBS.

OUTSTANDING COSTUME DESIGN FOR A DRAMA SERIES
• Kathi Nishimoto, *The Young and the Restless*. CBS.

OUTSTANDING COSTUME DESIGN
• Jeremy Railton, Lelan Berner, Victoria DeKaye Bodwell, *Zoobilee Zoo*. Syndicated.

OUTSTANDING MAKEUP FOR A DRAMA SERIES
• Joseph Cola, Sue Saccavino, *Guiding Light*. CBS.

OUTSTANDING MAKEUP
• Sharon Ilson Reed, *Pee-Wee's Playhouse*. CBS.

OUTSTANDING HAIRSTYLING FOR A DRAMA SERIES
• Linda Williams, Ralph Stanzione, *Guiding Light*. CBS.

OUTSTANDING HAIRSTYLING
• Sally Hershberger, Eric Gregg, *Pee-Wee's Playhouse*. CBS.

OUTSTANDING CINEMATOGRAPHY
• Don Lenzer, Chuck Levey, Dyanna Taylor, cinematographers. Howard Hall, Stan Waterman, George Waterman, underwater cinematographers, *3-2-1 Contact*. PBS.

OUTSTANDING FILM EDITING
• Harvey Greenstein, Wally Katz, Douglas W. Smith, *3-2-1 Contact*. PBS.

OUTSTANDING TECHNICAL DIRECTION/ELECTRONIC CAMERA/VIDEO CONTROL FOR A DRAMA SERIES
• Ervin D. Hurd, Jr., Harry Tatarian, technical directors. Mike Denny, Sheldon Mooney, Joseph Vicens, David Navarette, electronic camera. Dave Fisher, Scha Jani, video control, *The Young and the Restless*. CBS.

OUTSTANDING TECHNICAL DIRECTION/ELECTRONIC CAMERA/VIDEO CONTROL
• Dick Holden, technical director, *This Old House*. PBS.

OUTSTANDING VIDEO-TAPE EDITING FOR A DRAMA SERIES
• Joseph A. Mastroberti, Steven Shatkin, *As the World Turns*. CBS.

OUTSTANDING VIDEO-TAPE EDITING
• Paul Dougherty, Doug Jines, Joe Castellano, Les Kaye, Howard Silver, *Pee-Wee's Playhouse*. CBS.

OUTSTANDING FILM SOUND EDITING
• Greg Sheldon, Ira Speigel, editors, "The Gift of Amazing Grace," *ABC Afterschool Special*. ABC.

OUTSTANDING FILM SOUND MIXING
• Rolf Pardula, sound mixer. Ken Hahn, rerecording mixer, *Pee-Wee's Playhouse*. CBS.

OUTSTANDING LIVE AND TAPE SOUND MIXING AND SOUND EFFECTS FOR A DRAMA SERIES
• Scott A. Millan, preproduction mixer. Scott A. Millan, Tommy Persson, production mixers. Rafael O. Valentin, Donald D. Henderson, postproduction mixers. Larry Maggiore, Peter Romano, sound effects, *The Young and the Restless*. CBS.

OUTSTANDING LIVE AND TAPE SOUND MIXING AND SOUND EFFECTS
• Ken King, production mixer. David E. Fluhr, postproduction mixer. "God, the Universe and Hot Fudge Sundaes," *CBS Schoolbreak Special*. CBS.

OUTSTANDING LIGHTING DIRECTION FOR A DRAMA SERIES
• John Connolly, Candice Dunn, *Ryan's Hope*. ABC.

Outstanding Lighting Direction
• John Leay, lighting consultant. Chenault Spence, lighting designer, *The Damnation of Faust*. PBS.

Outstanding Special Class Program Area
(Area awards)
• "The Children of Ellis Island," *ABC Notebook*. Jane Paley, executive producer. ABC.
• *One to Grow on*. Charles Stepner, producer. NBC.
• *Taking Children Seriously*. Helen Marmor, executive producer. Patricia Mauger, producer. NBC.

Outstanding Achievement in Directing Special Class
(Area award)
• Dick Schneider, *Macy's 60th Annual Thanksgiving Day Parade*. NBC.

Outstanding Graphics and Title Design
• Prudence Fenton, Phil Trumbo, graphics, *Pee-Wee's Playhouse*. CBS.

(No award was bestowed in the area of outstanding writing in special class.)

NEWS & DOCUMENTARY AWARD WINNERS
Outstanding Coverage of Single Breaking News Story
(Programs)
• "Pan Am Flight 73 Hijack," *ABC News Nightline*. Richard N. Kaplan, executive producer. Ted Koppel, anchor/managing editor. William Moore, Robert Jordan, Betsy West, senior producers. Susan Mercandetti, Pam Kahn. Herb O'Connor, Julie Sertel, Marianne Kelley, Heather Vincent, Tara Sonenshine, producers. Bill Thomas, coordinating producer. Jed Duval, Mark Litke, correspondents. ABC.
• "Philippines: Two Inaugurations; Marcos Driven Out and the New Country," *ABC News Nightline*. Richard N. Kaplan, executive producer. Ted Koppel, anchor/managing editor. William Moore, Robert Jordan, Betsy West, senior producers. Phil Bergman, Tara Sonenshine, producers. Jim Laurie, Judd Rose, James Walker, correspondents. ABC.

Outstanding Coverage of a Single Breaking News Story
(Segments)
• "Reykjavek, Iceland," *The CBS Evening News with Dan Rather*. Linda Mason, executive producer. Terry Martin, senior producer. Jonathan Klein, broadcast producer. Rome Hartman, Susan Zirinsky, Peter Bluff, Roxanne Russel, Mary Martin, producers. Bill Plante, Wyatt Andrews, David Martin, Bill Moyers, Lem Tucker, correspondents. CBS.
• "Challenger Memorial Service," *NBC News Special Report*. Susan Butcher, Ann Kemp, producers. NBC.

Outstanding Investigative Journalism
(Programs)
• *MIAs — The Story That Would Not Die*. Janice Tomlin, producer. Tom Jarriel, correspondent. ABC.

Outstanding Investigative Journalism
(Segments)
• "Helicopter Dangers," *The CBS Evening News with Dan Rather*. Tom Bettag, executive producer. Peter Van Sant, Josh Howard, producers. Peter Van Sant, reporter/correspondent. CBS.
• "Heartbreak Hotel," *60 Minutes*. Allan Maraynes, producer. Ed Bradley, correspondent. CBS.
• "The McMartin Preschool," *60 Minutes*. Lowell Bergman, producer. Mike Wallace, reporter/correspondent. CBS.

Outstanding Background/Analysis of a Single Current Story
(Programs)
• "Holy War, Holy Terror," *Frontline*. David Fanning, executive producer. Stephanie Tepper, producer. Michael Kirk, senior producer. John Laurence, correspondent. PBS.
• "The Vanishing Family in a Crisis in Black America," *CBS Reports*. Perry Wolff, executive producer. Ruth C. Streeter, producer. Bill Moyers, correspondent. CBS.

Outstanding Background/Analysis of a Single Current Story
(Segments)
• "AIDS: A Bad Way to Die," *Jimmy Breslin's People*. Wayne Sherman, Hudson Meyer, producers. ABC.
• "By His Father's Hand: The Zumwalts," *20/20*. Ene Riisna, producer. Jack Laurence, correspondent. ABC.
• "Michele," *60 Minutes*. George Crile, producer. Ed Bradley, reporter/correspondent. CBS.

Outstanding Coverage of Continuing News Story
(Programs)
• "Sue the Doctor?." *Frontline*. David Fanning, executive producer. Graham Chedd, senior producer. Andrew Liebman, producer. PBS.

Outstanding Coverage of Continuing News Story
(Segments)
• "Ticket to Nowhere," *20/20*. Bob Lange, Kathy McManus, producers. John Stossel, correspondent. ABC.
• "Racism," *The CBS Evening News with Dan Rather*. Tom Bettag, executive producer. R. Cohen, senior producer. Marcia Henning, Marquita Poole, Cathy Olian, producers. Bob Faw, reporter/correspondent. CBS.

Outstanding Interview/Interviewers
(Programs)
• "The Burger Years," *A CBS News Special*. Perry Wolff, executive producer. Marianna C. Spicer, producer. Bill Moyers, correspondent. CBS.

Outstanding Interview/Interviewers
(Segments)
• "Charles Manson," *CBS News Nightwatch*. Carol Ross Joynt, producer. Charlie Rose, reporter/correspondent. CBS.
• "A Promise," *1986*. Mike Mosher, producer. Lucky Severson, correspondent. NBC.

Outstanding Informational, Cultural, or Historical Programming
(Programs)
• *The Global Assembly Line*. Lorraine Gray, Anne Bohlen, Maria Patricia, Fernandez Kelly, producers. PBS.

• "With Horowitz In Moscow," *Sunday Morning*. Robert Northshield, senior executive producer. Peter Gelb, executive producer. William Moran, senior producer. Charles Kuralt, reporter/ correspondent. CBS.
• *Before Stonewall: The Making of a Gay and Lesbian Community*. John Scagliotti, Greta Schiller, Robbie Rosenberg, producers. PBS.

Outstanding Informational, Cultural, or Historical Programming
(Segments)
• "East Africa: Changing," *Good Morning America*. Bill Geddie, producer. David Hartman, correspondent. ABC.

Outstanding Individual Achievement
(Writers)
• Mary Lou Teel, "We've Grown Accustomed," *Sunday Morning*. CBS.
• Richard Gerdau, Linda Ellerbee, Ray Gandolf, "Halloween 1983," *Our World*. ABC.
(Directors)
• Robert Gardner, *The Courage to Care*. PBS.
(Cinematographers)
• Hugh Miles, *Kingdom of the Ice Bear: The Frozen Ocean*. PBS.
(Researchers)
• Andrea Weiss, *Before Stonewall: The Making of a Gay and Lesbian Community*. PBS.
(Electronic camerapersons: Videographers)
• Mark Falstad, "Little Anthony," *West 57th*. CBS.
(Sound)
• Kenneth Love, Norman Andrews, sound recordists, "Realm of the Alligator," *National Geographic Special*. PBS.
(Film editors)
• Barry Nye, editor, "Realm of the Alligator," *National Geographic Special*. PBS.
(Tape editors)
• Tressa Anne Verna, video-tape editor, "Winnie Mandela," *1986*. NBC.
• Ed Delgado, Don Wahlberg, Charles Chinn, video-tape editors, *Wasted: Just Say No*. NBC.
(Music)
• John Scott, music director, "Cape Horn: Waters of the Wind," *The Cousteau Society*. Syndicated.

(Graphic Design)
• John Andrews, Judd Pillot, Todd Ruff, graphic design and electronic graphics, *Adam Smith's Money World*. PBS.

(There were no awards given for Special Classification for Outstanding Program Achievement—Programs or Segments.)

SPORTS AWARD WINNERS
OUTSTANDING LIVE SPORTS SERIES
• *NFL on CBS*. Ted Shaker, executive producer. Michael Burks, Bob Dekas, Robert Stenner, Mark Wolff, Rick LaCivita, Robert Mansbach, producers. Eric Mann, Scott Johnson, Steve Scheer, Robert Matina, associate producers. Larry Cavolina, Robert Fishman, Sandy Grossman, Craig Silver, directors. Daniel Forer, Richard Zyontz, Patti Gorsuch, Richard Drake, associate directors. CBS.

OUTSTANDING EDITED SPORTS SERIES
• *ABC's Wide World of Sports*. Curt Gowdy, Jr., Dennis Lewin, coordinating producers. Amy Sacks, associate coordinating producer. Bob Goodrich, Peter Lasser, Carol Lehti, Mike Pearl, Ken Wolfe, Joel Feld, producers. John DeLisa, Craig Janoff, Terry Jastrow, Jim Jennett, Larry Kamm, Andy Sidaris, Doug Wilson, Ned Simon, directors. Mary Ann Grabavoy, Ben Harvey, associate producers. Rob Beiner, Dick Buffinton, Jeff Cohan, Katherine Cook, Robert Cowen, Vince DeDario, Earl Freiman, Jack Graham, Joe Novello, Norm Samet, Toni Slotkin, Noubar Stone, associate directors. ABC.

OUTSTANDING LIVE SPORTS SPECIAL
• *Daytona 500*. Robert Stenner, producer. Dan Forer, pit producer. Robert Fishman, director. Cathy Barreto, Sherman Eagan, associate producers. Lance Barrow, Richard Drake, Diane Patterson, associate directors. CBS.

OUTSTANDING EDITED SPORTS SPECIAL
• *ABC's Wide World of Sports 25th Anniversary Special*. Doug Wilson, coordinating producer. Roger Goodman, coordinating director. Amy Sacks, associate coordinating producer. Rob Beiner, Joel Feld, Curt Gowdy, Jr., Mary Ann Grabavoy, George Greenberg, Ben Harvey, Chuck Howard, Larry Kamm, Peter Lasser, Carol Lehti, Mike Pearl, Ned

Simon, Ken Wolff, producers. Jeff Cohan, Robert Cowen, Vince DeDario, Earl Freiman, Jack Graham, Joe Novello, Norm Samet, Toni Slotkin, Stan Spiro, associate directors. ABC.

OUTSTANDING SPORTS PERSONALITY—HOST
• Al Michaels. ABC.

OUTSTANDING SPORTS PERSONALITY—ANALYST
• John Madden. CBS.

OUTSTANDING TECHNICAL TEAM—REMOTE
• *1986 World Series*. Lenny Stucker, technical director. Steven Cimino, replay technical director. Ken Harvey, N.S. Flagg, facilities technical directors. Ernie DeRosa, Bill Parinello, Keith Scammahorn, Ernie Thiel, technical managers. Ed McEwan, Dave Albiol, Larry Worster, Bill Kidd, Bruce Bodor, Bill Denis, Gino Guarna, Brian Lang, Mike Noseworthy, Ruben Quinones, John Russo, Hector Sarabiam, Bob Sazer, Joe Smeck, Joe Thornley, Jeffrey Wright, Red Roe, audio. John D. Marelli, Jerry Valdivia, senior video-tape replays. Leonard G. Basile, Mike Bennett, Phil Cantrell, Russ Diven, Eric A. Eisenstein, Rick Fox, Barry Frischer, Steve Gonzalez, Dave Hagen, John Hillyer, Bob Jaeger, Thomas Hogan, Buddy Joseph, Corey Leible, George Loomis, Brian Phraner, Jim Mott, Albert Rice, Jr., Steve Tacon, Vicki Walker, Harry Weisman, camera. Ken Baker, Jim Burt, Fernando Castro, Richard Leible, Lane Lucatorto, Ray Rivera, Bill Rose, Jack Sampsell, Stephen Skorupka, John Thomas, Rich Wedeking, video replay. NBC.

OUTSTANDING TECHNICAL TEAM—STUDIO
• *Major League Baseball: An Inside Look*. Steven Cimino, Salvatore Nigita, Skip Dresch, technical directors. Jim Blaney, Jr., Neil Goetz, Thomas Hyre, Joe Rocco, John Sullivan, Brian Wickham, audio. John Dolan, Bob Fraraccio, Bill Kenny, Bailey Stortz, Harry Weisman, camera. Scott Davis, Pamela Harris, Ernie Thiel, technical supervisors. Frances Cimino, Ed Delgado, James Grater, Howard Hirsch, Manuel Politis, Scott Rader, John Thomas, Susann Thomas, Mildred Wiggs,

Jeffrey Wurtz, video tape. NBC.
• *NFL '86*. Salvatore Nigita, technical director. Pamela Harris, technical manager. John Sullivan, Paul Johnston, Brian Wickham, audio. Bailey Stortz, Robert Fraraccio, Al Camoin, Carl Eckett, John Hillyer, John Dolan, Steve Tacon, camera. Francis Cimino, Jeffrey Wurtz, Jo-Anne Stathis, Harvey Telmar, James Grater, Melanie Rock, Steven Skorupka, Jose Alvarez-Ugarte, Joseph Bonanno, video tape. NBC.

OUTSTANDING VIDEO-TAPE CAMERAPERSONS
• Dan Wood, camera, *Race of Champions and Motocross*. PBS.
• Raphael Ortiz-Guzman, camera, "The 1986 Goodwill Games: Moscow Hippodrome," *Soviet Sports Page*. TBS.

OUTSTANDING VIDEO-TAPE EDITING
• Marvin Gench, Carlo Gennarelli, Michael Siegel, Ildefonso De Jesus, Conrad Kraus, Hector Kicelian, Alex Moskovic, Pamela Peterson, Joseph Longo, Michael Sclafani, Peter Mecca, James Holder, Lou Rende, Chris Von Benge, editors, *ABC's Wide World of Sports 25th Anniversary Special*. ABC.
• Helen Maier-Ruddick, Sean Mooney, John Bacchia, Roy Epstein, Greg Kiernan, David Israel, editors, *Light Moments in Sports—Major League Baseball*. Syndicated.
• Art David, editor, closing music piece, figure skating music piece, *The 1986 Goodwill Games*. TBS.

OUTSTANDING WRITING
• Bryan Polivka, Arthur Ashe, Bob Briner, writers, *A Hard Road to Glory*. Syndicated.

OUTSTANDING GRAPHIC DESIGN
• Stacey McDonough, Chyron. Wallace Colvard, Dubner. Barbara Trehubets, Ira Rappaport, paint box. Henry LaBounta, Bosch, *NBC Sports World*. NBC.

OUTSTANDING MUSIC COMPOSITION/DIRECTION
• Bill Tullis, music director, *The Goodwill Games Theme*. TBS.

OUTSTANDING TECHNICAL INNOVATION
• Don Ellis, executive producer. Jim Kitchell, technical producer, *The 1986 Goodwill Games: World's Largest Remote*. TBS.

OUTSTANDING INDIVIDUAL ACHIEVEMENT
• Amy Sacks, producer. Joel Feld, director, *Race Across America* (for creative use of "horror film style" in a television sports package). ABC.

OUTSTANDING PROGRAM ACHIEVEMENT
• *NBC Sports On-Air Promotion*. John Schipp, producer. NBC.

INTERNATIONAL AWARD WINNERS
OUTSTANDING DOCUMENTARY
• *Chasing a Rainbow: The Life of Josephine Baker*, Channel Four Television, U.K.

OUTSTANDING DRAMA
• *Shadowlands*, BBC, U.K.

OUTSTANDING PERFORMING ARTS
• Bejart's Kabuki Ballet, NHK Japan Broadcasting Corporation, Japan.

OUTSTANDING POPULAR ARTS
• *Spitting Image*, Central Independent Television, U.K.

OUTSTANDING CHILDREN'S PROGRAM
• *The Kids of Degrassi Street: Griff Gets a Hand*. Canadian Broadcasting Corp. Canada

INTERNATIONAL DIRECTORATE AWARD
• Herbert Schmertz

FOUNDERS AWARD
• Donald L. Taffner

SPECIAL AWARDS
OUTSTANDING ACHIEVEMENT IN THE SCIENCE OF TELEVISION ENGINEERING
• Dubner Computer Systems, Inc.
• Color Systems Technology, Inc.
• Colorization, Inc.
• NASA
• European Broadcasting Union
• SMPTE
• Public Broadcasting Service
• Communication Research Center (Canada)

**NATIONAL AWARDS
FOR COMMUNITY SERVICE**
• *Eye of the Beholder*, WPLG-TV, Miami,
Florida.
• *Getting in Touch*, KOTO-TV, Seattle,
Washington.

A.T.A.S. GOVERNORS AWARD
• Grant Tinker

Emmysomething
for the Upstarts

"These are the hippest Emmys I've ever seen!" roared comedian Tracey Ullman, whose critically acclaimed show was again up for best variety series. The *L.A. Times* added, "the hippest, headiest and happiest, from the opening campy Sweeney Sisters (actually Nora Dunn and Jan Hooks of *Saturday Night Live*) to Robin Williams's injection of inspired lunacy and a nine-letter dirty word to the wonderful weirdness of Penn and Teller, this was the Emmyest of Emmycasts."

Saturday Night Live's director/producer Lorne Michaels was in charge of the proceedings, which included such lighthearted touches as having Tony Danza act as the "designated accepter" for no-shows even though the *Who's the Boss?* star had never accepted an Emmy of his own. There turned out to be so many no-shows that the joke was eventually on Danza, who, after his seventh trek up to the podium to collect other people's awards, finally joked, "Now I'm mad! Boy, is my agent in trouble for getting me this gig!" The ceremony also included a moving tribute to the history of television involving clips from shows such as *I Love Lucy, All in the Family, The Defenders, Gunsmoke*, and *The Dick Van Dyke Show*.

The Emmys ceremony was historic in another respect: For the first time ever, cable TV productions were up for prime-time laurels. Cable began with 15 of the 337 total nominations and ended up with two awards, both for HBO's *Dear America: Letters Home from Vietnam*, which was acclaimed best informational special.

The radical changes and infusion of new blood were reflected in the results

MGM/UA

The upset winner of best drama series, thirtysomething, *explored the intimate yearnings of the new yuppie generation.*

of the voting. Emmy night would turn out to be an evening of endless surprises and one celebrating the triumph of a new bold, youthful spirit.

Nothing proved the point more than the winner of best drama series, which was expected to be either *L.A. Law* or *St. Elsewhere*, both established shows. The award went instead to those baby-boomers of *thirtysomething*, a show about the various relationships between seven Philadelphia yuppies as they reached the adult age of disillusionment. *thirtysomething* was either loved or loathed by the viewing public because of its success at capturing the sometimes petty woes and hopes of the generation it portrayed, but it was generally applauded by critics who appreciated its talky, intimate style. While accepting the series award, co-executive producer Edward Zwick acknowledged that there

"Designated accepter" Tony Danza, who has never won an Emmy, collected a hoarde on behalf of no-show winners.

trayed in the clichéd sympathetic way. Accepting the prize, the daring Drake called his victory "a wonderful moment."

But the most "wonder"-ful moment in the evening of continuous surprises occurred with the revelation of the best comedy series, which was supposed to be decided by a bout between the barroom brawlers of *Cheers* and those feisty *Golden Girls*, both champs in the past. Upstart youth again prevailed, though, when the prize went to *The Wonder Years*, which *Variety* called "a surprise hit that debuted at midseason" right after ABC's Super Bowl coverage in January. Jokingly called *twelvesomething* by cynics, the new series recreated the 1968 world of a suburban boy who was adjusting to the changing times around him with the same sassy self-appraisal that characterized the year's best drama series. Referring to both choices, the *L.A. Times* concluded, "It was a night when worthy underdogs came out winners."

The Golden Girls, however, was not totally down and out. This year it was Bea Arthur's turn to be named best comedy actress after costars Betty White and Rue McClanahan each claimed the honor over the two previous years. Arthur won the trophy once before, for *Maude* in 1977, and now thanked producer Norman Lear "for starting me off in this crazy, wonderful, delicious medium." When Estelle Getty was chosen best supporting actress, it meant that all four golden girls had finally struck gold. Getty, who played Arthur's smartcracker mother on the series, told reporters backstage that someday she hoped her character would become president of the Gray Panthers.

Being voted best comedy actor for a third time in as many years so surprised the twentysomething Michael J. Fox that he roared "Wow!" The newlywed then added, "I can't be happier than I am" and thanked his wife, actress Tracy Pol-

was a "whole group of people who tune in every week just to hate us." "But I'm more than a little thrilled by all the controversy we've generated," his partner Marshall Herskovitz added. "The fact that a lot of people can't stand the show won't change. The essence of this show is something about community."

thirtysomething also won the writing honors, a guest-performance award for Shirley Knight, and a supporting actress trophy for Patricia Wettig, who played, according to the Associated Press, "the struggling young mother with a rocky marriage." Defending the series, Wettig said up at the podium, "It cuts closer to the bone than most shows," then she slipped offstage and went back to the press room where she told reporters, "I don't know what a yuppie is."

L.A. Law started out with an impressive 19 nominations, but reaped only an editing award and a prize for best supporting actor Larry Drake as the law firm's mentally handicapped office boy, who was not always scripted or porlan. Another shocker came when John Larroquette of *Night Court* returned for his fourth supporting actor statuette and said, "Now I'm officially overwhelmed."

If *Cagney & Lacey*'s Tyne Daly was also overwhelmed by her own fourth prize as best drama series actress, she didn't express it at the Emmycast since she was one of Tony Danza's no-shows. Much to NBC's chagrin, however, the dark horse winner in the best actor category was not only on hand, but proved to be as upset as Danza pretended to be when he picked up Daly's trophy. Richard Kiley was honored for *A Year in the Life*, the new series based on last year's Outstanding Miniseries that didn't even last a year in Kiley's life. The winner said he had "nothing but sadness for the corporate myopia that killed a fine show."

Best actor in the year's best TV film: Jason Robards defends the Darwinian theory of evolution in Inherit the Wind.

This year's victorious miniseries was *The Murder of Mary Phagan*, the story of an innocent Atlanta businessman lynched for the murder of a 13-year-old girl. Executive producer George

Stevens, Jr., thanked his "wonderful" cast that included Jack Lemmon as Georgia's governor. Lemmon had been nominated for best actor, but the award went to Jason Robards (another no-show) for playing attorney Henry Drummond in a remake of the classic play *Inherit the Wind*, which was based on the infamous Scopes "monkey trial" of 1925 that pitted the scriptural account of mankind's creation against Charles Darwin's theory of evolution. When *Wind* swept up the award for best drama special, its breathless executive producer Peter Douglas said, "Before I came up here tonight, my mother said, 'Being nominated is the best.' This is better."

For the first time ever, cable shows were up for the prime-time laurels.

Jessica Tandy didn't quite agree when she accepted her statuette as best actress for *Foxfire*, in which she played an aging Appalachian woman opposite on- and off-screen husband Hume Cronyn. "I'm proud to be nominated," she said after a rousing ovation. "That would have been enough." The supporting actress award went to British-born Jane Seymour, who played opera diva Maria Callas in *Onassis: The Richest Man in the World*. "Thank you for letting me be an American actress," she said up at the podium. Danza was summoned up to the stage soon afterward to collect the supporting actor trophy for John Shea of *Baby M*, based on the famous New Jersey court battle involving surrogate motherhood. "I didn't prepare anything to say," an increasingly irritated Danza wisecracked, "because I didn't think he'd win."

Also not on hand was the ailing composer Irving Berlin whose 100th-birthday special was named best variety program. The night may have belonged to TV's young upstarts, but they remembered to pay tribute to show business veterans when the Governors Award was given to cartoon producers William Hanna and Joseph Barbera in honor of their 50th year of partnership. The Fox broadcasting network won no statuettes, but for the first time ever the youthful network finished number one in an evening's rankings, seeing its ratings share climb to 18 from 14 last year. *People* magazine scored its Emmys show a grade "A."

DAYTIME AWARDS

"This is our once-a-year self-indulgence," ceremony host Phil Donahue noted as the festivities began at the Waldorf-Astoria Hotel in New York, "and just as important to us is the opportunity to schmooz in a fancy ballroom with the pals we work with and compete against." The CBS broadcast would also include a record-setting ninth Emmy for its host's work hosting his own talk show, while *All My Children*'s "Susan Lucci's soap opera saga of dashed hopes extended to a ninth year," reported the Associated Press.

> *Helen Gallagher of Ryan's Hope now had the most lead acting awards in daytime.*

Lucci's disappointment over losing the best actress award yet again this year was offset by her series' success in three other categories. Costar David Canary (who played twins Adam and Stuart Chandler) received a standing ovation as he climbed the stage to accept his second trophy for best actor. "I am painfully aware that this belongs to my brother Stuart," he joked. He thanked two other cast members: "Julia Barr who keeps Adam on the ground and Ellen Wheeler who keeps Stuart well in the air."

Wheeler (who played character Cindy Parker) won as best supporting actress and began her acceptance remarks saying, "Golly! I know how much this is gonna mean to me later so this is really hard." When Donahue opened the Emmycast earlier that day, he made reference to the "long and painful labor action" then being conducted by the Writers Guild of America, so when *All My Children* took the writing honors the Emmys audience paid special attention. Head writer Lorraine Broderick expressed "a hope we all share that both sides will soon come to an agreement and we can all go back to work."

The best series award went to a show with low ratings and a high regard for the intrigue and woes of the California society set, *Santa Barbara*. The series represented a contemporary new kind of daytime drama that was generally considered more hip and witty than its competition. It also took a music award and supporting actor honors for Justin Deas (as Keith Thomas), who wasn't on hand to accept it.

Best lead actress Helen Gallagher (Maeve Ryan) also wasn't in attendance, but sent a note, which said, "What a happy and unanticipated honor this is in the 13th season of *Ryan's Hope*." What the actress failed to mention was that she was now the daytime performer with more Emmys than any other, having won twice before, in 1976 and 1977.

Another note-sender was the year's ingenue Julianne Moore (as twins Frannie and Sabrina Hughes) who said she had "spent three wonderful and extraordinary years on *As the World Turns*." The year's leading younger man was Billy Warlock (Frankie Brady on *Days of Our Lives*), who was on hand, but perhaps should have written down his remarks ahead of time, too. "I don't have a damn thing to say," he admitted. "I didn't expect to win."

"Here's an amazing statistic," Phil Donahue said when it came time to bestow the director's trophy. "There are approximately 3,640 episodes of daytime drama to direct every year. That's about 91,000 scenes. That a lot to direct!" He then awarded the prize to *The Young and the Restless*'s Rudy Vejar.

When Donahue accepted his ninth award for best talk show host, he acknowledged it as "a very proud moment" and thanked his production company, apparently for its patience and persistence, since he added, "It has not always been a picnic owning the *Donahue* show." Last year's triumphant talk program, *The Oprah Winfrey Show*, returned as the series winner. Executive producer Debra DiMaio spoke on behalf of the cast and crew when she claimed that the program's star "is our inspiration ... Against all odds Oprah Winfrey became somebody."

That same "somebody" was called upon to give away the prize for Outstanding Children's Special, which was claimed by the *CBS Schoolbreak Special* "Never Say Goodbye," about a "young girl who must tell her much-loved and hopelessly ill grandmother goodbye," Winfrey said, "and who learns in the process that love goes on forever." The Outstanding Children's Series prize was once again awarded to *Sesame Street*, which was approaching its 2,500th show in its upcoming 20th season.

1988 marked the 25th anniversary year of best game/ audience participation show winner *The Price is Right*, which was also honored for its host Bob Barker. Barker wasn't in attendance but sent the Emmycast watchers a love letter, which read: "You've made a gray-haired old man very happy."

SPORTS AWARDS

For the first time ever, the sports ceremony was broadcast nationally when Raycom and the Armed Forces Radio and Television Network jointly beamed the festivities to 125 stations as a fast-paced, two-hour prime-time special.

The athletic pace was set by celebrity hosts Alan Thicke and Joan Van Ark, who were assisted by such name presenters as actress Adrienne Barbeau, Indy 500 winner Danny Sullivan, and former Olympics stars Bruce Jenner and Brian Boitano. Entertainment at the Sheraton Center event in New York was provided by comedian Jerry Seinfeld and music groups Take 6, Pebbles, and the Fabulous Thunderbirds.

Old favorite *ABC's Wide World of Sports* returned as the Outstanding Edited Series as did past best sports analyst John Madden of CBS. ABC led the overall contest when it won two more of the top four program categories: Outstanding Live Special (Kentucky Derby coverage) and Outstanding Live Sports Series (*NFL Monday Night Football*). CBS's coverage of the Paris Roubaix Bike Race was voted Outstanding Edited Sports Special.

NEWS & DOCUMENTARY AWARDS

Dan Rather took some knocks from fellow journalists when he dressed up in native costume to investigate the Soviet military involvement in Afghanistan, but he and producer Perry Wolff ended up taking home Emmys for their courageous coverage of a continuing news story for their work, too. *CBS Reports* was likewise rewarded for its own probe into the Afghan conflict while *The CBS Evening News with Dan Rather* garnered one more major prize — for following the Vietnamese pullout from war-torn Cambodia.

The dinner ceremony attracted more than 300 news and television leaders to the ballroom of New York's Waldorf-

CBS producer Perry Wolff (left) and newsman Dan Rather were lauded for their coverage of the Afghanistan war.

Astoria Hotel (including Rather, Bill Moyers, Mary Alice Williams, and Connie Chung) to hear the names of 33 winners chosen from a list of 113 finalists. David and Julie Eisenhower were among the presenters.

As often occurred in previous years, PBS reaped the most awards. Its premier prize this year was for a *Frontline* investigation into what happened to the millions of dollars channeled out of the Philippines shortly before the fall of President Ferdinand Marcos. Bill Moyers had won a total of 14 news awards during his alternating careers at PBS and CBS, but he was back at PBS as of 1987 and now nabbed two more to add to his trophy case.

20/20 reaped the majority of ABC's Emmys. Prize-winning segments included "Death Knell for the Klan" and "The Woman Under the Crane."

While NBC continued participating in N.A.T.A.S.'s daytime and sports awards, it still declined to be involved officially in the news prize. Because the network still allowed its employees to participate independently, it won two statuettes, which included one of the two investigative journalism awards of the night for its drug probe on the nightly news broadcast.

1987–88

The prime-time ceremony was broadcast on the Fox network from the Pasadena Civic Auditorium on August 28, 1988, for prime-time programs telecast between July 1, 1987, and May 31, 1988. Daytime awards broadcast on CBS from New York's Waldorf-Astoria Hotel on June 29, 1988, for programs aired between March 6, 1987, and March 5, 1988. The sports awards for 1987 were presented July 13, 1988. News & documentary awards for 1987 were presented on September 8, 1988.

PRIME-TIME PROGRAM AWARDS
OUTSTANDING DRAMA SERIES
• *thirtysomething*. Edward Zwick, Marshall Herskovitz, executive producers. Paul Haggis, supervising producer. Edward Zwick, Scott Winant, producers. ABC.
Beauty and the Beast. Paul Junger Witt, Tony Thomas, executive producers. Ron Koslow, supervising producer. Stephen Kurzfeld, co-supervising producer. David Peckinpah, Kenneth Koch, George R.

Martin, Harvey Frand, Andrew Laskos, John David, producers. Lynn Guthrie, coproducer. CBS.
L.A. Law. Steven Bochco, executive producer. Gregory Hoblit, Rick Wallace, co-executive producers. Terry Louise Fisher, supervising producer. Scott Goldstein, producer. David E. Kelley, coproducer. Phillip M. Goldfarb, coordinating producer. NBC.
Rumpole of the Bailey, Mystery! Lloyd Shirley, executive producer. Jacqueline Davis, producer. Rebecca Eaton, series executive producer. PBS.
St. Elsewhere. Bruce Paltrow, Mark Tinker, executive producers. John Tinker, Channing Gibson, producers. Abby Singer, coordinating producer. NBC.

OUTSTANDING COMEDY SERIES
• *The Wonder Years*. Carol Black, Neal Marlens, executive producers. Jeff Silver, producer. ABC.
Cheers. James Burrows, Glen Charles, Les Charles, executive producers. Peter Casey,

David Lee, David Angell, producers. Tim Berry, coproducer. NBC.
Frank's Place. Hugh Wilson, Tim Reid, executive producers. Max Tash, David Chambers, producers. Richard Dubin, Samm-Art Williams, coproducers. CBS.
The Golden Girls. Paul Junger Witt, Tony Thomas, Susan Harris, executive producers. Kathy Speer, Terry Grossman, co-executive producers. Mort Nathan, Barry Fanaro, supervising producers. Winifred Hervey, producer. Marsha Posner Williams, Fredric Weiss, Jeffrey Ferro, coproducers. NBC.
Night Court. Reinhold Weege, executive producer. Jeff Melman, supervising producer. Tom Straw, Linwood Boomer, producers. Tim Steele, coproducer. NBC.

OUTSTANDING MINISERIES
• *The Murder of Mary Phagan*. George Stevens, Jr., producer. NBC.
Baby M. Ilene Amy Berg, executive producer. Gordon L. Freedman, producer. ABC.
Billionaire Boys Club. Donald March, executive producer. Marvin J. Chomsky, supervising producer. Marcy Gross, Ann Weston, producers. NBC.
The Bourne Identity. Alan Shayne, executive producer. Frederick Muller, Alfred R. Kelman, producers. Martin Rabbett, coproducer. ABC.
Gore Vidal's Lincoln. Sheldon Pinchuk, Bill Finnegan, Pat Finnegan, executive producers. Bob Christiansen, Rick Rosenberg, producers. NBC.

OUTSTANDING DRAMA/COMEDY SPECIAL
• *Inherit the Wind, AT&T Presents*. Peter Douglas, executive producer. Robert A. Papazian, producer. NBC.
The Ann Jillian Story. Andrea Baynes, executive producer. Peter Thompson, producer. NBC.
The Attic: The Hiding of Anne Frank, General Foods' Golden Showcase. Michael Lepiner, Kenneth Kaufman, executive producers. David Cunliffe, William Hanley, co-executive producers. John Erman, supervising producer. Marjorie A. Kalins, Timothy J. Fee, Nick Gillot, producers. CBS.
Foxfire, Hallmark Hall of Fame. Marian Rees, executive producer. Dorothea G. Petrie, producer. CBS.
The Taking of Flight 847: The Uli Derickson Story. Jim Calio, David Hume Kennerly, executive producers. Jay Benson, producer. NBC.

OUTSTANDING VARIETY, MUSIC, OR COMEDY PROGRAM
• *Irving Berlin's 100th Birthday Celebration*. Don Mischer, executive producer. Jan Cornell, David Goldberg, producers. Sara Lukinson, coproducer. CBS.
Late Night with David Letterman. Jack Rollins, David Letterman, executive producers. Robert Morton, producer. David Letterman, host. NBC.
Late Night with David Letterman 6th Anniversary Special. Jack Rollins, David Letterman, executive producers. Robert Morton, producer. David Letterman, host. NBC.
The Smothers Brothers Comedy Hour 20th Reunion. Tom Smothers, executive producer. Ken Kragen, producer. Tom and Dick Smothers, hosts. CBS.
The Tracey Ullman Show. James L. Brooks, Heide Perlman, Jerry Belson, Ken Estin, executive producers. Richard Sakai, Ted Bessell, producers. Marc Flanagan, Dick Blasucci, coproducers. Tracey Ullman, host. Fox.

OUTSTANDING CLASSICAL PROGRAM IN THE PERFORMING ARTS
(Winner)
• "Nixon in China," *Great Performances*. Jac Venza, executive producer. David Horn, series producer. Michael Bronson, producer. John Walker, coordinating producer. PBS.

OUTSTANDING INFORMATIONAL SPECIAL
(Winner)
• *Dear America: Letters Home from Vietnam*. Bill Couturie, Thomas Bird, producers. HBO.

OUTSTANDING INFORMATIONAL SERIES
(Winner)
• "Buster Keaton: Hard Act to Follow," *American Masters*. Kevin Brownlow, David Gill, producers. PBS.

OUTSTANDING ANIMATED PROGRAM
(Winner)
• *A Claymation Christmas Celebration*. Will Vinton, executive producer. David Altschul, producer. Will Vinton, director. Ralph Liddle, writer. CBS.

OUTSTANDING CHILDREN'S PROGRAM
(Winner)
• *The Secret Garden, Hallmark Hall of Fame*. Norman Rosemont, executive producer. Steve Lanning, producer. CBS.

OUTSTANDING VARIETY-MUSIC EVENTS PROGRAMMING
(Winner)
• *The 60th Annual Academy Awards*. Samuel Goldwyn, Jr., producer. ABC.

PERFORMANCE, DIRECTING, AND WRITING
OUTSTANDING LEAD ACTOR
IN A DRAMA SERIES
• Richard Kiley, *A Year in the Life*. NBC.
Corbin Bernsen, *L.A. Law*. NBC.
Ron Perlman, *Beauty and the Beast*. CBS.
Michael Tucker, *L.A. Law*. NBC.
Edward Woodward, *The Equalizer*. CBS.

OUTSTANDING LEAD ACTRESS
IN A DRAMA SERIES
• Tyne Daly, *Cagney & Lacey*. CBS.
Susan Dey, *L.A. Law*. NBC.
Jill Eikenberry, *L.A. Law*. NBC.
Sharon Gless, *Cagney & Lacey*. CBS.
Angela Lansbury, *Murder, She Wrote*. CBS.

OUTSTANDING LEAD ACTOR
IN A COMEDY SERIES
• Michael J. Fox, *Family Ties*. NBC.
Dabney Coleman, *The "Slap" Maxwell Story*. ABC.
Ted Danson, *Cheers*. NBC.
Tim Reid, *Frank's Place*. CBS.
John Ritter, *Hooperman*. ABC.

OUTSTANDING LEAD ACTRESS
IN A COMEDY SERIES
• Beatrice Arthur, *The Golden Girls*. NBC.
Kirstie Alley, *Cheers*. NBC.
Blair Brown, *The Days and Nights of Molly Dodd*. NBC.
Rue McClanahan, *The Golden Girls*. NBC.
Betty White, *The Golden Girls*. NBC.

OUTSTANDING LEAD ACTOR
IN A MINISERIES OR A SPECIAL
• Jason Robards, *Inherit the Wind, AT&T Presents*. NBC.
Hume Cronyn, *Foxfire, Hallmark Hall of Fame*. CBS.
Danny Glover, *Mandela*. HBO.
Stacy Keach, *Hemingway*. Syndicated.
Jack Lemmon, *The Murder of Mary Phagan*. NBC.

OUTSTANDING ACTRESS
IN A MINISERIES OR A SPECIAL
• Jessica Tandy, *Foxfire, Hallmark Hall of Fame*. CBS.
Ann Jillian, *The Ann Jillian Story*. NBC.
Mary Tyler Moore, *Gore Vidal's Lincoln*. NBC.
Mary Steenburgen, *The Attic: The Hiding of Anne Frank, General Foods' Golden Showcase*. CBS.
JoBeth Williams, *Baby M*. ABC.

OUTSTANDING SUPPORTING ACTOR
IN A DRAMA SERIES
• Larry Drake, *L.A. Law*. NBC.
Ed Begley, Jr., *St. Elsewhere*. NBC.
Timothy Busfield, *thirtysomething*. ABC.
Alan Rachins, *L.A. Law*. NBC.
Jimmy Smits, *L.A. Law*. NBC.

OUTSTANDING SUPPORTING ACTRESS
IN A DRAMA SERIES
• Patricia Wettig, *thirtysomething*. ABC.
Bonnie Bartlett, *St. Elsewhere*. NBC.
Polly Draper, *thirtysomething*. ABC.
Christina Pickles, *St. Elsewhere*. NBC.
Susan Ruttan, *L.A. Law*. NBC.

OUTSTANDING SUPPORTING ACTOR
IN A COMEDY SERIES
• John Larroquette, *Night Court*. NBC.
Kelsey Grammer, *Cheers*. NBC.
Woody Harrelson, *Cheers*. NBC.
Peter Scolari, *Newhart*. CBS.
George Wendt, *Cheers*. NBC.

OUTSTANDING SUPPORTING ACTRESS
IN A COMEDY SERIES
• Estelle Getty, *The Golden Girls*. NBC.
Rhea Perlman, *Cheers*. NBC.
Julia Duffy, *Newhart*. CBS.
Katherine Helmond, *Who's the Boss?* ABC.
Jackée, *227*. NBC.

OUTSTANDING SUPPORTING ACTOR
IN A MINISERIES OR A SPECIAL
• John Shea, *Baby M*. ABC.
Dabney Coleman, *Baby M*. ABC.
Anthony Quinn, *Onassis: The Richest Man in the World*. ABC.
Ron Silver, *Billionaire Boys Club*. NBC.
Bruce Weitz, *Baby M*. ABC.

OUTSTANDING SUPPORTING ACTRESS
IN A MINISERIES OR A SPECIAL
• Jane Seymour, *Onassis: The Richest Man in the World*. ABC.

Stockard Channing, *Joseph Wambaugh's "Echoes in the Darkness."* CBS.
Ruby Dee, *Gore Vidal's Lincoln*. NBC.
Julie Harris, *The Woman He Loved*. CBS.
Lisa Jacobs, *The Attic: The Hiding of Anne Frank, General Foods' Golden Showcase*. CBS.

OUTSTANDING GUEST PERFORMER
IN A DRAMA SERIES
• Shirley Knight, *thirtysomething*. ABC.
Imogene Coca, *Moonlighting*. ABC.
Lainie Kazan, *St. Elsewhere*. NBC.
Gwen Verdon, *Magnum, P.I.* CBS.
Alfre Woodard, *St. Elsewhere*. NBC.

OUTSTANDING GUEST PERFORMER
IN A COMEDY SERIES
• Beah Richards, *Frank's Place*. CBS.
Herb Edelman, *The Golden Girls*. NBC.
Geraldine Fitzgerald, *The Golden Girls*. NBC.
Eileen Heckart, *The Cosby Show*. NBC.
Gilda Radner, *It's Garry Shandling's Show*. Showtime.

OUTSTANDING INDIVIDUAL PERFORMANCE
IN A VARIETY OR MUSIC PROGRAM
• Robin Williams, *ABC Presents a Royal Gala*. ABC.
Billy Crystal, *All Star Toast to the Improv*. HBO.
Ray Charles, *Irving Berlin's 100th Birthday Celebration*. CBS.
Mikhail Baryshnikov, "Celebrating Gershwin," *Great Performances*. PBS.
Julie Kavner, *The Tracey Ullman Show*. Fox.

OUTSTANDING DIRECTOR
IN A DRAMA SERIES
• Mark Tinker, *St. Elsewhere*. NBC.
Kim Friedman, *L.A. Law*. NBC.
Rod Holcomb, *China Beach*. ABC.
Gregory Hoblit, *L.A. Law*. NBC.
Win Phelps, *L.A. Law*. NBC.
Sam Weisman, *L.A. Law*. NBC.

OUTSTANDING DIRECTOR
IN A COMEDY SERIES
• Gregory Hoblit, *Hooperman*. ABC.
James Burrows, *Cheers*. NBC.
Terry Hughes, *The Golden Girls*. NBC.
Alan Rafkin, *It's Garry Shandling's Show*. Showtime.
Jay Tarses, *The Days and Nights of Molly Dodd*. NBC.

OUTSTANDING DIRECTOR
IN A MINISERIES OR A SPECIAL
• Lamont Johnson, *Gore Vidal's Lincoln*. NBC.
Marvin J. Chomsky, *Billionaire Boys Club*. NBC.
John Erman, *The Attic: The Hiding of Anne Frank, General Foods' Golden Showcase*. CBS.
Glenn Jordan, *Joseph Wambaugh's "Echoes in the Darkness."* CBS.
Paul Wendkos, *The Taking of Flight 847: The Uli Derickson Story*. NBC.

OUTSTANDING DIRECTOR
IN A VARIETY OR MUSIC PROGRAM
• Patricia Birch, Humphrey Burton, "Celebrating Gershwin," *Great Performances*. PBS.
David Grossman, *The Smothers Brothers Comedy Hour 20th Reunion*. CBS.
Hal Gurnee, *Late Night with David Letterman 6th Anniversary Special*. NBC.
Walter Miller, *Irving Berlin's 100th Birthday Celebration*. CBS.

OUTSTANDING WRITING
IN A DRAMA SERIES
• Paul Haggis, Marshall Herskovitz, *thirtysomething*. ABC.
Ron Koslow, *Beauty and the Beast*. CBS.
John Sacret Young, *China Beach*. ABC.
Terry Louise Fisher, David E. Kelley, teleplay. Steven Bochco, Terry Louise Fisher, story. *L.A. Law*. NBC.
Terry Louise Fisher, David E. Kelley, *L.A. Law*. NBC.
Bruce Paltrow, Mark Tinker, teleplay. Tom Fontana, John Tinker, Gibson Channing, story. *St. Elsewhere*. NBC.

OUTSTANDING WRITING
IN A COMEDY SERIES
• Hugh Wilson, *Frank's Place*. CBS.
Glen Charles, Les Charles, *Cheers*. NBC.
Linda Bloodworth-Thomason, *Designing Women*. CBS.
Garry Shandling, Alan Zweibel, *It's Garry Shandling's Show*. Showtime.
Tom Gammill, Max Pross, Sam Simon, *It's Garry Shandling's Show*. Showtime.
Carol Black, Neal Marlens, *The Wonder Years*. ABC.

OUTSTANDING WRITING
IN A VARIETY OR MUSIC PROGRAM
• Jackie Mason, *The World According to Me*. HBO.
Steve O'Donnell, Joe Toplyn, Chris Elliott, Matt Wickline, Jeff Martin, Gerard Mulligan, Randy Cohen, Larry Jacobson, Kevin Curran, Fred Graver, Adam Resnick, Boyd Hale, David Letterman, *Late Night with David Letterman 6th Anniversary Special*. NBC.
Mason Williams, Bob Arnott, *The Smothers Brothers Comedy Hour 20th Reunion*. CBS.
James L. Brooks, Heide Perlman, Jerry Belson, Ken Estin, Sam Simon, Marc Flanagan, Matt Groening, Wallace Wolodarsky, Jay Kogen, Dick Blasucci, Tracey Ullman, *The Tracey Ullman Show*. Fox.

OUTSTANDING WRITING
IN A MINISERIES OR A SPECIAL
• William Hanley, *The Attic: The Hiding of Anne Frank*, *General Foods' Golden Showcase*. CBS.
James Steven Sadwith, *Baby M*. ABC.
Cy Waldron, *Billionaire Boys Club*. NBC.
Susan Cooper, *Foxfire*, *Hallmark Hall of Fame*. CBS.
Jeffrey Lane, George Stevens, Jr., teleplay. Larry McMurtry, story, *The Murder of Mary Phagan*. NBC.

OTHER AWARD WINNERS
OUTSTANDING DIRECTORS CLASSICAL MUSIC/DANCE PROGRAMMING
• Kirk Browning, *The Metropolitan Opera Presents: Turandot*. PBS.

OUTSTANDING WRITERS INFORMATIONAL PROGRAMMING
• Kevin Brownlow, David Gill, "Buster Keaton: Hard Act to Follow," *American Masters*. PBS.
• Bill Couturie, Richard Dewhurst, *Dear America: Letters Home from Vietnam*. HBO.

OUTSTANDING CHOREOGRAPHY
• Alan Johnson, *Irving Berlin's 100th Birthday Celebration*. CBS.

OUTSTANDING MUSIC AND LYRICS
• Larry Grossman, composer. Buz Kohan, lyricist. *Julie Andrews ... The Sound of Christmas*. Song: "The Sound of Christmas." ABC.

OUTSTANDING MUSIC COMPOSITION
FOR A SERIES
(Dramatic underscore)
• Lee Holdridge, *Beauty and the Beast*. CBS.

OUTSTANDING MUSIC COMPOSITION
FOR A MINISERIES OR A SPECIAL
(Dramatic underscore)
• Laurence Rosenthal, *The Bourne Identity*. ABC.

OUTSTANDING MUSIC DIRECTION
• Ian Fraser, music director. Chris Boardman, Alexander Courage, Ian Fraser, Angela Morley, principal arrangers, *Julie Andrews ... The Sound of Christmas*. ABC.

OUTSTANDING ART DIRECTION
FOR A SERIES
• John Mansbridge, art director. Chuck Korian, set decorator, *Beauty and the Beast*. CBS.

OUTSTANDING ART DIRECTION
FOR A MINISERIES OR A SPECIAL
• Jan Scott, production designer. Erica Rogalla, set decorator, *Foxfire*, *Hallmark Hall of Fame*. CBS.

OUTSTANDING ART DIRECTION
FOR A VARIETY OR MUSIC PROGRAM
• Charles Lisanby, production designer, *Barry Manilow: Big Fun on Swing Street*. CBS.

OUTSTANDING COSTUME DESIGN
FOR A SERIES
• William Ware Theiss, *Star Trek: The Next Generation*. Syndicated.

OUTSTANDING COSTUME DESIGN
FOR A MINISERIES OR A SPECIAL
• Jane Robinson, *Poor Little Rich Girl: The Barbara Hutton Story*. NBC.

OUTSTANDING COSTUME DESIGN
FOR A VARIETY OR MUSIC PROGRAM
• Pete Menefee, Ret Turner, *Las Vegas— An All-Star 75th Anniversary Special*. ABC.

OUTSTANDING COSTUMING FOR A SERIES
• Paula Kaatz, women's costumer. Darryl Levine, men's costumer, *China Beach*. ABC.

OUTSTANDING COSTUMING
FOR A MINISERIES OR A SPECIAL
• Eddie Marks, costume supervisor.
Deborah Hopper, costumer, *Shakedown on the Sunset Strip*. CBS.

OUTSTANDING MAKEUP FOR A SERIES
• Werner Keppler, Michael Westmore,
Gerry Quist, *Star Trek: The Next Generation*. Syndicated.

OUTSTANDING MAKEUP
FOR A MINISERIES OR A SPECIAL
• Ronnie Specter, key makeup. Linda De
Vetta, Pauline Heys, Farrah Fawcett's
makeup, *Poor Little Rich Girl: The Barbara Hutton Story*. NBC.

OUTSTANDING HAIRSTYLING FOR A SERIES
• Judy Crown, Monique De Sart,
Designing Women. CBS.

OUTSTANDING HAIRSTYLING
FOR A MINISERIES OR A SPECIAL
• Claudia Thompson, key hairdresser.
Aaron Quarles, Jan Archibald, Farrah
Fawcett's hairstylists. Stephen Rose, key
hairdresser, *Poor Little Rich Girl: The Barbara Hutton Story*. NBC.

OUTSTANDING GRAPHIC DESIGN
AND TITLE SEQUENCES
• Liz Friedman, "Strong Poison, A
Dorothy Sayers Mystery," *Mystery!* PBS.

OUTSTANDING SPECIAL VISUAL EFFECTS
• Will Vinton, Mark Gustafson, David
Altschul, *Moonlighting*. ABC.

OUTSTANDING CINEMATOGRAPHY
FOR A SERIES
• Roy H. Wagner, *Beauty and the Beast*.
CBS.

OUTSTANDING CINEMATOGRAPHY
FOR A MINISERIES OR A SPECIAL
• Woody Omens, *I Saw What You Did*. CBS.

OUTSTANDING TECHNICAL
DIRECTION/ELECTRONIC
CAMERAWORK/VIDEO CONTROL SERIES
• O. Tamburri, technical director. Jack
Chisholm, Stephen A. Jones, Ritch
Kenney, Ken Tamburri, camerapersons.
Robert G. Kaufmann, senior video control,
The Golden Girls. NBC.

OUTSTANDING TECHNICAL
DIRECTION/ELECTRONIC CAMERA/VIDEO
CONTROL FOR A MINISERIES
OR A SPECIAL
• Mike Spencer, technical director. David
"Rocket" Barber, Bob Keys, Ron Sheldon,
Gunter Degn, camerapersons. Mike
Spencer, senior video control, *Julie Andrews ... The Sound of Christmas*. ABC.

OUTSTANDING EDITING FOR A SERIES
(Single camera production)
• Elodie Keene, *L.A. Law*. NBC.
(Multicamera production)
• Andy Ackerman, *Cheers*. NBC.

OUTSTANDING EDITING FOR A MINISERIES
OR A SPECIAL
(Single camera production)
• John A. Martinelli, *The Murder of Mary Phagan*. NBC.
(Multicamera production)
• Andy Zall, Mark West, Bob Jenkis, *Julie Andrews ... The Sound of Christmas*. ABC.

OUTSTANDING SOUND EDITING
FOR A SERIES
• William Wistrom, supervising sound
editor. Wilson Dyer, Mace Matiosian,
James Wolvington, Keith Bilderbeck,
sound editors. Mace Matiosian,
supervising ADR editor. Gerry Sackman,
supervising music editor, *Star Trek: The Next Generation*. Syndicated.

OUTSTANDING SOUND EDITING
FOR A MINISERIES OR A SPECIAL
• Rich Harrison, supervising sound editor.
Tom Cornwell, Peter N. Harrison, Rich
Harrison, Tom McMullen, Stan Siegel,
sound editors. Tally Paulos, supervising
ADR editor. Allan K. Rosen, supervising
music editor, *The Murder of Mary Phagan*.
NBC.

OUTSTANDING SOUND MIXING
FOR A COMEDY SERIES OR A SPECIAL
• Michael Ballin, M. Curtis Price, Martin
P. Church, Lenora Peterson, *Frank's Place*. CBS.

OUTSTANDING SOUND MIXING
FOR A DRAMA SERIES
• Susan Chong, Thomas Huth, Tim
Philben, Sam Black, *Tour of Duty*. CBS.

OUTSTANDING SOUND MIXING FOR A VARIETY OR MUSIC SERIES OR A SPECIAL
• Doug Rider, Carroll Pratt, David E. Fluhr, Doug Nelson, *Dolly, Down in New Orleans*. ABC.

OUTSTANDING SOUND MIXING FOR A DRAMATIC MINISERIES OR A SPECIAL
• Don MacDougall, Grover Helsley, Joe Citarella, Russell Williams, *Terrorist on Trial: The United States vs. Salim Ajami*. CBS.

OUTSTANDING LIGHTING DIRECTION (ELECTRONIC) FOR A COMEDY SERIES
• Mark Buxbaum, *The Charmings*. ABC.

OUTSTANDING LIGHTING DIRECTION (ELECTRONIC) FOR A VARIETY/MUSIC OR DRAMA SERIES, A MINISERIES, OR A SPECIAL
• John Rook, *Julie Andrews ... The Sound of Christmas*. ABC.

OUTSTANDING LIGHTING— SPECIAL EVENTS PROGRAMMING
• Marc Palius, lighting director. Olin Younger, lighting consultant, *The 15th Annual American Music Awards*. ABC.

(No awards were bestowed in the areas of performers and directors in informational programming; performers, directors, costume designers, and art directors of special events programming; main title theme music; and performers and writers of classical music/ dance programming.)

DAYTIME AWARDS
OUTSTANDING DRAMA SERIES
• *Santa Barbara*. Jill Farren Phelps, Bridget Dobson, executive producers. Steven Kent, supervising producer. Leonard Friedlander, Julie Hanan, producers. NBC.
All My Children. Stephen Schenkel, producer. Thomas de Villiers, Kristen Laskas Martin, coordinating producers. ABC.
As the World Turns. Robert Calhoun, executive producer. Ken Fitts, supervising producer. Michael Laibson, Christine Banas, Lisa Anne Wilson, producers. CBS.
General Hospital. H. Wesley Kenney, executive producer. Bob Bardo, coordinating producer. Jerry Balme, producer. ABC.

The Young and the Restless. William J. Bell, Edward Scott, executive producers. Tom Langan, producer. CBS.

OUTSTANDING LEAD ACTOR
• David Canary, *All My Children*. ABC.
Larry Bryggman, *As the World Turns*. CBS.
Robert Gentry, *All My Children*. ABC.
Stephen Nichols, *Days of Our Lives*. NBC.
A Martinez, *Santa Barbara*. NBC.

OUTSTANDING LEAD ACTRESS
• Helen Gallagher, *Ryan's Hope*. ABC.
Elizabeth Hubbard, *As the World Turns*. CBS.
Susan Lucci, *All My Children*. ABC.
Erika Slezak, *One Life to Live*. ABC.
Marcy Walker, *Santa Barbara*. NBC.

OUTSTANDING SUPPORTING ACTOR
• Justin Deas, *Santa Barbara*. NBC.
Mark LaMura, *All My Children*. ABC.
David Lewis, *General Hospital*. ABC.
Bernie Barrow, *Ryan's Hope*. ABC.
Nicolas Coster, *Santa Barbara*. NBC.

OUTSTANDING SUPPORTING ACTRESS
• Ellen Wheeler, *All My Children*. ABC.
Lisa Brown, *As the World Turns*. CBS.
Eileen Fulton, *As the World Turns*. CBS.
Maeve Kinkead, *Guiding Light*. CBS.
Robin Mattson, *Santa Barbara*. NBC.
Arleen Sorkin, *Days of Our Lives*. NBC.

OUTSTANDING DRAMA SERIES DIRECTING TEAM
• Rudy Vejar, Frank Pacelli, Heather Hill, directors. Randy Robbins, Betty Rothenberg, associate directors, *The Young and the Restless*. CBS.
Paul Lammers, Jill Mitwell, Bob Schwarz, Maria Wagner, directors. Joel Aronowitz, Michael Kerner, associate directors, *As the World Turns*. CBS.
Joe Behar, Susan Orlikoff Simon, Herb Stein, Stephen Wyman, directors. Becky Greenlaw, Gay Linvill, Sheryl Harmon, associate directors, *Days of Our Lives*. NBC.
Larry Auerbach, Peter Miner, Gary Bowen, David Pressman, directors. Susan Pomerantz, Lisa Smith Hesser, Andrea Giles Rich, associate directors, *One Life to Live*. ABC.
Joe Behar, Hank Behar, directors. Aviva Jacobs, Christine Magarian, associate directors, *Superior Court*. Syndicated.

Outstanding Drama Series Writing Team

• Agnes Nixon, Clarice Blackburn, Lorraine Broderick, Susan Kirshenbaum, Kathleen Klein, Karen L. Lewis, Victor Miller, Megan McTavish, Elizabeth Page, Peggy Sloane, Gillian Spencer, Elizabeth Wallace, Wisner Washam, Mary K. Wells, Jack Wood, writers, *All My Children*. ABC.

Ann Aikman, Greg Ross, Claire Brush Sasano, James Goldin, John Cox, Ron Hoffman, Brady Rubin, Kris Hansen, Mike Lyons, writers, *The Judge*. Syndicated.

Anne Howard Bailey, Chuck Pratt, Jr., head writers. Linda Hamner, breakdown writer. Gary Tomlin, Courtney Simon, Patrick Mulcahey, script writers. Frank Salisbury, script/breakdown writer, *Santa Barbara*. NBC.

Bill Corrington, Joyce Corrington, head writers. Marvin Part, Ronald Part, Harry Boehm, Marcy Shaffer, writers, *Superior Court*. Syndicated.

OTHER DAYTIME AWARD WINNERS

Outstanding Younger Leading Man in a Drama Series
• Billy Warlock, *Days of Our Lives*. NBC.

Outstanding Ingenue in a Drama Series
• Julianne Moore, *As the World Turns*. CBS.

Outstanding Game/Audience Participation Show
• *The Price is Right*. Frank Wayne, executive producer. Phillip Wayne, Roger Dobkowitz, producers. CBS.

Outstanding Game Show Host
• Bob Barker, *The Price is Right*. CBS.

Outstanding Directing in a Game/Audience Participation Show
• Bruce Burmester, *The $25,000 Pyramid*. CBS.

Outstanding Talk/Service Program
• *The Oprah Winfrey Show*. Debra DiMaio, executive producer. Mary Kay Clinton, Dianne Atkinson Hudson, Ellen Sue Rakieten, Christine Tardio, producers. Syndicated.

Outstanding Talk/Service Show Host
• Phil Donahue, *Donahue*. Syndicated.

Outstanding Directing in a Talk/Service Show
• Russell Morash, *This Old House*. PBS.

Outstanding Children's Series
• *Sesame Street*. Dulcy Singer, executive producer. Lisa Simon, supervising producer. Arlene Sherman, coordinating producer. PBS.

Outstanding Children's Special
• "Never Say Goodbye," *CBS Schoolbreak Special*. Michael D. Little, executive producer. Susan Rohrer, producer. Craig S. Cummings, coproducer. CBS.

Outstanding Animated Program
• *Jim Henson's Muppet Babies*. Margaret Ann Loesch, Lee Gunther, Jim Henson, executive producers. Bob Richardson, supervising producer. John Ahern, Bob Shellhorn, producers. Margaret Nichols, director. Sindy McKay, Larry Swerdlove, writers. CBS.

Outstanding Performer in Children's Programming
• Philip Bosco, "Read Between the Lines," *ABC Afterschool Special*. ABC.

Outstanding Directing in Children's Programming
• Jeff Brown, "What If I'm Gay?" *CBS Schoolbreak Special*. CBS.

Outstanding Writing for a Children's Series
• Norman Stiles, head writer. Christian Clark, Sara Compton, Judy Freudberg, Tony Geiss, Emily Kingsley, David Korr, Sonia Manzano, Jeff Moss, Cathi Rosenberg-Turow, Mark Saltzman, Nancy Sans, Luis Santeiro, Jocelyn Stevenson, Jon Stone, Belinda Ward, John Weidman, writers, *Sesame Street*. PBS.

Outstanding Writing for a Children's Special
• Victoria Hochberg, "Just a Regular Kid: An AIDS Story," *ABC Afterschool Special*. ABC.

Outstanding Music Direction and Composition for a Drama Series
• Liz Lachman, music director. Dominic Messenger, composer. Rick Rhodes, principal arranger, *Santa Barbara*. NBC.

OUTSTANDING MUSIC DIRECTION AND COMPOSITION
• Bruce Hornsby, Peter Harris, music directors and composers, "Soldier Boys," *CBS Schoolbreak Special*. CBS.

OUTSTANDING ART DIRECTION/SET DECORATION/SCENIC DESIGN FOR A DRAMA SERIES
• Sy Tomashoff, Jack Forrestel, art directors. Jay Garvin, Randy Gunderson, set decorators, *The Bold and the Beautiful*. CBS.

OUTSTANDING ART DIRECTION/SET DECORATION/SCENIC DESIGN
• Gary Panter, production designer. Wayne White, Ric Heitzman, co-production designers. Jeremy Railton, art director. James Higginson, Paul Reubens, set decorators, *Pee-Wee's Playhouse*. CBS.

OUTSTANDING COSTUME DESIGN FOR A DRAMA SERIES
• Lee Smith, *Days of Our Lives*. NBC.

OUTSTANDING COSTUME DESIGN
• Lowell Detweiler, *Square One TV*. PBS.

OUTSTANDING MAKEUP FOR A DRAMA SERIES
• Carol Brown, head makeup artist. Keith Crary, Robert Sloan, Gail Hopkins, Lucia Bianca, makeup artists, *Days of Our Lives*. NBC.

OUTSTANDING MAKEUP
• Ve Neill, *Pee-Wee's Playhouse*. CBS.

OUTSTANDING HAIRSTYLING FOR A DRAMA SERIES
• Zora Sloan, Pauletta Lewis, *Days of Our Lives*. NBC.

OUTSTANDING HAIRSTYLING
• Bruce Geller, wig director. Victor Callegari, Luciano Pavarotti's wig, *Un Ballo in Maschera*. PBS.

OUTSTANDING CINEMATOGRAPHY
• Tom Hurwitz, director of photography, "Just a Regular Kid: An AIDS Story," *ABC Afterschool Special*. ABC.

OUTSTANDING TECHNICAL DIRECTION/ELECTRONIC CAMERA/VIDEO CONTROL FOR A DRAMA SERIES
• Chuck Guzzi, technical director. Ted Morales, Toby Brown, Gordon Sweeney, Mike Glenn, Pat Kenney, electronic camera. Roberto Bosio, Clive Bassett, video control, *The Bold and the Beautiful*. CBS.

OUTSTANDING TECHNICAL DIRECTION/ELECTRONIC CAMERA/VIDEO CONTROL
• Ray Angona, technical director. Joseph Arvizu, Cesar Cabreira, Keeth Lawrence, Martin Wagner, electronic camera. Allen Latter, video control, *The Price is Right*. CBS.

OUTSTANDING FILM EDITING
• John Craddock, "What If I'm Gay?" *CBS Schoolbreak Special*. CBS.

OUTSTANDING VIDEO-TAPE EDITING FOR A DRAMA SERIES
• Marc Beruti, Dan Brumett, *The Young and the Restless*. CBS.

OUTSTANDING VIDEO-TAPE EDITING
• John Ward Nielsen, *Pee-Wee's Playhouse*. CBS.

OUTSTANDING FILM SOUND EDITING
• Bruce Elliott, supervising editor. William Koepnick, sound effects. Richard Gannon, Gregory K. Bowron, ADR. Stuart Goetz, music editor, *ALF*, NBC.

OUTSTANDING FILM SOUND MIXING
• James Hodson, rerecording mixer, *ALF*. NBC.

OUTSTANDING LIVE AND TAPE SOUND MIXING AND SOUND EFFECTS FOR A DRAMA SERIES
• Scott A. Millan, preproduction and production mixer. Tommy Persson, production mixer. Rafael O. Valentin, Donald D. Henderson, postproduction mixers. Maurice "Smokey" Westerfeld, Peter Romano, sound effects, *The Young and the Restless*. CBS.

OUTSTANDING LIVE AND TAPE SOUND MIXING AND SOUND EFFECTS
• Blake Norton, Tim Lester, production mixers. Dick Maitland, sound effects, *Sesame Street*. PBS.

OUTSTANDING LIGHTING DIRECTION FOR A DRAMA SERIES
• Howard Sharrott, *Loving*. ABC.

OUTSTANDING LIGHTING DIRECTION
• Chenault Spence, lighting designer. Alan Adelman, lighting consultant, *Un Ballo in Maschera*. PBS.

OUTSTANDING GRAPHICS AND TITLE DESIGN
• Wayne Fitzgerald, David Pfeil, title designers, *The Bold and the Beautiful*. CBS.

OUTSTANDING SPECIAL CLASS PROGRAM AREA
(Area award)
• *American Bandstand*. Dick Clark, executive producer. Larry Klein, supervising producer. Barry Glazer, producer. Syndicated.

OUTSTANDING ACHIEVEMENT IN DIRECTING—SPECIAL CLASS
• Dick Schneider, *Macy's 61st Annual Thanksgiving Day Parade*. NBC.

OUTSTANDING ACHIEVEMENT IN WRITING—SPECIAL CLASS
• David Forman, Barry Adelman, *The 4th Annual Soap Opera Awards*. NBC.

SPORTS AWARD WINNERS
OUTSTANDING LIVE SPORTS SERIES
• *NFL Monday Night Football*. Ken Wolfe, producer. Larry Kamm, director. Mike Pearl, half-time producer. John McGuinness, associate producer. Rob Beiner, Ben Harvey, associate directors. ABC.

OUTSTANDING EDITED SPORTS SERIES
• *ABC's Wide World of Sports*. Curt Gowdy, Jr., coordinating producer. Amy Sacks, associate coordinating producer. Mike Pearl, Joel Feld, Ned Simon, Bob Goodrich, Peter Lasser, Carol Lehti, producers. Craig Janoff, Roger Goodman, Doug Wilson, Andy Sidaris, Jim Jennett, directors. John McGuinness, Jimmy Roberts, associate producers. Jeff Cohan, Norm Samet, Vince DeDario, Toni Slotkin, Katherine Cook, Earl Freiman, Robert Cowen, David Kiviat, associate directors. ABC.

OUTSTANDING LIVE SPORTS SPECIAL
• *Kentucky Derby*. Curt Gowdy, Jr., producer. Craig Janoff, director. Rob Beiner, Steve Nagler, associate producers. Earl Freiman, associate director. ABC.

OUTSTANDING EDITED SPORTS SPECIAL
• *Paris Roubaix Bike Race*. Ted Shaker, executive producer. David Michaels, producer/director. Andy Kindle, codirector. Victor Frank, associate producer. David Banks, associate director. CBS.

OUTSTANDING SPORTS PERSONALITY—HOST
• Bob Costas. NBC.

OUTSTANDING SPORTS PERSONALITY—ANALYST
• John Madden. CBS.

TECHNICAL TEAM—REMOTE
• *1987 World Series*. Tony Versley, Jerry Bobian, Loren Coltran, technical managers. Mike Blazo, Rich Gelber, Bob Bernthal, technical directors. Mel Handelsman, Brook Cuddy, lighting directors. Jack Cronin, Drew DeRosa, Dom Dragonetti, Roy Hutchings, Frank Melchiorre, Serf Menduina, George Montanez, John Morreale, Tom O'Connell, Luis Rojas, Jack Savoy, Bill Scott, Joseph Talosi, Rick Westlein, Mike Todd, Bill Sullivan, camera. Tom Wright, Martin Bell, Lou Rende, Ron Feszchur, Steve Iori, Dick Velasco, Hector Kicelian, Serena Pecararo, Dan Farrell, Al Dejesus, video-tape engineers. Mike Michaels, Dick Moller, Tony Capitano, Bill Triantafellow, Ken Arnow, Mike D'errico, Joe Lee, video operators. Tom Glazner, Bill Sandreuter, Chuck Eisen, Gene Mackvick, Jack Brandes, Joe Vernum, audio engineers. Lois Filippi, Sidney Lustgarten, Sandra York, Nancy Ross, Michael Finney, graphics operators. ABC.
• *Tour de France*. Peter Donlan, production coordinator. Raymond Ek, truck supervisor/editor. Mats Bergerren, engineer. Stig Johannson, audio/editor. Danielle Vandeeponsteele, video-tape operator. Ken Woo, Nigel Reynolds, Pascal Charpentier, Andy Kindle, David Michaels, Victor Frank, camera. Hans Oberg, technical supervisor. Joseph Flynn, graphics operator. CBS.

TECHNICAL TEAM—STUDIO
• *NFL Today*. Paul N. Cox, studio technical manager. Philip Selby, technical director. Jeffrey James, Elliot Gordon, Raymond Sills, Richard Brender, William Naeder, Jr., audio. Mike Snyder, James

Dima, video. David Cabano, David Dorsett, Al Loreto, Robert Higgins, James McCarthy, Frederick Rivera, camera. Roxanne Markline, Joe Davanzo, Tim Pendleton, Howard Steinkohl, graphics operators. CBS.

OUTSTANDING VIDEO-TAPE CAMERAPERSONS
• Ken Woo, Pascal Charpentier, Nigel Reynolds, Andy Kindle, David Michaels, Victor Frank, camera, *Tour de France.* CBS.
• Jim Douglas, camera, *America Today: Running for the Olympics, Dreams of a Comeback.* PBS.

OUTSTANDING VIDEO-TAPE EDITING
• Scott Cole, editor, *Pan Am Games Opening.* CBS.

FILM CINEMATOGRAPHERS
• John Schipp, creative director. Tom MacNeil, director. Kip Anderson, director of photography, *League Championship Series Prelude and Campaign.* NBC.

FILM EDITING
• Ted Winterburn, editor, *Race Across America.* ABC.

MUSIC
• John Tesh, composer, *Tour de France.* CBS.

WRITING
• Jim McKay, writer, *Indianapolis 500, British Golf Open, Kentucky Derby Open.* ABC.

GRAPHICS
• Stephen M. Anderson, director of production. Chip Dean, director. Mo Davenport, lead producer. Bill Feigenbaum, designer, *ESPN: NCAA Basketball Open.* ESPN.

SPECIAL CLASS: TECHNICAL ACHIEVEMENT
• John Wilcox, series producer. Bob Sloan, Stan Waterman, Howard Hall, technicians. Elwyn Gates, designer, underwater video, "Beneath the Sea: The Galapagos," *Mutual of Omaha Spirit of Adventure.* ABC.

SPECIAL CLASS: OUTSTANDING INDIVIDUAL ACHIEVEMENT
• Dick Schaap, writer/interviewer/narrator. Rob Wallace, producer, "To an Athlete Dying Young," *20/20.* ABC.

SPECIAL CLASS: OUTSTANDING PROGRAM ACHIEVEMENT
• *Promotion Campaign—ABC Reaching New Heights.* George Greenberg, director of advertising and promotion. ABC.

NEWS & DOCUMENTARY AWARD WINNERS
OUTSTANDING COVERAGE OF SINGLE BREAKING NEWS STORY
(Programs)
• "Tower Commission Report," *ABC News Nightline.* Richard Kaplan, executive producer. Terry Irving, Marie MacLean, Heather Vincent, Gil Pimenter, producers. Bill Moore, Robert Jordan, Betsy West, senior producers. Ted Koppel, anchor/managing editor. Sam Donaldson, correspondent. ABC.
(Segments)
• "The Vietnamese Withdraw from Cambodia," *The CBS Evening News with Dan Rather.* Larry Doyle, Tom Bettag, executive producers. Bob Simon, correspondent. CBS.

OUTSTANDING INVESTIGATIVE JOURNALISM
(Programs)
• "In Search of the Marcos Millions," *Frontline.* David Fanning, George Carey, executive producers. William Cran, Stephanie Tepper, producers. PBS.
(Segments)
• "Drug Investigations," *NBC Nightly News with Tom Brokaw.* Ira Silverman, Vic Walter, producers. Brian Ross, correspondent. NBC.

OUTSTANDING BACKGROUND/ANALYSIS OF SINGLE CURRENT STORY
(Programs)
• "The Kingdom Divided," *Moyers: God & Politics.* Joan Konner, executive producer. Bill Moyers, correspondent. Elena Mannes, producer. PBS.
• "The Secret Government ... The Constitution in Crisis," *Moyers: God & Politics.* Alvin Perlmutter, Joan Konner, executive producers. Bill Moyers, correspondent. Alan Levin, senior producer. Paul Budline, Leslie Clark, Mark Levin, Matthew Pook, producers. PBS.

(Segments)
• "Lest We Forget," *Sunday Morning*. Linda Mason, executive producer. Charles Kuralt, correspondent. James Houtrides, producer. CBS.
• "Death Knell for the Klan," *20/20*. Rob Wallace, producer. Tom Jarriel, correspondent. ABC.

OUTSTANDING INTERVIEW/INTERVIEWER
(Programs)
• "Jim and Tammy Faye Bakker," *ABC News Nightline*. Ted Koppel, anchor managing editor. ABC.
(Segments)
• "Arthur Miller," *60 Minutes*. Jim Jackson, producer. Mike Wallace, correspondent. CBS.
• "The Woman Under the Crane," *20/20*. Marc Goldbaum, producer. Barbara Walters, correspondent. ABC.

OUTSTANDING COVERAGE OF CONTINUING NEWS STORY
(Programs)
• "Battle for Afghanistan," *CBS Reports*. Perry Wolff, executive producer. Mike Hoover, producer. Dan Rather, correspondent. CBS.
(Segments)
• "Inside Afghanistan," *The CBS Evening News with Dan Rather*. Tom Bettag, executive producer. Dan Rather, correspondent. Alberto Ortiz, producer. CBS.

OUTSTANDING SPECIAL CLASSIFICATION FOR OUTSTANDING PROGRAM ACHIEVEMENT
(Programs)
• "Children of Apartheid," *CBS Reports*. Brian Ellis, producer/ reporter. CBS.

OUTSTANDING SPECIAL CLASSIFICATION FOR OUTSTANDING PROGRAM ACHIEVEMENT
(Segments)
• "Footsteps on the Sands of Time," *Sunday Morning*. Mary Lou Teel, producer. Linda Mason, executive producer. Charles Kuralt, correspondent. CBS.

OUTSTANDING INFORMATIONAL, CULTURAL, OR HISTORICAL PROGRAMMING
(Programs)
• "A Season in the Sun," *Nature*. David

Heeley, Alan Root, producers. George Page, reporter. PBS.

OUTSTANDING INFORMATIONAL, CULTURAL, OR HISTORICAL PROGRAMMING
(Segments)
• "Music Maestro Please," *20/20*. Dean Irwin, producer. Bob Brown, correspondent. ABC.
• "Triumph Over Darkness," *20/20*. Rob Wallace, producer. Tom Jarriel, correspondent. ABC.

OUTSTANDING INDIVIDUAL ACHIEVEMENT
(Outstanding writers)
• Steve Fayer, "Mississippi: Is This America? 1962–64," *Eyes on the Prize: America's Civil Rights Years, 1954–1965.* PBS.
• Callie Crossley, James Devinney, "Bridge to Freedom 1965," *Eyes on the Prize: America's Civil Rights Years, 1954–1965.* PBS.
(Outstanding directors)
• Ann Petrie, Jeanette Petrie, *Mother Teresa.* PBS.
(Outstanding cinematographers)
• David Hughes, Carol Hughes, "Lions of the African Night," *National Geographic Special.* PBS.
(Outstanding researchers)
• Teresa Koenig, "Secrets of the Titanic," *National Geographic Explorer.*TBS.
(Outstanding electronic camerapersons)
• Jon Alpert, "Russia—The Times Are Changing," *Today.* NBC.
(Outstanding videographers)
• James Douglas, "Dying Industry, the Deepies, Volunteer Firefighters," *America Today.* PBS.
(Outstanding technical directors)
• Gary Boyarsky, Vin Perry, Paul Glaser, Grahame Hadden, George Berger, *Capital to Capital.* ABC.
(Sound)
• David Hughes, *Lions of the African Night.* PBS.
(Outstanding tape editors)
• John Kuhrt, "Reflections, Elk Hunt, Frozen in Time," *America Today.* PBS. Ruth Iwano, "Wall Street Crash Week," *ABC World News Tonight.* ABC.
(Outstanding film editors)
• Joel Herson, "Music, Maestro, Please," *20/20.* ABC
• Tom Haneke, *Mother Teresa.* PBS.

N.A.T.A.S. president John Cannon (third from left) presented a Trustees Award to PBS president William Baker (center).

(Outstanding graphic designers)
• John Andrews, Todd Ruff, *Adam Smith's Money World*. PBS.
(Outstanding music composers)
• Jack Tillar, William Loose, "In the Shadow of Vesuvius," *National Geographic Special*. PBS.

INTERNATIONAL AWARD WINNERS
OUTSTANDING DOCUMENTARY
• *The Sword of Islam*. Granada Television, U.K.

OUTSTANDING DRAMA
• *Porterhouse Blue*. Channel 4 Television, U.K.

OUTSTANDING PERFORMING ARTS
• *The Belle of Amherst*. Thames Television, U.K.

OUTSTANDING POPULAR ARTS
• *Alias Smith and Jones*. BBC. U.K.

OUTSTANDING CHILDREN'S PROGRAM
• *It's Late: Degrassi Junior High*. CBC. Canada.

INTERNATIONAL DIRECTORATE AWARD
• Jeremy Isaacs

FOUNDERS AWARD
• Jacques-Yves Cousteau

SPECIAL AWARDS
OUTSTANDING ACHIEVEMENT IN THE SCIENCE OF TELEVISION ENGINEERING
• Quantel Inc.
• AVS Inc.
• Dr. Thomas G. Stockham
• Eastman Kodak
• BTS (Broadcast Television Systems)
• Barco Industries NV
• Textronix Inc.

OUTSTANDING ENGINEERING DEVELOPMENT
• Optical Disc Corporation
• Sony Corporation

NATIONAL AWARD FOR COMMUNITY SERVICE
• *AIDS Lifeline*. KPIX, San Francisco, California.

A.T.A.S. GOVERNORS AWARD
• William Hanna and Joseph Barbera

N.A.T.A.S. TRUSTEES AWARD
• William F. Baker (president, Public Broadcasting Systems)

The Old Timer's Game

Last year's triumph of youth was followed by the revenge of the old pros, which was manifest in a concentration on such serious, mature themes as abortion, alcoholism, Nazi atrocities, and the development of the atomic bomb.

Still, "upsets," noted *Broadcasting*, "were the order of the evening." *Cheers* had been named best comedy series in 1983 and 1984, but by decade's end was considered old news and an unlikely candidate for a rally, especially after the trouncing it took last year by *The Wonder Years*. When *Cheers* did manage to come roaring back during the final awards presentation of the 1980s, however, the climax of the Emmys night offered a hilarious moment worthy of a scene from the show. Milton Berle was standing nearby as producer Cheri Eichen accepted the series prize, obviously excited and noticeably pregnant. She "rattled on and on breathlessly," noted *The Washington Post* with its usual cynicism, "until Milton Berle came over to say, 'It's sounds like you're in labor!'"

One of the series' other two major awards went to supporting actress Rhea Perlman for a fourth time. "This could really put you in a good mood," she said up at the podium. Backstage, she told reporters, "I don't think anyone deserves to win this many times, but it's still wonderful. I'll have to build another press on my shelf for this one." Woody Harrelson, who plays the program's shy and spacy assistant bartender, was named Outstanding Supporting Actor. "Woody Harrelson of *Cheers* is good," commented the *L.A. Daily News*, "but his defeat of costar George Wendt and *Newhart*'s Peter Scolari was a stunner."

"Dad, this is for you!" Candice Bergen said. Her late father, Edgar, had been the first president of the TV academy.

The one award *Cheers* was considered likely to get was for its tavern owner and head bartender played by Ted Danson, who had been nominated for the best actor's prize every year since the show premiered. The *Cheers* star was now in the running for an eighth time and had a sizable cheering section among those watching the Emmycast at home, but instead the award went to a veteran winner. "In a major upset," noted the *L.A. Daily News*, "Richard Mulligan won his second Emmy (the first being for *Soap* in 1980) for his starring role in NBC's rookie series *Empty Nest*." Backstage in the news room, Mulligan, who played a befuddled widowed father on the new hit show spun off from *The Golden Girls*, said, "Maybe because I'm not a very funny person I can play a funny person. I had no expectations of winning at all."

Another rookie series, *Murphy Brown*, seized the best actress laurels for star Candice Bergen, whose character represented the new independent woman of the times. Bergen as Brown tossed off booze and cigarettes at the Betty Ford Clinic and excelled at her job (reporter for a fictional Washington, D.C., news-magazine program) thanks to an endless supply of nervous energy and an iron will. "I really wanted it a lot," Bergen said backstage holding the golden statuette. "I was dying for it." Part of the reason was sentimental, the rest historic. The actress's late father, legendary ventriloquist Edgar Bergen, never won an Emmy, but had been the first president of the original Academy of Television Arts and Sciences when it was founded in 1946–47. When his daughter accepted the TV academy's highest honor for a comedy series actress 43 years later, she held the trophy up triumphantly and said, "Dad, if you're watching, this is for you!"

Murphy's mother was played occasionally by Colleen Dewhurst, who won two Emmys this year, one for her guest role on *Murphy Brown*, and the other for best supporting actress in a TV film in which she portrayed the dying mother in *Those She Left Behind*. *Murphy* also won an editing award and one for writer/creator Diane English, who noted, "I was up against four wonderful episodes of *The Wonder Years*, and that's my favorite show!"

In a preview article published before the Emmycast, *The Hollywood Reporter* speculated, like so many others, "Can *thirtysomething* hold on to its title or will last year's big loser *L.A. Law* make a comeback? ... Last year *Law* went in cocky with a hefty 19 nominations, but slunk home with only two wins — one in a technical category. This year it has two fewer nominations, but it still leads in series nods with 17."

L.A. Law was acclaimed best drama series once before, in 1987, but when it returned as the winner this year, its executive producer and cocreator Steven Bochco (who also launched *Hill Street Blues*) was anything but cocky. "Of all the Emmys I've ever won this is the only one that took me totally by surprise," he said. "The feeling was we'd had our turn and there were many other deserving shows this year — *Wiseguy, thirtysomething*." Larry Drake, who played the law firm's mentally handicapped office boy, had had his turn as best supporting actor last year, but he also reprised his win. He said back in the press room: "The advantage of winning twice is I feel like less of a flash in the pan."

Four-time past Emmy winner for *All in the Family*, Carroll O'Connor, was now up for one more — for *In the Heat of the Night*, a new drama series based on the 1967 Academy Award–winning film about a crusty white sheriff in the South who is forced to team up with a black policeman from the north. Rod Steiger won the Best Actor Oscar for playing O'Connor's sheriff role in the movie, but O'Connor apparently didn't think he was a strong contender for the Emmy. On awards night, he wasn't even watching the ceremony on TV in Georgia where he was still on location shooting next year's episodes. Instead, he was dozing off in a chair while reading a book when his phone rang with the news that he was now only the second person in Emmy history to win best actor in both drama and comedy series. His predecessor was Robert Young, who struck gold for both *Father Knows Best* and *Marcus Welby, M.D.*

Dana Delany was hailed as best actress for *China Beach*, a new series that revisited the Vietnam war from the perspective of its female army nurses. "I'd like to thank the women who served in Vietnam," Delany said, accepting the honor. "I would like to thank you for sharing your experiences and allowing me to pay you the tribute you so greatly deserve."

Despite its victory as best drama series last year, *thirtysomething* was only 37th in the Nielsen rankings after its second season. This year it claimed four awards, however, to add to its previous four, including one for supporting actress Melanie Mayron, who was described by the Associated Press as the show's "unmarried manhunter." Her acceptance speech had "an infectious exuberance," observed *The Washington Post*. Mayron said, "Oh, God, I hope my dress stays up!" and then thanked "all the people who believed in me, no matter what I looked like."

Lonesome Dove began the miniseries competition with 18 nominations and was considered, said *Variety*, "the clear favorite" to take the top award. "The rustic tale of an epic cattle drive inspired critics to do handstands while America sat glued to the television for four nights last February," noted *American Film*. Based on the Pulitzer Prize–winning bestseller by Larry McMurtry and featuring a star-studded cast that included Robert Duvall and Anjelica Huston, *Lonesome Dove* became the most-watched miniseries since *North and South* in 1985. In all, it garnered seven Emmys, six in the creative arts categories and one for its director Simon Wincer. But when it went up for the prize for best miniseries, *Dove* was shot down by the mighty guns of *War and Remembrance*.

War and Remembrance is still the most expensive television program ever made, having cost an estimated $110 million. The 30-hour sequel to Herman Wouk's sweeping World War II novel *The Winds of War* (which had been made into a far more popular miniseries that was produced for nearly a third of the cost and ran only 18 hours) was so ambitious, in fact, that it was filmed in more than 10 countries and utilized more than 700 sets. (Its producer also admitted that it "took longer than World War II" to make.) Just based on its ratings, *Remembrance* could have been declared an unmemorable TV extravaganza had it not been for scattered critical praise and the Emmy for Outstanding Miniseries, "surely the evening's biggest surprise," commented the *L.A. Times*. Executive producer, director, and cowriter Dan Curtis acknowledged the award by admitting that it was "a major shock" and thanked ABC "for having the guts to pony up to the dough."

There was a tie in the best drama special category. Like *Remembrance*, one of the winners also dealt with World War II and took a staggeringly long time to make (four years). *Day One*, a dramatization of

Jolts and upsets were the order of the evening.

the U.S. development of the atom bomb, marked the first Emmy ever won by the producer of *Dynasty*, *Charlie's Angels*, and *The Love Boat*, Aaron Spelling. *Day One* tied with *Roe vs. Wade*, "one of the medium's most controversial TV movies," said the *L. A. Times*, since it had been based on the landmark 1973 Supreme Court decision that legalized abortion. *Roe vs. Wade* was such a sensitive endeavor that its script was reportedly rewritten 20 times and had the predictable problem of enlisting — and keeping — advertisers. Executive producer Michael Manheim thanked those sponsors who stuck with him, "each of whom stood up to be counted," he said, "when it would have been easier to run and hide." Holly Hunter was hailed as best actress and thanked the real "Jane Roe," Norma McCorney, whom she portrayed "for continuing to keep women from being second-class citizens and for refusing to give up her right for a repro-ductive choice."

Broadcasting was among those who considered *Lonesome Dove*'s Robert Duvall the inevitable choice for best actor. But throughout Emmys night, as the *L.A. Times* reminded its readers, "there were jolts." One of the biggest came when the 1987 winner for *Promise*, James Woods, was chosen for his lead role in *My Name is Bill W.*, the story of the founder of Alcoholics Anonymous. Woods said he considered it "truly an honor to play the man who I consider a saint."

The Fox network, still faithfully airing the festivities, finally won some Emmys of its own — four — when it was rewarded for the kind of innovative pro-gramming for which it was becoming famous. *The Tracey Ullman Show* was one of its earliest experiments, headed by *Taxi* and *The Mary Tyler Moore Show* producer/creator James L. Brooks and the British star who excelled at singing, dancing, and comic-tragic acting. Ullman showcased her diverse talents in a daring half-hour series that was characterized by skits full of irreverent wit and bawdy the-atrics. "While critics have looked favor-ably on the show and its star, ratings never have materialized," said *The Holly-wood Reporter*. "Maybe Tracey's time has come." It had. Among her show's four prizes was one for choreographer Paula Abdul and the top honor as best variety, music, or comedy program, which was accepted in part by Ullman. She said, "I think it's courageous of Fox not to sanitize the show and I don't feel sorry for anybody whom I beat."

Other notable awards of the night were two in the area of Outstanding Spe-cial Events. They honored *The 42nd Annual Tony Awards* and *The 11th Annual Kennedy Center Honors*, the lat-ter of which brought a 16th Emmy to the one person who still holds the most: pro-ducer/director Dwight Hemion. A Gov-ernors Award went to Lucille Ball, who had died in April. "A clip of Lucille Ball clowning with Elizabeth Taylor and Richard Burton — part of a Lucy tribute — was funny in a way that things don't seem to be funny anymore," said *The Washington Post*. The tribute was pre-sented to Ball's husband Gary Morton by Bob Hope, who said about Lucy, "She had a pretty face made for comedy."

DAYTIME AWARDS

Reporting on NBC's afternoon broad-cast of the festivities taking place at New York's Waldorf-Astoria Hotel, the *L.A. Times* said "NBC had something to crow about" when last year's top soap opera returned this year to claim a total of seven — the record.

Its top prize was announced by *Santa Barbara*'s best actress winner Marcy Walker, who screamed when she saw the contents of the envelope. "What a day!" cried senior supervising producer Steven Kent after racing up to the podium to claim the trophy. "Five years ago *Santa Barbara* was born. And against all odds, we're still here — and here we are again!"

Among the seven honors the sudser reaped were for writing, makeup, best juvenile male star Justin Gocke (as Bran-don Capwell), and the show's other Justin — Deas — who played Keith Timmons and won the supporting actor honor last year, too, but wasn't on hand at either ceremony. There was a tie in the supporting actress category, which was claimed in part by Nancy Lee Grahn (as Julia Wainwright), who said, "This is a really classy group of people and I really love you a lot." Best actress Marcy Walker (as Eden Capwell) also thanked "the generous and giving people at *Santa Barbara*," but began her remarks, saying, "First, because I never have had the opportunity to do so, I'd really love to thank the people I used to work with at *All My Children*" where she had once performed the role of bitchy Liza Colby.

Walker beat out perennial loser and former costar Susan Lucci (Erica Kane) of *All My Children,* who was up for the accolade for a 10th time. Lucci did participate in the awards, though, by giving away the costume prize to the team for *Another World.* "Being the fashion plate that Erica Kane is, I have the most spectacular wardrobe in the world," Lucci said, explaining her expertise in the field. "Otherwise, I'd be home dreaming about it while I looked through the pages of *Vogue* magazine" — and most likely dreaming about that Emmy, too.

Dreams were on the mind of the cowinner of the supporting actress honor, Debbi Morgan, who played Angie Baxter on *All My Children*. She referred to the early days of her career when she first became convinced, as she put it, that she could have "bigger dreams, bigger ambitions and, yes, they were within the realm of possibility." The series also won the director's trophy and a third one for last year's best actor David Canary (who played twins Adam and Stuart Chandler). He was now tied with Helen Gallagher of *Ryan's Hope* as the daytime performer with the most Emmys for leading roles. Canary said, "I don't deserve this any more than any of you, but I've got it and I'm thrilled." *The Young and the Restless* won four statuettes, including one for its director who said about the long-lasting *Y&R* cast and crew, "We're just as exuberant, but a little older."

In the first year of cable TV participation in the daytime honors, there were no network contenders in the category of Oustanding Talk/Service Show Host. Nominees included Lifetime's Linda Dano and Nancy Glass of *Attitudes,* plus all of the following, who appear on syndicated programs: Sally Jessy Raphael, Phil Donahue, Oprah Winfrey, and Regin Philbin and Kathie Lee Gifford. In a startling upset, the award went to Sally Jessy Raphael. Accepting her first Emmy, Raphael noted that she had been in TV for 33 years and then pointed to the sudden "nationwide explosion in talk" that helped make her a star. The series prize went to *The Oprah Winfrey Show* for the third consecutive year.

Multiple past Emmy winner *The $25,000 Pyramid* has experienced one of the most colossal struggles any game show has ever faced just to stay on the air. Back in the early 1970s, when the pyramid was only worth $10,000, the series was broadcast by CBS. The network dropped it in 1974, but the show managed to survive in syndication (and while the pyramid's value was hiked to $20,000). Then it was picked up and dropped by ABC, nearly shattering its hopes for survival. Back it went into syndication where the pyramid's value climbed to $50,000 in 1981 and a peak of $100,000 in 1985. Now it was back at a frugal CBS, which slashed the jackpot back to $25,000, but the program was again being canceled. When it was named best game show this year, producer David Michaels said, "Those of you who have been following *The $25,000 Pyramid* understand how much this one means." Another producer, Francine Michaels, added, "Thank you in advance to all the network executives who could possibly help us to be here again next year." Her appeal didn't work. Back the series went into syndication. Winner of the game show hosting honors was *Jeopardy!*'s Alex Trebek, who was not in attendance.

A record seven trophies for the struggling Santa Barbara: "What a day!"

All their Emmys: Marcy Walker of Santa Barbara *and alum of* All My Children *with former costar David Canary.*

Newton's Apple, the PBS science magazine program, was the surprise winner of the children's series award, topping *Sesame Street*, which had the most nominations among regular shows for the young set. The Outstanding Children's Special was the *ABC Afterschool Special* "Taking a Stand," which dealt with anti-black bigotry in an all-white neighborhood. *The New Adventures of Winnie the Pooh* was acknowledged as the best animated program.

Since it premiered on the air in 1969, *Sesame Street* had been hailed as best children's series on 11 occasions, the second-most times a show had been called best in its category in the history of the Emmys. (See sports awards section below for the number-one champ.) While *Sesame Street* failed to win its series trophy this year, a special one was nonetheless set aside for the woman who helped develop the show. A highlight of the Emmy ceremony included the presentation of the first Lifetime Achievement Award, which went to Joan Ganz Cooney, the head of Children's Television Workshop, which produces *Sesame Street* and other quality children's fare.

Appropriately, it was bestowed to her by Muppets creator Jim Henson.

SPORTS AWARDS

In its second year as a televised event, the sports awards ceremony was syndicated to 169 stations nationwide by Raycom. The show was hosted by comedian Robert Klein and featured presenters that included New York Knick Patrick Ewing, author George Plimpton, Olympic gymnast Mary Lou Retton, and *Sports Illustrated* swimsuit models Kathy Ireland and Kim Alexis.

Predictably, the top sports events of 1988 spawned the best sports coverage. NBC's *Games of the XXIV Olympiad* won the gold as Outstanding Live Sports Special (as well as an acknowledgment for sports journalism in the program area and four additional awards); *Road to the Superbowl '88*, syndicated by NFL Films, was the best edited sports special, and the CBS coverage of the NCAA basketball tournament was hailed as the best live sports series. In the category of Outstanding Edited Sports Series, old champ *ABC's Wide World of Sports* returned to claim its top prize for a 14th time. No other show in the history of the Emmys has ever been named best show in its category as many times. ABC's coverage of the winter Olympic events earned it a total of four Emmys.

Once again, John Madden returned as the year's top commentator (his sixth sports Emmy). NBC's Bob Costas won the laurels as host of sports play-by-play action and Harry Coyle of NBC was singled out for individual achievement.

NEWS & DOCUMENTARY AWARDS

It was a night of vindication for *West 57th Street*, CBS's newsmagazine program designed for younger, hipper audiences. The show that took its name from the address of the network's news division in New York was launched as an eventual successor to *60 Minutes* should the popular Sunday night show should ever slip from the Nielsen top ten, a ranking it's held since the late 1970s. *West 57th Street* premiered in 1985, but was tolerated only reluctantly by some CBS news officials who dismissed it as a lightweight imitator.

West 57th Street, however, grabbed the most news awards of the night — seven — including one for its investigative probe into the finances of leading religious figures and another for its coverage of the Reverend Pat Robertson's run for the U.S. presidency. *60 Minutes,* by comparison, received only two prizes — for interviews. The network's other newsmagazine series, *48 Hours,* hosted by Dan Rather, topped that with three winning episodes, which included "Faith Under Fire" and "48 Hours on Gang Street." ABC's imitator, *20/20,* outdid them both with four (including one for

investigative journalism).

Other strong showings came from *ABC News Nightline,* which was hailed three times for "*Nightline* in the Holy Land" and an interview with Austrian President Kurt Waldheim, who was suspected of involvement in Nazi horrors during his military service in World War II. *NBC Nightly News with Tom Brokaw* took three Emmys for segments such as "Palestinian Uprising."

But again it was a night when most of the news awards went to PBS — 18, compared to 16 for its closest competitor, CBS. PBS's most notable program prizes were bestowed for the *We Shall Overcome* and *Living with AIDS* specials, *Frontline*'s "Murder on the Rio San Juan," and a wrap-up of the 1988 elections.

History was made at the Emmys this year when cable programming won its first news award — for HBO's *JFK: In His Own Words.*

1988–89

The prime-time ceremony was broadcast on the Fox network from the Pasadena Civic Auditorium on September 17, 1989 for prime-time programs telecast between June 1, 1988 and May 31, 1989. The creative arts awards were bestowed on September 17, 1989. Daytime awards broadcast on NBC from New York's Waldorf-Astoria Hotel on June 29, 1989, for programs aired between March 6, 1988, and March 5, 1989. The sports awards for 1988 were presented April 10, 1989. News & documentary awards for 1988 were presented on September 12, 1989.

PRIME-TIME PROGRAM AWARDS
OUTSTANDING DRAMA SERIES
• *L.A. Law.* Steven Bochco, executive producer. Rick Wallace, co-executive producer. David E. Kelley, supervising producer. Scott Goldstein, Michele Gallery, producers. William M. Finkelstein, Judith Parker, coproducers. Phillip M. Goldfarb, Alice West, coordinating producers. NBC.
Beauty and the Beast. Paul Junger Witt,

Tony Thomas, Ron Koslow, executive producers. Stephen Kurzfeld, supervising producer. Kenneth R. Koch, George R. R. Martin, producers. Alex Gansa, Howard Gordon, Patricia Livingston, coproducers. David F. Schwartz, coordinating producer. CBS.
China Beach. John Sacret Young, executive producer. John Wells, producer. Patricia Green, supervising producer. Geno Escarrega, Christopher Nelson, coproducers. Fred Gerber, coordinating producer. ABC.
thirtysomething. Marshall Herskovitz, Edward Zwick, executive producers. Scott Winant, supervising producer. Richard Kramer, producer. Ellen S. Pressman, coproducer. Lindsley Parsons III, coordinating producer. ABC.
Wiseguy. Stephen J. Cannell, executive producer. Les Sheldon, co-executive producer. Jo Swerling, Jr., David J. Burke, Stephen Kronish, supervising producers. Alfonse Ruggiero, Jr., Alex Beaton, producers. CBS.

OUTSTANDING COMEDY SERIES
• *Cheers*. James Burrows, Glen Charles, Les Charles, executive producers. Cheri Eichen, Bill Steinkellner, Peter Casey, David Lee, producers. Tim Berry, Phoef Sutton, coproducers. NBC.
Designing Women. Harry Thomason, Linda Bloodworth-Thomason, executive producers. Pam Norris, supervising producer. Tommy Thompson, Douglas Jackson, producers. David Trainer, coproducer. CBS.
The Golden Girls. Paul Junger Witt, Tony Thomas, Susan Harris, executive producers. Kathy Speer, Terry Grossman, Mort Nathan, Barry Fanaro, co-executive producers. Eric Cohen, supervising producer. Martin Weiss, Robert Bruce, coproducers. NBC.
Murphy Brown. Diane English, Joel Shukovsky, executive producers. Korby Siamis, supervising producer. Tom Seeley, Norm Gunzenhauser, Russ Woody, Frank Pace, producers. Deborah Smith, coordinating producer. CBS.
The Wonder Years. Carol Black, Neal Marlens, executive producers. Bob Brush, coexecutive producer. Steve Miner, supervising producer. Jeffrey Silver, producer. ABC.

OUTSTANDING MINISERIES
• *War and Remembrance*. Dan Curtis, executive producer. Barbara Steele, producer. ABC.
I Know My First Name is Steven. Andrew Adelson, executive producer. Kim C. Friese, producer. NBC.
Lonesome Dove. Suzanne de Passe, Bill Wittliff, executive producers. Robert Halmi, Jr., co-executive producer. Dyson Lovell, producer. Michael L. Weisbarth, supervising producer. CBS.
A Perfect Spy, Masterpiece Theatre. Jonathan Powell, executive producer. Colin Rogers, producer. PBS.
The Women of Brewster Place. Carole Isenberg, Oprah Winfrey, executive producers. Karen Hall, supervising producer. Patricia K. Meyer, Reuben Cannon, producers. Barbara Black, line producer. ABC.

OUTSTANDING DRAMA/COMEDY SPECIAL
(Tie)
• *Day One, AT&T Presents*. Aaron Spelling, E. Duke Vincent, executive producers. David W. Rintels, producer. CBS.

• *Roe vs. Wade*. Michael Manheim, executive producer. Gregory Hoblit, producer. Alison Cross, coproducer. NBC.
David. Donald March, producer. John Erman, supervising producer. ABC.
Murderers Among Us: The Simon Wiesenthal Story. Robert Cooper, Abby Mann, Graham Benson, executive producers. John Kemeny, Robert Cooper, producers. HBO.
My Name is Bill W., *Hallmark Hall of Fame*. Peter K. Duchow, James Garner, executive producers. Daniel Petrie, producer. ABC.

OUTSTANDING VARIETY, MUSIC, OR COMEDY PROGRAM
• *The Tracey Ullman Show*. James L. Brooks, Jerry Belson, Heide Perlman, Ken Estin, Sam Simon, executive producers. Richard Sakai, Ted Bessell, producers. Marc Flanagan, coproducer. Tracey Ullman, host. Fox.
The Arsenio Hall Show. Arsenio Hall, executive producer. Marla Kell Brown, producer. Arsenio Hall, host. Syndicated.
"Gregory Hines' Tap Dance in America," *Great Performances*. Don Mischer, Jac Venza, executive producers. David J. Goldberg, Rhoda Grauer, producers. Gregory Hines, performer. PBS.
Late Night with David Letterman. Jack Rollins, David Letterman, executive producers. Robert Morton, producer. David Letterman, host. NBC.
Saturday Night Live. Lorne Michaels, executive producer. Jim Downey, producer. NBC.

OUTSTANDING CLASSICAL PROGRAM IN THE PERFORMING ARTS
(Winner)
• "Bernstein at 70!" *Great Performances*. Harry Kraut, Klaus Hallig, executive producers. Michael Bronson, Thomas P. Skinner, producers. PBS.

OUTSTANDING INFORMATIONAL SERIES
(Area award winner)
• *Nature*. David Heeley, executive producer. Fred Kaufman, series producer. PBS.

OUTSTANDING INFORMATIONAL SPECIAL
(Area award winner)
• "Lillian Gish: The Actor's Life for Me," *American Masters*. Freida Lee Mock, executive producer. Terry Sanders,

producer. William T. Cartwright, coproducer. Susan Lacy, executive producer. PBS.

OUTSTANDING SPECIAL EVENTS
(Area award winners)
• *Cirque du Soleil: The Magic Circus.* Helene Dufresne, producer. HBO.
• *The 11th Annual Kennedy Center Honors: A Celebration of the Performing Arts.* George Stevens, Jr., Nick Vanoff, producers. CBS.
• *The 42nd Annual Tony Awards.* Don Mischer, executive producer. David J. Goldberg, producer. Jeffrey Lane, coproducer. CBS.
• *The 17th Annual American Film Institute Film Achievement Award: A Salute to Gregory Peck.* George Stevens, Jr., producer. Jeffrey Lane, coproducer. NBC.

OUTSTANDING ANIMATED PROGRAM
(Winner—Less than one hour)
• *Garfield: Babes and Bullets.* Phil Roman, producer. Jim Davis, writer. Phil Roman, director. John Sparey, Bob Nesler, codirectors. CBS.

OUTSTANDING CHILDREN'S PROGRAM
(Winner)
• *Free to Be ... A Family.* Marlo Thomas, Christopher Cerf, executive producers, U.S.A. Robert Dalrymple, producer. U.S.A. Leonid Zolotarevsky, executive producer, U.S.S.R. Igor Menzelintsev, producer U.S.S.R. Vern T. Calhoun, coproducer. ABC.

(No award was bestowed in the area of Outstanding Animated Program of more than one hour in length.)

PERFORMANCE, DIRECTING, AND WRITING
OUTSTANDING LEAD ACTOR
IN A DRAMA SERIES
• Carroll O'Connor, *In the Heat of the Night.* NBC.
Ron Perlman, *Beauty and the Beast.* CBS.
Michael Tucker, *L.A. Law.* NBC.
Ken Wahl, *Wiseguy,* CBS.
Edward Woodward, *The Equalizer.* CBS.

OUTSTANDING LEAD ACTRESS
IN A DRAMA SERIES
• Dana Delany, *China Beach.* ABC.
Susan Dey, *L.A. Law.* NBC.
Linda Hamilton, *Beauty and the Beast.* CBS.

Angela Lansbury, *Murder, She Wrote.* CBS.
Jill Eikenberry, *L.A. Law.* NBC.

OUTSTANDING LEAD ACTOR
IN A COMEDY SERIES
• Richard Mulligan, *Empty Nest.* NBC.
Ted Danson, *Cheers,* NBC.
Michael J. Fox, *Family Ties.* NBC.
John Goodman, *Roseanne.* ABC.
Fred Savage, *The Wonder Years.* ABC.

OUTSTANDING LEAD ACTRESS
IN A COMEDY SERIES
• Candice Bergen, *Murphy Brown.* CBS.
Beatrice Arthur, *The Golden Girls.* NBC.
Blair Brown, *The Days and Nights of Molly Dodd.* Lifetime.
Rue McClanahan, *The Golden Girls.* NBC.
Betty White, *The Golden Girls.* NBC.

OUTSTANDING LEAD ACTOR
IN A MINISERIES OR SPECIAL
• James Woods, *My Name is Bill W.,* *Hallmark Hall of Fame.* ABC.
Robert Duvall, *Lonesome Dove.* CBS.
John Gielgud, *War and Remembrance.* ABC.
Ben Kingsley, *Murderers Among Us: The Simon Wiesenthal Story.* HBO.
Tommy Lee Jones, *Lonesome Dove.* CBS.

OUTSTANDING LEAD ACTRESS
IN A MINISERIES OR SPECIAL
• Holly Hunter, *Roe vs. Wade.* NBC.
Anjelica Huston, *Lonesome Dove.* CBS.
Diane Lane, *Lonesome Dove.* CBS.
Amy Madigan, *Roe vs. Wade.* NBC.
Jane Seymour, *War and Remembrance.* ABC.

OUTSTANDING SUPPORTING ACTOR
IN A DRAMA SERIES
• Larry Drake, *L.A. Law.* NBC.
Jonathan Banks, *Wiseguy.* CBS.
Timothy Busfield, *thirtysomething.* ABC.
Richard Dysart, *L.A. Law.* NBC.
Jimmy Smits, *L.A. Law.* NBC.

OUTSTANDING SUPPORTING ACTRESS
IN A DRAMA SERIES
• Melanie Mayron, *thirtysomething.* ABC.
Michele Greene, *L.A. Law.* NBC.
Lois Nettleton, *In the Heat of the Night.* NBC.
Amanda Plummer, *L.A. Law.* NBC.
Susan Ruttan, *L.A. Law.* NBC.

Outstanding Supporting Actor in a Comedy Series

• Woody Harrelson, *Cheers*. NBC.
Joe Regalbuto, *Murphy Brown*. CBS.
Peter Scolari, *Newhart*. CBS.
Meshach Taylor, *Designing Women*. CBS.
George Wendt, *Cheers*. NBC.

Outstanding Supporting Actress in a Comedy Series

• Rhea Perlman, *Cheers*. NBC.
Faith Ford, *Murphy Brown*. CBS.
Julia Duffy, *Newhart*. CBS.
Estelle Getty, *The Golden Girls*. NBC.
Katherine Helmond, *Who's the Boss?*
ABC.

Outstanding Supporting Actor in a Miniseries or Special

• Derek Jacobi, *The Tenth Man, Hallmark Hall of Fame*. CBS.
Armand Assante, *Jack the Ripper*. CBS.
James Garner, *My Name is Bill W.*,
Hallmark Hall of Fame. ABC.
Danny Glover, *Lonesome Dove*. CBS.
Corky Nemec, *I Know My First Name is Steven*. NBC.

Outstanding Supporting Actress in a Miniseries or Special

• Colleen Dewhurst, *Those She Left Behind*. NBC.
Peggy Ashcroft, *A Perfect Spy*,
Masterpiece Theatre. PBS.
Polly Bergen, *War and Remembrance*.
ABC.
Glenne Headly, *Lonesome Dove*. CBS.
Paula Kelly, *The Women of Brewster Place*. ABC.

Outstanding Individual Performance in a Variety or Music Program

• Linda Ronstadt, "Canciones De Mi Padre," *Great Performances*. PBS.
John Roarke puppet voices. Van
Snowden, Thom Fountain, Sandey
Grinn, John Lovelady, Steve Sherman,
Fred Spencer, Allan Trautman, Todd
Walcott, puppeteers, *D. C. Follies*.
Syndicated.
Dana Carvey, *Saturday Night Live*. NBC.
Maurice Lamarche, puppet voices. Van
Snowden, Thom Fountain, Sandey Grinn,
John Lovelady, Steve Sherman, Fred
Spencer, Allan Trautman, Todd Walcott,
puppeteers, *D.C. Follies*. Syndicated.
Julie Kavner, *The Tracey Ullman Show*.
Fox.

Outstanding Performance in Informational Programming
(Area award winner)

• Hal Holbrook, host, *Portrait of America*.
TBS.

Outstanding Performance in Special Events
(Area award winner)

• Billy Crystal, host, *The 31st Annual Grammy Awards*. CBS.

Outstanding Individual Performance in Classical Music/Dance Programming
(Area award winner)

• Mikhail Baryshnikov, performer,
"Baryshnikov Dances Balanchine," *Great Performances*. PBS.

Outstanding Guest Actor in a Drama Series

• Joe Spano, *Midnight Caller*. NBC.
Peter Boyle, *Midnight Caller*. NBC.
Jack Gilford, *thirtysomething*. ABC.
Michael Moriarty, *The Equalizer*. CBS.
Edward Woodward, *Hunted, Alfred Hitchcock Presents*. USA.

Outstanding Guest Actress in a Drama Series

• Kay Lenz, *Midnight Caller*. NBC.
Shirley Knight, *The Equalizer*. CBS.
Jean Simmons, *Murder, She Wrote*. CBS.
Maureen Stapleton, *B.L. Stryker, The ABC Monday Mystery Movie*. ABC.
Chloe Webb, *China Beach*. ABC.
Teresa Wright, *Dolphin Cove*. CBS.

Outstanding Guest Actor in a Comedy Series

• Cleavon Little, *Dear John...* NBC.
Sammy Davis, Jr., *The Cosby Show*. NBC.
Jack Gilford, *The Golden Girls*. NBC.
Leslie Nielsen, *Day by Day*. NBC.
Robert Picardo, *The Wonder Years*. ABC.

Outstanding Guest Actress in a Comedy Series

• Colleen Dewhurst, *Murphy Brown*. CBS.
Eileen Brennan, *Newhart*. CBS.
Diahann Carroll, *A Different World*. NBC.
Doris Roberts, *Perfect Strangers*. ABC.
Maxine Stuart, *The Wonder Years*. ABC.

Outstanding Directing in a Drama Series

• Robert Altman, *Tanner '88*. HBO.

Thomas Carter, *Midnight Caller*. NBC.
Eric Laneuville, *L.A. Law*. NBC.
John Pasquin, *L.A. Law*. NBC.
Scott Winant, *thirtysomething*. ABC.

OUTSTANDING DIRECTING
IN A COMEDY SERIES
• Peter Baldwin, *The Wonder Years*. ABC.
James Burrows, *Cheers*. NBC.
Michael Dinner, *The Wonder Years*. ABC.
Terry Hughes, *The Golden Girls*. NBC.
Barnet Kellman, *Murphy Brown*. CBS.
Steve Miner, *The Wonder Years*. ABC.

OUTSTANDING DIRECTING
IN A VARIETY OR MUSIC PROGRAM
• Jim Henson, *The Jim Henson Hour*.
NBC.
Debbie Allen, *The Debbie Allen Special*.
ABC.
Ted Bessell, *The Tracey Ullman Show*.
Fox.
Hal Gurnee, *Late Night with David
Letterman*. NBC.
Don Mischer, "Gregory Hines' Tap Dance
in America," *Great Performances*. PBS.

OUTSTANDING DIRECTING
IN A MINISERIES OR SPECIAL
• Simon Wincer, *Lonesome Dove*. CBS.
Larry Elikann, *I Know My First Name is
Steven*. NBC.
Daniel Petrie, *My Name is Bill W.*,
Hallmark Hall of Fame. ABC.
Gregory Hoblit, *Roe vs. Wade*. NBC.
Dan Curtis, *War and Remembrance*. ABC.

OUTSTANDING DIRECTING
FOR SPECIAL EVENTS
(Area award winner)
• Dwight Hemion, *The 11th Annual
Kennedy Center Honors: A Celebration of
the Performing Arts*. CBS.

OUTSTANDING WRITING
IN A DRAMA SERIES
• Joseph Dougherty, *thirtysomething*.
ABC.
David E. Kelley, *L.A. Law*. NBC.
Steven Bochco, David E. Kelley, William
M. Finkelstein, Michele Gallery, *L.A. Law*.
NBC.
David E. Kelley, William M. Finkelstein,
Michele Gallery, Judith Parker, *L.A. Law*.
NBC.
Edward Zwick, Marshall Herskovitz,
thirtysomething. ABC.

OUTSTANDING WRITING
IN A COMEDY SERIES
• Diane English, *Murphy Brown*. CBS.
Matthew Carlson, *The Wonder Years*.
ABC.
Todd W. Langen, *The Wonder Years*.
ABC.
David M. Stern, *The Wonder Years*. ABC.
Michael J. Weithorn, *The Wonder Years*.
ABC.

OUTSTANDING WRITING IN A VARIETY
OR MUSIC PROGRAM
• James Downey, head writer. John
Bowman, A. Whitney Brown, Gregory
Daniels, Tom Davis, Al Franken, Shannon
Gaughan, Jack Handey, Phil Hartman,
Lorne Michaels, Mike Myers, Conan
O'Brien, Bob Odenkirk, Herb Sargent,
Tom Schiller, Robert Smigel, Bonnie
Turner, Terry Turner, Christine
Zander, writers. George Meyer,
additional sketches. *Saturday Night Live*.
NBC.
Steve O'Donnell, head writer. Joe Toplyn,
Matt Wickline, Jeff Martin, Gerard
Mulligan, Randy Cohen, Larry
Jacobson, Kevin Curran, Fred Graver,
Adam Resnick, Boyd Hale, Bob Burnett,
David Letterman, writers. Chris Elliott,
additional sketches, *Late Night with David
Letterman's 7th Anniversary Special*.
NBC.
Matt Neuman, head writer. Larry Arnstein,
Steve Barker, David Hurwitz, Lane
Sarasohn, Billy Kimball, writers, *Not
Necessarily the News*. HBO.
Raymond Siller, head writer. Michael
Barrie, James Mulholland, Bob Keane,
Andrew Nicholls, Darrell Vickers, Tony
Desena, Patric Verrone, Bob Smith, Hal
Goodman, Larry Klein, Kevin
Mulholland, writers, *The Tonight Show
Starring Johnny Carson*. NBC.
James L. Brooks, Heide Perlman, Jerry
Belson, Ken Estin, Sam Simon, Marc
Flanagan, Jay Kogen, Wallace
Wolodarsky, Michael Sardo, Dick
Blasucci, Matt Groening, Tracey
Ullman, *The Tracey Ullman Show*. Fox.

OUTSTANDING WRITING IN A MINISERIES OR A SPECIAL
• Abby Mann, Robin Vote, Ron Hutchinson, *Murderers Among Us: The Simon Wiesenthal Story*. HBO.
William G. Borchert, *My Name is Bill W.*, *Hallmark Hall of Fame*. ABC.
Alison Cross, *Roe vs. Wade*. NBC.
JP Miller, Cynthia Whitcomb, teleplay. JP Miller, story, *I Know My First Name is Steven*. NBC.
Bill Wittliff, *Lonesome Dove*. CBS.

OUTSTANDING WRITING IN INFORMATIONAL PROGRAMMING
(Area award winner)
• John Heminway, *The Mind*. PBS.

OUTSTANDING WRITING FOR SPECIAL EVENTS
(Area award winner)
• Jeffrey Lane, *The 42nd Annual Tony Awards*. CBS.

(No awards were bestowed in the areas of directing classical music/dance programming or directing informational programming.)

OTHER AWARD WINNERS
OUTSTANDING CASTING FOR A MINISERIES OR SPECIAL
(Juried award)
• Lynn Kressel, *Lonesome Dove*. CBS.

OUTSTANDING CHOREOGRAPHY
• Walter Painter, *Disney/MGM Studios Theme Park Grand Opening*. NBC.
Paula Abdul, *The Tracey Ullman Show*. Fox.

OUTSTANDING MUSIC AND LYRICS
• Lee Holdridge, composer. Melanie, lyricist, "The First Time I Loved Forever," *Beauty and the Beast*. CBS.

OUTSTANDING MUSIC COMPOSITION FOR A SERIES
(Dramatic underscore)
• Joel Rosenbaum, *Falcon Crest*. CBS.

OUTSTANDING MUSIC COMPOSITION FOR A MINISERIES OR A SPECIAL
(Dramatic underscore)
• Basil Poledouris, *Lonesome Dove*. CBS.

OUTSTANDING MUSIC DIRECTION
• Ian Fraser, music director. Chris Boardman, J. Hill, principal arrangers, *Christmas in Washington*. NBC.

OUTSTANDING COSTUME DESIGN FOR A SERIES
• Judy Evans, *Beauty and the Beast*. CBS.

OUTSTANDING COSTUME DESIGN FOR A MINISERIES OR A SPECIAL
• Van Broughton Ramsey, *Lonesome Dove*. CBS.

OUTSTANDING COSTUME DESIGN FOR A VARIETY OR MUSIC PROGRAM
• Daniel Orlandi, *The Magic of David Copperfield XI: The Explosive Encounter*. CBS.

OUTSTANDING COSTUMING FOR A SERIES
• Patrick R. Norris, men's costumer. Julie Glick, women's costumer, *thirtysomething*. ABC.

OUTSTANDING COSTUMING FOR A MINISERIES OR SPECIAL
• Paula Kaatz, costume supervisor. Andrea Weaver, women's costumer, Los Angeles. Janet Lawler, women's costumer, Dallas. Stephen Chudej, men's costumer, *Pancho Barnes*. CBS.

OUTSTANDING MAKEUP FOR A SERIES
• Thomas R. Burman, Bari Dreiband-Burman, special makeup. Carol Schwartz, Robin Lavigne, makeup artists, *The Tracey Ullman Show*. Fox.

OUTSTANDING MAKEUP FOR A MINISERIES OR A SPECIAL
• Manlio Rocchetti, makeup supervisor. Carla Palmer, Jean Black, makeup artists, *Lonesome Dove*. CBS.

OUTSTANDING HAIRSTYLING FOR A SERIES
• Virginia Kearns, *Quantum Leap*. NBC.

OUTSTANDING HAIRSTYLING FOR A MINISERIES OR A SPECIAL
• Betty Glasow, chief hairstylist. Stevie Hall, Elaine Bowerbank, hairstylists, *Jack the Ripper*. CBS.

OUTSTANDING ART DIRECTION FOR A SERIES
• James J. Agazzi, production designer. Bill Harp, set decorator, *Moonlighting*. ABC.

**OUTSTANDING ART DIRECTION
FOR A MINISERIES OR A SPECIAL**
• Jan Scott, production designer. Jack
Taylor, art director. Edward J. McDonald,
set decorator, *I'll Be Home for Christmas.*
NBC.

**OUTSTANDING ART DIRECTION
FOR A VARIETY OR MUSIC PROGRAM**
• Bernie Yeszin, art director. Portia
Iversen, set decorator, *The Tracey Ullman
Show.* Fox.

**OUTSTANDING CINEMATOGRAPHY
FOR A SERIES**
• Roy H. Wagner, director of photography,
Quantum Leap. NBC.

**OUTSTANDING CINEMATOGRAPHY
FOR A MINISERIES OR A SPECIAL**
• Gayne Rescher, director of photography,
Shooter. NBC.

OUTSTANDING EDITING FOR A SERIES
(Single camera production)
• Steven J. Rosenblum, *thirtysomething.*
ABC.
(Multicamera production)
• Tucker Wiard, *Murphy Brown.* CBS.

**OUTSTANDING EDITING
FOR A MINISERIES OR SPECIAL**
(Single camera production)
• Peter Zinner, John F. Burnett, *War and
Remembrance.* ABC.
(Multicamera production)
• Mark D. West, "Gregory Hines' Tap
Dance in America," *Great Performances.*
PBS.

**OUTSTANDING TECHNICAL
DIRECTION/CAMERA/VIDEO FOR A SERIES**
• Robert G. Holmes, technical director.
Leigh V. Nicholson, John Repczynski,
Jeffrey Wheat, Rocky Danielson, Camera
operators. Thomas G. Timpidis, senior
video control, *Night Court.* NBC.

**OUTSTANDING TECHNICAL
DIRECTION/CAMERA/VIDEO
FOR A MINISERIES OR A SPECIAL**
• Ron Graft, technical director. Richard G.
Price, Kenneth Patterson, Greg Harms,
Camera operators. Mark Sanford, senior
video control, *The Meeting, American
Playhouse.* PBS.

OUTSTANDING SPECIAL VISUAL EFFECTS
• Charles Staffell, Martin Gutteridge,
effects supervisors. Bill Cruse, miniature
designer. Egil Woxholt, Bill Schrimer,
Godfrey Godar, directors of photography.
Simon Smith, Steve Anderson, Ed
Williams, miniature designers, *War and
Remembrance.* ABC.

**OUTSTANDING SOUND EDITING
FOR A SERIES**
• William Wistrom, supervising sound and
ADR editor. James Wolvington, Mace
Matiosian, Wilson Dyer, Guy Tsujimoto,
sound editors. Gerry Sackman, supervising
music editor, *Star Trek: The Next
Generation.* Syndicated.

**OUTSTANDING SOUND EDITING
FOR A MINISERIES OR A SPECIAL**
• David McMoyler, Supervising sound
editor. Joseph Melody, co-supervising
editor. Mark Steele, Rick Steele, Michael
J. Wright, Gary Macheel, Stephen Grubbs,
Mark Friedgen, Charles R. Beith, Scot A.
Tinsley, Karla Caldwell, George B. Bell,
G. Michael Graham, sound editors. Kristi
Johns, supervising ADR editor. Tom
Villano, Jamie Gelb, supervising music
editors, *Lonesome Dove.* CBS.

**OUTSTANDING SOUND MIXING
FOR A DRAMA SERIES**
• Chris Haire, rerecording mixer, dialogue.
Doug Davey, rerecording mixer, effects.
Richard Morrison, rerecording mixer,
music. Alan Bernard, sound mixer,
production, *Star Trek: The Next
Generation.* Syndicated.

**OUTSTANDING SOUND MIXING
FOR A COMEDY SERIES OR A SPECIAL**
• Klaus Landsberg, production mixer.
Craig Porter, Alan Patapoff, rerecording
mixers, *Night Court.* NBC.

**OUTSTANDING SOUND MIXING
FOR A VARIETY OR MUSIC SERIES
OR A SPECIAL**
• Robert Douglass, SFX mixer. David E.
Fluhr, rerecording mixer. Ed Greene,
production mixer. Larry Brown, music
mixer, *Kenny, Dolly, and Willie:
Something Inside So Strong.* NBC.

OUTSTANDING SOUND MIXING FOR A MINISERIES OR A SPECIAL
• Don Johnson, sound mixer. James L. Aicholtz, dialogue mixer. Michael Herbick, music mixer. Kevin O'Connell, sound effects mixer, *Lonesome Dove*. CBS.

OUTSTANDING SOUND MIXING FOR SPECIAL EVENTS
• Ed Greene, music production mixer. Don Worsham, dialogue production mixer. Carroll Pratt, production mixer audience reaction; Paul Sanweiss, production mixer, *The 31st Annual Grammy Awards*. CBS.

OUTSTANDING LIGHTING DIRECTION (ELECTRONIC) FOR A COMEDY SERIES
• Mark Levin, *Who's the Boss?* ABC.

OUTSTANDING LIGHTING DIRECTION (ELECTRONIC) FOR A DRAMA SERIES, VARIETY SERIES, MINISERIES, OR A SPECIAL
• Robert Andrew Dickinson, *The Magic of David Copperfield XI: The Explosive Encounter*. CBS.

(No awards were bestowed in the areas of engineering development, lighting direction for special events and achievement in graphic design, music for special events, or main title theme music.)

DAYTIME AWARDS
OUTSTANDING DRAMA SERIES
• *Santa Barbara*. Jill Farren Phelps, executive producer. Steven Kent, senior supervising producer. Charlotte Savitz, supervising producer. Julie Hanan Carruthers, Leonard Friedlander, producers. NBC.
All My Children. Stephen Schenkel, producer. Thomas de Villiers, Kristin Laskas Martin, coordinating producers. ABC.
As the World Turns. Robert Calhoun, Laurence Caso, executive producers. Kenneth Fitts, supervising producer. Christine S. Banas, John Valente, Lisa Anne Wilson, producers. CBS.
General Hospital. H. Wesley Kenney, executive producer. Jerry Balme, producer. Bob Bardo, coordinating producer. ABC.
Guiding Light. Joe Willmore, executive producer. Barbara Garshman, supervising producer. Robert Kochman, Kathlyn

Chambers, producers. Catherine Maher Smith, coordinating producer. CBS.
The Young and the Restless. William J. Bell, Sr., Edward Scott, executive producers. Tom Langan, producer. CBS.

OUTSTANDING LEAD ACTOR IN A DRAMA SERIES
• David Canary, *All My Children*. ABC.
Larry Bryggman, *As the World Turns*. CBS.
A Martinez, *Santa Barbara*. NBC.
James Mitchell, *All My Children*. ABC.
Douglass Watson, *Another World*. NBC.

OUTSTANDING LEAD ACTRESS IN A DRAMA SERIES
• Marcy Walker, *Santa Barbara*. NBC.
Jeanne Cooper, *The Young and the Restless*. CBS.
Elizabeth Hubbard, *As the World Turns*. CBS.
Susan Lucci, *All My Children*. ABC.

OUTSTANDING SUPPORTING ACTRESS IN A DRAMA SERIES
(Tie)
• Debbi Morgan, *All My Children*. ABC.
• Nancy Lee Grahn, *Santa Barbara*. NBC.
Jane Elliot, *Days of Our Lives*. NBC.
Robin Mattson, *Santa Barbara*. NBC.
Arleen Sorkin, *Days of Our Lives*. NBC.

OUTSTANDING SUPPORTING ACTOR IN A DRAMA SERIES
• Justin Deas, *Santa Barbara*. NBC.
Joseph Campanella, *Days of Our Lives*. NBC.
David Forsyth, *Another World*. NBC.
Quinn Redeker, *The Young and the Restless*. CBS.

OUTSTANDING DRAMA SERIES DIRECTING TEAM
• Frank Pacelli, Heather Hill, Randy Robbins, Rudy Vejar, directors. Betty Rothenberg, Kathryn Foster, associate directors, *The Young and the Restless*. CBS.
Paul Lammers, Jill Mitwell, Robert Schwarz, Maria Wagner, directors. Joel Aronowitz, Michael Kerner, associate directors, *As the World Turns*. CBS.
Joel Tator, director. Christine Magarian, Aviva Jacobs, associate directors, *Family Medical Center*. Syndicated.
Robert Scinto, Timothy Langtry, directors. Stuart Silver, associate director, *Loving*. ABC.
Larry Auerbach, Gary Bowen, Peter

Miner, David Pressman, directors. Andrea Giles Rich, Jim Sayegh, associate directors, *One Life to Live*. ABC.

OUTSTANDING DRAMA SERIES WRITING TEAM
• Charles Pratt, Jr., Anne Howard Bailey, head writers. Robert Guza, Jr., Courtney Simon, Lynda Myles, Patrick Mulcahey, Gary Tomlin, script writers. Josh Griffith, Jane Atkins, breakdown/script writers. Don Harary, breakdown writer, *Santa Barbara*. NBC.
Donna M. Swajeski, head writer. Chris Whitesell, breakdown writer. David Colson, Roger Newman, Fran Meyers, Carolyn Culliton, script writers, *Another World*. NBC.
Douglas Marland, head writer. Garin Wolf, John Kuntz, breakdown writers. Stephanie Braxton, Patti Dizenzo, Caroline Franz, Nancy Ford, associate writers, *As the World Turns*. CBS.
Pamela K. Long, head writer. Trent Jones associate head writer. Nancy Curlee, assistant head writer. Nancy Williams, Stephen Demorest, breakdown writers. Richard Culliton, Pete T. Rich, Melissa Salmons, N. Gail Lawrence, script writers, *Guiding Light*. CBS.

OTHER DAYTIME AWARD WINNERS
OUTSTANDING JUVENILE MALE IN A DRAMA SERIES
• Justin Gocke, *Santa Barbara*. NBC.

OUTSTANDING JUVENILE FEMALE IN A DRAMA SERIES
• Kimberly McCullough, *General Hospital*. ABC.

OUTSTANDING GAME/AUDIENCE PARTICIPATION SHOW
• *The $25,000 Pyramid*. Bob Stewart, executive producer. Anne Marie Schmitt, supervising producer. Francine Bergman, David Michaels, producers. CBS.

OUTSTANDING GAME SHOW HOST
• Alex Trebek, *Jeopardy!* Syndicated.

OUTSTANDING DIRECTING IN A GAME/AUDIENCE PARTICIPATION SHOW
• Dick Schneider, director, *Jeopardy!* Syndicated.

Sally Jessy Raphael credited the "nationwide explosion in talk" for her first Emmy after working 33 years in TV.

OUTSTANDING TALK/SERVICE PROGRAM
• *The Oprah Winfrey Show*. Debra DiMaio, executive producer. Oprah Winfrey, supervising producer. Ellen Rakieten, Dianne Hudson, Mary Kay Clinton, Angela Thame, Alice McGee, producers. Syndicated.

OUTSTANDING TALK/SERVICE SHOW HOST
• Sally Jessy Raphael, *Sally Jessy Raphael*. Syndicated.

OUTSTANDING DIRECTING IN A TALK/SERVICE SHOW
• Jim McPharlin, director, *The Oprah Winfrey Show*. Syndicated.

OUTSTANDING CHILDREN'S SERIES
• *Newton's Apple*. James Steinbach, executive producer. Lee Carey, Tacy Mangan, supervising producers. Lynne Reeck, producer. PBS.

OUTSTANDING CHILDREN'S SPECIAL
• "Taking a Stand," *ABC Afterschool Special*. Frank Doelger, executive producer. Roberta Rowe, producer. ABC.

OUTSAIND PERFORMER IN A CHILDREN'S SERIES
• Jim Varney, *Hey Vern, It's Ernest!* CBS.

OUTSTANDING DIRECTING IN A CHILDREN'S SERIES
• Matthew Diamond, director, *Shining Time Station*. PBS.
• Ozzie Alfonso, director, *3-2-1 Contact*. PBS.

OUTSTANDING WRITING IN A CHILDREN'S SERIES
• Norman Stiles, head writer. Nancy Sans, Luis Santeiro, Cathi Rosenberg-Turow, Belinda Ward, Sonia Manzano, Jeff Moss, Sara Compton, Judy Freudberg, David Korr, John Weidman, Tony Geiss, Emily Perl Kingsley, Mark Saltzman, Christian Clark, Jon Stone, writers, *Sesame Street*. PBS.

OUTSTANDING ANIMATED PROGRAM
• *The New Adventures of Winnie the Pooh*. Karl Geurs, producer/director. Mark Zaslove, story editor/writer. Bruce Talkington, Carter Crocker, writers. ABC.

SPECIAL CLASS PROGRAM AREA (Area award winners)
• *China: Walls and Bridges*. Jimmy R. Allen, Richard T. McCartney, executive producers. Robert Thornton, supervising producer and producer. ABC.
• *James Stewart's Wonderful Life*. Mary Frances Shea, executive producer. Phil Delbourgo, supervising producer. Dan Gurskis, producer. Cinemax.

OUTSTANDING MUSIC DIRECTION AND COMPOSITION
• Joe Raposo, music director/composer. Jeff Moss, Christopher Cerf, composers. Dave Conner, composer/arranger, *Sesame Street*. PBS.

OUTSTANDING MUSIC DIRECTION AND COMPOSITION FOR A DRAMA SERIES
• Jez Davidson, music director/composer. David Mathews, music director. David Kurtz, Jack Allocco, composers, *The Young and the Restless*. CBS.

OUTSTADING ART DIRECTION/SET DECORATION/SCENIC DESIGN
• Anthony Sabatino, William H. Harris, production designers. Phyllis Hofberg, Richard D. Bluhm, art directors, *Fun House*. Syndicated.

OUTSTANDING ART DIRECTION/SET DECORATION/SCENIC DESIGN FOR A DRAMA SERIES
• William Hultstrom, Norman Wadell, art directors. Joseph Bevacqua, Andrea Joel, Eric Fischer, set decorators, *The Young and the Restless*. CBS.

OUTSTANDING COSTUME DESIGN
• Calista Hendrickson, *Encyclopedia*. HBO.

OUTSTANDING COSTUME DESIGN FOR A DRAMA SERIES
• Margarita Delgado, Charles Schoonmaker, *Another World*. NBC.

OUTSTANDING MAKEUP
• Paul Gebbia, *Encyclopedia*. HBO.

OUTSTANDING MAKEUP FOR A DRAMA SERIES
• Carlos Yeaggy, John Maldonado, Dawn Marando, *Santa Barbara*. NBC.

OUTSTANDING HAIRSTYLING
• Andre Walker, *The Oprah Winfrey Show*. Syndicated.
• Yolanda Toussieng, Jerry Masone, *Pee-Wee's Playhouse*. CBS.

OUTSTANDING HAIRSTYLING FOR A DRAMA SERIES
• Janet Medford, Valerie Scott, *Santa Barbara*. NBC.

OUTSTANDING CINEMATOGRAPHY
• Ozzie Alfonso, Larry Engel, Howard Hall, Robert Leacock, Don Lenzer, Christophe Lanzenburg, Chuck Levey, Rick Malkames, Dyanna Taylor, Jeri Sopanen, *3-2-1 Contact*. PBS.

OUTSTANDING TECHNICAL DIRECTION/ELECTRONIC CAMERA/VIDEO CONTROL
• Ray Angona, technical director. Joseph Arvizu, Cesar Cabreira, Keeth Lawrence, Marnn Wagner, electronic camera. Allen Latter, video control, *The Price is Right*. CBS.

OUTSTANDING TECHNICAL DIRECTION/ELECTRONIC CAMERA/VIDEO CONTROL FOR A DRAMA SERIES
• Chuck Guzzi, technical director. Toby Brown, Ted Morales, Gordon Sweeney, Mike Glenn, electronic camera. Roberto Bosio, video control, *The Bold and the Beautiful*. CBS.

OUTSTANDING FILM EDITING
• Harvey Greenstein, Sam Pollard, Grace Tankersley, *3-2-1 Contact*. PBS.

OUTSTANDING FILM SOUND MIXING
• Jeff Haboush, Greg Russell, *Jim Henson's Muppet Babies*. CBS.

OUTSTANDING ACHIEVEMENT IN FILM SOUND EDITING
• Al Breitenbach, supervising editor. Ron Fedele, editor. Richard Allen, supervising music editor. Steve Williams, Ken Burton, sound effects editors. *Jim Henson's Muppet Babies*. CBS.
• Steve Michael, dialogue/ADR editor. Peter Cole, dialogue/music editor. Steve Kirklys, supervising sound effects editor. Ken Dahlinger, sound effects/ADR editor. Greg Teall, John Walker, sound effects editors, *Pee-Wee's Playhouse*. CBS.

OUTSTANDING IDEO-TAPE EDITING
• Charles Randazzo, Peter Moyer, David Pincus, Steve Purcell, *Pee-Wee's Playhouse*. CBS.

OUTSTANDING VIDEO-TAPE EDITING FOR A DRAMA SERIES
• Dan Brumett, Marc Beruti, *The Young and the Restless*. CBS.

OUTSTANDING LIVE & TAPE SOUND MIXING & SOUND EFFECTS
• Peter Miller, Rick Patterson, production mixers. Pam Bartella, Paul D. Collins, Ferne Friedman, Ken Hahn, Grant Maxwell, John Purcell, postproduction mixers, *3-2-1 Contact*. PBS.

OUTSTANDING LIVE & TAPE SOUND MIXING & SOUND EFFECTS FOR A DRAMA SERIES
• Scott Millan, Tommy Persson, audio mixers. Donald Henderson, Rafael O. Valentin, postproduction mixers. Maurice "Smokey" Westerfeld, Peter Romano, sound effects, *The Young and the Restless*. CBS.

OUTSTANDING LIGHTING DIRECTION
• Carl Gibson, lighting director, *Kids Incorporated*. Disney.

OUTSTANDING LIGHTING DIRECTION FOR A DRAMA SERIES
• Donna Larson, Alan Beacher, Dennis M. Size, lighting directors, *All My Children*. ABC.

OUTSTANDING GRAPHICS AND TITLE DESIGN
• Barbara Laszewski, animation designer. Joel Anderson, graphics artist, *Hey Vern, It's Ernest!* CBS.

(No awards were bestowed in the areas of writing or directing in special class.)

SPORTS AWARD WINNERS

OUTSTANDING LIVE SPORTS SERIES
• *1988 NCAA Basketball on CBS*. Ted Shaker, executive producer. Bob Dekas, lead producer. Robert Fishman, lead director. David Winner, studio producer. Michael Burks, Ed Goren, Bob Mansbach, Robert D. Stenner, George Veras, Mark Wolff, Stephanie Swafford, Daniel H. Forer, producers. Mike Arnold, Peter Bleckner, Larry Cavolina, Sandy Grossman, Andy Kindle, Bob Matina, John McDonough, directors. Richard Drake, Scott Johnson, Artie Kempner, Joan Papen, Suzanne Smith, Richard Zyontz, Eric Mann, Collen Kolibas, Michael Frank, Roy Hamilton, Steve Scheer, Lance Barrow, associate directors/associate producers. CBS.

OUTSTANDING LIVE SPORTS SPECIAL
• *Games of the XXIV Olympiad*. Michael Weisman, executive producer. Terry Ewert, coordinating producer. Bob Levy, coordinating director. David Banks, Doug Beeforth, Larry Cirillo, Rob Cowen, Peter C. Diamond, Ken Edmundson, Carla Engelman, John Filippelli, George Finkel, John Gilmartin, Stacey Gilmartin, John Gonzalez, Mickey Holden, Tom Huet, Jeff Hymes, Gary Jobson, Michael Klatt, Ralph Mellanby. Paul Miller, David Neal, Warren Pick, Ramon Plaza, Scott Rader, Tom Roy, Harriet Saltzman, Ellie Sanger-Keys, Ross Schneiderman, Jeff Simon, John Steele, producers. Frank Belmont, David Burchett, Mary Buta-Lomuscio, Dick Cline, John DeLisa, Jeff Goff, Bucky Gunts, J.D. Hansen, Tom Hastings, Bob Lanning, Jim Mellanby, Ralph Mole, Ted Nathanson, Andy Rosenberg, Leon Schweir, Brian Seip, Brian Sherriffe, Arlando Smith, Mark Warner, Mark Wolfson, directors. Glenn Adamo, Rick Diamond, video-tape producers. John LiBretto, David Hoffman, video-tape directors. Ken Aagaard, Jeff Kulliver, George Wenzel, operations producers. Rose Anderson, Karen

Beddingfield, Chris Bevilacqua, Jeff Blankman, Doug Brooker, Rob Buchanan, Tom Cheatham, Julie Chrisco, Joseph Fitzgerald, Lance Garrett, Kent Gordis, Lisa Hicks, Ted Howard, Jerome Ingram, Danny Meiseles, Gary Milkis, Rick Reed, Will Schwarz, Pam Shapiro, Jill Shepard, Lance Sherman, Kevin Smollon, Steve Turnberger, Shiela Vavasour, Howard Zryb, associate producers. Sharon Arnett, Steve Beim, Ray Bonasi, Peggy Burkhart, Paul Casey, Andrew Cheater, Margaret Collier, Kevin Cusick, Steve DeGroot, Dick Ellis, Susan Evans, Bob Gatley, Cary Ian Glotzer, Doug Grabert, Alan Kartun, Jay Kincaid, Mary Madeiras, Jim Mancuso, Dennis Mazzocco, Joe Michaels, Scott Moore, Douglas Myers, Joe Novello, Brian Orentreich, Sue Panisch, Norma Rios-Levy, Steve Rosen, Mike Sheehan, Hoard Singer, Ray Smaltz, Margaret Streeter-Lauck, Jennifer Walter, Al Wohl, Gail Zimmerman, Brooke Sessions, associate directors. NBC.

OUTSTANDING EDITED SPORTS SERIES
• *ABC's Wide World of Sports*. Geoffrey Mason, executive producer. Curt Gowdy, Jr., coordinating producer. Amy Sacks, associate coordinating producer. Mike Pearl, John Faratzis, Joel Feld, Peter Lasser, Bob Goodrich, Carol Lehti, Ned Simon, Kenneth Wolfe, producers. Craig Janoff, Jim Jennett, Larry Kamm, Bill Webb, Doug Wilson, Rob Beiner, directors. Bob Yalen, Steven Nagler, Margaret Streeter-Lauck, Emilie Deutsch, John McGuinness, Tony Tortorici, Jimmy Roberts, associate producers. Jamie Bravo, Dick Buffintop, Jeff Cohan, Katharine Cook, Vince DeDario, Earl "Woody" Freiman, Jack Graham, Ben Harvey, David Kiviat, Norm Samet, Toni Slotkin, Robert Cowen, Craig Bigelow, Cary Brown, associate directors. ABC.

OUTSTANDING EDITED SPORTS SPECIAL
• *Road to the Super Bowl '88*. Ed Sabol, executive producer. Steve Sabol, producer. Bob Angelo, Bob Smith, Phil Tuckett, Bob Ryan, Steve Seidman, Dave Douglas, Steve Sabol. Syndicated.

OUTSTANDING SPORTS PERSONALITY—HOST/PLAY BY PLAY
• Bob Costas. NBC.

OUTSTANDING SPORTS PERSONALITY—ANALYST/COMMENTARY
• John Madden. CBS.

SPECIAL CLASS: INDIVIDUAL ACHIEVEMENT
• Harry Coyle. NBC.

SPECIAL CLASS: PROGRAM ACHIEVEMENT
• *World Triathlon Championship—Nice, France*. Ted Shaker, executive producer. George Veras, coordinating producer. Daniel H. Forer, producer. Andy Kindle, director. Michael Frank, producer, features. David Banks, associate producer. CBS.
• *Iditarod Trail Sled Dog Race*. Ned Simon, producer. John Wilcox, director. David Kiviat, associate producer. ABC.
• *48 Hours: Showdown at Cheyenne*. Andrew Heyward, executive producer. Catherine S. Lasiewicz, senior producer. Lance Heflin, Brett Alexander, George Osterkamp, Nancy Solomon, John Blackstone, Victoria Corderi, Bernard Goldberg, Harry Smith, producers. Mary Foster, associate producer. CBS.

SPECIAL CLASS: INNOVATIVE TECHNICAL ACHIEVEMENT
• *XV Winter Olympic Games Special Camera Mount Project*. Larry Kamm, producer/director. Pierre de Lespinois, director. Joe DeBonis, technical consultant. Larry Gebhardt, Alan Teitel, cameramen. ABC.

PROGRAM AREA: FEATURES
• *Mike Tyson vs. Tony Tubbs* (feature: "The Tyson Invasion"). Ross Greenburg, executive producer. Rick Bernstein, producer. HBO.
• *Sportsworld Americana*. Michael Weisman, executive producer. Carla Engelman, coordinating producer. Harriet Saltzman, producer. J.D. Hansen, director. Dick Ellis, John Gilmartin, associate directors. NBC.

PROGRAM AREA: STUDIO SHOW
• *ESPN's "NFL Gameday."* Steven M. Bornstein, executive producer. Steve Anderson, director, production/coordinating producer. John A. Walsh, coordinating producer. Bob Rauscher, producer. Jeff Winn, director. Fred Christenson, Geoff Herman, Kevin Mihaly, Craig Mortali, Norbert Williamson, associate producers. ESPN.

PROGRAM AREA: SPORTS JOURNALISM
• *Games of the XXIV Olympiad*. Michael Weisman, executive producer. Terry Ewert, coordinating producer. Susan Adams, David Diaz, Paul Miller, Victor Solis, Sue Sprecher, John Steele, producers. Tom Cheatham, Julie Chrisco, Anthony Radizwill, associate producers. NBC.

PROGRAM AREA: PROMOTION
• *Calgary Olympic Campaign*. George Greenberg, executive producer. Robert G. Toms, coordinating producer. Cynthia Vannoy, Peter Van Roden, associate producers. Garland Simon, Audree Manley Rosburg, associate directors. ABC.

PROGRAM AREA: OPENINGS/CLOSES/TEASES
• *World Series Game Two*. Michael Weisman, executive producer. Harry Coyle, coordinating producer. Les Dennis, David Neal, producers. Doug Grabert, associate director. NBC.

ELECTRONIC CAMERAPERSONS
• *Tour de France*. Ken Woo, Pascal Charpentier, Andre Morize, Vic Frank, David Michaels, Nigel Reynolds. CBS.
• *1988 World Series*. Len Basile, Jim Bragg, Phil Cantrell, Eric Eisenstein, Rick Fox, Barry Frischer, Dave Hagen, John Hillyer, Tom Hogan, Cory Kimball, Cory Leible, Hugo Morelli, Jim Mott, Brian Phraner, Al Rice, Vickie Walker, Harry Weisman. NBC.

VIDEO-TAPE EDITING
• *XV Winter Olympic Games*. Harvey Beal, Martin Bell, William Bores, Stephan Cain, Steven Cali, Joseph Cangialosi, Vincent Catania, Natt Chomsky, Joseph Clark, Leo Cohen, Finbar Collins, Paul Colton, Robert Crump, Ildefonso Dejesus, Terri Edwards, Daniel Farrell, Ronald Feszchur, Joseph Finch, Robert Gaddey, Marvin Gench, Carol Gennarelli, Bruce Giarraffa, Barry Gingold, Nicholas Giordano, Frank Giugliano, Sal Giusto, Robert Grant, John Grella, Meribeth Hall, William Harris, James Holder, Steven Irori, Dean Irwin, Philip Jackson, Eddie Joseph, Frank Kaminski, Denise Kaufman, Hector Kicelian, Nicola Lepore, Patrick Malik, James McGiver, William McMillen, Thomas McMurray, Peter Mecca, Arthur Mireles, Francisco Morgan, Alex Moskovic, Manuel Moura, Dennis Murphy, Jesus O'Neil, Donald Palmore, Delores Palms, Paul Pecora, Donald Perhala, Pamela Peterson, Rory Reese, Louis Rende, Nathan Rogers, Rhonda Ruggieri, Rene Sanchez, Mario Schencman, Leonard Schneiderman, Michael Sclafani, Edward Seifert, Larry Shaw, Michael Siegel, Delmar Sills, Raymond Soroka, Ralph Soukis, William Stallone, Leo Stephan, George Stevens, Karen Stricherz, Patricia Sullivan, Louis Torino, John Tumino, Steve Ulrich, Arthur Volk, John Vuini, Badriyyah Waheed, Fredrick Weir, Michael Wenig, Thomas Wight, Glen Wolf, Leona Zeira, Henry Zimmer. ABC.

FILM CINEMATOGRAPHERS
• *Mutual of Omaha's Spirit of Adventure*. Mike Graber, Ron Peers, Beverly Johnson, Paul Sharpe, Gordy Waterman, camera. Dan Dominy, Mike Hoover, directors of photography. ABC.

FILM EDITING
• *Mutual of Omaha's Spirit of Adventure*. Angelo Bernarducci, Ted Winterburn, supervising film editors. Kris Liem, Tony Scandiffio, editors. ABC.

MUSIC
• *One Moment in Time*. John Bettis, composer. Narada Michael Walden, producer/arranger. Albert Hammond, lyricist. Whitney Houston, artist. NBC.

WRITING
• *Games of the XXIV Olympiad*. Michael Bass, Tom Brokaw, Jamie Carey, Jim Cefalo, Bob Costas, Frank Deford, Peter C. Diamond, Dick Enberg, Sam Flood, Gayle Gardner, Bryant Gumbel, Greg Lewis, Jane Pauley, Ahmad Rashad, Bruce Schoenfeld, Maria Shriver, Andrea Smith, Jeff Zucker, writers. NBC.

GRAPHICS
• *Games of the XXIV Olympiad*. Michael Weisman, executive producer. Terry Ewert, coordinating producer. Bob Levy, coordinating director. Scott Rader, director of graphic design. Stacey Gilmartin, manager of graphic design. Howard Zryb, associate producer-graphic design. Peter Savigny, lead artist. Terry Briegel, Wallace Covard, Paul Cormack, Ann

DeVilbiss, Ellen Denton, Steve Fastook, Dennis Gauthier, Michael Johnson, Peter Keating, Eileen Kim, Les Major, Paula Marass, Patrick McDonough, Irene Ostap, Kathryn Peaslee, Coleen Smith, graphic designers. NBC.

TECHNICAL TEAM REMOTE
• *XV Winter Olympic Games*. Technical supervisors team, technical directors team, electronic camerapersons team, video engineers team, video-tape operators team, audio engineers team, lighting directors team, graphics operators team. ABC
• *Tour de France*. Technical supervisors team, technical directors team, electronic camerapersons team, video engineers team, video-tape operators team, audio engineers team, lighting directors team, graphics operators team. CBS.
Games of the XXIV Olympiad. Technical supervisors team, technical directors team, electronic camerapersons team, video engineers team, video-tape operators team, audio engineers team, lighting directors team, graphics operators team. NBC.

TECHNICAL TEAM STUDIO
• *Games of the XXIV Olympiad*. Technical supervisors team, technical directors team, electronic camerapersons team, video engineers team, video-tape operators team, audio engineers team, lighting directors team, graphics operators team. NBC.

NEWS & DOCUMENTARY AWARD WINNERS
OUTSTANDING COVERAGE OF A SINGLE BREAKING NEWS STORY
(Programs)
• "The Tragedy of PanAm Flight 103," *CBS News*. Lane Venardos, executive producer. Steve Jacobs, Jack Kelly, Terrence Martin, senior producers. Allen Alter, Margery Baker, Steve Glauber, Carolyn Kresky, Jon Myerson, Marquita Pool, John Reade, Anne Reingold, Maureen Schoos, Doug Sefton, Pat Shevlin, Mary Walsh, Susan Zirinsky, producers. Dan Rather, anchor. CBS.

OUTSTANDING COVERAGE OF A SINGLE BREAKING NEWS STORY
(Segments)
• "Vincennes," *NBC Nightly News with Tom Brokaw*. Naomi Spinrad, producer. Fred Francis, correspondent. NBC.

OUTSTANDING BACKGROUND/ANALYSIS OF A SINGLE CURRENT STORY
(Programs)
• "Race for the Superconductor," *Nova*. Paula S. Apsell, executive producer. Linda Garmon, producer. PBS.
• *Burning Questions: The Poisoning of America*. Av Westin, executive producer. Stuart Schwartz, senior broadcost producer. Philip S. Bergman, senior producer. Clark Adams, Bryan Myers, Ann Opotowsky, Sylvia Patterson, Lisa Zeff, producers. Esther Zucker, coordinating producer. Mark Rosenwasser, editorial producer. Greg Dobbs, Jed Duvall, Tom Schell, John Quinones, Ken Kashiwahara, correspondents. Hugh Downs, anchor. ABC.
• "Nightmare Next Door," *48 Hours*. Andrew Heyward, executive producer. Catherine Lasiewicz, senior producer. Barbara Baylor, Lyne Bowens, Linda Martin, Stefan Moore, George Osterkamp, David Schneider, Ira Sutow, producers. Betsy Aaron, Bernard Goldberg, Bob McNamara, Terence Smith, correspondents. CBS.
• "*Nightline* in the Holy Land: Town Meeting," *ABC News Nightline*. Richard Kaplan, executive producer. Deborah Leff, William Moore, Betsy West, senior producers. Sigal Eadan, Lynn Eshel, Kyle Gibson, Jacques Grenier, Richard Harris, Ali Kaden, Marie MacLean, Herb O'Connor, Margaret Koval, Gil Pimentel, Dena Samach, Bill Seamans, Susan Sigel, Heather Vincent, Scott Willis, Terry Wrong, producers. Robert Jordan, project producer. Bill Blakemore, Barry Dunsmore, John Laurence, Dean Reynolds, Judd Rose, James Walker, correspondents. Ted Koppel, anchor/managing editor. ABC.

OUTSTANDING BACKGROUND ANALYSIS OF A SINGLE CURRENT STORY
(Segments)
• "Still on the Wrong Track," *20/20*. Martin Clancy, producer. Tom Jarriel, correspondent. ABC.
• "Fall from Grace," *20/20*. Janice Tomlin, producer. Tom Jarriel, correspondent. ABC.
• "A Formula for Tragedy," *20/20*. Rob Wallace, producer. Tom Jarriel, correspondent. ABC.

Outstanding Investigative Journalism (Programs)

• "Murder on the Rio San Juan," *Frontline*. David Fanning, executive producer. Charles Stuart, Marcia Izaguirre Vivancos, producers. PBS.

Outstanding Investigative Journalism (Segments)

• "Men of God: Borrowing on Faith," *West 57th*. Jane Stone, producer. Meredith Vieira, correspondent. CBS.
• "Cutting Corners, Costing Lives," *20/20*. Mary Whittington, Sharon Young, coproducers. Tom Jarriel, correspondent. ABC.

Outstanding Interview/Interviewers (Programs)

• "Masks of Eternity," *Joseph Campbell and the Power of Myth with Bill Moyers*. Joan Konner, Alvin H. Perlmutter, executive producers. Catherine Tatge, producer. Bill Moyers, correspondent. PBS.

Outstanding Interview/Interviewers (Segments)

• "Austrian President Kurt Waldheim," *ABC News Nightline*. Robert Jordan, senior producer. Kyle Gibson, producer. Ted Koppel, Pierre Salinger, reporters. ABC.
• "Soviet Dentist," *The CBS Evening News with Dan Rather*. Tom Bettag, executive producer. Robert Anderson, Peter Schweitzer, producers. Charles Kuralt, correspondent. CBS.
• "Edward Teller," *60 Minutes*. Ira Rosen, producer. Mike Wallace, correspondent. CBS.
• "Cara's Story," *60 Minutes*. Marti Galovic Palmer, producer. Morley Safer, correspondent.

Outstanding Coverage of a Continuing News Story (Programs)

• "Election '88 Wrapup," *CE Newsmagazine*. Harry Moses, executive producer. Marion Goldin, Allan Maraynes, producers. Laurel Barclay, Suki Cheong, Jonathan Zachary, corresponents. PBS.
• "48 Hours on Gang Street," *48 Hours*. Andrew Heyward, executive producer. Steve Glauber, senior producer. Brett Alexander, Tim Clifford, Lance Heflin,

David Schneider, Nancy Solomon, Ira Sutow, producers. Jerry Bowen, Victoria Corderi, David Dow, Bernard Goldberg, correspondents. CBS.
• "Faith Under Fire," *48 Hours*. Andrew Heyward, executive producer. Al Briganti, senior producer. Brett Alexander, Lyne Bowens, Tim Clifford, Linda Martin, George Osterkamp, Denise Schreiner, Ira Sutow, Clem Taylor, producers. Frank Currier, Bob Faw, Charlie Rosen, Bill Whitaker, correspondents. CBS.

Outstanding Coverage of a Continuing News Story (Segments)

• "Palestinian Uprising," *NBC Nightly News with Tom Brokaw*. Tom Keenan, Jim Maceda, Victor Solis, producers. Martin Fletcher, correspondent. NBC
• "Sudan Famine," *NBC Nightly News with Tom Bokaw*. Bishr Eltouni, Pat Thompson, producers. Jim Bitterman, corresponent. NBC.
• "Pat Robertson," *West 57th*. Jane Stone, producer. Meredith Vieira, correspondent. CBS.
• "Homeless in America: Suffer the Children," *West 57th*. Glen Silber, producer. Meredith Vieira, correspondent. CBS.

Outstanding Informational, Cultural, or Historical Programming (Programs)

• "Can the Vatican Save the Sistine Chapel?" *Nova*. Paula S. Apsell, executive producer. Susanne Simpson, producer. PBS.
• *JFK: in His Own Words*. Peter W. Kunhardt, producer. HBO.

Outstanding Informational, Cultural, or Historical Programming (Segments)

• "Marriage License Bureau," *West 57th*. Ray Farkas, producer. CBS.
• "Children in Crisis: Saving Face," *West 57th*. Alan B. Goldberg, producer. Meredith Vieira, corresponent. CBS.
• "Broadway Baby," *West 57th*. Pauline Canny, producer. Bob Sirott, correspondent. CBS.

SPECIAL CLASSIFICATION
FOR OUTSTANDING NEWS
AND DOCUMENTARY ACHIEVEMENT
• *We Shall Overcome.* Jim Brown, Ginger
Brown, Harold Leventhal, George Stoney,
producers. PBS.
• "Living with AIDS," *Point of View.* Marc
Weiss, executive producer. Tina
DeFeliciantonio, producer. PBS.

SPECIAL CLASSIFICATION
FOR OUTSTANDING NEWS
AND DOCUMENTARY ACHIEVEMENT
(Individuals)
• *The Unquiet Death of Eli Creekmore.*
David Davis, producer. PBS.

OUTSTANDING WRITING
• Anthony Potter, Eric Sevareid, "Eric
Sevareid: Not So Wild a Dream," *The
American Experience.* PBS.
• Stanley Breeden, "Australia's Twilight of
the Dreamtime," *National Geographic
Special.* PBS.

OUTSTANDING DIRECTING
• Roger Goodman, *"Nightline* in the Holy
Land: Town Meeting," *ABC News
Nightline.* ABC.

OUTSTANDING RESEARCHING
• Marlon T. Riggs, *Ethnic Notions.* PBS.

OUTSTANDING CINEMATOGRAPHY
• Norris Brock, "Inside the Soviet Circus,"
National Geographic Special. PBS.

OUTSTANDING ELECTONIC CAMERAWORK
• Jim Douglas, "Greetings from the North
Shore," *America Today.* PBS.

OUTSTANDING TAPE EDITING
• Warren Lustig, "1988: Year in Review,"
The CBS Evening News with Dan Rather.
CBS.
• Jess Bushyhead, "1988: The Year in
Review," *Today.* NBC.

OUTSTANDING FILM EDITING
• Holly K. Fine, "The Wall Within," *CBS
Reports.* CBS.
• Margot Francis, Joan Morris, *Sarafina!
Words of Freedom ... Songs of Hope.*
NBC.

OUTSTANDING SOUND
• Rick Patterson, "Inside the Soviet
Circus," *National Geographic Special.* PBS.

• Fred Burnham, Francis Daniel, Marc
Gilmartin, Ken King, Lawrence
Loewinger, Glen Marullo, David Mathew,
Allen Patapoff, Mark Roy, "The Geometry
of Life," *The Infinite Voyage.* PBS.

OUTSTANDING LIGHTING DIRECTION
• Martin S. Dick, *West 57th.* CBS.

OUTSTANDING GRAPHIC DESIGN
• John Andrews, Todd Ruff, *Adam Smith's
Money World.* PBS.

OUTSTANDING TITLE SEQUENCES
• Richard Greenberg, *USA Today: The
Television Show.* Syndicated.

OUTSTANDING ART DIRECTION
• Jeremy Conway, *USA Today: The
Television Show.* Syndicated.

OUTSTANDING MUSIC
• Charles Kuskin, *The American
Experience.* PBS.
• Lee Holdridge, "The Explorers: A
Century of Discovery," *National
Geographic Special.* PBS.

INTERNATIONAL AWARD WINNERS
OUTSTANDING DOCUMENTARY
• *The Last Seven Months of Anne Frank.*
Willy Lindwer, producer, audio visual arts,
writer, director. TROS-Television,
Netherlands.

OUTSTANDING DRAMA
• *A Very British Coup.* Ann Skinner, Sally
Hibbin, Skreba Films, producers. Mick
Jackson, director. Alan Plater, adapted
screenplay. Chris Mullin, author. Channel
Television, U.K.

OUTSTANDING PERFORMING ARTS
• *ABC of British Music.* Ken Russell,
producer/director.London Weekend Television (LWT), U.K.

OUTSTANDING POPULAR ARTS
• *The New Statesman.* Yorkshire
Television, U.K.

OUTSTANDING CHILDREN'S AND YOUNG
PEOPLE'S PROGRAM
• *Touch the Sun: Captain Johnno.* Jayne
Ballantyne, producer. Mario Andreacchio,
director. Rob George, writer. Australian
Children's Television Foundation,
Australia.

INTERNATIONAL DIRECTORATE AWARD
• Vittorio Boni

INTERNATIONAL FOUNDERS AWARD
• Goar Mestre

SPECIAL AWARDS
OUTSTANDING ACHIEVEMENT IN THE SCIENCE OF TELEVISION ENGINEERING
• TRW LSJ Products Inc
• Magni Systems, Inc.
• RTS Systems, Inc.
• Ray M. Dolby
• CBS
• Ampex Corporation
• Sony Corporation

NATIONAL AWARD FOR COMMUNITY SERVICE
• *Grief's Children.* WMAQ-TV, Chicago.

A.T.A.S. GOVERNORS AWARD
• Lucille Ball

N.A.T.A.S. TRUSTEES AWARD
• Peggy Charren, Children's Television.

Adhering to *Murphy* and *Law*

The comedy category was certainly no laughing matter this year.

Controversies abounded before the Emmycast. Headlines in the trade papers decried the omission of Roseanne Barr and her number one-rated sitcom *Roseanne* from the list of nominees. The press's favorite martyr of last year, Delta Burke of *Designing Women,* was nominated for comedy series actress this year unlike in past ones, but the show's militant fans wanted more. Rooting for her victory, they marched outside the Pasadena Civic Auditorium with campaign placards that insisted, "Delta Burke Always the Best!" *The Simpsons* had been named Outstanding Animated Series at the creative arts banquet held the day before the Emmycast, but its creators and vocal fans among the press weren't overly impressed: They wanted the show to compete against the "grown-up" comedies in prime time like *Cheers.* (An interesting irony might occur if it did: Nancy Cartwright, who plays the voice of Bart Simpson, could be nominated for best actor.) The show wasn't eligible to run for best comedy series, however, said A.T.A.S., because of the rules, which were established by Hollywood's leading animators. And, speaking of *Cheers*, its fans were also unhappy and wanted to know: When will the nine-time nominated Ted Danson ever get that Emmy?

Danson's costar Kirstie Alley made a point of ribbing him about the issue early on in the ceremony, likening his bad luck with Emmy to the misfortune of a guy who takes a "tease" to the drive-in movie. One hour later Danson had the last laugh when his nine-year quest for the gold was finally fulfilled.

His nine-year quest finally over, Cheers's Ted Danson said, "I guess you'll be saying 'you've been robbed' to some other boy."

He responded to one of the most rousing ovations ever given an Emmy champ by saying, "This is exactly what happened to me at the drive-in when I first got lucky. They all stood up and applauded." When the cheering died down, Danson said in a more serious tone, "I guess you'll be saying 'you've been robbed' to some other boy. I'll miss that."

Cheers held onto the supporting actress category from last year when Bebe Neuwirth, who plays an uptight psychiatrist among the clientele of Boston's craziest saloon, picked up where Rhea Perlman left off. But not returning was the most important award *Cheers* took last year (and in 1983 and '84): best comedy series.

In the second biggest upset of the night, *Murphy Brown* proved its might as a hit new humor program by taking both the series award and the best actress statuette — again — for star Candice Bergen, who plays a headstrong Washington, D.C., TV reporter. Bergen referred to her competition when she picked up her acting prize. "If a woman is known by the company she keeps, I can't imagine being in better company than with them," she said. Then remembering one of the other nominees in particular, she added, "Delta's going to be waiting for me in the parking lot." *Murphy* also won an acting prize for guest star Jay Thomas.

What *The Washington Post* called the "jaw dropper" of the night involved the year's most perplexing new show: the avant-garde cult sensation *Twin Peaks*, which dramatized director David Lynch's bizarre vision of life in a murderous logging town in the Pacific Northwest. *Peaks* was the most talked-about new show of its day, a darling of the arts crowd and a sensation at the Television Critics Association's Awards. It was clearly the favorite to take the most Emmys, too, having started out with the most series nods: 14, compared to 13 for runner-up *L.A. Law*.

But in the tradition of *Miami Vice*'s and *Moonlighting*'s first date with Emmy some years earlier, the soon-to-be-canceled *Twin Peaks* ended up unlucky. "Emmy Voters Uphold the *Law*," was the towering headline in *The Hollywood Reporter* the next day, announcing the return of last year's champ instead. Critics like John J. O'Connor of *The New York Times* were outraged: "This year they shortchanged *Twin Peaks*. Last year it was *Lonesome Dove* ... and the continuing refusal to recognize even the existence of Roseanne Barr smacks of middle-class stuffiness."

When *L.A. Law* ended up making a molehill out of *Twin Peaks*, it was an act of sweet revenge. Since it went on the air in 1986, *L.A. Law* had never been surpassed by another show in total number of nominations. Now it was not only topped by *Peaks*, but *Peaks* was so weird and controversial that it was getting most of the headlines. "Anytime a show goes into its fourth year you begin to get ignored by the press," acknowledged *L.A. Law*'s executive producer David Kelley as he accepted the series honor, "so we weren't surprised to see the attention go elsewhere." The fact that the award came back despite the huge media pressure in *Peaks*'s favor, made the Emmy, he added, "all the more reward." Also honored were the show's writers and four-time supporting actor nominee Jimmy Smits as the firm's firebrand Hispanic lawyer. "I have to thank God, my higher power," Smits said while accepting it, "for giving me the strength." *Peaks*, by comparison, won only two awards — for editing and costume design.

L.A. Law *made a* molehill *out of* Twin Peaks.

Also welcomed back from the ranks of past winners was Peter Falk, who returned to claim his fourth Emmy as *Columbo* and the fifth of his career. "It's my birthday," the 63-year-old champ informed the audience while up at the podium. "This morning I got three shirts and a dozen golf balls. To get this thing at any age is a nice thing, but when you hit 41 ..." Falk also said he considered himself an underdog, but then added, "Ma, you were right! I'll never argue with you again!" Backstage, when asked what he has done with all his statuettes at home, he said, "My wife uses them for wig racks."

thirtysomething's Patricia Wettig was named best supporting actress in 1987,

The Simpsons *was hailed as Outstanding Animated Series, but fans continued to press for its chance at best comedy show.*

---

but now returned as best lead actress since her character's role had been expanded to accommodate a dramatic bout with ovarian cancer. In what *The Washington Post* called "one of the most emotional moments of the evening," Wettig said, "I would really like to thank all the women with cancer who have shared their stories with me so wholeheartedly. I shared their insights and their fears. I truly salute their courage." *thirtysomething* also won a director's honor.

Women sharing intimate life-and-death experiences also contributed to the victory of *China Beach*'s Marg Helgenberger, who modeled her performance as an army nurse in Vietnam on the insights offered her by those who served on the battlelines. She thanked them all and then ABC and Warner Bros. "for keeping us on another season," adding, "You won't regret it." One year later

China Beach was canceled.

The year's best miniseries was *Drug Wars: The Camarena Story*, which dramatized the tragedy of slain drug enforcement agent Enrique Camarena. Accepting the award, producer Michael Mann (formerly of *Miami Vice*) spoke of Camarena, saying, "In his work as a D.E.A. agent, he was just a man, but in his martyrdom he came to mean so much more. This is a victory for him, too."

Just like last year, there was a tie for best drama special. The joint winners were *The Incident,* which starred Walter Matthau as a small-town attorney who must defend a German prisoner-of-war suspected of murder during World War II, and *Hallmark Hall of Fame*'s *Caroline?*, a mystery about a young woman, presumed dead, who returns to her family after a 15-year absence in order to claim an inheritance. Performance awards went to Hume Cronyn (best actor) and Vincent Gardenia (best supporting actor) for *Age-Old Friends*, which offered hope, said Gardenia, to seniors who feel "old, lonely, and frightened."

Barbara Hershey was voted best actress for her role as a woman who murders her neighbor with an axe in *A Killing in a Small Town.* "When I first read the script I was amazed it was going to be on television," Hershey said in her acceptance remarks. "It is uncompromisingly dark." She added that she hoped its success would encourage producers to do "other films of an unusual nature." Eva Marie Saint was hailed as best supporting actress for her role in the TV adaptation of Dominique Dunne's bestseller *People Like Us*, about low deeds in high society. Saint thanked her daughter, "who works at NBC, read the script, and thought of her mom to play Lil." Backstage, the former Oscar winner for *On the Waterfront*, said, "It's a nice change to play a rich bitch."

"One major surprise" of the night,

according to *The New York Times*, was the winner of best variety series, *In Living Color*, Fox's irreverent hit show that featured a mostly black cast spoofing hot issues such as racial prejudice and gay stereotypes. *In Living Color* was the creation of Keenen Ivory Wayans, who includes his talented siblings in the show's ensemble cast. "Above all, I'd like to thank my family," Wayans said, appropriately, while clutching his Emmy. "My mother and father are here tonight. This is for you, Ma!"

It was last year's winner, *The Tracey Ullman Show*, which had been considered the favorite again. The *Ullman Show* was a precursor of variety show hipness: it even launched *The Simpsons*, which was shown on the program originally as a series of cartoon vignettes. Now that her series was canceled, Ullman at least salvaged a performance trophy for herself and three crafts awards for her show. "Oh, blimey, this brings it all full circle," Ullman said accepting her performance award. "I miss the show a whole lot. Maybe I should have taken that two minutes in the middle of *The Simpsons*. I breast-fed the little devils."

Winner of the best variety special was *Sammy Davis, Jr.'s 60th Anniversary Celebration*, a tribute to the singer involving so many legendary showbiz names that its producers said they had to turn down President Reagan's request to participate, too.

"All in all, not a bad show," said *The New York Times* about the Emmys. It "was smartly paced, each of the three hours featuring a different host: Candice Bergen, Jay Leno and Jane Pauley ... There was no formal comedy monologue, but Mr. Leno managed to score nicely with his scattershot quips. [Supreme Court nominee] Judge David H. Souter, he said, was sent an Emmy ballot but didn't have an opinion." Other highlights included a tribute to the recently deceased Muppeteer Jim Henson and the bestowal of a Governors Award to former ABC Chairman Leonard Goldenson.

Fox scored a coup by signing another three-year agreement to broadcast the Emmy ceremony despite the fact that it had just delivered the award show's lowest viewership ever: a 8.2 rating and 14 share. The once-a-year spectacle celebrating the best of professional TV entertainment was even beaten by, of all things, a weekly episode of *America's Funniest Home Videos*.

DAYTIME AWARDS

As its appointed host, Oprah Winfrey explained what the daytime Emmycast was to anyone witnessing the event for the first time. It's "the show with more tears than a soap," she said, "more prizes than a game show, more thanks than a prayer meeting, and more people with more things to say about other people than even *The Oprah Winfrey Show*."

In an unprecedented winning streak, *Santa Barbara* retained its crown for the third year in a row as the best daytime drama series (only *The Young and the Restless* had more total series wins: four), while also picking up honors for its lead actor A Martinez (as Cruz Castillo), supporting actor Henry Darrow (as Rafael Castillo), and its director. What made *Santa Barbara* such a surefire hit? Humor, *TV Guide* once said, calling the lighthearted soaper "unquestionably the liberating force in daytime comedy." Its characters, the magazine noted, included "a cross-dressing mobster; a one-eyed, peg-legged psychopath; a Shakespeare-spouting boozehead; a 4'3" phony psy-

"If my daughter Allison is watching: Yes, mom won the enemy award."

A record third award for Guiding Light*'s Kim Zimmer: "They have to control me every so often. I like to chew the scenery."*

chic; and a white-trash mama who robbed a sperm bank."

"Humor is no joke to us," cocreator and head writer Bridget Dobson told *TV Guide*. "We take it *very* seriously."

A very serious moment of the daytime competition came when *Guiding Light* star Kim Zimmer (as Reva Shayne Lewis) was named best actress for a third time, tying the record for most wins by a lead performer previously held by Helen Gallagher (Maeve Ryan of *Ryan's Hope*) and David Canary (Adam and Stuart Chandler on *All My Children*). She thanked "all the men in Reva's life because they helped me win this thing," then went on to pay tribute to the rest of the cast and crew, particularly the writers and director "for letting me do the things that I do," she said. "They have to control me every so often. I like to chew the scenery." The award marked a fond farewell for Zimmer. "I'm leaving *Guiding Light*," she noted, "but I've always

said 'never say never again' and I will be back someday."

All My Children's Julia Barr was considered a strong candidate for supporting actress because her character, Brooke English, "was at the center of a tortuous love triangle," noted *TV Guide*. When the magazine was proved right, Barr gave one of the most touching acceptance speeches in Emmy history: "Because life is not a soap opera — thank God — I want to thank my husband Richie," she said, adding, "and if my daughter Allison is watching: yes, mom won the enemy award." *All My Children* also took the prize for best juvenile female for Cady McClain (as Dixie Martin).

The winner of last year's statuette for best talk show, Sally Jessy Raphael, saw her eponymous program take the top series prize while she lost the hosting trophy to first-time Emmy winner Joan Rivers, who broke down and cried as she accepted it.

"Probably no award has done so much for any person in the history of these awards," N.A.T.A.S. president John Cannon once said, commenting on Rivers's acceptance speech. Those who witnessed it, like Cannon, say they will never forget it. "Her winning was a surprise against stiff competition," he added. "Her husband had committed suicide a year and half before. Her [late night talk] show on Fox had just been canceled. Winning it meant so much to her."

"Two years ago I couldn't get a job in this business," Rivers said after cutting short her cheerful opening remarks. "My income dropped to 1/16th of what it was before I was fired and people said I would never work again and my husband, as you know, had a breakdown. It's so sad that he's not here because it was my husband, Edgar Rosenberg, who always said, 'You can turn things around' and except for one terrible moment in a hotel room in Philadelphia when he forgot that ..." Her voice trailed off as she choked back tears, adding, "This is really for him because he was with me from the beginning and I'm so sorry he's not here." She then hurried off the stage, sobbing.

The emcee of this year's best game show, *Jeopardy!*, won the honors as best host last year, but came back this year with *two* nominations — one for *Jeopardy!* and the other as host of *Master Concentration*. When he tied (for *Jeopardy!*) with *The Price is Right*'s Bob Barker (who wasn't in attendance), Alex Trebek said, "I can't tell you how scared I was today with two out of the three nominations. If I hadn't won, I don't think I'm a good enough actor to sit out there and put a smile on my face." Trebek noted that his Emmy capped a banner year: 1990 marked his 30th anniver-

Best lead actor A Martinez of Santa Barbara, *voted best daytime series for an unprecedented three years in a row.*

sary of being in television; he just turned 50 — and just got married, too.

Sesame Street took six awards, but not the most prestigious. The program prize went to *Reading Rainbow*, the innovative series hosted by LeVar Burton that encouraged children to read. A *CBS Schoolbreak Special*, "A Matter of Conscience," was acclaimed best children's special.

A Lifetime Achievement Award was bestowed to Mark Goodson, the creator of such hit game shows as *I've Got a Secret* and *What's My Line?* Accepting his statuette, Goodson said that he'd "dedicated a lifetime to a genre of television that has often been underestimated and misunderstood — the game show."

SPORTS AWARDS

Veteran broadcaster Jim McKay was no stranger to Emmy trophies, but he was now given one more at the festivities staged at New York's Sheraton Center — the first Lifetime Achievement Award ever bestowed in sports. It was a salute to McKay's distinguished career at *ABC's Wide World of Sports* and his coverage of the Olympics that once even earned him a news award when he was one of the few reporters on the scene as terrorists attacked Israeli athletes at the Munich games in 1972. Following an introductory tribute by producer Roone Arledge, "a short retrospective biography of McKay with video clips of memorable broadcasts brought an appreciative audience to their feet," reported the N.A.T.A.S. newsletter. "A highlight of the video was Jim singing a memorable rendition of 'The Same Ol' Shillelagh My Father Brought From Ireland.'"

ABC's coverage of the Indianapolis 500 was the winner as best live sports special, while there was a tie for the first time in the category of live sports series, with the trophy being shared by *ABC's NFL Monday Night Football* and ESPN's *Speedworld*. ESPN's victory was especially sweet since America's largest cable network would be broadcasting the sports awards for the first time next year. (This year, Raycom continued to syndicate its broadcast.) In all, ESPN won three statuettes, compared to one for NBC, five for CBS, and 15 for ABC.

The syndicated show *This is the NFL* was voted Outstanding Edited Series, and the prize for edited sports special went to *Trans-Antarctica! The International Expedition.*

For the fourth year in a row, John Madden was chosen Outstanding Sports Personality/Analyst, bringing his total of Emmy wins to seven. Al Michaels's Emmy as Outstanding Sports Personality/ Host was his second.

NEWS & DOCUMENTARY AWARDS

The most newsworthy of all the news awards was the first ever won by the Cable News Network — for its coverage of the student uprising in Beijing, China's Tiananmen Square. Accepting the prize, anchor Bernard Shaw dedicated it to "the people who lived and bled an event that their government still says did not exist." He shared the award for Outstanding Instant Coverage of a Single Breaking News Story with the *NBC News Special* "China in Crisis."

The black-tie dinner at the ballroom of the Waldorf-Astoria in New York was the first news awards show in years that wasn't dominated by PBS programs. CBS, in fact, led in nominations with 37 to 27 for PBS, but they both ended up with 10 awards. Among CBS's most notable wins were two for *The CBS Evening News with Dan Rather* (includ-

ing one for its segment "China: The Ancient, The New") and another for *48 Hours*'s "Hurricane Watch." Co-executive producer Andrew Heyward accepted the latter prize in the memory of the recently deceased CBS News chief David Burke, who, he said, "knew a good hurricane when he saw one." CBS was also awarded for its interviews with film star Marlon Brando and former Texas senator John Tower.

The Hollywood Reporter noted: "Perennial Emmy collector *60 Minutes* was left out in the cold although it was nominated for six segments, including its November 1989 broadcast 'Hollywood and the Mob.'"

PBS's top winning programs and segments included its *AIDS Quarterly*, hosted by Peter Jennings, and two acknowledgments for Bill Moyers's thoughtful specials.

ABC's top-rated nightly news program failed to nab any prizes at all while its five-month-old *Primetime Live* series garnered three, including one for its investigative coverage of "PanAm Flight 103" and "Prisoners of Care," a probe into private care facilities for mental patients. The network's *20/20* was honored for its interview with actress Patty Duke, who talked frankly about her bout with psychological depression.

In addition to the statuette for *China in Crisis*, NBC was also rewarded for its *NBC News* interview with President Reagan and its *Nightly News* coverage of the fall of communism in Romania.

1989–90

The prime-time ceremony was broadcast on the Fox network from the Pasadena Civic Auditorium on September 16, 1990, for prime-time programs telecast between June 1, 1989, and May 31, 1990. The creative arts awards were bestowed on September 15, 1990. Daytime awards broadcast on ABC from New York's

Marriott Marquis Hotel on June 28, 1990, for programs aired between March 6, 1989, and March 5, 1990. The sports awards for 1989 were presented April 23, 1990. News & documentary awards for 1989 were presented on September 12, 1990.

PRIME-TIME PROGRAM AWARDS
OUTSTANDING DRAMA SERIES

• *L.A. Law*. David E. Kelley, executive producer. Rick Wallace, co-executive producer. William M. Finkelstein, supervising producer. Elodie Keene, Michael M. Robin, producers. Alice West, coordinating producer. Robert M. Breech, coproducer. NBC.

China Beach. John Sacret Young, executive producer. John Wells, Georgia Jeffries, supervising producers. Mimi Leder, Fred Gerber, Geno Escarrega, producers. ABC.

Quantum Leap. Donald P. Bellisario, executive producer. Deborah Pratt, Michael Zinberg, co-executive producers. Paul M. Belous, Robert Wolterstorff, Scott Shepherd, Harker Wade, supervising producers. Chris Ruppenthal, Paul Brown, Jeff Gourson, coproducers. NBC.

thirtysomething. Edward Zwick, Marshall Herskovitz, executive producers. Scott Winant, supervising producer. Richard Kramer, producer. Ellen S. Pressman, coproducer. Lindsley Parsons III, coordinating producer. ABC.

Twin Peaks. Mark Frost, David Lynch, executive producers. Gregg Fienberg, David J. Latt, producers. ABC.

OUTSTANDING COMEDY SERIES

• *Murphy Brown*. Diane English, Joel Shukovsky, executive producers. Korby Siamis, consulting producer. Tom Seeley, Norm Gunzenhauser, Russ Woody, Gary Dontzig, Steven Peterman, Barnet Kellman, producers. Deborah Smith, coproducer. CBS.

Cheers. James Burrows, Glen Charles, Les Charles, executive producers. Cheri Eichen, Bill Steinkellner, Phoef Sutton, co-executive producers. Tim Berry, producer. Andy Ackerman, coproducer. NBC.

Designing Women. Linda Bloodworth-Thomason, Harry Thomason, executive producers. Pam Norris, supervising producer. Douglas Jackson, Tommy Thompson, producers. David Trainer, coproducer. CBS.

The Golden Girls. Paul Junger Witt, Tony Thomas, Susan Harris, executive producers. Marc Sotkin, Terry Hughes, co-executive producers. Tom Whedon, Philip Jayson Lasker, supervising producers. Gail Parent, Martin Weiss, Robert Bruce, producers. Tracy Gamble,

Richard Vaczy, coproducers. NBC.

The Wonder Years. Bob Brush, executive producer. Bob Stevens, Jill Gordon, co-executive producers. Matthew Carlson, Michael Dinner, Ken Topolsky, producers. Kerry Ehrin, coproducer. ABC.

OUTSTANDING MINISERIES

• *Drug Wars: The Camarena Story*. Michael Mann, executive producer. Richard Brams, co-executive producer. Christopher Canaan, Rose Schacht, Ann Powell, supervising producers. Branko Lustig, producer. Mark Allan, coproducer. NBC.

Blind Faith. Susan Baerwald, Dan Wigutow, executive producers. Daniel Franklin, coproducer. NBC.

Family of Spies. Jennifer Alward, Gerald W. Abrams, executive producers. Jonathan Bernstein, producer. William Dunne, coproducer. CBS.

The Kennedys of Massachusetts. Edgar J. Scherick, Susan G. Pollock, executive producers. Gary Hoffman, co-executive producer. Lynn Raynor, producer. Michael Barnathan, coproducer. ABC.

Small Sacrifices. Suzanne de Passe, Louis Rudolph, executive producers. S. Bryan Hickox, producer. ABC.

OUTSTANDING DRAMA/COMEDY SPECIAL (Tie)

• *Caroline? Hallmark Hall of Fame*. Dan Enright, Les Alexander, Don Enright, executive producers. Barbara Hiser, Joseph Broido, co-executive producers. Dorothea G. Petrie, producer. CBS.

• *The Incident, AT&T Presents*. Robert Halmi, executive producer. Bill Brademan, Edwin Self, producers. CBS.

The Final Days, AT&T Presents. Stu Samuels, executive producer. Richard L. O'Connor, producer. Susan Weber-Gold, coproducer. ABC.

A Killing in a Small Town. Bruce Sallan, executive producer. Dan Witt, Courtney Pledger, producers. Cynthia Cidre, coproducer. CBS.

Murder in Mississippi. David L. Wolper, Bernard Sofronski, executive producers. Tova Laiter, co-executive producer. Mark M. Wolper, producer. NBC.

OUTSTANDING VARIETY, MUSIC, OR COMEDY SERIES

• *In Living Color*. Keenen Ivory Wayans, executive producer. Kevin S. Bright,

Patricia Wettig of thirtysomething *thanked the female cancer victims who "shared their insights and their fears."*

supervising producer. Tamara Rawitt, producer. Michael Petok, coproducer. Fox.
The Arsenio Hall Show. Arsenio Hall, executive producer. Marla Kell Brown, producer. Arsenio Hall, host. Syndicated.
Late Night with David Letterman. Jack Rollins, David Letterman, executive producers. Robert Morton, producer. David Letterman, host. NBC.
Saturday Night Live. Lorne Michaels, executive producer. James Downey, producer. NBC.
The Tracey Ullman Show. Jerry Belson, James L. Brooks, Heide Perlman, Sam Simon, executive producers. Marc Flanagan, supervising producer. Marilyn Suzanne Miller, senior producer. Richard Sakai, Ted Bessell, Dinah Kirgo, producers. Jay Kogen, Wallace Wolodarsky, coproducers. Tracey Ullman, host. Fox.

OUTSTANDING VARIETY, MUSIC, OR COMEDY SPECIAL
• *Sammy Davis, Jr.'s 60th Anniversary Celebration.* George Schlatter, producer. Jeff Margolis, Buz Kohan, Gary Necessary, Maria Schlatter, coproducers. ABC.
The 62nd Annual Academy Awards. Gilbert Cates, producer. ABC.
The Best of the Tracey Ullman Show. Jerry Belson, James L. Brooks, Heide Perlman,

Sam Simon, executive producers. Marc Flanagan, supervising producer. Marilyn Suzanne Miller, senior producer. Richard Sakai, Ted Bessell, Dinah Kirgo, producers. Jay Kogen, Wallace Wolodarsky, coproducers. Fox.
Billy Crystal: Midnight Train to Moscow. Billy Crystal, David Steinberg, executive producers. Robert Dalrymple, producer. Carmi Zlotnik, coproducer. Jay Roewe, line producer. HBO.
The 43rd Annual Tony Awards. Don Mischer, executive producer. David J. Goldberg, producer. CBS.

OUTSTANDING CLASSICAL PROGRAM IN THE PERFORMING ARTS (Winner)
• *Aida, The Metropolitan Opera Presents.* Peter Gelb, executive producer. PBS.

OUTSTANDING INFORMATIONAL SERIES (Area award winner)
• *Smithsonian World.* Adrian Malone, executive producer. Sandra W. Bradley, producer. PBS.

OUTSTANDING INFORMATIONAL SPECIAL (Area award winners)
• "Dance in America: Bob Fosse Steam Heat," *Great Performances.* Jac Venza, executive producer. Judy Kinberg, producer. PBS.
• "Broadway's Dreamers: The Legacy of the Group Theatre," *American Masters.* Jac Venza, Susan Lacy, executive producers. Joan Kramer, David Heeley, Joanne Woodward, producers. PBS.

OUTSTANDING ANIMATED PROGRAM (Winner — One hour or less)
• *The Simpsons.* James L. Brooks, Matt Groening, Sam Simon, executive producers. Richard Sakai, producer. Al Jean, Mike Reiss, Larina Jean Adamson, coproducers. Margot Pipkin, animation producer. Gabor Csupo, supervising animation director. David Silverman, director. John Swartzwelder, writer. Fox.

OUTSTANDING CHILDREN'S PROGRAM (Winner)
• "A Mother's Courage: The Mary Thomas Story," *The Magical World of Disney.* Ted Field, Robert W. Cort, executive producers. Patricia Clifford, Kate Wright, co-executive producers. Richard L. O'Connor, producer.

Chet Walker, coproducer. NBC.

PERFORMANCE, DIRECTING, AND WRITING
OUTSTANDING LEAD ACTOR
IN A DRAMA SERIES
• Peter Falk, *Columbo, The ABC Monday Mystery Movie*. ABC.
Scott Bakula, *Quantum Leap*. NBC.
Robert Loggia, *Mancuso F.B.I.* NBC.
Kyle MacLachlan, *Twin Peaks*. ABC.
Edward Woodward, *The Equalizer*. CBS.

OUTSTANDING LEAD ACTRESS
IN A DRAMA SERIES
• Patricia Wettig, *thirtysomething*. ABC.
Dana Delany, *China Beach*. ABC.
Jill Eikenberry, *L.A. Law*. NBC.
Angela Lansbury, *Murder, She Wrote*. CBS.
Piper Laurie, *Twin Peaks*. ABC.

OUTSTANDING LEAD ACTOR
IN A COMEDY SERIES
• Ted Danson, *Cheers*. NBC.
John Goodman, *Roseanne*. ABC.
Richard Mulligan, *Empty Nest*. NBC.
Craig T. Nelson, *Coach*. ABC.
Fred Savage, *The Wonder Years*. ABC.

OUTSTANDING LEAD ACTRESS
IN A COMEDY SERIES
• Candice Bergen, *Murphy Brown*. CBS.
Kirstie Alley, *Cheers*. NBC.
Blair Brown, *The Days and Nights of Molly Dodd*. Lifetime.
Delta Burke, *Designing Women*. CBS.
Betty White, *The Golden Girls*. NBC.

OUTSTANDING LEAD ACTOR
IN A MINISERIES OR A SPECIAL
• Hume Cronyn, *Age-Old Friends*. HBO.
Michael Caine, *Jekyll & Hyde*. ABC.
Art Carney, *Where Pigeons Go to Die*. NBC.
Albert Finney, *The Image*. HBO.
Tom Hulce, *Murder in Mississippi*. NBC.

OUTSTANDING LEAD ACTRESS
IN A MINISERIES OR A SPECIAL
• Barbara Hershey, *A Killing in a Small Town*. CBS.
Farrah Fawcett, *Small Sacrifices*. ABC.
Christine Lahti, *No Place Like Home*. CBS.
Annette O'Toole, *The Kennedys of Massachusetts*. ABC.
Lesley Ann Warren, *Family of Spies*. CBS.

Alfre Woodard, "A Mother's Courage: The Mary Thomas Story," *The Magical World of Disney*. NBC.

OUTSTANDING SUPPORTING ACTOR
IN A DRAMA SERIES
• Jimmy Smits, *L.A. Law*. NBC.
Timothy Busfield, *thirtysomething*. ABC.
Larry Drake, *L.A. Law*. NBC.
Richard Dysart, *L.A. Law*. NBC.
Dean Stockwell, *Quantum Leap*. NBC.

OUTSTANDING SUPPORTING ACTRESS
IN A DRAMA SERIES
• Marg Helgenberger, *China Beach*. ABC.
Sherilyn Fenn, *Twin Peaks*. ABC.
Melanie Mayron, *thirtysomething*. ABC.
Diana Muldaur, *L.A. Law*. NBC.
Susan Ruttan, *L.A. Law*. NBC.

OUTSTANDING SUPPORTING ACTOR
IN A COMEDY SERIES
• Alex Rocco, *The Famous Teddy Z*. CBS.
Kelsey Grammer, *Cheers*. NBC.
Woody Harrelson, *Cheers*. NBC.
Charles Kimbrough, *Murphy Brown*. CBS.
Jerry Van Dyke, *Coach*. ABC.

OUTSTANDING SUPPORTING ACTRESS
IN A COMEDY SERIES
• Bebe Neuwirth, *Cheers*. NBC.
Julia Duffy, *Newhart*. CBS.
Faith Ford, *Murphy Brown*. CBS.
Estelle Getty, *The Golden Girls*. NBC.
Rhea Perlman, *Cheers*. NBC.

OUTSTANDING SUPPORTING ACTOR
IN A MINISERIES OR A SPECIAL
• Vincent Gardenia, *Age-Old Friends*. HBO.
Ned Beatty, *Last Train Home*. Family Channel.
Brian Dennehy, *A Killing in a Small Town*. CBS.
Anthony Hopkins, *Great Expectations*. Disney.
James Earl Jones, *By Dawn's Early Light*. HBO.
Max Von Sydow, *Red King, White Knight*. HBO.

OUTSTANDING SUPPORTING ACTRESS
IN A MINISERIES OR A SPECIAL
• Eva Marie Saint, *People Like Us*. NBC.
Stockard Channing, *Perfect Witness*. HBO.
Colleen Dewhurst, *Lantern Hill*. Disney.
Swoosie Kurtz, *The Image*. HBO.

Irene Worth, *The Shell Seekers, Hallmark Hall of Fame*. ABC.

OUTSTANDING INDIVIDUAL PERFORMANCE IN A VARIETY OR MUSIC PROGRAM
• Tracey Ullman, *The Best of the Tracey Ullman Show*. Fox.
Dana Carvey, *Saturday Night Live*. NBC.
Billy Crystal, *Billy Crystal: Midnight Train to Moscow*. HBO.
Julie Kavner, *The Tracey Ullman Show*. Fox.
Angela Lansbury, *The 43rd Annual Tony Awards*. CBS.

OUTSTANDING PERFORMANCE IN INFORMATIONAL PROGRAMMING
(Winner)
• George Burns, host, *A Conversation with ....* Disney Channel.

OUTSTANDING PERFORMANCE IN CLASSICAL MUSIC/DANCE PROGRAMMING
(Area award winners)
• Brian Boitano, *Carmen on Ice*. HBO.
• Brian Orser, *Carmen on Ice*. HBO.
• Katarina Witt, *Carmen on Ice*. HBO.

OUTSTANDING GUEST ACTOR IN A DRAMA SERIES
• Patrick McGoohan, *Columbo, The ABC Monday Mystery Movie*. ABC.
Peter Frechette, *thirtysomething*. ABC.
Harold Gould, *To the Chicago Abyss, Ray Bradbury Theater*. USA.
William Hickey, *The Switch, Tales from the Crypt*. HBO.
Bruce Weitz, *Midnight Caller*. NBC.

OUTSTANDING GUEST ACTRESS IN A DRAMA SERIES
• Viveca Lindfors, *Life Goes On*. ABC.
Ruby Dee, *China Beach*. ABC.
Colleen Dewhurst, *Avonlea*. Disney Channel.
Shirley Knight, *thirtysomething*. ABC.
Kay Lenz, *Midnight Caller*. NBC.

OUTSTANDING GUEST ACTOR IN A COMEDY SERIES
• Jay Thomas, *Murphy Brown*. CBS.
David Huddleston, *The Wonder Years*. ABC.
Darren McGavin, *Murphy Brown*. CBS.
Jerry Orbach, *The Golden Girls*. NBC.
Dick Van Dyke, *The Golden Girls*. NBC.

OUTSTANDING GUEST ACTRESS IN A COMEDY SERIES
• Swoosie Kurtz, *Carol & Company*. NBC.
Georgia Brown, *Cheers*. NBC.
Morgan Fairchild, *Murphy Brown*. CBS.
Alexis Smith, *Cheers*. NBC.
Liz Torres, *The Famous Teddy Z*. CBS.

OUTSTANDING DIRECTING IN A DRAMA SERIES
(Tie)
• Thomas Carter, *Equal Justice*. ABC.
• Scott Winant, *thirtysomething*. ABC.
David Lynch, *Twin Peaks*. ABC.
Win Phelps, *L.A. Law*. NBC.
Rick Wallace, *L.A. Law*. NBC.

OUTSTANDING DIRECTING IN A COMEDY SERIES
• Michael Dinner, *The Wonder Years*. ABC.
James Burrows, *Cheers*. NBC.
Terry Hughes, *The Golden Girls*. NBC.
Barnet Kellman, *Murphy Brown*. CBS.
Harry Thomason, *Designing Women*. CBS.
Hugh Wilson, *The Famous Teddy Z*. CBS.

OUTSTANDING DIRECTING IN A MINISERIES OR A SPECIAL
• Joseph Sargent, *Caroline? Hallmark Hall of Fame*. CBS.
Gilbert Cates, *Do You Know the Muffin Man?* CBS.
Stephen Gyllenhaal, *A Killing in a Small Town*. CBS.
Lamont Johnson, *The Kennedys of Massachusetts*. ABC.
Richard Pearce, *The Final Days, AT&T Presents*. ABC.

OUTSTANDING DIRECTING IN A VARIETY OR MUSIC PROGRAM
• Dwight Hemion, *The Kennedy Center Honors: A Celebration of the Performing Arts*. CBS.
Paul Flaherty, *Billy Crystal: Midnight Train to Moscow*. HBO.
Jim Henson, *The Jim Henson Hour*. NBC.
Jeff Margolis, *Sammy Davis Jr.'s 60th Anniversary Celebration*. ABC.
Chuck Workman, *The 62nd Annual Academy Awards*. ABC.

OUTSTANDING DIRECTING IN CLASSICAL MUSIC/DANCE PROGRAMMING
(Area award winner)
• Alan Skog, director of concert performances. Peter Rosen, director, *The Eighth Van Cliburn International Piano Competition: Here to Make Music*. PBS.

OUTSTANDING DIRECTING IN INFORMATIONAL PROGRAMMING
(Area award winner)
• Gene Lasko, "W. Eugene Smith: Photography Made Difficult," *American Masters*. PBS.

OUTSTANDING WRITING IN A DRAMA SERIES
• David E. Kelley, *L.A Law*. NBC.
David E. Kelley, William M. Finkelstein, *L.A. Law*. NBC.
Joseph Dougherty, *thirtysomething*. ABC.
Mark Frost, David Lynch, *Twin Peaks*. ABC.
Harley Peyton, *Twin Peaks*. ABC.

OUTSTANDING WRITING IN A COMEDY SERIES
• Bob Brush, *The Wonder Years*. ABC.
Ken Levine, David Isaacs, *Cheers*. NBC.
Diane English, *Murphy Brown*. CBS.
Mark Egan, Mark Solomon, Bob Bendetson, *Newhart*. CBS.
Hugh Wilson, *The Famous Teddy Z*. CBS.

OUTSTANDING WRITING IN A MINISERIES OR A SPECIAL
• Terrence McNally, "Andre's Mother," *American Playhouse*. PBS.
Michael De Guzman, *Caroline? Hallmark Hall of Fame*. CBS.
Hugh Whitemore, *The Final Days, AT&T Presents*. ABC.
Michael Norell, James Norell, *The Incident, AT&T Presents*. CBS.
William Hanley, *The Kennedys of Massachusetts*. ABC.

OUTSTANDING WRITING IN A VARIETY OR MUSIC PROGRAM
(Tie)
• Billy Crystal, *Billy Crystal: Midnight Train to Moscow*. HBO.
• James L. Brooks, Heide Perlman, Sam Simon, Jerry Belson, Marc Flanagan, Dinah Kirgo, Jay Kogen, Wallace Wolodarsky, Ian Praiser, Marilyn Suzanne Miller, Tracey Ullman, *The Tracy Ullman Show*. Fox.

Steve O'Donnell, head writer. Joe Toplyn, Matt Wickline, Jeff Martin, Gerard Mulligan, Randy Cohen, Larry Jacobson, Fred Graver, Adam Resnick, Rob Burnett, Dave Rygalski, David Letterman, writers. Chris Elliott, additional sketches, *Late Night with David Letterman 8th Anniversary Special*. NBC.
Franklyn Ajaye, Jeanette Collins, Barry "Berry" Douglas, Rob Edwards, Sandy Frany, Mimi Friedman, Jeff Joseph, Howard Kuperberg, Buddy Sheffield, Joe Toplyn, Damon Wayans, Keenen Ivory Wayans, Matt Wickline, *In Living Color*. Fox.
James Downey, head writer. A. Whitney Brown, Gregory Daniels, Tom Davis, Al Franken, Jack Handey, Tom Hymes, Lorne Michaels, Mike Myers, Conan O'Brien, Bob Odenkirk, Herb Sargent, Tom Schiller, Rob Schneider, Robert Smigel, David Spade, Bonnie Turner, Terry Turner, Christine Zander, writers, *Saturday Night Live*. NBC.

(No awards were bestowed for outstanding writing in the areas of informational programming or classical music/dance programming.)

OTHER AWARD WINNERS
OUTSTANDING CASTING FOR A MINISERIES OR A SPECIAL
(Juried award)
• Randy Stone, Holly Powell, *The Incident, AT&T Presents*. CBS.

OUTSTANDING MUSIC AND LYRICS
• Larry Grossman, composer. Buz Kohan, lyricist, *From the Heart ... The First International Very Special Arts Festival*. NBC.

OUTSTANDING MUSIC COMPOSITION FOR A MINISERIES OR A SPECIAL
(Dramatic underscore)
• James Di Pasquale, *The Shell Seekers, Hallmark Hall of Fame*. ABC.

OUTSTANDING MUSIC DIRECTION
• Ian Fraser, music director. Chris Boardman, Bill Byers, Bob Florence, J. Hill, Angela Morley, arrangers, "Julie Andrews in Concert," *Great Performances*. PBS.

OUTSTANDING CHOREOGRAPHY
• Paula Abdul, Michael Darrin, Dean Barlow, *The 17th Annual American Music Awards.* ABC.

OUTSTANDING ART DIRECTION FOR A SERIES
• Richard D. James, production designer. James J. Mees, set decorator, *Star Trek: The Next Generation.* Syndicated.

OUTSTANDING ART DIRECTION FOR A MINISERIES OR A SPECIAL
• Timian Alsaker, Jacques Bufnoir, production designers, *The Phantom of the Opera.* NBC.

OUTSTANDING ART DIRECTION FOR A VARIETY OR MUSIC PROGRAM
• Roy Christopher, production designer. Greg Richman, art director, *The 62nd Annual Academy Awards.* ABC.

OUTSTANDING COSTUME DESIGN FOR A SERIES
• Patricia Norris, *Twin Peaks.* ABC.

OUTSTANDING COSTUME DESIGN FOR A MINISERIES OR A SPECIAL
• Shelley Komarov, *The Kennedys of Massachusetts.* ABC.

OUTSTANDING COSTUME DESIGN FOR A VARIETY OR MUSIC PROGRAM
• Pat Field, *Mother Goose Rock 'n' Rhyme, Think Entertainment.* Disney Channel.

OUTSTANDING COSTUMING FOR A SERIES
• Frances H. Hays, costume supervisor, *The Young Riders.* ABC.

OUTSTANDING MAKEUP FOR A SERIES (Tie)
• Rick Stratton, makeup effects supervisor. Michelle Burke, head makeup artist. Richard Snell, Katalin Elek, Ken Diaz, makeup artists. *Alien Nation.* Fox.
• Thomas R. Burman, Bari Dreiband-Burman, Dale Condit, Ron Walters, Greg Nelson, *The Tracy Ullman Show.* Fox.

OUTSTANDING MAKEUP FOR A MINISERIES OR SPECIAL
• Ken Chase, *Billy Crystal, Midnight Train to Moscow.* HBO.

OUTSTANDING HAIRSTYLING FOR A SERIES
• Linle White, Peggy Shannon, *The Tracey Ullman Show.* Fox.

OUTSTANDING HAIRSTYLING FOR A MINISERIES OR A SPECIAL (Tie)
• Janice Alexander, Dorothy Andre, hairstylists. *Fall from Grace.* NBC.
• Cedric Chami, *The Phantom of the Opera.* NBC.

OUTSTANDING CINEMATOGRAPHY FOR A SERIES
• Michael Watkins, director of photography, *Quantum Leap.* NBC.

OUTSTANDING CINEMATOGRAPHY FOR A MINISERIES OR A SPECIAL
• Donald M. Morgan, director of photography, *Murder in Mississippi.* NBC.

OUTSTANDING TECHNICAL DIRECTION/CAMERA/VIDEO FOR A SERIES
• Terry Rohnke, technical director. Steve Jambeck, Joe Debonis, Jan Kasoff, John Pinto, Robert Reese, camera operators, Bruce Shapiro, senior video control, *Saturday Night Live.* NBC.

OUTSTANDING TECHNICAL DIRECTION/CAMERA/VIDEO FOR A MINISERIES OR A SPECIAL
• Keith Winikoff, technical director. Gary Childs, Dave Banks, Sam Drummy, Hank Geving, Dean Hall, Dave Levisohn, Bill Philbin, Hector Ramirez, camera operators. Keith Winikoff, senior video control, *The Magic of David Copperfield XII: The Niagara Falls Challenge.* CBS.

OUTSTANDING SPECIAL VISUAL EFFECTS (Area award winners)
• Craig Barron, special visual effects supervisor. Michael Pangrazio, effects art direction supervisor. Charlie Mullen, motion control camera. Bill Mather, matte artist, *By Dawn's Early Light.* HBO.
• William Mesa, visual effects supervisor. Tony Tremblay, visual effects art director. Tim Donahue, matte supervisor. John Coats, technical director. David B. Sharp, miniatures supervisor, *Miracle Landing.* CBS.
• Zbig Rybczynski (conceived and directed). John O'Connor, visual effects editor. Ryszard Welnowski, ultimatte

operator. Paul Bachman, motion control operator, "The Orchestra," *Great Performances*. PBS.

OUTSTANDING EDITING FOR A SERIES
(Single camera production)
• Duwayne Dunham, *Twin Peaks*. ABC.
(Multicamera production)
• Douglas Hines, M. Pam Blumenthal, film editors, *The Tracey Ullman Show*. Fox.

OUTSTANDING EDITING FOR A MINISERIES OR A SPECIAL
(Single camera production)
• Paul Lamastra, film editor. *Caroline? Hallmark Hall of Fame*. NBC.
(Multicamera production)
• M. Pam Blumenthal, Douglas Hines, Brian K. Roberts, *The Best of the Tracey UllmanShow*. Fox.

OUTSTANDING SOUND EDITING FOR A SERIES
• Willlam Wistrom, supervising sound editor. James Wolvington, Mace Matiosian, Wilson Dyer, Rick Freeman, sound editors. Gerry Sackman, supervising music editor, *Star Trek: The Next Generation*. Syndicated.

OUTSTANDING SOUND EDITING FOR A MINISERIES OR A SPECIAL
(Tie)
• Vince Gutierrez, supervising sound editor. Randal S. Thomas, Ken Gladden, Mace Matiosian, Joseph A. Johnston, T.W. Davis, Douglas Gray, John Orr, Gary Gelfand, Andre Caporaso, Russell Brower, David Scharf, sound editors. Philip Jamtaas, supervising ADR editor. John Caper, Jr., supervising music editor, *Challenger*. ABC.
• Burton Weinstein, Michael Guttierrez, supervising sound editors. Randal S. Thomas, Joseph A. Johnston, Ken Gladden, George R. Groves, Philip Jamtaas, Sam Black, Andre Caporaso, Clark Conrad, Gary Gelfand, John Orr, David Scharf, Terence Thomas, T.W. Davis, sound editors. Abby Treloggen, supervising music editor, *Family of Spies*. CBS.

OUTSTANDING SOUND MIXING FOR A COMEDY SERIES OR A SPECIAL
• Robert Crosby, Jr., production mixer. Thomas J. Huth, Sam Black, Bobby Douglass, rerecording mixers, *Cheers*. NBC.

OUTSTANDING SOUND MIXING FOR A VARIETY OR MUSIC SERIES OR A SPECIAL
• Gordon Klimuck, Barton Michael Chiate, production mixers, *The Arsenio Hall Show*. Syndicated.

OUTSTANDING SOUND MIXING FOR A DRAMA MINISERIES OR A SPECIAL
• Fred Schultz, production mixer. William McCaughey, Richard D. Rogers, Grover Helsley, rerecording mixers, *Cross of Fire*. NBC.

OUTSTANDING LIGHTING DIRECTION (ELECTRONIC) FOR A COMEDY SERIES
• George Spiro Dibie, director of photography, *Just the Ten of Us*. ABC.

OUTSTANDING LIGHTING DIRECTION (ELECTRONIC) FOR A DRAMA SERIES, VARIETY SERIES, MINISERIES OR A SPECIAL
(Tie)
• Olin Younger, lighting designer, *The 17th Annual American Music Awards*. ABC.
• John Rook, director of photography, *Time Warner Presents "The Earth Day Special."* ABC.

(No awards were bestowed for main title theme music, music composition for a series, or graphic design.)

DAYTIME AWARDS
OUTSTANDING DRAMA SERIES
• *Santa Barbara*. John Conboy, senior executive producer. Jill Farren Phelps, executive producer. Steve Kent, senior supervising producer. Charlòtte Savitz, supervising producer. Julie Hanan Carruthers, producer. NBC.
All My Children. Felicia Minei Behr, executive producer. Thomas de Villiers, Terry Cacavio, coordinating producers. ABC.
Guiding Light. Robert Calhoun, executive producer. Barbara Garshman, supervising producer. Catherine Maher Smith, coordinating producer. Robert Kochman, Kathlyn Chambers, producers. CBS.
The Young and the Restless. William J. Bell, senior executive producer. Edward J. Scott, executive producer. Tom Langan, producer. Nancy Bradley Wiard, coordinating producer. CBS.

Joan Rivers with her first Emmy after 25 years in television: "I always had a fantasy as a child that I'd win one of these."

OUTSTANDING LEAD ACTOR IN A DRAMA SERIES
• A Martinez, *Santa Barbara*. NBC.
David Canary, *All My Children*. ABC.
Stephen Schnetzer, *Another World*. NBC.
Peter Bergman, *The Young and the Restless*. CBS.
Eric Braeden, *The Young and the Restless*. CBS.

OUTSTANDING LEAD ACTRESS IN A DRAMA SERIES
• Kim Zimmer, *Guiding Light*. CBS.
Susan Lucci, *All My Children*. ABC.
Elizabeth Hubbard, *As the World Turns*. CBS.
Finola Hughes, *General Hospital*. ABC.
Jeanne Cooper, *The Young and the Restless*. CBS.

OUTSTANDING SUPPORTING ACTOR A DRAMA SERIES
• Henry Darrow, *Santa Barbara*. NBC.
Robert Gentry, *All My Children*. ABC.

Kin Shriner, *General Hospital*. ABC.
Kristoff St. John, *Generations*. NBC.
Jerry ver Dorn, *Guiding Light*. CBS.
Roscoe Born, *Santa Barbara*. NBC.
Quinn Redeker, *The Young and the Restless*. CBS.

OUTSTANDING SUPPORTING ACTRESS IN A DRAMA SERIES
• Julia Barr, *All My Children*. ABC.
Lynn Herring, *General Hospital*. ABC.
Mary Jo Catlett, *General Hospital*. ABC.
Michelle Forbes, *Guiding Light*. CBS.
Jess Walton, *The Young and the Restless*. CBS.

OUTSTANDING DRAMA SERIES DIRECTING TEAM
• Michael Gliona, Rick Bennewitz, Robert Schiller, directors. Pamela Fryman, Jeanine Guarneri-Frons, associate directors, *Santa Barbara*. NBC.
Jack Coffey, director. Christopher Goutman, Henry Kaplan, Conal O'Brien, directors. Barbara Martin Simmons, Shirley Simmons, associate directors, *All My Children*. ABC.
Paul Lammers, Jill Mitwell, Bob Schwarz, Maria Wagner, directors. Joel Aronowitz, Michael Kerner, associate directors, *As the World Turns*. CBS.
Bruce S. Barry, Scott McKinsey, Jo Anne Sedwick, directors. Susan Dansby, Joanne Goodhart, Angela Tessinari, John O'Connell, associate directors, *Guiding Light*. CBS.
Heather Hill, Frank Pacelli, Randy Robbins, Mike Denney, directors. Betty Rothenberg, Dan Brumett, Kathryn Foster, associate directors, *The Young and the Restless*. CBS.

OUTSTANDING DRAMA SERIES WRITING TEAM
• Pamela K. Long, head writer. Nancy Curlee, Trent Jones, associate head writers. Jeff Ryder, story consultant. Stephen Demorest, script editor. Garrett Foster, Peter Brash, Nancy Williams, breakdown writers. Patty Gideon Sloan, Richard Culliton, breakdown/script writers. N. Gail Lawrence, Pete T. Rich, Melissa Salmons, script writers, *Guiding Light*. CBS.
Agnes Nixon, Lorraine Broderick, Margaret De Priest, Susan Kirshenbaum, Kathleen Klein, Karen L. Lewis, Megan McTavish, Victor Miller, Elizabeth Page, Elizabeth Smith, Gillian Spencer, Wisner

Washam, Mary K. Wells, writers, *All My Children*. ABC.
S. Michael Schnessel, head writer. Craig Carlson, Leah Laiman, co-head writers. Ethel M. Brez, Mel Brez, Addie Walsh, associate head writers. Dorothy Ann Purser, Lloyd Gold, Norman Hart, Lanie Bertram, writers, *One Life to Live*. ABC. Charles Pratt, Jr., head writer. Robert Guza, Jr., Sam Hall, associate head writers. Patrick Mulcahey, story editor. Courtney Simon, Gary Tomlin, Linda Myles, script writers. Josh Griffith, breakdown writer, *Santa Barbara*. NBC. William J. Bell, head writer. Kay Alden, associate head writer. Jerry Birn, John F. Smith, Eric Freiwald, Enid L. Powell, Rex M. Best, writers, *The Young and the Restless*. CBS.

OTHER DAYTIME AWARD WINNERS
OUTSTANDING JUVENILE MALE IN A DRAMA SERIES
• Andrew Kavovit, *As the World Turns*. CBS.

OUTSTANDING JUVENILE FEMALE IN A DRAMA SERIES
• Cady McClain, *All My Children*. ABC.

OUTSTANDING GAME/AUDIENCE PARTICIPATION SHOW
• *Jeopardy!* Merv Griffin, executive producer. George Vosburgh, producer. Syndicated.

OUTSTANDING GAME SHOW HOST
(Tie)
• Alex Trebek, *Jeopardy!* Syndicated.
• Bob Barker, *The Price is Right*. CBS.

OUTSTANDING DIRECTING IN A GAME/AUDIENCE PARTICIPATION SHOW
• Joseph Behar, *Fun House*. Syndicated.

OUTSTANDING TALK/SERVICE SHOW
• *Sally Jessy Raphael*. Burt Dubrow, executive producer. Karl Sagin, senior producer. Linda Finnell, Alex Williamson, Donna Benner Ingber, Mary Duffy, producers. Syndicated.

OUTSTANDING TALK/SERVICE SHOW HOST
• Joan Rivers, *The Joan Rivers Show*. Syndicated.

OUTSTANDING DIRECTING IN A TALK/ SERVICE SHOW
• Russell Morash, *This Old House*. PBS.

OUTSTANDING CHILDREN'S SERIES
• *Reading Rainbow*. Twila Liggett, Tony Buttino, executive producers. Cecily Truett, supervising producer/producer. Larry Lancit, supervising producer. Orly Berger, Jill Gluckson, Ronnie Krauss, producers. LeVar Burton, contributing producer. PBS.

OUTSTANDING CHILDREN'S SPECIAL
• "A Matter of Conscience," *CBS Schoolbreak Special*. Eve Silverman, executive producer. Susan Aronson, producer. CBS.

OUTSTANDING DIRECTING IN A CHILDREN'S SERIES
• Mike Gargiulo, series director. Charles S. Dubin, series director (Mathnet), *Square One TV/Mathnet*. PBS.

OUTSTANDING ANIMATED PROGRAM
(Tie)
• *The New Adventures of Winnie the Pooh*. Ken Kessel, Karl Geurs, producers/directors. Ed Ghertner, producer. Terence Harrison, director. Bruce Talkington, Mark Zaslove, story editors. Carter Crocker, Steven Sustarsic, writers. ABC.
• *Beetlejuice*. David Geffen, Tim Burton, executive producers. Lenora Hume, supervising producer. Stephen Hodgins, coordinating producer. Michael Hirsh, Patrick Loubert, Clive A. Smith, producers. Robin Budd, director. Patsy Cameron, Tedd Anasti, story editors. ABC.

OUTSTANDING WRITING IN A CHILDREN'S SERIES
• Norman Stiles, series head writer. Judy Freudberg, Cathi Rosenberg-Turow, Nancy Sans, Tony Geiss, Luis Santeiro, Jeff Moss, Sara Compton, Belinda Ward, John Weidman, Josh Selig, Emily Perl Kingsley, David Korr, Sonia Manzano, Mark Saltzman, Jon Stone, series writers, *Sesame Street*. PBS.

OUTSTANDING WRITING IN A CHILDREN'S SPECIAL
• Paul Cooper, "A Matter of Conscience," *CBS Schoolbreak Special*. CBS.

Producer Mark Goodson (center) received the Lifetime Achievement award from A.T.A.S. president Leo Chaloukian (left) and N.A.T.A.S. chairman Michael Collyer.

**OUTSTANDING PERFORMER
IN A CHILDREN'S SERIES**
• Kevin Clash, *Sesame Street*. PBS.

**OUTSTANDING PERFORMER
IN A CHILDREN'S SPECIAL**
• Greg Spottiswood, *Looking for Miracles*. Disney Channel.

**OUTSTANDING MUSIC DIRECTION
AND COMPOSITION FOR A DRAMA SERIES**
• Marty Davich, music director/composer. Amy Burkhard, music supervisor. Ken Corday, composer, *Days of Our Lives*. NBC.

**OUTSTANDING MUSIC DIRECTION
AND COMPOSITION**
• Christopher Cerf, Jeff Moss, Tony Geiss, Sarah Durkee, composers. Stephen Lawrence, Cheryl Hardwick, Paul Jacobs, David Conner, composers/arrangers, *Sesame Street*. PBS.

OUTSTANDING MAKEUP
• David Abbott, Gil Mosko, makeup artists, *The Munsters Today*. Syndicated.

**OUTSTANDING MAKEUP
FOR A DRAMA SERIES**
• Mark Landon, Steve Artmont, Ed Helm, makeup artists, *The Young and the Restless*. CBS.

OUTSTANDING HAIRSTYLING
• Andre Walker, *The Oprah Winfrey Show*. Syndicated.

**OUTSTANDING HAIRSTYLING
FOR A DRAMA SERIES**
• Angel De Angelis, head hairstylist. John Quaglia, Annette Bianco, Joyce Sica, hairstylists, *Another World*, NBC.

**OUTSTANDING GRAPHICS
AND TITLE DESIGN**
• Penelope Gottlieb, title designer, *Generations*. NBC.

**OUTSTANDING ART DIRECTION/SET
DECORATION/SCENIC DESIGN**
• Victor DiNapoli, art director. Mike Pantuso, scenic designer. Nat Mongioi, set decorator, *Sesame Street*. PBS.

**OUTSTANDING ART DIRECTION/SET
DECORATION/SCENIC DESIGN
FOR A DRAMA SERIES**
• Lawrence Icing, art director. Elmon Webb, scenic designer. Holmes Easley, David Harnish, Paul W. Hickey, set decorators, *As the World Turns*. CBS.

**OUTSTANDING DIRECTING—SPECIAL
CLASS AREA**
• Victoria Hochberg, "Sweet 15," *Wonderworks*. PBS.

**OUTSTANDING WRITING—
SPECIAL CLASS AREA**
• Glenn Kirschbaum, *Remembering World War II—Hitler: Man & Myth*. Syndicated. Robert Kirk, *Remembering World War II—Pearl Harbor*. Syndicated.

OUTSTANDING COSTUME DESIGN
• Bill Kellard, costume designer—live actors. Caroly Wilcox, Kermit Love, Connie Peterson, Paul Hartis, Barry Link, Peter MacKennan, Stephen Rotondaro, Mark Zeszotek, costume designers—muppet costumes, *Sesame Street*. PBS.

**OUTSTANDING COSTUME DESIGN
FOR A DRAMA SERIES
(Tie)**
• Carol Luiken, Charles Clute, *All My Children*. ABC.
• Margarita Delgado, Charles Schoonmaker, *Another World*. NBC.

OUTSTANDING CINEMATOGRAPHY
• James Carter, "Torn Between Two Fathers," *ABC Afterschool Special*. ABC.

Outstanding Technical Direction/Electronic Camera/Video Control

• Ray Angona, technical director. Jose Arvizu, Cesar Cabreira, Keeth Lawrence, Martin Wagner, electronic camera. Allen Latter, senior video, *The Price is Right*. CBS.

Outstanding Technical Direction/Electronic Camera/Video Control for a Drama Series

• Janice Bendiksen, Ervin D. Hurd, Jr., technical directors. Sheldon Mooney, Joel Binger, Joseph Vicens, Dave Navarette, electronic camera. Roberto Bosio, Scha Jani, video control, *The Young and the Restless*. CBS.

Outstanding Film Editing

• Stan Salfas, editor, "All That Glitters," *ABC Afterschool Special*. ABC.

Outstanding Video-Tape Editing

• Robert J. Emerick, supervising editor. Evamarie Keller, editor, *Sesame Street*. PBS.

Outstanding Video-Tape Editing for a Drama Series

• Dan Brumett, Marc Beruti, *The Young and the Restless*. CBS.

Outstanding Film Sound Editing

• Charles King, supervising editor. Rick Hinson, Richard Harrison, sound editors, *Ducktales*. Syndicated.

Outstanding Film Sound Mixing

• Kim Ornitz, productionmixer. Douglas Gray, T.W. Davis, rerecording mixers. Brian Risner, sound effects, "The Girl with the Crazy Brother," *CBS Schoolbreak Special*. CBS.

Outstanding Live and Tape Sound Mixing and Sound Effects

• Galen Handy, production sound mixer. David E. Fluhr, rerecording mixer, "Torn Between Two Fathers," *ABC Afterschool Special*. ABC.

Outstanding Live and Tape Sound Mixing and Sound Effects for a Drama Series

• Pat Lucatorto, Tommy Persson, audio mixers. Don Henderson, music mixer. Rafael O. Valentin, Harold Linstrot,

postproduction mixers. Maurice "Smokey" Westerfeld, Peter Romano, sound effects, *The Young and the Restless*. CBS.

Outstanding Lighting Direction for a Drama Series

• Brian McRae, Ted C. Polmanski, *Santa Barbara*. NBC.

Outstanding Lighting Direction

• Jim Tetlow, Bill Berner, *Sesame Street*. PBS.

SPORTS AWARD WINNERS

Outstanding Live Sports Series (Tie)

• *ABC's NFL Monday Night Football*. Geoffrey Mason, executive producer. Ken Wolfe, producer. Craig Janoff, director. John McGuinness, associate producer. Earl "Woody" Freiman, Ben Harvey, associate directors. ABC.

• *Speedworld*. Steven M. Bornstein, executive producer. Steve Anderson, director of production. Peter Englehart, coordinating producer. Neil Goldberg, senior producer. Conrad Piccirillo, producer. Mike Wells, director. Chevy Ferland, Jeff Hallas, Danny Laycock, Pamela Miller, Jenny Nickell, associate producers. ESPN.

Outstanding Live Sports Special

• *Indianapolis 500*. Geoffrey Mason, executive producer. Bob Goodrich, Ben Harvey, producers. Don Ohlmeyer, Roger Goodman, directors. Debbie Cole, associate producer. Jaime Bravo, Jeff Cohan, Vince DeDario, Norman Samet, associate directors. ABC.

Outstanding Edited Sports Series

• *This is the NFL*. Steve Sabol, executive producer. Jay Gerber, Denine Bergey, coordinating producers. Steve Seidman, Bob Ryan, Jonathan Hock, Bob Smith, Dave Douglas, David Swain, Phil Tuckett, Kenneth Sheil, producers. Ed Sherrier, Rene Hangley, Brad Perch, associate directors. Syndicated.

Outstanding Edited Sports Special

• *Trans-Antarctica! The International Expedition*. Geoffrey Mason, executive producer. Ben Harvey, Emilie Deutsch, producers. John Wilcox, director. Angelo Bernarducci, Patty Rodilosso, associate directors. ABC.

Outstanding Sports Personality/Host
(Play-by-Play)
• Al Michaels. ABC.

Outstanding Sports Personality/Analyst
(Commentary)
• John Madden. CBS.

Special Class: Individual Achievement
• Geoffrey Mason, Roger Goodman, Bill Conti, coordination of live music at the New York City Marathon. ABC.

Special Class: Program Achievement
• *NBC Sportsworld — February 25, 1964: The Championship*. Michael Weisman, executive producer. Carla Engelman, coordinating producer. J.D. Hansen, coordinating director. David Neal, producer. Sheila Vavasour, Charlene Zalis, associate producers. John Gilmartin, associate director. NBC.

Special Class: Innovative Technical Achievement
• *New York City Marathon* , Live music with Juilliard Orchestra. Martin Slutsky, technical operations manager. Lee DeCarlo, audio and music consultant. Wayne Wilfong, technical manager. ABC.

Program Area: Features
• *ESPN SportsCenter: Tim Burke Adoption*. Steven M. Bornstein, executive producer. John A. Walsh, managing editor. Bill Shanahan, Noubar Stone, Mike Bogard, Mike Matters, coordinating producers. John Hamlin, producer. Chris Myers, producer/reporter. ESPN.

Program Area: Studio Show
• *The NFL Today*. Ted Shaker, executive producer. David Winner, senior producer. Eric Mann, coordinating producer. Duke Struck, director. David Blatt, Allan Brum, Victor Frank, Richard Gentile, feature producers. Lance Barrow, Steve Milton, Steve Scheer, associate producers. Scott Johnson, Colleen Kolibas, associate directors. CBS.

Program Area: Sports Journalism
• *1989 World Series Game #3, Earthquake Coverage*. Geoffrey Mason, executive producer. Curt Gowdy, Jr., coordinating producer. Craig Janoff, director. Robert Beiner, pregame producer. Michael Rosen, associate producer. Toni Slotkin, David Kiviat, Earl "Woody" Freiman, associate directors. ABC.

Program Area: Promotion
• *ABC's NFL Monday Night Football "All My Rowdy Friends."* Geoffrey Mason, executive producer. Robert G. Toms, Thomas Remiszewski, coordinating producers. David Seeger, Richard Getz, David Vos, George Greenberg, producers. Bruce Logan, director. Mary Schiarizzi, Lenore Ballard, associate producers. Cynthia J. Vannoy, Audrees Manley Rosburg, associate directors. ABC.

Program Area: Opens/Closes/Teases
• *ABC's NFL Monday Night Football 20th Anniversary Show*. Dennis Lewin, show producer. Robert Toms, feature producer. ABC.

Craft Area: Video-Tape Editing
• *Western Open Tease*. Joe Malecki, editor. CBS.
• *Insport: Paula Abdul*. Paul Prisco, Meredith Paige, editors. Syndicated.

Craft Area: Film Editing
• *Calgary '88: 16 Days of Glory*. Andrew Squicciarini, Michael Schanzer. Disney Channel.

Craft Area: Writing
• *Trans-Antarctica! The International Expedition*. Sam Posey, writer. ABC.

Craft Area: Music
• *New York City Marathon*. Bill Conti, composer/conductor. ABC.

Craft Area: Electronic Camerapersons
• *ABC's Wide World of Sports: Iditarod Sled Dog Race*. D'Arcy Marsh, Peter Henning, Gary Russell. ABC.

Craft Area: Film Cinematographers
• *Tim McCarver's World of Adventure*. Gordon Brown, Ron Kanter, D'Arcy Marsh, Norman W. Nelson, Tyler S. Nelson, film cinematographers. Pierre de Lespinois, director/camera. Larry Gebhardt, Howard Hall, directors of photography. ABC.

CRAFT AREA: AUDIO
• *New York City Marathon*. Jack Brandis, Tom Blazner, Dennis Hernandez, Norm Kiernan, Dana Kirkpatrick, Morley Lang, Eugene Mackvick, Vinnie Perry, John Sherrand, Bob Smith, audio. Martin Slutsky, technical operations manager. ABC.

CRAFT AREA: TECHNICAL TEAM REMOTE
• *Speedworld*. Jim Dullaghan, vice president. Joe Commare, director, remote engineering. Reggie Thomas, senior vice president of operations and engineering. Frank Casarella, technical supervisor. Rick McDowell, Doug Dodson, technical managers. John Tomlinson, Bill Dillehay, Joe Signorino, Gib White, Al Taylor, technical maintenance. Steve Laxton, Greg Borbas, technical directors. Sam Abousamra, Dan Ortiz, Dennis Lamb, Ron Scalise, audio engineers. Chuck Mills, Tom Hladik, Paul Vogel, Gordie Saiger, Frank Vilics, Terry Hester, Keith Hobleman, Jeff Zachary, Chuck Whitfield, Mike Ratusz, Dick Price, Alan Merriweather, Barry Hogenauer, John Boeddedker, Bob Sloan, Don McCluskey, electronic camerapersons. Doug Coffland, Jon Lunceford, Keith Buttleman, Chuck Reilly, Steve Gaughen, Jim Dove, Steve Ulrich, Ernie Flotto, R.D. Willis, Leo Fournier, Mark Charon, Scott Geyer, Steve Lawrence, video-tape engineers. Bob Smicz, RF technician. Fred Clow, Susan Sandt, international coordinators. Joe Eaton, Phil Tollefsen, Don Hale, international audio. ESPN.

CRAFT AREA: TECHNICAL TEAM REMOTE
• *1989 World Series*. Joe Alvarado, Arthur Boodaghian, Jack Coffey, Ralph Gerrard, Ken Michel, Ed Muller, Marty Slutsky, Mark Smith, Anthony Versley, technical operations managers. Michael Ferrell, telecommunications manager. Mike Blazo, Werner Gunther, technical directors. Tom Glazner, Ken Hoffman, John Lory, Bill Sandreuter, Dick Sloan, Robert Smith, audio engineers. Brook Cuddy, lighting director. Sid Lustgarten, Nancy Ross, Sandy York, graphics operators. Tony Capitano, Mike Stefanidis, Cyril Tywang, Martin Bell, Joe Clark, Dan Farrell, Ron Feszchur, Raymond Hughes, Hector Kicelian, Wes Quon, Lou Rende, Mike Shore, Tom Wright, Henry Zimmer, video operators. Jack Cronin, Drew DeRosa,

James Dos Santos, Dom Dragonetti, Roy Hutchings, Jim Lynch, Paul Martens, Ed Martino, Frank Melchiorre, Serf Menduina, George Montanez, John Morreale, Tom O'Connell, Luis Rojas, Jack Savoy, Bill Scott, Bruce Smith, William Sullivan, Mike Todd, Rich Westlein, Steve Wolff. ABC.

CRAFT AREA: TECHNICAL TEAM STUDIO
• *The NFL Today*. Phil Selby, technical director. Jim Dima, Bob Squiltieri, video engineers. Dave Dorsett, Dave Cabano, Angel Herrera, Tim Patryk, electronic cameras. Rich Brender, Ray Sills, Irving Elias, Kevin Rogers, audio engineers. Roxanne Markline, Tracy Morris, Howard Steinkohl, graphics operators. CBS.

CRAFT AREA: GRAPHIC DESIGN
• *Dream Season Promo*. Mitch Friedman, designer. Joe Shingelo, animator. Dan Spech, Eric Altit, assistant animators. Robb Wyatt, Doug Towey, creative directors. CBS.

NEWS & DOCUMENTARY AWARD WINNERS
OUTSTANDING GENERAL COVERAGE OF A SINGLE BREAKING NEWS STORY (Programs)
• "48 Hours: Hurricane Watch," *48 Hours*. Andrew Heyward, Lane Venardos, executive producers. Al Briganti, Steve Glauber, Steve Jacobs, Jack Kelly, Terence Martin, senior producers. Lance Heflin, Liza McGuirk, Rand Morrison, Nancy Solomon, Andrew Tkach, Jonathan Klein, Ira Sutow, Ed Alpern, Margery Baker, Al Berman, Peter Goodman, Madelyn Greenberg, Sharon Houston, Donna Inserra, Carolyn Kresky, Jim McGlinchy, Anne Reingold, Stacy Richman, Lisa Sanders, Laurie Singer, Clem Taylor, Michael R. Whitney, Thomas Flynn, producers. Dan Rather, Bernard Goldberg, Ron Allen, Frank Currier, David Martin, Bob McNamara, Richard Roth, Richard Schlesinger, Harry Smith, Terrence Smith, Kathleen Sullivan, correspondents. CBS.

OUTSTANDING GENERAL COVERAGE OF A SINGLE BREAKING NEWS STORY (Segments)
• "Romanian Revolution Coverage," *NBC Nightly News with Tom Brokaw, Weekend Nightly News*. Bill Wheatley, Dennis Sullivan, Cheryl Gould, executive producers. Bernie Brown, Bruce

Cummings, senior producers. Marc Kusnetz, Don Morfoot, foreign producers. Denise Baker, Charles Sabine, David Page, Joe Alicastro, Tom Aspell, Phil Smith, Barbara Conroy, Debra Pettit, producers. Tom Brokaw, Garrick Utley, Mary Alice Williams, John Cochran, Deborah Norville, Katherine Couric, anchors. Dennis Murphy, George Lewis, Arthur Kent, Tom Aspell, correspondents. NBC.

OUTSTANDING INSTANT COVERAGE OF A SINGLE BREAKING NEWS STORY (Programs)
• "China in Crisis," *NBC News Special.* Bill Wheatley, executive producer. Paul Greenberg, Marc Kusnetz, Jack Chesnutt, Jon Entine, Anne Binford, Robin Skolnick, Paul Hammons, Susan Farkas, Mary Ellen Meehan, Bruce Cummings, producers. Linda Ellman, Denise Baker, Annie Pong, Bud Pratt, Eric Baculiano, Maralyn Gelefsky, Madeline Lewis, producers in China. Keith Miller, George Lewis, Arthur Kent, John Dancy (in Washington), Robert Abernethy (in Moscow), Jim Maceda, Robert Hager (in Washington), Charles McLean, John Chancellor (in New York), correspondents. Tom Brokaw, anchor. NBC.
• *CNN's China Coverage.* Alec Miran, executive producer (China). Jane Maxwell, Eason Jordan, executive producers (Atlanta). Larry Register, Vito Maggiolo, Jim Miller, producers (China). Nancy Lane, Donna Liu, Clair Shipman, field producers (China). Bernard Shaw, anchor. Mike Chinoy (Beijing), Steve Hurst (Moscow), John Lewis (Toyko), Jeanne Moss, correspondents. CNN.

OUTSTANDING BACKGROUND/ANALYSIS OF A SINGLE CURRENT STORY (Programs)
• "Tragedy at Tiananmen: The Untold Story," *The Koppel Report.* Dorrance Smith, executive producer. Lionel Chapman, William Moore, senior producers. Tara Sonenshine, Bob Haberl, Terry Irving, Marianne Keeley, Louis Hepp, producers. Ted Koppel, anchor. ABC.

OUTSTANDING BACKGROUND/ANALYSIS OF A SINGLE CURRENT STORY (Segments)
• "Tragedy at Pine Ridge," *NBC Nightly News with Tom Brokaw.* Mary Laurence Flynn, producer. Betty Rollin, correspondent. NBC.
• "The Education of Admiral Watkins," *The AIDS Quarterly.* Sherry Jones, producer. Elizabeth Sams, coproducer. Margo Reid, field producer. Peter Jennings, correspondent. PBS.

OUTSTANDING INVESTIGATIVE JOURNALISM (Programs)
• "PanAm Flight 103," *Primetime Live.* Richard Kaplan, executive producer. Betsy West, senior broadcast producer. Ira Rosen, senior producer. Neal Shapiro, David Doss, Marc Burstein, broadcast producers. Rudy Bednar, Bob Calo, Terri Lichstein, Lisa Hsia, Sheila Hershow, Albert Oetgen, Roger Goodman, producers. Pierre Salinger (in Europe), Chris Wallace, senior correspondents. Judd Rose, correspondent, Diane Sawyer, Sam Donaldson, anchors/correspondents. ABC.

OUTSTANDING INVESTIGATIVE JOURNALISM (Segments)
• "Prisoners of Care," *Primetime Live.* Ira Rosen, senior producer. Robbie Gordon, producer. Chris Wallace, senior correspondent. ABC.

OUTSTANDING INTERVIEW/INTERVIEWER(S) (Programs)
• "The Living Language," *The Power of the Word with Bill Moyers.* David Grubin, producer. Bill Moyers, executive editor. PBS.
• "Ronald Reagan ... An American Success Story," *NBC News.* Paul W. Greenberg, executive producer. Lelia Bundles, Julie Chrisco, Susan Farkas, Martin Phillips, Polly Powell, Thomas Tomizawa, field producers. Tom Brokaw, interviewer. NBC.

OUTSTANDING INTERVIEW/INTERVIEWER(S) (Segments)
• "Interview with John Tower," *CBS News Face the Nation.* Karen M. Sughrue, executive producer. Carin F. Pratt, producer. Lesley Stahl, interviewer. CBS.
• "Marlon Brando," *Saturday Night with Connie Chung.* Andrew Lack, executive producer. Michael Rubin, senior producer. Christopher Dalrymple, producer. Connie Chung, interviewer. CBS.
• "Patty Duke: Out of the Black Hole," *20/20.* Susan Lester, producer. Hugh Downs, interviewer. ABC.

**OUTSTANDING COVERAGE
OF A CONTINUING NEWS STORY
(Programs)**
• "Women Doing Time," *48 Hours*. Andrew
Heyward, executive producer. Catherine S.
Lasiewicz, senior producer. Nancy Duffy,
Alan Goldberg, Denise Schreiner, Judy
Tygard, producers. Dan Rather, anchor.
Victoria Corderi, Faith Daniels, Harold
Dow, Erin Moriarty, correspondents. CBS.

**OUTSTANDING COVERAGE
OF A CONTINUING NEWS STORY
(Segments)**
• "China: The Ancient, The New," *The
CBS Evening News with Dan Rather*. Tom
Bettag, executive producer. Joel Bernstein,
producer. Bob Simon, correspondent. CBS.

**OUTSTANDING INFORMATIONAL,
CULTURAL, OR HISTORICAL
PROGRAMMING
(Programs)**
• "Search for Battleship Bismarck,"
National Geographic Explorer. Tim Kelly,
Tom Simon, co-executive producers.
Christine Weber, Peter Schnall, producers.
Julia Mair, series producer. TBS.
• *Remembering World War II—Hitler:
Man and Myth*. Craig Haffner, executive
producer. Glenn Kirschbaum, Donna
Lusitana, producers. Steven Lewis,
executive in charge of production. Scott
Paddar, coordinating producer. Edward
Woodward, correspondent. Syndicated.

**OUTSTANDING INFORMATIONAL,
CULTURAL, OR HISTORICAL
PROGRAMMING
(Segments)**
• "Free to Be Wild," *20/20*. Fred Peabody,
producer. Roger Caras, correspondent.
ABC.

OUTSTANDING PROGRAM ACHIEVEMENT
• "Illusions of News," *The Public Mind
with Bill Moyers*. Alvin H. Perlmutter,
executive producer. Richard Cohen,
producer. Bill Moyers, executive editor.
PBS.

OUTSTANDING INDIVIDUAL ACHIEVEMENT
• Chris Beaver, Judy Irving, Ruth Landy,
producers, "Dark Circle," *P.O.V.* PBS.
• Perry Wolff, producer, *The Moon Above,
The Earth Below*. CBS.

**OUTSTANDING INDIVIDUAL
ACHIEVEMENT IN WRITING**
• Perry Wolff, *The Moon Above, The Earth
Below*. CBS.
• Charles Kuralt, Peter Freundlich,
"Milepost —Student Stopping Tank in
Beijing," *Sunday Morning*.

**OUTSTANDING INDIVIDUAL
ACHIEVEMENT IN DIRECTING**
• Jon Else, "Yosemite—The Fate," *The
American Experience*. PBS.

**OUTSTANDING INDIVIDUAL
ACHIEVEMENT IN RESEARCHING**
• Marjorie M. Mooney, "Elephant,"
National Geographic Special. PBS.
Bruce Norfleet, Margaret Bauer, Lisa
Manning, "Search for Battleship
Bismarck," *National Geographic
Explorer*. TBS.

**OUTSTANDING INDIVIDUAL
ACHIEVEMENT IN CINEMATOGRAPHY**
• Gordy Waterman, Stan Waterman,
"Dancing with Stingrays," *National
Geographic Explorer*. TBS.

**OUTSTANDING INDIVIDUAL ACHIEVEMENT
IN ELECTRONIC CAMERAWORK**
• Mark Falstad, "Yellowstone Under Fire,"
Frontline. PBS.
• Craig B. White, "America Works:
Window-Washer," *Today*. NBC.

**OUTSTANDING INDIVIDUAL ACHIEVEMENT
IN TAPE EDITING**
• Warren Lustig, "The '80s Remembered,"
The CBS Evening News with Dan Rather.
CBS.

**OUTSTANDING INDIVIDUAL ACHIEVEMENT
IN FILM EDITING**
• Sara Fishko, "No Applause, Just Throw
Money," *P.O.V.* PBS.
• Mary Alfieri, "Mountains of Fire,"
National Geographic Explorer. TBS.

**OUTSTANDING INDIVIDUAL ACHIEVEMENT
IN LIGHTING DIRECTION**
• Martin S. Dick, *Saturday Night with
Connie Chung*. CBS.

**OUTSTANDING INDIVIDUAL ACHIEVEMENT
IN GRAPHIC DESIGN**
• Chris Harvey, *Decade*. MTV.
Roger Goodman, Ben Blank, Frank Sveva,

Katherine Dillon, Brett Holey, Victoria Hunter, Barbara Gil, Lou Castellar, *Primetime Live*. ABC.

OUTSTANDING INDIVIDUAL ACHIEVEMENT IN TITLE SEQUENCES
• Joachim Blunck, Scott Miller, Ellen Kahn, Peter Faiman, *The Reporters*. Fox.

OUTSTANDING INDIVIDUAL ACHIEVEMENT IN ART DIRECTION/SCENIC DESIGN
• Robert Thayer, scenic designer, *The AIDS Quarterly*. PBS.

OUTSTANDING INDIVIDUAL ACHIEVEMENT IN MUSIC
• Bobby McFerrin, *Common Threads: Stories from the Quilt*. HBO.

OUTSTANDING INDIVIDUAL ACHIEVEMENT IN SOUND
• Kenneth Love, Clifford Hoelscher, Paul Schremp, Mark Linden, "Serengeti Diary," *National Geographic Special*. PBS.

INTERNATIONAL AWARD WINNERS
DRAMA
• *Traffic*. Picture Partnership producer for Channel 4. U.K.

DOCUMENTARY
• *Four Hours in My Lai.* Yorkshire TV. U.K.

ARTS DOCUMENTARY
• *Gwen — A Juliet Remembered*. A Saffron Production for BBC Television.

POPULAR ARTS
• *Alexei Sayles's Stuff: Fun with Magnets*. BBC. U.K.

PERFORMING ARTS
• *La Bohème*. ABC, Australia.

CHILDREN AND YOUNG PEOPLE
• *My Secret Identity*. Sunrise Films, Ltd., in association with Scholastic Productions, the CTV Television Network, MCA Television and with the participation of Telefilm Canada. Canada.

SPECIAL AWARDS
OUTSTANDING ACHIEVEMENT IN THE SCIENCE OF TELEVISION ENGINEERING
• Gregory Frazier, codirector of the AudioVision Institute, San Francisco State University's School of Creative Arts.

• Dr. Margaret R. Pfanstiehl, president, Washington Ear.
• Narrative Television Network
• Glen Southworth, founder, Colorado Video, Inc.
• Sony Corporation
• Eastman Kodak
• Odetics Broadcast
• Panasonic Broadcast Systems Company
• Ampex Corporation
• Sony Corporation
• Fuji Photo Film Corp.
• F/X, Inc.
• Pinnacle Systems
• Grass Valley Group, Inc.
• Accom, Inc.

OUTSTANDING ACHIEVEMENT IN ENGINEERING DEVELOPMENT (Statuettes)
• Comark Communications, Inc. and Varian/Eimac (and its creative team members Merald Shrader, Don Preist, and Nat Ostroff) for the Klystrode UHF High Power Amplifier Tube and Transmitter.
• Zaxcom Video, Inc. (and Glenn Sanders) for the TBC Control System
(Engineering plaques)
• Samuelson Alga Cinema (and its creative team members Jean Marie Lavalou, Alain Masseron, David Samuelson, Herve Theys) for the Louma Camera Crane.
• Alan Gordon Enterprises (and Grant Loucks and Geoff Williamson) for the Image 300 35mm High Speed Camera.

NATIONAL AWARD FOR COMMUNITY SERVICE
• *Colorblind*, WEWS-TV. Cleveland, Ohio.
• *Eye to Eye*, KSTP-TV. St. Paul, Minnesota.

LIFETIME ACHIEVEMENT AWARD FOR DAYTIME TELEVISION
• Mark Goodson

A.T.A.S. GOVERNORS AWARD
• Leonard Goldenson

N.A.T.A.S. TRUSTEES AWARD
• Lawrence Fraiberg, president, MCA Television stations.

Cheers and *L.A. Law* Score
The Biggest One

At first glance, this awards show looked almost identical to the one two years earlier with *Cheers* and *L.A. Law* back as series champs. It was only the fifth time in Emmys history that the victorious comedy and drama series returned together in a later year: *The Dick Van Dyke Show* and *The Defenders* did it in 1962–63 and 1963–64, *The Mary Tyler Moore Show* and *Upstairs, Downstairs* in 1974–75 and 1976–77, *Lou Grant* and *Taxi* in 1978–79 and 1979–80 and *Cheers* and *Hill Street Blues* in 1982-83 and 1983-84.

The latest victories by *Cheers* and *L.A. Law* were the stuff of showbiz history. Both now joined four other programs tied for the honor of winning best prime-time series the most times (four): *The Dick Van Dyke Show*; *All in the Family*; *Upstairs, Downstairs;* and *Hill Street Blues*. When *Cheers* nabbed three additional statuettes in other categories, it even tied *HSB*'s number of total awards — 26 — second only to *The Mary Tyler Moore Show*'s record tally of 29. With the barroom comedy continuing to fly high in the ratings and in the regard of admiring TV critics and Emmy voters, it suddenly seemed inevitable that it would soon topple *MTM*'s 16-year-old reign as the overall Emmys champ. Also, like the still-popular *L.A. Law, Cheers* could establish itself as the sole winner of the most series awards by just copping one more in a future year. Accepting this year's series prize, *Cheers* executive producer and cocreator James Burrows (who also won an Emmy for directing) bowed to his team's success so far with the words, "I said we were good, but now we're venerable, I guess."

A.T.A.S.

Best actress Kirstie Alley of Cheers *set a racy tone for the Emmycast when she thanked her husband for "the big one."*

The 1991 ceremony also distinguished itself in other ways: black actors and dramas did particularly well ("It's about time!" cried actress Lynn Whitfield backstage), cable programming did better than ever (taking eight out of 76 awards), and it was another X-rated event. "It was the dirtiest Emmys show since Joan Rivers and Eddie Murphy emceed in 1983," *Emmy Magazine* editor and past A.T.A.S. president Hank Rieger said in an interview after the ceremony.

As the Emmycast begin, the night was billed as a tribute to comedy with cartoon hellion Bart (or "brat" but for an obvious transposition of letters) Simpson welcoming home viewers to *"The Bart Simpson Show!"* and James Earl Jones getting a cream pie in his face.

Veteran actor James Earl Jones introduced the prime-time ceremony and its tribute to TV comedy by taking an ignominious pie in the face.

The last laugh turned out to be Jones's, however, when he won two Emmys as the evening's trend toward appreciating blacks gained momentum — one for lead actor in the troubled crime show *Gabriel's Fire* (later renamed *Pros and Cons*) and the other for best supporting actor in *Heat Wave*, a TNT cable dramatization of the 1965 race riots in the Watts district of Los Angeles. Backstage, the veteran actor held up both awards and said, smiling, "These things are glorious because they help you get other things done."

Gabriel's Fire also garnered a best supporting actress trophy for Madge Sinclair (as Jones's longtime friend on the show — her first Emmy) and for guest performer David Opatoshu who played a Holocaust survivor searching for a family portrait once seized by Nazis.

When *L.A. Law* executive producer David Kelley accepted the statuette for best drama series, he warmly acknowledged his competition when he singled out the two canceled series *China Beach*

and *thirtysomething*. "We know that when we win this, we never win it by default," he said. "We will miss seeing you."

1988's best drama series *thirtysomething* went out in a blaze of glory by scoring threesomething awards: one for costuming, another for supporting actor Timothy Busfield (as the restless, sometimes immature advertising executive Elliot Weston), and one for Patricia Wettig — her third. Wettig played Elliot's wife Nancy who battled ovarian cancer. She had been voted best supporting actress in 1988 and best lead actress last year, but this was her most emotional victory yet. She was close to tears as she accepted her second trophy as lead actress saying, "It's a little sad. It's my last time to say goodbye to this character."

In the comedy category, the awards proved to be just as dramatic. For a second year in a row, Bebe Neuwirth was voted best supporting actress for her role as a pyschiatrist on *Cheers* while Jonathan Winters won the first Emmy of his long TV career for his role as Gunny Davis on *Davis Rules*.

Murphy Brown began the night with 13 nominations (the same number as *Cheers*). Its most touching victory went, posthumously, to Colleen Dewhurst, the 67-year-old stage actress who also won an award for portraying Murphy's mother in a guest appearance on the show in 1989. She died just two days prior to winning her fourth career Emmy.

TV Guide said Candice Bergen was a cinch for the actress's statuette because the episode she submitted to the blue-ribbon panel for consideration was an especially dramatic one involving a near-fatal plane crash. Her closest challenger was considered to be *Cheers*'s Kirstie Alley, who entered an episode that dramatized her character's bout with alcoholism.

It was the third time that Alley was up for the honor. When she won it this time, she referred to her costar Ted Danson's recent nine-year quest for the equivalent male trophy, saying, "I only thank God I didn't have to wait as long as Ted!" She then thanked her husband, actor Parker Stevenson, for being "the man who has given me the big one for the last eight years." When a moment of quiet embarrassment followed, Emmys cohost Jerry Seinfeld tried to keep the tempo light by feigning innocence and gasping, "The big one? That could be anything!" Soon thereafter Burt Reynolds was named best lead actor for playing a high-school football coach on *Evening Shade* and, in an obvious reference to her breasts, thanked his wife Loni Anderson for giving him *two* big ones. And so the ceremony degenerated quickly into an evening full of sexual innuendo.

It might not have been a major issue if it hadn't been for an inane comedy routine delivered by Gilbert Gottfried that ended up threatening to turn the Emmycast into a raunchy burlesque show. Gottfried pounced on the recent news of children's star Pee-Wee Herman being arrested for allegedly masturbating in a Florida porn theater. If masturbation were a crime, Gottfried said, "I should already be on death row!" He then tripped through an annoying series of variations on the same gag ("To think, by age 14, I was already Al Capone!") that weren't particularly funny and went on ad nauseam. Meantime, irritated viewers jammed the A.T.A.S. switchboard with protest calls while Fox, hoping to minimize the damage, immediately edited the routine out of delayed broadcasts to some parts of southern California. Right after the show the network issued a public apology calling the unscripted remarks "irresponsible and insulting" while newspapers like *The New York Times* referred the next day to "the outrage from many critics and viewers over the perceived tastelessness and vulgarity of this year's Emmy Awards telecast."

> *It was "the dirtiest Emmy show" in years.*

This was the first year that miniseries competed directly against made-for-TV films and it was the docu-drama *Separate But Equal* that prevailed. ABC's *Separate* was based on the Supreme Court's landmark 1954 decision to desegregate schools and starred Sidney Poitier as Thurgood Marshall,

Later on Jones won two Emmys: for best actor in Gabriel's Fire *(above, presented by Jason Priestley) and a supporting honor for TV film* Heat Wave.

who was then a lawyer for the N.A.A.C.P. Legal Defense Fund (before serving as a justice on the high court himself). Poitier was considered a likely choice to be the year's best actor, but he was upset by Sir John Gielgud of *Masterpiece Theatre*'s *Summer's Lease*, who had been nominated for, and lost, four Emmys in the past. Gielgud also beat out another front runner, James Garner of *Decoration Day*, a *Hallmark Hall of Fame* drama (costarring Ruby Dee) about a black winner of the Congressional Medal of Honor who refuses to accept the award. Dee, an accomplished stage performer, was named best supporting actress and said backstage about her victory, "There's a whole new generation discovering me now and that's exciting."

It was HBO's *The Josephine Baker Story* that was expected to take the most awards in the category — and did — even though the top prize was elusive. Baker was the sexy black American dancer who became the toast of Paris in between the two World Wars, and she was played with panache by the relatively unknown actress Lynn Whitfield. Whitfield won the trophy for best actress for her efforts, director Brian Gibson was given the director's statuette, and together their wins were considered "a victory for romance," said *The Washington Post*. The duo fell in love while shooting the film, got married soon afterward, and had a baby just three weeks before the Emmys.

The awards for *The Josephine Baker Story* were also considered a significant victory for cable TV. The HBO production began with 12 nominations, the most ever received by a cable program, and ended up with five honors, including Emmys for costume design, hairstyling, and art direction. The lavish and daring TV movie, said *The Hollywood Reporter*, "broke new ground for cable honors."

The Emmycast had many other serious moments that included a well-orchestrated farewell to the TV stars who had died that year, such as Dewhurst, Michael Landon, Danny Thomas, and Lee Remick. A Governors Award was given to *Masterpiece Theatre*. Throughout the night presenters and winners alike sported bright red ribbons with their formal attire to demonstrate their support for the fight against AIDS.

Viewership was up dramatically compared to last year, reaching a 12.5 rating and 22 share, but the numbers were still less than those enjoyed by the daytime Emmys.

DAYTIME AWARDS

"This is a very special occasion," noted host Bob Barker. "For the first time in 18 years, the telecast about the people who make up daytime TV gets a chance for a prime-time celebration."

The idea had been around for many years, but no network dared to try it earlier. TV executives just weren't convinced that a salute to daytime programs could pull a respectable prime-time rating, but the results that CBS received were staggering. Not only did the daytime awards top the viewership numbers for both last and this year's prime-time Emmys, the show finished second in the week's overall Nielsen lineup, topped only by *60 Minutes*.

Eleven-time past loser of the best actress award, Susan Lucci of *All My Children*, introduced the evening's most effective vignette when she opened "the family album of soaps." Inside were the photos of the many celebrities who starred in both daytime and prime-time television, including all of the following Emmy winners: Dana Delany (*As the World Turns/China Beach*), Jimmy Smits (*All My Children/L.A. Law*), Judith Light (*One Life to Live/Who's the*

Boss?) Daniel J. Travanti (*General Hospital/ Hill Street Blues*), and this year's best supporting actor for *thirtysomething*, Timothy Busfield, who once starred on *All My Children*.

Lucci proved to have a championship sense of humor about her amazing losing streak by starring in commercials that ran during the Emmycast for a new artificial sweetener called Sweet One. ("Twelve years without an Emmy!" she ranted and raved at the conclusion of it, in a scene worthy of her TV character, Erica Kane. "What does a person have to do?!") Proof that the issue was reaching high camp proportions, presenter Joan Rivers offered her own comments on the matter. "Maybe tonight, please God!" she started out saying about Lucci's chances. "I think Erica deserves a million Emmys — just for being the trampiest person on daytime TV. Her purse folds out into a Murphy bed. She's got the hottest set of thighs since Joan of Arc ...."

Lucci lost this year to British actress Finola Hughes, who played Anna Lavery on *General Hospital*. Hughes reportedly flew to New York from London for the Emmys show, but had to return to England just prior to the show for what Hughes called a family emergency and the tabloid press called trouble with her immigration status that could affect her work on the soap.

The rest of the daytime drama awards were split among a half dozen shows. The 1987 winner of best series, *As the World Turns*, returned to reap the same honor again. Its executive producer Laurence Caso accepted it, saying, "An award like this is not only a pat on the back. It's a kick in the head and all of us thank you mightily for it." *Santa Barbara* took the directing and writing prizes while *The Young and the Restless* took a total of five, including two performance awards. "I've never spent hap-

Susan Lucci displayed a new sense of humor about her losing streak, but was defeated again after a twelfth nomination.

pier years!" exclaimed Jess Walton (Jill Foster Abbott) as she claimed the trophy for best supporting actress. Peter Bergman (Jack Abbott) was voted best actor and thanked the cast, crew, his mother and father, and "my conscience, my best friend and my dearest love — my wife, Mary Ellen."

Bernie Barrow (Louie Slavinski) of *Loving* had the best acceptance speech of all when he was revealed as the year's best supporting actor. "It's nice to be in daytime," he said, "where every living day is an opening night, and all the actors out there know what I'm talking about." Almost as eloquent, but surely more dramatic was the thank-you from the year's top young actor, Rick Hearst (Alan-Michael Spaulding) of *Guiding Light*. "I would say this is the single greatest moment of my life," he began, "but I can't say that because at 11:42 last night, my son Nicholas Charles was born."

Emmys host and animal rights activist Bob Barker won his sixth award for hosting *The Price is Right.* "I want to read the inscription to you," he said to the audience as he held the statuette, pretending to read the wee print: "Have you had your pet spayed or neutered?" *Jeopardy!* won the trophy as game show of the year, which was accepted by producer George Vosburgh, who noted proudly that *Jeopardy!*'s writers recently won their first Emmy.

Sesame Street once again was voted best children's series while *Lost in the Barrens,* about a group marooned in the Artic cold, was named best children's special. *Tiny Toon Adventures,* which was produced in part by Steven Spielberg, was acclaimed the animated program of the year. One of its other producers plugged Spielberg's latest film and made reference to the famed Hollywood producer/director's failure ever to win an Oscar, saying, "Spielberg couldn't be here tonight because he's shooting *Hook.* He's not going to worry about those Oscars anymore because he's got a daytime Emmy."

> **The success of the new daytime Emmys, aired at night, was staggering.**

Last year's best talk show host, Joan Rivers, introduced the category this time with a montage of old clips showing talk show greats of yore. ("And could they talk!" the queen of the same said in her intro remarks.) Included were kids saying some of the darnedest things on *Art Linkletter's House Party,* Jack Benny giving the silent treatment to Merv Griffin, and Muhammad Ali telling David Frost, "You're not as dumb as you look!"

The winner of both the host and program awards this year was *The Oprah Winfrey Show.* Producer Debra DiMaio thanked the "once-in-a-lifetime spirit" of Winfrey while Winfrey herself thanked Truddi Chase, a victim of sexual abuse who also suffered from multiple personality disorder. It was the episode with Winfrey's interview with Chase that was submitted to Emmy's judging panels. "During that show," Winfrey said, "a lot of victims of sexual abuse were able to release some of their own personal shame."

For the first time in its history, the Lifetime Achievement Award went to a company, Procter & Gamble, the longtime sponsor of such series as this year's best, *As the World Turns,* and others such as *Guiding Light* and *The Edge of Night.* "Because they made soap products," Bob Barker said of the company's leaders, "daytime dramas became known as soap operas."

Throughout their history the regular prime-time Emmys seldom came close to finishing on time. The daytime Emmys in prime time, by comparison, ran just 20 seconds over, qualifying it for an entry in the *The Guinness Book of World Records* for the awards show coming closest to its anticipated length.

SPORTS AWARDS

It was a championship night for the sports awards, broadcast nationally by ESPN for the first time, and featuring celebrity cohosts Joan Van Ark and Dennis Miller (Miller had also served as a cohost of the prime-time awards). Star participants included Heisman Trophy winner Doug Flutie, Green Bay Packer Paul Hornung, America's Cup winner Dennis Conner, and model Cheryl Tiegs.

ABC won the most awards, including ones for its live coverage of the Indianapolis 500, a writing award for Jack Whitaker for his eloquence on the subject of the PGA golf tour, and a program prize for *ABC's Wide World of Sports* as best anthology series ("a genre it created," claimed *The Hollywood Reporter*). CBS's coverage of the NCAA basketball tournament was declared Outstanding Live Sports Series while the syndicated preview *Road to the Super Bowl XXIV* was hailed as best edited sports special.

Ted Turner received a Trustees award for his success in cable TV. With him was his future wife and past Emmy champ Jane Fonda (for The Dollmaker, *1983-84).*

NBC won only one trophy, which went to Dick Enberg as Outstanding Sports Personality/ Host Play-by-Play. Accepting the honor, Enberg said, "Play-by-play people, the sportscasters, we're the obstetricians of the business. We deliver the baby while many others do the work." (Winning another Emmy, Enberg told N.A.T.A.S. President John Cannon afterward, always feels to him like hitting a home run in the bottom of the ninth inning with the bases loaded.) John Madden won his eighth career award — and fifth in a row as Outstanding Sports Personality/Analyst.

After ABC, the night's biggest winner was broadcaster ESPN, which reaped only four trophies during its first four years of eligibility, but took a total of five this year. "The network's *Sports-Center* was the biggest winner," noted *The Sporting News*, "topping NBC's *NFL Live* and CBS's *NFL Today* as Outstanding Studio Show. *SportsCenter* spinoff *Outside the Lines* deservedly won the Outstanding Sports Journalism category for its investigative look at the sports autograph business."

The Sporting News was less happy about an omission from the lineup of program nominees, even claiming that

the TV academy "overlooked the most compelling piece of TV sports in 1990."

"Remember ABC's coverage of last year's Kentucky Derby," the paper asked, "when Unbridled's trainer, Carl Nafzger, provided an emotional call of the stretch run for the horse's 92-year-old owner Frances Genter? Producer Curt Gowdy's brilliant decision to wire Nafzger inexplicably failed to merit a nomination in the Outstanding Live Sports Special category."

The most heartfelt moment of the Emmy evening was the presentation of a Lifetime Achievement Award to "the man behind the mike" Lindsey Nelson, also known as "he of the signature sports coat with the wild patterns and colors," said *The Hollywood Reporter*. Nelson gained fame for providing animated play-by-play commentary for games played by Notre Dame, the New York Giants, and the New York Mets. "Never has such a profession ever been so dominated by one man," Paul Hornung said.

NEWS & DOCUMENTARY AWARDS

"It seems to be Romania's night!" cried Janice Tomlin, an executive producer who won two top awards for covering

Connie Chung and producer Hal Gessner were honored for their interview with Paul Newman and Joanne Woodward.

post-Communist Romania for ABC's *20/20*. One of them was even the plum prize for investigative journalism that went to reward "Shame of a Nation," Tomlin's probe into the horrors she discovered in that country's mental and medical institutions. Coincidentally, among the celebrity speakers and presenters that night at the Waldorf-Astoria Hotel in New York was Aurel Dragos Munteanu, Romania's representative to the United Nations.

The other prize for investigative journalism went to *Frontline*'s coverage of the Iran-Contra scandal in "High Crimes and Misdemeanors." *Frontline* received more Emmys than any other series this year, including one for its coverage of "Seven Days in Bensonhurst," about continuing racial tensions in a working-class section of Brooklyn, New York. PBS's *Eyes on the Prize II* won the second-largest number — four, including two for writing the 14-part series chronicling the history of the civil rights movement from 1965 to 1985.

Among the night's other winners was the easy-going anchor of *CBS This Morning*, Harry Smith, who was honored for writing a meditation on the fall of Communism called "The Party's Over." Backstage, Smith said that winning a writing award "is an incredible high," and then offered his advice on how to get into the news business: "write, write, write and read, read, read."

Connie Chung talked candidly backstage about her Emmy for interviewing Paul Newman and Joanne Woodward. "It was a particularly difficult assignment because they never do interviews," Chung said. The show worked out well in the end, though, she said, because "Joanne made the interview — by making it free, easy, and relaxed."

The biggest news event of the year — Iraq's invasion of Kuwait — was the subject of only one award out of the more than 40 given away for news coverage. It went to *ABC News Nightline,* which was also hailed for its "Town Meeting in South Africa." CNN's close-up coverage of the war seemed like a natural to have been included, but the new network received no nominations this year, a matter of some controversy.

1990–91

The prime-time ceremony was broadcast on the Fox network from the Pasadena Civic Auditorium on August 25, 1991, for prime-time programs telecast between June 1, 1990, and May 31, 1991. The creative arts awards were bestowed on August 24, 1991. Daytime awards broadcast on CBS from New York's Marriott Marquis Hotel on June 27, 1991, for programs aired between March 6, 1990, and March 5, 1991. The sports awards for 1990 were presented April 3, 1991, and were broadcast on ESPN. News & documentary awards for 1990 were presented at New York's Waldorf-Astoria Hotel on September 11, 1990.

PRIME-TIME PROGRAM AWARDS
OUTSTANDING DRAMA SERIES
• *L.A. Law*. David E. Kelley, Rick Wallace, executive producers. Patricia Green, supervising producer. Elodie Keene, James C. Hart, Alan Brennert, Robert Breech, John Hill, producers. Alice West, coordinating producer. NBC.
China Beach. John Sacret Young, executive producer. John Wells, co-executive producer. Mimi Leder, supervising producer. Lydia Woodward, Carol Flint, producers. Geno Escarrega, line producer. ABC.
Northern Exposure. Joshua Brand, John Falsey, executive producers. Andrew Schneider, co-executive producer. Diane Frolov, Robin Green, Charles Rosin, supervising producers. Cheryl Bloch, Matthew Nodella, Robert T. Skodis, producers. CBS.
Quantum Leap. Donald P. Bellisario, executive producer. Deborah Pratt, Michael Zinberg, co-executive producers. Harker Wade, Robert Wolterstorff, supervising producers. Chris Ruppenthal, producer. Paul Brown, Jeff Gourson, coproducers. NBC.
thirtysomething. Edward Zwick, Marshall Herskovitz, executive producers. Scott Winant, supervising producer. Ellen Pressman, Richard Kramer, Ann Lewis Hamilton, Joseph Dougherty, producers. Lindsley Parsons III, coproducer. ABC.

OUTSTANDING COMEDY SERIES
• *Cheers*. James Burrows, Glen Charles, Les Charles, Cheri Eichen, Bill Steinkellner, Phoef Sutton, executive producers. Tim Berry, producer. Andy Ackerman, Brian Pollack, Mert Rich, Dan O'Shannon, Tom Anderson, Larry Balmagia, coproducers. NBC.
Designing Women. Harry Thomason, Linda Bloodworth-Thomason, executive producers. Pam Norris, co-executive producer. Douglas Jackson, Tommy Thompson, supervising producers. David Trainer, producer. CBS.
The Golden Girls. Paul Junger Witt, Tony Thomas, Susan Harris, Marc Sotkin, executive producers. Tom Whedon, Philip Jayson Lasker, co-executive producers. Gail Parent, Richard Vaczy, Tracy

Gamble, Don Seigel, Jerry Perzigian, supervising producers. Nina Feinberg, coproducer. NBC.
Murphy Brown. Diane English, Joel Shukovsky, executive producers. Gary Dontzig, Steven Peterman, supervising producers. Tom Palmer, co-supervising producer. Barnet Kellman, producer. Korby Siamis, consulting producer. Deborah Smith, coproducer. CBS.
The Wonder Years. Bob Brush, executive producer. Jill Gordon, co-executive producer. Ken Topolsky, supervising producer. David Chambers, Michael Dinner, producers. ABC.

OUTSTANDING DRAMA/COMEDY SPECIAL OR MINISERIES
• *Separate But Equal*. George Stevens, Jr., Stan Margulies, executive producers. ABC.
Decoration Day, Hallmark Hall of Fame. Marian Rees, executive producer. Anne Hopkins, producer. Dick Gallegly, line producer. Joyce Corrington, coproducer. NBC.
The Josephine Baker Story. Robert Halmi, David Puttnam, executive producers. John Kemeny, producer. HBO.
Paris Trout. Diane Kerew, executive producer. Frank Konigsberg, Larry Sanitsky, producers. Showtime.
Sarah, Plain and Tall, Hallmark Hall of Fame. William Self, Glenn Close, executive producers. Edwin Self, supervising producer. Glenn Jordan, producer. CBS.
Switched at Birth. Michael O'Hara, Lawrence Horowitz, Barry Morrow, Richard Heus, executive producers. Mark Sennet, supervising producer. Ervin Zavada, producer. NBC.

OUTSTANDING VARIETY, MUSIC, OR COMEDY PROGRAM
• *The 63rd Annual Academy Awards*. Gilbert Cates, producer. ABC.
In Living Color. Keenen Ivory Wayans, executive producer. Tamara Rawitt, producer. Michael Petok, coproducer. Fox.
The Kennedy Century Honors: A Celebration of the Performing Arts. George Stevens, Jr., Nick Vanoff, producers. CBS.
Late Night with David Letterman. Jack Rollins, David Letterman, executive producers. Robert Morton, producer. David Letterman, host. NBC.

The Muppets Celebrate Jim Henson. Don Mischer, producer. Martin G. Baker, David J. Goldberg, coproducers. CBS.
The Tonight Show Starring Johnny Carson. Fred DeCordova, Peter Lassally, executive producers. Jeff Sotzing, producer. Jim McCawley, coproducer. Johnny Carson, host. NBC.

OUTSTANDING INFORMATIONAL SERIES
(Area award winner)
• *The Civil War*. Ken Burns, Ric Burns, producers. Stephen Ives, Julie Dunfey, Mike Hill, coproducers. Catherine Eisele, coordinating producer. PBS.

OUTSTANDING INFORMATIONAL SPECIAL
(Area award winner)
• "Edward R. Murrow: This Reporter," *American Masters*. Susan Lacy, executive producer. Susan Steinberg, producer. Elizabeth Kreutz, Harlene Freezer, coproducers. PBS.

OUTSTANDING CHILDREN'S PROGRAM
(Winner)
• *You Can't Grow Home Again: A 3-2-1 Contact Extra*. Anne MacLeod, executive producer. Tom Cammisa, producer. PBS.

OUTSTANDING ANIMATED PROGRAM
(Winner — One hour or less)
• *The Simpsons*. James J. Brooks, Matt Groening, Sam Simon, executive producers. Al Jean, Mike Reiss, supervising producers. Jay Kogen, Wallace Wolodarsky, Richard Sakai, Larina Jean Adamson, producers. George Meyer, coproducer. Gabor Csupo, executive animated producer. Sherry Gunther, animation producer. Steve Pepoon, writer. Rich Moore, director. Fox.

OUTSTANDING CLASSICAL PROGRAM
IN THE PERFORMING ARTS
(Winner)
• *Tchaikovsky's 150th Birthday Gala from Leningrad*. Peter Gelb, executive producer. Helmut Rost, producer. Anne Cauvin, Laura Mitgang, coordinating producer. PBS.

PERFORMANCE, DIRECTING, AND WRITING
OUTSTANDING LEAD ACTOR
IN A DRAMA SERIES
• James Earl Jones, *Gabriel's Fire*. ABC.
Scott Bakula, *Quantum Leap*. NBC.
Peter Falk, *Columbo, The ABC Monday Mystery Movie*. NBC.

Kyle MacLachlan, *Twin Peaks*. ABC.
Michael Moriarity, *Law and Order*. NBC.

OUTSTANDING LEAD ACTRESS
IN A DRAMA SERIES
• Patricia Wettig, *thirtysomething*. ABC.
Dana Delany, *China Beach*. ABC.
Sharon Gless, *The Trials of Rosie O'Neill*. CBS.
Angela Lansbury, *Murder, She Wrote*. CBS.

OUTSTANDING LEAD ACTRESS
IN A COMEDY SERIES
• Kirstie Alley, *Cheers*. NBC.
Candice Bergen, *Murphy Brown*. CBS.
Blair Brown, *The Days and Nights of Molly Dodd*. Lifetime.
Delta Burke, *Designing Women*. CBS.
Betty White, *The Golden Girls*. NBC.

OUTSTANDING LEAD ACTOR
IN A COMEDY SERIES
• Burt Reynolds, *Evening Shade*. CBS.
Ted Danson, *Cheers*. NBC.
John Goodman, *Roseanne*. ABC.
Richard Mulligan, *Empty Nest*. NBC.
Craig T. Nelson, *Coach*. ABC.

OUTSTANDING LEAD ACTOR
IN A MINISERIES OR SPECIAL
• John Gielgud, *Summer's Lease, Masterpiece Theatre*. PBS.
James Garner, *Decoration Day, Hallmark Hall of Fame*. NBC.
Dennis Hopper, *Paris Trout*. Showtime.
Sidney Poitier, *Separate But Equal*. ABC.
Christopher Walken, *Sarah, Plain and Tall, Hallmark Hall of Fame*. CBS.

OUTSTANDING LEAD ACTRESS
IN A MINISERIES OR SPECIAL
• Lynn Whitfield, *The Josephine Baker Story*. HBO.
Glenn Close, *Sarah, Plain and Tall, Hallmark Hall of Fame*. CBS.
Barbara Hershey, *Paris Trout*. Showtime.
Suzanne Pleshette, *Leona Helmsley: The Queen of Mean*. CBS.
Lee Purcell, *Long Road Home*. NBC.

OUTSTANDING SUPPORTING ACTOR
IN A COMEDY SERIES
• Jonathan Winters, *Davis Rules*. ABC.
Charles Durning, *Evening Shade*. CBS.
Woody Harrelson, *Cheers*. NBC.
Michael Jeter, *Evening Shade*. CBS.
Jerry Van Dyke, *Coach*. ABC.

**OUTSTANDING SUPPORTING ACTRESS
IN A COMEDY SERIES**
• Bebe Neuwirth, *Cheers*. NBC.
Elizabeth Ashley, *Evening Shade*. CBS.
Faith Ford, *Murphy Brown*. CBS.
Estelle Getty, *The Golden Girls*. NBC.
Rhea Perlman, *Cheers*. NBC.

**OUTSTANDING SUPPORTING ACTOR
IN A DRAMA SERIES**
• Timothy Busfield, *thirtysomething*. ABC.
David Clennon, *thirtysomething*. ABC.
Richard Dysart, *L.A. Law*. NBC.
Jimmy Smits, *L.A. Law*. NBC.
Dean Stockwell, *Quantum Leap*. NBC.

**OUTSTANDING SUPPORTING ACTRESS
IN A DRAMA SERIES**
• Madge Sinclair, *Gabriel's Fire*. ABC.
Marg Helgenberger, *China Beach*. ABC.
Piper Laurie, *Twin Peaks*. ABC.
Melanie Mayron, *thirtysomething*. ABC.
Diana Muldaur, *L.A. Law*. NBC.

**OUTSTANDING SUPPORTING ACTOR
IN A MINISERIES OR SPECIAL**
• James Earl Jones, *Heat Wave*. TNT.
Ruben Blades, *The Josephine Baker Story*.
HBO.
David Dukes, *The Josephine Baker Story*.
HBO.
Richard Kiley, *Separate But Equal*. ABC.
Leon Russom, *Long Road Home*. NBC.

**OUTSTANDING SUPPORTING ACTRESS
IN A MINISERIES OR SPECIAL**
• Ruby Dee, *Decoration Day, Hallmark
Hall of Fame*. NBC.
Olympia Dukakis, *Lucky Day*. ABC.
Doris Roberts, *The Sunset Gang, American
Playhouse*. PBS.
Vanessa Redgrave, *Young Catherine*.
TNT.
Elaine Stritch, *An Inconvenient Woman*.
ABC.

**OUTSTANDING GUEST ACTOR
IN A DRAMA SERIES**
• David Opatoshu, *Gabriel's Fire*. ABC.
Dabney Coleman, *Columbo, The ABC
Monday Mystery Movie*. ABC.
Peter Coyote, *Avonlea*. Disney Channel.
John Glover, *L.A. Law*. NBC.

**OUTSTANDING GUEST ACTRESS
IN A DRAMA SERIES**
• Peggy McCay, *The Trials of Rosie
O'Neill*. CBS.

Eileen Brennan, *thirtysomething*. ABC.
Colleen Dewhurst, *Avonlea*. Disney
Channel.
Penny Fuller, *China Beach*. ABC.

**OUTSTANDING GUEST ACTOR
IN A COMEDY SERIES**
• Jay Thomas, *Murphy Brown*. CBS.
Sheldon Leonard, *Cheers*. NBC.
Alan Oppenheimer, *Murphy Brown*. CBS.
Tom Poston, *Coach*. ABC.
Danny Thomas, *Empty Nest*. NBC.

**OUTSTANDING GUEST ACTRESS
IN A COMEDY SERIES**
• Colleen Dewhurst, *Murphy Brown*. CBS.
Whoopi Goldberg, *A Different World*.
NBC.
Frances Sternhagen, *Cheers*. NBC.
Sada Thompson, *Cheers*. NBC.
Brenda Vaccaro, *The Golden Girls*. NBC.

**OUTSTANDING DIRECTING
IN A DRAMA SERIES**
• Thomas Carter, *Equal Justice*. ABC.
Gregory Hoblit, *Cop Rock*. ABC.
Mimi Leder, *China Beach*. ABC.
Tom Moore, *L.A. Law*. NBC.

**OUTSTANDING DIRECTING
IN A COMEDY SERIES**
• James Burrows, *Cheers*. NBC.
Peter Baldwin, *The Wonder Years*. ABC.
Tom Cherones, *Seinfeld*. NBC.
Barnet Kellman, *Murphy Brown*. CBS.
Jay Tarses, *The Days and Nights of Molly
Dodd*. Lifetime.

**OUTSTANDING DIRECTING
IN A MINISERIES OR A SPECIAL**
• Brian Gibson, *The Josephine Baker
Story*. HBO.
Gilbert Cates, *Absolute Strangers*. CBS.
Glenn Jordan, *Sarah, Plain and Tall,
Hallmark Hall of Fame*. CBS.
Robert Markowitz, *Decoration Day,
Hallmark Hall of Fame*. NBC.

**OUTSTANDING DIRECTING
IN A VARIETY OR MUSIC PROGRAM**
• Hal Gurnee, *Late Night with David
Letterman*. NBC.
Dwight Hemion, *The Kennedy Center
Honors: A Celebration of the Performing
Arts*. CBS.
Jeff Margolis, *The 63rd Annual Academy
Awards*. ABC.

Burt Reynolds and wife Loni Anderson:
He acknowledged "two big ones" and a
best actor Emmy for Evening Shade.

OUTSTANDING WRITING IN DRAMA SERIES
• David E. Kelley, *L.A. Law*. NBC.
Judith Feldman, Sarah Woodside
Gallagher, *L.A. Law*. NBC.
David E. Kelley, Patricia Green, Alan
Brennert, *L.A. Law*. NBC.
Joshua Brand, John Falsey, *Northern
Exposure*. CBS.
Ann Lewis Hamilton, *thirtysomething*.
ABC.

**OUTSTANDING WRITING
IN A COMEDY SERIES**
• Gary Dontzig, Steven Peterman, *Murphy
Brown*. CBS.
Jay Tarses, *The Days and Nights of Molly
Dodd*. Lifetime.
Diane English, *Murphy Brown*. CBS.
Larry David, Jerry Seinfeld, *Seinfeld*. NBC.
Larry David, *Seinfeld*. NBC.

**OUTSTANDING WRITING
IN A MINISERIES OR A SPECIAL**
• Andrew Davies, *House of Cards,
Masterpiece Theatre*. PBS.
Robert W. Lenski, *Decoration Day,
Hallmark Hall of Fame*. NBC.
Pete Dexter, *Paris Trout*. Showtime.
Patricia MacLachlan, Carol Sobieski,
*Sarah, Plain and Tall, Hallmark Hall of
Fame*. CBS.

George Stevens, Jr., *Separate But Equal*.
ABC.

**OUTSTANDING WRITING IN A VARIETY
OR MUSIC PROGRAM**
• Hal Kanter, Buz Kohan, writers. Billy
Crystal, David Steinberg, Bruce Vilanch,
Robert Wuhl, special material, *The 63rd
Annual Academy Awards*. ABC.
John Bowman, Buddy Sheffield, head
writers. Keenen Ivory Wayans, Fax Bahr,
Kim Bass, Les Firestein, Greg Fields,
Becky Hartman, J.J. Paulsen, Adam
Small, Steve Tompkins, Pam Veasey,
Damon Wayans, *In Living Color*. Fox.
Stephen M. O'Donnell, head writer.
Rob Burnett, Spike Feresten, Larry
Jacobson, David Letterman, Gerard
Mulligan, Maria Pope, Paul Simms, Steven
Young, *Late Night with David Letterman*.
NBC.
Jerry Juhl, Sarah Lukinson, Bill Prady, *The
Muppets Celebrate Jim Henson*. CBS.
A. Whitney Brown, Tom Davis, James
Downey, Al Franken, Jack Handey, Lorne
Michaels, Conan O'Brien, Bob Odenkirk,
Andrew Robin, Adam Sandler, Herb
Sargent, Rob Schneider, Robert Smigel,
David Spade, Bonnie Turner, Terry
Turner, Christine Zander, *Saturday Night
Live*. NBC.

**OUTSTANDING INDIVIDUAL PERFORMANCE
IN A VARIETY OR MUSIC PROGRAM
(Winner)**
• Billy Crystal, host, *The 63rd Annual
Academy Awards*. ABC.

**OUTSTANDING INDIVIDUAL
ACHIEVEMENT—CLASSICAL
MUSIC/DANCE PROGRAMMING
(Area award winners)**
• Kurt Moll, "The Ring of Nibelung," *The
Metropolitan Opera Presents*. PBS.
• Yo-Yo Ma, performer, *Tchaikovsky's
150th Birthday Gala from Leningrad*.
PBS.

OTHER AWARD WINNERS
OUTSTANDING MUSIC AND LYRICS
• Randy Newman, composer and lyricist,
Cop Rock. ABC.

**OUTSTANDING MUSIC COMPOSITION
FOR A SERIES
(Dramatic underscore)**
• John Debney, *The Young Riders*.
ABC.

OUTSTANDING MUSIC COMPOSITION FOR A MINISERIES OR A SPECIAL (Dramatic underscore)
• Richard Bellis, *Stephen King's "It."* ABC.

OUTSTANDING MUSIC DIRECTION
• Ian Fraser, music director. Bill Byers, Chris Boardman, J. Hill, principal arrangers, *The Walt Disney Company Presents "The American Teacher Awards."* Disney.

OUTSTANDING CHOREOGRAPHY
• Debbie Allen, *Motown 30: What's Goin' ON!* CBS.

OUTSTANDING CASTING FOR A MINISERIES OR A SPECIAL (Juried award)
• Alixe Gordon, *Separate But Equal.* ABC.

OUTSTANDING COSTUMING FOR A SERIES
• Patrick R. Norris, costume supervisor. Linda Serijan-Fasmer, women's costume supervisor, *thirtysomething.* ABC.

OUTSTANDING COSTUMING FOR A MINISERIES OR A SPECIAL
• Michael T. Boyd, military costume supervisor. Cathy A. Smith, American Indian Costume supervisor. Bud Clark, civilian costume supervisor, *Son of the Morning Star.* ABC.

OUTSTANDING COSTUME DESIGN FOR A MINISERIES OR A SPECIAL
• Maria Hruby, Gyorgyi Vidak, *The Josephine Baker Story.* HBO.

OUTSTANDING COSTUME DESIGN FOR A VARIETY OR MUSIC PROGRAM
• Ret Turner, costume designer. Bob Mackie, costume designer for Carol Burnett, *Carol & Company.* NBC.

OUTSTANDING COSTUME DESIGN FOR A SERIES
• Bill Hargate, *Murphy Brown.* CBS.

OUTSTANDING MAKEUP FOR A SERIES
• Gerald Quist, Michael Mills, Jeremy Swan, Douglas D. Kelly, *Quantum Leap.* NBC.

OUTSTANDING MAKEUP FOR A MINISERIES OR A SPECIAL
• Joe McKinney, Hank Edds, makeup supervisors. Paul Sanchez, key makeup.

T.C. Williams, American Indian makeup, *Son of the Morning Star.* ABC.

OUTSTANDING HAIRSTYLING FOR A SERIES
• Dee Dee Petty, Jan Van Uchelen, Susan Boyd, *Dark Shadows.* NBC.

OUTSTANDING HAIRSTYLING FOR A MINISERIES OR A SPECIAL
• Aldo Signoretti, Lynn Whitfield's hairstylist. Ferdinando Merolla, Katalin Kajtar, hairstylists, *The Josephine Baker Story.* HBO.

OUTSTANDING ART DIRECTION FOR A SERIES
• John C. Mula, production designer. Kevin Pfeiffer, art director, Brian Savegar, set decorator, *Dinosaurs.* ABC.

OUTSTANDING ART DIRECTION FOR A MINISERIES OR A SPECIAL
• Jozsef Romvari, production designer. Dean Tschetter, art director, *The Josephine Baker Story.* HBO.

OUTSTANDING ART DIRECTION FOR A VARIETY OR MUSIC PROGRAM
• John Shaffner, Joe Stewart, production designers, *The Magic of David Copperfield XIII: Mystery on the Orient Express.* CBS.

OUTSTANDING GRAPHIC DESIGN AND TITLE SEQUENCES (Area award winner)
• Steve Martino, Jeff Doud, designers/directors. Jon Townley, creative director. Thomas Barham, designer, *ABC World of Discovery.* ABC.

OUTSTANDING CINEMATOGRAPHY FOR A SERIES
• Michael Watkins, director of photography, *Quantum Leap.* NBC.

OUTSTANDING CINEMATOGRAPHY FOR A MINISERIES OR A SPECIAL
• Gayne Rescher, director of photography, *Jackie Collins' "Lucky Chances."* NBC.

OUTSTANDING TECHNICAL DIRECTION/CAMERA WORK/VIDEO FOR A SERIES
• Jerry Weiss, technical director. Marty Brown, Dave Owen, Marvin Shearer, Mark Warshaw, electronic camera operators. Rich Rose, senior video control, *Married People.* ABC.

OUTSTANDING TECHNICAL DIRECTION/CAMERA WORK/VIDEO FOR A MINISERIES OR A SPECIAL
• Keith Winikoff, technical director/senior video control. Sam Drummy, Dave Levisohn, Bill Philbin, Hector Ramirez, electronic camera operators, *The Magic of David Copperfield XIII: Mystery on the Orient Express*. CBS.

OUTSTANDING INDIVIDUAL ACHIEVEMENT IN ANIMATION
• Terese Drilling, Jeff Mulcaster, animators, *Will Vinton's Claymation*. CBS.

OUTSTANDING EDITING FOR A SERIES
(Single camera production)
• Joe Ann Fogle, *Cop Rock*. ABC.
(Multicamera production)
• Tucker Wiard, *Murphy Brown*. CBS.

OUTSTANDING EDITING FOR A MINISERIES OR A SPECIAL
(Single-Camera production)
• John Wright, *Sarah, Plain and Tall, Hallmark Hall of Fame*. CBS.
(Multicamera production)
• David Gumpel, Girish Bhargava, *The Muppets Celebrate Jim Henson*. CBS.

OUTSTANDING SOUND EDITING FOR A SERIES
• William Wistrom, supervising editor/supervising ADR editor. James Wolvington, Mace Matiosian, Wilson Dyer, Masanobu "Tomi" Tomita, Dan Yale, sound editors. Gerry Sackman, supervising music editor, *Star Trek: The Next Generation*. Syndicated.

OUTSTANDING SOUND EDITING FOR A MINISERIES OR A SPECIAL
• G. Michael Graham, Joseph A. Meolody, supervising editors. Rick Steele, Mark Steele, Gary Macheel, Charles Beith, Jr., Mark Freidgen, Dan Luna, Michael J. Wright, Bob Costanza, Chris Assells, David McMoyler, Bill Bell, Scot Tinsley, Philip Jamtaas, Andre Caporaso, Stephen Grubbs, sound editors. Kristi Johns, supervising ADR editor. John Caper, supervising music editor, *Son of the Morning Star*. ABC.

OUTSTANDING SOUND MIXING FOR A DRAMA SERIES
• Alan Bernard, production mixer. Doug Davey, Chris Haire, Richard Morrison, rerecording mixers, *Star Trek: The Next Generation*. Syndicated.

OUTSTANDING SOUND MIXING FOR A COMEDY SERIES OR A SPECIAL
• Joe Kenworthy, production mixer. Dean Okrand, William Thiederman, Michael Getlin, rerecording mixers, *Doogie Howser, M.D.* ABC.

OUTSTANDING SOUND MIXING FOR A DRAMA MINISERIES OR A SPECIAL
• Nelson Stoll, production mixer. Thomas J. Huth, Sam Black, Anthony Costantini, rerecording mixers, *Son of the Morning Star*. ABC.

OUTSTANDING SOUND MIXING FOR A VARIETY OR MUSIC SERIES OR SPECIAL
• Ed Greene, Terry Kulchar, production mixers, *Carnegie Hall: Live at 100*. PBS.

OUTSTANDING LIGHTING DIRECTION (ELECTRONIC) FOR A COMEDY SERIES
• George Spiro Dibie, director of photography, *Growing Pains*. ABC.

OUTSTANDING LIGHTING DIRECTION (ELECTRONIC) FOR A DRAMA SERIES, VARIETY SERIES, MINISERIES, OR A SPECIAL
(Tie)
• William M. Klages, lighting director, *The 33rd Annual Grammy Awards*. CBS.
• Bob Dickinson, director of photography, *The Magic of David Copperfield XIII: Mystery on the Orient Express*. CBS.

OUTSTANDING INDIVIDUAL ACHIEVEMENT—INFORMATIONAL PROGRAMMING
(Area award winners)
• Geoffrey C. Ward, Ric Burns, Ken Burns, writers, *The Civil War*. PBS.
• Todd McCarthy, writer, "Preston Sturges: The Rise and Fall of an American Dreamer," *American Masters*. PBS.
• Peter Gelb, Susan Froemke, Albert Maysles, Bob Eisenhardt, directors, *Soldiers of Music: Rostropovich Returns to Russia*. PBS.

(No awards were bestowed in the areas of outstanding animated program more than one hour, special visual effects, or main title theme music.)

DAYTIME AWARD WINNERS

OUTSTANDING DRAMA SERIES

• *As the World Turns*. Laurence Caso, executive producer. Kenneth L. Fitts, supervising producer. Christine S. Banas, David Domedion, producers. Lisa Anne Wilson, coordinating producer. CBS.

All My Children. Felicia Minei Behr, executive producer. Terry Cacavio, coordinating producer. ABC.

Guiding Light. Robert Calhoun, executive producer. Barbara Garshman, supervising producer. Robert Kochman, Kathlyn Chambers, Roy Steinberg, producers. Catherine Maher Smith, coordinating producer. CBS.

The Young and the Restless. William J. Bell, senior executive producer. Edward Scott, executive producer. Tom Langan, producer. Nancy Bradley Wiard, coordinating producer. CBS.

OUTSTANDING LEAD ACTOR IN A DRAMA SERIES

• Peter Bergman, *The Young and the Restless*. CBS.

David Canary, *All My Children*. ABC.

Nicolas Coster, *Santa Barbara*. NBC.

A Martinez, *Santa Barbara*. NBC.

James Reynold, *Generations*. NBC.

OUTSTANDING LEAD ACTRESS IN A DRAMA SERIES

• Finola Hughes, *General Hospital*. ABC.

Jeanne Cooper, *The Young and the Restless*. CBS.

Julia Barr, *All My Children*. ABC.

Elizabeth Hubbard, *As the World Turns*. CBS.

Susan Lucci, *All My Children*. ABC.

OUTSTANDING SUPPORTING ACTOR IN A DRAMA SERIES

• Bernie Barrow, *Loving*. ABC.

William Christian, *All My Children*. ABC.

Stuart Damon, *General Hospital*. ABC.

Kin Shriner, *General Hospital*. ABC.

William Roerick, *Guiding Light*. CBS.

Jerry ver Dorn, *Guiding Light*. CBS.

OUTSTANDING SUPPORTING ACTRESS IN A DRAMA SERIES

• Jess Walton, *The Young and the Restless*. CBS.

Darlene Conley, *The Bold and the Beautiful*. CBS.

Maureen Garrett, *Guiding Light*. CBS.

Jill Larson, *All My Children*. ABC.

Kathleen Widdoes, *As the World Turns*. CBS.

OUTSTANDING DRAMA SERIES DIRECTING TEAM

• Rick Bennewitz, Peter Brinckerhoff, Michael Gliona, Robert Schiller, directors. Jeanine Guarneri-Frons, Pamela Fryman, Robin Raphaelian, associate directors, *Santa Barbara*. NBC.

Jack Coffey, Christopher Goutman, Henry Kaplan, Conal O'Brien, directors. Barbara Martin Simmons, Shirley Simmons, associate directors, *All My Children*. ABC.

Bruce Barry, Jo Anne Sedwick, Scott McKinsey, Sherrell Hoffman, directors. John O'Connell, Matthew Lagle, Angelea Tessinari, associate directors, *Guiding Light*. CBS.

Heather Hill, Randy Robbins, Frank Pacelli, Mike Denney, directors. Betty Rothenberg, Kathryn Foster, Dan Brumett, associate directors, *The Young and the Restless*. CBS.

OUTSTANDING DRAMA SERIES WRITING TEAM

• Chuck Pratt, Jr., head writer. Sheri Anderson, Sam Ratcliffe, Maralyn Thoma, co-head writers. Josh Griffith, Robert Guza, associate head writers. Linda Hamner, breakdown writer. Lynda Myles, Frank Salisbury, script writers. Richard Culliton, script writer/editor, *Santa Barbara*. NBC.

Agnes Nixon, Lorraine Broderick, Susan Kirshenbaum, Kathleen Klein, Karen L. Lewis, Megan McTavish, Michelle Patrick, Elizabeth Smith, Gillian Spencer, Wisner Washam, Mary K. Wells, writers, *All My Children*. ABC.

Douglas Marland, head writer. John Kuntz, Juliet Packer, Meredith Post, breakdown writers. Patti Dizenzo, Caroline Franz, Penelope Koechl, script writers. Stephanie Braxton, Nancy Ford, Richard Backus, script/breakdown writers, *As the World Turns*. CBS.

William J. Bell, head writer. Kay Alden, co-head writer. Jerry Birn, John F. Smith, James E. Reilly, Eric Freiwald, Rex M. Best, Enid Powell, writers, *The Young and the Restless*. CBS.

OTHER DAYTIME AWARDS

**OUTSTANDING YOUNGER ACTOR
IN A DRAMA SERIES**
• Rick Hearst, *Guiding Light*. CBS.

**OUTSTANDING YOUNGER ACTRESS
IN A DRAMA SERIES**
• Anne Heche, *Another World*. NBC.

OUTSTANDING CHILDREN'S SERIES
• *Sesame Street*. Dulcy Singer, executive producer. Lisa Simon, producer. Arlene Sherman, coordinating producer. PBS.

OUTSTANDING CHILDREN'S SPECIAL
• *Lost in the Barrens*. Michael MacMillan, Michael Scott, executive producers. Seaton McLean, Derek Mazur, Joan Scott, producers. Disney.

**OUTSTANDING PERFORMER
IN A CHILDREN'S SERIES**
• Tim Curry, *Fox's Peter Pan and the Pirates*. Fox.

**OUTSTANDING DIRECTING
IN A CHILDREN'S SERIES**
• Brian Henson, Michael J. Kerrigan, series directors, *Jim Henson's Mother Goose Stories*. Disney Channel.

**OUTSTANDING WRITING
IN A CHILDREN'S SERIES**
• Norman Stiles, head writer. Judy Freudberg, Nancy Sans, Tony Geiss, Jeff Moss, Cathi Rosenberg-Turow, David Korr, Belinda Ward, Lou Berger, Josh Selig, Sonia Manzano, Sara Compton, Luis Santeiro, John Weidman, Emily Perl Kingsley, Mark Saltzman, Jon Stone, series writers, *Sesame Street*. PBS.

**OUTSTANDING WRITING
IN A CHILDREN'S SPECIAL**
• Courtney Flavin, teleplay and story. Tracey Thompson, Beth Thompson, story, "A Question About Sex," *ABC Afterschool Special*. ABC.

**OUTSTANDING PERFORMER
IN A CHILDREN'S SPECIAL**
• Joanne Vannicola, "Maggie's Secret," *CBS Schoolbreak Special*. CBS.

**OUTSTANDING ACHIEVEMENT
IN DIRECTING—SPECIAL CLASS**
• Kristoffer Tabori, "The Perfect Date," *ABC Afterschool Special*. ABC.

OUTSTANDING ANIMATED PROGRAM
• *Tiny Toon Adventures*. Steven Spielberg, executive producer. Tom Ruegger, producer. Ken Boyer, Art Leonardi, Art Vitello, directors. Paul Dini, story editor. Sherri Stoner, writer. Syndicated.

OUTSTANDING TALK/SERVICE SHOW
• *The Oprah Winfrey Show*. Debra Di Maio, executive producer. Ray Nunn, senior producer. Oprah Winfrey, supervising producer. David Boul, Mary Kay Clinton, Rudy Guido, Dianne Hudson, Alice McGee, Sally Lou Oaks, Ellen Rakieten, producers. Syndicated.

OUTSTANDING TALK/SERVICE SHOW HOST
• Oprah Winfrey, host, *The Oprah Winfrey Show*. Syndicated.

**OUTSTANDING DIRECTING
IN A TALK/SERVICE SHOW**
• Peter Kimball, *The Oprah Winfrey Show*. Syndicated.

**OUTSTANDING GAME/AUDIENCE
PARTICIPATION SHOW**
• *Jeopardy!* Merv Griffin, executive producer. George Vosburgh, producer. Syndicated.

OUTSTANDING GAME SHOW HOST
• Bob Barker, *The Price is Right*. CBS.

**OUTSTANDING DIRECTING IN A GAME/
AUDIENCE PARTICIPATION SHOW**
• Dick Schneider, *Jeopardy!* Syndicated.

**OUTSTANDING ACHIEVEMENT
IN WRITING—SPECIAL CLASS**
• Harry Eisenberg, Steven Dorfman, Kathy Easterling, Frederik Pohl IV, Steve D. Tamerius, Debbie Griffin, Michele Johnson, Carol Campbell. *Jeopardy!* Syndicated.

OUTSTANDING SPECIAL CLASS PROGRAM
• "Yo-Yo Ma in Concert," *Live from Lincoln Center*. John Goberman, executive producer. Marc Bauman, coordinating producer. Hugh Downs, host. PBS.

OUTSTANDING ORIGINAL SONG
• A.J. Gundell, composer and lyrist, "Love Like This," *Guiding Light*. CBS.
• Bruce Broughton, composer and lyricist. Wayne Kaatz, Tom Ruegger, lyricists, Main Title Theme, *Tiny Toon Adventures*. Syndicated.

**OUTSTANDING MUSIC DIRECTION
AND COMPOSITION**
• William Ross, composer, "Fields of Honey," *Tiny Toon Adventures*. Syndicated.

**OUTSTANDING MUSIC DIRECTION
AND COMPOSITION FOR A DRAMA SERIES**
• Barbara Miller-Gidaly, music director/supervisor. Andrew J. Gundell, music director. Rob Mounsey, John Henry, Richard Hazard, Barry DeVorzon, Theodore Irwin, composers. James Elliot Lawrence, composer/arranger, *Guiding Light*. CBS.

OUTSTANDING MAKEUP
• David Abbott, Gil Mosko, Carlos Yeaggy, makeup artists, *The Munsters Today*. Syndicated.

**OUTSTANDING MAKEUP
FOR A DRAMA SERIES**
• Carol Brown, head makeup artist. Keith Crary, Robert Sloan, Gail Hopkins, Lucia Bianca, makeup artists, *Days of Our Lives*. NBC.

OUTSTANDING HAIRSTYLING
• Jody Ann Lawrence, *The Munsters Today*. Syndicated.

**OUTSTANDING HAIRSTYLING
FOR A DRAMA SERIES**
• Janet Medford, Valerie Scott, *Santa Barbara*. NBC.

OUTSTANDING COSTUME DESIGN
• Jacqueline Mills, Jill Thraves, *Jim Henson's Mother Goose Stories*. Disney Channel.

**OUTSTANDING COSTUME DESIGN
IN A DRAMA SERIES**
• Sandra Bojin-Sedlik, *The Bold and the Beautiful*. CBS.

**OUTSTANDING ART DIRECTION/SET
DECORATION/SCENIC DESIGN
FOR A DRAMA SERIES**
• Sy Tomashoff, production designer. Jack Forrestel, art director. Jay Garvin, Randy Gunderson, set decorators, *The Bold and the Beautiful*. CBS.

**OUTSTANDING ART DIRECTION/SET
DECORATION/SCENIC DESIGN**
• Gary Panter, production designer. Ric Heitzman, Wayne White, co-production

designers. Jimmy Cuomo, art director. Debbie Madalena, Paul Reubens, set decorators, *Pee-Wee's Playhouse*. CBS.

**OUTSTANDING GRAPHICS
AND TITLE DESIGN**
• Paul Reubens, title designer. Prudence Fenton, Dorne Huebler, codesigner, *Pee-Wee's Playhouse*. CBS.

OUTSTANDING CINEMATOGRAPHY
• Hanania Baer, director of photography, "But He Loves Me," *CBS Schoolbreak Special*. CBS.

**OUTSTANDING TECHNICAL
DIRECTION/ELECTRONIC CAMERA/
VIDEO CONTROL FOR A DRAMA SERIES**
• Janice L. Bendiksen, Ervin D. Hurd, Jr., technical directors. Sheldon L. Mooney, Joseph M. Vicens, David Navarrette, Joel D. Binger, electronic camera. Roberto A. Bosio, Scha Jani, senior video, *The Young and the Restless*. CBS.

**OUTSTANDING TECHNICAL
DIRECTION/ELECTRONIC CAMERA/
VIDEO CONTROL**
• Ray Angona, technical director. Jose Arvizu, Cesar Cabreira, Wayne Getchell, Keeth Lawrence, Martin Wagner, electronic camera. Allen Latter, video control, *The Price is Right*. CBS.

OUTSTANDING FILM EDITING
• Barbara Pokras, "The Perfect Date," *ABC Afterschool Special*. ABC.

OUTSTANDING VIDEO-TAPE EDITING
• James C. Wright, *Reading Rainbow*. PBS.

**OUTSTANDING VIDEO-TAPE EDITING
FOR A DRAMA SERIES**
• Dan Brumett, Marc Beruti, Steve Pierron, *The Young and the Restless*. CBS.

OUTSTANDING FILM SOUND EDITING
• Peter Cole, dialogue/ADR editor. Chris Trent, dialogue editor. Glenn Jordan, supervising music editor. Steve Kirklys, supervising sound effects editor. Ken Dahlinger, John Walker, sound effects editors, *Pee-Wee's Playhouse*. CBS.

OUTSTANDING FILM SOUND MIXING
• Bo Harwood, production sound mixer. Peter Cole, Chris Trent, Troy Smith, rerecording mixers, *Pee-Wee's Playhouse*. CBS.

Young and the Restless *best actor Peter Bergman with his "conscience, best friend and dearest love," wife Mary Ellen.*

N.A.T.A.S.

OUTSTANDING LIVE AND TAPE SOUND MIXING AND SOUND EFFECTS
• David E. Fluhr, rerecording mixer. Mark Bovos, production mixer, "A Question About Sex," *ABC Afterschool Special.* ABC.

OUTSTANDING LIVE AND TAPE SOUND MIXING AND SOUND EFFECTS FOR A DRAMA SERIES
• Otto Svoboda, Tommy Persson, mixers. Donald D. Henderson, music mixer/sound effects. Harold "Lanky" Linstrot, postproduction mixer. Bob Marencovich, postproduction mixer. Jack Tenhoor, Maurice "Smokey" Westerfeld, sound effects, *The Young and the Restless.* CBS.

OUTSTANDING LIGHTING DIRECTION
• Bill Berner, *Sesame Street.* PBS.

OUTSTANDING LIGHTING DIRECTION FOR A DRAMA SERIES
• Brian McRae, Ted C. Polmanski, *Santa Barbara.* NBC.

LIFETIME ACHIEVEMENT AWARD FOR DAYTIME TELEVISION
• Procter & Gamble Productions

SPORTS AWARD WINNERS
OUTSTANDING LIVE SPORTS SPECIAL
• *The Indianapolis 500.* Geoffrey Mason, executive producer. Bob Goodrich, Ned Simon, producers. Roger Goodman, Don Ohlmeyer, director. Emilie Deutsch, Bruce Clark, Debbie Cole, associate producers. Norman Samet, Vince DeDario, Jaime Bravo, Jeff Cohan, associate directors. ABC.

OUTSTANDING LIVE SPORTS SERIES
• *NCAA Tournament.* Ted Shaker, executive producer. David Winner, senior producer. Bob Dekas, coordinating producer. David Blatt, Mike Burks, Dan Forer, Ed Goren, Jim Gray, Bob Mansbach, George Veras, David Winner, Mark Wolff, Richie Zyontz, producers. Bob Fishman, Mike Arnold, Cathy Barreto, Larry Cavolina, Sandy Grossman, Scott Johnson, Andy Kindle, Eric Mann, Bob Matina, Duke Struck, directors. Lance Barrow, Vin DeVito, Richard Drake, Marcy Gause, Rich Gentile, Roy Hamilton, Artie Kempner, Colleen Kolibas, Pete Macheska, Steve Milton, Joan Papen, Rich Russo, Steve Sheer, Suzanne Smith, Rob Silverstein. CBS.

OUTSTANDING EDITED SPORTS SPECIAL
• *Road to the Super Bowl XXIV.* Ed Sabol, executive producer. Jay Gerber, Vicky Denenberg, Kennie Smith, coordinating producers. Steve Sabol, producer. Steve Sabol, Phil Tuckett, Bob Ryan, Dave Douglas, Steve Seidman, Bob Smith, directors. Louis Schmidt, associate producer. Don Thompson, associate director. Syndicated.

OUTSTANDING EDITED SPORTS SERIES/ANTHOLOGIES
• *ABC's Wide World of Sports.* Geoffrey Mason, executive producer. Curt Gowdy, Jr., coordinating producer. Kimberly C. Belton, Katharine Cook, Emilie Deutsch, Joel Feld, Robert Goodrich, Carol Lehti, Stephen Nagler, Ned Simon, producers. George Greenberg, Larry Kamm, Bruce Treut, Bill Webb, Doug Wilson, Jim Jennett, directors. Jim Ressler, Nancy Stern, Tony Tortorici, Bob Yalen, Robin Stratton, William Kunz, Mike Rosen, associate producers. Dick Buffinton, Bruce Clark, Vince DeDario, David Kiviat, Patrick McManus, Patty Rodilosso, Norman Samet, Toni Slotkin, Cary Brown,

Craig Bigelow, Earl "Woody" Freiman, Robin Horlick. ABC.

OUTSTANDING SPORTS PERSONALITY/HOST (Play-By-Play)
• Dick Enberg. NBC.

OUTSTANDING SPORTS PERSONALITY/ANALYST (Commentary)
• John Madden. CBS.

SPECIAL CLASS: INDIVIDUAL ACHIEVEMENT
• Jimmy Roberts, David Brofsky, *Sports and the Prospect of War*. ESPN. Geoffrey Mason, Emilie Deutsch, Jim McKay, *Athletes and Addiction: It's Not a Game*. ABC.

SPECIAL CLASS: PROGRAM ACHIEVEMENT
• *Let Me Be Brave*. Ted Shaker, executive producer. George Veras, coordinating producer (Sports Saturday/Sunday). Vin DeVito, coordinating producer. Mike Tollin, producer. George Bell, remote producer. CBS.

SPECIAL CLASS: INNOVATIVE TECHNICAL ACHIEVEMENT
• *Expedition Earth—'Cocos—Treasure Island.'* (Underwater Communication System.) Michael R. Pelissier, designer. Jerry Peck, designer/engineer. John Wilcox, executive producer. ESPN.

SPECIAL CLASS: INNOVATIVE TECHNICAL ACHIEVEMENT
• *Speedworld*. Peter Englehart, coordinating producer. Neil Goldberg, producer. Todd Hamilton, Craig Palmer, David Brooks, engineers. Telemetry. ESPN.

PROGRAM AREA: FEATURES
• *This is the NFL/Christian Okoye "They Grow Pros."* Steve Sabol, executive producer. Jay Gerber, Denine Bergey, Vicky Denenberg, Kennie Smith, coordinating producers. Phil Tuckett, producer. Syndicated.
• *Spike Lee Presents Mike Tyson*. Ross Greenburg, executive producer. Spike Lee, producer/director. HBO.

PROGRAM AREA: PROMOTION
• *ABC Monday Night Football "All My Rowdy Friends II."* Geoffrey Mason, executive producer. Tom Remiszewski, Robert Toms, coordinating producers. Richard Getz, Glenn Chalek, producers. Brian Coyne, director. Mary Schiarizzi, Brian Fahey, Carlo Gennarelli, associate producers. Audree Manley-Rosburg, Lenore Ballard, Elliot Mendelson, associate directors. ABC.

PROGRAM AREA: OPENS/CLOSES/TEASES
• *ABC's Wide World of Sports/Preakness Stakes Opening*. Geoffrey Mason, executive producer. Curt Gowdy, Jr., producer. David Kiviat, associate director. ABC.

PROGRAM AREA: SPORTS JOURNALISM
• *Outside the Lines "Autograph Game" (Autograph Fraud)*. Steven M. Bornstein, executive producer. John A. Walsh, managing editor. Bob Rausher, coordinating producer. Steve Anderson, director of production. Steve Wilson, producer/reporter. Chris Martens, producer. Bob Ley, reporter. ESPN.

PROGRAM AREA: STUDIO SHOW
• *SportsCenter*. Steven M. Bornstein, executive producer. John A. Walsh, managing editor. Steve Anderson, director of production. Michael S. Bogad, Michael Matters, Bob Rausher, Robert Eaton, Noubar Stone, coordinating producers. Steve Vecchione, Jeff Schneider, Scott Ackerson, Barry Sacks, Chris Martens, Dave Miller, Jean McCormick, producers. Denis Sedory, David Williams, Martha Walker, Debra Ward, Calvin Haywood, Dan Glovach, directors. ESPN.

TECHNICAL TEAM REMOTE
• *Post Season Major League Baseball*. CBS.
• *ABC's Wide World of Sports—The Kentucky Derby*. ABC.

TECHNICAL TEAM STUDIO
• *The NFL Today*. CBS.

FILM CINEMATOGRAPHERS
• John Armstrong, David Breashears, D'Arcy Marsh, Gregory Poschman, Paul Sharpe, Marty Snyderman, Stan Waterman, *ESPN's Expedition Earth*. ESPN.

Doug Flutie (left) and Dabney Coleman (right) with Jim McKay, who was hailed for his probe of "Athletes and Addiction."

Howard Neff, Hank McElwee, Ernie Ernst, Dave Dart, Bob Angelo, Don Marx, Art Spieller, Bob Smith, Phil Tuckett, Lonnie Balat, Joe Orlando, Craig Johnson, Dave Paul, Jeff Lotierzo, Scott Scharf, *Road to the Super Bowl*. Syndicated.

ELECTRONIC CAMERAPERSONS
• Bill Philbin, D'Arcy Marsh, Gene Kois, Mike Culp, Jeff Grouwinkle, Randy Tomiuk, Steve Bennett, *Ironman Triathlon*. ABC.
• D'Arcy Marsh, Peter Henning, Todd Hardesty, "Iditarod Sled Dog Race," *ABC's Wide World of Sports*. ABC.

FILM EDITING
• Sam Pollard, *Spike Lee Presents Mike Tyson*. HBO.

VIDEO-TAPE EDITING
• Joseph Longo, Dave Seeger, Ildefonso DeJesus, *Athletes and Addiction: It's Not a Game*. ABC.

GRAPHIC DESIGN
• Ted Shaker, executive producer. Duke Struck, producer/director. Cliff Garbutt, Robert Kirkpatrick, David Woodward, designers. Roger Tyrell, editor, *Super Bowl Today*. CBS.
• Geoffrey Mason, executive producer. George Greenberg, Don Gialanellam, producers. Les Hunter, associate producer. Scott Miller, designer, *ABC Sports NFL Graphics*. ABC.

MUSIC
• Hank Williams, Jr., composer/lyricist. Randy Thornton, Brian Blosil, Byran Hofheins, *ABC's Monday Night Football "All My Rowdy Friends II."* ABC.

AUDIO
• Jerry Mahler, Vince Caputo, *Road to the Super Bowl*. Syndicated.
• Peter Englehart, coordinating producer. Neil Goldberg, producer. Mike Wells, director. Peter Larsson, engineer. Ron Scalise, head audio. Bobby Carter, Bill Fuchs, Al Connal, Bill Robinson, audio, *Speedworld*. ESPN.

WRITING
• Jack Whitaker, *ABC Sports Essay: Golf Tour*. ABC.

LIFETIME SPORTS ACHIEVEMENT AWARD
• Lindsey Nelson

NEWS & DOCUMENTARY AWARD WINNERS
OUTSTANDING GENERAL COVERAGE OF A SINGLE BREAKING NEWS STORY (Programs)
• "48 Hours: The Search for Matthew," *48 Hours*. Andrew Heyward, executive producer. Catherine Lasiewicz, senior producer. Barbara Baylor, Lyne Bowens, Nancy Duffy, Linda Martin, Mary Murphy, Mitchell Weitzner, producers. Erin Moriarty, Jacqueline Adams, John Blackstone, correspondents. Dan Rather, anchor. CBS.
• "The Struggle for South Africa," *Frontline*. Peter Horrocks, executive producer for BBC. David Fanning, executive producer for *Frontline*. David Harrison, producer. David Dimbleby, correspondent. PBS.

OUTSTANDING GENERAL COVERAGE OF A SINGLE BREAKING NEWS STORY (Segments)
• "Soldiers' Stories," *Sunday Morning*. James Houtrides, Michael Rosenbaum, Robert J. Shattuck, producers. Bob Simon, correspondent. CBS.

OUTSTANDING INSTANT COVERAGE OF A SINGLE BREAKING NEWS STORY (Programs)
• "Bulletin: Iraq Invades Kuwait," *ABC News Nightline*. Dorrance Smith, Lauren Block, Tracy Day, Gil Pimentel, Richard Harris, Bryan Myers, Robert LeDonne,

Margaret Murphy, Deanna Lee, Sandra Mayer, Herb O'Connor, Grey McCown, Artis Waters, Katherine Kross, Jeff Milstein, Reid Orvedahl, producers. David Tabacoff, Mark Nelson, William Moore, senior producers. Ted Koppel, Jackie Judd, Dean Reynolds, correspondents. ABC.

OUTSTANDING BACKGROUND ANALYSIS OF A SINGLE CURRENT STORY (Programs)
• "Seven Days in Bensonhurst," *Frontline.* David Fanning, executive producer. Thomas Lennon, producer. Shelby Steele, correspondent. PBS.

OUTSTANDING BACKGROUND ANALYSIS OF A SINGLE CURRENT STORY (Segments)
• "Children of Terror," *20/20.* Victory Neufeld, executive producer. Janice Tomlin, producer. Tom Jarriel, correspondent. ABC.
• "Nobody's Children/ The Greatest Gift of All," *20/20.* Victor Neufeld, executive producer. Janice Tomlin, producer. Tom Jarriel, correspondent. ABC.

OUTSTANDING INVESTIGATIVE JOURNALISM (Programs)
• "High Crimes and Misdemeanors," *Frontline.* David Fanning, executive producer. Sherry Jones, Elizabeth Sams, producers. Bill Moyers, correspondent. PBS.

OUTSTANDING INVESTIGATIVE JOURNALISM (Segments)
• "Shame of a Nation," *20/20.* Victor Neufeld, executive producer. Janice Tomlin, producer. Tom Jarriel, correspondent. ABC.

OUTSTANDING INTERVIEW/INTERVIEWER(S) (Programs)
• "Guns," *ABC News/Time Forum.* Tom Yellin, executive producer. Heidi Berenson, Lisa Cohen, Craig Leake, Pam Ridder, Carrie Cook, Susan Robinson, Stephanie Swafford, Susanna Aaron, Andrea Blaugrund, producers. Stuart Schwartz, senior broadcast producer. Peter Jennings, interviewer. ABC.
• "Abortion — The New Civil War," *ABC News/Time Forum.* Tom Yellin, executive producer. Heidi Berenson, Alison Craiglow, Carrie Cook, Marylin Fletcher, Shari Levine, Jonathan Talmadge, Andrea

Blaugrund, Carole DiFalco, Ray Farkas, producers. Stuart Schwartz, senior broadcast producer. Peter Jennings, interviewer. ABC.

OUTSTANDING INTERVIEW/INTERVIEWER(S) (Segments)
• "The Walkers," *60 Minutes.* Richard Bonin, producer. Mike Wallace, interviewer. CBS.
• "Paul Newman and Joanne Woodward," *Face to Face with Connie Chung.* Hal Gessner, producer. Connie Chung, interviewer. CBS.

OUTSTANDING COVERAGE OF A CONTINUING NEWS STORY (Programs)
• "A Town Meeting in South Africa," *ABC News Nightline.* Dorrance Smith, executive producer. Bob Haberl, David Tabacoff, William Moore, Lionel Chapman, senior producers. Tracy Day, Terry Irving, Herb O'Connor, F.D. Wilkinson III, Reid Orvedahl, Roger Goodman, producers. Tara Sonenshine, Richard Harris, editorial producers. Artis Waters, Lori Beecher, Scott Sforza, Amy Rosenthal, Perry Ascher, Regina Egan, associate producers. Ted Koppel, James Walker, Jeff Greenfield, Carole Simpson, Don Kladstrup, correspondents. ABC.

OUTSTANDING COVERAGE OF A CONTINUING NEWS STORY (Segments)
• "Murder in Beverly Hills," *Primetime Live.* Richard N. Kaplan, executive producer. Betsy West, senior broadcast producer. Ira Rosen, senior producer. Neal Shapiro, David Doss, Marc Burstein, broadcast producers. Shelly Ross, Jonathan Talmadge, Phyllis McGrady, Anthony Radziwill, producers. Diane Sawyer, correspondent. ABC.

OUTSTANDING INFORMATIONAL, CULTURAL, OR HISTORICAL PROGRAMMING (Programs)
• *Chimps: So Like Us.* Karen Goodman, Kirk Simon, Carol Wilson, producers. HBO.

OUTSTANDING INFORMATIONAL, CULTURAL, OR HISTORICAL PROGRAMMING (SEGMENTS)

• "Blue Period—Manic Depression," *The MacNeil-Lehrer Newshour*. Lee Koromvokis, producer. JoAnna Simon, correspondent. PBS.
• "Thy Brother's Keeper," *60 Minutes*. Suzanne St. Pierre, producer. Meredith Vieira, correspondent. CBS.
• "Window on the Past," *Primetime Live*. Richard N. Kaplan, executive producer. Betsy West, senior broadcast producer. Ira Rosen, senior producer. Marc Burstein, broadcast produce. Lisa Hsia, producer. John Quinones, correspondent. ABC.
• "The Soviet Union Series," *World Monitor*. Sandra Allik, producer. Don McNeill, correspondent. Discovery Channel.
• "See No Evil," *20/20*. Rob Wallace, producer. John Stossel, correspondent. ABC.

SPECIAL CLASSIFICATION FOR OUTSTANDING NEWS AND DOCUMENTARY PROGRAM ACHIEVEMENT

• "High Crimes and Misdemeanors," *Frontline*. David Fanning, executive producer. Sherry Jones, producer. Elizabeth Sams, coproducer. Bill Moyers, correspondent. PBS.
• "Chernobyl," *60 Minutes*. William McClure, producer. Steve Kroft, correspondent. CBS.

OUTSTANDING INDIVIDUAL ACHIEVEMENT IN A CRAFT: WRITERS

• James A. DeVinney, Madison Davis Lacy, Jr., "The Time Has Come," *Eyes on the Prize II*. PBS.
• Harry Smith, "The Party's Over," "Flag Burning," Death Penalty," *CBS This Morning*. CBS.
• Sam Pollard, Sheila Bernard, "Ain't Gonna Shuffle No More," *Eyes on the Prize II:* PBS.

OUTSTANDING INDIVIDUAL ACHIEVEMENT IN A CRAFT: DIRECTORS

• Elena Mannes, *Amazing Grace with Bill Moyers*. PBS.

OUTSTANDING INDIVIDUAL ACHIEVEMENT IN A CRAFT: RESEARCHERS

• Elizabeth Sams, Scott Armstrong, Morrow Cater, Kristin Schneeman, "High Crimes and Misdemeanors," *Frontline*. PBS.

OUTSTANDING INDIVIDUAL ACHIEVEMENT IN A CRAFT: CINEMATOGRAPHERS

• Peter Schnall, "Don't Even Think of Parking Here," *National Geographic Explorer*. TBS.

OUTSTANDING INDIVIDUAL ACHIEVEMENT IN A CRAFT: ELECTRONIC CAMERAPERSONS

• Nick Bond, Simon Bray, Dave Barber, Howard Badger, John Landi, "Inside the Kremlin," *Primetime Live*. ABC.

OUTSTANDING INDIVIDUAL ACHIEVEMENT IN A CRAFT: VIDEO-TAPE EDITORS

• Charles Scott, "The Time Has Come," *Eyes on the Prize II*. PBS.
• Betty Ciccarelli, "Ain't Gonna Shuffle No More," *Eyes on the Prize II*. PBS.
• David Ewing, Cliff Hackel, John J. Martin, Mitch Udoff, Bob Fahringer, "Death of a Dictator," *The Koppel Report*. ABC.

OUTSTANDING INDIVIDUAL ACHIEVEMENT IN A CRAFT: FILM EDITORS

• Connie Rinehart, "Don't Even Think of Parking Here," *National Geographic Explorer*. TBS.

OUTSTANDING INDIVIDUAL ACHIEVEMENT IN A CRAFT: LIGHTING DIRECTORS

• Daniel A. Kinsley, *Primetime Live*. ABC. Daniel A. Kinsley, " Live from the Houston Economic Summit," *This Week with David Brinkley*. ABC.

OUTSTANDING INDIVIDUAL ACHIEVEMENT IN A CRAFT: GRAPHICS

• Angela Fernan, Laura Vaccaro-Seeger, "Opening Animation," *NBC Special—Summit*. NBC.
• Alex Weil, *National Geographic on Assignment*. TBS.

OUTSTANDING INDIVIDUAL ACHIEVEMENT IN A CRAFT: TITLE SEQUENCES

• Alex Weil, Jaime Bernanke, Vicky Lemont, *National Geographic on Assignment*. TBS.
• Glenn Lazzaro, Don Duncan, Tim Miller, *Exposé*. NBC.

OUTSTANDING INDIVIDUAL ACHIEVEMENT IN A CRAFT: ART DIRECTION AND SCENIC DESIGN

• Robert Thayer, *Primetime Live*. ABC.

OUTSTANDING INDIVIDUAL ACHIEVEMENT IN A CRAFT: MUSIC
• Scott Harper, "Amazon, Land of the Flooded Forest," *National Geographic Special*. PBS.

OUTSTANDING INDIVIDUAL ACHIEVEMENT IN A CRAFT: SOUND
• Beverly Joubert, Paul Schremp, Mark Linden, Clifford Hoelscher, Chuck White, "Journey to the Forgotten River," *National Geographic Special*. PBS.

INTERNATIONAL AWARD WINNERS
DRAMA
• *First and Last*. BBC. U.K.

DOCUMENTARY
• *J'ai Douze Ans et Je Fais La Guerre*. CAPA Production with Canal Plus and FR3. France.

ARTS DOCUMENTARY
• *Bookmark: From Moscow to Pietushki*. BBC Television. U.K.

PERFORMING ARTS
• *The Mahabharata,* produced by Les Productions du 3EME Etage in association with the Brooklyn Academy of Music and Channel 4 Television. U.K.

CHILDREN AND YOUNG PEOPLE
• *Living with Dinosaurs*. TVS Films production in association with Jim Henson Productions for Channel 4 Television. U.K.

POPULAR ARTS
• *Norbert Smith – A Life*. Hat Trick Productions for Channel 4 Television. U.K.

SPECIAL AWARDS
TECHNICAL ACHIEVEMENT AND SCIENTIFIC DEVELOPMENT ENGINEERING AWARDS
• Accom, Inc.
• Abekas Video Systems
• Faroudja Laboratories
• Grass Valley Group
• Magni Systems
• Mr. Masahiko Morizono
• NEC (two awards)
• Matsushita Electronic Corp. (Panasonic)
• Philips
• Ramadec EPO Ltd.
• Sony Corporation (three awards)
• Teletra USA
• Tektronix Television Division
• Toshiba Corporation
• T.S.M. Corporation
• Vineten Broadcast Inc.

CHARLES F. JENKINS LIFETIME TECHNICAL ACHIEVEMENT AWARD
• Harry Lubcke

SYD CASSYD FOUNDER'S AWARD
• Syd Cassyd

N.A.T.A.S. TRUSTEES AWARD
• Ted Turner

GOVERNORS AWARD
• Mobil Oil
• Masterpiece Theatre

Emmy Extras

How Emmy Award
Winners Are Chosen Today

Members of the two television academies vote to select the nominees each year in the prime-time and daytime competitions, then the winners are determined by blue-ribbon panels, which are comprised mostly of the academies' members. The two-tiered system thus invites the broad participation of A.T.A.S. and N.A.T.A.S. members in the eventual determination of winners while ensuring that the work of all nominated shows and individuals is seen and evaluated carefully. It also explains how shows like *Miami Vice, Moonlighting,* and *Twin Peaks* can head into the prime-time Emmys show with a sackful of nominations, but once the auditorium lights dim, are left standing at the door holding an empty bag. The members en masse and the judges, gathered in small groups, frequently disagree.

Approximately three months before the prime-time and daytime ceremonies, academy members receive ballots in the mail to begin the nomination process. All members vote their choices for outstanding programs, but then determine nominees according to craft. (Only directors can suggest names for outstanding directors; animators select the top contenders among eligible animators; and so on. The same holds true for the blue-ribbon judging panels, which are comprised of experts in each related field.) Only A.T.A.S. members can participate in the prime-time honors, and only N.A.T.A.S. members can vote for sports and news & documentary award nominees. Many members of both academies, however, vote jointly for the daytime prizes, since the two academies produce those awards together.

When members' votes are tallied, the nominations are submitted to peer-group panels comprised of as few as 6 panelists or as many as 75 in the major program categories. (An official maximum is not set.) The academies actively recruit as many members as they can to join the panels, but there's seldom a stampede to sign up once members learn what commitment is involved in terms of time and energy. Non-academy members are therefore sometimes permitted to participate, too.

After the stars and other individual nominees submit the episodes of shows they believe are examples of their best work, the judges go into seclusion, usually at a hotel in New York or Los Angeles over several days, to view all the contending footage. For the 1990–91 prime-time awards, a total of 1,200 panelists viewed more than 10,000 hours of nominated work. The judges are screened for potential conflicts of interest ahead of time and are asked not to react noticeably to the material they view so they don't influence other judges' decisions. The votes are then tallied in secret by an accounting firm.

The practice of nominees choosing the material on which they will be judged has led to more than a few controversies. *Dragnet*'s Jack Webb once withdrew his nomination for best director because the episode for which he was

> *Academy members choose the nominees, while winners are selected by judging panels.*

being considered was a repeat, but then-academy president Johnny Mercer maintained that the fault was the director's since Webb himself submitted the wrong show (see 1955 awards). In the early 1980s, best actress nominee Veronica Hamel's submission of an episode of *Hill Street Blues* in which she appeared for only 10 minutes was blamed for her subsequent loss. Critics who decry the fact that *The Bionic Woman*'s Lindsay Wagner was named best drama series actress of 1976–77 should know that the favored nominee that year, Sada Thompson of *Family*, entered a particularly weak episode for consideration, narrowing the field significantly for Wagner, who did give a strong performance in her own episode.

Entries for Emmy consideration are submitted by producers, networks, and craftspeople who usually pay fees ranging from $50 to $250 per submission, which is applied toward the expense of setting up the judging process. At A.T.A.S., the first individual achievement entry made by a member is free. Subsequent ones are $50 ($75 to non-members).

Prime-time, daytime, and sports awards all have categories in which one winner is chosen, as well as "areas" in which material is judged by an ideal standard of excellence resulting in the selection of one winner, multiple winners, or no winner. (The news awards are chosen exclusively on an area basis.) For the N.A.T.A.S. category awards, which generally include one winner from among 5 nomineess, panelists rank the shows in order of their preference, 1 to 5, with number 1 being the best score. The winner, therefore, receives the lowest total score. For N.A.T.A.S. area awards, panelists assign an ideal value of 1 to 5 to each submission they view, with 1, again, being the highest value. Because of the larger volume of contending shows, panelists can prescribe a 1 or 4 vote, for example, to many different shows when determining the area prizes. An accounting firm then tallies the results and recommends what the numerical cutoff points should be to determine nominees and winners. The judges then consider the issue among themselves and determine the outcome.

At A.T.A.S., the voting procedure was changed in early 1992 to have all prime-time awards determined on a ratings score system. When evaluating each nominee, panelists respond to a series of questions with votes of 1 to 10 (10 is the best score). In the categories, that means that the nominees are now judged on their own merits instead of by comparison to other shows and the nominee with the highest tally wins. (In the recent past, as per N.A.T.A.S., panelists had sized up the five nominees in each category by ranking them by their preference, 1 to 5.) In the areas, the panelists go through a similar procedure and wait until the votes have been tallied by the accounting firm. They then take each award area on a case-by-case basis, deciding if there will be one winner, many, or none.

AUTHOR'S NOTE: A diligent effort was made to make this book's lists of nominees and winners as accurate as possible. I regret any misspellings or omissions that may have occurred and will try to correct them in subsequent editions.   — T.O.

Fast Emmy Facts

• *ABC's Wide World of Sports* holds the record for being voted best series the most times (15). *Sesame Street* comes in second with 12 best series Emmys.

• The soap opera that's been voted best daytime series more than any other is *The Young and the Restless*, which has won four times. *All My Children* and *One Life to Live* have never won. *Santa Barbara* holds the record for the most Emmys nabbed in a single year: seven.

• On five occasions the winners of a year's best comedy and drama series came back together in a later year: *The Dick Van Dyke Show* and *The Defenders* did so in 1962–63 and 1963–64, *The Mary Tyler Moore Show* and *Upstairs, Downstairs* in 1974–75 and 1976–77, *Lou Grant* and *Taxi* in 1978–79 and 1979–80, *Cheers* and *Hill Street Blues* in 1982–83 and 1983–84, and *Cheers* and *L.A. Law* in 1988–89 and 1990–91.

• Only three shows have held onto the best series award continuously for as many as four years in a row: *The Dick Van Dyke Show*, *All in the Family*, and *Hill Street Blues*.

• Shows saved by the Emmy Awards: *Hill Street Blues*, *Cagney & Lacey*, *Mission: Impossible*, and *The $20,000 Pyramid*.

• The Emmy statuette is covered with 24-karat gold plate, is 16 inches high, weighs 4 pounds, and costs about $150 to manufacture.

• Only two actors have been voted the best in both drama and comedy series: Robert Young (*Father Knows Best* and *Marcus Welby, M.D.*) and Carroll O'Connor (*All in the Family* and *In the Heat of the Night*).

• Helen Gallagher (Maeve Ryan of *Ryan's Hope*), David Canary (Adam and Stuart Chandler of *All My Children*), and Kim Zimmer (Reva Shayne of *Guiding Light*) are tied with most best-acting honors in daytime TV with three wins each.

• Three actors are tied for winning the most Emmys (five) for playing the same character in one or more series. Ed Asner won two best actor awards and three supporting ones as newsman Lou Grant on *Lou Grant* and *The Mary Tyler Moore Show*. Art Carney's Emmys for playing sewer worker Ed Norton on *The Honeymooners* and *The Jackie Gleason Show* were all supporting honors. Don Knotts received five supporting awards as the bungling deputy Barney Fife on *The Andy Griffith Show*.

• Two people have won more than one best-acting Emmy for playing the same part in different TV films: Judith Anderson in 1954 and 1961 for *Hallmark Hall of Fame*'s two versions of *Macbeth*, and Geraldine Page for portraying the spinster character Miss Sookie in *A Christmas Memory* (1967) and *The Thanksgiving Visitor* (1969), both written by Truman Capote.

• Glenda Jackson is the only person to win two Emmys for the same role in the same production in the same year (1972) — for *Elizabeth R*. Jackson was honored for giving the Outstanding Single Performance by an Actress in a Leading Role and the Outstanding Continued Performance by an Actress in a Leading Role in a Dramatic Series.

• Only once were the winners of best actor and actress in a drama and comedy series repeated in a subsequent year. In 1967 and 1968 the winners were Bill Cosby for *I Spy*, Barbara Bain for *Mission: Impossible*, Don Adams for *Get Smart*, and Lucille Ball for *The Lucy Show*.

• The most nominated actors never to win an Emmy are Susan Lucci of *All My Children* with 12 nominations and Angela Lansbury of *Murder, She Wrote* with 11 nods.

• William Daniels and Bonnie Bartlett of *St. Elsewhere* are the only husband and wife in real life to win Emmys for playing husband and wife on TV, which they did in 1986.

• Jackie Gleason never won an Emmy, but his costar Art Carney won five for *The Honeymooners* and *The Jackie Gleason Show*. Andy Griffith shared Gleason's sad fate, never having won for his comedy series either, while costar Don Knotts of *The Andy Griffith Show*, like Carney, won five times.

• *M*A*S*H*'s Alan Alda is the only person to win Emmys for acting, writing, and directing.

• The person with the most Emmy nominations (37) is also the person with the most awards (16) — Dwight Hemion, the producer/director of such specials as *Frank Sinatra: A Man and His Music, Barbra Streisand ... and Other Musical Instruments*, and *The Kennedy Center Honors*.

• Director Bob Fosse is the only person ever to win an Emmy, Oscar, and Tony in the same year (1973) for, respectively, *Liza with a "Z," Cabaret*, and *Pippin*.

• The first black to win a major award was Harry Belafonte for giving the best performance in a variety show in his 1959–60 special *Tonight with Belafonte*.

• The longest prime-time Emmycast was in 1987, the Fox network's first year of airing the ceremony. (Its executives wanted a complete show and got it.) The ceremony ran just 20 seconds short of four hours. The shortest Emmys program was the 1971 ceremony, which was kept to half the time.

• The highest-rated prime-time ceremony was the 1957 telecast, which had 73.4 percent of the nation's viewing audience tuned in. (In more recent times, the most-watched ceremony was 1971 Emmycast, which had a 30.3 rating and 59 share.) The lowest-rated show was in 1990, which had an 8.2 rating and 14 share.

The largest audience to view a daytime awards telecast was in 1991 when the ceremony was aired in prime time for the very first time, receiving a 13.5 rating and 25 share (79% higher than 1990's prime-time awards show). It also ran just 20 seconds overtime, qualifying it for an entry in *The Guinness Book of World Records* for the awards show that came closest to its anticipated length.

Emmy Champs

BIGGEST PRIME-TIME WINNERS

(All names are those of actors unless otherwise noted)

Dwight Hemion (producer, director)	16
Jan Scott (art director, production designer)	10
Steven Bochco (producer, writer)	10
Ian Fraser (composer, music conductor)	9
Carl Reiner (actor, writer)	9
Dinah Shore	8
Edward Asner	7
Art Carney	6
Cloris Leachman	6
Mary Tyler Moore	6
Lily Tomlin	6
Alan Alda	5
Carol Burnett	5
Dick Van Dyke	5
Peter Falk	5
Don Knotts	5
Laurence Olivier	5
Lucille Ball	4
Tyne Daly	4
Valerie Harper	4
Hal Holbrook	4
Bob Hope	4
Harvey Korman	4
John Larroquette	4
Michael Learned	4
Carroll O'Connor	4
Rhea Perlman	4
Peter Ustinov	4
Betty White	4

STARS WHO HAVE WON BOTH EMMYS AND OSCARS

Jack Albertson
Bette Davis
Ingrid Bergman
Shirley Booth
Marlon Brando
Art Carney
Melvyn Douglas
Patty Duke
Sally Field
Jane Fonda
Louis Gossett, Jr.
Ruth Gordon
Lee Grant
Helen Hayes
Katharine Hepburn
Dustin Hoffman
William Holden
Glenda Jackson
Cloris Leachman
Karl Malden
Rita Moreno
Laurence Olivier
Geraldine Page
Vanessa Redgrave
Jason Robards
Cliff Robertson
Eva Marie Saint
Paul Scofield
George C. Scott
Simone Signoret
Maureen Stapleton
Meryl Streep
Barbra Streisand
Jessica Tandy
Claire Trevor
Peter Ustinov
Shelley Winters
Joanne Woodward
Loretta Young

HUSBANDS AND WIVES WHO HAVE BOTH WON EMMYS

Hume Cronyn & Jessica Tandy
William Daniels & Bonnie Bartlett
Danny DeVito & Rhea Perlman
Phil Donahue & Marlo Thomas
Alfred Lunt & Lynn Fontanne
George C. Scott & Colleen Dewhurst

PRIME-TIME SERIES WITH THE MOST EMMYS

The Mary Tyler Moore Show	29
Cheers	26
Hill Street Blues	26
The Carol Burnett Show	22

MOST WINS AS OUTSTANDING DRAMA SERIES

Hill Street Blues	4
L.A. Law	4

MOST WINS AS OUTSTANDING COMEDY SERIES

All in the Family	4
Cheers	4
The Dick Van Dyke Show	4

PRIME-TIME SERIES WITH THE MOST EMMY WINS IN ONE YEAR

Hill Street Blues	8

MOST EMMYS WON BY A NEW PRIME-TIME SERIES IN ITS FIRST SEASON

Hill Street Blues	8

PRIME-TIME SERIES WITH THE MOST NOMINATIONS

Cheers	101
*M*A*S*H*	99
Hill Street Blues	98

MINISERIES WITH THE MOST EMMYS

Roots	9

MOVIE-OF-THE-WEEK WITH THE MOST EMMYS

Eleanor and Franklin	11

MOST PRIME-TIME EMMYS WON BY A NETWORK IN A YEAR

CBS (1973–74)	44

TOP-RATED SHOWS OF THE YEAR THAT ALSO WON AN OUTSTANDING SERIES AWARD

Texaco Star Theater
I Love Lucy
The $64,000 Question
Gunsmoke
Rowan and Martin's Laugh-In
All in the Family
60 Minutes
The Cosby Show

MOST WINS AS OUTSTANDING DAYTIME DRAMA SERIES

The Young and the Restless	4
Santa Barbara	3
As the World Turns	2
General Hospital	2
Guiding Light	2
Ryan's Hope	2
The Doctors	2

MOST WINS AS OUTSTANDING GAME SHOW

*The $20,000 Pyramid**	9
The Hollywood Squares	4
Jeopardy	2
Password	2

(* Plus *The $50,000 Pyramid*, etc.)

MOST WINS AS OUTSTANDING DAYTIME TALK OR VARIETY SHOW

Donahue	6
The Merv Griffin Show	4
The Oprah Winfrey Show	4
Dinah!/ Dinah's Place	3

MOST WINS AS OUTSTANDING CHILDREN'S SERIES

(Informational/ Instructional/ Entertainment)

Sesame Street	12
Captain Kangaroo	5
30 Minutes	3

All-Time Emmy Losers

NOTABLE PEOPLE WHO HAVE NEVER WON AN EMMY

Harry Ackerman (producer)
Gracie Allen
Desi Arnaz
Roseanne Arnold
Ed Begley, Jr.
Edgar Bergen
Blair Brown
Susan Dey
Julia Duffy
Charles Durning
Judy Garland
Dave Garroway
Jackie Gleason
Peter Graves
Andy Griffith
William Frawley
Martin Landau
Angela Lansbury
Susan Lucci
Ed Sullivan *
Nancy Walker

* Ed Sullivan was given a Trustees Award in 1971, but never prevailed in a competitive category despite having one of the most popular shows in TV history and having been president of the TV academy.

NUMBER ONE-RANKED SHOWS OF THE YEAR THAT NEVER WON AN OUTSTANDING SERIES AWARD

Arthur Godfrey's Talent Scouts
Wagon Train
The Beverly Hillbillies
Bonanza
The Andy Griffith Show
Marcus Welby, M.D.
Happy Days
Laverne & Shirley
Three's Company
Dallas
Dynasty
Roseanne

ALL-TIME LOSING NUMBER ONE-RANKED SHOW

Dynasty was nominated for 24 awards, but never won.

A.T.A.S. Hall of Fame

The Hall of Fame was established in 1984 to acknowledge those "persons who have made outstanding contributions in the arts, science, or management of television based upon either cumulative contributions and achievements or a singular and extraordinary contribution or achievement." In 1991, *I Love Lucy* broke new ground when a program was admitted to the Hall of Fame for the first time.

Steve Allen
Roone Arledge
Desi Arnaz
Fred Astaire
Lucille Ball
Jack Benny
Milton Berle
Leonard Bernstein
Carol Burnett
George Burns and Gracie Allen
Sid Caesar
Johnny Carson
Paddy Chayefsky
Fred Coe
Perry Como
Joan Ganz Cooney
Jacques-Yves Cousteau

Walter Cronkite
James Garner
Jackie Gleason
Leonard Goldenson
Joyce C. Hall
Jim Henson
Don Hewitt
Bob Hope
Chet Huntley and David Brinkley
I Love Lucy — The Program
Ernie Kovacs
Norman Lear
Mary Tyler Moore
Edward R. Murrow
Carroll O'Connor
William S. Paley
David Sarnoff
Rod Serling
Eric Sevareid
Red Skelton
Frank Stanton
Ed Sullivan
David Susskind
Danny Thomas
Burr Tillstrom
Mike Wallace
Barbara Walters
Sylvester ("Pat") Weaver, Jr.
David L. Wolper

Academy Presidents

1947	Edgar Bergen
1948	Charles R. Brown
1949	Harry Lubcke
1950	Syd Cassyd
1951	Mike Stokey
1952	Hal Roach, Jr.
1953	Charles Ruggles
1954–55	Don DeFore
1956–57	Johnny Mercer
1957–58	Ed Sullivan
1958–59	Harry Ackerman
1959–60	Walter Cronkite
1960–61	Harry Ackerman
1961–63	Robert Lewine
1963–64	Mort Werner
1965–66	Rod Serling
1967–68	Royal Blakeman
1969–70	Seymour Berns
1971–72	Sonny Fox
1973–74	Thomas W. Sarnoff
1975–77	Larry Stewart
1976-	John Cannon*
1977–80	Hank Rieger
1980–83	John H. Mitchell
1983–85	Diana Muldaur
1985–87	Richard Frank
1987–89	Doug Duitsman
1989–91	Leo Chaloukian

N.A.T.A.S. CHAIRMEN
The following persons have served as chairmen of the board of the National Academy of Television Arts and Sciences since its inception in 1977.

John Cannon
Joel Chaseman
Irwin "Sonny" Fox
Lee Polk
Richard Rector
Thomas W. Sarnoff
Robert Wussler

* After the academy split in two in 1977, John Cannon served as president of the New York-based National Academy of Television Arts and Sciences. Persons listed chronologically after Cannon have been president of the Academy of Television Arts and Sciences based in Los Angeles.

Index

365, 382, 383, 392, 402, 425, 448, 449, 471, 472
Mr. Novak, 93, 99
Mr. Peepers, 35, 38, 41
Mrs. Delafield Wants to Marry, 356
Mudd, Roger, 180, 262
Muldaur, Diana, 437, 461, 485
Mulligan, Richard, 256, 273, 405, 413, 437, 460
Mulligan, Robert, 72
Muni, Paul, 65
Muppet Show, The, 214, 225, 228, 242, 255, 272
Murder in Mississippi, 435
Murder of Mary Phagan, The, 389, 393
Murder, She Wrote, 337, 355, 373, 480
Murderers Among Us: The Simon Wiesenthal Story, 412
Murphy Brown, 406, 412, 428, 429, 435, 453, 459
Murphy, Anthony, 161, 164
Murphy, Eddie, 301, 303, 307, 323
Murphy, Rosemary, 196, 202
Murrow, Edward R., 33, 35, 36, 38, 46, 49, 54, 58, 60, 62, 66, 103, 285, 303, 354, 484
Mutual of Omaha's Wild Kingdom, 116
"My Mom's Having a Baby," *ABC Afterschool Special*, 221
My Mother the Car, 98
My Name is Barbra, 97, 98, 99, 100, 101
My Name is Bill W., 408, 412
My Sweet Charlie, 132, 133, 135, 136
My World and Welcome to It, 3, 133, 135
Myrne, Martha, 370
NET Journal, 138
NET Playhouse, 120, 125, 127, 128, 135
Naked City, 64, 76, 87
Name of the Game, The, 125, 128, 135
Nancy Astor, 321
NASA, 139
National Endowment for the Arts, 349
National Geographic, 181, 225, 228, 254, 262, 330, 347, 403, 449
Nature, 402, 412
Natwick, Mildred, 54, 171, 175
NBC News Special, 434, 448
NBC News, 148, 329, 448
NBC Nightly News (also *NBC Nightly News with Tom Brokaw*), 148, 157, 180, 241, 248, 262, 288, 298, 336, 347 348, 355, 364, 402, 411, 424, 424, 425, 434, 447, 448, 458, 470
NBC Opera, 87
NBC Reports, 168
NBC Weekend, 248, 249
NBC White Paper, 93, 100, 147, 158, 168
NCAA basketball championship coverage, 287, 296, 410, 421, 457, 468

NCAA College Football, 263
Neal, Patricia, 154, 217, 257, 285
Nelson, Craig T., 437, 460
Nelson, Lindsey, 241, 457, 470
Nesbit, Cathleen, 178
Neuwirth, Bebe, 428, 437, 453, 461
"Never Say Goodbye," *CBS Schoolbreak Special*, 391, 399
New York Philharmonic Young People's Concerts with Leonard Bernstein, 82, 93, 99, 106
Newhart, 306, 321
Newhart, Bob, 3, 4, 69, 70, 80, 81, 250, 338, 350, 357, 375
Newman, Randy, 462
Newton's Apple, 410, 419
NFL Football, 287, 296
NFL Game of the Week, 254, 263
NFL Monday Night Football, 198, 205, 212, 241, 248, 391, 401, 433, 445
NFL on CBS, 372, 384
NFL Today, 212, 221, 235
Nicholas Nickleby, 303, 306
Nielsen, Leslie, 290, 414
Night Court, 333, 337, 351, 374, 393
Night of 100 Stars, 285, 289
Nightline (*ABC News Nightline*), 262, 271, 288, 297, 298, 330, 331, 337, 346, 355, 364, 373, 382, 402, 411, 425
Nightwatch (*CBS News Nightwatch*), 373
Nimoy, Leonard, 115, 121, 129, 291
Niven, David, 42, 54
Nixon, Agnes, 282
"Nixon in China," *Great Performances*, 393
Nixon, Richard, 64
No Time for Sergeants, 47
Nobody's Child, 352
Nolan, Lloyd, 48
Noone, Kathleen, 370, 379
North, Sheree, 256
Northern Exposure, 459
Norville, Deborah, 448
Nova, 281, 354, 364, 365, 424, 425
Novak, Kim, 63
Nutcracker: Money, Madness, Murder, 374
O'Brien, Hugh, 54
O'Brien, Pat, 172, 178
O'Connor, Carroll, 140, 144, 149, 154, 159, 164, 175, 187, 195, 209, 212, 213, 215, 224, 229, 238, 243, 406, 413, 479, 481, 484
O'Connor, Donald, 37, 49
O'Connor, John, J., 429
O'Toole, Annette, 437
O'Toole, Peter, 268, 273
Odd Couple, The, 140, 143, 153, 174, 184

184, 187
Rape of Richard Beck, The, 334
Raphael, Sally Jessy, 409, 419, 432
Rather, Dan, 167, 180, 213, 288, 320, 329, 347, 364, 372, 391, 392, 403, 411, 424, 447, 449, 470
Razzmatazz, 240, 247
Reading Rainbow, 433
Reagan, Ronald, 73
Reasoner, Harry, 122, 173, 181, 281, 298, 330
Red Pony, The, 163
Red Skelton Hour, The, 106
Red Skelton Show, The, 30, 32, 64, 71, 82
Redgrave, Lynn, 273
Redgrave, Vanessa, 268, 273, 351, 357, 357, 461, 481
Reed, Donna, 65, 70, 71, 77, 83
Rees, Roger, 307
Reeves, Richard, 262
Reggie Jackson, 287, 297
Regis Philbin Show, The, 287, 294
Reilly: Ace of Spies, 321
Reiner, Carl, 33, 38, 48, 51, 52, 54, 58, 60, 80, 85, 88, 91, 95, 109, 115, 149, 481
Reiner, Rob, 149, 154, 164, 175, 188, 224, 229
Remick, Lee, 229, 250, 256, 375, 454
Requiem for a Heavyweight, 4, 52, 53, 54, 55
Reynold, James, 465
Reynolds, Burt, 453, 460, 462
Reynolds, Dean, 471
Reynolds, Frank, 262
Reynolds, Gene, 184
Rhoda, 183, 184, 187
Rich Man, Poor Man, 195, 200, 208
Richard Boone Show, The, 93
Richard Simmons Show, The, 294
Richards, Beah, 395
Rickles, Don, 97, 119
Rieger, Hank, xi, 12, 15, 250, 253, 485
Rifleman, The, 65
Rigg, Diana, 114, 121, 188
Ritchard, Cyril, 48
Ritter, John, 229, 238, 273, 317, 394
Rivera, Geraldo, 262, 281
Rivers, Joan, 16, 301, 303, 369, 432, 442, 443, 455, 456
Roach, Jr., Hal, 485
Robards, Jr., Jason, 94, 201, 229, 251, 256, 389, 394, 481
Robert Kennedy and His Times, 337
Robert Montgomery Presents, 32, 35, 38
Robert Q. Lewis, 42
Roberts, Doris, 301, 302, 307, 339, 414, 461
Roberts, Pernell, 273

Robertson, Cliff, 73, 74, 77, 103, 106, 481
Rocco, Alex, 437
Rockford Files, The, 5, 210, 224, 227, 239, 241, 255
Rodgers, Richard, 84
Roe vs. Wade, 407, 412
Rogers, Fred, 261, 344
Rogers, Suzanne, 240, 246
Rogers, Wayne, 169
Rogosin, Joel, 124
Rolle, Esther, 243
Ronstadt, Linda, 414
Room 222, 132, 135
Rooney, Andy, 130, 241, 271, 281, 298
Rooney, Mickey, 59, 65, 83, 285, 290, 322
Roots, 15, 208, 214, 237, 302, 482
Roots: The Next Generations, 237, 242
Rose, Charlie, 383
Rose, Reginald, 39, 43, 55, 75, 79, 84, 85, 89
Roseanne, 2, 428, 483
Rowan, Dan, 5, 117
Rowlands, Gena, 238, 357, 370, 375
Roy Rogers Show, The, 41
Ruben, Aaron, 124
Rubinstein, Artur, 139, 359
Rubinstein, John, 229
Rudie, Evelyn, 54
Ruggles, Charles, 485
Rukeyser, Bud, xi, 287
Rule, Elton H., 282
Rumpole of the Bailey, 272, 392
Run for Your Life, 113, 120
Russell, Kurt, 243
Russom, Leon, 461
Ryan's Hope, 212, 220, 233, 240, 245, 276, 293, 390, 479
Sacco-Vanzetti, 76
Safer, Morley, 213, 249, 298, 330, 364, 365, 425
Saga of Western Man, The, 93
Saint James, Susan, 125, 129, 136, 145, 154, 164, 188, 316, 322, 338
Saint, Eva Marie, 42, 48, 216, 229, 430, 437, 481
Salant, Richard, 173
Salinger, Pierre, 329, 425, 448
Sally Jessy Raphael, 443
Sammy Davis Jr.'s 60th Anniversary Celebration, 431, 436
Sanford and Son, 153, 163
Sanford, Isabel, 243, 256, 267, 273, 290, 307, 322, 338
Santa Barbara, 379, 390, 398, 408, 409, 418, 431, 441, 479
Sarah, Plain and Tall, 459
Sarnoff, David, 84, 303, 484
Sarnoff, Thomas, 11, 485

FOR THE BEST IN PAPERBACKS, LOOK FOR THE 🐧

In every corner of the world, on every subject under the sun, Penguin represents quality and variety—the very best in publishing today.

For complete information about books available from Penguin—including Pelicans, Puffins, Peregrines, and Penguin Classics—and how to order them, write to us at the appropriate address below. Please note that for copyright reasons the selection of books varies from country to country.

In the United Kingdom: For a complete list of books available from Penguin in the U.K., please write to *Dept E.P., Penguin Books Ltd, Harmondsworth, Middlesex, UB7 0DA.*

In the United States: For a complete list of books available from Penguin in the U.S., please write to *Dept BA, Penguin*, Box 120, Bergenfield, New Jersey 07621-0120.

In Canada: For a complete list of books available from Penguin in Canada, please write to *Penguin Books Canada Ltd, 10 Alcorn Avenue, Suite 300, Toronto, Ontario, Canada M4V 3B2.*

In Australia: For a complete list of books available from Penguin in Australia, please write to the *Marketing Department, Penguin Books Ltd, P.O. Box 257, Ringwood, Victoria 3134.*

In New Zealand: For a complete list of books available from Penguin in New Zealand, please write to the *Marketing Department, Penguin Books (NZ) Ltd, Private Bag, Takapuna, Auckland 9.*

In India: For a complete list of books available from Penguin, please write to *Penguin Overseas Ltd, 706 Eros Apartments, 56 Nehru Place, New Delhi, 110019.*

In Holland: For a complete list of books available from Penguin in Holland, please write to *Penguin Books Nederland B.V., Postbus 195, NL-1380AD Weesp, Netherlands.*

In Germany: For a complete list of books available from Penguin, please write to *Penguin Books Ltd, Friedrichstrasse 10-12, D-6000 Frankfurt Main 1, Federal Republic of Germany.*

In Spain: For a complete list of books available from Penguin in Spain, please write to *Longman, Penguin España, Calle San Nicolas 15, E-28013 Madrid, Spain.*

In Japan: For a complete list of books available from Penguin in Japan, please write to *Longman Penguin Japan Co Ltd, Yamaguchi Building, 2-12-9 Kanda Jimbocho, Chiyoda-Ku, Tokyo 101, Japan.*

FOR THE BEST IN PAPERBACKS, LOOK FOR THE

☐ **AMUSING OURSELVES TO DEATH**
Public Discourse in the Age of Show Business
Neil Postman

In this eloquent, persuasive book, Postman outlines the dangers of handing over politics, education, religion, and journalism to the show-business demands of the television age and offers compelling suggestions for withstanding the media onslaught.

"A brilliant, powerful and important book"—*Washington Post Book World*
184 pages   ISBN: 0-14-009438-5

FOR THE BEST IN REFERENCE, LOOK FOR THE 🐧

☐ **INFORMATION U.S.A.**
Revised Edition
Matthew Lesko

Dedicated to bureaucrats everywhere, *Information U.S.A.* is the key to obtaining direct access to federal government agencies, boards, branches, commissions, committees, and departments. This completely revised and updated edition of the national bestseller provides the most up-to-date, accurate information on virtually any subject, from consumer product safety to missing persons.
1254 pages   ISBN: 0-14-046745-9

☐ **THE NEW PENGUIN GUIDE TO COMPACT DISCS AND CASSETTES**
Edward Greenfield, Robert Layton and Ivan March

This guide is an invaluable tool for the serious collector, both as a reference work of extraordinary depth and as a practical guide to making quality selections in a rapidly expanding market. Each recording, including all released since the publication of the first Penguin Guide, is discussed individually, with ratings and expert comments.   *1200 pages   ISBN: 0-14-046829-3*

☐ **YOUR WEDDING**
Making It Perfect
Yetta Fisher Gruen

Witty, informative, and thoroughly reassuring, *Your Wedding* is the definitive guide to wed-iquette.   *370 pages   ISBN: 0-14-046755-6*

FOR THE BEST IN REFERENCE, LOOK FOR THE 🐧

☐ **THE BEST**
Peter Passell

A discerning selection for the quality-obsessed, Passell's collection highlights an incredibly varied list of superlatives, from the Best Chinese Restaurant in America to the Best Market for Prune Juice.

320 pages   ISBN: 0-14-009420-2

☐ **THE LOVER'S QUOTATION BOOK**
A Literary Companion
Helen Handley, Editor

No lover should be without this light-hearted collection of every important and ridiculous idea about love that ever sprang from great and not-so-great minds.

76 pages   ISBN: 0-14-051192-X